PARKER AND EVANS'S INSIDE LAWYERS' ETHICS

Fourth edition

Parker and Evans's Inside Lawyers' Ethics provides a practical and engaging introduction to ethical decision-making in legal practice in Australia.

Underpinned by four theoretical concepts – adversarial advocacy, responsible lawyering, moral activism and ethics of care – this text analyses legal and professional frameworks in the Australian context. Relevant parts of the *Australian Solicitors' Conduct Rules* are highlighted, and the accompanying text provides guidance on professional obligations. Case studies and discussion questions offer contemporary, practical examples of the application of ethics in legal practice for both students and practising lawyers. The book also addresses the challenge of ethical action and offers skills and techniques to deal with ethical conflicts.

The fourth edition has been comprehensively updated and discusses the implications of advances in legal technology, mental ill-health in the profession and the complexities of government legal practice. A new chapter covers lawyers' ethical obligation to address the legal challenges posed by climate change and environmental damage.

Written by an expert author team, *Parker and Evans's Inside Lawyers' Ethics* empowers readers to identify ethical challenges and resolve them through good decision-making practices.

Vivien Holmes is a Professor in the ANU College of Law at the Australian National University.

Francesca Bartlett is an Associate Professor in the TC Beirne School of Law at the University of Queensland.

PARKER AND EVANS'S INSIDE LAWYERS' ETHICS

Fourth edition

Vivien Holmes

Francesca Bartlett

CAMBRIDGE
UNIVERSITY PRESS

CAMBRIDGE
UNIVERSITY PRESS

Shaftesbury Road, Cambridge CB2 8EA, United Kingdom

One Liberty Plaza, 20th Floor, New York, NY 10006, USA

477 Williamstown Road, Port Melbourne, VIC 3207, Australia

314–321, 3rd Floor, Plot 3, Splendor Forum, Jasola District Centre, New Delhi – 110025, India

103 Penang Road, #05–06/07, Visioncrest Commercial, Singapore 238467

Cambridge University Press is part of Cambridge University Press & Assessment, a department of the University of Cambridge.

We share the University's mission to contribute to society through the pursuit of education, learning and research at the highest international levels of excellence.

www.cambridge.org
Information on this title: www.cambridge.org/highereducation/isbn/9781009045636

First published 2007
Second edition 2014
Third edition 2018
Fourth edition 2023

Cover designed by Tanya de Silva
Typeset by Integra Software Services Pvt. Ltd
A catalogue record for this publication is available from the British Library

A catalogue record for this book is available from the National Library of Australia

ISBN 978-1-009-04563-6 Paperback

Additional resources for this publication at www.cambridge.org/highereducation/isbn/9781009045636/resources

Please be aware that this publication may contain several variations of Aboriginal and Torres Strait Islander terms and spellings; no disrespect is intended. Please note that the terms 'Indigenous Australians', 'Aboriginal and Torres Strait Islander peoples' and 'First Nations peoples' may be used interchangeably in this publication.

CONTENTS

PREFACE

It is a privilege to build on the work of Christine Parker and Adrian Evans and offer a fourth edition of this groundbreaking book. The challenges facing the legal profession have not diminished since the last edition and we have written this new edition cognisant of the impact on lawyers of the digital revolution, ongoing challenges to mental health, sexual harassment in the profession, the need for more diversity and a healthier relationship with Australia's First Nations Peoples and their Law, and the challenge to our legal system of climate change and environmental destruction. To this last challenge we devote a whole new Chapter 10. For the first time, we address the ethical complexity of government legal practice, exploring the similarities it shares with corporate practice. We also consider for the first time some of the perennial and newer challenges to maintaining competency in practice. This edition includes substantially revised chapters and new case studies, and addresses in more detail the skills needed to *act* on what we know to be ethical.

As in previous editions, the book analyses and critiques lawyer regulation, conduct rules and case law on lawyers' professional responsibilities. The *Legal Profession Uniform Law* is in force in New South Wales, Victoria and Western Australia and its key legislative provisions are cited and explained throughout the book. We expand upon previous editions to refer to relevant provisions applying in other Australian jurisdictions and note differences in approach across the country. The *Australian Solicitors' Conduct Rules* remain the model for all the States' and the Australian Capital Territory's conduct rules. Recent amendments to these Rules that have been adopted in New South Wales, Victoria and Western Australia are included and considered in this edition. This edition also refers to conduct rules governing barristers that apply in most jurisdictions. An expanded section of Chapter 3 considers the historical development and distinctions in professional duties and orientation of barristers and solicitors in Australia.

We retain the original authors' central concern to connect a lawyer's humanity and values to competent, caring and reflective practice. Whether working as adversarial advocates, responsible officers of the court, champions of justice and/or caring professionals, lawyers will most effectively fulfil their duty to the administration of justice if they are guided by professional values and conscious of the ethical import of their work. This book aims to strengthen the ethical sensibilities and skills of students and lawyers, to enable them to contribute positively to the legal system, to healthy professional cultures, to the clients and other parties involved in the system and to their own wellbeing and career satisfaction.

Vivien Holmes and Francesca Bartlett
July 2022

ABOUT THE AUTHORS

Vivien Holmes is a Professor at the ANU College of Law where she teaches and researches in the fields of legal ethics, legal education and the legal profession. Prior to joining ANU, Vivien worked as a litigation solicitor in private and government practice, a government legal policy officer, a Court Registrar and Judicial Registrar, a Registrar of Probates and a Deputy Coroner. She has been a member of the Social Security Appeals Tribunal and is a member of the ACT Law Society's Professional Standards Committee.

Vivien's research has explored how to best equip law students to meet ethical challenges in practice. With colleagues, Vivien has researched the transition of new lawyers into legal practice and the links between lawyer wellbeing and ethics, including the impact of the ethical climate of legal workplaces. She is currently exploring with colleagues the potential overlap between unethical practice climates and incidents of sexual harassment and bullying. Vivien is passionate about lawyers using their skills to contribute to the change needed to address climate change and environmental destruction; Chapter 10 in this new edition explores this topic.

Francesca Bartlett is an Associate Professor and Director of Teaching and Learning in the Law School at the University of Queensland. She teaches and researches in the fields of legal ethics and the legal profession, and women and the law. Prior to joining academia, Francesca worked as a solicitor in a large law firm and at a community legal centre.

Francesca's research has explored admission to legal practice, professional discipline and apologies, and pro bono legal practice. Her work has also considered how to achieve diversity within the legal profession and the judiciary and how law impacts women. She was a Chief Investigator on the ARC Discovery–funded Australian Feminist Judgments Project and has received funding to undertake projects on technology and access to justice, and innovation and change in the Queensland legal profession. In addition to these projects considering the context of modern legal practice, Francesca is working with colleagues to develop best practices for lawyering in domestic and family violence cases and modelling pro bono within law schools.

ACKNOWLEDGEMENTS

Vivien Holmes would like to give her heartfelt thanks to her partner Greg Roche for all his support and to Lara and Erica for encouragement along the way. Thanks also to the ANU College of Law for the research leave that enabled her to dig her teeth into the project at its outset and to Des Lane and Anthony Hopkins for long conversations about criminal practice ethics. Deep thanks to her co-author Francesca Bartlett for being so great to work with and so committed to wrangling with the complexities of lawyer regulation, conduct rules and the multiple ethical questions that arise in legal practice.

Francesca Bartlett extends her thanks always to her partner Robert Colvin for listening and support, and doing all the cooking. Thanks and love to Arthur and Anna for bringing the fun and being her critics and conscience. Thank you to Monica Taylor for insightful comments on environmental lawyering. Finally, her great thanks to her co-author for welcoming her onto the project and the kindness, collegiality, and intellectual clarity she brought to their collaboration.

The authors and Cambridge University Press would like to thank the following for permission to reproduce material in this book.

Earlier versions of Chapters 1 and 2 were published in Christine Parker, 'A Critical Morality for Australian Lawyers and Law Students' (2004) 30 *Monash University Law Review* 49–74.

Some of the material in Chapter 3 is based on work previously published in Christine Parker, 'Competing Images of the Legal Profession: Competing Regulatory Strategies' (1997) 25(4) *International Journal of the Sociology of Law* 385–409.

Some of the material in Chapter 9 is partly based on Christine Parker et al, 'The Ethical Infrastructure of Legal Practice in Larger Law Firms: Values, Policy and Behaviour' (2008) 31 *University of New South Wales Law Journal* 158, 172, 174–5.

Extracts from David Luban, *Lawyers and Justice: An Ethical Study* (1988) republished with permission of Princeton University Press through Copyright Clearance Center, Inc.

Extract from Liz Curran, *Better Law for a Better World*: republished with permission of Taylor & Francis (Books) Limited UK, from Liz Curran, *Better Law for a Better World: New Approaches to Law Practice and Education*, 2021; permission conveyed through Copyright Clearance Center, Inc.

Victoria accepts no responsibility for the accuracy and completeness of any legislation contained in this product or provided through this service.

Extract from *Prosecution Guidelines* © Copyright 2021 The Office of the Director of Public Prosecutions, reproduced with permission.

Extracts from *Legal Profession Uniform Admission Rules 2015*, *National Conduct Rules* and *Australian Solicitors' Conduct Rules*: sourced from the NSW Legislation website. For the latest information on New South Wales Government legislation please go to https://www.legislation.nsw.gov.au. Reproduced under a CC BY 4.0 licence: https://creativecommons.org/licenses/by/4.0/.

Extract from *AWB Ltd v Cole (No 5)* (2006) 155 FCR 30: reproduced with permission of Thomson Reuters (Professional) Australia Limited, https://legal.thomsonreuters.com.au.

Extract from *R v Szabo* [2000] QCA 194 reproduced with permission of Supreme Court Library Queensland and Queensland Courts.

Every effort has been made to trace and acknowledge copyright. The publisher apologises for any accidental infringement and welcomes information that would redress the situation.

ABBREVIATIONS

AAT	Administrative Appeals Tribunal
ABA	American Bar Association
ABC	Australian Broadcasting Corporation
ACC	Association of Corporate Counsel
ACT	Australian Capital Territory
ADR	alternative dispute resolution
AFP	Australian Federal Police
AG	Attorney-General
AI	artificial intelligence
APP	Australian Privacy Principles
ASCR	*Australian Solicitors' Conduct Rules 2015*
ASIC	Australian Securities and Investment Commission
ASIS	Australian Security and Intelligence Service
ASX	Australian Securities Exchange
ATO	Australian Taxation Office
AWB	Australian Wheat Board
BATAS	British American Tobacco Australia Services
CLP	client legal privilege
CP Act	*Civil Procedure Act 2010* (Vic)
DPP	Director of Public Prosecutions
EDO	Environmental Defenders Office
ESG	environmental, social and governance
GVV	Giving Voice to Values
IBA	International Bar Association
ILP	incorporated legal practice
JH	James Hardie Industries Ltd
JHIL	James Hardie Industries Ltd
JHINV	James Hardie Industries NV

LACC	Law Admissions Consultative Committee
LCA	Law Council of Australia
LPBT	Legal Profession Board of Tasmania
LSC	Legal Services Commissioner
MRCF	Medical Research and Compensation Foundation
NGO	non-government organisation
NSW	New South Wales
ODPP NSW	NSW Office of the Director of Public Prosecutions
PILCH	Public Interest Law Clearing House
QC	Queen's Counsel
QLS	Queensland Law Society
SCAG	Standing Committee of Attorneys-General
SEC	Securities Exchange Commission
TLS	Tasmanian Law Society
UK	United Kingdom
UN	United Nations
US	United States of America

FIGURES AND TABLES

Figures

Tables

CASE STUDIES

TABLE OF CASES

TABLE OF STATUTES

Northern Territory

Queensland

South Australia

Tasmania

Victoria

Western Australia

United States of America

United Kingdom

International instruments

TABLE OF ASCR

1

INTRODUCTION: VALUES IN PRACTICE

Introduction: an overview of this book

Previous editions of this book have explained how an individual lawyer's preference for a particular approach to making ethical decisions (for example, *adversarial* or *zealous advocacy*) influences their thinking about 'the right thing to do' in any particular situation. The third edition explained how good ethical decisions involve not just the application of a legal framework – such as the professional conduct rules and case law – but also a working understanding of moral philosophy, otherwise known as general morality. It also noted the importance of being able *to act* on ethical decisions. This fourth edition is structured around these same themes, while updated to take into account recent case law and legislative changes, and broader issues currently affecting the profession.

In this introductory chapter we first provide an overview of the whole book and discuss some global issues affecting legal practice and lawyers' ethics. We then explore insights from general morality as an underlying framework for the four approaches to lawyers' ethics explored in Chapter 2. This framework compensates, to some extent, for the lack of an explicit statement of values in our current rules of professional conduct. We consider the professional imperatives for ethical action (legal and cultural norms) and the ethical decision-making process, including the skills we need to put our ethics into action.

In Chapter 2 we describe four approaches to lawyers' ethics, and explore the strengths and limitations of each approach. The first two approaches are expressions of 'role morality – that is, what is the proper role of lawyers in our system of justice? A common answer to this question is *adversarial advocate*, which understands the lawyer primarily as agent for the client, advocating for the client's interests. Increasingly, however, lawyers are required to adopt a different role – *responsible lawyering*. *Responsible lawyering*, like *adversarial advocacy*, is based on the lawyer's role in the adversary system, but sees the lawyer as having more of a mediating role between the law and clients. We then consider two other approaches that apply more general ethics to the legal profession – the *moral activist* and *ethics of care* approaches. Both are underpinned by the general moral theory of virtue ethics. *Moral activism* sees social ethics, and particularly social justice, as the final arbiter of what lawyers' ethics should be, since the legal system should be concerned with advancing the virtue of justice. The *ethics of care* approach, which includes the idea that we ought to care for the earth community, sees relational ethics, the virtue of compassion and the minimisation of harm as the most important principles that should govern lawyers' behaviour.

Responsible lawyering suggests alternatives to, and limits on, excessive adversarialism within the terms of the adversary system itself, by proposing that lawyers behave as officers of the court as well as client advocates. Existing professional conduct regulation attempts (at least half-heartedly) to put this into practice, as we shall see in the chapters that follow. *Moral activism* and the *ethics of care*, by contrast, provide completely external critiques to adversarialism. They propose virtue ethics–based alternatives to the partisanship and non-accountability of *adversarial advocacy* and even at times question the appropriateness of the adversarial legal system itself as a method of resolving disputes and doing justice.

In each succeeding chapter we examine in more detail what the four ethical approaches and underlying general morality might mean, and which values would be appropriate to apply, in different contexts. In doing so we critique the extent to which the rules and regulations, particularly the *Australian Solicitors' Conduct Rules*[1] as they currently stand, do a good job of demonstrating appropriate values, and how these rules and regulations influence individual lawyers' capacity to put values into action. We argue that common law approaches might at times align more closely with the ethical approaches than with the rules. But while the approach in this text may seem to undervalue the conduct rules, we do not say that they are pointless or of no value; on the contrary, they are in themselves a reflection of the underlying general moral principles we describe. They indicate a commitment to ethical practice and provide a framework for professional regulation through the disciplinary system. We have emphasised the conduct rules in separate text boxes in all relevant chapters, so that they stand out; but we maintain the view, expressed in earlier editions, that a compliance-like attitude to their observance will never be enough for good decision-making.

In each chapter, we make extensive use of case studies to illustrate our points and to provide an opportunity for students (and other readers) to develop their own values-based judgements and apply the law of lawyering in respect of the topics covered.

The broad topics covered are as follows. Chapter 3 discusses the regulatory systems that govern Australian lawyers and some of the history of its evolution and likely future trajectory. Chapter 4 explores lawyers' fundamental duty of client confidentiality, and the place of whistleblowing in our system of justice. Chapter 5 deals with the ethics of criminal justice, for both defence and prosecution lawyers. Chapter 6 addresses the issues that arise in civil justice resolution, from litigation to alternative dispute resolution, and provides new perspectives on the challenges of technology and competency in this area of law. Chapter 7 covers the complex issue of conflicts of interest. Although conflicts are now seen as a broad social issue not limited to lawyers, lawyers have particularly complex principles and conduct rules to apply when confronted with conflicts. Perceived and actual conflicts of interest have led to much case law and are a consistent source of client complaint. However, the largest area of client complaint concerns fees and costs, and the whole of Chapter 8 is dedicated to these challenges in the context of the detailed regulatory environment lawyers must understand in order to bill their clients ethically. Chapter 9 deals with corporate lawyers and, for the first time in this fourth edition, we also explore the ethical responsibilities of government lawyers: both these groups of lawyers act for powerful clients and there are interesting overlaps in the ethical issues they face. In a wholly new Chapter 10, we examine the role of lawyers in one of the defining challenges of our times – climate change and environmental degradation. We conclude in Chapter 11 by examining the connection between personal values and professional practice. We finish that chapter with further discussion of how case studies and ethics assessment can be used to build lawyers' and law students' values awareness and strengthen their ethical resolve.

1 We also refer to the ethical conduct rules applying to barristers across the country. The Australian Bar Association drafted model rules that were adopted in most jurisdictions in 2011. In 2015, these rules with amendments were enacted (as part of the *Legal Profession Uniform Law* in New South Wales and Victoria) as the *Legal Profession Uniform Conduct (Barristers) Rules 2015*. In the book we refer to the *Legal Profession Uniform Conduct (Barristers) Rules 2015* (*'Barristers' Conduct Rules'*) as these represent the approach in the majority of jurisdictions, but will indicate where there is significant local variation.

Global issues affecting legal practice and lawyers' ethics

Some of the global trends noted in the last edition as impacting on legal practice have accelerated significantly. One such trend is the use of legal technology, with the COVID-19 pandemic seeing a wholesale shift online in many areas of practice, including court hearings. The extent to which these changes are transformative is yet to be seen, but it is unlikely that the profession will return to work practices that were normal before the pandemic but have been replaced by digital innovations. These developments underscore the importance of lawyers being digitally competent. We discuss what the greater use of legal technology means for lawyers' duties of both confidentiality and competence in Chapters 4 and 6.

The legal profession continues to deal with the serious issue of mental illness within its ranks – an issue exacerbated for some by lengthy COVID-19 lockdowns. The profession has taken steps to address this challenge, which is certainly discussed more openly now than it was a decade ago. Law societies offer resources and assistance to lawyers experiencing mental health problems. We applaud these moves; however, we consider that there is a lot more work to be done by the profession to address the structural issues that affect the wellbeing of lawyers, such as long working hours, pressure to 'make budget' and secondary trauma. We also draw attention to research shedding light on the links between workplace ethical climate,[2] mental wellbeing, and job and career satisfaction. Research by Stephen Tang, Vivien Holmes and Tony Foley[3] shows that new lawyers have a clear perception of the values of their workplace, and this affects them in significant ways. New lawyers' positive sense of professional wellbeing is enhanced in workplaces characterised by both integrity and an ethic of care. Conversely, their wellbeing suffers in workplaces where power and self-interest are the prevailing norms, and also in workplaces with little ethical awareness or relational engagement. These findings support the view that lawyers' mental wellbeing cannot be simply reduced to an individual's personal experiences, disconnected from the ethical climate of the organisation in which they work.

Another deeply concerning issue with which the profession is grappling is the high incidence of sexual harassment and bullying within its ranks. A 2019 report by the International Bar Association ('IBA')[4] drew attention to the global nature of the problem. In the same year, a report by the Victorian Legal Services Board and Commissioner[5] noted that nearly two-thirds of women surveyed indicated they had experienced sexual harassment

2 Employee perceptions of the 'ethical climate' of an organisation are their perceptions of 'how the members of an organization typically make decisions concerning "events, practices, and procedures requiring ethical criteria"': John B Cullen et al, 'The Ethical Climate Questionnaire: An Assessment of Its Development and Validity' (1993) 73(1) *Psychological Reports* 667, 669.

3 Stephen Tang, Vivien Holmes and Tony Foley, 'Ethical Climate, Job Satisfaction and Wellbeing: Observations from an Empirical Study of New Australian Lawyers' (2020) 33(4) *Georgetown Journal of Legal Ethics* 1035.

4 Kieran Pender, *Us Too? Bullying and Sexual Harassment in the Legal Profession* (IBA Legal Policy and Research Unit, Report, 2019).

5 Victorian Legal Services Board and Commissioner, *Sexual Harassment in the Victorian Legal Sector* (Report, 2019).

at work. Reports on sexual harassment in Victorian courts[6] and in the South Australian profession[7] generally confirm these findings. These reports indicate that the problem of sexual harassment in the legal profession is worse than in workplaces generally, and has particular features.[8] Importantly, the IBA report reminds us that '[b]ullying and sexual harassment do not occur in a vacuum'. It emphasises that 'mental health challenges, a lack of workplace satisfaction and insufficient diversity are all related issues' and that these aspects of a legal culture also need to be understood and addressed.[9]

In relation to gender diversity, as Margaret Thornton and others have long documented, women were long the 'fringe-dwellers'[10] in law, due to many interlocking structural and social barriers erected against women's acceptance as equal members of the profession. These barriers ranged from indirect factors such as an expectation to show 'commitment' to the firm by working very long hours, or direct discrimination in promotion and career opportunities.[11] While women now represent more than half the practising profession[12] (53%, although this is in the more numerous solicitors' branch) they still lag behind in most places of seniority such as equity partnership and senior counsel (often called Queen's Counsel).[13] Given that male-dominated hierarchies are a risk factor for sexual harassment, it is important that the profession continues efforts to advance women in its ranks.[14]

While the profession has begun to address the issue of sexual harassment and bullying, it will take sustained efforts by all levels of the profession to significantly minimise or eliminate the problem. Given what we know about the cultures in which sexual harassment thrives (cultures with little regard for integrity, fairness or an ethic of care), we suggest that, as part of the profession's efforts, a focus on the ethical culture of a workplace may produce dividends.[15]

---

6 Helen Szoke, *Preventing and Addressing Sexual Harassment in Victorian Courts and VCAT: Report and Recommendations* (Report and Recommendations, March 2021).

7 Government of South Australia, Equal Opportunity Commission, *Review of Harassment in the South Australian Legal Profession* (Report, 2021).

8 Vivien Holmes et al, 'Sexual Harassment: Is Strengthening Ethical Culture the Answer?' (2021) 95(10) *Law Institute Journal* 20, 21.

9 Pender (n 4) 10.

10 Margaret Thornton, *Dissonance and Distrust: Women in the Legal Profession* (Oxford University Press, 1996).

11 Hilary Sommerlad, '"A Pit to Put Women in": Professionalism, Work Intensification, Sexualisation and Work–Life Balance in the Legal Profession in England and Wales' (2016) 23(1) *International Journal of the Legal Profession* 61–82.

12 Urbis, *2020 National Profile of Solicitors* (Final Report, July 2021).

13 More than half of all female solicitors have been admitted for 10 years or less, and are overrepresented in the younger brackets compared to male solicitors: ibid 2. While there are no recent national reports on seniority by gender, our desktop reviews of barristers lists indicate that women represent approximately 9% of senior counsel. See the report on the recent appointment of 12 new female senior counsel in New South Wales raising the percentage of women senior counsel from 6.7% to 9.4%: 'Record Number of Female Silks Appointed', Women Lawyers Association of NSW (Web page) <https://womenlawyersnsw.org.au/press/record-number-of-female-silks-appointed/>. In recent years, the solicitors' branch has done far better through concerted campaigns for equality. For example, within the large law firm sector over 30% of partners are women: Hanna Wootton, 'Female Law Partners Breach Through 30pc Barrier' (The Australian Financial Review (online at 10 December 2020) <https://www.afr.com/companies/professional-services/women-partners-break-through-30pc-barrier-20201130-p56j7u>.

14 We acknowledge the need for broad diversity in the profession. See, eg, Law Society of New South Wales, *Diversity and Inclusion in the Legal Profession: The Business Case* (October 2021). Below we discuss the need for greater representation of First Nations Peoples.

15 See further Holmes et al (n 8).

Another area of important focus for the profession is the justice system's relationship with Australia's First Nations Peoples. As the Uluru Statement From The Heart reminds us, Aboriginal and Torres Strait Islander sovereignty 'has never been ceded or extinguished and co-exists with the sovereignty of the Crown'.[16] The Statement calls for constitutional change and structural reform, including establishment of a Voice to Parliament. The Law Council of Australia supports the call for constitutional recognition; its 2021 President, Dr Jacoba Brasch QC, noted:

> The discrimination and intergenerational trauma that Aboriginal and Torres Strait Islander peoples face on a day-to-day basis cannot be alleviated unless and until their rightful place in this country is recognised and the legacy of colonialism confronted. The legal and justice system has played an undeniable part in this history of colonisation, discrimination and trauma.[17]

The legal profession has much work to do to redress that history. Some important work has begun – for example, in Aboriginal Circle Sentencing Courts[18] – but much remains to be done, including ensuring that First Nations Peoples are properly represented in the profession. Further, as Canadian scholar Pooja Parma argues, 'the ethical practice of law requires attention to Indigenous laws, legal practices, and epistemologies as sources of ethics and professionalism'.[19] We suggest that that an *ethics of care* approach (see Chapter 2) may help facilitate the necessary dialogue between the profession and First Nations Peoples about sources of ethics. We have much to learn about ethics from First Nations Peoples. For example, 'dadirri', or 'deep listening' to Country to discern right ways of living, is an Aboriginal ethic taught by Dr Miriam Rose Ungunmerr-Baumann, Aboriginal Elder and 2021 Senior Australian of the Year.[20] We consider in Chapter 7 what difference an *ethics of care* approach might make in dealing with conflicts (a significant issue in remote Aboriginal communities)[21] and in Chapter 10 we discuss the *ethics of care* underpinning 'earth jurisprudence', which is itself informed by First Nations legal systems.

Taking into account all of the issues covered in this book, and being aware of the wider social, economic and political concerns described above, our focus on the general morality that underlies ethical type and choice can only do so much. We cannot directly advance the careers of ethical lawyers, eliminate sexual harassment in the profession or improve lawyers' mental health issues, let alone address environmental destruction. But we can suggest that law students and lawyers who are ethically aware are better equipped to

16 The Uluru Statement, 'The Uluru Statement From The Heart' <https://ulurustatement.org/the-statement>.

17 Law Council of Australia, 'Time to Enshrine a First Nations Voice to Parliament' (Media Release, 10 December 2021).

18 See, eg, *Owen Patterson v Wendy Brookman* [2021] ACTMC 16.

19 Pooja Parma, 'Reconciliation and Ethical Lawyering: Some Thoughts on Cultural Competence' (2019) 97(3) *Canadian Bar Review* 526, 557.

20 'Dadirri', *Miriam Rose Foundation* (Web Page) <https://www.miriamrosefoundation.org.au/dadirri/>.

21 Judy Harrison submission to Law Council of Australia's Review of the ASCR (8 December 2020). Copy on file with authors.

improve the profession and to provide greater value to clients, in a manner that addresses the longer-term interests of those clients, our system of justice and indeed our society. We also believe that attention to ethics underpins profitable and sustainable legal practice. At a time dubbed the 'great resignation' in many industries, including the legal sector across the common law world, attention to engendering a firm culture that is ethical and promotes lawyer wellbeing seems to make very good business sense.[22] And we suggest that lawyers' greater awareness of general morality, and the choices this awareness enables, will help them to step back from daily practice and make informed choices about whose interests they serve. This in turn may well help inoculate them against the depression that affects some members of the profession.

It is to this last, very personal, issue that we now turn. In the next section we want to emphasise that mental health and communication problems are not fringe issues for the profession and that, apart from distorting ethical behaviours, poor communication and abusive conduct can affect client relationships very powerfully. The 2021 Annual Report of the NSW Office of the Legal Services Commissioner notes:

> Once again, this year a significant proportion of the consumer complaints have dealt with communication issues. In [some instances] it has become clear that the lawyer may be suffering with mental health problems. ... This Office ... commends the considerable resources offered by the Law Society to lawyers who may be suffering work or life stresses.[23]

We therefore begin our case studies with a disciplinary case that confrontingly illustrates how lawyers' personal wellbeing – upon which all of their productivity, service and justice impacts ultimately depend – is in need of pre-emptive attention.

CASE STUDY 1.1 STAYING ON THE RAILS

In many if not most cases, the wider impact of a lawyer's work is beneficial and adds to justice. But to illustrate what can happen to lawyers under stress and to make the point that failures of legal ethics are neither trivial nor uncommon, this case study takes extracts from a disciplinary tribunal decision that graphically describes the breakdown of a lawyer–client relationship.

It concerns a lawyer with a small regional practice and 13 years' experience who was charged with three counts of misconduct in relation to 'conduct which would be beyond the contemplation of reasonable practitioners'. The first count related to the 'discourteous, unprofessional and abusive tone and content of his correspondence with his clients'.[24]

The transcript of the Tribunal's decision includes these paragraphs:

22 Thomson Reuters Institute and Georgetown Law, *2022 A Report on the State of the Legal Market: A Challenging Road to Recovery* (Thomson Reuters, 2022).

23 Office of the Legal Services Commissioner (NSW), *Annual Report 2020–2021* (Report, 2021) 12.

24 *Legal Services Commissioner v Lynch* [2015] VCAT 772, [1].

Charge 1 – Unprofessional Language

6. Charge 1 is as follows:

   Professional misconduct within the meaning of section 4.4.3(1) of the [*Legal Profession Act 2004* (Vic) ('the Act')], namely misconduct at common law, as the Respondent's conduct in communicating with his client, Mr Marshall and with members of Mr Marshall's family in a manner that was discourteous, unprofessional; and/or abusive would be reasonably regarded as disgraceful and dishonourable by professional brethren of good repute and competency.

7. Attached to the Application for Order are 18 emails and one letter from Mr Lynch to his client. Most were sent to Adam Marshall, but some were sent to his father Ronald Marshall.

8. This correspondence was frequently hectoring, aggressive, disrespectful and abusive in tone towards his clients. The language was quite informal and unprofessional. The emails were peppered with profanities and intemperate language. They generally did not contain salutations or sign offs (although sometimes they ended 'me'). There was liberal use of capitalisation, bolding and varied font sizes. There were threats to cease acting.

9. The following examples are illustrative:

   - email of 17 October 2011

     3 THINGS:

     1. THE F ... CONCILIATION IS GOING ON. LISTEN TO ME AT SOME STAGE;
     2. I WILL MEET YOU AT 2.15 PM IN THE FOYER. I DO9 [sic] NOT NEED MY HEAD FILLED WITH EXTANEOUS [sic] CRAP I KNOW WHAT I AM DOOING [sic] AND
     3. THE PRICK THAT PUT MY ATTACHMENTS OUT OF ORDER IS GOING TO DIE LIKE A DOG. THINGS GO 11 12 13 NOT 13 11 12.

   - email of 19 October 2011:

     sweet jesus. Don't you buggers ever learn. What in the hell are you writing to the Commissioner for

   - email of 5 December 2011:

     Adam;

     YOU HAVE 10 MINUTES TO ANSWER THIS STARTING NOW On the basis of appropriate lawyering, I send the attached. Based on this, DO YOU WANT TO CHANGE ANYTHING. NOTE if your instructions remain the same, then I shall give it to her with both barrels.

     ANSWER BY 4:30 PM TODAY AS AT 4:31 I DO THE ABOVE.

   - email of 22 April 2012:

     Here is the bloody thing. You have until I get back from dinner (in about 3 hours) to advise of any spelling mistakes and or info I need provided. I WILL NOT BE F ... AMENDING ANY STUPID SHIT AS IT HAS ALREADY COST U A FORTUNE TO DO WHAT I HAVE DONE NOR WILL IN [sic] BE

EXPLAINING AGAIN ANY STUFF 6X IS ENOUGH IF NO CHANGES TONITE IT WILL BE AT YOUR PLACE FOR DELIVERY TOMORROW AND YES YOU DO HAVE TO GIVE THE ATTACHMENTS AGAIN.

ME.

10. Mr Lynch had a personal relationship with the Marshall family before he acted for Adam Marshall in this proceeding. He indicated their relationship was characterised by robust language. For example, Ronald Marshall had on one occasion encouraged the use of such language, in a jocular email in July 2011.
11. In the hearing, whilst on the one hand acknowledging his communications were discourteous and 'out of order', on the other hand, Mr Lynch also suggested that the LSC's concerns about language were out of touch with the modern world. He also said his clients were 'hard work'. They expected to be able to speak with him at any time or place, and came to his house.
12. ...
13. Amongst other things, this case is obviously illustrative of the inadvisability of a practitioner acting professionally for friends.
14. I reject Mr Lynch's suggestion that the LSC's concern about the use of such language is out of date. Yes, times have changed, and communication is generally more informal nowadays. But practitioners must be careful not to slip down the path towards communication which could be construed as overly aggressive, disrespectful, abusive, imprecise or otherwise unprofessional.
15. Obviously, this case is an extreme example. I have no hesitation in finding the conduct in this case constitutes misconduct at common law. Applying the well known test, it is conduct which colleagues of good repute and competency would reasonably regard as disgraceful and dishonourable. As such, it falls within the inclusive definition of professional misconduct in s 4.4.3 of the Act.[25]

The lawyer gave evidence in his defence that he suffered from bipolar disorder, but offered no medical report in support, despite maintaining that the disorder was controlled by medication under the supervision of a psychiatrist and his general practitioner. He was effectively friendless, appearing before the Tribunal without anyone to represent him. The Tribunal recognised that the case itself had eventually been settled on terms favourable to the clients, but found that the lawyer lacked insight into his offences.[26] In other words, whatever the truth of his condition he was not able to effectively control his outbursts, because to some extent he did not accept he had behaved poorly.[27]

25 Ibid [6]–[15] (citations omitted).

26 Ibid [31], [35].

27 Lynch was reprimanded, prevented from obtaining a practising certificate for 12 months, required to obtain a mental health assessment before being granted a practising certificate in the future and ordered to pay the costs of the Legal Services Commissioner: ibid [30], [35]–[36]. Chapter 3 discusses professional discipline, specifically its regulatory structures and common law principles.

A lawyer who is chronically ill will have an uphill battle holding everything together. When you are ill it is common to lose the ability to recognise and act when things are going off the rails. Yet the capacity to 'know yourself' is critical to a successful legal career, not just in terms of your own health but also, as we will see throughout this book, in relation to taking an ethical stance on many different issues. In all of these issues our objective must be to develop and maintain an ethical reputation for integrity – something that usually takes years to acquire, but is easily lost in a few emails.

DISCUSSION QUESTIONS

1. Do you know any lawyers who have little insight into the way they are perceived by others, or who are suffering from 'hidden' health issues (such as alcoholism, gambling addictions or other mental health issues) that you think are affecting them, even if they do not think so?
2. What can you do about anyone you have identified who needs help but who is reluctant to 'own' their issue? Did you know that the legal profession is very aware of the risks to lawyers' health and is now publicising resources designed to help?
3. Can you safely talk to your friend or colleague and let them know that there are pathways to health that may help?

Being unwell but not realising it is a particular hazard. But just as risky is *self-aware* conduct that has repercussions for reputations and lives far wider than a single case. In these matters the debate is the one more central to this book – the question of allegiance. To whom are we accountable for our intentional actions?

In Case study 1.2 we see a different example of the challenge of how to link our personal and professional lives in an integrated ethical manner. It raises some important questions about the role of lawyers and about limits to the dominant lawyering type of *adversarial advocacy*, and asks: 'When is it just too hot for a lawyer to take a different stand in their personal life, compared to their paid professional work?'

What is the role of lawyers?

CASE STUDY 1.2 THE CASE OF THE PHILANTHROPIST QC AND THE TOBACCO COMPANY

In 2012 a leading commercial and constitutional law barrister and supporter of the arts, higher education, civil liberties and medical research was appointed to the Board of the fundraising arm of Australia's highest-profile cancer hospital. He was a prominent Queen's Counsel ('QC') who had previously acted in many important and high-profile cases for a great variety of private clients, both for and against government agencies and in royal commissions. He was also a highly successful businessman in his own right and among

Australia's wealthiest individuals. He had used his prominence and wealth for many philanthropic purposes, focused particularly on supporting higher education, including through scholarships, promoting well-informed public policy debate, and medical research. He had donated generously to public art galleries and served on the Boards of the most prominent art galleries in Australia and of various other non-profit organisations.

The barrister's appointment to the Board of the cancer foundation was, however, criticised because he had previously represented a prominent tobacco company in its constitutional challenge to the Australian government's plain packaging legislation for cigarettes. The plain packaging law requires that cigarettes be sold without any branding (that is, no images, colours, logos or trademarks) and with only the name of the brand (in plain lettering and standardised size) and mandated health warnings and other information on a dull brown packet. Plain packaging was recommended in guidelines for implementation of the *WHO Framework Convention on Tobacco Control* (to which Australia is a signatory) to reduce tobacco consumption, especially the uptake of smoking by young people, and therefore reduce the negative health impacts of smoking. Australia was the first country in the world to introduce plain packaging laws, and the three major international tobacco companies (Philip Morris, British American Tobacco and Imperial Tobacco) joined together to challenge the legislation in the High Court of Australia, arguing that it was an unconstitutional usurping of their property rights in their brands and trademarked logos without just compensation. British American Tobacco, unlike the other companies, accepted for the purposes of the case that smoking causes serious health consequences but argued that the plain packaging laws were nonetheless an unjust appropriation of its property.[28] The High Court challenge was unsuccessful and plain packaging became law.[29]

In the previous year the QC had acted for British American Tobacco in the High Court case and also appeared and spoke on behalf of British American Tobacco executives in hearings before a parliamentary committee inquiring into views as to whether the legislation should go ahead. The QC had also previously acted for British American Tobacco in its successful appeal against the Supreme Court of Victoria decision in favour of Rolah McCabe. McCabe died from lung cancer in 2002, just before that appeal was decided. She had earlier been successful in arguing that the tobacco companies had destroyed evidence relevant to determining whether her lung cancer had been caused by smoking cigarettes sold by British American Tobacco. (The *McCabe* case is discussed further in Chapter 9.)

The important question in 2012 was whether it was proper for the QC to sit on the Board of the fundraising arm of the cancer hospital while also actively supporting the interests of tobacco manufacturers. The chief executive of the cancer hospital argued that the QC had a 'strong anti-tobacco stance', and that the High Court challenge 'wasn't about smoking,

28 Lenore Taylor, 'Health Issue Irrelevant, Tobacco Firms Tell Court', *The Sydney Morning Herald* (Sydney, 13 March 2012) 4.

29 *JT International SA v Commonwealth* (2012) 250 CLR 1. See Matthew Rimmer, 'The High Court and the Marlboro Man: The Plain Packaging Decision', *The Conversation* (online at 18 October 2012) <https://theconversation.com/the-high-court-and-the-marlboro-man-the-plain-packaging-decision-10014>.

it was about whether aspects of the *Tobacco Plain Packaging Act 2011* were inconsistent with the *Constitution* ... It was about intellectual property, appropriation of trademark and potential compensation'. He went on to comment that '[t]he key clinical staff involved in our anti-smoking areas were consulted and were respectful of [the QC's] right to advocate on behalf of his client. They felt it absolutely did not undermine our collective work, which is very strong on tobacco'.[30]

A professor of public health at the University of Melbourne, on the other hand, argued that 'advocating for the tobacco industry was indefensible':

> I can't think of why people would want to work for an organisation whose products kill half of the people who use them, particularly if you have alternative forms of employment. It certainly does seem odd that you would have someone so intimately involved in doing good for a hospital which is trying to cure people from tobacco-related disease, working for the industry that directly causes so many people to be in that hospital.[31]

In other notable cases, a top criminal law barrister, the son of Holocaust survivors and a prominent member of Melbourne's Jewish community, received media attention when he was asked to represent an alleged Nazi war criminal facing extradition proceedings.[32] Another successful QC was labelled anti-Semitic for having taken on the representation of the same accused. Further afield, in late 2012 a 23-year-old Indian student was raped and bashed by six men on a Delhi bus, before being thrown off and left to die. When she died some days later and the six alleged murderers were charged with her rape and murder, members of the Saket Bar Association refused en masse to represent the defendants and heatedly berated another lawyer in the Court for offering to do so.[33]

These situations raise a range of discussion questions about the proper role and conduct of lawyers.

DISCUSSION QUESTIONS

1. To what extent is it our role as lawyers to act as zealous advocates for any client that comes along? Looking at the tobacco case above, would you be comfortable defending British American Tobacco and sitting on the Cancer Council Board?
2. Can we be overzealous in our work for causes we believe in?
3. Should we advocate for clients and causes that we personally believe to be morally repugnant or socially irresponsible? Return to this question again after you have finished reading this chapter and Chapter 2.

30 Quoted in Jill Stark, 'Peter Mac Denies Tobacco Conflict', *The Sunday Age* (Melbourne, 2 September 2012) 8.

31 Quoted in ibid.

32 Darrin Farrant, 'Leading QC May Defend Kalejs', *The Age* (Melbourne, 23 January 2001) 1; Richard C Paddock, 'Case Tests Australian Protection of Nazi War Criminal', *The Washington Post* (Washington, DC, 21 January 2001) A21. The case study relating this story was in the first edition of *Inside Lawyers' Ethics*. It is now in the online material for the book.

33 Ben Doherty, 'Secret Trial for Delhi Accused', *The Age* (Melbourne, 8 January 2013) 6.

4. Can we trust the legal system to sort out issues of truth and justice and to determine important questions of public policy?
5. To what extent should we consider our duties to society, our relationships with our own families and communities, and our personal, social and political commitments outside of our legal practice in deciding what clients to take on, or how to advise and represent them?
6. Is it appropriate for others, including sometimes the government of the day,[34] to criticise us for the clients and causes we advocate for?

Many of the questions raised by these scenarios are ethical questions. They raise issues like:

- Is it possible to be a good person *and* a good lawyer?
- What interests do we want to spend our life serving as a lawyer?
- How should we relate to clients?
- To what extent should we consider non-legal factors, particularly moral, relational and spiritual ones, in attempting to solve clients' problems?
- What obligations do we, as lawyers, owe to others beyond our clients (for example, opposing parties, colleagues, the public interest, the courts, our families) and the communities (of social interest, faith, ethnic identity, sexuality etc) that we are a part of?

We might find answers to these questions in various ways that do not invoke ethics – our own financial interests, what others expect of us, what we find most convenient or fulfilling, and so on. *Ethics* is concerned with deciding what is the good or right thing to do – the right or wrong action; and with the moral evaluation of our own and others' character and actions – what does it mean to be a good person? In deciding what to do and how to be, ethics requires that we look for coherent reasons for our actions and character – reasons that explain why it is right or wrong to act according to our financial interests, or to do what others expect in certain situations, etc. It asks us to examine the competing interests and principles at stake in each situation and the reasons why one should trump the other, or how they can be reconciled.

In Case study 1.2 it is not enough to say that the QC should not represent tobacco companies because he finds it distasteful to do so, or because he might anger his friends and those with whom he wishes to work on philanthropic purposes or that he might suffer reputational loss in the wider community. The anger of friends and associates or personal distaste are not independent ethical reasons for refusing to do something. Similarly, we cannot simply say that the QC needs to earn a living and therefore should take every paying client. We need to look more deeply to determine whether an ethical principle is at stake. For example, when does the 'cab rank' rule – the rule that barristers

34 See, eg, Michelle James, 'I'm Proud to Be a Lawyer, Premier Campbell Newman', *Brisbane Times* (online, 7 February 2014) <https://www.brisbanetimes.com.au/national/queensland/i-am-proud-to-be-a-lawyer-premier-campbell-newman-20140207-326xl.html>. See also the discussion in Chapter 4 of the prosecution of Bernard Collaery, lawyer for the whistleblower Witness K.

should be available to any client who asks (through a solicitor)[35] – apply? Even if there is no possibility whatsoever that the tobacco company will be unrepresented if the QC does not act for it, should he still say 'no'? Is the possibility of disloyalty to the QC's philanthropic commitments and the undermining of important public health goals more or less important in this situation, for this QC, than the values that might be furthered by representing the client? These would include ensuring that important public policy questions and constitutional issues are fully argued before the High Court so that an authoritative public decision can be made.

We need to consider whether there is any justification for a socially conscious lawyer, or indeed any lawyer, to earn money to feed themselves and their family by working for a firm whose products have killed millions of people and may be more likely to kill more people if the lawyer's arguments succeed. Does the need to earn money override the commitment to a charity researching a 'cure' for cancer? Is a lawyerly commitment to assisting the High Court to decide important cases more important than a personal commitment as a philanthropist and humanist? What about a personal commitment to earning money or arguing challenging cases? Are these good reasons for choosing certain cases over others? Is it appropriate to take on cases such as these that might pit lawyerly identity against personal identity, and do so in a way that influences the client or the court towards what the lawyer personally believes to be a better way of doing things?

Most of us have our own ideas about the right thing to do or what good character is. Our personal ideas about values and ethics are likely to have come from our family upbringing, our friends and colleagues, and any political or faith commitments we might have – our *personal ethics*. There are also more public or shared expectations that go along with our various roles. For example, the community has ideas about what it means to be a good friend, a good parent, a good citizen or a good doctor. Why not what it means to be a good lawyer? Some of these public ideas about ethics go formally unstated. Other ethical norms are codified in legal rules and regulations. Sometimes our personal ideas about ethics (for example, on issues like euthanasia or recreational drug use) can come into conflict with community ethical norms and/or legal rules, to the point where much can appear to be relative and little is settled.[36] Good ethical reasoning demands that none of these assumptions about the right thing to do or the right way to be should go unexamined.

For lawyers, apart from our own personal ethics, there are two potential sources of ethical expectations that might affect the way we do, or *should*, behave: professional conduct principles and general morality.

35 Legal Services Council, *Legal Profession Uniform Conduct (Barristers) Rules 2015* (at 4 March 2022) r 17. These rules apply in substance (numbering might be different) around the country – see generally Chapter 3 for the relevant provisions. Note that the 'cab rank' rule requires a barrister to accept a brief in certain circumstances, where they are not obliged or permitted to refuse the brief under r 101, 103, 104 or 105. This is an instance where, regardless of a personal understanding of general morality or an identifiable preferred lawyer type, compliance with the rules is simply required: see generally at r 4(f).

36 See, eg, Alasdair MacIntyre, *After Virtue: A Study in Moral Theory* (University of Notre Dame Press, 3rd ed, 2007).

Professional conduct

Professional conduct is the law of lawyering – the published rules and regulations and the disciplinary decisions that apply to lawyers and the legal profession. In Australia the rules and regulations can be found in the legal profession statutes in each State, in the various professional conduct and practice rules and in the way the general law (particularly contract, tort and equity) applies to lawyers and their relationships with clients. In this book, when it is necessary to refer to the statutory rules governing Australian lawyers we will generally cite the *Legal Profession Uniform Law Application Act 2014* (Vic) sch 1, as amended ('*Legal Profession Uniform Law*' or '*Uniform Law*') and the *Legal Profession Uniform Law Australian Solicitors' Conduct Rules 2015*, as amended in 2022 ('*Australian Solicitors' Conduct Rules*' or '*ASCR*').[37] Both the *Uniform Law* and the *ASCR* apply in New South Wales, Victoria and Western Australia[38] but are closely emulated in other jurisdictions and are likely over the long term to be followed in those other jurisdictions, because these three States cover the majority of practising lawyers.[39]

Much teaching and practical discussion of lawyers' 'ethics' in the legal profession is dominated by legalism. Legalism treats legal ethics as a branch of law – 'professional responsibility' or 'professional conduct' law. The professional conduct approach caters to the need for certainty, predictability and enforceability in a context where people often consider ethics to be subjective and relative. The law of lawyering is significant as one way in which lawyers' ethics are institutionally enforced or regulated, and can certainly be helpful in guiding behaviour. We refer to and visually highlight in this book the rules of conduct as being one of the sources of information that lawyers can and should use to make ethical judgements about what is the right thing to do in different situations, but as mentioned previously, these rules do not provide a complete basis for considering what values should motivate a lawyer's behaviour and choices about what kind of lawyer to be.

This is not to say that it is not important for society to have and enforce a law of lawyering. However, lawyers must also have an ethical perspective on being a lawyer in order to judge what rules should be made (on a professional level) and also to decide (on a personal level) what the rules mean, how to obey them, what to do when there are gaps or conflicts in the rules and whether, in some circumstances, it may even be necessary to consciously disobey a particular rule for ethical reasons. This book, therefore, focuses on the ethical underpinnings of professional conduct rules and principles.[40]

37 New South Wales and Western Australia have adopted the provisions of the Victorian Act. Throughout the text we also refer to the current provisions of States and Territories not governed by the *Uniform Law* and note particular differences. Similar versions of the *ASCR* have been adopted across the country with the exception of the Northern Territory.

38 The *Legal Profession Uniform Law Application Act 2014* (NSW) s 4 applies the *Uniform Law* as a law of New South Wales. The *Legal Profession Uniform Law Application Act 2022* (WA) s 6 applies the *Uniform Law* as a law of Western Australia.

39 Urbis (n 12). According to Urbis there are now 83,643 solicitors nationally.

40 Other books already provide strong coverage of the law of lawyering, particularly GE Dal Pont, *Lawyers' Professional Responsibility* (Lawbook, 7th ed, 2020).

General morality

The second source of ethics for lawyers (apart from their own personal ethics) is general philosophical theories of *social ethics* or general morality. Social ethics come from general moral theory or ethical theory – philosophical work devoted to understanding what it means for something to be good or right or a duty.[41] Particularly relevant for lawyers are general moral ideas about justice, social and environmental responsibility, minimising harm and respecting others.

Some commentators on lawyers' ethics go to the opposite extreme from legalism, and propose that general and abstract moral theories or methodologies should be applied, without elaboration or modification, to the practice of law. These fundamental moral theories generally divide into 'deontological' or rule-based theories, on the one hand, and 'teleological' or consequentialist (sometimes known as utilitarian) theories, on the other. In what follows, deontological ethics and utilitarian ethics have been used, respectively, as the main examples of these two approaches. Other theories that have enjoyed significant attention include virtue ethics and ethics of care.

The most famous philosophical formulation of deontological ethics is Immanuel Kant's 'categorical imperative': 'Act only according to that maxim whereby you can, at the same time, will that it should become a universal law.'[42] This is similar to the Golden Rule in the Judaeo-Christian tradition and other religious traditions, which requires people to always treat others as they would want to be treated themselves.[43] Religious formulations of ethics based on divine command are generally deontological because they set absolute rules that tend to emphasise the idea of *fairness* as important to deciding individuals' rights and entitlements. According to Kant, 'right' actions or policies are those that primarily respect individual autonomy by promoting fairness. Kantian methods refute the notion that 'the end justifies the means'. Hence it is a 'categorical imperative' – an absolute and unconditional requirement – that people never be treated merely as means to an end, but always as ends in themselves. Kantian theory argues that the means, since they often involve what happens to individuals, are at least as ethically significant as outcomes.

In a teleological approach, by contrast, right actions or policies are those that maximise good consequences and minimise bad consequences; the (good) ends of an action can justify the means used to obtain those ends, even if they involve otherwise unfair treatment of individuals or organisations. Utilitarianism proposes that ethical actions are those that produce the greatest good (defined as happiness) for the greatest number of those affected by a situation.[44] Jeremy Bentham and John Stuart Mill developed utilitarianism as a way for legislators and public policy makers particularly to decide what laws to make. A famous

41 For a good overview see Noel Preston, *Understanding Ethics* (Federation Press, 4th ed, 2014); Russ Shafer-Landau, *The Fundamentals of Ethics* (Oxford University Press, 4th ed, 2017).

42 Immanuel Kant, *Grounding for the Metaphysics of Morals*, tr James W Ellington (Hackett Publishing, 3rd ed, 1993) 30 [tr of: *Grundlegung zur Metaphysik der Sitten* (first published 1785)].

43 See, eg, *Holy Bible* (King James Version), Matthew 7:12.

44 Bhikhu Parekh (ed), *Bentham's Political Thought* (Routledge, 2017); John Stuart Mill, 'On Liberty' in JM Robson (ed), *Collected Works of John Stuart Mill – Volume XVIII: Essays on Politics and Society* (University of Toronto Press, 1977) 213; John Stuart Mill, 'Utilitarianism' in JM Robson (ed), *Collected Works of John Stuart Mill – Volume X: Essays on Ethics, Religion and Society* (University of Toronto Press, 1969) 203.

contemporary utilitarian ethicist, Peter Singer, argues that animals should be included in the calculation of the greatest good for the greatest number as they can suffer.[45]

Standard deontological and teleological moral theories can be contrasted with both virtue ethics and the ethics of care. The ethics of care focuses attention on people's responsibilities to maintain relationships and communities, and to show caring responsiveness to others in specific situations. It was developed by feminists, particularly Carol Gilligan, in the second half of the 20th century as a correction to the traditional emphasis in deontological and utilitarian ethical theories on individual rights and duties and formal, abstract, universalist reasoning.[46] It has now been developed by theorists well beyond feminism who emphasise the interdependence of humans and the importance of sensitivity and emotional response in ethical action. Deontological and consequential ethics tend to assume that each person decides on their actions individually, in isolation from others, and that the choices they make then impact others. The ethics of care, however, points out that most of the time our actions are so intertwined with our relationships with other people and our emotional responses to them that the most important ethical questions are about how we relate with and respond to others, rather than how our actions impact on them. The ethics of care recognises the importance of modern psychology in understanding the intricacies of human relationships, and would stress that interpersonal skill and sensitivity are crucial tools for ethical decision-making.

Virtue ethics shifts the focus of ethical attention from particular conduct and its impact to the inherent quality or character of the actor. Virtue ethics approaches derive from ancient philosophy and especially Aristotle's emphasis on right character as a personal virtue. A virtue ethics approach is not necessarily inconsistent with deontological, consequentialist and ethics of care approaches, but rather asks a different and more difficult question.

Virtue ethics asks: What kind of person should I be in order to be a good person? The other theories by contrast ask: What is a good action? A central virtue for Aristotle was therefore 'phronesis' – practical wisdom, or the ability to choose wisely. It sits alongside 'sophia' – theoretical wisdom – and other virtues such as courage, generosity, gentleness, honesty about oneself, justice and fairness, magnanimity and fortitude. Like the ethics of care, virtue ethics sees how one relates to others as being central to ethics, but looks beyond this and asks us to consider our identity, character and motivations at a profoundly personal level.[47] Virtue ethicists assert that intentional, ethically defensible behaviour is more likely to emerge from the ongoing process of genuine personal reflection about our virtues (and our lack of some of them) than if we attempt to act without regard to our inner virtues (values).

General moral theories are in their nature abstract. It can be difficult to apply them to concrete situations. But making an effort to analyse what to do according to general morality usually sharpens our reasons behind our final decision, subject to the following preliminary point. Applying general moral theories to legal practice begs one of the main questions debated in lawyers' ethics, which is: To what extent should lawyers' ethics be determined by the idea that lawyers should play a special and unique role in society? Or to what extent should lawyers be held to the same general ethical standards as anyone else? These two

45 Peter Singer, *Animal Liberation* (Harper Collins, updated ed, 2009).

46 Carol Gilligan, *In a Different Voice: Psychological Theory and Women's Development* (Harvard University Press, 1982).

47 See Justin Oakley and Dean Cocking, *Virtue Ethics and Professional Roles* (Cambridge University Press, 2001). See also Robert Eli Rosen, 'Ethical Soap: *LA Law* and the Privileging of Character' (1989) 43 *University of Miami Law Review* 1229.

questions sum up the central 'meta-ethical' dilemma for lawyers. Do we owe our primary allegiance to our clients or to society? Which approach ought to take priority? We need to decide this initial question in each case, before attempting further analysis. Case study 1.3 asks you to consider how general moral principles apply to a situation when you are 'just' a concerned sibling and then when you are a lawyer.

CASE STUDY 1.3 UNDERSTANDING DIFFERENT ETHICAL APPROACHES IN PRACTICE

You are very close to your older sister, Lee, who, like you, is a university student. You have always felt able to discuss your secrets with each other without other friends or family members finding out.

For the last few years Lee has been indulging regularly in alcohol binges and certain illegal drugs. This does not appear to be seriously affecting her study or part-time work yet, but she has exhibited increasingly erratic behaviour in the last few months. Last week Lee was found lying in the middle of the road after a party and there have been a number of times in recent months when friends had to make sure she got home safely before doing something that might harm herself or others.

Lee tells you that she is probably indulging 'a bit too much' but is planning to 'pull back' and has the situation 'under control'. Lee says she does not need your concern or help, and demands that whatever happens, you do not let other members of your family know anything about the situation until she is 'out the other side'. You feel that Lee may need professional help to find her way 'out the other side'.

DISCUSSION QUESTIONS

1. Role-play (or imagine) how a conversation between yourself and Lee, after the lying in the middle of the road incident, might play out. What approach might you take to trying to get help for Lee? Should you talk to other friends or family members if you feel that Lee is not going to be able to get through to 'the other side' on her own? How would Lee view the different approaches you might take?
2. What arguments might each of you use to support or explain your preferred approach? Can you identify how the different potential approaches draw on deontological, utilitarian, care or virtue-based ethical arguments? Can you identify to yourself which of these approaches are most attractive to you, and why?
3. Now imagine that rather than Lee being your older sibling, you are a criminal defence lawyer and Lee is not a friend or relation but another lawyer who is your *client*. Lee has been charged in relation to the incident where she lay down in the middle of the road, but you believe you can probably persuade the police to drop the charges. Lee insists that you do everything you can to get the police to drop the charges and completely hush up the whole situation. As before, Lee insists that she has her substance use under control and needs no help or intervention.

Once again, role-play the conversation between yourself and Lee. Does your role as lawyer for Lee (and not just as a layperson) mean that you are bound by a relevant professional conduct rule more than general morality, and therefore make you think differently about your ethical obligations in this situation? As we saw in Case study 1.1 in relation to the mentally unwell lawyer, Lee's level of insight into her situation is crucial. How would you begin the conversation with her about her behaviour in such a way as to engage rather than repel her? How do the arguments and considerations change when you are Lee's lawyer rather than her sibling? What about the fact that Lee is a lawyer? Does this make things different? How?

4. What if, rather than being Lee's lawyer or sibling, you were Lee's general practitioner, rabbi, pastor, priest, imam or meditation teacher, or a friend who also happens to be a psychologist specialising in drug abuse problems? Do these different roles that you play in society change your conception of your ethical obligations in the situation?

As Case studies 1.2 and 1.3 illustrate, thinking about the ethical standards and principles that should apply in legal practice raises many questions. We can group these into four main questions, which we outline here and will discuss in more depth throughout the text in relation to different practice contexts.

1. **To what extent should lawyers' ethics be determined by a special and particular social role that lawyers should play?**

   As mentioned above, this is a central issue of 'meta ethics'. Should our conduct be prescribed solely by the role of zealous (and often adversarial) advocate for clients' interests in a complex and adversarial legal system? Or is there some alternative role that prescribes how we should behave as lawyers – perhaps as an officer of the court or as a trustee of the legal system with a special responsibility for ensuring compliance? Or should we, in our professional lives, be held to the same general moral standard as anyone else? Is the good lawyer good enough if they adhere to the *ASCR*, or is there a higher goodness to which they need to be aspiring?

2. **How should lawyers and clients relate to one another in relation to ethical issues?**

   Should we consider the justice or morality of our clients' causes in choosing whether and how to represent them? Should ethical considerations – such as our assessment of the public interest; our personal moral, social or religious beliefs (or those of our clients); and the impact of various options on our clients' relationships or psyches or on the opponent – be explicitly discussed in legal advice and counselling? Should either our or our clients' views of morality prevail over the other's in deciding what to do? When there is disagreement over ethical issues, when can or should we act, refuse to act or cease to act?

3. **What are lawyers' obligations towards law and justice?**

   Is it justifiable to help our clients test the limits of the law, provided we can argue that we, and they, are not breaching the letter of the law? Or should we preserve the spirit and integrity of the law against client interests? For example, is the effort that specialist tax minimisation lawyers put into the creation and maintenance of opaque shelf companies in overseas tax havens preserving the spirit and integrity of the tax system? How would such lawyers define the virtue of integrity in their work? Should we work to reform the law and legal institutions to improve their substantive social justice – for example, by actively seeking out test cases or lobbying politically for legislative reform? How much should we need to find out about a client's honesty, guilt or innocence before advocating for them? Are there any circumstances in which we could be considered ethically justified in resisting or breaking the law or helping our clients to do so?

4. **To what extent should lawyers in their daily work make sure they care for people and relationships, including themselves?**

   Is not the care of one human for another and for themselves the central ethical imperative? Should we pursue the moral goodness and/or best interests of our clients in the context of their relationships despite what the law says, perhaps despite even the broader dictates of social justice? How should we determine what is in the best interests of clients – is it material and financial, is it power and prestige, or is it psychological, relational or spiritual? What about our own selves? Should we work long hours in the law even if it means neglecting ourselves, our family and our relationships? Will we wish on our deathbeds that we had spent more time at the office? Or are there alternative ways of practising law and preserving our own psyche?

We return to these questions throughout the book, but first it is important to ground our ethical deliberations by way of a practical and applied approach to ethical decision-making.

An applied ethics approach

Our approach in this book accepts that lawyers must first know where they fit in relation to the social theories of ethics discussed above, but asserts that more is needed, because lawyers must operate as everyday 'judges' inside fairly well-defined roles, as a part of the justice system. Our aim is to enable lawyers and law students to critique and evaluate professional conduct and lawyers' behaviour in practice by applying their own personal ethics (described above) to the professional conduct rules and social considerations. We do this in recognition that the conduct rules will often be inadequate for their purpose, even though they are or ought to be grounded in general moral notions of fairness (Kantianism) and balance (consequentialism). Our focus will be on using real-life case studies to help enliven an ethical evaluation process that involves awareness of the ethical issues likely to arise for lawyers in practice, the standards and values available to resolve those issues, and consideration of how we might implement our ethical decision-making.

In the next chapter we introduce four main ethical approaches, derived from the theories mentioned above, that can provide further help for lawyers when making ethical decisions. Each approach draws its legitimacy from different and sometimes overlapping traditions of general morality, as indicated in Figure 1.1.

Figure 1.1 Relationships between lawyers' ethical types and underlying moral frameworks[48]

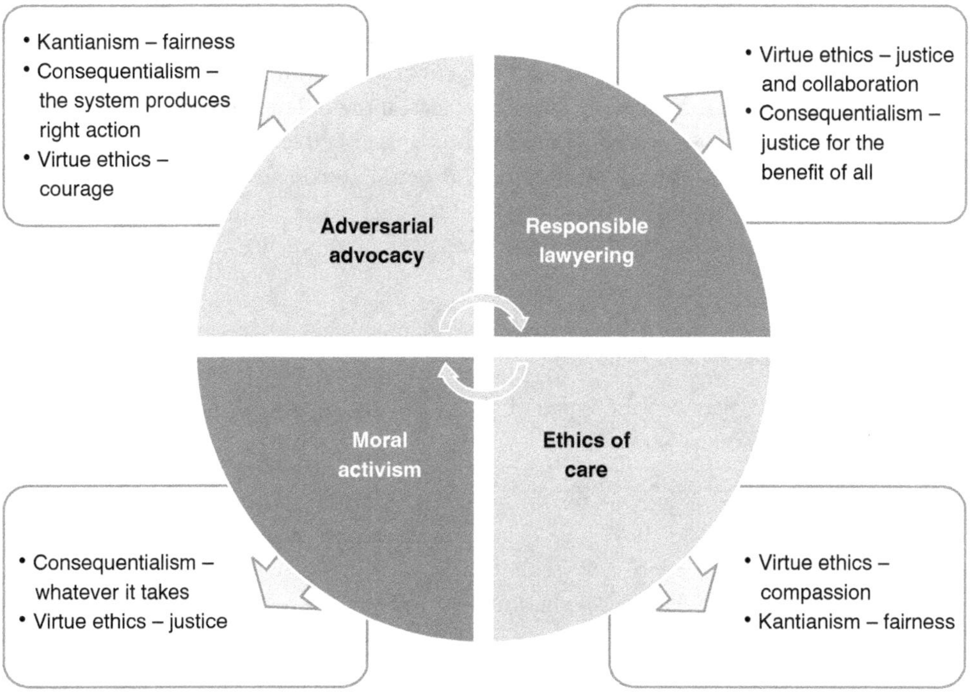

In Chapters 3–10 we examine a number of substantial topics in lawyers' ethics through case studies and analyse the professional conduct principles and ethical approaches that might apply. In each chapter we will introduce some of the major ethical issues facing lawyers in relation to the chapter's topic and set out the conventional ('current') values that are commonly applied to resolving those issues. We will then compare current approaches with alternatives derived from our four ethical approaches ('alternative values'), as understood in the light of general morality. We give readers a chance to work through the current and alternative approaches that might apply to the topic by means of specific case studies (usually based on real cases) and questions designed to clarify and challenge the reader's own stance on each area. Our aim is to make explicit the sort of values awareness and decision-making processes we go through (or ought to go through) in order to make decisions about what is the right thing to do or the right sort of person to be in legal practice.

In real life, ethical issues often arise in complex and ambiguous circumstances. They cannot be resolved by a rote application of a mechanical process applying abstract principles. Ethical behaviour is a matter of skill and character, of practical wisdom, or 'virtue', that is consciously developed over time. It involves ethical *action*, to which we now turn.

48 Adapted with permission from Adrian Evans, *The Good Lawyer* (Cambridge University Press, 2014) 104.

Ethical decision-making and ethical action

In order for ethical considerations to make a real difference to lawyers' behaviour, it is helpful to think about the components of decision-making involved in applying ethical considerations to real-life situations. It has been suggested that in any practical endeavour, ethically responsible decision-making requires at least three different components. It is very well for theorists to propose certain theories or principles of ethics to guide people's actions (the second step below). But in practice ethical decision-making also requires us to be aware that an ethical dilemma or choice exists in the first place (the first step), and to have the creativity, skills and will to put our ethical principles into practice (the third step). Thus, we must

1. be aware of the ethical issues that arise in practice, and of our own values and predispositions;
2. make a choice between the range of standards and values that are available to help resolve those ethical issues; and
3. implement that resolution in practice.[49]

Keep in mind that, while the above 'model' of ethical decision-making gives the impression that the decision-making process is sequential and 'logical', in reality the components may overlap or occur simultaneously. In addition, research in behavioural ethics indicates that ethical decision-making is not simply a conscious, cognitive process. Our decisions are influenced by a range of non-conscious processes, such as heuristics and biases and situational pressures (for example, our overconfidence bias, peer pressure, time pressures). Nonetheless, the model is useful because it focuses our attention on different aspects of ethical decision-making.

The substantive content of this book (of necessity) focuses on and critically examines the second component of the model – the standards and values that should apply to different ethical issues that arise in practice. But learning to reason ethically also involves practising the identification of ethical issues in the first place and creating practical resolutions to ethical dilemmas that respect ethical values (the first and third components). That is one of the reasons that we have included a number of scenarios throughout this book. These case studies are designed to help us learn to become aware of ethical issues, to reflect and decide on what ethical standards and values should apply to those issues, and to consider how we might put those resolutions into practice. We will often learn more about these aspects of ethical reasoning if we can discuss case studies with other people with different knowledge, values and experiences from our own.

The three components of ethical decision-making in the above model are explained in further detail below, and illustrated with a case study. While the case study raises a fairly straightforward ethical issue, it is an opportunity to try out the proposed model of ethical decision-making, and it draws attention to the challenge of implementation.

49 Based on Kenneth E Goodpaster, 'The Concept of Corporate Responsibility' (1983) 2(1) *Journal of Business Ethics* 1, 7–9. These three steps combine the third and fourth steps (moral inclination and moral implementation) in James Rest's foundational model described in James R Rest, 'A Psychologist Looks at the Teaching of Ethics' (1982) 12(1) *The Hastings Center Report* 29.

We also encourage readers to investigate the insights of behavioural ethics into the many non-rational influences on our ethical decision-making,[50] discussed briefly below.

CASE STUDY 1.4 **THE UNWITNESSED AFFIDAVIT**[51]

You are a second-year solicitor at a medium-sized commercial firm. The partner to whom you report (Janice Spencer) is required to travel overseas on urgent business and asks you to 'look after' an important file concerning a contractual dispute. The client is a small business (a company) in financial hardship. Spencer has indicated that she thinks the client has a very good case. Counsel has been briefed and the matter is currently listed for an interlocutory hearing.

Counsel contacts you in the afternoon before the interlocutory hearing to tell you that one of the affidavits prepared by Janice Spencer (which is on your firm's file; he has a copy) needs to be filed at court today. You find the affidavit – it has been signed by the client but not witnessed by anyone. You ring counsel to tell him. He tells you to 'witness' it and file it at court before 5 pm.

Step one: Awareness of ethical issues

What ethical issues arise in this situation?

- What principles or values are at stake in this scenario?
- Who are the stakeholders? That is, whose interests are affected?
- What interests or values are at stake in this situation from the perspective of each of these stakeholders?
- Are there any conflicts between the interests or values of the different stakeholders?
- What are your own interests and values (as the lawyer) in this scenario?

Step two: Application of ethical standards or principles

- What professional conduct principles (the law of lawyering) might apply to this situation, including any relevant professional code of ethics?
- What general ethical principles might apply to this scenario (for example, justice and the public interest, conflicts of interest, respect for the spirit of the law, non-harm and respect for others)?
- What are the particular responsibilities of a lawyer in this scenario, because of their role as a lawyer and officer of the court?
- If there are conflicts between these various ethical standards and principles that could apply to the situation, how should they be resolved?

50 See, eg, Jennifer K Robbennolt, 'Behavioral Ethics Meets Legal Ethics' (2015) 11 *Annual Review of Law and Social Science* 75; Milton C Regan and Nancy L Sachs, 'Ain't Misbehaving: Ethical Pitfalls and Rest's Model of Moral Judgment' (2017) 51(1) *New England Law Review* 53.

51 The case study is based on experiences reported by lawyers to one of the authors.

Step three: Moral imagination and practical implementation

How might the 'right thing to do' be put into action in the current situation? *Doing* the 'right thing' can be the most difficult step. This is especially so if there are situational pressures (such as being at the bottom of a hierarchy) working against ethical action. Milton C Regan and Nancy Sachs remind us that we tend to overestimate the impact of our character and reasoning on our behavior – and underestimate the impact of situational influences. Because of this overconfidence bias,[52] we are very poor at predicting our future ethical behavior and consistently overestimate how ethically we will behave.[53]

Mary Gentile's Giving Voice to Values ('GVV')[54] approach addresses this implementation challenge. GVV suggests that, when we have decided what the right thing to do is, we *assume* that we will do it (which removes any internal 'will I / won't I' debate before we explore possibilities) and consider:

- (As above) What is at stake for the key parties/stakeholders (including ourselves);
- What arguments or rationalisations will be used to dissuade us from acting on our values; and
- What strategies we can use to counter these rationalisations, keeping in mind what has facilitated us acting on our values in the past.

Another important aspect of the GVV approach is to prepare for and *practise* our strategy for acting on our values (we can draw on the diplomacy, communication, negotiation and persuasion skills we use in other areas of life). If we have a plan in our heads for what we can say in response to others' arguments, we are more likely to feel empowered and speak up.[55] Practice a GVV approach by considering the following questions in relation to Case study 1.4.[56]

DISCUSSION QUESTIONS

1. What rules or principles of professional conduct apply here?
2. What practical alternatives (to 'witnessing' the affidavit) are available? What are likely to be the consequences of different alternatives?
3. Do I feel disinclined to act, and, if so, how might I reframe the issue so that I feel more likely to act, keeping in mind my own values and the kinds of things that have motivated me to act ethically in the past?

52 'The overconfidence bias is the tendency people have to be more confident in their own abilities, such as driving, teaching, or spelling, than is objectively reasonable. This overconfidence also involves matters of character. Generally, people believe that they are more ethical than their competitors, co-workers, and peers': 'Overconfidence Bias', *Ethics Unwrapped – UTexas* (Web Page) <https://ethicsunwrapped.utexas.edu/glossary/overconfidence-bias>.

53 Regan and Sachs (n 50) 73.

54 Mary Gentile, *Giving Voice to Values: How to Speak Your Mind When You Know What's Right* (Yale University Press, 2010); 'Giving Voice to Values', *University of Virginia – Darden School of Business* (Web Page) <https://www.darden.virginia.edu/ibis/initiatives/gvv>.

55 See further Vivien Holmes, '"Giving Voice to Values": Enhancing Students' Capacity to Cope with Ethical Challenges in Legal Practice' (2015) 18(2) *Legal Ethics* 115; Carolyn Plump, *Giving Voice to Values in the Legal Profession: Effective Advocacy with Integrity* (Routledge, 2018).

56 Holmes (n 55) 130.

4. What personal and systemic or organisational resources could I access in order to do the right thing (for example, collegial support, an ethics policy, character, will)?
5. What might happen if I do not speak up in this situation and simply comply with counsel's request? How this might affect me and the other stakeholders?
6. What are the possible rationalisations/motivations of counsel in asking me to act unethically?
7. What are the most powerful and persuasive responses to those rationalisations?
8. What skills would I need to put it into practice (for example, negotiation and communication skills, the exercise of moral courage)?
9. To whom will I 'speak', and when? (Plan what you will say, including how you will respond to any objections from the other party to the conversation. Then practise the conversation, inviting feedback from a fellow student.)

While the ethical issues in Case study 1.4 may seem clear, there are many disciplinary cases involving lawyers who bowed to pressure to falsely 'witness' or certify documents.[57] Developing the 'moral muscle' to withstand similar pressures is important.

Conclusion

This chapter introduced the main themes of the book. After an overview of the topics addressed in later chapters and discussion of several global issues affecting legal practice, we considered how ethical standards and principles (from both professional conduct codes and general morality) provide a basis for deciding what values and interests should prevail in different circumstances. Case studies 1.2 and 1.3 raised questions about the proper role of lawyers, which will be explored in more detail in the following chapters, as we consider four different approaches to legal ethics that seek to answer the 'role' question in different ways and with different priorities. Case study 1.4 introduced the challenge of how to act on ethical decisions.

The invitation of this book is to look systematically *behind* the rules and the case law applying to professional conduct. Behind them are deeply held personal differences of approach, the knowledge of which will enrich legal practice and help to make it both more satisfying and less vulnerable to public criticism.

RECOMMENDED FURTHER READING

Adrian Evans and Josephine Palermo, 'Australian Law Students' Perceptions of Their Values: Interim Results in the First Year – 2001 – of a Three-Year Empirical Assessment' (2002) 5 *Legal Ethics* 103

Vivien Holmes, "'Giving Voice to Values'': Enhancing Students' Capacity to Cope with Ethical Challenges in Legal Practice' (2015) 18(2) *Legal Ethics* 115

57 Gino Dal Pont, 'Under Pressure to Falsely Certify' (2021) 95(12) *Law Institute Journal* 57.

Vivien Holmes et al, "Sexual Harassment: Is Strengthening Ethical Culture the Answer?' (2021) 95(10) *Law Institute Journal* 20

Pooja Parma, 'Reconciliation and Ethical Lawyering: Some Thoughts on Cultural Competence' (2019) 97(3) *Canadian Bar Review* 526

Carolyn Plump, *Giving Voice to Values in the Legal Profession: Effective Advocacy with Integrity* (Routledge, 2018)

Noel Preston, *Understanding Ethics* (Federation Press, 4th ed, 2014)

Milton C Regan and Nancy L Sachs, 'Ain't Misbehaving: Ethical Pitfalls and Rests's Model of Moral Judgment' (2017) 51(1) *New England Law Review* 53

Jennifer K Robbennolt, 'Behavioral Ethics Meets Legal Ethics' (2015) 11 *Annual Review of Law and Social Science* 75

Stephen Tang, Vivien Holmes and Tony Foley, 'Ethical Climate, Job Satisfaction and Wellbeing: Observations from an Empirical Study of New Australian Lawyers' (2020) 33(4) *Georgetown Journal of Legal Ethics* 1035

2

APPROACHES TO ETHICAL LAWYERING

Introduction

Lawyering in the 21st century is a complex mix of skills, knowledge, experience and ethics. While all these are obviously important for successful practice, it is the ethical zone that ultimately defines reputable lawyers and separates them from those who are merely successful in financial terms. Reputation is an elusive concept and hard to analyse in a short introduction. But one vital element of reputation is the notion of sound ethical judgement – the capacity of a lawyer to understand and choose wisely between contrasting ethical frameworks before making a difficult decision. In this task it is vital to appreciate that there are several possible approaches to legal ethics. In this chapter we explore those different approaches and explain why it is frequently appropriate to assess all alternatives for their possible impact.

Different approaches to lawyers' ethics

There are four main strands of ethical reasoning or considerations specific to lawyers in the context of Australian legal institutions: *adversarial advocacy*, *responsible lawyering*, *moral activism* and *ethics of care*.[1] These four types are set out in this book as 'ideal types' that emphasise what is distinctive about each approach. (Table 2.1 sets out a summary of the four types.) These four types are reflected in applied ethics scholarship and in the commonsense 'folk practices' of lawyers, and share concepts with more general methods of moral reasoning. Each emphasises a different value (or bundle of values) that lawyers could or should serve in legal practice.

It would be oversimplistic to seek to brand most individual lawyers or applied legal ethics scholars as following one type or another. Just as many of us call unconsciously on more than one moral framework to guide our behaviour, the four different types tend to complement one another and build on an understanding of the moral frameworks introduced in Chapter 1. In order to develop ethical judgement, it is good to consider a scenario or issue from all points of view, and the four types, augmented by general moral analyses, are helpful in doing that. In many situations all four types will lead to agreement on the right thing to do. In some situations the considerations mandated by another type might temper and improve the way in which we might have approached a situation had we applied only one approach. In other situations careful analysis using underlying moral concepts will show that some ethical considerations should carry more weight than others because of the surrounding circumstances.

Importantly, the four specific lawyer types contain no inbuilt reasoning process for use in deciding difficult ethical problems, though they do tend to assist in predicting where a lawyer starts from. To add analytical capacity, we need to understand how general morality helps. One objective of this chapter is to set out the justifications for the four

1 For a similar typology of three possible underlying values that legal practice should serve, see Charles Sampford and Christine Parker, 'Legal Regulation, Ethical Standard-Setting, and Institutional Design' in Stephen Parker and Charles Sampford (eds), *Legal Ethics and Legal Practice: Contemporary Issues* (Clarendon Press, 1995) 11, 21–4.

different types of ethical approaches so that it is clear what assumptions each makes about the circumstances in which it should apply.

Ultimately, however, each of us will have to make hard choices about values and ethical considerations in difficult situations (like the case studies in this book). It is these choices that give each of us our distinctive ethical character, and it is in knowing and consistently following through on our ethical character that we develop virtue. For most lawyers the ethical choices we make (or want to be able to make) in those 'hard' cases will tend to fall into one or other of the four types set out here (or perhaps some combination of them). In practice, the first and second – the *adversarial advocacy* and *responsible lawyering* types – are the most dominant ethical types cited in public statements about lawyers' ethics. Many lawyers probably unthinkingly follow the dictates of these two types to ethical lawyering, without ever clarifying their own ethical beliefs, or the values that lie beneath them. However we believe that, to practise law successfully over the long term, it is necessary to understand our own values and ethical beliefs, then apply moral reasoning to the highly individual circumstances in which legal practice dilemmas arise and also to consider the same in the context of the *Australian Solicitors' Conduct Rules* ('*ASCR*').

Have a look at Table 2.1. Can you identify an approach (or approaches) and a general moral reasoning that tend to appeal to you most consistently?

Table 2.1 Four lawyer types and their underlying moral methods

Legal ethical type	Social role of lawyers	Relationship to client and law	Underlying moral methods'
Adversarial advocate (The traditional conception)	Lawyers' ethics are governed by role as advocate in adversarial legal process and complex legal system. Partisanship: loyalty and non-accountability for morality of actions as lawyer.	Lawyers' duty is to advocate clients' interests as zealously as possible within the bounds of the law without regard for other impacts or interests. Extends beyond adversary role to ensuring client autonomy in a complex legal system as required by the rule of law.	Kantianism – fairness Virtue ethics – courage Consequentialism – the system produces right action
Responsible lawyer (Officer of the court and trustee of the legal system)	Lawyers' ethics governed by role of facilitating the public administration of justice according to law in the public interest.	Duties of advocacy are tempered by duty to ensure integrity of and compliance with the spirit of the law; to ensure that issues are not decided on purely procedural or formal grounds but substantive merits. Lawyer is responsible to make law work as fairly and justly as possible. May need to act as gatekeeper of law and advocate of legal system against client.	Virtue ethics – justice and collaboration Consequentialism – justice for the benefit of all

Table 2.1 (cont.)

Legal ethical type	Social role of lawyers	Relationship to client and law	Underlying moral methods*
Moral activist (Agent for justice through law reform, public interest lawyering and client counselling)	General ethics, particularly social and political conceptions of justice, moral philosophy and promotion of substantive justice define lawyers' responsibilities.	Lawyers should take advantage of their position to improve justice in two ways: (1) public interest lawyering and law reform activities to improve access to justice and change the law and legal institutions to make the law more substantively just (in the public interest); (2) client counselling to seek to persuade clients of the moral thing to do, or withdraw if client wants something else.	Consequentialism – whatever it takes Virtue ethics – justice
Ethics of care (Relational lawyering)	Responsibilities to people, communities and relationships should guide lawyers (and clients) as everybody else.	Preserving relationships and avoiding harm are more important than impersonal justice. The value of law, legal institutions and institutional roles of lawyers and others are derivative of relationships. People and relationships are more important than institutions such as law. The goal of the lawyer–client relationship (like all relationships) should be the moral worth and goodness of both lawyer and client, or at least the nurturing of relationships and community.	Virtue ethics – compassion Kantianism – fairness

* A complete explanation of these three underlying methods or approaches can be found in Marcia W Baron, Philip Pettit and Michael Slote, *Three Methods of Ethics: A Debate* (Blackwell, 1997).

All four types set out in Table 2.1 have attractive aspects, and these are brought into sharper relief when considered alongside moral frameworks. The considerations of *adversarial advocacy* and *responsible lawyering* will tend to be the starting point for ethical practice in most ordinary situations. Commonly, the strength of the adversarial advocate is and ought to be tempered by the paramount duty to the court and by the other three types.

The authors of this book believe that ultimately lawyers are responsible for improving the way justice is done between individuals and the world at large. Our aim in this book is not, however, to persuade readers of our personal and particular views of ethics or lawyering trends.

Rather, our aim is to emphasise the importance of, and help improve, the clarity and integrity of current ethical reasoning in lawyering. We recognise that each reader will find a different type (or combination of the types), or one of the underlying moral frameworks, the most attractive and convincing way to organise their own career and practices. We suggest, however, that all lawyers can use the four ideal types and moral frameworks set out here (see Table 2.1) as a self-diagnostic aid in clarifying and critically examining their own ethical preferences as a lawyer, and also in making sure they have explored all the facts of any situation they might face as a lawyer, considered all the relevant ethical considerations, and responded appropriately.[2] Appendix: Part I contains a self-assessment tool or scale to allow individual lawyers to determine the relative importance of each ethical type for their own decision-making.

The remainder of this chapter describes each of the four approaches to legal ethics and their connections to underlying morality. At the end of this chapter we set out several case studies that could form the basis for application of the four ethical types and three general moral methods, and for reflection and discussion with others.

Adversarial advocacy: the traditional conception of legal ethics

Adversarial advocacy is the predominant conception of what lawyers' role and ethics ought to be in most common law countries including Australia. It is also the simplest, most clear-cut of the four approaches. It gives a reasonably clear answer as to what to do in most situations; that is, a lawyer should advance their client's partisan interests with the maximum zeal permitted by law. This approach to legal ethics is often termed an 'amoral' one because it sees general morality – that is, consequentialism, Kantianism and virtue ethics – as being irrelevant to the detail of lawyers' ethics.[3] In fact, adversarial advocacy sees the suppression of one's own individual moral opinions and consideration of general ethical concerns as a moral act in itself. The lawyer must 'turn off' these other ethical considerations in order to fulfil their proper moral role as advocate for their client. The moral basis for lawyers' ethics within adversarial advocacy is found in the social role that lawyers play in the adversarial legal system.

Adversarial advocacy combines the 'principle of partisanship' and the 'principle of non-accountability'.[4] The principle of partisanship means that the lawyer should do all for the client that the client would do for themselves, if the client had the knowledge of the lawyer. This is because the adversarial system is based on party control of the proceedings, with each party ensuring that all legitimate arguments in their own favour are put forward. The principle of non-accountability follows on from this and says that the lawyer is not morally responsible for either the means or the ends of representation, provided both are lawful.

2 As per Preston's 'ethics of response' following H Richard Niebuhr: Noel Preston, *Understanding Ethics* (Federation Press, 2nd ed, 2001) ch 4.

3 Gerald J Postema, 'Moral Responsibility in Professional Ethics' (1980) 55 *New York University Law Review* 63; Richard Wasserstrom, 'Lawyers as Professionals: Some Moral Issues' (1975) 5 *Human Rights* 1.

4 David Luban, *Lawyers and Justice: An Ethical Study* (Princeton University Press, 1988) 7.

Ultimately, the justification for non-accountability depends on accepting that lawfulness is a good enough proxy for justice/morality and on recognising that if the lawyer were morally responsible for their actions on behalf of clients, they may not be willing to act zealously to represent the client's interests.

This approach is most clearly justified in the case of trial lawyers, especially criminal defence advocates who must vigorously assert the rights of the accused against the superior power and resources of the state. By corollary, the adversarial advocate approach is least justifiable if applied to a criminal prosecutor who represents the state against the accused. It is well accepted that prosecutors should act as 'ministers of justice', pay keen attention to fairness and candour and only present to the court those facts and arguments that they believe to be well grounded (see Chapter 5).

Historically, the adversarial advocate approach was essentially liberal, motivating lawyers to pursue client interests primarily against the power of the state. It was dependent on a conception of the rule of law that puts the courts between citizens and governments, and requires lawyers to be independent of the state and available to help those who want to use the law to challenge or defend themselves against the government. However, the approach has extended beyond representing client interests against state interests to representing client interests against other private interests and in any situation where a lawyer is necessary. Since ours is a complex legal system, lawyers must be readily available to empower those who need to use the law to organise their affairs, settle a dispute, defend themselves against the powers of the state or establish a right against some private interest, without pre-judging their clients or being held accountable for what the client chooses to do (provided it is within the bounds of law).

Lord Brougham's 1820 defence of Queen Caroline before the House of Lords is a favourite example of the ideal in action. King George IV was trying to rid himself of his wife, Caroline, by alleging that she had committed adultery, but it was well known that the King himself had been unfaithful. Lord Brougham implied that although he did not yet need to defend the Queen by attacking her husband, if such a defence did become necessary, neither he nor

> even the youngest member in the profession, would hesitate to resort to such a course and fearlessly perform his duty … [A]n advocate, in the discharge of his duty, knows but one person in all the world, and that person is his client. To save that client by all means and expedients, and at all hazards and costs to other persons, and, amongst them, to himself, is his first and only duty; and in performing this duty he must not regard the alarm, the torments, the destruction which he may bring upon others. Separating the duty of a patriot from that of an advocate, he must go on reckless of consequences, though it should be his unhappy fate to involve his country in confusion.[5]

These words were controversial at the time, but the same philosophy can still be found today. In the case of *McCabe v British American Tobacco Australia Services Ltd*,[6] at first instance the Supreme Court of Victoria found that Clayton Utz, the solicitors for the defendant British American Tobacco Australia Services Ltd ('BATAS'), had advised the company on a 'document

5 Quoted in David Mellinkoff, *The Conscience of a Lawyer* (West Publishing, 1973) 188–9.
6 [2002] VSC 73 (Eames J).

retention policy' that intentionally resulted in the destruction of thousands of documents. These documents would have been relevant and favourable to McCabe's negligence case against the company for her terminal cancer. The Court found that the defendant and its legal advisers had misled the plaintiff and the Court about the fact and the extent of BATAS's document destruction. The judge struck out the defendant's defence and ordered judgment for the plaintiff, without a trial, on the basis that the destruction of documents had unfairly prejudiced the plaintiff's chances of success. This decision was later overturned on appeal.[7] But in the meantime, the lawyers for BATAS were severely criticised in the media. The following comments by the then chief partner of Clayton Utz in defence of their position illustrate the traditional, adversarial conception of the responsibility and role of the lawyer well:

> [He said:] 'The clients are entitled obviously to avail themselves of the full protection of the law and the lawyers are there to advance their clients' interests subject to the constraints of their professional duties and, in particular, their duties to the court. But if they operate within those constraints then they are acting appropriately'. He said a lawyer might advise on the 'appropriateness' of different strategies, but it was wrong for a lawyer to make moral judgments. 'We don't take a moral stance and it's not up to us, as advocates for a client, to take a moral stance. Ultimately that comes to a decision by the client, not the lawyer.' ... [He continued:] 'We operate for a range of clients and make decisions based on a business assessment. What we aspire to ensures that we act with integrity at all times, but I don't think that involves bringing moral judgment to who we act for and who we don't act for.'[8]

In the case of barristers, the adversarial advocate approach is taken as far as the 'cab rank' rule, which requires that a barrister take on and vigorously defend a brief in any area in which they practise, if they are available and the client can pay. While solicitors do not have such an onerous duty to take on clients, once they do have a client they, like barristers, owe duties of loyalty to take instructions from the client, to pursue their client's case vigorously, and to keep them fully informed. Indeed, most of the rules of law and ethics governing lawyers that are taught in legal ethics and professional responsibility courses relate to the lawyer's duty to the client, including the duties of confidentiality, diligence and fidelity or loyalty. These duties are limited only by the general requirements of the law: a lawyer must represent their client to the full extent of the law.

For some lawyers the explicit nature of the adversarial advocate approach can help them to work for clients who might otherwise miss out on representation because other lawyers find them or their cause distasteful, or because they lack resources to pay for a lawyer. Hence, in Case study 1.2 'The case of the philanthropist QC and the tobacco company' the adversarial advocate approach permits the barrister to take on cases for tobacco companies when asked, and to pursue all arguable claims. According to the adversarial advocate

7 *British American Tobacco Australia Services Ltd v Cowell* (2002) 7 VR 524. For an account of the first-instance judgment, including discussion of some of the ethical issues involved, see Camille Cameron, 'Hired Guns and Smoking Guns: *McCabe v British American Tobacco Australia Ltd*' (2002) 25 *University of New South Wales Law Journal* 768.

8 Margaret Simons, 'Lawyers Not Moral Judges: Clayton Utz Chief', *The Sunday Age* (Melbourne, 4 August 2002) 3.

approach, this should not be seen as reflecting the QC's personal opinions or tarnishing his personal and philanthropic reputation in any way, since he would simply be acting as a representative for whichever client came along. On an adversarial advocate approach, the barrister's personal anti-smoking stance and support for medical research to prevent and cure cancer would be seen as a matter of personal loyalties and values that were irrelevant to his role as a lawyer in advocating without discrimination for any client. It would be his ethical duty to his client to not allow those loyalties to affect the quality of his representation, and there should be no implication that his lawyerly activities representing tobacco companies would affect his anti-cancer activities.

Limitations of adversarial advocacy

Although proponents of the adversarial advocate approach generally state that client advocacy should extend only as far as the law allows, the lawyer's duty to the law is usually left vaguely defined. And there is minimal effort to measure up actions against the considerations of justice. Rather it is assumed that there is enough justice in being faithful to a client's demands, if they are within the law and if the duty to the court is not ignored. Indeed, taken to its logical extreme, the adversarial advocate approach requires lawyers to resolve ambiguity in the law or the duty to the court and their own ethical duties, in favour of the client. One criticism of the adversarial advocate approach is that it prescribes only the barest obligations to the legal framework and is therefore a recipe for sabotage. While the legal system works on the basis that people will generally internalise norms and comply voluntarily, under the adversarial advocate approach, even the version of it practised in Australia, there is admiration for lawyers who find loopholes that allow clients' interests to precede those of less tangible duties to the court:

> [Lawyers] are expected and even encouraged to exploit every loophole in the rules, take advantage of every one of their opponents' tactical mistakes or oversights, and stretch every legal or factual interpretation to favour their clients. The guiding premise of the entire system is that maintaining the integrity of rights-guarding procedures is more important than obtaining convictions or enforcing the substantive law against its violators.[9]

There is little room, within the relationship between an adversarial advocate and their client, for the idea that the law might make legitimate claims on a client, that people might have *responsibilities* as well as rights under the law, that a democratic state might 'have a role as guarantor of freedom where liberty is most at peril from the actions of individuals or private institutions'.[10] As mentioned, individual lawyers and their clients operating under an adversarial advocacy approach do not have to concern themselves directly with justice or the public interest. This is said to be ethically justified because, as long as all the lawyers for all the parties in any action or deal act in the narrow interests of their own client, the legal

9 Robert W Gordon, 'The Independence of Lawyers' (1988) 68(1) *Boston University Law Review* 1, 10.
10 David Weisbrot, *Australian Lawyers* (Longman Cheshire, 1990) 44–5.

system will make sure that the right (that is, just) outcome ensues. Indeed, the adversarial advocate believes that it would be a presumptuous denial of justice by lawyers to refuse on moral grounds to act for a person who is endeavouring to use the legal system for lawful activities. However, the fact that the advocacy ideal prescribes devoted service to clients' ends, whatever they may be, is problematic where the market functions so that the rich can buy up most legal services. For example, while our criminal defence system is supported by legal aid, many of the best criminal lawyers will not work consistently for the fees offered by legal aid, and legal aid itself is increasingly inaccessible because of very restrictive means and matter tests. The advocacy ideal is also problematic when it creates a culture in which 'good' advocacy means a culture of excessive adversarialism that raises the costs and length of litigation, making it more and more unaffordable (see Chapter 6).

A number of legal ethics scholars have defended the adversarial advocate idea against these criticisms by modifying it to some extent. Tim Dare argues that the standard conception of lawyers' ethics as requiring adversarial advocacy has been mischaracterised (and perhaps misapplied) as requiring 'hyper-zeal': an all-out approach to win at all costs. In Dare's view, an obligation of 'mere-zeal', rather than hyper-zeal, is morally justified: adversarial advocacy requires a lawyer to zealously pursue a client's *legal* rights and entitlements, but not 'to pursue any advantage attainable for the [client] through the law'.[11]

Alice Woolley reminds us that law itself, including the law of lawyering, reflects social values (that is, morality):

> [T]here is a multiplicity of values relevant to a lawyer's decision about what to do, and about a client's legal position, but those values are the ones contained in the law, not ones that exist outside the law. The lawyer must assess those values through legal analysis, interpretation, and application, not through moral analysis, interpretation, and application.[12]

According to Woolley, if, on analysis, a lawyer's actions on behalf of a client are legal but unjust, it is the law, not the lawyer, who should be subject to critique. Such a lawyer may choose to step outside their role and work for law reform; or in extreme cases they may decide to comply with what they see as their moral, rather than their role, obligations.[13]

The values that Woolley speaks of as 'contained in the law' sometimes explicitly moderate the 'hyper-zeal' of adversarial advocacy. For example, the *ASCR* clearly sets out the hierarchy of a lawyer's duties:

ASCR r 3 Paramount duty to the court and the administration of justice[14]

3.1 A solicitor's duty to the court and the administration of justice is paramount and prevails to the extent of inconsistency with any other duty.

11 Tim Dare, *The Counsel of Rogues? A Defence of the Standard Conception of the Lawyer's Role* (Ashgate, 2009) 7.

12 Alice Woolley, 'Is Positivist Legal Ethics an Oxymoron' (2019) 32(1) *Georgetown Journal of Legal Ethics* 77, 89–90.

13 Ibid 90.

Another example, which we discuss in Chapter 6, is legislation governing civil procedure in some jurisdictions, which now specifically requires lawyer and parties to facilitate the just, quick and cheap resolution of the real issues in the proceedings. This limits the opportunities for adversarially minded lawyers to exploit loopholes and run up costs to wear down the other side. In contrast, we discuss in Chapter 5 an area of practice where the law needs reform to more successfully rein in hyper-zeal: the cross-examination of fragile witnesses, such as victims of sexual assault or family violence.

Another critically important limitation of the adversarial advocate approach is its assumption that lawyers practise in a rule of law context. In other words, they practise in a pluralistic society in which the legislature and courts are democratic institutions that treat citizens fairly and equally: legislatures enact laws that reflect generally accepted values and courts adjudicate disputes. When lawyers work for clients who operate in societies in which these institutional and legal safeguards cannot be assumed, this precondition for adversarial advocacy falls away: a lawyer cannot appeal to role morality to justify acting on a client's instructions simply because those instructions are 'legal', or even 'not illegal'.[15] Consider global lawyers who act for transnational corporations. Such clients wield enormous economic power, often in circumstances in which '[t]here is no one … playing … the role of judge, jury, prosecutor, opposing party, or supervising [a]gency'[16] – that is, there are no institutions of the state impartially administering the rule of law. In such circumstances, as César Arjona argues, lawyers *are* morally responsible for the interests to which they apply their expertise, and for the arrangements they legitimise through such expertise.[17]

There are two main alternative ways of thinking about lawyers' ethics in contrast to the adversarial ideal. The first is to accept that lawyers' ethics should be defined by their particular role in the adversarial legal system and in society but to define that role differently from the traditional adversarial advocate approach, and the second is to abandon role morality for lawyers and argue instead that general ethics should apply to lawyers.[18] We turn to these alternatives now.

Responsible lawyering: officer of the court and trustee of the legal system

The *adversarial advocate* approach focuses on the lawyer's role as representative of the client in the legal system. The *responsible lawyer* approach, by contrast, focuses more on the lawyer's role as an officer of the court and guardian of the legal system, as opposed to

14 We note that the relationship between duty to the court and duty to the client is conceptualised differently in the United States and this strict hierarchy does not apply. See Abbe Smith, 'Defending the Unpopular Down-Under' (2006) 30(2) *Melbourne University Law Review* 495, 502.

15 Vivien Holmes and Simon Rice, 'Our Common Future: The Imperative for Contextual Ethics in a Connected World' in Francesca Bartlett, Reid Mortensen and Kieran Tranter (eds), *Alternative Perspectives on Lawyers and Legal Ethics: Reimagining the Profession* (Routledge, 2011) 56, 70.

16 César S Arjona, 'The Usage of What Country: A Critical Analysis of Legal Ethics in Transnational Legal Practice' (2019) 32(2) *Canadian Journal of Law and Jurisprudence* 259, 280.

17 Ibid 282.

18 See Justin Oakley and Dean Cocking, *Virtue Ethics and Professional Roles* (Cambridge University Press, 2001) 121–36.

their role of agent for the client. The responsible lawyer is still an advocate for the client, but they have an overriding duty to maintain the justice and integrity of the legal system, even against client interests, in the public interest. According to this approach to lawyers' ethics:

> [T]he wellspring of a lawyer's duties to clients and to the public flows from the legal profession's unique role in society as the trustee for the forms of social order. The forms of social order include not only legislative, judicial and administrative forums, but also the process of private ordering through contract, and the negotiation and drafting of the constitutions of private organisations. Thus what the lawyer does in the privacy of the office may be seen as part of the *public* administration of justice because law is made and applied through lawyer counselling and planning, and often this 'private' law has public impacts as great as any ruling of a high court in a litigation matter. To keep *all* the forms of social order working fairly and with integrity is the obligation of the profession, and each lawyer must place that obligation above any particular client interest contrary to it. Loyalty to the fair process of law is primary and constrains lawyer behaviour on behalf of clients.[19]

Unlike the adversarial advocate, who can be seen to be acting out an extreme version of the Kantian's sense of fairness to the individual, the responsible lawyer focuses on maintaining the institutions of law and justice in their best possible form. Some would argue that obedience to the rules of the legal system is important in itself. But the underlying justification for *responsible lawyering*, as with *adversarial advocacy*, is preserving the social goods that the legal system attempts to serve. Such a concern is strongly consequentialist, because it recognises that these social goods – summed up in the rule of law, but including notions of fair trials, access to legal representation, adequate investigative resources and the rejection of corruption – are all contributors to our willingness to cooperate and flourish as human beings.

It is generally beyond contention that lawyers should obey the letter of the law and should not assist clients in breaking it. The rules of professional responsibility – essentially, in Australia, the *ASCR* and the *Barristers' Conduct Rules* – also include rules designed to ensure that lawyers do not abuse the court process on behalf of their clients. But in legal practice there are also many 'grey' areas where lawyers and their clients have choices about how to interpret the law, the rules of professional responsibility, and whether to act in accordance with the purpose of the law or solely in the interests of the client. In choosing how to navigate those grey areas, the responsible lawyer will act in such a way as to contribute to the effectiveness and enforcement of the substantive law. They will not unhesitatingly use loopholes, procedural rules or barely arguable points to frustrate the substance and spirit of the law. Responsible lawyers see the practice of law as a 'public profession' in which lawyers have a mediating function between the client and the law.[20]

19 Alvin Esau, 'What Should We Teach? Three Approaches to Professional Responsibility' in Donald E Buckingham et al (eds), *Legal Ethics in Canada: Theory and Practice* (Harcourt Brace, 1996) 178, 178–9 (emphasis in original).

20 See, eg, Robert W Gordon, 'Corporate Law Practice as a Public Calling' (1990) 49(2) *Maryland Law Review* 255.

They certainly advocate for clients' interests, but they also represent the law to their clients, and help clients comply with the law. Responsible lawyering is often to be found among those lawyers who help plan business strategies for clients in such a way that the clients' affairs are in tune with the overall regulatory environment of the business. These lawyers act as 'go-betweens' and help to keep clients and the state in greater harmony than a purely adversarial lawyer might achieve.

Thus, according to the responsible lawyer approach, it is desirable not only for lawyers to be independent of the state but also to show some autonomy from clients and powerful private interests. Lawyers should not be too dependent on, or too close to, clients. As one legal ethicist has argued:

> If lawyers do not moderate their clients' tendency to extract the maximum advantage from the legal system, we can expect legal outcomes to become increasingly skewed in favour of resourceful parties, thus undermining the legitimacy of legal institutions.[21]

Since the market will always be such that some people will be able to buy more than others, there must be some limits to what they can buy. Responsible lawyers will say no to those who are prepared to use their economic power to compromise the integrity of the justice system. Because the legal system depends on shared ideas about justice, lawyers who exercise ethical judgements that go beyond 'pure' legal advice in order to interpret and apply the law might also provide more prescient and strategic advice about how the law is likely to be enforced and interpreted than lawyers who do not consider the ethical perspective.

For the traditional responsible lawyer, like the adversarial advocate, personal moral beliefs are generally irrelevant. Instead the responsible lawyer will look to the ethics inherent in their role as officer of the court and in the law itself. This classic approach does not see lawyers as responsible for positively pursuing substantive justice according to some external standard (unlike the moral activist approach, below). The responsible lawyer generally looks for justice within the framework of the existing legal system and commonly does not set out to challenge it or highlight its inadequacies. The approach requires that lawyers take those actions that seem likely to promote 'legal justice' – that is, the basic values of the legal system. It sees the lawyer's role as helping clients to pursue justice according to law, no more and no less.[22]

For example, Brad Wendel argues that the ethical significance of lawyering revolves around law's political authority as a way of coordinating compliance with the demands of morality in complex communities. This requires lawyers to maintain 'fidelity to law' as a moral enterprise in and of itself. This ethical approach puts the morality of law at the centre of lawyering, as opposed to both adversarial advocacy, which puts client

21 Robert L Nelson, *Partners with Power: The Social Transformation of the Large Law Firm* (University of California Press, 1988) 234.

22 See William H Simon, *The Practice of Justice: A Theory of Lawyers' Ethics* (Harvard University Press, 1998) 9–11, 138–69 for an excellent account of this type of approach.

autonomy and access to law at the centre of the lawyer's role, and traditional critiques of adversarial advocacy that argue for general accounts of justice and morality to trump the lawyer's role as partisan.[23]

Thus in Case study 1.2 'The case of the philanthropist QC and the tobacco company' the responsible lawyer would have no trouble with representing tobacco companies in putting any fair arguments to the court that might protect their interests. However, the responsible lawyer might pull back from running arguments all the way to the highest court in Australia if they have little prospect of success. The responsible lawyer might also endeavour to avoid the conflict of interest involved in regularly acting for tobacco companies over many years on the one hand while also taking on a public role on the Board of an anti-cancer organisation that is clearly anti-smoking on the other hand.

Responsible lawyering need not require lawyers to self-righteously force rigid interpretations of the law on unwilling clients. It does mean lawyers who creatively combine technical skill, a sense of social and legal responsibility and the vigorous pursuit of clients' interests. This would include corporate lawyers who do not demand 'dumb, literal obedience to every rule but creative forms of compliance that, although aiming to minimise cost and disruption to the company, effectively still realise the regulation's basic purposes'.[24] Over the last few decades many corporate lawyers, especially in-house counsel, in Australia and elsewhere have recognised that this type of stance for advising corporate clients is not only more personally satisfying but also more helpful to their corporate clients than a purely adversarial approach to lawyering.[25] Lawyers of this type engage in the creative task of designing systems for ensuring legal compliance and public legitimacy that add value to corporate products and services, improve business efficiency and enhance corporate image. Consider the way that the in-house counsel at the Australian headquarters of a multinational waste management firm considered his role. Following some issues concerning price-fixing and market-sharing conduct in the waste management industry in the United States, one of his major areas of responsibility became compliance with competition and consumer protection law. This covered issues such as making sure the company's sales people and operatives were not dividing up the market with other firms and not misleading potential customers about their services. He described his role in a way consonant with the responsible lawyer approach:

> You need a fair and just outlook in how a business should be operated … There must be an underlying sense of fairness in your character … that you shouldn't be overly opportunistic, smart and technical. It needs to be in your character to go looking for fair solutions to problems rather than just technical legal ones. A lot of lawyers love

23 W Bradley Wendel, *Lawyers and Fidelity to Law* (Princeton University Press, 2010). See also W Bradley Wendel, 'Pluralism, Polarization, and the Common Good: The Possibility of *Modus Vivendi* Legal Ethics' (2021) 131 *Yale Law Journal Forum* 89.

24 Gordon (n 20) 277.

25 See, eg, Adrian Evans, 'The Climate for Whistleblowing: Climate Deterioration Will Challenge the Courage of Corporate Lawyers' (2017) 27(2) *Australian Corporate Lawyer* 34.

> to be wise guys and to hit people over the head with the technical stuff. But in this work it is not a question of whether something is right or wrong in the [technical] legal sense but of whether it could be perceived right or wrong [in the spirit of the law]. In a competitive industry it is to our detriment in the long run if we are seen as a bunch of wise guys.[26]

The responsible lawyering approach clearly addresses the problem of lawyers helping clients to escape, manipulate or abuse the legal system. It does so out of the concern to approach legal problems collaboratively, in the interests of an overall stability within the justice system. Yet it also puts lawyers in danger of not adequately serving clients' goals and interests. As Katherine Kruse observes, zealous partisanship 'occurs too *infrequently* among lawyers whose clients are unable to pay handsomely for hourly work; and it is received with too much suspicion by even well-heeled clients when they get their billing statements'.[27] Probably for this reason there is no strong tradition in Australian or other common law legal systems that emphasises the responsible lawyering ideal of duty to the justice of law without also emphasising the advocacy ideal of duty to the client.

The *responsible lawyering* and *adversarial advocacy* types are often held in tension with one another in professional conduct rules and widely accepted ideas of legal ethics. This is reflected in the way that debates about ethical issues for lawyers are frequently framed as a question of how to balance the lawyer's duty to the client with the lawyer's duty to the court or, more broadly, to the integrity of the law. Yet the two types are also recognised as complementing one another. Both derive a role for the lawyer from the system for administration of justice and, in a sense, both roles are required by our system of administration of justice. Radically adversarial, 'loophole' lawyering, untempered by the duty to the law and the court (Dare's 'hyper-zeal'), cannot ultimately be justified by the legal system because it is destructive of the legal system, and we do not consider it an ethical approach to lawyering.

Yet neither the adversarial advocacy approach, with its focus on individual client rights, nor the responsible lawyer approach, with its emphasis on preserving the justice of the law, encourages critique of the law[28] in accordance with standards of social justice external to the law. In that sense they are essentially conservative ethical approaches. The two remaining approaches to lawyers' ethics seek to more fully recognise the breadth and plurality of ethically significant factors relevant to the exercise of lawyers' professional, personal and moral judgement in their work. These alternatives thus re-admit general morality to lawyers' decision-making on the basis that it is not appropriate for lawyers to have a special ethics defined by role. Rather, lawyers should abide by ordinary ethics, although the application of

26 Lawyer quoted in Christine Parker, *The Open Corporation: Effective Self-Regulation and Democracy* (Cambridge University Press, 2002) 172. Also on preventive lawyering by in-house corporate lawyers, see Robert W Gordon and William H Simon, 'The Redemption of Professionalism?' in Robert L Nelson, David M Trubek and Rayman L Solomon (eds), *Lawyers' Ideals / Lawyers' Practices: Transformations in the American Legal Profession* (Cornell University Press, 1992) 230, 252–3; Robert Eli Rosen, 'The Inside Counsel Movement, Professional Judgment and Organizational Representation' (1989) 64(3) *Indiana Law Journal* 479.

27 Katherine Kruse, 'Client-Centered Answers to Legal Ethics Questions' (2010) 13(2) *Legal Ethics* 186, 187 (emphasis added).

28 Though see Woolley (n 12).

those ethics to their practice as lawyers may have particular features. Two types of lawyers' ethics that propose different ways in which general ethics should apply to legal practice are the *moral activist* and *ethics of care* types. We discuss moral activism first.

Moral activism: agents for justice with clients and the law

Moral activism requires that mainstream theories of ethics, and of justice in particular, should be applied to legal practice. It focuses on social critique and promoting reform of the law in the public interest. It argues that lawyers should do good according to general theories of ethics – whichever theory (consequentialist, deontological, etc) the individual lawyer finds attractive. Of course, this need not be a formal philosophical theory – it may simply be the lawyer's personal ethics and philosophy of life. In particular, because the legal system is intended to do justice, lawyers should be particularly concerned with doing justice. Thus moral activism encourages lawyers to have their own convictions about what it means to do justice in different circumstances and to seek out ways to act out those convictions as lawyers. They cannot escape moral accountability for their actions by playing the role of adversarial advocate or even responsible lawyer. American legal ethicist David Luban, who coined the term 'moral activism', describes what it is likely to mean in practice in the following way:

> Moral activism … involves law reform – explicitly putting one's *phronesis*, one's savvy, to work for the common weal – and client counselling … And client counselling in turn means discussing with the client the rightness or wrongness of her projects, and the possible impact of those projects on 'the people,' in the same matter-of-fact and (one hopes) un-moralistic manner that one discusses the financial aspects of a representation. It may involve considerable negotiation about what will and won't be done in the course of a representation; it may eventuate in a lawyer's accepting a case only on condition that it takes a certain shape, or threatening to withdraw from a case if a client insists on pursuing a project that the lawyer finds unworthy. Crucially, moral activism envisions the possibility that it is the lawyer rather than the client who will eventually modify her moral stance … But, ultimately, the encounter may result in a parting of ways or even a betrayal by the lawyer of a client's projects, if the lawyer persists in the conviction that they are immoral or unjust.[29]

Unlike the responsible lawyer approach, moral activism is not confined by the idea of justice set out in the legal system – instead it contemplates that the legal system may need to be changed to become more just, and that lawyers may have a responsibility to change it. Moral activists argue that lawyers should use legal practice to change people, institutions and the law to make them conform more to general ideals of social and political justice. It is a tradition of active citizenship by lawyers – to actively improve justice in ways that simply doing their duty for paying clients and the legal system, as per the adversarial advocate and

29 Luban (n 4) 173–4.

responsible lawyer types, leaves untouched. To the extent that the law and legal processes as they stand coincide with the lawyer's ideals of justice, then the moral activist lawyer will behave similarly to the responsible lawyer. But the moral activist lawyer does not see themselves as necessarily confined by a duty to the law where the law is unjust. They see themselves as responsible for doing justice *even if* that involves changing or challenging the law and, from time to time, its practitioners.

A moral activist lawyer will sometimes go further and suffer the consequences of their activism where that involves a necessary disobedience to law, and possible punishment. There is a strong tradition of lawyers' deliberate disobedience to law in the overriding interests of civil and human rights, particularly in the 20th-century examples of Mahatma Gandhi[30] and Nelson Mandela.[31] More commonly, where a moral activist lawyer believes in the justice of a particular client's cause, then they will behave like an adversarial advocate to the extent of exploiting loopholes and testing the limits of the law to establish their client's cause. But a moral activist will not advocate zealously for clients if they believe their cause is not just.

Many of the obvious examples of moral activist lawyers are those from the social democratic left (for example, those lawyers who worked for little or for free to represent Indigenous clients in groundbreaking native title claims or Stolen Generation cases). However, a lawyer could equally be a moral activist for other causes and political beliefs. For example, in the case of the philanthropist QC and the tobacco company, a moral activist lawyer might have a strong belief that it would be wrong to act for a company that makes money out of selling a product that is addictive and fatal to a large proportion of its customers, to help it defeat public health–oriented government policies such as plain packaging laws, and refuse to act. Another moral activist lawyer might take a different view and see the liberty of individuals to choose to use drugs that might harm themselves – and themselves only – as of the essence of a liberal democracy even though the lawyer themselves does not do so for health reasons. A lawyer taking this view might see this as an important test case for the *Australian Constitution* about whether a government can completely prohibit a certain product or not. In such a case, a moral activist approach would suggest that a lawyer should make a choice about which justice principles are most compelling and most important to pursue in the circumstances.

As is evident in the quotation from Luban above, a moral activist approach to legal practice can manifest itself in several ways. First, a moral activist lawyer may try to represent only those clients with 'worthy causes' or those who are often the subject of injustice. Lawyers who choose to do legal aid work for a reduced fee, to pursue a career in the legal aid or community legal centre sectors, or to volunteer their time for poor clients are common examples of moral activism.

Are there causes and cases that lawyers ought to take on because they are important to the wider community? Many lawyers, including those who would identify most strongly with the adversarial advocate or responsible lawyering approach in their own practice, agree with this ideal. It's called *pro bono publico* (from the Latin, 'for the public good') or just pro bono.

30 See, eg, Camille Bergsrud, 'Civil Disobedience', *Gandhi's Struggle for Independence* (Web Page, 6 April 2009) <http://mgandhi.weebly.com/civil-disobedience.html>.

31 Nelson Mandela, *Long Walk to Freedom: The Autobiography of Nelson Mandela* (Little Brown, 1995).

The Australian Pro Bono Centre promotes the idea that all lawyers have an ethical obligation to volunteer their time in a morally positive manner;[32] the Centre's National Pro Bono Target is a 'voluntary and aspirational target of at least 35 hours of pro bono legal services per lawyer per year'.[33] There are many organisations that practise pro bono and deliver access to justice to many client groups. Law students are often closely involved in these programs.[34]

Moral activism might lead lawyers to become involved in more politicised law reform activities and representation of people and causes to create legal and social change. In this type of public interest lawyering, the lawyer is as likely to seek out the client to fit the cause as the client is to seek out the lawyer. In extreme cases the participation of individual clients is almost subordinated to the bigger cause such as a class action (against a corporation in a product liability case) or constitutional challenge (to government actions). There have been many challenges over the last two decades to immoral refugee policies of successive federal governments, but one of the first is the most instructive. Consider the litigation concerning the Australian government's actions in 2001 in preventing 433 asylum seekers on board the Norwegian vessel, MV *Tampa*, from disembarking on Australian soil. Justice Connect, formerly the Public Interest Law Clearing House ('PILCH'), organised a team of private lawyers (a commercial law firm and senior and junior barristers) to act for free in seeking the release and delivery onto Australian soil of the asylum seekers. Because it was impossible to contact the asylum seekers on board the ship, the Victorian Council for Civil Liberties (Liberty Victoria, itself acting through public interest lawyers) became the client. In effect the public interest lawyers themselves defined the cause and the shape of the litigation in the absence of instructions from the asylum seeker clients. The Directors of PILCH commented about the case:

> Striking were the roles of the lawyers, and how they were perceived both within the legal profession and more broadly. 'How much money do you make out of defending these worthless scum?' senior counsel was asked by a member of the public. On another occasion it was '[w]hy don't you and all of your tree-hugging, libertarian, do-gooder, wanker buddies go to Afghanistan and practise your law?' In contrast, his Honour Justice French (one of the judges in the majority in the Full Court [who denied the application]) characterised the lawyers as 'acting according to the highest ideals of the law' and of '[serving] the rule of law and so the whole community' ... The actions of the lawyers were bold. Amongst other things, these were proceedings against the highest echelons of government. They involved a challenge to executive power to ensure the lawful exercise of discretion and concerned conspicuous and controversial government policy. The issues were highly politicised, as the events unfolded in the weeks leading up to a federal election campaign. There is a hunger [amongst lawyers] for public interest work that is interesting, challenging, even confronting and political,

32 The Australian Pro Bono Centre, located in Sydney. See, eg, 'About the Centre', *Australian Pro Bono Centre* (Web Page) <https://www.probonocentre.org.au/about-the-centre/>.

33 'Provide Pro Bono Assistance', *Australian Pro Bono Centre* (Web Page, November 2021) <https://www.probonocentre.org.au/provide-pro-bono/target/>.

34 See, eg, Francina Cantatore, 'Pro Bono in Law Schools: Tracking the Effect of Pro Bono Service in an Australian University Law Clinic' (2020) 27(1) *International Journal of Clinical Legal Education* 101.

> and involves direct contact with 'real' people. There is also a desire to see an outcome or a challenge to the status quo, not just on a micro level for individual clients, but also on a larger scale.[35]

Of course, not every lawyer has the time and opportunity to get involved in public interest cases for justice causes that they really believe in. A second way in which moral activism can manifest itself is in the way that lawyers represent and advise their clients, even those clients who have not necessarily been chosen because they have a just cause. As proposed in the quotation from Luban above, moral activist lawyers seek to argue with and persuade clients to do what the lawyer considers the just thing, always bearing in mind the possibility that the *client* might also persuade the *lawyer* about what justice involves. Luban illustrates this style of law practice by invoking a famous instance of Abraham Lincoln's advice to one of his law practice clients:

> Yes, we can doubtless gain your case for you; we can set a whole neighbourhood at loggerheads; we can distress a widowed mother and her six fatherless children and thereby get you six hundred dollars to which you seem to have a legal claim, but which rightfully belongs, it appears to me, as much to the woman and her children as it does to you. You must remember that some things legally right are not morally right. We shall not take your case, but will give you a little advice for which we will charge you nothing. You seem to be a sprightly energetic man; we would advise you to try your hand at making six hundred dollars in some other way.[36]

Contrast this quotation with Lord Brougham's defence of Queen Caroline, quoted earlier in the chapter.

As its label suggests, moral activism gives lawyers a much more proactive role in ensuring justice than either responsible lawyering or adversarial advocacy. Indeed the justice of our current legal system is at least partially dependent on the fact that there are lawyers (motivated by moral activism) who are willing to work for reduced fees or voluntarily for clients and causes who cannot afford any other lawyer; lawyers who seek out and are committed to public interest causes; lawyers who will fight battles no one else will fight; and lawyers who seek to reform the law, the legal system and their own profession in the interests of justice. Yet moral activism as a total approach to legal practice can also be criticised for neglecting the wisdom of adversarial advocacy – that anyone should be entitled to legal representation and the chance to argue their case in court, without first having to persuade a lawyer that their case is worthwhile. Furthermore, moral activism runs the risk of encouraging lawyers to act without regard to law and procedural fairness when they do find a client they believe in.

Another critique of moral activism is that it perverts the lawyer's role in a pluralist democracy, for at least two reasons. First, the client's interests, which should be the lawyer's paramount concern, are subordinated to the cause (and therefore to the *lawyer's*

35 Samantha Burchell and Emma Hunt, 'From Conservatism to Activism: The Evolution of the Public Interest Law Clearing House in Victoria' (2003) 28(1) *Alternative Law Journal* 8, 11 (citations omitted).

36 Luban (n 4) 174.

interests, setting up a clear conflict of interests). Second, where moral activism seeks to change government policy, lawyers are asking courts to take on the role of government: in a representative democracy, it is the role of policy decision-making bodies to negotiate and mediate between competing interests, while courts 'serve a fundamentally different role: resolving concrete disputes between particular parties'.[37] (Of course, the line between litigating a recognised legal right and litigating for policy change is sometimes a fine one.) In the US context Noah Rosenblum suggests these criticisms can be addressed by courts (1) assessing whether plaintiffs' interests are being genuinely served by their lawyers and (2) considering whether plaintiffs need access to the courts because they are unlikely to receive an appropriate hearing through the ordinary political process (history being very relevant to this inquiry).[38] We note that recent public interest litigation against the Australian government would meet Rosenblum's suggested tests – for example, the class action by welfare recipients seeking compensation for unlawful debts raised by the Commonwealth Government through the Robodebt system;[39] and a class action by teenagers seeking to prevent the Commonwealth Environment Minister from approving a coal mine extension project.[40] In contrast, the tobacco industry's legal challenge to Australia's tobacco plain packaging laws[41] would not meet the test, because the tobacco lobby has historically been well funded and powerful. However, we doubt that Australian courts are likely to adopt such a test.

Moral activist lawyering in practice is sometimes criticised as a demonstration of a lawyer's ego that undermines their commitment to justice. It is for this reason that moral activist lawyers must rightly be challenged to justify their actions independently of any personal gratification or desire for the public notoriety that goes with running a high-profile public interest case. The final approach – the *ethics of care* – puts the focus back on the lawyer's responsibilities to the client and their relationships.

Ethics of care: relational lawyering

The ethics of care, like moral activism, emphasises the integration of personal ethics with legal practice. While moral activism proposes that lawyers should act in a way calculated to best promote social and political justice, the ethics of care, by contrast, is more concerned with personal and relational ethics. The ethics of care focuses on lawyers' responsibilities to

37 Noah A Rosenblum, 'Power-Conscious Professional Responsibility: Justice Black's Unpublished Dissent and a Lost Alternative Approach to the Ethics of Cause Lawyering' (2021) 34(1) *Georgetown Journal of Legal Ethics* 125, 146.

38 Ibid 190.

39 This was a class action by people who had been required to repay welfare payments, because they had been 'overpaid', and so owed a debt to the Commonwealth. The litigants argued that the debts were invalid because they were calculated incorrectly. In approving settlement in the matter, the Court noted the serious stress and anxiety caused by the debt collection and said that the case 'has exposed a shameful chapter in the administration of the Commonwealth social security system and a massive failure of public administration': *Prygodicz v Commonwealth (No 2)* (2021) FCA 634, [5].

40 *Sharma by her litigation representative Sister Marie Brigid Arthur v Minister for the Environment* (2021) 391 ALR 1. This case is discussed further in Chapter 10.

41 *JT International SA v Commonwealth*; *British American Tobacco Australasia Limited v Commonwealth* (2012) 250 CLR 1.

people, communities and relationships. Often this approach is linked to the work of Carol Gilligan, who proposes that traditional rights-oriented theories of the development of moral reasoning privileged typically male forms of ethical reasoning and ignored the care-based ethics that many women tend to use:[42]

> Whereas the ethic of justice is founded on the idea that everyone should be treated equally, the ethic of care requires that no one should be hurt. Whereas men tend to stand on principle and act according to people's rights irrespective of the consequences, women are more pragmatic, being more concerned to uphold relationships and protect their loved ones from harm. Whereas the ethic of justice assumes that one can resolve moral dilemmas by abstract and universalistic moral reasoning, the ethic of care requires due attention to context and the specific circumstances of each moral dilemma. And in resolving such dilemmas, men tend to rank ethical principles, whereas women attempt to address the concrete needs of all and to ensure that if anyone is going to be harmed it should be those who can best bear the harm.[43]

The empirical claim made by Gilligan as to whether an ethics of care is a typically female ethics has been controversial.[44] But the general contours of an ethics of care have developed a life beyond the gender debate and beyond settled law. The ethics of care has been generally accepted as an alternative approach to ethical reasoning in general, and to the application of ethics in legal practice in particular.[45]

The ethics of care approach focuses on trying to serve the best interests of both clients and others in a holistic way that incorporates moral, emotional and relational dimensions of a problem into the legal solution. It is particularly concerned with preserving or restoring (even reconciling) relationships and avoiding harm, including to oneself. Lawyer

42 Carol Gilligan, *In a Different Voice: Psychological Theory and Women's Development* (Harvard University Press, 1982). For influential applications of Gilligan's work to lawyers' ethics, see Rand Jack and Dana Crowley Jack, *Moral Vision and Professional Decisions: The Changing Values of Women and Men Lawyers* (Cambridge University Press, 1989); Carrie Menkel-Meadow, 'Portia in a Different Voice: Speculations on a Women's Lawyering Process' (1985) 1 *Berkeley Women's Law Journal* 39. For further discussion see Carrie Menkel-Meadow, 'Portia Redux: Another Look at Gender, Feminism and Legal Ethics' in Stephen Parker and Charles Sampford (eds), *Legal Ethics and Legal Practice: Contemporary Issues* (Clarendon Press, 1995) 25. For evidence that there is a difference between the values orientation of male and female law students in Australia on some issues, see Adrian Evans and Josephine Palermo, 'Australian Law Students' Perceptions of Their Values: Interim Results in the First Year – 2001 – of a Three-Year Empirical Assessment' (2002) 5 *Legal Ethics* 103. See also Richard Moorhead et al, 'The Ethical Identity of Law Students' (2016) 23(3) *International Journal of the Legal Profession* 235, 250, 257.

43 Caroline Maughan and Julian Webb, *Lawyering Skills and the Legal Process* (Butterworths, 1995) 36.

44 See Francesca Bartlett and Lyn Aitken, 'Competence in Caring in Legal Practice' (2009) 16(2–3) *International Journal of the Legal Profession* 241. The authors conclude from their empirical work that 'some women purposely adopt a lawyering ethic of care', which is 'a valid approach to lawyering'. They call for caring roles and skills to be revalued in the legal professional context. Such a revaluing is evident in the models discussed later in this chapter.

45 See Peter Quinlan CJ, 'Primum Non Nocere: What Might the Justice System Learn from Hippocrates?' (Speech, Piddington Society, 4 June 2021) <https://www.supremecourt.wa.gov.au/S/speeches_2018_2022.aspx>. See also Thomas L Shaffer, *On Being a Christian and a Lawyer: Law for the Innocent* (Brigham Young University Press, 1981); Thomas L Shaffer and Robert F Cochran Jr, *Lawyers, Clients and Moral Responsibility* (West Publishing, 1994); Reid Mortensen, 'The Lawyer as Parent: Sympathy, Care and Character in Lawyers' Ethics' (2009) 12(1) *Legal Ethics* 1.

self-care is a part of this approach, which resonates with more contemporary and holistic notions of wellbeing, in the sense that an ethics of care allows us to focus on our own needs and take steps to avoid the overwork and mental illness that can characterise some types of legal practice. The ethics of care approach prioritises relationships, including both the client's network of relationships and the lawyer's own relationships with colleagues, family and community, rather than the institutions of the law or systemic and social ideas of justice and ethics, although some advocates of relational lawyering see it as a framework that 'enables lawyers to enhance their contribution to the public good *at the same time as* more effectively representing clients'.[46] Eli Wald and Russell Pearce, for example, envisage relational lawyering (that is, ethics of care) as also imposing obligations on the profession as a whole to promote 'institutional arrangements that will best advance a just society and [support] lawyers in their efforts to live up to their individual obligations'.[47]

An ethics of care can be as radical as moral activism in its own way, because it will discard fundamental rules of professional conduct if circumstances seem to demand it. Consider the following scenario:

> You are acting for a mother of three small children in a divorce and intervention order matter. Your client has previously shown you some old photographs of bruises and marks on the children that she claims were inflicted not by their father but by her new boyfriend.
>
> One of the children now has blurred vision. Your client now instructs you to stop all legal proceedings as she intends to return to the children's father with her children. You believe the children will be at risk if this happens, but you know 'mandatory reporting' does not apply to lawyers in your state. Would you break client confidentiality and inform the relevant welfare department of your fears?[48]

You might consider whether you could bring such a disclosure within the exceptions to the duty of confidentiality (which we discuss in detail in Chapter 4).[49] But disclosure would probably be considered by your client to be a significant breach of trust and she may find another lawyer (or go without legal assistance). Perhaps there is some way to ensure the client receives the support she needs to stay separated or, at the very least, to better protect her children?[50] There are no easy answers to this dilemma.

46 Eli Wald and Russell G Pearce, 'Being Good Lawyers: A Relational Approach to Law Practice' (2016) 29(3) *Georgetown Journal of Legal Ethics* 601, 636.

47 Ibid.

48 Evans and Palermo (n 42) 114.

49 See *ASCR* r 9.2.4 (disclosure for the sole purpose of avoiding the probable commission of a serious criminal offence); *ASCR* r 9.2.5 (disclosure to prevent imminent serious physical harm to another).

50 Leslie Levin surveyed lawyers in the US state of New Jersey to ascertain what they did when confronted with a client threatening to harm others. (Mandatory disclosure provisions were in place in New Jersey, *requiring* lawyers to disclose in the circumstances envisaged by *ASCR* rr 9.2.4 and 9.2.5.) Levin found that many lawyers were uncomfortable with mandatory disclosure (and many did not comply with the rule), but most displayed 'a real commitment to attempting to dissuade their clients from committing wrongful acts': Leslie C Levin, 'Testing the Radical Experiment: A Study of Lawyer Response to Clients Who Intend to Harm Others' (1994) 47(1) *Rutgers Law Review* 81.

The concerns that motivate academic discussion of the ethics of care have also been tremendously influential in legal practice in incremental, if not revolutionary, ways. There are at least three practical ways in which ethics of care concerns have influenced legal practice in recent times.[51]

A holistic understanding of law and clients

First, the ethics of care encourages lawyers to take a more *holistic* view of clients and their problems. Thus, lawyers following the ethics of care are likely to spend more time listening to and discussing the broader concerns of clients and the way that legal issues are likely to impact on other aspects of their lives and relationships. At the very least, the ethics of care encourages lawyers and clients to consider the non-legal and non-financial consequences (for example, reputational, relational and psychological) of different legal options. Good lawyers refer clients for advice or counselling for the non-legal aspects of their legal problems, or incorporate relational and psychological wellbeing more explicitly into legal representation (for example, through movements such as therapeutic jurisprudence).[52] Holistic lawyering is also a feature of many clinical approaches to legal education. More particularly, the ethics of care encourages lawyers and clients to see ethics and the moral goodness of the client and lawyer as an explicit part of the lawyer–client relationship. It assumes that lawyers and clients will want to discuss the ethical implications of different courses of action, as well as the social, psychological, financial and other consequences. But it does not presume that the lawyer's initial view of the ethics of a client's situation is automatically correct. Rather, it emphasises dialogue about ethics and respect for each other's positions. In this sense, an ethics of care approach is somewhat optimistic, in that it celebrates conversation and respectful listening over and above legal outcomes. It also implicitly recognises that legal outcomes often take many years to achieve and, when achieved, are then too costly and therefore relatively empty and even damaging.

Dialogue and participation

Second, the ethics of care emphasises dialogue between lawyer and client and *participatory* approaches to lawyering. The lawyer–client relationship is built on mutual trust and shared knowledge. At the most mundane level this means that lawyers have a responsibility to make sure that clients understand the consequences, costs and uncertainties associated with the various alternative courses of action available to them so that the client can choose which option to pursue in an informed way (see discussion in Chapter 8). More ambitiously, the ethics of care puts a premium on the lawyer spending time listening to the broader concerns of the client so that the legal solution they offer fits in with the other aspects of the client's life. It requires the lawyer and client to agree on any course of action that is taken: neither can decide for the other – the (fully informed, authentic) consent of both to any course of action is considered necessary, because the lawyer–client relationship is seen as

51 The three ways are based on Maughan and Webb (n 43) 118–20.

52 See, eg, David B Wexler et al, 'Current Issues in Therapeutic Jurisprudence Guest Editorial' (2016) 16(3) *QUT Law Review* 1.

a partnership in which both parties are equally responsible. Therefore, legal advice is likely to be offered in dialogue with the client rather than the client being told what to do. But at the same time, the lawyer will not take actions in representing a client that the lawyer does not feel ethically (and generally) comfortable with.

Appropriate dispute resolution and relationship preservation

Thirdly, because the ethics of care asks lawyers (and clients) to see themselves within a network of relationships and to understand the feelings and experiences of others within those relationships, they are likely to look for *non-adversarial* ways to resolve disputes and preserve relationships. Therefore, lawyers will recommend dialogic, non-litigious means to resolve disputes such as negotiation, mediation and other forms of alternative dispute resolution. There will be less emphasis on positional bargaining and more on creative, 'win-win' resolutions. It has been suggested (though not yet verified) that following an ethics of care, cases that do go to court 'would be conducted on the basis of "good faith" principles. These would suggest a need for: (a) more dialogue and fuller disclosure between parties; (b) respect for the interests of other parties, resulting in avoidance of trial and pretrial adversarial tactics; and (c) less intimidating advocacy when in court'.[53] Outside of the dispute resolution context, the ethics of care lawyer is also likely to take a collaborative and preventive problem-solving approach to deals and transactions.

Each of these three aspects of an ethics of care legal practice – holism, lawyer–client participation, and a collaborative and preventive problem-solving approach – are now regularly advised in books, seminars and, to an extent, conduct rules on legal interviewing, advising and 'client care'. Many lawyers have chosen to devote themselves to advocating and promoting alternative dispute resolution precisely because they (and their clients) are disenchanted with adversarialism as a way of resolving disputes and prefer to be part of a problem-solving, relationship-preserving way of practising law, whether the concern is with business or family relationships.[54] Similarly, the profession as a whole has also recognised that 'client care' – effective communication with clients and participation by clients in decision-making – is necessary for delivering legal services effectively, and preventing client complaints and public disenchantment with the profession. These are everyday ways in which the ethics of care have influenced legal practice.

In the case of the philanthropist QC and the tobacco company – Case study 1.2 – an ethics of care approach would require the barrister to consider not only what was in the best interests (including for the moral worthiness) of his potential client, but also the ramifications of taking on this client for his own relationships within his family and community. In relation to the client, the ethics of care is concerned with compassion for humans and human feelings, not artificial, legal persons such as companies. So an ethics of care approach would not concern itself with the economic rights of a company to keep marketing a product. In relation to his family and community, the ethics of care requires a

53 Maughan and Webb (n 43) 119.

54 An example of this is collaborative law which involves all parties to a dispute and their lawyers agreeing to constructively negotiate an outcome without resorting to litigation. See, eg, 'Collaborative Law', *The Law Society of New South Wales* (Web Page) <https://www.lawsociety.com.au/advocacy-and-resources/publications-and-resources/my-practice-area/collaborative-law>.

potential lawyer to ask what impact the representation would have on these relationships. In this case the QC does indeed do a lot of caring in his personal life through involvement with various charitable purposes to which he gives substantially and encourages others to give. In deciding whether to act for tobacco companies, from an ethics of care perspective such a lawyer might consider whether that representation would be a betrayal of those charitable causes and the people he has worked with and helped as part of his charity efforts. For example, he might want to consider how his relationships with the fundraising Board of the cancer hospital would function, if on the one hand he continues to represent tobacco companies, and on the other hand he happens to be sitting on the Board alongside a representative of the hospital's patients who had lung cancer caused by smoking and is a passionate anti-smoking activist.

The ethics of care, in line with a virtue ethics approach, suggests that a lawyer's fundamental moral character carries through from their work as a lawyer to their relationships and activities outside of work. An ethics of care lawyer would not want to do legal work (or to do it in such a way) that they would not feel comfortable explaining to their friends or children, or associates in a charitable, political or religious community. The QC in Case study 1.2 would therefore need to think through whether it was possible to continue acting for tobacco companies in a way that he could 'own' and explain without embarrassment to people at the cancer hospital, or whether this would be, practically speaking, impossible.

The ethics of care approach is more focused on the client's best interests – understood broadly – than the moral activist or responsible lawyer types. However, unlike the adversarial advocate approach, it sees the client's best interests in the context of the client's network of relationships. The moral activist regards the individual client as more dispensable in the cause of justice and social change. The ethics of care approach is often more interested in personal change than social change, and can be sceptical about social change. The caring lawyer wants the client to become the best person they can be and intends to be active in that relationship. In that sense the ethics of care is as concerned with the ethics of the client as with the ethics of the lawyer, and it sees them as being interdependent. However, the approach can have quite a conservative impact. Because the emphasis is on the worth of the individual client and preserving relationships, caring does not necessarily focus on the systemic injustices in a situation; and because a caring lawyer can tend to avoid conflict, they might downplay the importance of activism and adversarialism to achieve larger-scale legal and political change. Yet, in the final analysis, lawyers who address larger-scale and systemic injustices are necessary to create the conditions in which caring relationships can flourish between autonomous people who can choose their own goals and values.

Many of the best examples of ethical lawyering *combine* an ethics of care for the client with work on systemic injustice. Liz Curran identifies several of these approaches:[55]

- **Empowerment models** focus on lawyers working alongside individuals and communities to empower them. Curran gives an example:

55 Liz Curran, *Better Law for a Better World: New Approaches to Law Practice and Education* (Routledge, 2021). See also *Integrative Law Movement* (Web Page) <https://integrativelaw.com/>.

> [W]hen I was working as a lawyer assisting residents of public housing in Victoria, I used human rights legislation and other legislative provisions to get the Department of Housing to address their legal responsibilities to maintain public housing. One client had an instance of mould growing on their infant's basinet, which caused asthma, resulting in frequent visits to the children's hospital for life-threatening asthma attacks. Other housing issues included instances of asbestos crumbling, indoor temperatures for the elderly in summer of up to 52 °C and violent intrusions and/or attacks due to unsafe premises in high crime neighbourhoods.
>
> Working side by side with the residents/clients, I learned that while I had the legal technical skills, my clients were the experts in life on a public housing estate. At night, I would return to my safe and comfortable existence. By contrast, my clients had to live daily with stress, poor income support and lack of control in their lives on the housing estate with a recalcitrant public authority who had ignored their plight for 40 years. ... I worked with the residents to use our joint expertise to hold the public authority to account through legal channels (albeit a slow, unwieldy and expensive process), media exposure, community-based action and mutual skill development. By recognising different critical players and each person's expertise, we started to make inroads and finally gained the ear of the parliament.[56]

- **Multidisciplinary practices** bring together multiple service professions to provide a holistic and cohesive service for clients/patients.[57] Examples are the Consumer Law Action Centre and the Asylum Seeker Resource Centre, which provide holistic assistance in areas of client need (including legal need) while also advocating for policy change. Another example is Health Justice Partnerships, which recognises that 'unresolved legal problems lead to stress and anxiety which in turn causes poor health outcomes'[58] but that disadvantaged people are unlikely to consult a lawyer; they are more likely to consult a health professional. Working in a multidisciplinary practice, health professionals can introduce a patient to a lawyer, who can then assist with legal needs. Curran notes that most multidisciplinary models both in Australia and the United States incorporate a systemic perspective – seeking to make a positive impact on the social determinants of health.[59]
- **Restorative practice** brings together all the parties involved in a particular issue or conflict, in an attempt 'to resolve collectively how to deal with the issue or aftermath of the conflict and its implications for the future'.[60] Examples include cultural courts, drug courts and institutional abuse group conferencing. As Curran explains, one of the benefits of restorative practice is that it allows room for a greater range of perspectives on an issue/harm/conflict, thus increasing the chances of finding solutions that are 'sustainable, compassionate and enable healing and, even on occasion, restoration of relationships'.[61]

56 Curran (n 55) 57.
57 Ibid 79.
58 Ibid 85.
59 Ibid 86.
60 Ibid 102.
61 Ibid 104.

Being explicit about our ethics

Most lawyers are unlikely to talk in terms of *adversarial advocacy*, *responsible lawyering*, *moral activism* or the *ethics of care*, unless this conceptual language is explored in law school. They are even less likely to talk about character and virtue. But who we happen to be in a character sense and who we are trying to be are nevertheless live issues as we struggle to reconcile, for example, why we might help a tobacco company to sell its toxic product while advocating for better lung cancer care through sitting on the Board of a cancer hospital.

Knowing what makes your life worth living and, for example, what values are important to you are powerful tools in the self-understanding required to practise law in a fulfilling and therefore successful manner. We all implicitly act on intuitions and personal philosophies of life and lawyering. The challenge is to turn our implicit understandings into explicit and discussed self-knowledge, by one means or another. The logic in one or more of these four types provides one such avenue. Because they are based on applied legal ethics theory as well as underlying moral frameworks, these four ethical types have some theoretical coherence and are capable of providing us with a principled set of considerations that allow us to position or 'locate' ourselves when we need to analyse a new ethical situation.

These four types can be seen as options on an à la carte menu – each of us could choose which type we prefer for the purpose of grounding our own lives as lawyers and for valuing others. Or they could be seen as the tools and ingredients available for creating our own individual dishes – there are a range of arguments and considerations available that can be combined and used in a variety of ways, each unique to each of us in the circumstances of our own lives. But each approach requires a conscious response from us – a decision about whether to accept it in each situation and, if not, why not; or if so, how? Some of the most thoughtful commentators on legal ethics and the skill of teaching legal ethics argue that the key to understanding and learning legal ethics is a process of judgement: 'Moral decision making involves identifying which principle is most important given the particularities of the situation … [Simply] reducing judgement to rules or formulas lands us in an infinite regress of rules.'[62]

Moral judgement that goes beyond rules and formulas is likely to be messy. It is not reducible to a set of algorithms or a code, particularly where virtue ethics is concerned, and, as far as we can see, is not therefore susceptible to replacement by an artificial intelligence ('AI'). Proponents of AI in the law have not yet attempted to design algorithms that can make decisions for lawyers on ethical bases, but it is only a matter of time before AI seeks to make inroads here, as it has in many other aspects of legal practice.[63] It is not inconceivable that such algorithms will attempt to reduce such decision-making to a computation process, but, at least in the short term, we are confident that each lawyer will need to be truly conscious of making their own ethical decisions. Apart from anything else, the premises behind any algorithm – that is, how particular choices are to be classified and prioritised according to ethical type,

62 David Luban and Michael Millemann, 'Good Judgment: Ethics Teaching in Dark Times' (1995) 9 *Georgetown Journal of Legal Ethics* 31, 39 (citations omitted).

63 See, eg, Richard Susskind, *Tomorrow's Lawyers: An Introduction to Your Future* (Oxford University Press, 2nd ed, 2017).

moral framework, applicable conduct rules and case law – will need to be acceptable to the profession and regulators in order for the outputs to be credible.[64] And it is certain, in both the short and long term, that a human lawyer's failure to enquire as to the premises, algebraic coherence and reputation of the 'decision-maker' algorithm itself will be unethical. In that light, and unless AI evolves to the point where it literally takes over, we cannot see how human engagement in legal ethical decision-making is about to become redundant.

Perhaps the capacity for moral judgement will be a central differentiator of future lawyers from the machines that are rapidly replacing some of the traditional functions of legal practitioners. Whether that is correct or not, the types set out here provide a series of questions and considerations that can help us structure the mess. But it is up to each of us to decide what to 'cook' with them. What combination of ethical types or moral approaches resonates most strongly with you in the following case studies?

CASE STUDY 2.1 SEEKING JUSTICE FOR A CLIENT WITH A TRAUMATIC HISTORY[65]

Your firm is renowned for fighting for clients who have suffered as a result of institutional failings. You are acting for a young person (represented by a litigation guardian) who was detained in a State detention centre and subjected to illegal strip searches, punishment by solitary confinement and other treatment that, you will argue, breaches the State's duty of care. Your client suffers from trauma as a result of his experiences. He has instructed you to sue the State. You also want the State to amend the guidelines for strip searches, which you consider to be vague and in need of amendment to reflect international law, which prohibits routine strip searches of children.[66]

CASE STUDY 2.2 PROBLEMS IN THE NEIGHBOURHOOD

A client is seeking your advice. His home faces directly onto an easement that doubles as a driveway for his property and the property of his immediate neighbour. The land on the other side of the easement belongs to a well-endowed private school. The school land has been unfenced for decades and people living nearby regularly walk across

64 See Monika Zalnieriute, Lyria Bennett Moses and George Williams, 'The Rule of Law and Automation of Government Decision-Making' (2019) 82(3) *Modern Law Review* 425. The authors note: 'Converting rule of law values into design specifications that can be understood by system designers, and enforced through regulation, professional standards, contracts, courts or other mechanisms represents a formidable technical and legal challenge' (at 455).

65 Case studies 2.1 to 2.4 are all based on real events.

66 See, eg, the work of Shine Lawyers: 'Sexual Abuse During Strip Searches: Your Rights', *Shine Lawyers* (Blog Post, 3 June 2021) <https://www.shine.com.au/blog/abuse-law/strip-search-rights>.

the easement and the school land to reach a popular recreational area. The school is concerned 'to secure its property' and plans to fence its land, but it has agreed that it won't fence along the driveway/easement because this would spoil your client's view. The plan is to put a gate at the entrance to the easement/driveway for which the school, your client and his immediate neighbour will have the access code. Other residents will have to walk a long way (around neighbourhood streets) to reach the recreational area. Your client is concerned about security so is pleased that access to the area will be restricted, but some residents are irate about the school's proposal and have physically threatened your client.

CASE STUDY 2.3 ENABLING A CLIENT TO TELL HER STORY

Your client is now 18 years old and wants control of money that the Public Advocate has been managing on her behalf. You are preparing for a tribunal hearing requesting an order that control of your client's funds be returned to her. The tribunal member who will be hearing the case has a reputation for listening carefully to self-represented litigants. You think that the client telling her own story is powerful; however, she is prone to get angry and lose focus when communicating about things she cares deeply about.

CASE STUDY 2.4 GREENWASHING?

In 2021 the Australian energy company AGL sued Greenpeace in the Federal Court for infringing its intellectual property rights.[67] Greenpeace had used the AGL logo in a campaign in which it accused AGL of being Australia's biggest climate polluter. This campaign followed a Greenpeace report that accused AGL of 'greenwashing' its image and of taking no meaningful action to reduce emissions from its activities. Greenpeace argued in court that its actions were covered by the 'fair dealing' defence and the freedom of speech safeguard in the *Copyright Act 1968* (Cth), which together allow for freedom of expression and expression for the socially useful purposes of parody, satire and criticism. Greenpeace and several other environmental charities accused AGL of attempting to stifle free speech and intimidate its critics. Imagine you were asked, as AGL's senior in-house counsel, to advise on Greenpeace's campaign when AGL first became aware of it. What approach to your role do you think you would adopt?

67 *AGL Energy Ltd v Greenpeace Australia Pacific Ltd* (2021) 395 ALR 275. The Federal Court generally accepted the Greenpeace 'fair dealing' defence (except in relation to three social media posts, and some photos and placards) but did not agree that it included a public interest component.

DISCUSSION QUESTIONS

1. Do you prefer to work with general moral methods, or to consider only the four different approaches to lawyers' ethics when considering these and similar scenarios?
2. Can you identify which of the four ethical approaches is more attractive to you?
3. Can you justify that preference to your peers?
4. Which approach to legal ethics might you adopt if you were the lawyer in the scenarios detailed above?
5. How might the four different approaches to a lawyers' ethical responsibilities in these scenarios conflict with each other?
6. What difference, if any, do you think your preferred approach might make to the outcome for your client and/or for the wider society (if you think this is relevant)?

Conclusion

Remember that the four ethical lawyer types are constructs of personality–experience–values and that, when clarified through the self-assessment scale at the end of the book (see Chapter 11 and Appendix: Parts 1 and 2), they can help you identify a personal preference for particular priorities in legal ethical decision-making. But remember also that together these types represent only preferences, not a compliance manual. Their strength is in enabling us to understand our own entrenched priorities and values – so that we and all lawyers can be aware of and allow for our biases in such decision-making.

RECOMMENDED FURTHER READING

César S Arjona, 'The Usage of What Country: A Critical Analysis of Legal Ethics in Transnational Legal Practice' (2019) 32(2) *Canadian Journal of Law and Jurisprudence* 259

Tim Dare, *The Counsel of Rogues* (Ashgate, 2009)

Monroe H Freedman, *Lawyers' Ethics in an Adversary System* (Bobbs-Merrill, 1975)

David Luban, *Lawyers and Justice: An Ethical Study* (Princeton University Press, 1988)

David Luban, 'The Adversary System Excuse' in David Luban (ed), *The Good Lawyer: Lawyers' Roles and Lawyers' Ethics* (Rowman & Allanheld, 1983) 83

David Luban and Bradley Wendel, 'Philosophical Legal Ethics: An Affectionate History (2017) 30(3) *Georgetown Journal of Legal Ethics* 337

Daniel Markovits, *A Modern Legal Ethics: Adversary Advocacy in a Democratic Age* (Princeton University Press, 2008)

Donald Nicolson and Julian Webb, *Professional Legal Ethics: Critical Interrogations* (Oxford University Press, 1999) ch 7

Christine Parker, 'Forum: Philosophical Legal Ethics: Ethics, Morals and Jurisprudence: Introduction' (2010) 13(2) *Legal Ethics* 165

Stephen L Pepper, 'The Lawyer's Amoral Ethical Role: A Defense, A Problem and Some Possibilities' (1986) 11(4) *American Bar Foundation Research Journal* 613

William H Simon, *The Practice of Justice: A Theory of Lawyers' Ethics* (Harvard University Press, 1998)

Eli Wald and Russell G Pearce, 'Being Good Lawyers: A Relational Approach to Law Practice' (2016) 29(3) *Georgetown Journal of Legal Ethics* 601

W Bradley Wendel, *Lawyers and Fidelity to Law* (Princeton University Press, 2010)

W Bradley Wendel, 'Pluralism, Polarization, and the Common Good: The Possibility of *Modus Vivendi* Legal Ethics' (2021) 131 *Yale Law Journal Forum* 89

Alice Woolley, 'Is Positivist Legal Ethics an Oxymoron?' (2019) 32(1) *Georgetown Journal of Legal Ethics* 77

3

PROFESSIONALISM AND THE REGULATION OF LAWYERS' ETHICS

Introduction

This chapter considers how the structure and processes of the regulatory systems that govern the legal profession are relevant to lawyers' ethics and behaviour – that is, the significance of 'institutions' for lawyers' ethics. Traditionally, the legal profession was self-regulated on the basis of confidence that any misbehaviour by lawyers was an *individual* anomaly, while the culture and practices of the profession as a *whole* were ethical.[1] But the ethical character of lawyers' practices does not depend on personal factors alone. In practice, personal ethical decisions will either be supported or undermined by the surrounding 'institutional' ethical culture and processes in which they are embedded. Personal ethics will be influenced by institutional constraints such as who sets and enforces the rules that govern the legal profession; what ethical and conduct issues the rules address; which values are represented in the rules; and whose interests are promoted, and whose are ignored, in those rules.

In this chapter we consider ways in which the ethics demonstrated by the legal profession as a whole are likely to affect lawyers' individual and personal ethics. We first consider the ethical dimensions of different models of regulation of the legal profession – self-regulation, co-regulation and independent regulation. We then trace the development of these regulatory approaches across Australia and map today's landscape. We examine the specific effects of these regulatory approaches on how we admit people to the legal profession, the formulation of rules of ethical conduct, and professional discipline processes and principles.

The previous chapter introduced different ways of thinking about which values should characterise legal practice – and therefore any regulatory system for lawyers. This chapter begins the discussion about how our current approaches to regulating the legal profession might, or might not, embody and engender these values. In the following chapters we will look at key topics for legal practice, the relevant legal and professional ethical rules, and which values would be appropriate to apply in these different contexts. In doing so we will critique the extent to which the rules and regulations as they currently stand do a good job of demonstrating the right values, and how these rules and regulations can influence individual lawyers' capacity to put different values into action in practice.

We highlight a number of examples where current regulation fails to give lawyers adequate guidance on how to put values into action, such as the lack of clarity about the public interest exceptions to confidentiality obligations to facilitate whistleblowing in Chapter 4 and what is expected in 'fair and reasonable' billing in Chapter 8. The book also points to examples of regulation that in our view runs contrary to appropriate professional values, such as some of the conduct rules relating to conflicts of interest discussed in Chapter 7. We describe a number of examples where 'cultural', taken-for-granted assumptions and practices of the legal profession probably promote unethical conduct by individual lawyers that has

1 Christine Parker, 'Regulation of the Ethics of Australian Legal Practice: Autonomy and Responsiveness' (2002) 25(3) *University of New South Wales Law Journal* 676.

not been addressed by rules and regulation, such as the rationalisation of unethical conduct on behalf of clients in commercial lawyering discussed in Chapter 9. Finally, this book notes that, as lawyers are regulated by their local State or Territory, there is a diversity of regulatory approach to certain issues, which can result in differing values being emphasised or enforced. This chapter provides a high-level mapping of the regulatory regime across the country to inform these later specific analyses.

In this chapter we focus on the 'law of lawyering' – rules and regulatory regimes that have been created to apply specifically to lawyers under the legislation and case law governing the legal professions of each of the States and Territories. In particular, we focus on the largely *self-regulatory* and character-based system for admission to the profession and for the issue and renewal of practising certificates, and the *co-regulatory* complaints handling and disciplinary systems for lawyers (except in the Australian Capital Territory, the Northern Territory and South Australia).[2] However, as with any other occupation or business, a wide range of laws and regulations apply to legal practice.[3] The most important of these are the duty of care owed by lawyers to clients in negligence and contract at common law, the fiduciary duties and trustee duties to account for and manage client money, and confidentiality owed by lawyers to their clients in common law and equity. Other areas of law, such as anti-discrimination, corporate, environmental, and consumer protection regulation, also apply to legal practice, just as they apply to other businesses, and can be enforced against lawyers and law firms by regulatory agencies. These aspects of regulating lawyers are not forgotten in this book. We examine the effect of these laws and their interpretation by courts on lawyers as they arise in the key areas examined.

Why have a 'law of lawyering' or a specific regime applying only to lawyers? The next section provides a brief history of the development of Australian legal professional regulation. This provides one answer to the above question: because lawyers want specific regulation, as long as they create and enforce it themselves. The chapter then contrasts this perspective with a very different regulatory approach that sees market competition as the fairest and most efficient form of professional regulation. In the second part of the chapter we describe the predominant approach to regulation in Australia today – co-regulation – which retains some self-regulation (for instance, in admission and certification) and independent regulation (for instance, professional discipline).

2 The Australian Capital Territory and Northern Territory are *self-regulating*, whereas South Australia is *independently* regulated.

3 See David Wilkins, 'Who Should Regulate Lawyers?' (1992) 105(4) *Harvard Law Review* 799; David Wilkins, 'Afterword: How Should We Determine Who Should Regulate Lawyers? Managing Conflict and Context in Professional Regulation' (1996) 65(1) *Fordham Law Review* 465. Wilkins divides enforcement/regulatory controls for the legal profession into four categories: (1) disciplinary controls (traditional self-regulation), (2) liability controls (negligence etc) (3) institutional controls (enforced by courts and state administrative agencies on lawyers who practise before them) and (4) legislative controls (enforced by a special independent regulator or commission or even by the government).

Self-regulation: professional community and social trustee professionalism

The regulatory structures for the legal profession in the various States and Territories in Australia are still heavily influenced by the fact that historically the English legal profession regulated itself.[4] Under this approach in most common law countries, professional associations promulgate and enforce standards of professional conduct, investigate and prosecute complaints, and establish the disciplinary tribunals to hear charges. They decide on qualifications for admission, issue practising certificates, police compliance with trust account rules, and administer fidelity funds and insurance schemes. They also protect lawyers' monopolies on legal work, set standard fees and prohibit most forms of competition between lawyers, including any form of advertising or price competition.[5]

Today in Australia many aspects of this control held by the profession have been removed and assigned to independent authorities through regulatory intervention as described in the second part of the chapter. However, the historical origins continue to influence how courts and the profession interpret modern legislation – for example, in applying disciplinary principles described below – and law societies still regulate many areas in practice. This story of regulatory change can also tell us things about how future change may occur and why.

It is useful to begin with a basic regulatory distinction in Australian legal practice inherited from English structures of a divided (if only by culture and practice) legal profession – the distinct branches of barristers and solicitors.[6]

Barristers

Barristers were and largely remain specialists in advocacy. As specialists they are the smaller branch of the profession.[7] Historically, they had exclusive audience in the courts, although

---

4 We note that this chapter, and most of this book, concerns the regulation and practices of Australian lawyers applying law and traditions imported by colonial settlers. We acknowledge the laws, and those who practised them, of First Nations Peoples of Australia. For an authoritative account, see Irene Watson, *Aboriginal Peoples, Colonialism and International Law: Raw Law* (Routledge, 2014). For accounts of how the English model developed historically see Julian Disney et al, *Lawyers* (Lawbook, 2nd ed, 1986) 6; William S Holdsworth, *A History of English Law* (Sweet & Maxwell, 1937) vol 6, 443. For Australian adoption see further Christine Parker, 'Competing Images of the Legal Profession: Competing Regulatory Strategies' (1997) 25(4) *International Journal of the Sociology of Law* 385.

5 Edward Shinnick, Fred Bruinsma and Christine Parker, 'Aspects of Regulatory Reform in the Legal Profession: Australia, Ireland and the Netherlands' (2003) 10(3) *International Journal of the Legal Profession* 237, 242. See further Chapter 8.

6 In *Ex parte Bateman* (1845) 115 ER 322, the Court of Queen's Bench held that at common law one person cannot practise as both a barrister and an attorney. However, as early as 1892, Victoria had a model where all qualified applicants were admitted as either a barrister or solicitor, as was the case historically in Western Australia and South Australia. New South Wales and Queensland maintained formal division of admission of barristers and solicitors until more recently (1993 and 2004 respectively). See Francesca Bartlett and Linda Haller 'Australia: Legal Services Regulation in Australia – Innovative Co-regulation' in Andrew Boon (ed), *International Perspectives on the Regulation of Lawyers and Legal Services* (Hart, 2017) 161.

7 Today barristers represent approximately 8% of the legal profession nationally. In 2020 there were 83,643 solicitors: Urbis, *2020 National Profile of Solicitors* (Final Report, July 2021) 1. A desktop review of bar association membership lists reveals that there are approximately 6,800 barristers.

now all lawyers can appear in all courts. From at least the end of the 15th century, English barristers were self-regulated by the strict hierarchies of Inns of Court where students, barristers and benchers (senior barristers) lived together. This was an apprenticeship model of learning a trade, initially available to the privileged class only. Today barristers are educated, like other lawyers, at universities and subject to the same regulatory controls described later in the chapter. However, there are additional entry requirements to practise as a barrister that require demonstration of specific knowledge and advocacy training (generally, passing a bar exam and then an advocacy course in order to be certified to practise). This specialised group of professionals also impose tight restrictions on the scope of their own work. According to their own conduct rules, barristers are limited in the work they can perform[8] and work as individuals rather than in an organisation.[9] However, collegial bonds are strong in this community and many barristers choose to work in traditional work hubs – barristers' chambers.[10] Australian barristers have abided to this day by the English code of the 'cab rank rule' – to take all work offered without discrimination – which is often regarded as a defining professional ethos.[11] Only recently have other inherited legal rules and traditions been removed by legislation,[12] such as barristers having no legal relationship with the client,[13] or challenged,[14] such as the observation of strict protocols about a professional uniform in court (wearing a wig and robes). While legislation now permits barristers to receive work directly from clients, they still typically enter legal relationships with solicitors to act on behalf of the solicitors' clients (see Chapters 6 and 8). These ways of operating continue, in some form, centuries-old traditional practices from England. This is not to imply that such approaches to practice are necessary for common law advocacy. For instance, in the United States there are no formal divisions of practice as described above. Rather, the organisation of the Australian Bar reflects a continued professional preference permitted by self-regulation or co-regulation described later in this chapter.

Solicitors

Solicitors are lawyers who have direct contact with clients inside and outside the courts. They are not limited as to the nature and type of practice and can now appear in all courts. Solicitors may practise as solo practitioners, in partnerships with other solicitors, as employees or as the principal of a firm. As described later in the chapter, recent legislation

8 *Legal Profession Uniform Conduct (Barristers) Rules 2015* rr 11–13.

9 Ibid rr 12 and 13, which prohibit barristers acting as agents of the client and generally conducting business on behalf of a client, and require barristers to work as sole practitioners.

10 In Victoria, clerks administer barristers' lists as inherited from the English tradition.

11 *Legal Profession Uniform Conduct (Barristers) Rules 2015* r 17. The rule is often thought to originate from Thomas Erskin's statement in *R v Thomas Paine* (1792) 22 St Tr 357. It has now been adopted in modern Australian jurisprudence as the basis of the barrister's role: see, eg, *Giannarelli v Wraith* (1988) 165 CLR 543, 580 (Brennan J).

12 As described below, barristers are now regulated by legislation in much the same way as solicitors in relation to entering into relationships with clients, costs and billing.

13 *Moor v Row* (1629) 1 Ch Rep 38; 21 ER 501. Any payment due for service was not a debt of contract but a debt of honour.

14 In 2016 the Victorian Supreme Court decided that neither judges nor lawyers appearing in their civil courts would wear traditional wigs: Victorian Supreme Court, 'Notice to the Profession: Wearing of Wigs in Common Law Division Proceedings' (1 May 2016). At the date of writing this move has not been followed by other jurisdictions.

has deregulated the organisational structures in which solicitors can work, allowing incorporation of firms and the ability to work with non-lawyers in multidisciplinary practices (with various ethical controls). More recently, there have been reports of a large growth in in-house or corporate counsel and government lawyers.[15] These are solicitors who work for just one client (also their employer). Chapter 9 considers some of the specific ethical challenges facing these lawyers.

The solicitors of the English profession organised themselves into professional associations in the 18th century in a direct attempt to emulate the success of the English Inns of Court in acquiring political influence and in inculcating common standards of professional conduct and ethics through a self-regulatory community.[16] In Australia a similar approach can be seen in the 1800s. For instance, in 1828 the NSW Supreme Court was granted powers of admission and regulation over the NSW legal profession.[17] In 1884 the Incorporated Law Institute of New South Wales was established and later became known as the Law Society of New South Wales, which remains its name today. It first acquired significant statutory powers of regulation of solicitors in 1935.[18] In Queensland a specific statutory disciplinary tribunal was set up as early as 1927 to police misconduct by individual solicitors.[19] Certification by a law society to practise as a solicitor became compulsory around the country.

Thus, solicitors have actively organised and acted to self-regulate from the first colonial practice. This approach has provided stability and power over professional practice, and the profession has argued strongly for the maintenance of this regulatory approach. We turn now to the basis of the argument for self-regulation.

The social bargain: social trustee professionalism

Self-regulation is justified by the ideal of a profession as a coherent moral community that socialises its members into appropriate and ethical behaviour as it teaches and maintains the craft of lawyering.[20] In the case of the legal profession, lawyers as a community are responsible for ensuring that all lawyers play their important twin roles as adversarial advocates and responsible lawyers with the important social function of establishing and maintaining the rule of law.

This conception of a professional and how they should be regulated is distinguished from both the apparent chaos and self-interest of businesses competing in the market and the bureaucracy of government organisations.[21] Christine Parker explains that, by

15 Urbis (n 7) reported over 80% growth over 10 years.

16 See Alan Paterson, 'Professionalism and the Legal Services Market' (1996) 3(1) *International Journal of the Legal Profession* 137; Brian Abel-Smith and Robert Stevens, *Lawyers and the Courts: A Sociological Study of the English Legal System 1750–1965* (Heinemann, 1967) 23, 187–92.

17 David Weisbrot, *Australian Lawyers* (Longman Cheshire, 1990) 166.

18 Under amendments of the *Legal Practitioners Act 1898* (NSW). See NSW Law Reform Commission, *The Legal Profession: General Regulation* (Discussion Paper No 1, 1979) 43.

19 Under legislation such as the *Queensland Law Society Act 1927* (Qld). See Reid Mortensen and Linda Haller, 'Legal Practice Reform in Queensland' (2004) 23(2) *University of Queensland Law Journal* 280, 285.

20 Emile Durkheim, *Professional Ethics and Civic Morals*, tr Cornelia Brookfield (Routledge, 2nd ed, 1992) [tr of: *Leçons de sociologie: Physique des mœurs et du droit* (first published 1950)].

21 See Talcott Parsons, *Essays in Sociological Theory* (Free Press, rev ed, 1954) ch 2; Eliot Freidson, *Professionalism Reborn: Theory, Prophecy and Policy* (Polity, 1994).

this account, professional self-regulation of ethics is necessary because we can trust neither market forces nor state regulation to inculcate ethics.[22] Rather, ethics must be the concern of self-regulating occupations that teach each member to look away from their self-interest and towards the whole professional community and the role it is supposed to serve for the legal system and thus for society. The more protection given to these groups, the better their ethics will be.[23] In juxtaposing professionalism with markets and bureaucracies, these foundational accounts of professionalism in social theory conceptualise professionalism as a construct that cultivates ethical responsibility, and autonomy, in a way that capitalist, commercial, bureaucratic and hierarchical business modes of organising work cannot do.[24]

The self-regulating profession then enters a bargain with the state and community, which allows the profession to self-regulate because of its obscure but expert knowledge and its superior institutions of socialisation and social control. On this view, lawyers (and members of the other traditional professions such as medicine, the clergy and the military) are seen as different from members of other occupations or markets, because they are 'trained in and integrated with, a distinctive part of our cultural tradition, having a fiduciary responsibility for its maintenance, development and implementation'.[25] That is, the profession is a social trustee for the rule of law.[26]

The regulation of the profession can thus be understood as a social bargain characterised by trust: the legal professional community takes on the burden of regulating itself since it alone is competent to do so. In return, the theory argues, society at large and clients trust the legal profession and protect it from interference, supervision and competition, as well as allowing lawyers higher remuneration and social status. But these privileges can be withdrawn if the profession fails to regulate itself in the public interest:

> [T]he larger society has obtained an *indirect* social control by yielding *direct* social control to the professional community, which thus can make judgments according to its own norms ... Thus it is that the social control of the professional community over its members may be seen as a response to the threat of the larger lay society to control it. Failure to discipline would mean both a loss of prestige in the society, and a loss of community autonomy.[27]

22 Christine Parker, *Just Lawyers: Regulation and Access to Justice* (Oxford University Press, 1999).

23 See Durkheim (n 20) 12–13, 23–4.

24 Julia Evetts, 'The Sociological Analysis of Professionalism: Occupational Change in the Modern World' (2003) 18(2) *International Sociology* 395, 404.

25 Parsons (n 21) 381.

26 Terence Halliday and Lucien Karpik (eds), *Fates of Political Freedom: The Legal Complex in the British Post-Colony* (Cambridge University Press, 2011); Terence Halliday, Lucien Karpik and Malcolm Feeley (eds), *Fighting for Political Freedom: Comparative Studies of the Legal Complex and Political Change* (Hart Publishing, 2007); Terence Halliday and Lucien Karpik (eds), *Lawyers and the Rise of Western Political Liberalism: Europe and North America from the Eighteenth to Twentieth Centuries* (Oxford University Press, 1997). Cf Ronen Shamir, *Managing Legal Uncertainty: Elite Lawyers in the New Deal* (Duke University Press, 1995); Yves Dezalay and Bryant Garth, *Dealing in Virtue: International Commercial Arbitration and the Construction of a Transnational Legal Order* (University of Chicago Press, 1996).

27 William J Goode, 'Community Within a Community: The Professions' (1957) 22 *American Sociological Review* 194, 198 (emphasis in original).

Of itself, this social bargain may not be sufficient to make every individual professional altruistic, but it means that the profession as a whole will be motivated to organise, regulate and socialise individual lawyers to serve and not exploit clients.[28] The state and broader community might enter into dialogue with the profession to make adjustments to the social bargain from time to time, but overall the value of professional community must be recognised for its role in advocating for and sustaining the integrity of the legal process and the rule of law.[29]

There are three main justifications for a continuing self-regulatory bargain proposed by the social trustee view of professionalism, and each of them draws on the twin roles of lawyers as adversarial advocates and responsible lawyers.[30]

First, it is asserted that only lawyers are knowledgeable enough about the law to set standards for their own practice. Clients and the general public lack the expertise to participate in setting and enforcing the ethics and standards of the legal profession. The whole point of law being a profession is that clients need to trust lawyers to serve their interests in the legal system, because they do not know how to do so themselves. The public likewise need to trust lawyers to act honourably as responsible lawyers by advocating vigorously for clients without breaching their duties to the court and the law. Only lawyers and courts have the experience and expertise to understand how that delicate balance should be maintained; thus, self-regulation is necessary.

It follows that since professions are responsible for, and learned in, bodies of knowledge and practice of great value to society, they must be specially regulated to ensure they are suitably trained and certified to interpret, develop, improve and practically apply this tradition for the benefit of others.[31] This also justifies unusually restrictive rules such as the fiduciary duties to avoid conflicts of interest and preserve confidentiality (discussed in Chapters 4 and 7) to protect individual clients from being dominated by professionals who would usually know so much more than they do.

Economists have shown that failure occurs in the market for professional services because of 'informational asymmetry, in which the seller knows the quality of his service or product, but the buyer does not'.[32] Intervention in the market to ensure minimum quality standards is thus necessary.[33] The functionalists argue that since unqualified persons are not competent

28 This theory of a social bargain between the profession and both the community and the state has also received contemporary support from Bernard Barber, *The Logic and Limits of Trust* (Rutgers University Press, 1983) and Terence Halliday, *Beyond Monopoly: Lawyers, State Crises and Professional Empowerment* (University of Chicago Press, 1987).

29 See generally Halliday, *Beyond Monopoly* (n 28); Andrew Boon, 'Professionalism Under the *Legal Services Act 2007*' (2010) 17(3) *International Journal of the Legal Profession* 195; Alan Paterson, 'Self-Regulation and the Future of the Profession' in David Hayton (ed), *Law's Future(s): British Legal Developments in the 21st Century* (Hart Publishing, 2000) 29. See also Parker (n 22) ch 7 (assessing this literature and suggesting a revision to the approach it takes, in order to better make the legal profession accountable to broader access to justice concerns).

30 See Harry Arthurs, 'The Dead Parrot: Does Professional Self-Regulation Exhibit Vital Signs?' (1995) 33(4) *Alberta Law Review* 800; Parker (n 22) 112–14.

31 Parsons (n 21) 372.

32 Hayne E Leland, 'Quacks, Lemons and Licensing: A Theory of Minimum Quality Standards' (1979) 87(6) *Journal of Political Economy* 1328, 1329.

33 George A Akerlof, 'The Market for "Lemons": Quality Uncertainty and the Market Mechanism' (1970) 84(3) *Quarterly Journal of Economics* 488; Kenneth J Arrow, 'Uncertainty and the Welfare Economics of Medical Care' (1963) 53(5) *American Economic Review* 941.

to meddle in professional affairs, professionals must be trusted to do this special regulation themselves: 'Professionals *profess*. They profess to know better than others the nature of certain matters, and to know better than their clients what ails them or their affairs ... Since the professional does profess, he asks that he be trusted.'[34]

Second, the profession traditionally argued, the state should not be involved in regulating lawyers. This is because it is necessary that lawyers remain completely independent of government, so that they can defend individuals and society against the state where necessary without bias or fear of reprisal. Separation is also important because lawyers need to be able to defend the rule of law and use their expertise to maintain and gradually reform the legal system from a disinterested, rather than a party political, perspective as responsible lawyers.

Third, it was argued that just as the state should not directly regulate lawyers because this might corrupt the justice system with partisan interests, nor should the profession be thrown open to the competitive forces of the market because this might corrupt the justice system with self-interest. It should be in the nature of all the professions to be trusted to self-regulate, because the members of professions are motivated by higher goals beyond self-interest in a competitive marketplace. If they fail to self-regulate for the benefit of the public, so the argument went, their monopoly on legal practice and/or the right to self-regulate can be removed by government. This threat of loss of privileges is supposed to be a sufficient incentive to make sure the legal profession (and also other professions) regulate themselves properly.[35]

These arguments still hold considerable force in regulating common law lawyers around the world, and many countries' legal professions consequently remain largely self-regulating. However, there are some strong counterarguments to self-regulation that have been accepted by governments, and resulted in legislative interventions that have changed the way the Australian[36] legal profession is regulated. Yet there remain aspects of Australian law that adhere to the arguments for self-regulation, such as the monopoly lawyers have over legal advice and representation.

CASE STUDY 3.1 MONOPOLY OF PRACTICE

The trust in, and protection of, legal professionals can be seen today in a number of ways. A key example in Australia and many other common law countries[37] is that lawyers have a monopoly – or a reserve – over practising law.[38] This protectionism is justified on the following grounds:

34 Everett C Hughes, 'Professions' (1963) 92(4) *Daedalus* 655, 656 (emphasis in original).

35 See Paterson (n 16) 137.

36 The regulation of the English legal profession has arguably made the biggest move away from the traditional social bargain: Boon (n 29).

37 This market protection similarly applies in the United States. See, eg, Deborah Rhode, 'Policing the Professional Monopoly: A Constitutional and Empirical Analysis of Unauthorised Practice Prohibitions' (1981) 34(1) *Stanford Law Review* 1. There has been a differing traditional approach in England where only specific tasks have been reserved to lawyers: Andrew Boon, *The Ethics and Conduct of Lawyers in England and Wales* (Hart, 3rd ed, 2014) chs 5, 7.

38 There are other professionals who lawfully practise across areas of law such as migration agents, patent and trade mark attorneys, industrial advocates and (in most jurisdictions) conveyancers.

> [I]f the public is to be adequately protected from those lacking relevant qualifications, then, in the context of a regulated legal profession, the giving of legal advice professionally is, I think, to be regarded as exclusively the province of those properly trained in the law and having the necessary expertise. It is thus something required to be undertaken only by the legally qualified, and not by those not properly qualified.[39]

Modern legislation continues the tradition of permitting only qualified lawyers – usually called 'Australian legal practitioners' or solicitors and barristers – to practise law, because of the fear that an unskilled person will provide poor legal services and may even imperil the proper working of the justice system. Much like other professions, this reserve of practice is enforced by strong legal means imposing a criminal sanction on unqualified practice, as well as on an unqualified person holding themselves out as able to engage in legal practice.[40]

> ***Legal Profession Uniform Law, or 'Uniform Law'***[41]
>
> **10 Prohibition on engaging in legal practice by unqualified entities**
>
> **(1)** An entity[42] must not engage in legal practice in this jurisdiction, unless it is a qualified entity.
>
> Penalty: 250 penalty units or imprisonment for 2 years, or both.
>
> **(2)** An entity is not entitled to recover any amount, and must repay any amount received, in respect of anything the entity did in contravention of subsection (1). Any amount so received may be recovered as a debt by the person who paid it.
>
> **(3)** Subsection (1) does not apply to an entity or class of entities declared by the Uniform Rules to be exempt from the operation of subsection (1), but only to the extent (if any) specified in the declaration.

---

39 *Cornall v Nagle* [1995] 2 VR 188. See also *Uniform Law* s 9.

40 *Uniform Law* ss 10, 11; *Legal Profession Act 2007* (Qld) s 24; *Legal Profession Act 2007* (Tas) s 13. In the Australian Capital Territory, Northern Territory and South Australia it is an offence to practise when not entitled but these legislatures do not provide for a possible term of imprisonment.

41 This is contained in the *Legal Profession Uniform Law Application Act 2014* (Vic) sch 1. As stated in Chapter 1, New South Wales and Western Australia have adopted the provisions of the Victorian Act.

42 *Uniform Law* s 6 defines a 'qualified entity' as follows:
(a) an Australian legal practitioner; or
(b) a law practice; or
(c) either –
  (i) an Australian-registered foreign lawyer; or
  (ii) a foreign lawyer who is not an Australian-registered foreign lawyer but only to the extent that the foreign lawyer's legal practice is limited to the practice of foreign law and is carried out in accordance with the applicable requirements of Part 3.4; or
(d) an individual engaged in legal practice under the authority of a law of the Commonwealth or of a jurisdiction, other than this Law or the Uniform Rules; or
(e) an entity engaged in legal practice of a kind specified in the Uniform Rules for the purposes of this definition, but only while the entity engages in the legal practice in accordance with any applicable requirements of the Uniform Rules;

In other states there is some variation in who can engage in the practice of law without admission and/or certification.

11 Prohibition on advertisements or representations by or about unqualified entities

(1) An entity must not advertise or represent, or do anything that states or implies, that it is entitled to engage in legal practice, unless it is a qualified entity.

Penalty: 250 penalty units.

(2) A director, partner, officer, employee or agent of an entity must not advertise or represent, or do anything that states or implies, that the entity is entitled to engage in legal practice, unless the entity is a qualified entity.

Penalty: 50 penalty units.

However, 'engage in legal practice' is not defined in any Act. The widely cited definition applied by courts is from *Cornall v Nagle* [1995] 2 VR 188, 210:

> (1) by doing something which, though not required to be done exclusively by a solicitor, is usually done by a solicitor and by doing it in such a way as to justify the reasonable inference that the person doing it is a solicitor;
>
> (2) by doing something that is positively proscribed by the Act or by Rules of Court unless done by a duly qualified legal practitioner; or
>
> (3) by doing something which, in order that the public may be adequately protected, is required to be done only by those who have the necessary training and expertise in the law.

This rather circular reasoning – it should be done by a lawyer if it *is* usually done by a lawyer – makes for a broad monopoly. However, there has been pressure for some time to further justify why lawyers are granted a strong economic monopoly, and claims that changes are needed to assist access to justice.[43] Indeed, empirical studies in several jurisdictions have questioned claims that lawyers are best able to provide certain legal services; it seems that specialised non-lawyers provide superior service in certain areas.[44] A range of technological interventions into the legal market – like chatbots and automated forms for a non-lawyer to submit to an authority or court to contest fines – test the edges of the legal definition of 'practising law'. More significantly, these technologies often promise access to the law that might be cheaper and easier than accessing a lawyer.[45] However, for the moment, the traditional social bargain approach protects the Australia lawyer (or law firm) from market competition.

43 A recently filed lawsuit in the United States has claimed the monopoly is unjustifiable when there is an access to justice crisis: *Upsolve Inc and Rev John Udookon v Letitia James in her official capacity as Attorney General of the State of New York*, filed on 25 January 2022 in the United States District Court, Southern District of New York. Many argue other skilled providers could at the very least be licensed to do certain legal work. For instance, Jessica K Steinberg et al, 'Judges and the Deregulation of the Lawyer's Monopoly' (2021) 89(4) *Fordham Law Review* 1315 describe how non-lawyers work in domestic violence courts to provide essential assistance to the functioning of these jurisdictions.

44 Richard Moorhead, 'Lawyers and Other Legal Service Providers' in Peter Cane and Herbert Krizer (eds), *The Oxford Handbook of Empirical Legal Research* (2010) 798; Leslie Levin, 'The Monopoly Myth and Other Tales about the Superiority of Lawyers' (2014) 82(6) *Fordham Law Review* 2611.

45 Dana Remus and Frank Levy, 'Can Robots Be Lawyers? Computers, Lawyers and the Practise of Law' (2017) 30(3) *Georgetown Journal of Legal Ethics* 501; Benjamin Barton and Deborah Rhode, 'Access to Justice and Routine Legal Services: New Technologies Meet Bar Regulators' (2019) 70(4) *Hastings Law Journal* 955.

DISCUSSION QUESTIONS

1. Discuss the reasoning behind self-regulation. Do you agree that this is important or necessary? What might the counterarguments be?
2. Should lawyers be the only professionals permitted to undertake legal work?
3. If there was a technology, such as an online form, that could assist thousands of people to successfully contest fines without needing a lawyer, should we prohibit this, if the form was not created or overseen by a lawyer?
4. Should law students be allowed to perform certain legal work?

Competition regulation and the legal profession as a business

The legal profession as a conspiracy against the laity

In contrast to the traditional image of the legal profession as a self-regulating moral community, since the early 1980s government policy in Australia (also in England and Wales, Canada and New Zealand) regards the profession as a business that must be regulated in a way that ensures competition and a consumer service orientation. The Trade Practices Commission (now the Australian Competition and Consumer Commission) decided in 1989 to review the legal profession and determine the extent to which it complied with antitrust principles. In 1993 the *Hilmer Report* into gaps in implementation of competition policy reform in Australia identified the legal profession as a problem area.[46] The thrust of the Trade Practices Commission's criticisms is illustrated in the following passage from its final report in 1994:

> The Australian legal profession is heavily over-regulated and in urgent need of comprehensive reform. It is highly regulated compared to other sectors of the economy and those regulations combine to impose substantial restrictions on the commercial conduct of lawyers and on the extent to which lawyers are free to compete with each other for business. As a result, the current regulatory regime has adverse effects on the cost and efficiency of legal services and their prices to business and final consumers ...[47]

Competition reformers see the legal profession as no different from any other industry that must be subject to microeconomic reform. Their image of the legal profession is of a cartel that managed in the 20th century to achieve monopoly rents and privileges by exploiting self-regulation. At its most extreme, the picture of the legal profession as a cartel is justified by the neoclassical economics of Milton Friedman. In his theory, special regulation always

46 National Competition Policy Review Committee, *National Competition Policy* (1993) ('*Hilmer Report*'). For a fuller account of this process and its consequences, see Parker (n 22) 121–39.

47 Trade Practices Commission, *Study of the Professions: Legal – Final Report* (1994) 3–4. See also *Hilmer Report* (n 46) 133–7.

becomes 'a tool in the hands of a special producer group to obtain a monopoly position at the expense of the rest of the public'.[48] Social critiques of the professions in the 1980s and 1990s were also dominated by a perspective that complements this economic critique. Sociologists have seen professions as occupational groups organised to maximise their power by claiming the status of 'profession' and the privileges that go with it. Magali Sarfatti Larson described the 'professional project' as the use of claims to special knowledge and skills to strive both for market control (economic power) through monopolisation, and social status (social power) through a collective mobility project.[49]

This theory sees traditional self-regulation and its justifications as nothing more than support for the self-interested professional project. It is suggested that traditional professional claims of disinterested public service and of a social bargain mandating self-regulation form part of an ideology that justifies and obscures the social structural inequalities caused by professionalism. Furthermore, self-regulation is actually aimed at ensuring that competition between members is minimised and the profession acts in solidarity to advance the collective goals of monopoly and status. The profession provides a clear path for individual members to achieve power and prestige within this tightly regulated structure, so that they remain committed to a unified profession and contribute, deliberately or not, to its collective project.[50] On this view, the legal profession is an autonomous collective organisation aimed and organised to secure its economic and social self-interest through the control of entry, competition and internal regulation.

Regulation of the legal profession as a business

If we accept that self-regulation of the legal profession is questionable, is opening it to market forces a better alternative? It is ironic 'that much of the criticism of professionalism by radicals seems to advance the implicit alternative of the individualistic free market that underlies capitalism'.[51] But the policy consequence of accepting the market control theory of the profession is to 'reform' lawyers by breaking down professional organisation and self-regulation, forcing more competition and treating law more like a business. As mentioned above, one of the profession's arguments for self-regulation was that law is a profession with ethical values beyond those of the market. Some scholars of the legal profession, however, have pointed out that if we examine the nature of the way law is actually practised these days, it is subject to such strong market pressure that it is hard to see how the case can be made that it is a profession with different values to those of general business. Richard Abel,

48 Milton Friedman, *Capitalism and Freedom* (University of Chicago Press, 1962) 148.

49 Magali Sarfatti Larson, *The Rise of Professionalism: A Sociological Analysis* (University of California Press, 1977) xvi.

50 Ibid 70–7. A number of studies published in the 1980s and 1990s supported the application of Larson's theory to the legal profession: Abel shows how this theory explains the history and behaviour of the legal profession in the United Kingdom in Richard Abel, *The Legal Profession in England and Wales* (Basil Blackwell, 1988) and the United States in Richard Abel, *American Lawyers* (Oxford University Press, 1989). Weisbrot (n 17) and Pat O'Malley, *Law, Capitalism and Democracy* (Allen & Unwin, 1983) have attempted to do the same for Australia.

51 Eliot Freidson, 'Professionalism as Model and Ideology' in Robert L Nelson, David M Trubek and Rayman L Solomon (eds), *Lawyers' Ideals/Lawyers' Practices: Transformations in the American Legal Profession* (Cornell University Press, 1992) 215, 219.

who has studied the legal professions in England and Wales and the United States for many years, is one who takes this view:

> The lawyer today (and even more tomorrow) is an entrepreneur selling his services to an increasingly competitive market, an employee whose labor is exploited, an employer exploiting subordinates – all increasingly dependent on state or capital for business and therefore increasingly subject to their control. Although the ideal of professionalism undoubtedly will linger on as an ever more anachronistic warrant of legitimacy, as an economic, social, and political institution the profession is moribund.[52]

Even if we are not as cynical as Abel, the profession's arguments in favour of self-regulation are not persuasive. Harry Arthurs, another scholar of the legal profession, has shown how the three classic arguments for self-regulation (set out in the previous section) fail.[53] His ideas may be expressed as follows:

- *First*, self-regulation is not necessary to defend individuals and society from the power of the state – other countries like Sweden manage well without it. Just because the profession does not self-regulate does not mean it must be controlled by the state – it can be independently regulated.
- *Second*, although lawyers claim to be the only ones who know how to regulate themselves, the legal profession has effectively failed to regulate itself properly. Individual lawyers with appropriate expertise can be part of the regulatory process without having to hand over all regulation to self-regulatory professional associations.
- *Finally*, the argument that professions have always been self-governing is circular. Just because it has been so in the past does not mean it must be so in the future. Indeed, the argument for self-regulation belies the reality that occupational groups have been trying for nearly 200 years to claim 'professional' status for themselves as a means of controlling the market for their services.[54] The self-regulating 'professions' are really just those occupations that have succeeded in establishing a monopoly that they control.

It is also possible that the burden of self-regulation may be more onerous than any of its supposed advantages. The need for the profession to constantly defend its independence in complaints handling, investigation and prosecution against charges of bias is demoralising and distracting. Consider these two Australian examples of where the public and government considered self-regulation as self-interested and in need of radical reform:

- In Queensland, self-regulation by the two professional associations for solicitors and barristers ended in 2004 after major criticisms by the State Attorney-General, the Legal Ombudsman and the press of the way the Queensland Law Society ('QLS') carried out its regulatory responsibilities. The event that sparked the furore was allegations that Brisbane law firm Baker Johnson had been guilty of unprofessional, unethical and fraudulent conduct in relation to its 'no-win, no-fee' clients. Most dramatically, in one

52 Richard L Abel, 'Toward a Political Economy of Lawyers' (1981) (5) *Wisconsin Law Review* 1117, 1186–7.

53 Arthurs (n 30).

54 Richard Abel, 'Why Does the ABA Promulgate Ethical Rules?' (1981) 59(4) *Texas Law Review* 639; Larson (n 49); Parker (n 22) 109–12, 112–21 (for critique of this approach).

instance Baker Johnson had won a case for a client but then effectively diverted to itself the entire compensation payout for the payment of fees, and proceeded to sue the client for additional fees under a 'no-win, no-fee' arrangement.[55] Complaints about Baker Johnson's conduct had been made to the QLS, but the local newspaper and the Attorney-General criticised the QLS for failing to either investigate or prosecute Baker Johnson, and for generally inadequate complaints-handling procedures, leading to numerous unresolved complaints.[56]

The then Queensland Legal Ombudsman, Jack Nimmo, investigated and concluded that the QLS's complaints-handling service was 'nothing but a post office box'. He found that complainants were unhappy with the fact that QLS's practice was to merely refer a copy of their complaint to the solicitor for response, and then send that response back to the complainant. He considered it inadequate that 'the complainant [would] be forwarded a copy of the solicitor's response, the contents of which have already been disputed, [with QLS merely] stating that 'on the face of it the response appears to answer your complaint'.[57] The inactivity and delay in the QLS's investigation and prosecution of Baker Johnson and other legal practitioners was described by Mr Nimmo as the consequence of an unacceptable conflict of interest between the QLS's role as a union and its complaints-handling role. This allowed those lawyers to remain in practice, and continue to avoid scrutiny for acts that were subsequently criticised severely in both civil and disciplinary proceedings.[58] When the Attorney-General announced that he was stripping the QLS of its powers and handing them to a new Legal Services Commissioner,[59] no one was surprised.[60]

- The Tasmanian government became determined to shake up the Tasmanian Law Society ('TLS') after the collapse of a number of solicitors' mortgage schemes that ultimately led to criminal proceedings against some lawyers. One firm apparently lost up to $20 million of clients' funds.[61] The government was convinced that the TLS had mismanaged the regulatory framework for solicitors' mortgage practices so that the losses went undiscovered until it was too late.[62] The government divested the Tasmanian profession of most self-regulatory functions by establishing a new Legal Profession Board, consisting of two non-lawyers and four legal practitioners (to be appointed by the Attorney-General from a list of nominations from the profession).

55 *Baker Johnson v Jorgensen* [2002] QDC 205. Ethical issues concerning billing are discussed further in Chapter 8.

56 Jack Nimmo, Queensland Legal Ombudsman, *The Queensland Law Society and Baker Johnson Lawyers, the Queensland Law Firm* (Report, 2002) 2–3.

57 Ibid 6–7.

58 Ibid 3. The newly created Legal Services Commission, as its first prosecution, sought, and achieved, the removal from practice of the principal of Baker Johnson: *Legal Services Commissioner v Baker (No 2)* [2006] 2 Qd 249.

59 Sam Strutt, 'Watchdog Set to End Self-Regulation', *The Australian Financial Review* (Sydney, 16 May 2003) 57.

60 Chris Griffith, 'Law Society Hits Reform Process', *The Courier-Mail* (Brisbane, 7 May 2003) 5. However, the *Legal Profession Act 2007* (Qld) s 435 allows the Commissioner to refer investigations back to the QLS or the Bar. Today, the Commissioner only refers matters to the Bar for investigation.

61 'Lawyers Could Lose Power to Investigate Complaints', *The Advocate* (Burnie, 22 June 2000) 4; Anne Barbeliuk, 'Move to Shake up Law Society', *Mercury* (Hobart, 21 May 2000) 3.

62 Martine Haley, 'New Watchdog to Regulate Lawyers', *Mercury* (Hobart, 18 April 2003) 5.

Any professional association will find it hard to represent the interests of all members politically, while at the same time choosing to prosecute some of those members. This must at some level eventually operate to confuse the priorities and concentration of its leadership. Sometimes, the prosecution of peers by peers can be subverted for internal political purposes. At the least, the trust of the membership in the leadership is undermined by the threat of such prosecutions, and personal ethics too are likely to be undermined by institutionally suspect practices.

Regulation of the Australian legal profession today

Charles Sampford and Christine Parker argue that individual development of a 'positive morality' (that is, a morality actually accepted and shared by a group, as opposed to an ideal standard) is *the* important part of the answer to the diverse range of values that lawyers encounter in practice.[63] The view that a personal morality shared by others is essential to deal with the numerous (morally) significant situations that are encountered in legal practice seems obvious. The conduct rules will not be enough. Below we will examine the way self-regulation has been altered in each of the States and Territories by incorporating co-dependent and independent regulators into the system for governing the legal profession, while retaining aspects of self-regulation.

But Sampford and Parker's point in critiquing rules and their enforcers in this way is not necessarily to argue about *who* should be regulating the profession. The key point is *what* values should be represented in the regulation of the profession (whoever does it) and about how well that regulation facilitates ethical conduct in everyday legal practice. This is not to say, of course, that we do not need regulators, but rather that watchdogs can make us cringe and act furtively rather than more transparently and in a public-spirited manner.

Today, Australian legislators have rejected 'stand-alone' self-regulation except in the Australian Capital Territory. Yet it is not necessarily the case that independent regulation or regulation via the market would be any better. Consider, for example, the fact that competition policy is probably the external regulatory force that has had most impact on the regulation of the legal profession in Australia.[64] Federal and State and Territory governments and an independent regulator, the Australian Competition and Consumer Commission, have all imposed regulation (and deregulation) promoting competition on the profession. Yet, Jim Spigelman, former Chief Justice of New South Wales, has argued that essential public protections that are bound up in the current concerns of legal regulation may be abandoned to the market in competition regulation:[65]

63 Charles Sampford and Christine Parker, 'Legal Regulation, Ethical Standard-Setting, and Institutional Design' in Stephen Parker and Charles Sampford (eds), *Legal Ethics and Legal Practice: Contemporary Issues* (Clarendon Press, 1995) 11.

64 Christine Parker, 'Converting the Lawyers: The Dynamics of Competition and Accountability Reform' (1997) 33(1) *Australian and New Zealand Journal of Sociology* 39. See earlier discussion in this chapter.

65 Chief Justice JJ Spigelman, 'Are Lawyers Lemons? Competition Principles and Professional Regulation' (Speech, St James Ethics Centre Lawyers' Lecture Series, Sydney, 29 October 2002).

> The role of the profession in the administration of justice cannot be characterised simply as the provision of services to consumers. There are structural and institutional issues here of great significance. Competition regulators tend not to understand, or if they understand tend not to value, rival institutional traditions to that of the market. A market does not value history and tradition. As I said at my swearing-in, a market wakes up every morning with a completely blank mind, like Noddy.[66]

If Spigelman is correct, rationalist economics provides little help for us in deciding whether or not and how to implement ethical regulatory structures. In the end, the moral stance of those structures is important. If self-regulation fails the fairness test and is consequentially ineffective because it does not diminish the level of complaints or increase public satisfaction with the profession, is it worth keeping nonetheless because it trusts lawyers as professionals to show courage and judgement in regulating their peers?

It has been suggested that the profession and the community might be able to renegotiate legal professionalism so that the profession still maintains a role in its own regulation and is also more responsive to other values – that is, some sort of co-regulation.[67] This is the predominant approach in Australia. It may be that a wise government will encourage some self-regulation, particularly within areas of specialisations, if for no other reason than to harness natural interest in self-improvement and self-respect as a consolidating force in professional formation.[68] This might be seen in the self-regulation of legal education and standards for admission to legal practice. But whoever the regulator, the important things are the extent to which any regulatory system seeks to institutionalise agreed-upon values and virtues (not just that of prohibiting obvious dishonesty). It must also be effective in regulating individual lawyer wrongdoing, as well as critiquing current professional practices and cultures.

Towards a national approach to setting standards and values

Traditionally the regulation of lawyers was controlled by the States and Territories. But a nationally agreed regulatory structure for the legal profession is gradually evolving, although it contains significant flaws and there is by no means universal commitment to a country-wide approach. The first version was the *Model Laws*, and the next version was the *Uniform Law*. While these approaches were developed at a national level, and with the objective of conformity of regulation around the country, they are implemented at the State and Territory level, with consequent jurisdictional differences.

66 Ibid.

67 Parker (n 22) ch 7; Paterson (n 16); William H Hurlburt, *The Self-Regulation of the Legal Profession in Canada, and in England and Wales* (Law Society of Alberta and Alberta Law Reform Institute, 2000) 140.

68 Parker (n 1) 702 argued: '[I]f we wish to make legal practice more responsive to ethical concerns and community values, then a fruitful strategy might be to bypass the traditional professional associations and look to more specific groups of lawyers to elaborate their own standards of ethical responsiveness.' This insight was accepted by Australian law societies, many of whom have promoted self-regulating specialist accreditation, often with success.

There is more uniformity in the application of ethical standards: there has been wide adoption of the conduct rules for solicitors, the *Australian Solicitors' Conduct Rules 2015* ('*ASCR*').[69] As a result of a long-running consultation to update and amend these rules, a new version of the *ASCR* was produced in 2022 and adopted in the *Uniform Law* States. This book refers to the 2022 version of the rules, which is likely to be adopted in other jurisdictions in time. The Australian Bar Association drafted a template set of conduct rules for barristers in 2010 that have been adopted and updated, with some local variation across the country. The version applying in most jurisdictions forms part of the *Uniform Law,* or, more specifically, the *Legal Profession Uniform Conduct (Barristers) Rules 2015* to which we refer in this book.

The following sections of this chapter will sketch the legislative approaches (*Model Laws* and *Uniform Law,* and other jurisdictional approaches) and ethical rules, and then describe in more detail the key aspects of regulation of the profession – admission and certification to practise, regulation of trust accounts and complaints handing and discipline.

The *Model Laws* and *Uniform Laws* project

In 2004 the States and Territories, prompted by the Law Council of Australia ('LCA'),[70] agreed on a model law framework for regulation of the legal profession, which consisted of model provisions for legislation governing the legal profession in all jurisdictions – the *Legal Profession Model Laws Project Model Provisions* ('*Model Laws*').[71] While there are jurisdictional differences, the *Model Laws* approach substantively aligned standards for law degrees and practical legal training, introduced a national scheme for certification and consistent rules for trust accounting and fidelity funds, provided clear definitions of lawyer misconduct, and required costs disclosure and systematised approaches to regulation of law firm entities.

The *Model Laws* approach was applied in all jurisdictions except South Australia, and still applies in the Australian Capital Territory, the Northern Territory, Queensland and Tasmania. The legal profession in South Australia is *independently* regulated by a Legal Profession Conduct Commissioner. To the extent that the *Model Laws* approach is applied, there is differing implementation when it comes to complaints handling and discipline. Queensland has a *co-regulatory* approach such that the profession is governed both by law societies that, for example, issue practising certificates, govern trust accounts and make conduct rules, and externally by a government-appointed and independent regulator – the Legal Services Commissioner – that investigates and prosecutes lawyers for disciplinary offences. The legal professions in the Australian Capital Territory, the Northern Territory and Tasmania still essentially *self-regulate* (with the law societies in charge of regulation and prosecution), with some layperson representation in their processes.

The *Model Laws* approach was competition oriented in terms of how solicitors' organisations could be organised – it removed the traditional restraints that firms could

69 An earlier version of the *ASCR* (2012) is adopted in Queensland and South Australia. The Northern Territory retains a previous conduct code: *Rules of Professional Conduct and Practice* (2002). Some jurisdictions also provide a commentary to the rules.

70 The Law Council of Australia is the national umbrella association for State and Territory legal professional associations.

71 This was in fact a lengthy process beginning in 2001. See Daryl Williams, Standing Committee of Attorneys-General ('SCAG'), 'Communiqué: Historic Agreement on National Legal Profession' (Press Release, 7 August 2003) announcing agreement to proceed with the SCAG Legal Profession – Model Laws Project.

only exist as a partnership.[72] The *Model Laws* regime introduced the concept of an 'incorporated legal practice' ('ILP') that allows firms to be companies, including listing on the stock exchange.[73] However, this market-based approach is tempered by specific regulatory constraints that seek to address ethical concerns about non-lawyers influencing the way legal work is performed and impairing the independence expected of a lawyer.[74] In particular, ILPs must have a legal practitioner director who has responsibility for the proper legal and ethical functioning of the firm and its lawyers. ILPs are also required to undertake 'self-assessment audits' when establishing the firm, as a way to institute an appropriate internal 'ethical infrastructure'.[75] This regulatory approach seeks to manage ethics from the ground up, so that a firm internalises ethical practices rather than reacting to rules imposed from on high.

The *Model Laws* initiative was shepherded by the LCA over many years towards greater national uniformity. The (now defunct) Council of Australian Governments ('COAG') commenced a new round of nationalising laws in 2009 when it established the National Legal Profession Taskforce. In 2011 the Taskforce produced template legislation to be implemented by States and Territories. In July 2015, Victoria legislated the *Legal Profession Uniform Law Application Act 2014* (Vic) ('*Victorian Application Act*'), which was followed by New South Wales legislating the *Legal Profession Uniform Law Application Act 2014* (NSW) ('*NSW Application Act*'). Schedule 1 to the *Victorian Application Act* contains the common or 'uniform' provisions (the *Uniform Law*), the idea being that these would be enacted across the country.[76] Western Australia joined the *Uniform Law* in April 2022.[77] Collectively, this represents a uniform regime for approximately 75% of Australia's practising lawyers.[78]

Figure 3.1[79] sets out the functional relationships between the different bodies that govern regulation in New South Wales, Victoria and Western Australia under the *Uniform Law*, in

72 Susan Fortney and Talia Gordon, 'Adopting Law Firm Management Systems to Survive and Thrive: A Study of the Australian Approach to Management-Based Regulation' (2012) 10 *University of St Thomas Law Journal* 152.

73 Law firms Slater & Gordon and Shine Lawyers are examples of this. It is noted that a version of corporation had been permitted in a number of states since 1990s but a uniform approach to this can be seen in the *Model Laws* (and the *Uniform Law* in pt 3.2 div 2) regimes: *Legal Profession Act 2007* (Qld) pt 2.7 divs 2–7; *Legal Profession Act 2006* (ACT) div 2.6.2; *Legal Practitioners' Act 1981* (SA) sch 1; *Legal Profession Act 2006* (NT) pt 2.6 div 2; *Legal Profession Act 2007* (Tas) pt 2.5 div 2.

74 Fortney and Gordon (n 72). These, and other concerns about conflicting duties to shareholders and clients, were the traditional ethical concerns that justified prohibiting lawyers working collectively except as a partnership where the partners each had civil and professional liability. See Christine Parker, 'Law Firms Incorporated: How Incorporation Could and Should Make Law Firms More Ethically Responsible' (2004) 23(2) *University of Queensland Law Journal* 347.

75 This operates in Queensland and for all regulated legal entities in the *Uniform Law* States of New South Wales, Victoria and Western Australia. See S Fortney, 'The Role of Ethics Audits in Improving Management Systems and Practices: An Empirical Examination of Management-Based Regulation of Law Firms' (2014) 4 *St Mary's Journal on Legal Malpractice and Ethics* 112. See also further discussion in Chapter 9.

76 The *NSW Application Act* s 4 applies the *Uniform Law* as a law of New South Wales.

77 This was through the enactment of the *Legal Profession Uniform Law Application Act 2021* (WA) and the Legal Profession Uniform Application (Levy) Bill 2021 (WA). The regime came into force from 1 July 2022.

78 Urbis (n 17) 6.

79 Adapted from a diagram prepared by the Legal Services Council. For more detail, see Legal Services Council and Commissioner for Uniform Legal Services Regulation, *Role of Bodies Under the Legal Profession Uniform Law* <https://www.legalservicescouncil.org.au/Documents/Role-of-Bodies-Under-the-Uniform-Law-February2021.pdf> © State of NSW (Department of Justice).

relation to the supervision of lawyers' professional conduct. Essentially, the State-based Legal Services Commissioners ('LSCs') are at the coalface of investigation and prosecution in their respective States but are supervised by and defer to the Commissioner for Uniform Legal Services Regulation and Legal Services Council on aspects of overarching *Uniform Law* policy.[80] An Admissions Committee also develops rules to be implemented by these local admissions bodies.

Figure 3.1 Relationships between key regulators under the *Uniform Law* in New South Wales and Victoria.*

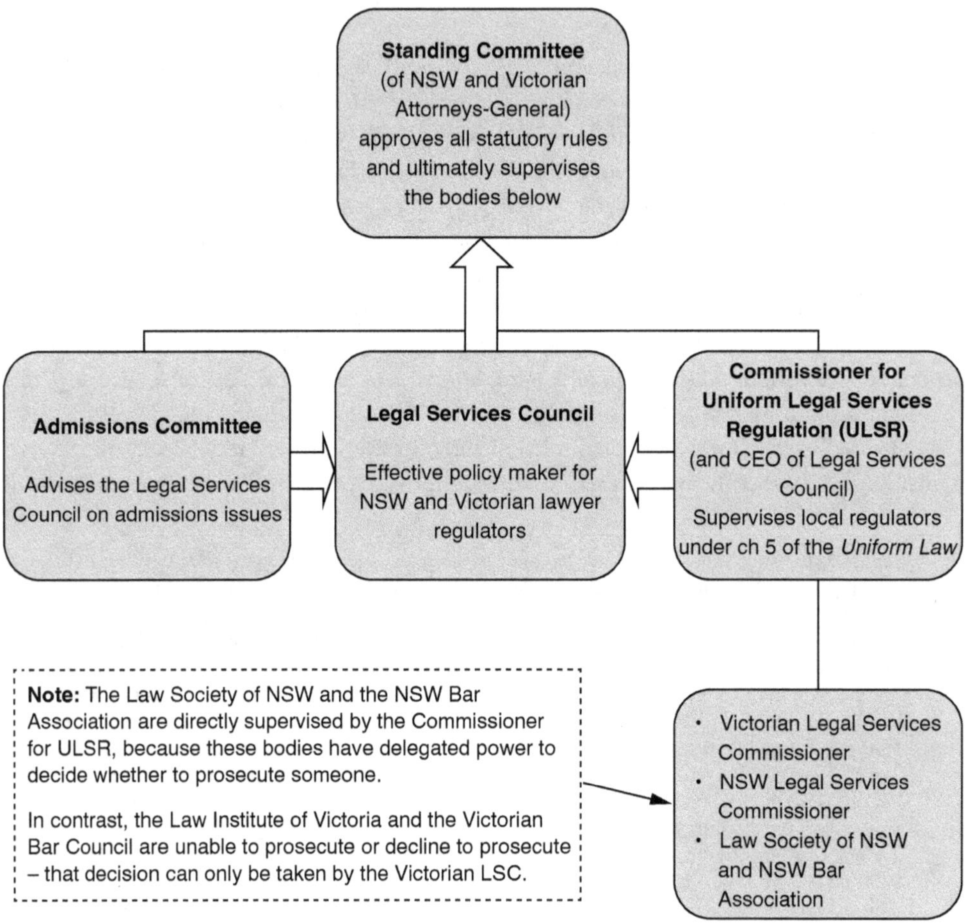

*These will likely be reflected in the regulatory structure in Western Australia.

80 In Victoria a seven-member Legal Services Board and Legal Services Commissioner ('LSC') sits at the apex of professional regulation. The Legal Services Board issues practising certificates, administers and manages the trust accounting system and the fidelity fund, and can make and approve legal professional rules. The LSC is also chief executive officer of the Legal Services Board. This function necessarily involves taking direction from the Board, the composition of which includes at least three lawyers elected by the profession. However, in the LSC's other roles as complaints handler, investigator and prosecutor, it is to operate 'independently' of the Legal Services Board.

National ethical rules

Professional ethical guidance through conduct rules has been a more successful national campaign than the campaign for uniform regulation. As noted, model professional conduct rules for solicitors – the *ASCR* – have been adopted by legislation in all jurisdictions except the Northern Territory. Amendments made in 2022 have been, at the time of writing, adopted in the *Uniform Law* jurisdictions. The first and second versions of the *ASCR* were drafted by the LCA and based on its earlier *Model Rules*, but with significant changes in two vital areas of professional ethics: confidentiality (see Chapter 4) and conflicts of interest (see Chapter 7). In these and other respects the impact of continuing self-regulation of the profession is evident. As discussed in Chapter 7, changes to earlier conduct rules[81] to legitimate and license certain conflicts of interest that most benefit large firms may be the result of lobbying by Law Firms Australia, a group of global law firms. The national rules could therefore be seen more as a compromise than as driven by common values in a diverse profession servicing a range of clients. However, the 2022 amendments to these conflict rules (new *ASCR* r 11A), as described in Chapter 7, better reflect this diversity of practice and a stronger commitment to access to justice. Community legal services and small firms servicing individuals argued that modification of the conflict rules was required to address a severe lack of access to justice for many people. Modification, they said, would not diminish the competency and ethicality of their services but would allow more people to access an affordable lawyer when they need one – surely an important goal of the profession.

This raises a question about the best form of ethical rules. Should there be one set of rules to cover all practitioners or specific rules for specific areas or contexts of practice? Another approach is to simply set out key values or principles that must be observed and leave lawyers to interpret these for themselves. Scholars debate whether ethical rules are most effective as comprehensive codes or as principle-based standards.[82] There is no perfect solution, we suggest; rather, we should evaluate the rules for any positive guidance as to ethical daily practice. This we do throughout the book.

As mentioned, the Australian Bar Association drafted template conduct rules for barristers that were adopted in most jurisdictions in 2011. In 2015, these rules with amendments were enacted (as part of the *Uniform Law* in New South Wales, Victoria and Western Australia) as the *Legal Profession Uniform Conduct (Barristers) Rules 2015* ('*Barristers' Conduct Rules*'). While the conduct rules governing barristers in other jurisdictions vary in name and do not contain identical provisions, there is generally a common ethical code applying across Australia.[83]

81 *ASCR* rr 10, 11.

82 England and Wales take an 'outcome-based' approach that comes from a consequentialist approach to regulation (what it calls 'risk-based'). This requires certain outcomes from solicitors and authorised firms observing seven key ethical principles. The firm or individual is expected to exercise judgement in applying the standards to the situation. See, eg, Fred Zacharias, 'Steroids and Legal Ethics Codes: Are Lawyers Rational Actors' (2010) 85(2) *Notre Dame Law Review* 671.

83 Tasmania adopts these rules in 2023. In Queensland the 2011 *Barristers Rules*, as amended in 2018, are made by the local Bar Association pursuant to the legislation but are binding only on its members. The South Australian *Legal Practitioners' Conduct Rules* (from 1 January 2022) contain rules for all legal practitioners in that State as a fused profession. The conduct rules for barristers are contained in pt B and numbered according to the rules under the *Uniform Law* with minor variations. In the book we refer to the *Legal Profession Uniform Conduct (Barristers) Rules 2015* ('*Barristers' Conduct Rules*') as these represent the approach in the majority of jurisdictions, but we indicate where there is significant local variation.

The *Barristers' Conduct Rules*, like the *ASCR*, set out relatively detailed ethical practice requirements for barristers. Unlike the *ASCR,* they also regulate the scope of practice. The current form of the rules can be seen as implementing competitive regulation that removes previous restrictive practices, such as requiring that a junior barrister also be briefed if a senior barrister is briefed (thereby increasing costs for the client).[84]

In the following chapters of this book we refer to the *ASCR* and the *Barristers' Conduct Rules* as the national standards for professional conduct and practice rules. We do so because these rules have achieved considerable acceptance across Australia rather than because they are an improvement on any prior rules or are superior to any of the local versions of the *Model Rules* made by State and Territory professional associations and regulators in particular jurisdictions. Accordingly, we will critique the details of many specific provisions of the *ASCR* and the *Barristers' Conduct Rules*, pointing out any gaps or ambiguities in their coverage.

Continuing self-regulation – admission and certification

Prior to the current regulatory regimes, self-regulation set strict entry, or 'admission', requirements to the profession in the attempt to ensure that only well-qualified people of good character entered the profession – lawyers that clients could trust. Lawyers were, and still are, admitted into practice on the basis of academic legal qualifications, practical training and 'good fame and character'.[85]

Admission to practice still reflects the historical self-regulatory ideal of the profession as a moral community that socialises its members into the appropriate role and character. Admission to the profession is largely controlled by the Supreme Courts of the various States and Territories, and these courts also retain their inherent jurisdiction to remove from the roll – or 'strike off' – practitioners who fail to live up to the standards of a fit and proper person. There is now national consensus about requirements for admission, although the processes are somewhat different.[86]

In order to practise law lawfully,[87] a person must be admitted and certified. Once admitted, the step of certification is a formality for solicitors (absent another issue arising), but barristers are generally expected to undertake a bar examination and some further training in advocacy before being issued with a practising certificate.[88] In most jurisdictions, except Victoria, control of the administrative licensing process is in the hands of the law societies. Even in Victoria, the Legal Services Board has delegated the licensing process back to the profession.

Linda Haller argues that the power to control practising certificates may be even more important for regulatory authority than is the power of disciplinary control, because

84 Other traditionally restrictive practices of barristers have been swept away through competition regulation described earlier in the chapter.

85 See *Re Davis* (1947) 75 CLR 409; *Ex parte Lenehan* (1948) 77 CLR 403; *Re B* [1981] 2 NSWLR 372. Under most legislation in Australia, 'good fame and conduct' is a subset of other criteria for determining the 'fitness to practice' of an applicant as described further in this chapter.

86 Francesca Bartlett and Linda Haller, 'Disclosing Lawyers: Questioning Law and Process in the Admission of Australian Lawyers' (2013) 41 *Federal Law Review* 227.

87 See above discussion of this.

88 Renewal of certification must be done annually and the same requirements for ongoing disclosure about matters going to a practitioner's 'character' (described below) apply.

administrative withdrawal of a right of practice is immediate and less expensive for regulators than the commencement of contested disciplinary proceedings.[89] As can be seen in Case study 3.3, there are considerable powers in certification: a law society can quickly remove the licence of a lawyer with questionable 'fitness' to practise, so as to both allay public concerns and protect current clients.

Today, for admission and certification, only those who have the required knowledge (the law degree),[90] have completed a practical legal training requirement, have proficiency in English, and are 'fit and proper'[91] to be admitted can be admitted to, and remain in, the legal profession.[92] Usually, it is only the last of these requirements that causes any difficulty or contention.[93] The words 'fit and proper' are not defined in any legislation and those that decide admission (courts and admission bodies issuing compliance certificates) are given wide discretion to decide what might be relevant to consider, although there is a list of things that must be considered, if raised.[94] One of these considerations is the old common law concept of 'good fame and character', although the aspect of 'fame' – how someone is publicly regarded – seems of less importance than it initially was.[95]

Being 'fit and proper' could mean almost anything: for potential lawyers, it is generally demonstrated by the absence of anything that would cast doubt on the suitability of the person for admission to the profession, such as a prior criminal history, deliberate rule breaking or any other indication of dishonesty.[96] Courts have been particularly concerned about student academic misconduct where this relates to dishonest behaviour.[97] Legislation directing decision makers (set out below) now provides some guidance about relevant matters and explicitly includes the concept of 'capacity' – whether the applicant is 'currently unable satisfactorily to carry out the inherent requirements of practice as an Australian legal practitioner'. This consideration takes into account any evidence of mental illness.[98] One of

89 Linda Haller, 'Discipline vs Regulation: Lessons from the Collapse of Tasmania's Legal Profession Reform Bill' (2005) 12(1) *eLaw Journal: Murdoch University Electronic Journal of Law* [1].

90 The requirement around the country is to complete the required 'Priestley 11' subjects, plus statutory interpretation: Law Admissions Consultative Committee, Law Council of Australia, *Prescribed Academic Areas of Knowledge* (December 2016) <https://www.legalservicescouncil.org.au/Documents/prescribed-academic-areas-of-knowledge.pdf>. The areas are criminal law and procedure, torts, contracts, property, equity (including trusts), company law, administrative law, constitutional law, civil dispute resolution, evidence, and ethics and professional responsibility. A process of review and a newly framed list in 2020 was scrapped by the Law Admissions Consultative Committee.

91 Bartlett and Haller (n 86); Alice Woolley, 'Tending the Bar: The Good Character Requirement for Law Society Admission' (2007) 30(1) *Dalhousie Law Journal* 27.

92 In New South Wales, Victoria and Western Australia, see the *Uniform Law* s 17 and the *Legal Profession Uniform Admission Rules 2015* r 10. This is replicated in other States and Territories.

93 While the character test is applied at the admission and certification stage, generally this will be considered by a court or admission body on application for admission.

94 *Legal Profession Uniform Admission Rules, 2015* r 10.

95 Bartlett and Haller (n 86).

96 Law Admission Consultative Committee, *Disclosure Guidelines for Applicants for Admission to Legal Practice* ('*LACC Guidelines*'). These guidelines have been subject to minor amendments by local State and Territory admission authorities where they are adopted and applied. They are not binding law but provide guidance to applicants on how the law and procedure is to be understood.

97 *Re OG (A Lawyer)* (2007) 18 VR 164; *Re Liveri* [2006] QCA 152.

98 *Victorian Lawyers RPA Ltd v X* (2001) 3 VR 601; *Re Legal Practitioners Act 1970* [2003] ACTSC 11; *XY v Board of Examiners* [2005] VSC 250.

the authors has argued that listing 'capacity' among moral considerations about the person's character is questionable.[99] Nevertheless, admissions boards and courts have indicated that the relevant inquiry about a person's mental state is directed to ascertain whether a person is simply incapable of practising law due to a serious and untreated mental illness. Practically, this means that, if a mental health condition is adequately treated, it would not prevent the person from being admitted.[100]

The legislatively prescribed list of matters to be taken into account in relation to fitness appears below (this list is similar around the country). While the list is long, case law indicates that admission authorities regularly raise other matters (as above) as indicating a concern about a person's 'character'. The profession is chiefly interested in whether an applicant is honest and has a respect for law.

> ***Legal Profession Uniform Admission Rules 2015***
>
> **10. Determining whether someone is a fit and proper person**
>
> **(1)** For the purposes of section 17(2)(b) of the *Uniform Law*, the following matters are specified as matters to which the Board must have regard –
>
> **(a)** any statutory declaration as to the person's character, referred to in rule 16;
> **(b)** any disclosure statement made by the person under rule 17;
> **(c)** any police report provided under rule 18;
> **(d)** any student conduct report provided under rule 19;
> **(e)** any certificate of good standing provided under rule 20;
> **(f)** whether the person is currently of good fame and character;
> **(g)** whether the person is or has been a bankrupt … or has been an officer of a corporation that has been wound up in insolvency or under external administration;
> **(h)** whether the person has been found guilty of an offence including a spent offence in Australia or in a foreign country, and if so –
> **(i)** the nature of the offence; and
> **(ii)** how long ago the offence was committed; and
> **(iii)** the person's age when the offence was committed;
> **(i)** whether the person has been the subject of any disciplinary action, howsoever expressed, in any profession or occupation in Australia or in a foreign country;
> **(j)** whether the person has been the subject of disciplinary action, howsoever expressed, in any profession or occupation that involved a finding adverse to the person;
> **(k)** whether the person is currently unable satisfactorily to carry out the inherent requirements of practice as an Australian legal practitioner; …

99 Bartlett and Haller (n 86).

100 For instance, in Victoria the Legal Admissions Board has issued a 'Guide for Applicants for Admission as an Australian Lawyer' (2022) that provides detailed guidance on admission requirements including disclosures regarding 'capacity' to practise law. This guide also annexes the *LACC Guidelines* that similarly indicate that managed illness does not have to be disclosed and would not be a basis for refusing someone entry into the profession: at 29–32. See also *S v Legal Practice Board of Western Australia* (2004) 29 WAR 173.

In practice, the above factors usually arise for consideration only when the practitioner draws them to the attention of the admission board.[101] While at law the onus of proof rests on the applicant to establish their fitness to practise,[102] in reality there is a presumption of good character. The majority of admission cases are about inappropriate non-disclosure by the applicant – *not* telling an admission board about a matter listed above or about something else that the applicant should know reflects on their honesty or obedience to law. When this occurs, or the applicant is seen as inappropriately playing down the moral nature of disclosed conduct – 'it wasn't that bad' – the court interprets this as reflecting poorly on the applicant's present ethical awareness and thus their personal character (that is, is the person dishonest?). The test is whether the applicant is *currently fit and proper* (*Uniform Law* s 17(2)(b)). Consider the example in Case study 3.2.

CASE STUDY 3.2 PLAYING DOWN MORAL RESPONSIBILITY IN A CROWD[103]

The following facts were described by a court about an application for admission:

> In his application for admission the applicant provided the Board with a disclosure statement relating to [his] offending and also with the sentencing remarks from the Court of Summary Jurisdiction. He disclosed that he had been convicted of five counts of engaging in conduct as a result of which he obtained a financial advantage, knowing or believing that he was not eligible to receive that financial advantage, contrary to the provisions of s 135(2)(1) of the *Criminal Code* (Cth). On 30 March 2009 he was dealt with in the Court of Summary Jurisdiction when he was convicted on each count and released on a bond in the sum of $2,000 in his own recognisance to be of good behaviour for a period of 12 months.
>
> The applicant advised that the offending occurred when, for the period from August 2006 to April 2008, he received Austudy benefits from Centrelink pursuant to an entitlement arising from his course of study at Charles Darwin University. During the relevant period he also worked in casual employment and he failed to declare his earnings from that employment to Centrelink contrary to his obligations. He thereby received more in the way of benefits than would be his entitlement had he disclosed his earnings.

101 Applicants must also advertise their intention to be admitted to practice, and there is provision for a member of the public to contact the admitting authority about any matters that might be relevant to that person's suitability or eligibility. See, eg, *Uniform Law* s 17(2).

102 *Re OG (A Lawyer)* (2007) 18 VR 164.

103 This case study is based on *In the Matter of an Application by TJS* [2011] NTSC 63. After a few years, this person applied for admission in New South Wales and was admitted because he was judged to have sufficiently understood his previous wrongdoing and engaged in rehabilitation that demonstrated his *current* fitness to practise law: *S v Legal Profession Admission Board* [2015] NSWSC 1839.

> At the end of the period the applicant commenced full-time work. He stated that he was aware he had accumulated a large debt and he approached Centrelink and informed an officer that he had been overpaid. He provided his pay slips to the officer and requested that the amount to be repaid be calculated so that he could make the necessary repayments. The calculation revealed the applicant had been paid $9,236.46 to which he was not entitled. He subsequently repaid the amount in full.
>
> In his affidavit the applicant explained that he had previously been in receipt of benefits and had terminated those benefits whilst he took a break from studies. When he resumed his study in 2006 he suffered delay in having benefits restored. Once the benefits were restored, and when he started to receive income, he said he approached Centrelink and informed an officer that he had commenced working and requested that appropriate declaration forms be provided to him. He was advised by the officer to declare his income on the Centrelink website, but he was unsuccessful in his attempts to do so. Thereafter he said he approached the Centrelink office on two further occasions requesting that the appropriate declaration forms be sent to his address. The forms did not arrive.

When the applicant applied for admission, he revealed his conviction and explained it in this way:

> Following the frustration of having to reapply for my benefits, the month long process therein involved, and having attempted three times to declare my income unsuccessfully I felt worn down by Centrelink. Each time I was directed to the correct procedures for declaring income and each time Centrelink had failed to send me the appropriate documentation to comply with these procedures. I waited for a while for the fortnightly form to arrive with fading attentiveness. I felt that I had made a concerted and genuine attempt to do the right thing only to be frustrated by Centrelink. My focus was on my studies, my new job, my new home, and getting by. The frustration and stress was magnified by my financial need. I was struggling to meet costs even receiving the extra money and foresaw difficulties ahead. I was aware that many students failed to declare their income. The usual outcome is that they are caught at some later stage and forced to repay the money. In fact I had never heard of a student not being caught up with eventually. It is extremely common behaviour within the student body and I felt some comfort in this fact. However I had never heard of a student being prosecuted for this type of behaviour. I genuinely believed that by failing to declare my income I would receive a slightly higher sum of money each week that I would be able to pay back with interest at a later stage but with no other penalty. I conceived of the money as a loan which I always intended to declare and repay. Moreover as I had the financial record of an average student I did not believe I could approach a financial lending institution for a loan.[104]

104 *In the Matter of an Application by TJS* [2011] NTSC 63, [9]–[12].

The Law Society of the Northern Territory opposed the applicant's admission on the basis that the impressions he conveyed about the context were false:

> The Society submitted that information subsequently obtained from Centrelink revealed that the applicant was notified on 16 April 2008 that an overpayment had occurred and would be investigated. Shortly thereafter he received a letter confirming that to be the case. His co-operation by volunteering information came about in circumstances where he was aware that an investigation into an aspect of his entitlement had been commenced. Of the prospect that the investigation would reveal the overpayments made to him the applicant said in evidence, 'it was certainly something I considered at that time but I dismissed it'. He said he made a conscious decision not to reveal the payments immediately because he still had financial difficulties. The applicant did not reveal to the Court of Summary Jurisdiction or to the Board that any enquiry was under way, that it had caused him initial concern or that, because of his financial position, he had made a conscious decision to continue to receive payments to which he was not entitled for a further period.[105]

The Court found the applicant's account was implausible and 'reflect[ed] an effort on his part to minimise his culpability. [The account] demonstrates that, at the time of giving evidence, he was not fully accepting of responsibility for the course of criminal conduct he had undertaken. ... This finding impacts upon my assessment of whether or not he is now a fit and proper person to be admitted as a local lawyer'.[106] The application was refused.

Discussion questions

1. The applicant described the nature of his breach as 'one of omission' – being a failure to inform Centrelink of his earnings. (The Court did not agree with this on the evidence.) Is an action morally less concerning if it was an act of 'omission' rather than a positive act?
2. The Court found that the applicant 'has been convicted of offences of dishonesty which, at the time of commission, demonstrated that he was not a fit and proper person for admission. There has been no evidence placed before the Court to enable a conclusion to be drawn that he is now a fit and proper person for admission.'[107] What might change a court's mind about his 'fitness' between receiving a conviction and applying for admission?
3. What do you think about the applicant describing his underreporting of income to Centrelink as 'extremely common behaviour'? Does it make it more acceptable behaviour?

105 Ibid [31]–[33].
106 Ibid [24].
107 Ibid [42].

Courts have increasingly adopted a strict approach to disclosure of matters relating to an applicant's character. As Pagone J stated in *Frugtniet v Board of Examiners:*

> [The applicant's] obligation was to disclose matters that could inform a judgment about whether he was a fit and proper person for admission to practice. It was not an obligation merely to list convictions or charges, but was an obligation to inform the decision maker of everything that could bear upon the judgment that needed to be made about him and his character. His task was not to select or edit from his life's experiences only some events that might be relevant to the question, but to disclose every matter that might fairly assist in deciding whether the applicant was a fit and proper person at the time of admission. *Revealing more than might strictly be necessary counts in favour of an applicant; especially where the disclosure still carries embarrassment or discomfort. Revealing less than may be necessary distorts the proper assessment of the applicant and may itself show an inappropriate desire to distort by selection and screening of relevant facts.*[108]

Given the breadth of judicial interest in an applicant's life, it might be difficult for an applicant to decide what to include in an application for admission. While a 'when in doubt put everything in' approach is probably the safest, those with a background of minor indiscretions might find the application process unnecessarily daunting.[109] This might not simply be a case of wanting to hide their past but a concern that they will be unfairly judged. The expectation of the test of 'fitness' is that applicants ethically reflect on their past and what is required for legal practice. It might be a worthy reflective exercise for all applicants to consider their values and personal weaknesses, and honestly reveal their past misdeeds, when entering the profession. Yet we doubt whether such an exercise is genuinely undertaken by most applicants who have no criminal convictions or other findings of dishonesty. We note also that there is little evidence that the past deeds of a person will predict whether they will engage in unethical conduct in practice.[110] Indeed, one might question, based on a wealth of social psychology,[111] the assumption that we have stable character traits that will dictate our behaviour into the future.

A final concern is that a 'fitness' test at admission can simply be used to exclude those with whom the profession, being senior lawyers and judges at the time, disagrees. Across the common law world, there have been critiques of admission tests as masking discriminatory intentions.[112] While Australian courts have rejected the notion that they would exclude anyone for their religious or political beliefs,[113] Australia has a history of refusing entry to

108 [2002] VSC 140, [11] (emphasis added).

109 This might be particularly the case for applicants with a history of minor rule breaking that might have resulted from mental health issues. This is further discussed in Bartlett and Haller (n 86).

110 Woolley (n 91); Leslie Levin, 'The Folly of Expecting Evil: Reconsidering the Bar's Character and Fitness Requirement' (2014) (4) *Brigham Young University Law Review* 775.

111 See, eg, Mitt Regan, 'Legal Ethics and the Situated Lawyer' (2017) 30(2) *Georgetown Journal of Legal Ethics* 415.

112 See, on the United States, Deborah Rhode, 'Moral Character as a Professional Credential' (1985) 94(3) *Yale Law Journal* 491.

113 *Re B* [1981] 2 NSWLR 372, 380.

women – a practice that required legislative intervention to reverse.[114] Indeed, in one case where the court adamantly declared that no person would be excluded for their political belief, they refused to admit a feminist activist, Wendy Bacon.[115] Excluding women may be a thing of the past, but it illustrates that social context can influence the 'at large' assessment of suitability for admission. For instance, sedition legislation introduced into Australia could, over time, swing the balance against the admission of lawyers who, for example, argue for non-violent civil disobedience.[116] As discussed in Chapter 11, active campaigning in relation to climate change, where there is an increasing array of legislative restraints on peaceful protest, could not only result in a conviction that must be revealed but chill the expression of opinion by future lawyers.

Independent and co-regulation: complaints and discipline

Once entry to the profession had been attained, under the traditional model, lawyers were assumed to be sufficiently expert, competent and capable of serving clients well. The ongoing regulation of lawyers' practice focused on maintaining standards of character, not competence.[117] The community of lawyers was the relevant judge of the moral character of the lawyer and their impugned behaviour. The *Allison* test, still applied by Australian courts, defines professional misconduct as 'disgraceful or dishonourable conduct' as judged by other lawyers of 'good repute and competency'.[118] The assumption is that unethical conduct is the result of dishonest behaviour by individual lawyers of bad character, who must be cast out of the profession or have their character reformed.

Thus, traditional self-regulation focused on discovering and sanctioning failures of character such as knowingly or deliberately misleading a court or tribunal, or falsifying a document, serious breaches of trust account rules and other fiduciary breaches such as acting on personal conflicts of interests. Traditional self-regulation did little to make sure that lawyers maintained an appropriate standard of competence or client service. It was assumed that competence would take care of itself through individual lawyers' steadily increasing experience. Only in the case of 'gross negligence' could a lawyer be sanctioned for lack of care and competence.[119] This was despite the fact that the vast majority of complaints

114 *Re Edith Haynes* (1904) 6 WAR 209.

115 *Re B* [1981] 2 NSWLR 372. In this case Wendy Bacon was refused admission to practice after the majority of the Court considered that she had not been honest in relation to her actions in assisting a person by providing money for bail. Bacon provided a scathing account of her experience that suggests that she was considered unfit on the basis of her activism: Wendy Bacon, 'I Fought the Law … ', *The Sydney Morning Herald* (Sydney, 22 November 2003).

116 *Re B* [1981] 2 NSWLR 372 is arguably an example of this.

117 This is a function of the court's duty to administer the law in the interests of justice and of its authority to admit lawyers to practice: *Myers v Elman* [1940] AC 282. See William Felstiner, 'Professional Inattention: Origins and Consequences' in Keith Hawkins (ed), *The Human Face of Law: Essays in Honour of Donald Harris* (Clarendon, 1997) 121; Parker (n 1) 689–93.

118 *Allison v General Council of Medical Education and Registration* [1894] 1 QB 750.

119 See *Re Moseley* (1925) 25 SR (NSW) 174. While the legislation governing lawyers around the country now refers to a failure to comply with a standard of 'competence and diligence' expected by the public of a reasonably competent lawyer (below), mere negligence is rarely prosecuted and, when it has been, disciplinary tribunals have tended to refer to common law standards.

clients make about lawyers concern poor service – delay, incompetence, overcharging and discourtesy or failure to communicate.[120] These complaints were rarely seriously investigated by disciplinary authorities. Overcharging was generally only disciplined where it was blatant and dishonest. Indeed, price fixing was entrenched by self-regulatory rules, and competition of any kind that might lower fees was discouraged or prohibited, as discussed in Chapter 8. Self-regulatory authorities were unlikely to act against lawyers in relation to conduct that was against the public interest but in the interests of clients, such as abuse of the court process by frivolous or vexatious claims or claims for an ulterior purpose, or for excessive adversarialism that wastes the resources of the court and/or the parties.[121]

Traditional approaches to professional discipline are now incorporated into the Australian regulatory regimes. The common law tests are applied for serious charges, alongside statutory terminology (set out below).[122] But regimes around the country add to the common law approach by introducing a less serious category of wrongdoing than 'disgraceful or dishonourable conduct' – 'unsatisfactory professional conduct'. This represents a shift from the traditional approach to expand the disciplinary regime to better meet consumer complaints.[123] The following is a description of the regulatory charges in lawyer discipline that are used around the country.

DISCIPLINARY CHARGES – *UNIFORM LAW* ss 296–298[124]

Unsatisfactory professional conduct includes conduct in relation to practice that 'falls short of the standard of competence and diligence that a member of the public is entitled to expect of a reasonably competent Australian legal practitioner'.

Professional misconduct is a more serious form of conduct, including a 'substantial or consistent failure to reach or maintain a reasonable standard of competence and diligence'.

Certain types of conduct are expressly included that could constitute professional misconduct or unsatisfactory professional conduct: namely, charging of excessive legal fees; a finding of guilt for a serious offence, tax offence or offence involving dishonesty; becoming insolvent under administration; becoming disqualified from management or being involved in a corporation; failure to comply with an order of a professional disciplinary body or a compensation order.

120 See, eg, Office of the Legal Services Commissioner (NSW), *Annual Report 2020–2021* (Report, 2021) 25.

121 Chapter 6 considers how the procedural powers of courts, augmented by legislation in some States, have been used by courts to address these concerns in recent years.

122 Some have argued that this is a somewhat incongruous approach: Chris Edmonds, 'Misconduct of Australian Lawyers under Legislation Based on the National Model – Aligning the Common Law Tests with the New Statutory Regime' (2013) 39(3) *Monash University Law Review* 776. Recently, the NSW Court of Appeal confirmed that the '*Allison* test' is useful in deciding whether a practitioner remains 'fit' to practise but does not constitute a separate category of professional misconduct: *Council of the New South Wales Bar Association v EFA (A Pseudonym)* (2021) 106 NSWLR 383, [151].

123 However, some have argued that the implementation of this parliamentary intention is less than satisfactory: Linda Haller, 'Professional Discipline for Incompetent Lawyers? Developments in the UK and Australia' (2010) 17(1) *International Journal of the Legal Profession* 83.

124 *Legal Profession Act 2006* (ACT) ss 386–9; *Legal Profession Act 2006* (NT) ss 464–6; *Legal Profession Act 2007* (Qld) ss 418–20; *Legal Practitioners Act 1981* (SA) ss 68–70; *Legal Profession Act 2007* (Tas) ss 420–2.

The main sanctions imposed under current legislation for findings by a court of professional misconduct are also consistent with traditional conceptions: namely, expulsion of the lawyer from the profession, suspension from practice, a reprimand and monetary fines. Yet, in addition to the traditional sanctions, legislation has introduced more therapeutic approaches such as restrictions on practice, removal of a right to manage a trust account or need for senior lawyer supervision, a requirement to attend continuing legal education, and strategies to manage personal challenges such as assistance in maintaining mental health.

The courts were and remain clear that the purpose of these sanctions is to *protect the public* from professionals who are not worthy of their trust, and to *protect the reputation and privileges of the whole profession* by ridding the profession of unethical individuals: 'A disbarring order is in no sense punitive in character. When such an order is made, it is made, from the public point of view, for the protection of those who require protection and, from the professional point of view, in order that abuse of privilege may not lead to loss of privilege.'[125] The 'abuse of privilege' to which the court was referring in that case concerned unfounded allegations of fraud made by a barrister in open court. Consider the disciplinary action in Case study 3.3.

CASE STUDY 3.3 **REGULATING DISHONESTY IN PRACTICE**

A solicitor was found guilty of professional misconduct due to behaviour in the course of practice, and for his conduct when he was subject to criminal investigation,[126] in relation to a 'scheme' with colleagues to avoid reporting income from clients. The solicitor asked a number of clients to pay $600,000 in cash, which was not deposited into the firm's trust account (as it should have been, because it was trust money) and did not comply with anti-money laundering[127] reporting requirements. Neither was it reported to the trustee in bankruptcy (which the solicitor was obliged to do, because he was bankrupt).[128] For many client files there were no written agreements (costs agreements and costs disclosure are required by legislation as is described in Chapter 8) and some agreements were falsified. When subject to inquiry by the Crime and Corruption Commission, the solicitor created false records to provide to the Commission.

In sentencing the solicitor for various criminal convictions in 2017, Atkinson J remarked:

> There is an expectation that all citizens will obey the law. However, as a legal practitioner, you have specifically sworn or affirmed that you will, as it says in the

125 *Clyne v New South Wales Bar Association* (1960) 104 CLR 186, 201–2. See also Linda Haller, 'Disciplinary Fines: Deterrence or Retribution?' (2002) 5(1–2) *Legal Ethics* 152; Linda Haller, 'Smoke and Mirrors: Public Health or Hazard?' (2005) 8(1) *Legal Ethics* 70.

126 *Legal Services Commissioner v Meehan* [2019] QCAT 17. In the criminal case he pleaded guilty to one count of aggravated fraud and eight counts of fraudulently falsifying records after a Crime and Corruption Commission investigation into a Brisbane law firm.

127 Lawyers must report cash received of $10,000 or more to the Australian Transaction Reports and Analysis Centre: *Financial Transaction Reports Act 1988* (Cth) s 15A.

128 The trust account duties are briefly outlined later in the chapter.

> oath or affirmation of office which you took in this court when you became a legal practitioner – that you will truly and honestly conduct yourself in the practice of a lawyer of this court according to law and to the best of your knowledge and ability. You have grossly breached that solemn promise that you made. A legal practitioner is afforded a number of privileges, including a favourable presumption concerning honesty and integrity in your professional conduct. Members of the public, other legal practitioners and the court are entitled to rely on the honesty and integrity of legal practitioners, no less is expected of any legal practitioner, and it is a presumption that lies at the heart of the effective and efficient administration of justice, both civil justice and, in particular, criminal justice. Unfortunately, your conduct has breached that important presumption of honesty and integrity. That means that your conduct is regarded more seriously than conduct by someone who is not a legal practitioner.[129]

In 2018 the Queensland Legal Services Commissioner brought disciplinary proceedings against the solicitor for 'dishonest and disreputable conduct'[130] and a breach of *ASCR* r 5 relating to the multiple findings of fraud. The solicitor was found guilty of professional misconduct and removed from the role.

The Tribunal found that the solicitor was currently not 'fit to practice' and that the solicitor was 'probably permanently unfit to practice' (this being the common law test for deciding to remove a name from the roll).[131]

DISCUSSION QUESTIONS

1. The President of the Queensland Law Society said of the criminal proceedings:

> There are more than 11,000 ethical, dedicated and hardworking solicitors across Queensland whose reputation is no doubt called into question in the very rare occasion where a lawyer participates in criminality. QLS take matters such as this very seriously and the public deserve answers when a lawyer is charged with committing criminal acts.[132]

The President emphasised that there was swift action taken by the Society to ensure the lawyer surrendered his practising certificate while the criminal prosecution was continuing[133] and was auditing the trust accounts of the firm. What was the

129 Transcript of Proceedings, *R v Timothy Vincent Charles Meehan* (Supreme Court of Queensland, Indictment No 873/2017, 14 July 2017) 8, cited in *Legal Services Commissioner v Meehan* [2019] QCAT 17, [21]. Meehan was sentenced to five and a half years in prison.

130 *Legal Services Commissioner v Meehan* [2019] QCAT 17.

131 *Prothonotary v Richard* (New South Wales Court of Appeal, McHugh JA, 31 July 1987).

132 David Hunt, 'Morcombe Killer's Lawyer Tim Meehan Pleads Guilty to More than $30k Fraud, Falsifying Invoices in Brisbane Court', *ABC News* (online at 22 June 2017) <https://www.abc.net.au/news/2017-06-22/criminal-solicitor-tim-meehan-pleads-guilty-fraud-brisbane-court/8641666>.

133 Cited in Kate McKenna, 'Paroled Former Criminal Lawyer Tim Meehan's Bid to be Reinstated on the Legal Role Denied', *ABC News* (online at 15 February 2019) <https://www.abc.net.au/news/2019-02-18/tim-meehan-brett-cowan-lawyer-bid-reinstated-legal-role/10822686>.

President trying to communicate to the public in these statements? It took about two years after the solicitor's criminal convictions for him to be removed from the roll. Is this concerning in terms of the responsiveness of the system?

2. Do you think a lawyer will always be found to be 'unfit to practice' law, if they are convicted of a criminal offence? If not, are there certain offences that might be more likely to result in this finding?

In Case study 3.3 the Tribunal weighed a number of factors in sentencing the solicitor, including that he had been punished for his actions (receiving a five-and-a-half-year custodial sentence) and had cooperated with the authorities and expressed his remorse.[134] Nonetheless, the nature of the behaviour – sustained dishonesty – was enough to require his name to be removed from the roll. In other cases tribunals have taken into consideration, in relation to sanction, that a practitioner is completely candid with the profession and the court about their past misbehaviour, acknowledges that it was wrong and shows remorse, contrition and a demonstrated change of behaviour.[135] Courts are also increasingly recognising evidence of serious mental illness, and treatment, as relevant to whether a lawyer can show that they are 'fit' to practise again.[136]

In Case study 3.3 the Tribunal considered convictions relating to his professional practice. However, other disciplinary cases raise difficult questions about what aspects of a lawyer's life should relate to their 'fitness' to practise. The starkest example is the High Court of Australia decision in the case of *A Solicitor v Law Society of New South Wales*.[137] Here a solicitor was convicted of four counts of aggravated indecent assault on persons under 16. The assaults were against his stepdaughters. There was a disciplinary application a few years later, where the solicitor failed to reveal that he had been convicted of further similar charges (and then acquitted on appeal), and he was removed from the roll. He appealed this sanction, and by the time his appeal was heard by the High Court in 2004 he had served five years in prison. The Court considered that his conduct 'did not occur in the course of the practice of his profession, and it had no connection with such practice'.[138] This reflects other decisions of that Court that there needs to be a nexus between the conduct in a lawyer's personal life and legal practice. It is not enough that the lawyer breaks the law – their transgression must have relevance for practice.[139] However, as Reid Mortensen

134 Such factors were equally considered as important in sanctioning in *A Solicitor v Council of the Law Society of New South Wales* (2004) 216 CLR 253 where the Court considered the contrition and rehabilitation of the solicitor as significant in deciding he should have been suspended and his time in prison was a sufficient period.

135 Francesca Bartlett, 'The Role of Apologies in Professional Discipline' (2011) 14(1) *Legal Ethics* 49; Stephen Tang, Tony Foley and Vivien Holmes, 'Ethical Misconduct by New Australian Lawyers: Prevalence and Prevention' (2020) 27(3) *International Journal of the Legal Profession* 245.

136 Tara Sklar et al, 'Vulnerability to Legal Misconduct: A Profile of Problem Lawyers in Victoria, Australia' (2020) 27(3) *International Journal of the Legal Profession* 269.

137 *A Solicitor v Council of the Law Society of New South Wales* (2004) 216 CLR 253. See also Haller, 'Smoke and Mirrors' (n 125); Suzanne Le Mire, 'Striking Off: Criminal Lawyers and Disclosure of Their Convictions' (2005) 79(10) *Australian Law Journal* 641.

138 *A Solicitor v Council of the Law Society of New South Wales* (2004) 216 CLR 253, 273 [32].

139 *Prothonotary of the Supreme Court of New South Wales v P* [2003] NSWCA 320.

has argued, a virtue-based conception of character for lawyers might approach this issue very differently.[140] The behaviour in this case is ethically concerning, because the lawyer can be understood to have acted in gross breach of trust towards his stepdaughters. Lawyers are expected to act as fiduciaries and bear considerable responsibilities, and a breach of trust can be seen as akin to an act of dishonesty.

An equally ethically concerning recent decision of a NSW disciplinary tribunal concerned an incident at a Bar social function, where two male barristers greeted each other with a parody of oral sex in front of a female clerk. It was found that one of the male barristers then pushed the female clerk's head towards his crotch and said the words 'suck my dick'.[141] The Tribunal found that this behaviour was not a sexual advance but 'horseplay', was 'unwelcome conduct of a sexual nature towards H', and was 'poorly judged, vulgar and inappropriate'.[142] Further, the Tribunal characterised the conduct as one without a real or sensible connection with professional practice.[143] The conduct was held to be unsatisfactory professional conduct and the barrister received a reprimand. We disagree that a professional function is not related to the course of practice and we suggest that the characterisation of this behaviour as 'horseplay' reflects a lack of concern about deeply concerning cultures at the Bar.[144] There is ample evidence of sexual harassment within the legal profession, which appears to have been historically ignored or tacitly accepted.[145] It is only more recently that the profession, lagging behind society, has taken this issue seriously.[146]

140 Reid Mortensen, 'The Lawyer as Parent: Sympathy, Care and Character in Lawyers' Ethics' (2009) 12(1) *Legal Ethics* 1.

141 *Council of the New South Wales Bar Association v EFA* [2021] NSWCATOD 21, [49].

142 Ibid [58], [76].

143 On appeal, in *Council of the New South Wales Bar Association v EFA (A Pseudonym)* [2021] NSWCA 339 the Court of Appeal upheld the decision of the Tribunal. It noted 'the significant financial penalty already levelled against the respondent by his insurer' such that a fine was not necessary and would be punitive, and cited at length the public commentary on the case: at [184], [186]–[192]. The Court did not need to decide the factual question of the connection between a Bar function and the practice of law, but described it as 'at a quasi (at least) professional function': at [181].

144 This is not necessarily to argue that the case should have resulted in a different sanction imposed upon this lawyer. The *Barristers' Conduct Rules* r 123 applying in New South Wales now specifically provide that breaches of anti-discrimination law are unethical and that 'conduct at social functions connected with the bar' are covered by the rule. This rule does not appear in the Queensland *2011 Barristers Rules*, as amended, and there are differing versions of this rule in other States, such as South Australia.

145 Law Council of Australia, *National Attrition and Re-engagement Study Report* (Report, 2013); Kieran Pender, *Us Too? Bullying and Sexual Harassment in the Legal Profession* (IBA Legal Policy and Research Unit, Report, 2019).

146 Most State and Territory regulators have announced special telephone hotlines and other ways to encourage reporting, and issued guidance around workplace behaviour. See also the International Bar Association report on international regulatory responses to sexual harassment and bullying in the legal profession, entitled *Beyond Us Too?* (April 2022). Australian regulatory responses to this issue were cited as exemplars. Nevertheless, the *EFA* case (including on appeal) arguably provides an example of narrow legalistic judicial approaches to professional discipline in the context of sexual harassment. While not referring to the case, an amendment to the *Barristers' Conduct Rules* r 123 was proposed by the Australian Bar Association in 2021, citing the reports in n 145: 'Proposed Amendments to the *Legal Profession Conduct (Barristers) Rules 2015*', *ABA – Australian Bar Association* (Blog Post, 24 June 2021) <https://austbar.asn.au/news-media/proposed-amendments-to-the-legal-profession-conduct-barristers-rules-2015>.

Dealing with a complaint and disciplinary tribunals

Legislation has introduced concepts of 'consumer' and 'disciplinary' matters to distinguish between types of complaints against lawyers and to create distinct pathways for addressing them. A consumer matter is one relating to a dispute about legal costs or failures of service, such as poor communication or lack of competency – these matters comprise about half of all complaints.[147] In *Uniform Law* jurisdictions, Legal Services Commissioners ('LSCs') have summary powers to investigate and decide these matters and to mandate that lawyers and clients mediate their disputes.[148] In other jurisdictions, regulators have fewer powers to require mediation and determine such matters; regulators may have to determine that a matter is 'disciplinary' to have power to deal with it.

'Disciplinary' matters are complaints about lawyer conduct that is a breach of regulations, conduct rules or otherwise 'dishonest and disreputable' behaviour as discussed above. The LSC in New South Wales refers complaints that involve allegations about professional conduct back to the two professional organisations – the Law Society (solicitors) and the Bar Association (barristers) – to investigate *and* prosecute any disciplinary action.[149] In Queensland, Victoria and Western Australia, the LSC, not the lawyers' associations, decides who is or is not to be investigated and prosecuted for a disciplinary matter.

South Australia and the Territories have a different regulatory approach. In the case of South Australia there is no self-regulation. The Legal Profession Conduct Commissioner investigates and prosecutes in a specialist disciplinary tribunal.[150] This State did not formally adopt the *Model Laws* approach but adopted much of its core aspects. Again, this approach resulted partly from public scandals involving a huge misappropriation from a trust account and a lawyer who, when involved in a hit and run incident that killed a cyclist and left the scene, was not removed from the profession for this conduct in his personal life.[151] Both Territories have always maintained entirely self-regulatory mechanisms for complaints-handling and disciplinary procedures.[152] Their practitioners have maintained that the small size of these jurisdictions compels a cost-sensitive, self-regulatory approach,[153] and this view

147 See, eg, Office of the Legal Services Commissioner (NSW) (n 120) 25.

148 *Uniform Law* s 299. This summary power is to make a finding of unsatisfactory professional conduct and impose a penalty such as a caution, require an apology or work redone or resolve a costs dispute.

149 This constitutes about 20% of the complaints: Office of the Legal Services Commissioner (NSW) (n 120) 25. The LSC can recall a complaint investigation from the profession. The LSC can also review complaints that the professional associations have dismissed without taking any action.

150 *Legal Practitioners Act 1981* (SA).

151 These incidents are summarised in Kellie Toole and Suzanne Le Mire, 'From Failure to Hope? Lawyer Regulation in South Australia' (2014) 39(1) *Alternative Law Journal* 63. Parliament responded to the cases by passing the *Legal Practitioners (Miscellaneous) Amendment Act 2013*. This brought South Australia in line with the *Model Laws* approaches to disciplinary charges and access to fidelity fund payments for lawyer wrongdoing while other civil avenues are being pursued.

152 *Legal Profession Act 2006* (ACT) ch 4, s 577; *Legal Profession Act 2006* (NT).

153 Josh Massoud, 'Profession Trades Blows as Regulation Debate Hits ACT', *Lawyers Weekly* (Sydney, 15 August 2003) 4.

has dominated despite the implicit pressure of the *Uniform Law* for nationally consistent complaints-handling structures.[154]

Disciplinary offences are prosecuted in specialist tribunals dominated by practising lawyers in the Australian Capital Territory, Northern Territory, South Australia and Tasmania. In Queensland they are prosecuted in a specialist tribunal constituted by a current Supreme Court judge and a lawyer and layperson. Courts of superior jurisdiction in Australia also have an inherent jurisdiction to discipline lawyers and jurisdiction to hear appeals on disciplinary decisions from the lower tribunals.

Finally, the LSCs in many jurisdictions can investigate of their own motion an individual lawyer or a firm. In *Uniform Law* States, all LSCs have powers to conduct an audit of the firm, if there is a systemic problem inside a firm, to ascertain whether or not the firm, and not just individual lawyers, are complying fully with the law.[155] Most audits are consensual and intended to highlight for the firm which policies and practices could be improved, to the benefit of both firm and clients. This approach is designed to be 'responsive' rather than 'reactive' regulation, allowing early interventions to assess how the firm is going wrong and proactively address problems. Yet, compliance audits remain a limited tool, because they only permit an LSC to audit where the Commissioner has 'reasonable grounds' to do so.[156] An LSC will first need to be presented with a formal complaint or contacted by a whistleblower.[157] This limitation on LSCs' powers might be affected by differing structural approaches. In New South Wales, compliance audits are conducted jointly by the LSC and the Law Society, but in Victoria the Law Institute can conduct the whole audit, subject to LSC oversight.[158] In theory, therefore, a NSW compliance audit is less likely to be dominated by the professional association than is the case in Victoria, though there is no evidence either way to date.

Table 3.1 summarises the different approaches taken to complaints handling and the prosecution of disciplinary action in each State and Territory, according to whether the profession functionally controls its own complaints and prosecutions (*self-regulation*), shares control with some external body (*co-regulation*) or is *independently regulated*.[159]

154 Williams (n 71).

155 *Uniform Law* s 374(2)(c)(i). Note that the power to enter a law firm's office without warning or warrant requires the investigator to form the opinion that 'on reasonable grounds … it is urgently necessary to do so in order to prevent the destruction of or interference with relevant material'.

156 *Uniform Law* s 256. In the former LSC of Queensland's view this change to the *Model Laws* approach, albeit only for ILPs, was to render the regulator 'impotent': John Briton, 'Between the Idea and the Reality Falls the Shadow' (Presentation Paper, Australian and New Zealand Legal Ethics Colloquium, 3–4 December 2015).

157 Such whistleblowers (see Chapter 4) are almost unheard of inside the legal profession. Indeed, in the largest jurisdiction, the busy LSC conducted only four audits in 2020–21: Office of the Legal Services Commissioner (NSW) (n 120) 15.

158 *Uniform Law* s 256(2). It is as yet unclear what approach will be adopted in Western Australia.

159 For more detail on each jurisdiction see Gino Dal Pont, *Lawyers' Professional Responsibility* (Thomson Reuters, 7th ed, 2021) ch 1.

Table 3.1 Different regulatory arrangements for complaints handling and prosecuting disciplinary action in Australia

Jurisdiction	Regulatory approach	Regulating bodies	Composition of external prosecutor/regulator and limits to independence
New South Wales	Co-regulation	Law Society of New South Wales/NSW Bar Association/Legal Services Commissioner	A single Legal Services Commissioner, but it refers some investigations to Law Society and Bar Association.
Queensland	Co-regulation	Law Society of Queensland/ Bar Association of Queensland/Legal Services Commissioner	A single Legal Services Commissioner but refers investigation of barristers to Bar Association. Law Society governs trust accounts. Judicial officer presides over disciplinary prosecutions in specialist tribunals.
Tasmania	Self-regulation	Legal Profession Board Tasmania/Law Society of Tasmania	6 Legal Profession Tasmania Board members appointed by the Governor, 4 of whom are practising lawyers. The Tasmanian approach is still essentially self-regulatory because the Board is chiefly governed by lawyers.
Victoria	Co-regulation	Legal Services Board/ Legal Services Commissioner/Law Institute of Victoria/ Victorian Bar Council	Legal Services Board: 1 Chair (originally a lawyer), 3 elected lawyers and 3 non-lawyers nominated by the Attorney-General. A single Legal Services Commissioner who is also the Chief Executive of the Legal Services Board.
South Australia	Independent regulation	Legal Profession Conduct Commissioner	A single Legal Profession Conduct Commissioner, appointed by government. The inaugural and current Commissioner is a former lawyer, but does not report to any Board or committee.
Western Australia	Co-regulation	Under the *Legal Profession Act 2008* (WA) until end of 2022 the bodies are Legal Profession Complaints Committee/Legal Services Board/Law Society/ Western Australian Bar Association[160]	Legal Profession and Complaints Committee is an independent statutory committee of the Legal Practice Board. Together they carry out complaints and investigation functions, grant practising certificates and provide professional development.

160 The regulatory bodies and their functions will change and will reflect the regulatory approach in New South Wales and Victoria.

Table 3.1 (cont.)

Jurisdiction	Regulatory approach	Regulating bodies	Composition of external prosecutor/regulator and limits to independence
Northern Territory	Self-regulation	Law Society of the Northern Territory	The Law Society is a statutory body under the *Legal Profession Act 2006* (NT), and fully controls the affairs of the legal profession in the Territory.
Australian Capital Territory	Self-regulation	Law Society of the Australian Capital Territory/ACT Bar Association	The ACT Law Society and ACT Bar Association are statutory bodies under the *Legal Profession Act 2006* (ACT), and are responsible for the discipline of ACT lawyers.

Regulation of solicitor trustee duties

One type of lawyer behaviour that is both sadly common and dealt with sternly by regulators is inappropriately dealing with money held on trust for clients. In the normal business of conducting transactions, solicitors frequently hold large amounts of client money on trust, such as the proceeds of a sale of land or assets of a disputed estate. Lawyers also frequently ask clients to deposit money to be held in trust for the future payment for the lawyer's services (described in Chapter 8). There are detailed regulatory regimes in place governing what is considered trust money and how money is to be received and paid from a trust account.[161] In short, the solicitor or firm must hold client money on trust and deal with it *only* in accordance with client instructions.

Trust accounts have been described as 'sacred' and even minor defaults, not causing the client financial loss, are dealt with harshly. Most disciplinary cases concern a solicitor – as only solicitors can receive and deal with trust money – who has dishonestly accessed trust funds for personal use. The courts have described such behaviour as not only an individual failing but as betraying the confidence of the public in the profession.[162] Indeed, scandals involving major misappropriations of trust funds have affected the profession to the extent that the local law society has been stripped of self-regulatory powers. The sanction for individual lawyers is usually removal from the profession.

Generally, trust account regulation is overseen by the profession, even under the *Uniform Law* that has largely removed self-regulation. In New South Wales the Law Society itself

161 The concept of 'trust money' is now legislatively defined: 'money entrusted to a law practice in the course of or in connection with the provision of legal services by the practice', which includes 'money received by the practice on account of legal costs in advance of providing the services', 'controlled money', 'transit money' and 'power money': *Uniform Law* s 129. There are specific regulations regarding dealing with defined trust money, including how a lawyer can pay their bill when entitled: *Uniform Law* pt 4.2; *Legal Profession Uniform Law Application Regulation 2015* pt 3. These are replicated in States and Territories applying *Model Laws* legislation.

162 *Re a Practitioner* (1982) 30 SASR 27.

decides whether it should investigate a report of a breach of trust accounting duties. In Victoria, by contrast, while the Law Institute can also investigate such reports, it remains subject to Legal Services Board supervision in those decisions.

Despite the strong emphasis on regulating the way solicitors handle trust moneys – whether by self-regulation or an independent regulator – solicitors continue to regularly appear in the disciplinary records for breaching these duties. Thus, specific, detailed and punitive regulation has not resolved this concerning behaviour. As discussed in Chapter 8 in relation to the pressures of meeting billing targets, it might be that the context of practice and cultural failures within firms continue to influence such behaviour and regulation does little to address it. It may also be opportunity or pure greed. A lawyer's willingness to behave well might not be affected by rules.

Mandatory reporting by lawyers

One way to approach this problem is to expect the profession itself – individual lawyers – to be proactive in early identification of the issue to deal with underlying problems rather than simply punish a lawyer for a breach afterwards. Regulation around the country imposes a requirement for *lawyers* to inform the professional body if they become aware that there is a problem with a trust account anywhere.[163] This approach, while demonstrating the depth of concern of the legislature about this behaviour, has not resulted in an end to trust account defaults. However, it is conceded that mandatory reporting, and direct oversight by law societies, might result in more breaches being reported and acted upon by regulators.

The requirement that lawyers report wrongdoing by other lawyers in respect of trust money is a unique feature of modern regulation – there are no other similar compulsory reporting duties imposed on lawyers. However, the Victorian Government, as a response to a recent public scandal concerning a barrister breaching client secrets[164] is considering implementing a duty for lawyers to report other lawyer wrongdoing.[165] How extensive this duty will be – about what sorts of lawyer wrongdoing – is yet to be determined. Perhaps unsurprisingly, the Law Institute of Victoria has expressed 'serious concerns' and opposes the move, characterising it as an over-response to a scandal involving a lawyer in that State.[166] Mandatory reporting of breaches of professional ethics (other than trust account defaults) has been introduced in many countries including the United States, England and Wales and most recently New Zealand. While there is limited international evidence of the efficacy of mandatory reporting, the requirement aims to ensure that ethical breaches are identified

163 *Uniform Law* s 154: *Legal Profession Act 2006* (ACT) s 231; *Legal Profession Act 2006* (NT) s 256; *Legal Profession Act 2007* (Qld) s 260; *Legal Practitioners Act 1981* (SA) sch 2 cl 24; *Legal Profession Act 2007* (Tas) s 254.

164 In a well-publicised case, Nicola Gobbo, a criminal barrister, was a long-time police informant. Her actions gave rise to serious concerns about conflicts of interest, breaches of client confidentiality and legal professional privilege. This case is described in detail in Chapter 4. As a result of this case, the Victorian Government instituted a Royal Commission into the Management of Police Informants in 2018 and the Commissioner delivered her report in 2020: *Royal Commission into the Management of Police Informants* (Final Report, November 2020).

165 Office of the General Council, Department of Justice and Community Safety (Vic), *Construction of Mandatory Reporting for Lawyers* (Consultation Paper, July 2021).

166 Law Institute of Victoria, *Submission to the Department of Justice and Community Consultation: Construction of Mandatory Reporting for Lawyers* (2021).

and efficiently and promptly notified to the regulator.[167] Lawyers are in the best position to learn of, and understand, ethical breaches by other lawyers, and yet are acculturated not to blow the whistle.[168] On the other hand, mandatory reporting may decrease toleration of poor ethical cultures in which behaviours such as sexual harassment or bullying take place. Still, an obligation to simply report breaches of the governing Act or conduct rules would provide little guidance on ethical values underlying the requirement. Legislating such an obligation is an opportunity to expressly state the underlying values to which lawyers should aspire and/or to change cultures that might be protected by traditional secrecy.

Conclusion

Ongoing consideration of, and reform to, the regulation of lawyers as described above is important because ethical behaviour is a function of individual values as well as the social and market context of lawyers' practices. Legal regulation and ethical standard setting are part of the moral economy of the whole profession that supports or detracts from the right values being adopted and practised by lawyers.

The *Uniform Law* might be the newest version of regulation in Australia, but it is not necessarily the best. In particular, it makes very little attempt to set out what substantive values should animate legal practice or be reflected in the codes of professional conduct promulgated for the profession. The legislation asserts that one of its objectives is to 'ensur[e] lawyers are competent and maintain high ethical and professional standards in the provision of legal services',[169] but nothing more. There is no commentary on the principles underlying these objectives or guidance as to how to apply them in practice.[170] It is as if the Attorneys-General of each State and the LCA considered that the regulation of the legal profession is a purely technical, neutral matter in which no particular values are significant. In reality, the *Uniform Law* lacks a 'positive morality' (in the sense advocated by Sampford and Parker).

The law societies and bar associations that make up the institutional membership of the LCA, and the other States and Territories that govern them, have all been encouraged to adopt the *Uniform Law* without substantial local modification. While it is always possible

167 Gino Dal Pont, 'Mandating Lawyer Reporting of Their Peers' Misconduct: Should Australia Follow Suit?' (2014) 17(1) *Legal Ethics* 23, 38. In contrast, critiques of mandatory reporting in the United States have included the lack of observation of the obligation by attorneys and a consequent failure to identify of misconduct: see, eg, the discussion in Arthur Greenbaum, 'The Attorney's Duty to Report Professional Misconduct: A Roadmap for Reform' (2002) 16(2) *Georgetown Journal of Legal Ethics* 261.

168 There might also be reasonable fear, particularly held by junior lawyers, that reporting will result in repercussions should they be identifiable.

169 *Uniform Law* s 3(b).

170 The now repealed *Legal Practice Act 1996* (Vic) s 64 set out several guiding principles for legal practice that were to be reflected in any code of practice promulgated by legal professional associations. They included acting 'with honesty and candour in all dealings with courts and tribunals and otherwise discharg[ing] all duties owed to courts and tribunals': at s 64(f). But such general principles were omitted from the *Uniform Law*.

171 *Legal Profession Uniform Law Application Act 2022* (WA).

that an Attorney-General in another State or Territory will adopt the *Uniform Law* provisions in their jurisdiction and strengthen them with legislation expressing positive morality, there is not currently any significant agitation for such reform. The recent adoption of the *Uniform Law* in Western Australia made no such modification.[171] The impending change in Victoria to require mandatory reporting of lawyers by lawyers is an opportunity to express what values are particularly important.

But regulation is just one aspect of the whole story.

In 1986 the American Bar Association Commission on Professionalism urged lawyers to adopt higher standards than those required by disciplinary rules and named a devotion to public service as the *dominant* feature of professionalism.[172] The objective of this chapter has been to examine legal regulatory structures from an ethical perspective – that is, with professionalism in mind. We have provided examples of those structures that affect, or seek to affect, a lawyer's personal ethics. As we have briefly documented, regulatory approaches and structures change over time, often because of public concern about a perceived lack of efficacy of regulation to make lawyers behave appropriately.

The traditional approach was self-regulation. It is possible to conclude that significant self-regulation is fundamental to lawyers' self-respect and hence to their *willingness* to 'behave'. However, a contrary, increasingly accepted view is that external regulation is required to keep self-interest in check. Even where there is external regulation (at least co-regulation), changes such as mandatory reporting requirements are proposed to address perceived shortfalls.

In the end, attitudes to these contrasting positions about lawyer regulation ought to be guided by the question 'Which viewpoint will best assist me to practise ethically?' In answering this question, lawyers will be acting in their local environment but must also consider what is happening nationally and internationally. Lawyers are entitled to practise in an economically efficient manner, yet clients and society more broadly must not be denied ethical lawyers and transparent, value-specific ethical standards in lawyering.

RECOMMENDED FURTHER READING

Francesca Bartlett and Linda Haller, 'Disclosing Lawyers: Questioning Law and Process in the Admission of Australian Lawyers' (2013) 41(2) *Federal Law Review* 227

Gino Dal Pont, *Lawyers' Professional Responsibility* (Lawbook, 7th ed, 2021) chs 1, 2, 24

Susan Fortney and Talia Gordon, 'Adopting Law Firm Management Systems to Survive and Thrive: A Study of the Australian Approach to Management-Based Regulation' (2012) 10(1) *University of St Thomas Law Journal* 152

Linda Haller, 'Professional Discipline for Incompetent Lawyers? Developments in the UK and Australia' (2010) 17(1) *International Journal of the Legal Profession* 83

172 Commission on Professionalism, American Bar Association, *'In the Spirit of Public Service': A Blueprint for the Rekindling of Lawyer Professionalism* (Report, 1986) 10, 50.

Christine Parker, *Just Lawyers: Regulation and Access to Justice* (Oxford University Press, 1999) chs 6, 7

Christine Parker, 'Regulation of the Ethics of Australian Legal Practice: Autonomy and Responsiveness' (2002) 25(3) *University of New South Wales Law Journal* 676

Deborah Rhode, *In the Interests of Justice: Reforming the Legal Profession* (Oxford University Press, 2000) especially ch 6

Charles Sampford and Christine Parker, 'Legal Regulation, Ethical Standard-Setting, and Institutional Design' in Stephen Parker and Charles Sampford (eds), *Legal Ethics and Legal Practice: Contemporary Issues* (Clarendon Press, 1995) 11

David Wilkins, 'Who Should Regulate Lawyers?' (1992) 105(4) *Harvard Law Review* 799

4

CONFIDENTIALITY: BOUNDARIES AND DISCLOSURE

Introduction

The profession, the legal system and society have all traditionally seen loyalty, confidentiality, care and competence as cornerstones of professional responsibility. Lawyers are in a fiduciary relationship with their clients – clients need to be able to trust their lawyers to provide advice and represent them *loyally* in the legal system, uninfluenced by any concern other than the client's interests. We examine lawyers' obligations to avoid conflicts of interest in Chapter 7 and their general duty of *care* and *competence* in Chapter 6. The topic for this chapter is the duty of *confidentiality*: the obligation to keep secret all communications made by the client to the lawyer about their affairs and all the information learned about the client directly or indirectly during the professional relationship (subject to various exceptions to be discussed below).[1]

The first part of the chapter argues that strong obligations of confidentiality support the lawyer's role as zealous advocate and officer of the court, but that there must be ethical limitations to this obligation in some circumstances. Next, we show that the concept of confidentiality has become quite tenuous in a world of surveillance, wired for instant disclosure and based on a communication and business model that feeds on demolishing all secrecy. Lawyers, as much as anyone, are caught up in the demand for instant, widely accessible communication, and can forget that their primary stock-in-trade is confidentiality. We discuss cloud computing as a case in point. We then examine the ideals of confidentiality and client legal privilege ('CLP'). We evaluate them as both an essential support for the process of legal representation, and as a tool used by some unscrupulous lawyers, as well as perhaps by other lawyers who lose sight of their need for courage and independence.

Finally, we consider whether lawyers should sometimes blow the whistle on their own clients or colleagues in order to fulfil their professional obligations as gatekeepers of justice. The absolute nature of lawyer–client confidentiality is challenged by increasing expectations that lawyers will act as gatekeepers of justice in the legal system and advocates for the public interest, not just zealous advocates for individual clients. There are exceptions to confidentiality in the *Australian Solicitors' Conduct Rules ('ASCR')* for certain practical and public interest reasons (discussed below). Even the strongest protection for confidentiality, CLP, does not attach to communications for the purpose of facilitating or furthering the commission of a crime, fraud or civil offence.[2] We argue below that these exceptions to confidentiality obligations and the narrower concept of CLP support (at least weakly) the possibility that lawyers may act as whistleblowers and disclose confidential information to appropriate authorities in compelling circumstances. Should the *ASCR* provide a clearer and stronger encouragement for lawyers to blow the whistle in certain circumstances? For example, the Victorian Royal Commission into the Management of Police Informants recommended that lawyers be required to report suspected misconduct of other lawyers.[3]

1 See *Baker v Campbell* (1983) 153 CLR 52, 65 (Gibbs CJ).

2 *R v Cox* (1884) 14 QBD 153, 158.

3 *Royal Commission into the Management of Police Informants* (Final Report, 2020) recommendations 86, 87. The Victorian Government has conducted a public consultation on this recommendation: see 'Mandatory Reporting Requirement for Lawyers', *Engage Victoria* (Web Page) <https://engage.vic.gov.au/mandatory-reporting-requirement-lawyers>. See also Chapters 3 and 5.

We note, though, that it will take more than rules to prompt lawyers to blow the whistle – this can only come from the inculcation of values based on an understanding of the role of the profession as both confidant of clients' secrets and gatekeeper of justice.

Rationale for confidentiality

Confidentiality (privacy) is important for individuals' humanity and freedom. We all deserve to keep some secrets – that is, to have a private life – if we are to remain psychologically healthy. Sissela Bok[4] has suggested that there are three ethical principles that generally require us to preserve the confidences of others, all of which would apply to many professional–client relationships and also much more broadly to family relationships, friendships and collegial relationships in the workplace. These are as follows:

1. *Respect for individual autonomy over personal information*: People should generally be able to keep control over whether they want to keep their own thoughts, plans and actions secret or open, and others should respect this.
2. *Respect for the secrets of intimates*: Human relationship and intimacy in which secrecy can be shared is a good thing that should be respected.
3. A pledge of silence (maintaining confidentiality) creates an obligation beyond the respect due to personal autonomy and relationships: where one person has promised secrecy to another, extra weight is added to the obligation of confidentiality.

Yet, the obligation of confidentiality is not generally considered to be absolute. As Bok points out, in general thinking and practical ethics each of the principles above has limits. The first two principles have limits, such as when secrecy would allow violence to be done to innocent persons or would turn someone into an unwitting accomplice to crime. The third principle, where secrecy has been promised, adds moral weight but should still only be a prima facie ground of obligation. We need to go on to ask whether one was right to make the pledge, whether the promise is binding and, if so, what circumstances might nevertheless justify overriding it.

A fourth rationale for confidentiality applies only to professionals and carries a heavier weight. According to Bok, *professional* confidentiality is stronger and breaches are harder to excuse, because there is some public interest in confidentiality above and beyond ordinary obligations of confidentiality. In the case of the legal profession, the duty of confidentiality at general law and in professional conduct rules is supposed to encourage full and frank disclosure between client and lawyer, so that clients can seek and obtain legal advice without apprehension of prejudice by disclosure. This is said to be necessary to help lawyers provide effective advice and representation, to allow lawyers a chance to dissuade clients from illegal or immoral conduct, and to ensure long-term trust in lawyers and the legal system.[5] It is suggested that the justice system would not operate effectively if parties could not freely disclose information to the court and to the other side without the promise that it

4 See Sissela Bok, *Secrets: On the Ethics of Concealment and Revelation* (Random House, 1983).

5 Leslie C Levin, 'Testing the Radical Experiment: A Study of Lawyer Response to Clients Who Intend to Harm Others' (1994) 47(1) *Rutgers Law Review* 81.

will not be used for purposes other than the resolution of the dispute.[6] But, as we will see, the lawyer's role as gatekeeper of justice also puts limits on the idea that lawyers should treat the protection of confidential information as always overriding even the public interest in the values of truth and justice.[7]

Lawyers' obligations of confidentiality

Subject to some significant exceptions (which we discuss below), Australian lawyers have obligations to

- keep their clients' affairs *confidential*; and
- preserve their clients' *legal privilege*.

Lawyers' confidentiality obligations to clients are enshrined in the professional conduct rules enforced by the disciplinary system (*ASCR* r 9), are implied into the terms of every lawyer–client contract, and are also enforceable under equitable principles of confidentiality.[8] The professional duty of confidentiality requires all lawyers to keep secret all information received in the course of acting for their client.[9] Equity can also enforce confidentiality in any situation (including lawyer–client communications) where information was communicated confidentially with an expectation that confidentiality would be maintained, providing it is not public knowledge.[10] This equitable obligation continues after the retainer ends and even after the client dies.[11]

Client legal privilege ('CLP') protects lawyer–client confidentiality from disclosure enforced by courts and various statutory authorities.[12] This means that the privilege applies in all settings in which an authority purports to have power to require the disclosure of information. CLP covers confidential communications from the client to the lawyer for the dominant purpose of legal advice or use in litigation, and also confidential communications to the lawyer by third-party experts for the purposes of preparation for litigation. There are also obligations of confidentiality, akin to CLP, to opposing parties for material disclosed for the purposes of litigation.[13]

Confidentiality deals with the broad class of secrets, whereas privilege is a narrower subset of those secrets (confidential communications for the dominant purposes of legal advice or litigation) that are often particularly related to court proceedings. The distinction between the

6 For a more critical perspective on these assumptions, see William H Simon, 'Attorney-Client Confidentiality: A Critical Analysis' (2017) 30(3) *Georgetown Journal of Legal Ethics* 447.

7 Bok (n 4) 123.

8 *Legal Practitioners Complaints Committee and Trowell* [2009] WASAT 42.

9 Including the name of the client, which is particularly important in family and criminal law. Even if a client's information is 'public', it would be unwise for a lawyer to discuss it publicly without specific instructions to do so.

10 See generally, GE Dal Pont, *Law of Confidentiality* (LexisNexis, 2nd ed, 2020). Lawyers have been injuncted from acting against a party on the other side on the basis of confidentiality obligations: see Chapter 7.

11 See *Gartside v Sheffield Young & Ellis* [1983] NZLR 37.

12 *Baker v Campbell* (1983) 153 CLR 52.

13 *Hearne v Street* (2008) 235 CLR 125. See also *Sapphire (SA) Pty Ltd v Barry Smith Grains Pty Ltd (in liq)* [2011] NSWSC 1451 (material from an arbitration).

two concepts is important, and although the terms are often used interchangeably they should never be equated. Privileged communications are not compellable (that is, disclosure cannot be required by a court or other statutory authority). Communications that are confidential only are compellable. Figure 4.1 sets out the differences between the two concepts.

Figure 4.1 Confidentiality distinguished from privilege[14]

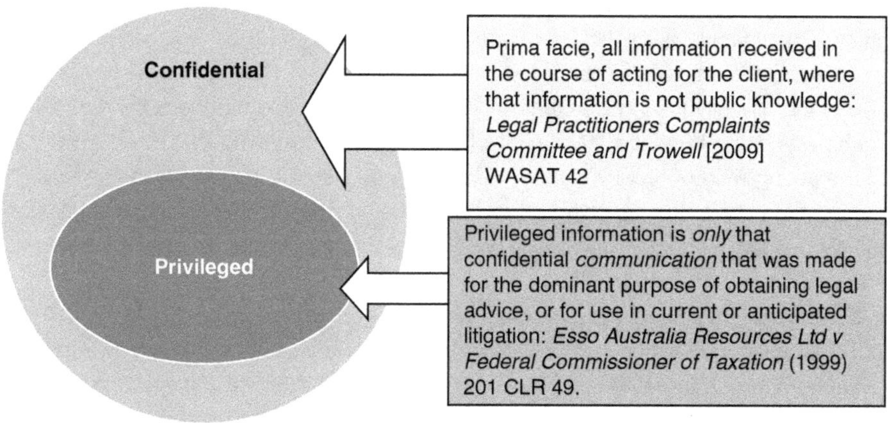

The obligation of confidentiality and its rationale can be simply stated, but its practical and relational implications are not so easily comprehended. When a client comes in to see their lawyer, or telephones them late at night, they sometimes mention something, or hint at something, that they are embarrassed about. Often these disclosures can seem minor on first telling – for example, a client mentioning that they are very late in paying a significant debt or are having difficulty in getting planning permission for a contentious subdivision. But sometimes there is more at stake. Consider, for example, Case study 4.1, a true story told by criminal lawyer Bill Potts.[15]

CASE STUDY 4.1 THE CLIENT WITH A TERRIBLE SECRET

Many years ago a young man came to see me. He was charged with relatively minor property offences involving possession of stolen tools, parts from cars and various pieces of property that had been stolen from various places. The offences in and of themselves were not serious and, as he was a young man with no previous convictions, he was more likely than not to get a sentence of probation or community service.

14 Extracted from Adrian Evans, *The Good Lawyer* (Cambridge University Press, 2014) 139.

15 'The Ethics of Criminal Lawyers', *Law Report* (ABC Radio National, 12 November 2002) <http://www.abc.net.au/radionational/programs/lawreport/the-ethics-of-criminal-lawyers/3527274>. Reproduced here with permission.

But he was very, very worried, and kept hinting to me that there was something more serious going on ... After some time in getting to know him, I eventually tried to get to the nub of what his real problem was. And what he revealed to me, haltingly, was that he was in fact in possession of a stolen car, and not just any stolen car ... [but] the key piece of evidence in a murder investigation ...

[Potts went on to explain that his new client was in possession of information that would exculpate another young man who had confessed to a murder he did not commit. But his own client would quite likely implicate himself in stealing the car and possibly the murder, if he told the truth to the police.]

... Now the difficulty I faced was that my young fellow who told me these things, told me that he was going to destroy this piece of evidence, and this thing that could literally have got a young man off a very serious murder charge. And he told me when he was going to do it, and how he was going to do it. And the ethical dilemma I faced was 'Do I in those circumstances contact the police with a view to effectively putting my client in?' The effect of me telling the police these things is that he would have been charged with offences relating to the murder vehicle, and indeed it may well have been that there were [murder] charges in the background. So the other alternative was to do nothing, in which case a young and possibly innocent man could have stayed in jail for the rest of his life, because the case was certainly overwhelming, given his written and signed admissions.

DISCUSSION QUESTIONS

1. How would you decide what to do in these circumstances?
2. Potts says: 'After some time in getting to know him, I eventually tried to get to the nub of what his real problem was.' In this situation, would you have probed into your client's real worries?
3. In the end, Potts did convince his client to go to the police with the story and it turned out his client (in cohort with others) had killed the man. The client was of a very young mental age and had other psychiatric problems. In all the circumstances, and knowing how the case ended, would convincing the client to go to the police and tell the full story be consistent with any or all of the four ethical approaches – *adversarial advocacy*, *responsible lawyering*, *moral activism* and *ethics of care*?

In situations like Case study 4.1 the lawyer must offer advice, but is immediately confronted with the classic conflict between 'knowing too much', which might prevent them from advising a client to plead not guilty to any later charge, and knowing too little, which makes them ineffective as a client representative. It is arguably unethical to be wilfully blind to a situation in which the client may be breaching their duty to the court and the law, because it means that the lawyer is assisting in the breach. It may also be a breach of the duty to the client to not be fully aware of the client's situation, as a matter of care for the client. The rationale for lawyer–client confidentiality does not mean the lawyer should just accept the first version of the story that the client provides. In principle at least, the obligation of confidentiality is supposed to provide the lawyer and client with the 'confidence' for the lawyer to probe further and understand the client's story more fully – the facts and the emotional, social and financial significance of those facts for the client – in order to give appropriate advice.

A lawyer who chooses to disclose confidential, and especially privileged, information faces a number of consequences (all designed to discourage such disclosure) in contract law, equity and professional discipline: injunction, liability for breach of contract, liability for equitable compensation and account of profits, an order to hand over or destroy materials, loss of clients, the loss of their job, damage to reputation, and even disciplinary proceedings. Whether any or all of these consequences actually occur depends on the circumstances and the presence of any mitigating factors. These real-life cases provide some examples:

- Alton Logan was released from an Illinois prison in 2009 after being imprisoned for 26 years for the murder of a security guard – a murder he did not commit.[16] The fact that he was, and always had been, innocent was known by two lawyers (Dale Coventry and Jamie Kunz). At the time of Logan's trial, Coventry and Kunz acted for another man, Wilson, who was charged with the unrelated murder of two police officers and who confessed to them that he had also murdered the security guard. Coventry and Kunz kept this knowledge secret for 26 years, because they considered themselves bound by the local Illinois Bar (and American Bar Association) rule of attorney–client privilege. Wilson was sentenced to life in prison for the murder of the police. They feared Wilson would be sentenced to death, if he was tried and found guilty of the crime for which Logan was convicted. Both lawyers sought advice from legal ethics experts. They prepared an affidavit setting out what Wilson had told them and convinced Wilson to give them permission to speak out once he died (otherwise they would have been bound by confidentiality forever). When Wilson died in prison, Coventry and Kunz revealed his confession.

  What should the lawyers have done if Logan had been sentenced to death (instead of life imprisonment) or Wilson had died without giving permission to tell his secret?[17] What would you do in this situation? Would it make a difference if the information received by the lawyers from Wilson was confidential only (and not privileged), because it was not disclosed for the dominant purpose of legal advice or litigation?

- In 2005 one of the lawyers for Schapelle Corby, who had been charged in Bali (and was later convicted) of a number of serious offences concerning drug smuggling, appeared on the popular Channel Nine TV program *Sunday* and disclosed that there had been previous convictions for drug offences in Schapelle Corby's family. He also commented that Mercedes Corby, Schapelle's sister, had lied to him about these matters in the course of preparation for Schapelle's trial. Later, in another TV documentary, he made a number of derogatory remarks about the whole family. When challenged about

16 Logan has written a book about his experiences: Alton Logan, *Justice Failed: How 'Legal Ethics' Kept Me in Prison for 26 Years* (Counterpoint, 2018). See also '26-Year Secret Kept Innocent Man in Prison', *CBS News* (online at 6 March 2008) <https://www.cbsnews.com/news/26-year-secret-kept-innocent-man-in-prison/>.

17 See Peter A Joy and Kevin C McMunigal, 'Confidentiality and Wrongful Incarceration' (2008) 23(2) *Criminal Justice* 46, which discusses whether there should be a new exception to the duty of client confidentiality to prevent the wrongful incarceration of another.

these disclosures by the disciplinary authorities, the lawyer, Robin Tampoe, said he did not believe that Schapelle Corby was his client, as he had been hired by Ron Bakir, a Gold Coast entrepreneur who was trying to help Schapelle Corby, and not directly by Schapelle Corby, and that anyway he believed the information about the Corby family was public knowledge and therefore not confidential. The Queensland Legal Practice Tribunal found that it did not matter how he had been hired in the first place – he was in fact acting as a legal representative, held himself out in that way and was believed to be acting for Schapelle Corby by all her family. When Schapelle's sister told him about previous convictions, she believed she was telling him in confidence to aid her sister's defence. The Tribunal commented that it was hard to imagine a more 'egregious' breach of lawyer–client confidentiality than one on national television! Tampoe was struck off for professional misconduct for his breach of confidentiality and for bringing the profession into disrepute by stating that as a criminal defence lawyer he could 'provide' Schapelle Corby with a defence and then 'take it away' if it was not working.[18] (We consider the proper role of the criminal defence lawyer in Chapter 5.) This is in part an example of a lawyer succumbing to enormous pressure to comment about his infamous client to journalists. How should he have handled the media?

- JK Rowling, the celebrated author of the *Harry Potter* series, tried her hand at crime fiction and published *The Cuckoo's Calling* under the pseudonym of Robert Galbraith. Her lawyer disclosed this confidential information in a private conversation with a trusted friend, but the friend then revealed it in a Twitter exchange with a journalist and soon it was general knowledge. Rowling, who was angry and disappointed at the breach of confidence,[19] sued the law firm. The firm apologised to Rowling and paid her substantial damages (which she donated to charity). The UK Solicitors Regulation Authority fined Rowland's lawyer 1,000 pounds. The Authority found that, by disclosing confidential client information to a third party, the lawyer had breached several principles of its rules and code of conduct: fundamentally he had failed to act in the best interests of the client and to behave in a manner that upholds public trust in the legal profession.[20] This case underlines how quickly confidentiality can be compromised in an interconnected world, and the dangers of telling even a 'trusted friend' a client's confidential information.

Maintaining confidentiality in an interconnected world

In practice the obligation of confidentiality is not as simple and straightforward as it might appear. Lawyers may still be very concerned with maintaining confidentiality, but social media like TikTok, Instagram, LinkedIn and YouTube, as well as traditional broadcast media, thrive on completely trivial breaches of confidence, sometimes with tragic consequences. Less obvious, but perhaps more relevant to confidentiality and privacy, are the increasingly pervasive CCTV cameras, mobile phone tracking, failed passwords, Google maps and many

18 *Legal Services Commissioner v Tampoe* [2009] LPT 14.

19 'JK Rowling Lawyer Fined over Robert Galbraith Leak' *BBC News* (online at 2 January 2014) <https://www.bbc.com/news/entertainment-arts-25575269>.

20 Ibid.

other avenues of electronic surveillance. Once information has been uploaded to the internet, it is potentially recoverable forever. 'Cloud' servers, where much of our data is now stored, may not be as secure as we assume them to be. What we think is confidential is increasingly vulnerable to the prying eyes of those who want to put the time or money into finding it.[21]

Community attitudes towards confidentiality and privacy are contradictory. On the one hand, advances in technology are generally welcomed even though they favour disclosure and openness over confidentiality and privacy.[22] When children are groomed on the internet by paedophiles, when scammers steal from unsuspecting web users or when mafia hijack thousands of credit card identities, the dangers of internet transparency are obvious. But when Julian Assange's Wikileaks publishes huge volumes of secret diplomatic communications, reactions are far more mixed. Depending on who is embarrassed, there is both public approval and/or political condemnation for breaching confidentiality.

Lawyers are involved in these debates at every level. Is national security endangered by the disclosure of classified military information on a publicly accessible website? Or is the resilience and strength of that society actually improved by such disclosures, because greater public discussion will make it less likely that its key institutions – parliament, the courts and the media – will be undermined from within?

The technological and cultural developments described in this chapter mean that as time goes by, much information that would otherwise be both confidential and privileged is likely to have been disclosed publicly or privately to others, without the permission of those directly affected. However, a party who seeks to deny confidentiality or CLP must *prove* that the information in question is public knowledge.[23] If that public knowledge is only likely or suspected, confidentiality and CLP obligations remain intact. Clients may not initially appreciate the realities of the (lack of) privacy of much of their information, but lawyers carry a heavy obligation of confidentiality, and therefore ought to be particularly conscious of the practical problems of security of information.

CASE STUDY 4.2 **LIVING IN THE CLOUDS: THE REAL LEVELS OF CONFIDENTIALITY AND PRIVACY**

As technology advances, computing in 'the cloud' is now inevitable. A lot of sensitive information is stored on anonymous servers located who-knows-where and only partially controlled by the corporations who originally contract with many parties, including lawyers, to provide computing services. Often, servers will be located in politically unstable countries, because the server providers are offered a low tax environment by shaky governments desperate for investment. Confidentiality of cloud-stored data in such countries is unlikely to be secure, despite what might be promised in the head contract between an Australian lawyer and their IT provider.

21 Nicole Perlroth, *This Is How They Tell Me the World Ends: The Cyberweapons Arms Race* (Bloomsbury Publishing, 2021).

22 See Jane Lee, 'You're Being Closely Watched', *The Age* (Melbourne, 17 September 2012) 4.

23 *Legal Practitioners Complaints Committee and Trowell* [2009] WASAT 42.

Yet despite the fairly obvious risks, many of us are choosing to deposit our documents, photographs and drawings through our mobile phones and internet-connected tablets onto the servers of any number of social and other media providers. Our access devices have relatively small internal storage capacity – most of what we really value goes straight to cyberspace. That information is then no longer in our physical control, though we convince ourselves that that does not matter – the important thing is convenience of access.

But the internet is not a benign environment and while access may be relatively certain, privacy (and hence confidentiality) is now an endangered concept. It seems that many governments' security services, not to mention mercenary hackers, have access to enormous numbers of datasets and communications.[24] Apart from whatever protection we derive from the law of contract, we cannot assume that anything placed in cloud 'care' will be retained, remain uncorrupted and, most importantly, kept private and confidential.

Law firms have been particularly vulnerable to cyber-attacks, because (certainly in the past) their security has been lax, but also because the limited amount of data they keep contains information such as financial details that is valuable to hackers.[25] Professional bodies have emphasised that lawyers must take reasonable steps to prevent unauthorised disclosure of client data and have provided guidance as to how this might be done.[26] This includes encrypting data and using a cloud provider that holds the data in Australia, because other countries may allow their government to review data in the cloud.[27] The *Privacy Act 1988* (Cth) now requires all private sector organisations with an annual turnover of more than $3 million (that is, many law firms) to comply with 13 Australian Privacy Principles ('APP') that address the handling, use and management of personal information. In addition, if a firm has reasonable grounds to suspect that an 'eligible data breach' has occurred, it must notify the Office of the Australian Information Commissioner and affected individuals (that is, clients). Even if a law firm is not regulated under the *Privacy Act*, the Law Council of Australia ('LCA') advises that it is nonetheless best practice to take steps to comply with the APP.[28] Smaller law practices holding the details of clients' tax file numbers are required by the *Privacy Act* to report certain data breaches.

Some commentators argue that the existing conduct rules requiring competent representation in clients' best interests and the general duty of confidentiality (*ASCR* rr 4 and 9 – see below) add up to a duty to keep clients' data secure. In theory this may be so, but we concur with the view that client confidentiality is so important that it warrants the

24 Perlroth (n 21).

25 Ahmet Goksu, 'Cyber-Attacks Against Law Firms' (2021) 24 *GSI Articletter* [iii].

26 See, eg, 'Cyber Precedent', *Law Council of Australia* (Web Page) <http://lca.lawcouncil.asn.au/lawcouncil/cyber-precedent-tools>.

27 'Checklist: Cloud Provider Security', *Law Council of Australia* (Web Page) <http://lca.lawcouncil.asn.au/lawcouncil/cyber-precedent-tools>.

28 'Cyber Precedent on the Australian Privacy Principles and Cyber Security' (prepared by Law Society of New South Wales for Law Council of Australia) <https://lca.lawcouncil.asn.au/lawcouncil/images/Privacy_Principles.pdf>.

imposition of explicit data security obligations on lawyers. These obligations would include a positive duty on lawyers to adopt robust cybersecurity plans for all clients, and to advise clients of any unauthorised access to their confidential information.[29]

Other ethical issues that arise relating to the capacity of cloud computing to protect both professional and personal secrets include the following:[30]

- Even when client data is encrypted both for transmission and cloud storage, it is protected for only as long as the integrity of the encryption and the pace of computing innovation allow. As quantum computing becomes more viable, it will massively increase processing power, to the point that stable encryption (that is, confidentiality) is simply not possible and confidential information becomes vulnerable.
- Because lawyers' cloud storages are well known to contain information that is likely to be commercially valuable, their servers are 'high-risk' hacking targets. As such, clients need to be *fully* informed of the firm's cloud provider details and the reality of their lawyer's actual supervision of their head contractor. Local storage alternatives should be discussed, if a client has concerns about cloud storage.

DISCUSSION QUESTIONS

1. How should lawyers discuss these issues with their clients? Would you see it as sensible to discuss every risk with every client, to gloss over the risks of cloud storage since it is ubiquitous anyway, or approach the subject in some other way?
2. If you were a client with highly confidential information, would you be comfortable about placing that information in the cloud?
3. Do you think that the current general rules (*ASCR* rr 4 and 9) addressing competence and confidentiality are sufficient to encompass the lawyer's duty to stay up to date with current risks and appropriate security measures to maintain client confidentiality, or would more targeted rules better protect clients?

Client legal privilege

The law on CLP (or 'legal professional privilege', as it is also known)[31] is sufficiently broad to ensure that most confidential communications between a lawyer and their client remain private, even before a court that would otherwise have the authority to compel disclosure.

29 Eli Wald, 'Legal Ethics' Next Frontier: Lawyers and Cybersecurity Symposium: Cyberwars: Navigating Responsibilities for the Public and Private Sector' (2016) 19(2) *Chapman Law Review* 501. Despite a review of the *ASCR*, such an obligation was not inserted into the rules by the 2022 amendments: see Law Council of Australia, *Review of the Australian Solicitors Conduct Rules* (2018) 41–2.

30 Michael Park (Partner, Norton Rose) and Ka-Chi Cheung (Senior Associate, Norton Rose) raised these issues in a presentation on 'The Ethics of Cloud Computing' to the Law Institute of Victoria in May 2012. They remain relevant.

31 We prefer the term 'client legal privilege' as it makes clear that the privilege lies with the client, and not the lawyer.

But there are a few caveats. As discussed above, there must be a clearly identified 'dominant purpose'[32] in the communication, and that dominant purpose must be either

- to obtain legal advice (the 'advice privilege'); or
- for use in actual, pending or contemplated court proceedings (the 'litigation privilege').

In many cases, communications between lawyers and their clients will have *ancillary* purposes – for example, to provide general assistance in the establishment of all manner of commercial transactions, or their restructure – but the relevant communications will remain privileged so long as a bona fide dominant purpose can still be identified.

There are, however, a number of collateral 'principles' that apply to privilege. All are important in understanding the limitations placed on the concept by the common law. The following paraphrased extract of those principles is from the judgment of Young J in a case concerning AWB's claims to privilege over various documents it was asked to produce for the Royal Commission inquiring into payments made by AWB to the Iraqi regime (see Case studies 4.4 and 9.1):[33]

- The party claiming privilege carries the onus of proving that the communication or document was made for the dominant purpose of giving or obtaining legal advice.
- The purpose for which a document is brought into existence is a question of fact that must be determined objectively. Evidence of the intention of the document's maker, or of the person who authorised or procured it, is not necessarily conclusive. It may be necessary to examine the evidence concerning the purpose of other persons involved in the hierarchy of decision-making or consultation that led to the creation of the document and its subsequent communication.
- A claim of privilege is not established by mere assertion that privilege applies to particular communications, or that communications are undertaken for the purpose of obtaining or giving 'legal advice'.
- Where communications take place between a client and their independent legal advisers, or between a client's in-house lawyers and those legal advisers, it may be appropriate to assume that legitimate legal advice was being sought, absent any contrary indications.
- CLP protects the disclosure of documents that record legal work carried out by the lawyer for the benefit of the client, such as research memoranda, collations and summaries of documents, chronologies and the like, whether or not they are actually provided to the client.
- Subject to meeting the dominant purpose test, CLP extends to notes, memoranda or other documents made by officers or employees of the client that relate to information sought by the client's legal adviser to enable [them] to advise. The privilege extends to drafts, notes and other material brought into existence by the client for the purpose of communication to the lawyer, whether or not they are themselves actually communicated to the lawyer.
- CLP is capable of attaching to communications between a salaried legal adviser and [their] employer, provided that the legal adviser is consulted in a professional capacity

32 *Esso Australia Resources Ltd v Federal Commissioner of Taxation* (1999) 201 CLR 49. See generally GE Dal Pont, *Lawyers' Professional Responsibility* (Thomson Reuters, 7th ed, 2021) ch 11.

33 *AWB Ltd v Cole (No 5)* (2006) 155 FCR 30, 44 (references omitted).

in relation to a professional matter and the communications are made in confidence and arise from the relationship of lawyer and client.

- CLP protects communications rather than documents, as the test for privilege is anchored to the purpose for which the document was brought into existence. Consequently, CLP can attach to copies of non-privileged documents, if the purpose of bringing the copy into existence satisfies the dominant purpose test.

In the dominant purpose test and subsidiary principles lies much ongoing disquiet about the proper limits to CLP, as some of the case studies in this chapter demonstrate. It is clear that some clients do seek to keep out of court advice received that is not bona fide within the 'privilege protection zone'. For example, lawyers may provide advice that is not necessarily legal advice – it may be financial planning advice, accounting advice, or even strategic business advice that is only secondarily of a legal nature. In these cases they may also provide legal advice, but not as the dominant purpose of the communication.

For example, a client may ask for an analysis of the best capital market in which to issue a prospectus for a new manufacturing process to 'print' machinery in China. Their lawyer may offer an opinion that prefers the Shanghai stock exchange to the Melbourne exchange because there is more capital available in China. At the time that opinion is provided, the lawyer may also comment that the manufacturing regulatory environment is less restrictive in Shanghai, and that specific employment rules that apply in Australia do not apply in China. The latter piece of advice is legal in nature, but might not be privileged, if it is clear that the lawyer was primarily retained for their overall capital market opinion. The distinction would be important and embarrassing for the client and their lawyer if, in later proceedings concerning a workplace accident, it was alleged that their lawyer had encouraged location in China because the client would get away with employment practices that were unsafe by Australian standards.

Although the central protections of privilege are reinforced by the law of evidence,[34] there are also some more general exceptions to the veil of silence erected around otherwise privileged communications. Importantly, privilege is the right of the lawyer's client and can be demolished by the client, even if their lawyer simultaneously takes other action on their behalf. Privilege does not cover confidential communications

- directed *against* the public interest;[35]
- when legislation has specifically removed the privileged status of those communications[36] – for example, where the federal parliament considers there is a risk that some lawyers will connive at setting up tax evasion schemes;[37]
- where the client has acted inconsistently (even on a single occasion) with the exercise of that privilege;[38]

34 See, eg, *Evidence Act 1995* (Cth) and similar provisions in the *Evidence Acts* of the Australian Capital Territory, New South Wales, Northern Territory, Tasmania and Victoria. For litigation privilege see s 119 (*Mitsubishi Electric Australia Pty Ltd v Victorian Workcover Authority* (2002) 4 VR 332) and for advice privilege see s 118.

35 See *Evidence Act 1995* (Cth) s 125.

36 There must be a clear, unambiguous statutory intention to remove the exception. See *Daniels Corporation International Pty Ltd v Australian Competition and Consumer Commission* (2002) 213 CLR 543.

37 See generally Stephen Barkoczy, *Foundations of Taxation Law* (Cambridge University Press, 14th ed, 2022) 'Part N: Tax Avoidance'.

38 See, eg, *Evidence Act 1995* (Cth) s 122.

- where the client knowingly and voluntarily disclosed the substance of the communication;
- where the communication is disclosed with the express or implied consent of the client; or
- if the client has acted in a way that would make it unfair to then claim privilege.[39]

For all purposes, while the *communication* is privileged, the information it contains is not. Accordingly, if that information is available elsewhere, a claim of CLP is irrelevant. This was graphically illustrated by the High Court case of *Glencore International AG v Commissioner of Taxation (Cth)*.[40] Following a massive data hack affecting a law firm in Bermuda (a tax haven), over 13 million documents (the 'Paradise Papers') were released into the public domain.[41] The Commissioner of Taxation obtained a copy of legal advice relating to a proposed restructure of mining giant Glencore International ('Glencore'). Glencore sought to prevent the Commissioner's use of the advice, on the grounds that the advice was privileged. Noting there was no suggestion that the documents containing the advice were improperly obtained, the High Court rejected Glencore's argument, holding that CLP is a 'shield' to protect a party from having to disclose documents, not an actionable legal right (a 'sword') that could found a cause of action, such as an injunction to prevent the Commissioner having further access to documents already in the public domain. This case underscores the importance of ensuring the security of clients' data; CLP will be lost if the data is hacked and disclosed by a third party.

Where privileged documents are mistakenly disclosed to an opposing side's lawyer, *ASCR* r 31 requires the lawyer to return, destroy or delete the material (as appropriate) and notify the other side's lawyer of both the disclosure and the steps taken to prevent inappropriate misuse of the material.[42]

Case study 4.3 illustrates the significance of limitations to CLP.

CASE STUDY 4.3 **BIG TOBACCO PRIVILEGE**

It is now well known that tobacco products kill up to one half of all their users. The harm is seriously compounded by the highly addictive nature of cigarette smoking and the fact that many users start young. Serious global efforts are underway to restrict the marketing and sale of cigarettes, especially to children, to avoid others being exposed to second-hand

39 *A-G (NT) v Maurice* (1986) 161 CLR 475.

40 *Glencore International AG v Commissioner of Taxation (Cth)* (2019) 265 CLR 646.

41 Four Corners and the International Consortium of Investigative Journalists, 'Paradise Papers. What Is the Leak and Who Is the Firm Behind Appleby?', *ABC News* (online at 6 November 2017) <https://www.abc.net.au/news/2017-11-06/what-are-the-paradise-papers-and-what-is-the-firm-appleby/9075640?nw=0>. See also 'Paradise Papers: Secrets of the Global Elite', *ICIJ (International Consortium of Investigative Journalists)* (Web Page) <https://www.icij.org/investigations/paradise-papers/>. See also 'The Panama Papers: Exposing the Rogue Offshore Finance Industry, *ICIJ (International Consortium of Investigative Journalists)* (Web Page) <https://www.icij.org/investigations/panama-papers/>.

42 See also *Expense Reduction Analysts Group Pty Ltd v Armstrong Strategic Management and Marketing Pty Ltd* (2013) 250 CLR 303 and the *Civil Procedure Act 2010* (Vic). It may become necessary for a lawyer who has seen a document by way of inadvertent disclosure to cease to act: see Chapter 7.

smoke, and to implement various other measures under the auspices of the *WHO [World Health Organization] Framework Convention on Tobacco Control*, a treaty that has been signed by 180 parties representing more than 90% of the world's population.[43]

Yet there is a long history of lawyers assisting tobacco companies to avoid public and legal scrutiny of their culpability in relation to the marketing of cigarettes, their addictiveness and harm. In the 1990s it was revealed that tobacco companies in the United Kingdom and United States had, with the help of their lawyers, hidden or destroyed many relevant documents about the health effects of smoking.[44] Tobacco industry lawyers in the United States devised schemes to ensure that it was *lawyers* who commissioned and controlled scientific evidence about the health effects of smoking. When litigants sued tobacco companies, they then claimed CLP over reports that showed smoking was dangerous. However, they made sure that reports prepared by 'sympathetic' scientists that were positive for the tobacco industry were well publicised. Eventually, the claim of privilege over these reports was struck down as an abuse of privilege. But in the meantime, lawyers had kept hidden for years scientific reports showing the dangers and addictiveness of smoking, and revealing that the tobacco companies knew about this. It was not until whistleblowers alerted plaintiff lawyers to the existence of these reports and devices that these claims of privilege could be attacked.[45]

In Australia, the NSW Dust Diseases Tribunal heard the evidence of former British American Tobacco Australian Services ('BATAS') in-house legal counsel Fred Gulson that BATAS and law firm Clayton Utz participated in a 'contrivance' to hide evidence behind CLP. BATAS would give Clayton Utz copies of its documents (including those that might harm it, if discovered in litigation), ostensibly for legal advice. The originals were destroyed under the document retention policy while Clayton Utz kept the copies but claimed that they were protected by privilege.[46] The Tribunal found that there was evidence that BATAS had dishonestly concealed the true nature of its document policy from the other side, and ordered disclosure of the documents.[47]

DISCUSSION QUESTIONS

1. The reputation of a number of Big Tobacco law firms was damaged by adverse judicial reflection on the lawyers' use of privilege in defending litigation against their clients. How could the lawyers have advised their clients differently in relation to privilege claims? Assuming that the advice in fact given was from an *adversarial advocacy* perspective, how might advice from a *responsible lawyering*, *moral activism* or *ethics of care* perspective have differed?

43 See, 'Tobacco', *World Health Organization* (Fact Sheet, 26 July 2021) <https://www.who.int/news-room/fact-sheets/detail/tobacco>.

44 Stanton A Glantz et al (eds), *The Cigarette Papers* (University of California Press, 1998).

45 Ralph Nader and Wesley J Smith, *No Contest: Corporate Lawyers and the Perversion of Justice in America* (Random House, 1996) 18–31; Richard Kluger, *Ashes to Ashes: America's Hundred-Year Cigarette War, the Public Health, and the Unabashed Triumph of Philip Morris* (Alfred A Knopf, 1996).

46 Susannah Moran, 'Cloaks of Privilege and Smoking Guns', *The Australian Financial Review* (Sydney, 19 May 2006) 57; Vanda Carson, 'Smoke Clearing on Big Tobacco as Insurers Fight' and 'Policy Failed the Smell Test: Whistleblower', *The Australian* (Sydney, 19 May 2006) 24.

47 *(Re Mowbray) Brambles Australia Ltd v British American Tobacco Australia Services Ltd* [2006] NSWDDT 15. See also Elisabeth Sexton, 'Ifs, Butts and Big Bucks', *Insight, The Age* (Melbourne, 3 June 2006) 4. The case, however, then settled and the documents therefore did not have to be disclosed: Vanda Carson, 'Tobacco Company Sidesteps Ruling', *The Australian* (Sydney, 6 July 2006) 8.

2. Other large industries and sectors – for example, fast food, confectionery, sugar-sweetened beverages, gaming, alcohol and fossil fuel extractors – are in danger of being sued in respect of the effects of their products on consumers, particularly very young consumers, and the ecosystem. These large industry sectors will have the results of numerous internal investigations (for example, into the impacts of fossil fuel consumption on climate change) and marketing polls (for example, about how best to target advertising directed at children). How would you advise them, if they seek to exert claims to privilege in respect of that information?
3. Should large corporate and government clients whose actions affect thousands of lives be able to claim absolute confidentiality over their own investigation of the impacts of their products and marketing strategies?

The Australian Law Reform Commission has suggested that the problem of regulatory and judicial scrutiny of CLP is likely to be inevitably and perennially insoluble, not least because

> [t]he difficult issue of weighing up when an expansive claim of privilege becomes an improper one … is compounded by potential breadth of a test which requires the assessment of the 'dominant purpose' of the communications in question.[48]

The Commission therefore recommended better legal education and general enforcement of existing disciplinary standards by the courts and regulators, rather than specific penalties for abuse of privilege, but it was sufficiently concerned to observe as follows:

> The ALRC acknowledges that identifying when the assertion of a claim of client legal privilege amounts to 'abuse' may be problematic … [W]here a lawyer is testing the boundaries of the doctrine of privilege with an arguable case, this is different from maintaining a hopeless claim as a tactic in order to frustrate or delay an investigation. While there is no clear evidence of chronic abuse of claims of client legal privilege, there are some cases that cause concern, and also evident distrust on the part of federal investigatory bodies that claims are not being made legitimately in every case.[49]

Most claims of privilege will not be challenged by the opposing party, given the cost of additional interlocutory proceedings to resolve the claim. This puts the onus squarely on a lawyer preparing a claim to keep in mind their overriding duty to the court and the administration of justice and not encourage or acquiesce in a claim for privilege over communications to which privilege does not attach. When the opposing party does have the resources to contest a privilege claim, lawyers who advise clients to make improper claims put the reputation of their clients and themselves at risk.[50]

48 Australian Law Reform Commission, *Privilege in Perspective: Client Legal Privilege in Federal Investigations* (Report No 107, 2008) 493 [9.19] (citations omitted).

49 Ibid 33.

50 As Jeremy Hirschhorn Second Commissioner, Client Engagement, Australian Tax Office has indicated: 'If … privilege is claimed over documents which could never be privileged, and the ATO ultimately demonstrates that they were not privileged, there is the potential for significant downside for both the taxpayer and the adviser': Jeremy Hirschhorn, 'Reflections on Being a Large Market Tax Adviser', *Australian Tax Office* (Web Page/Paper Delivered to Large Market Tax Advisory Firms,

Alongside these concerns about the proper 'use' of confidentiality and CLP, we note the trend within civil and family justice to early and full disclosure of otherwise 'secret' evidence in the interest of fairer, cheaper dispute resolution. This trend is being embraced by courts and governments, which cannot afford to keep funding an expensive trial system where lengthy disputes about privilege continue for many months. But courts and governments are also interested in shorter, more principled dispute resolution because it is perceived to be fairer to the parties. As discussed in Chapter 6, the concept of an 'overarching obligation' on lawyers and their clients to conduct civil proceedings with integrity signifies, in part, a policy-driven frustration with the inappropriate recourse to privilege by some lawyers and their clients.

CASE STUDY 4.4 **AWB**

The AWB (formerly the Australian Wheat Board) case offers a clear example of the abuse of CLP. Its claim for CLP was the subject of litigation, and adverse comments by a royal commissioner. After reviewing the discussion of the case in Case study 9.1, consider the following.

According to newspaper reports of evidence given at the Australian government's Commission of Inquiry ('Cole Royal Commission'), as soon as AWB became aware of allegations of corruption and bribery in June 2003, two months after the fall of Saddam Hussein, the company set up an internal investigation into the allegations, codenamed 'Project Rose', under the control of their in-house counsel. The in-house counsel in turn called in three external law firms and two barristers to review emails and documents and to advise on whether AWB had paid illegal bribes. At the Royal Commission in 2006, the AWB Board members claimed privilege over all the legal advice they had received, and also all internal records that related in any way to the advice received from external lawyers. AWB's in-house counsel also claimed privilege to prevent him from answering any questions on his own opinion about any of the documents the external lawyers had been asked to advise on since, he said, even his own opinion would be based in part on the outside advice, which was privileged. Since hundreds of emails and other documents had been handed over to the external lawyers, this left very little that the in-house lawyer could be questioned about. AWB Board members and staff also refused to answer questions on the basis of their claims of privilege.[51]

12 September 2019) <https://www.ato.gov.au/Media-centre/Speeches/Other/Reflections-on-being-a-large-market-tax-adviser/>. See also Charlotte Grieve, '"Very Uncomfortable Position": ATO Won't Rule Out Criminal Charges in PwC Legal Stoush', *The Age* (online at 3 February 2021) <https://www.theage.com.au/business/banking-and-finance/very-uncomfortable-position-ato-won-t-rule-out-criminal-charges-in-pwc-legal-stoush-20210203-p56z2e.html>.

51 Richard Ackland, 'That's Privileged, Sir, and Go Scratch', *The Sydney Morning Herald* (Sydney, 3 March 2006) 13; Marian Wilkinson, 'Lawyers Swept Up Files, Inquiry Told', *The Sydney Morning Herald* (Sydney, 24 February 2006) 1.

AWB also tried (unsuccessfully) to claim privilege over a document accidentally given to the Commission that recorded a draft 'statement of contrition' prepared in a teleconference with external lawyers, and a corporate image and crisis management consultant.[52] This consultant had advised that AWB should apologise 'sooner rather than later', and an apology had been drafted. But AWB decided it did not want to admit that level of responsibility. Some of the statements made by the AWB chief executive in the draft apology were inconsistent with what he later told the Commission about AWB senior management's awareness of, and responsibility for, bribery.[53]

During the Royal Commission, Commissioner Terence Cole commented that, although it might have been *legal* to claim privilege in some of the circumstances in which AWB claimed privilege, the AWB Board should have been careful to consider the 'wisdom' of making the claim, from a 'corporate governance' point of view.[54] In other words, clients always have a choice about whether or not to claim privilege or enforce confidentiality. There may be a number of considerations in making this decision, other than the mere fact that both options are legally possible. For example, it might be desirable to not claim privilege so as to fully cooperate with a Commission or regulator in order to indicate an attitude of taking ethical responsibility for past wrongdoing.

Commissioner Cole also made this comment regarding AWB's claims for CLP:

> The claim for legal professional privilege [by AWB] in respect of the Project Rose brief to Mr Tracey QC, abandoned on day 62 of the hearings, resulted in great delay and expense to the Inquiry. Had AWB produced the brief earlier, with most of the relevant documents contained in it, the course of this Inquiry would have been different, and its duration and expense much less. Whatever may be said about legal professional privilege flowing from the skill of compiling a brief, it is plain that the original documents copied in the brief were all material to this Inquiry, would have had to be produced in response to notices, and would, after the expenditure of significant time and money, be compiled by the Inquiry to give a chronological picture of the involvement of AWB and its officers in the payment of monies by way of trucking fees. Had there been frankness or real cooperation on the part of AWB, most material documents could have been produced in November 2005.[55]

52 *AWB Ltd v Cole (No 5)* (2006) 155 FCR 30.

53 Caroline Overington, 'I'm Deeply Sorry: AWB Chief's Apology', *The Australian* (Sydney, 19 May 2006) 1, 8. In the Supreme Court of Victoria the former AWB chief executive Andrew Lindberg was fined $100,000 and disqualified from being a company director until 1 September 2014. See Ben Butler, 'Iraq Scandal: Former AWB Boss Fined', *The Age* (Melbourne, 10 August 2012) 2.

54 Transcript of Proceedings, Inquiry into Certain Australian Companies in Relation to the UN Oil-for-Food Programme (Commissioner Terence RH Cole, 6 March 2006) 4042. Subsequently the Federal Court decided that a number of the documents over which AWB claimed privilege were not privileged: *AWB Ltd v Cole (No 5)* (2006) 155 FCR 30. We note that a court cannot make an adverse inference from a claim of privilege.

55 *Royal Commission into Certain Australian Companies in Relation to the UN Oil-for-Food Programme* (Final Report, 2006) vol 1, 189 [7.64].

Discussion questions

ASCR r 17.1 states:

> A solicitor representing a client in a matter that is before the court must not act as the *mere mouthpiece* of the client or of the instructing solicitor (if any) and must exercise the forensic judgments called for during the case independently, after the appropriate consideration of the client's and the instructing solicitor's instructions where applicable.[56]

If you were an advocate representing a large corporation such as AWB, and believed that the claim of CLP (on behalf of your client) was spurious and could result in very critical comment by a judge at a later date:

1. Would you be prepared to make that claim?
2. Would you feel able to argue that your reputation is worth as much as, if not more than, the client's?
3. Would you be prepared never to receive a brief from the client again, as a consequence of a single instance where you considered a claim for CLP to be disingenuous and not to be pursued?

Public interest exceptions to confidentiality: should lawyers' obligations of confidentiality be absolute?

There are a number of examples given throughout this book of lawyers and clients using the cloak of confidentiality to cover up misconduct and obstruct justice. These include the way in which tobacco industry lawyers devised schemes to try and claim CLP over reports that showed smoking was dangerous (Case study 4.3); and the response by AWB to the Royal Commission into whether it paid 'kickbacks' to former Iraqi dictator Saddam Hussein in order to make sure the Iraqi government bought wheat from Australia under the United Nations' Oil-for-Food Programme (Case study 4.4; see also Case study 9.1).

It is clearly improper for a lawyer and client to 'use' confidentiality to cover up misconduct. Leaving such cases aside, there tends to be a strong presumption in the Australian legal system that lawyer–client confidentiality and privilege are absolute. Deane J has explained the rationale this way:

> That general principle is of great importance to the protection and preservation of the rights, dignity and freedom of the ordinary citizen … and to the administration of justice … in that it advances and safeguards the availability of full and unreserved communication between the citizen and his or her lawyer and in that it is a precondition of the informed and competent representation of the interests of the ordinary person

56 Emphasis added.

> before the courts and tribunals of the land. Its efficacy as a bulwark against tyranny and oppression depends upon the confidence of the community that it will in fact be enforced. That being so, *it is not to be sacrificed even to promote the search for justice or truth in the individual case* or matter and extends to protect the citizen from compulsory disclosure of protected communications or materials to any court or person with authority to require the giving of information or the production of documents or materials.[57]

This rationale sees truth and justice in a particular case as subordinate to the protection of client confidences via the overall system of privilege. That is, the existence of the privilege protecting certain lawyer–client communications is considered such an essential bulwark against tyranny and oppression in the society as a whole that it is *more important than truth and justice in a particular case.* Yet the notion that lawyers' obligations of confidentiality and of protecting clients' legal privilege are absolute is not borne out in the rules of confidentiality (we discuss exceptions to the rules and in the law of privilege and confidentiality below), nor in ethical theory.

Bok argues that we need to look at the roots of professional confidentiality in order to spell out the limits of its application. She claims that confidentiality should only extend as far as necessary to achieve the benefit the profession is supposed to secure, and that it cannot override greater injustice. She takes an essentially moral activist and consequentialist approach, arguing that the role-based morality of professional confidentiality can be overridden where there is a higher public interest.[58] One legal ethicist has argued:

> Part of the difficulty [with confidentiality] lies in the tendency of lawyers to present and of courts and commentators to accept that confidentiality is some kind of absolute, preferably never to be overridden and pragmatically to be overridden rarely and then only in cases where the justification is little short of overwhelming. Given self-regulation by the legal profession, the ethos of those charged with the duty of maintaining ethical standards is likely to share and reflect the general respect for confidentiality as some kind of absolute. On that view, the professional duty of confidentiality necessarily restricts access to information about lawyer conduct including lawyer misconduct, if any. Socially responsible and effective regulation of lawyers' conduct requires not only balancing of confidentiality and access to information but also devising and sustaining institutional arrangements that permit critical and informed scrutiny of lawyer conduct where appropriate without damaging the legitimate interests of clients.
>
> In addressing these issues, legal education and theory should resist the lawyer's ideological and self-serving account of confidentiality as some kind of absolute and demonstrate that the doctrines of confidence and privilege in a society at any one time represent a compromise between conflicting principles and values … A recognition that confidentiality and disclosure are of equal status leads to serious questions about limiting confidentiality in the interests of disclosure. Both confidentiality and disclosure can reasonably lay claim to being essential to the interests and administration of justice … Confidentiality does not necessarily mandate non-disclosure – it merely

57 *A-G (NT) v Maurice* (1986) 161 CLR 475, 490 (emphasis in original).

58 Bok (n 4).

> provides a reason for non-disclosure which may or may not be outweighed by other considerations.[59]

This suggests that we should direct attention to the goal of confidentiality obligations – that is, the public interest in the administration of justice – and what it requires, not just certain means of attaining it (that is, the privilege and confidentiality rules).

Lawyers should also be aware of broader public interests that may justify disclosure of otherwise secret information disclosed to lawyers. Legal ethics scholar and business regulation expert William Simon argues[60] that confidentiality between corporations and their lawyers could no longer be justified on public interest grounds: many corporate lawyers and accountants have become so conditioned to the culture of zealous advocacy that they have transformed appropriate lawyer–client confidentiality (a traditional loyalty) into anti-social secrecy. This secrecy has become so bad that these professionals' perceptions of what is in clients' interests, protected by that secrecy, became literally destructive to much of wider society.

The International Bar Association ('IBA') offers guidance on professional expectations regarding confidentiality through its *International Principles on Conduct for the Legal Profession*,[61] which provide:

> A lawyer shall at all times maintain and be afforded protection of confidentiality regarding the affairs of present or former clients, unless otherwise allowed or required by law and/or applicable rules of professional conduct.[62]

The Commentary also makes clear that

> no statement of principles or code of ethics can provide for every situation or circumstance that may arise. Consequently, lawyers must act … in accordance with the *dictates of their conscience*, in keeping with the general sense and ethical culture that inspires these International Principles.[63]

The IBA's recognition of the importance of conscience for lawyers faced with deciding matters of confidentiality is significant, because it supports the fundamental obligation of all lawyers to look to their own internal morality in weighing up the ethical alternatives that may be before them. In respect of confidentiality, the Commentary goes on to remind lawyers that confidentiality is always conditional, and that there 'are manifest situations in which the principles of confidentiality and professional secrecy of lawyer–client communications no longer apply in full or in part'.[64] Indeed *responsible lawyering*, *moral activism* and *ethics of*

59 Richard Tur, 'Confidentiality and Accountability' (1992) 1(1) *Griffith Law Review* 73, 83–4. See also Simon (n 6).

60 William H Simon, 'After Confidentiality: Rethinking the Professional Responsibilities of the Business Lawyer' (2006) 75(3) *Fordham Law Review* 1453, 1454.

61 International Bar Association, *International Principles for the Conduct of the Legal Profession* (25 May 2019) (includes 'Commentary on IBA International Principles on Conduct for the Legal Profession').

62 See International Principle 4, 'Confidentiality/Professional Secrecy' in ibid 6.

63 Ibid 11 (emphasis added).

64 Ibid 21. The Commentary notes that '[l]awyers should also take care to ensure that confidentiality and professional secrecy are maintained in respect of electronic communications, and data stored on computers': at 23.

care approaches all see some limits to confidentiality. The remainder of this chapter discusses the limits to confidentiality and privilege on public interest grounds and finishes with a discussion of whether it is ever appropriate for lawyers to blow the whistle on their clients.

ASCR r 9 uses mandatory language in its primary prohibition of disclosure of confidential information ('must not disclose'); however, it uses permissive language for its exceptions ('may disclose'). That is, the exceptions are available to lawyers, but lawyers are not compelled to disclose. The distinction between the two illustrates the fact that, from the profession's point of view, loyalty to clients (confidentiality) tends to weigh more heavily in the balance than wider public responsibilities (disclosure, especially for the purposes of whistleblowing).

ASCR r 9 Confidentiality

9.1 A solicitor must not disclose any information which is confidential to a client and acquired by the solicitor during the client's engagement to any person who is not:

9.1.1 a solicitor who is a partner, principal, director, or employee of the solicitor's law practice; or

9.1.2 a barrister or an employee of, or person otherwise engaged by, the solicitor's law practice or by an associated entity for the purposes of delivering or administering legal services in relation to the client,

EXCEPT as permitted in Rule 9.2.

9.2 A solicitor may disclose confidential client information if:

9.2.1 the client expressly or impliedly authorises disclosure;

9.2.2 the solicitor is permitted or is compelled by law to disclose;

9.2.3 the solicitor discloses the information in a confidential setting, for the sole purpose of obtaining advice in connection with the solicitor's legal or ethical obligations;

9.2.4 the solicitor discloses the information for the sole purpose of avoiding the probable commission of a serious criminal offence;

9.2.5 the solicitor discloses the information for the purpose of preventing imminent serious physical harm to the client or to another person; or

9.2.6 the information is disclosed to the insurer of the solicitor, law practice or associated entity.

Three of the exceptions essentially support the lawyer in the normal ethical running of client matters:

- *ASCR* r 9.2.1 recognises that clients themselves need to authorise disclosure of confidential information in their own interests and in the ordinary course of legal matters. But this can also go beyond normal and routine matters. Ethical clients might be willing to authorise disclosure of otherwise confidential information in the public interest. For example, a company that manufactures garden chemicals might agree through its lawyer to reveal the exact contents of that chemical to a doctor, if a toddler accidentally drank the chemical, in order to save the toddler's life more quickly – even if the contents of the product had only been disclosed to the lawyer for regulatory compliance purposes, were strictly confidential and might raise questions of whether the company had taken enough care in the composition and manufacture of the chemical. Implied authorisation by the client under *ASCR* r 9.2.1 is also important, because it permits a lawyer to make a judgement about circumstances that might justify disclosure. For example, when a client goes missing in the middle of a difficult and financially damaging negotiation with other parties of dubious motives, their lawyer might go to the police with more confidence, if they thought that their discussion with detectives would be sanctioned by the client, given the client might have met with 'foul play'. Note that this situation is not as obvious or compelling as that envisaged by *ASCR* r 9.2.5 ('imminent … physical harm') discussed below.

- *ASCR* r 9.2.3 wisely encourages lawyers to seek confidential advice about their obligations and their options, where needed. This encourages competent and ethical decision-making.
- *ASCR* r 9.2.6 grants an exception to confidentiality for the purposes of a lawyer telling their insurer about client matters. This is a limited exception and does not allow for more general disclosure of a client's matters.
- The opening part of *ASCR* r 9 also recognises that an individual lawyer will need to share confidential client information with a range of employees and other professionals in order to serve their client well.

The other three exceptions set out in *ASCR* r 9 all allow lawyers to consider a wider public interest when discharging their duty of confidentiality, and may allow lawyers to blow the whistle on their own clients and colleagues in the public interest. These are as follows:

- where the solicitor discloses the information for 'the sole purpose of avoiding the probable commission of a serious criminal offence' (*ASCR* r 9.2.4);
- where the solicitor discloses the information for the purpose of preventing imminent serious physical harm to the client or to another person (*ASCR* r 9.2.5); and
- where 'the solicitor is permitted or is compelled by law to disclose' (*ASCR* r 9.2.2). This suggests and probably even affirms, that the conduct rules may track any exceptions included in the general law of contract, equity and privilege, such as the iniquity rule discussed below.

The exceptions for avoiding serious criminal offences and preventing physical harm acknowledge that, just because a lawyer owes a strong obligation of confidentiality to an individual client, this should not prevent the lawyer speaking where to do so would save another individual from imminent physical harm or prevent a serious criminal offence. However, the substance of the exceptions is quite narrowly constrained. There must be either a 'serious criminal offence' or 'imminent physical harm'. They clearly envisage the situation where an individual client informs their lawyer that they intend to commit a crime or injure or kill someone. The narrowness of the wording makes it difficult to apply to any situation where the client is an organisation such as a corporation or government. The attribution of criminal activity to a corporation is difficult and in many cases relies on a close consideration of the degree of knowledge of the executives. The harm caused by a large corporate client that is slowly killing a large proportion of its customers via a carcinogenic product, for example, would not be considered 'imminent' enough, even if it were to be considered inevitable and criminal.[65] Hence, the uncertainty in relation to these exceptions is likely to mitigate against a lawyer exercising the discretion to disclose in any but the clearest cases involving individuals with clear murderous intent and capability.

In contrast to the approach of the *ASCR* (and the US *Model Rules*), which provide categorical exceptions to the duty of confidentiality, US scholar William Simon argues for a duty of 'moderate confidentiality'. Such a duty would require lawyers to keep client information confidential unless such confidentiality threatens to work 'injustice', in which case the lawyer 'must weigh the value of … loyalty [to the client] against the harm disclosure would avert'.[66] While determining what might be unjust would require lawyers to exercise complex professional judgement, Simon argues that this is not beyond the skill of lawyers (and is regularly required of many lawyers) and is preferable to categorial definitions that struggle to cover all appropriate cases.

As noted, abuse of confidentiality and CLP is of serious concern. Lawyer involvement in client corruption of the administration of justice (including hiding evidence and avoiding transparency) is one of the most important ethical issues for lawyers (see Case study 4.3 and the discussion in Chapter 6 on ethics in civil litigation and dispute resolution). For example, the 'Panama Papers' and 'Paradise Papers' leak of millions of documents (referred to earlier in this chapter) exposed the way tax haven law firms assist rich clients, including celebrities, government figures and global corporations, to avoid paying tax in their home countries by using shelf companies in tax havens such as Panama and Bermuda. This leak of confidential lawyer–client documents opened up the issue of injustice and inequality in terms of who pays taxes and who does not, and has provided evidence to support criminal investigations.[67] In an era where wealth inequality is growing everywhere and we know that that inequality contributes profoundly to so much future crime and poverty, it is appropriate to suggest that lawyers who aid tax avoidance by artificial means are directly implicated in the abuse of confidentiality. The IBA's Commentary to its Principles on conduct notes:

> As governments take further action on tax evasion, tax avoidance and financial crimes, an increasing number of decision-makers have been expressing disquiet about the extent to which confidentiality/professional secrecy shields wrong-doers from discovery, or hides behaviour of which governments disapprove (even if it is not illegal). This in turn exposes lawyers to accusations that their long-held values facilitate criminality or behaviour that is considered by some decision-makers to be socially harmful, even if the lawyer is an unwitting party, and even if those values underlie other aspects of due process and fairness in the legal system. Of course, lawyers are forbidden from aiding criminality or fraud, but much of the recent discussion has been around client conduct which is lawful [citing lawyers helping clients minimise their tax obligations through off-shore structures, which may follow the letter but not the spirit of the law and

65 Tom Lininger argues that the ABA *Model Rules* should allow disclosure of confidential information 'to prevent imminent, substantial and irremedial environmental damage'. While retaining the 'imminent' test, this proposal recognises harm to the environment as a harm in itself (ie not just as possibly leading to harm to humans). See Tom Lininger, 'Green Ethics for Lawyers' (2016) 57(1) *Boston College Law Review* 61, 77 and Chapter 10.

66 Simon (n 6) 448.

67 Including against the mining company Glencore: see 'The Panama Papers: Exposing the Rogue Offshore Finance Industry' (n 41).

> which could be depriving governments of valuable tax income]. Bars are encouraged to ensure that they have measures in place to satisfy themselves that the public can have full confidence that lawyer-client confidentiality is not being abused.[68]

The wording of *ASCR* r 9.2.2 (which makes an exception to confidentiality where the solicitor is 'permitted' by the law to disclose) is particularly vague. We suggest that it should be recognised as incorporating into the professional conduct rules both the crime-fraud exception to privilege and the iniquity rule defence to breach of confidence in equity. That is, where the crime-fraud exception or the iniquity defence would apply, we suggest that r 9.2.2 would also excuse the lawyer who blows a whistle.

The crime-fraud 'exception' means that privilege does not apply to communications that facilitate or further a crime, fraud or civil offence.[69] It extends to communications made with the intention of frustrating the processes of law, and that may be described as a 'fraud on justice'.[70] It applies whether or not the lawyer is aware of the (wrongful) purpose of the communication: the relevant issue is the client's intention. The courts recognise that the privilege does not apply in such circumstances, because clients should not be able to rely on privilege to facilitate actions against the public interest.

The 'iniquity rule' defence to breach of confidence was originally quite narrow, stating that where iniquitous information (at that stage confined to crimes and frauds) was disclosed, confidentiality could not attach to this information.[71] By 1967 the defence had broadened to extend to 'crimes, frauds and misdeeds'[72] that could have already occurred, or may occur in the future; and '[t]he courts [had] adopted a flexible approach to the nature of "frauds and misdeeds", being prepared to consider almost any civil wrong as falling within the category'.[73] Kaaren Koomen labels this the 'broad' iniquity rule, which she defines as applying

> to cases where an iniquity is involved, but the existence of an iniquity will not *automatically* justify disclosure. If an iniquity is involved the court must then balance the competing interests to determine whether disclosure is justified.[74]

This approach was accepted by Kaye J in a case involving the disclosure of confidential information by Christopher Dale, a former partner of law firm Clayton Utz, concerning that firm's internal investigation of its own lawyers' conduct in tobacco litigation. Kaye J stated that there is 'a public interest in the disclosure of the relevant wrongdoing to a person who has a relevant interest in redressing that wrongdoing'.[75] However, it is important to note that Australian courts have not accepted the much broader English 'public interest

68 International Bar Association (n 61) 22–3.
69 *R v Cox* (1884) 14 QBD 153, 158.
70 *A-G (NT) v Kearney* (1985) 158 CLR 500, 514 (Gibbs CJ). See also *R v Bell; Ex parte Lees* (1980) 146 CLR 141, 156 (Stephen J).
71 *Gartside v Outram* (1857) 26 LJ Ch 113.
72 *Initial Services Ltd v Putterill* [1968] 1 QB 396.
73 Tanya Aplin et al, *Gurry on Breach of Confidence: The Protection of Confidential Information* (Oxford University Press, 2nd ed, 2012) [16.09], [16.14], [16.12]. See also Kaaren Koomen, 'Breach of Confidence and the Public Interest Defence: Is It in the Public Interest? A Review of the English Public Interest Defence and the Options for Australia' (1994) 10 *Queensland University of Technology Law Journal* 56, 58.
74 Koomen (n 73) 76 (emphasis in original).
75 *British American Tobacco Australia Ltd v Gordon (No 3)* [2009] VSC 619, [118].

defence' to breach of confidentiality that merely requires a balancing of interests without the need for any 'iniquity' or wrongdoing. In the case of *privileged* communications, Australian courts consider that 'the public interest favours maintenance of the confidence of the communication unless the communication comes within one of the established exceptions to legal professional privilege'.[76]

Considerations of the public interest were relevant in the case of Stephen Keim QC, who represented Indian doctor Mohammad Haneef in Queensland when he was charged by the Australian Federal Police ('AFP') with terrorism-related offences in 2007. Glasgow Airport had just been bombed by a distant cousin of Haneef. The AFP case against Haneef was weak and, *before* the case was decided, the AFP leaked to the media selected and misleading extracts of its record of interview with him, in order to sway public opinion against him.

Keim faced the barristers' equivalent of *ASCR* r 28.1, which states: 'A solicitor must not publish or take steps towards the publication of any material concerning current proceedings which may prejudice a fair trial or the administration of justice.' He nevertheless decided to publish the *full* record of interview (which showed how unlikely it was that Haneef was connected to his terrorist cousin), to balance the adverse effects of the AFP's selective publication, asserting later that his decision was essential to a fair trial and the administration of justice. The prosecution case against Haneef was withdrawn and although Keim was investigated by regulators after an AFP complaint was lodged against him, he (and his virtuous commitment to justice) was found to be justified.[77]

A contrasting case in which public interest was absent is the 2009 Western Australia State Administrative Tribunal decision of *Legal Practitioners Complaints Committee and Trowell*,[78] another case concerning Schapelle Corby's legal representatives. The Australian government requested that Mr Trowell represent Corby while she was incarcerated in Bali, Indonesia, in relation to drug offences. Trowell later made allegations to the media that a member of the Bali legal team suggested that the government should provide funds to bribe the appeal judges.[79] The Tribunal rejected the possibility that a broad public interest defence could excuse breaches of confidence via disclosure to the media in Australia (in contrast to the United Kingdom).[80] It did accept the iniquity rule and held that the disclosure of

> a serious proposal to bribe the judiciary ... would likely avoid any finding of unprofessional conduct. However, in our opinion, disclosure by a lawyer of such confidential information could only be justified if made to the appropriate authority ... It is difficult to see how it could ever justify publication to the press.[81]

76 *Cowell v British American Tobacco Australia Services Ltd* [2007] VSCA 301.

77 See Rachel Spencer, 'Legal Ethics and the Media: Are the Ethics of Lawyers and Journalists Irretrievably at Odds?' (2012) 15(1) *Legal Ethics* 83; Stephen Keim, 'Disciplinary Processes from the Inside' [2008] *Precedent AULA* 63.

78 [2009] WASAT 42.

79 Ibid [375]–[376].

80 Ibid [388]. The Tribunal cited a passage from *Gartside v Outram* (1857) 26 LJ Ch 113 before stating, '[t]his passage has been developed in England as an independent "public interest" defence to justify publication of an otherwise confidential publication. Moreover, the English doctrine has in certain circumstances allowed for the possibility of disclosure to the media': at [378]–[379]. However, the Tribunal went on to state that 'the doctrine has received limited theoretical recognition in Australia' and cite Gummow J's decision in *Corrs Pavey Whiting & Byrne v Collector of Customs (Vic)* (1987) 14 FCR 434: at [381].

81 [2009] WASAT 42, [384].

Nicola Gobbo has become a notorious example of a lawyer breaching confidentiality (including privilege), purportedly in the public interest. Ms Gobbo was a criminal defence barrister at the time of Melbourne's violent 'gangland war'.[82] The Victoria Police was under significant political and public pressure to dismantle the criminal syndicates behind the violence. From 2005 to 2009, Gobbo provided the Police with information about her clients, their associates and other people, some of whom were involved in the gangland war. This information helped the Police secure convictions against people accused of serious violent and drug-related offences. However, in 2016, when the Director of Public Prosecutions ('DPP') became aware that the Police had used a barrister as an informant, he considered it his duty to disclose this information to the convicted persons. The Police objected to such disclosure. The High Court in effect endorsed the Supreme Court decision that the DPP should be permitted to disclose, and in doing so said:

> [Ms Gobbo's] actions in purporting to act as counsel for the Convicted Persons while covertly informing against them were fundamental and appalling breaches of [her] obligations as counsel to her clients and of [her] duties to the court. Likewise, Victoria Police were guilty of reprehensible conduct in knowingly encouraging [Ms Gobbo] to do as she did and were involved in sanctioning atrocious breaches of the sworn duty of every police officer to discharge all duties imposed on them faithfully and according to law without favour or affection, malice or ill-will. As a result, the prosecution of each Convicted Person was corrupted in a manner which debased fundamental premises of the criminal justice system.[83]

A Royal Commission was set up to investigate whether criminal cases had been affected by Gobbo's conduct as a 'human source' (that is, informant) and, more generally, the use of human sources by Victoria Police. The Commission made a suite of recommendations about Police use of informants with the aim of 'strengthening the operation of, and public confidence in, Victoria's criminal justice system'.[84] It also noted the importance of lawyers understanding their duty of confidentiality to their clients and the need for appropriate professional boundaries.[85] A number of convictions secured on the basis of intelligence supplied by Ms Gobbo have been overturned.[86] Ms Gobbo was struck off the Supreme Court roll of practitioners in 2020.[87]

Issues of confidentiality and disclosure in the public interest are often complex. Lawyers can protect themselves in these situations by prior consultation with legal profession ethics advisers or other acknowledged ethics exponents, pursuant to *ASCR* r 9.2.3, and making sure they go through a holistic consideration of all the competing interests and concerns, clearly documenting their decision-making process. At the very least this type of consultation and consideration will make regulatory action less likely, should a client complain at a later date. It's not always a good idea to take advice only from inside the firm. And in deciding where

82 See 'Chronology of Melbourne's Gangland War', *ABC News* (online at 9 April 2014) <https://www.abc.net.au/news/2010-04-19/chronology-of-melbournes-gangland-war/401850>.
83 *AB (A Pseudonym) v CD (A Pseudonym)* (2018) 362 ALR 1, 4 [10].
84 *Royal Commission into the Management of Police Informants* (n 3) 7.
85 Ibid 34.
86 See generally *Royal Commission into the Management of Police Informants* (n 3).
87 *Victorian Legal Services Board v Gobbo* [2020] VSC 692.

the appropriate balance of private and public interests lies in a particular case, lawyers will benefit from considering the various ethical categories discussed in Chapter 2 and their own moral beliefs.

Why blow a careful whistle?

Although lawyers will increasingly find that what they thought was private has leaked into the public domain, there remains plenty of client information that clients and lawyers at least *believe* is private. In the face of the primary and usually legitimate requirement for lawyers to keep client information confidential, and to preserve CLP where appropriate, it is unlikely that many lawyers will consider themselves able or obliged to engage in 'pro-social behaviour' as 'internal witnesses'[88] or whistleblowers against their clients. Nevertheless, *responsible lawyering*, *moral activism* and *ethics of care* approaches all suggest that lawyers should be permitted to blow the whistle in some situations. We suggest that lawyers should be able to blow the whistle – with care and consideration – where they have information about clients or other lawyers using legal services to subvert the administration of justice, and in circumstances where there is misconduct analogous to situations where courts or regulatory authorities would refuse to uphold CLP on the basis of the crime-fraud exception to privilege or where the iniquity defence to confidentiality applies.[89]

Reinier Kraakman and Ronald Gilson pointed out in the 1980s that lawyers and other private professionals could supplement government regulation, and discourage corporations and their managements from engaging in misconduct, by withholding their support from illegal or unethical actions.[90] As John Coffee Jr explains in his influential book on gatekeepers, professionals (including lawyers) lend corporations their 'reputational capital' and 'thus enable investors or the market to rely on the corporation's own disclosures or assurances where they otherwise might not'.[91] It follows that the market relies on professionals to act as gatekeepers and not pledge their reputation to clients who act dishonestly or illegally, and that it is in gatekeepers' own interests to preserve their reputation.

Where lawyers *assist* in illegal conduct, lawyers are held legally responsible. An Australian example is the lawyer who advised company directors to breach their duties under the *Corporations Act 2001* (Cth) ('*Corporations Act*') by phoenixing their companies (that is, winding up the original company and reconstituting a new company) to avoid paying properly due debts. The lawyer was sanctioned for being 'involved' in the contravention.[92]

88 On whistleblowers as 'internal witnesses' and whistleblowing as 'pro-social behaviour', see generally AJ Brown (ed), *Whistleblowing in the Australian Public Sector: Enhancing the Theory and Practice of Internal Witness Management in Public Sector Organisations* (ANU E Press, 2008).

89 See also Evans (n 14) ch 6; Christine Parker, Suzanne Le Mire and Anita Mackay, 'Lawyers, Confidentiality and Whistleblowing: Lessons from the *McCabe* Tobacco Litigation' (2017) 40(3) *Melbourne University Law Review* 999. This section is based in part on the latter article.

90 Reinier H Kraakman, 'Corporate Liability Strategies and the Costs of Legal Controls' (1984) 93(5) *Yale Law Journal* 857; Reinier H Kraakman, 'Gatekeepers: The Anatomy of a Third-Party Enforcement Strategy' (1986) 2(1) *Journal of Law, Economics, and Organization* 53; Ronald Gilson and Reinier H Kraakman, 'The Mechanisms of Market Efficiency' (1984) 70(4) *Virginia Law Review* 549.

91 John C Coffee Jr, *Gatekeepers: The Professions and Corporate Governance* (Oxford University Press, 2006) 2.

92 *Australian Securities and Investments Commission v Somerville* (2009) 77 NSWLR 110.

This is a rare example in Australia, but in the United States, agencies such as the Securities Exchange Commission ('SEC') and Inland Revenue Service have pursued lawyers, and encouraged lawyer regulatory authorities to discipline lawyers, when they have failed to meet agency views of acceptable standards.[93] Lawyer participation in or instigation of a client's illegal conduct is a clear failure of the lawyer's obligation as gatekeeper of the justice system.

Whistleblowing lies at the other end of the spectrum of lawyer responses to client wrongdoing, and may be the most appropriate response in some circumstances. In the United States the corporate regulator, the SEC, requires lawyers who practise corporate law to engage in internal whistleblowing should they become aware of 'a material violation of securities law or breach of fiduciary duty'.[94] The more ambitious requirement initially proposed as part of *Sarbanes-Oxley* reforms (but not legislated) completed the picture by explicitly requiring lawyers to notify their 'noisy withdrawal' externally to the SEC where internal reporting did not lead to an adequate response, thus actually mandating a form of whistleblowing.[95]

There are a few instances where Australian lawyers have a mandatory obligation to report to an external body, regardless of duties of confidentiality owed to the firm or the client. These provide implicit exceptions to confidentiality. These include trust account breaches,[96] reporting of cash transactions over a certain amount (to prevent money laundering)[97] and, in some jurisdictions, reporting of some criminal conduct.[98] At present, the most proactive monitoring and strictest enforcement occurs in relation to trust accounting regulatory requirements. As noted above, the Victorian Royal Commission into the Management of Police Informants has recommended that lawyers be required to report the suspected misconduct of other lawyers to regulatory bodies.[99]

There were serious proposals to require lawyers (and other finance-related providers such as accountants and real estate agents) not only to report any suspicions about clients'

93 Robert J Wilczek, 'Corporate Confidentiality: Problems and Dilemmas of Corporate Counsel' (1982) 7(2) *Delaware Journal of Corporate Law* 221, 226. For example, lawyers can be caught within the ambit of the *Sarbanes-Oxley Act* if they mislead an auditor engaged in the preparation of financial statements: *Sarbanes-Oxley Act of 2002* § 303, 15 USC § 7242 (Supp 2003); John C Coffee Jr, 'Can Lawyers Wear Blinders? Gatekeepers and Third Party Opinions' (2005) 84(1) *Texas Law Review* 59, 67–8.

94 *Sarbanes-Oxley Act of 2002* § 307, 15 USC § 7245 (Supp 2003) and 17 CFR § 205.3(b)(1) (2003).

95 David Waters, 'The Wisdom of Whistleblowing: The *Sarbanes-Oxley Act of 2002* and the "Noisy Withdrawal" Provision' (2010) 34(2) *Journal of the Legal Profession* 411.

96 *Legal Profession Uniform Law* (NSW; Vic; WA) ss 154 (obligation to report irregularities), 466 (suspending CLP and failure to comply may amount to unsatisfactory conduct or misconduct); *Legal Profession Act 2006* (ACT) ss 231 (obligation to report irregularities), 525 (failure to provide information or documents is an offence); *Legal Profession Act 2006* (NT) ss 256 (obligation to report irregularities), 620 (obligation to provide information and documents); *Legal Profession Act 2007* (Qld) ss 260 (obligation to report irregularities), 544 (failure to comply may amount to unsatisfactory conduct or misconduct); *Legal Profession Act 2007* (Tas) ss 254 (obligation to report irregularities), 571 (person failing to provide information or documents may incur penalty); *Legal Practitioners Act 1981* (SA) sch 2 cl 24 (obligation to report irregularities), sch 4 cl 4 (obligation to provide information and documents), s 95C (suspending CLP).

97 *Financial Transaction Reports Act 1988* (Cth) s 15A.

98 *Crimes Act 1900* (NSW) s 316(1).

99 *Royal Commission into the Management of Police Informants* (n 3) recommendations 86, 87.

possible money laundering, but in some circumstances to keep those reports a secret from their clients in order that ongoing regulatory investigations could occur without those clients' knowledge.[100] Amendments to the anti-money laundering and counterterrorism financing regime that took effect in 2021[101] will not implement this reform, which was opposed by the Law Council of Australia ('LCA'). The LCA's opposition stems from a number of concerns, including there being no evidence that the facilitation of money laundering by lawyers is a significant problem; the effect on CLP; erosion of client confidentiality; a change in the role of lawyer from trusted adviser to informant; imposition of dual regulation on the legal profession; and the cost of compliance with the anti-money laundering regime (particularly significant for sole and small practices).[102]

The literature on gatekeeping generally stops short of advocating that lawyers should be mandated to blow the whistle in relation to organisational misconduct.[103] The gatekeeper role can only be carried out effectively if whistleblowing is available as the last step in a process of prevention of wrongdoing. Without the whistleblowing possibility, the lawyer gatekeeper is constrained to persuasion or withdrawal of services, neither of which may be effective. As Waters suggests, '[a]ll a silent withdrawal does is pass the problem along to another securities lawyer, possibly one who is not as concerned with ethics and professional responsibility'.[104] We, therefore, suggest that the justice system is only just when lawyers can act on their gatekeeper of justice obligations by speaking out when they see or strongly suspect their clients or others are abusing justice and they are unable to prevent it by other means.

There is certainly a danger that lawyer whistleblowing could be over-encouraged and that clients would lose faith in lawyer confidentiality, undermining frankness between lawyer and client, and thus promoting inefficiency and the loss of opportunities for lawyers to assist clients to act legally and ethically. We argue that it is crucial to the administration of justice that lawyers be careful about the circumstances in which they blow the whistle. There are three elements that must be considered:

100 The so-called second tranche of anti-money laundering and terrorist financing legislation, as proposed by the international Financial Action Task Force ('FATF'), contemplates these secret reporting obligations. In so doing, the FATF is consciously advocating the breach of the fundamental principle of client loyalty, but justifies this on the basis (disputed by the LCA) that global money laundering and terrorist financing are likely to be actively abetted by finance-related professionals in Australia. See generally Financial Action Task Force and Asia/Pacific Group on Money Laundering, *Anti-Money Laundering and Counter-Terrorist Financing Measures – Australia – Mutual Evaluation Report* (April 2015) <http://www.fatf-gafi.org/media/fatf/documents/reports/mer4/Mutual-Evaluation-Report-Australia-2015.pdf>, especially recommendation 21 at 167.

101 *Anti-Money Laundering and Counter-Terrorism Financing and Other Legislation Amendment Act 2020* (Cth).

102 Dr Jacoba Brasch QC, 'Opening Statement – Senate References Committee on Legal and Constitutional Affairs Inquiry on the Adequacy and Efficacy of Australia's Anti-money Laundering and Counter Terrorism Financing (AML/CTF) Regime', *Law Council of Australia* (Web Page, 10 November 2021) <https://www.lawcouncil.asn.au/media/speeches/opening-statement-inquiry-on-the-adequacy-and-efficacy-of-australias-anti-money-laundering-and-counter-terrorism-financing-aml-ctf-regime>. For a counter perspective see Nathan Condoleon, 'Risky Business: AML Regulation and Legal Ethics', *The Proctor* (November 2019) 26. The debate continues.

103 Coffee Jr, for instance, focuses on a duty to enquire and withdrawal of service as the consequence where the law firm identifies wrongdoing: Coffee Jr (n 93) 72.

104 Waters (n 95) 423.

- Only certain types of wrongdoing are serious enough to be disclosed.
- A lawyer whistleblower faced with misconduct must use an appropriate *process* to seek both to prevent the wrongdoing before blowing the whistle and to blow the whistle as quietly as possible, in a manner consistent with effectively addressing the wrongdoing.
- Lawyer whistleblowers will need *protection* from potential retaliation.

The *nature of the wrongdoing* is an important factor in determining whether it is appropriate for people to blow the whistle.[105] It has been argued that a broad definition of the type of wrongdoing that justifies whistleblowing as simply any 'illegal, immoral and illegitimate acts is problematic'.[106] We suggest that where misconduct is analogous to conduct that would fall within the crime-fraud exception to CLP, then gatekeeper of justice obligations are triggered and external whistleblowing may be permitted if other measures to address the misconduct fail. Similarly, if the iniquity defence to breach of confidentiality would apply, then whistleblowing may also be permitted, bearing in mind that the iniquity defence only applies where (1) there is misconduct, (2) it is, on balance, in the public interest to disclose the misconduct to an appropriate agency or authority and (3) the matter is disclosed to that agency/authority. Examples of the kind of wrongdoing that could justify whistleblowing on the part of the lawyer under this exception include situations where the courts or other regulatory authorities have been misled or deceived by either the lawyer's own client, or a lawyer or client on the other side.

An example would be AWB's subversion of the United Nations' Oil-for-Food Programme to illegally channel funds to Saddam Hussein's regime.[107] In such a situation the lawyer would have a clear duty not to counsel or assist in illegal conduct;[108] however, should the client persist with the wrongdoing, the pressure on the lawyer to conceal the wrongdoing is likely to be high. Moreover, the client may embroil the lawyer in its illegal purpose by expecting the lawyer to defend and even further the client's purpose. This type of wrongdoing falls within the crime-fraud exception, and thus it is desirable to make the conduct rules clear about when and how lawyers can blow the whistle in such a situation, and to provide them with protection from retaliation if they do so.

The *process* to be followed when whistleblowing is just as important as the type of wrongdoing. Whistleblowing is ethically problematic because it breaches shared understandings of loyalty and confidentiality within a relationship or organisation.[109] It is, therefore, important that lawyer whistleblowers disclose confidential information only when it is ethically justified to do so and do not unnecessarily breach other ethical obligations in the process.[110] In order to encourage appropriate use of a whistleblowing exception, the

105 Richard Wortley, Peter Cassematis and Marika Donkin, 'Who Blows the Whistle, Who Doesn't and Why?' in Brown (ed) (n 88) 53, 66.

106 Marit Skivenes and Sissel C Trygstad, 'Wrongdoing: Definitions, Identification and Categorizations' in AJ Brown et al (eds), *International Handbook on Whistleblowing Research* (Edward Elgar, 2014) 95, 99.

107 Caroline Overington, *Kickback: Inside the Australian Wheat Board Scandal* (Allen & Unwin, 2007).

108 See, eg, *Law Society of New South Wales v Dennis* (1981) 7 Fam LR 417; *Australian Competition and Consumer Commission v Real Estate Institute of Western Australia Inc* (1999) 161 ALR 79. See also Dal Pont (n 32) 653 (citations omitted): 'Lawyers must not engage in conduct that is dishonest, illegal, unprofessional, that may otherwise bring the profession into disrepute or that is prejudicial to the administration of justice. Lawyers must not therefore seek to advance their client's causes by unfair or dishonest means.'

109 Bok (n 4) 120.

110 Ibid 219–25.

conduct rules should set out the circumstances when whistleblowing is permissible and the process that should be followed. The following are the relevant circumstances.

First, lawyer whistleblowers should use judgement and ensure they are accurate in their assessment of any wrongdoing. That is, they should verify that they have accurate and sufficient evidence to at least prompt a further investigation by a regulatory authority before whistleblowing.

Second, lawyer whistleblowers should ensure the breach of loyalty is minimised by exploring appropriate alternative options for preventing wrongdoing (such as strong advice and persuasion) before sounding the alarm. Any disclosure should be as narrow as possible and directed to the party who can rectify or prevent the wrong – usually, first, an authoritative figure within the firm or company, and then a regulatory authority or court. Public disclosure, such as via the media, should only be a last resort because it carries with it a complete loss of control over the information.

Third, lawyer whistleblowers should disclose only the information necessary to address the wrongdoing. They should not, for example, disclose extraneous personal matters or hide what evidence they have. Rather, the whistleblowing should put matters of significance to an appropriate forum for investigation and accountability.

In relation to process, the principle is that the lawyer should start by raising issues of ethics and misconduct with the person concerned in a private and confidential way, and only gradually move on to more public and coercive ways of resolving the issues as each previous option fails. This process respects the confidentiality and sensitivity of the information, by only revealing the information to the extent absolutely necessary to prevent unethical conduct. Nevertheless, the process is likely to be draining for the lawyer, since it will involve sensitive, often tense, communications and negotiations, and the constant possibility of open conflict. In some cases the disclosure will be time sensitive and the whole process must occur very quickly, requiring that an instant judgement be made about whether to blow the whistle or not. Figure 4.2 provides a short guide to proper process.

It is best practice for lawyers to be respectful but clear with their clients from the beginning by explaining what can be kept secret and what might be disclosable in some future court or hearing, should government, media, competitors, whistleblowers or police learn of their actions. This is a difficult but necessary discussion between lawyer and client and requires courage, respect and determination. A lawyer may need to show courage in warning their client that their current or proposed practices are illegal or immoral and may not remain confidential. They will have to choose their words carefully, arguing that their clients' business or safety is better served in the long run by avoiding questionable behaviour, and the lawyer may need to be determined not to back down, if threatened with 'find yourself another job'. Lawyers truly do their clients a service when this kind of advice is listened to.

Amendments to the *Corporations Act* significantly strengthened the protections afforded corporate whistleblowers. The Act now protects corporate employees and service providers from civil or criminal liability, or victimisation, where the whistleblower has 'reasonable grounds' to suspect that the information they are disclosing concerns 'misconduct, or an

Figure 4.2 Checklist of issues to consider before blowing the whistle[111]

1. Find out if the local (State-based) whistleblower legislation protects you. This legislation could cover public sector lawyers and private sector lawyers where the *Corporations Act* protection can be invoked. The local legislation ideally will protect you from retribution. Make sure that, when ready, you are revealing something that is sufficiently in the public interest, and that you are revealing it to the designated person/authority.

2. See if you can find others in the organisation who will support you, and get them to come to any meetings that are called to discuss the matter.

3. Talk the issues over first with family and close friends and then gather as much independently supported evidence of the wrongdoing as you can, before you reveal anything.

4. Use *ASCR* r 9.2.3 (permitting disclosure 'for the sole purpose of obtaining advice in connection with the solicitor's legal or ethical obligations') to get confidential advice from your local law society or legal ethicist on the right course of action and its implications.

5. Prepare a 'script' and raise the issue internally with a sense of personal confidence, in the presence of a trusted witness, and send a record of the discussion to an appropriate superior(s).

6. Be prepared for rejection and retaliation inside the organisation – it will be very unusual if it does not come. Senior managers will resent the implication that they have been ineffective, some of them may even be involved in the wrongdoing; and colleagues will resent you as a threat to the security of the organisation. If the harassment continues, record all details and threaten legal action. If necessary, take legal action. Most State Acts give you the right to do so. Or seek a new job. Early consideration of this possible need will probably be in your best interests.[a]

7. Keep notes.

8. If the harassment continues, determine what other relief your Act offers you (relocation, for instance). Complain to a higher level if possible, but in the final analysis, seek legal advice and take action for damages. If you complain about harassment, place your emphasis on the public interest disclosure; any harassment or ill-will is a result of that disclosure. Also follow up on the investigation of your complaint, as most jurisdictions are obliged to tell you what the outcome is. And finally, if you do not win, if the wrongdoing is covered over, and no action is taken, try not to allow any sense of injustice to dominate your life. Remember that you have had a personal moral victory in making the disclosure. Attempt, as far as is possible, to recreate a new life and a new job.[b]

9. Try to take into account that, should you do nothing and the wrongdoing eventually be revealed, the loss to your personal reputation may be irrecoverable.

[a] See Bowden's 'ten point process'.
[b] See Bowden's 'ten point process'.

111 This guide is adapted by the authors from Peter Bowden's 'ten point process' for maximising chances of successful whistleblowing: see Peter Bowden, 'Our Ten Point Process for Protecting Yourself from Retaliation', *Whistleblowing Ethics* (Blog Post, 28 April 2011) <http://whistleblowingethics.blogspot.co.uk/2011_04_28_archive.html>.

improper state of affairs or circumstances'.[112] Disclosures are made within the company to the Board or to the corporate regulator, although certain emergency disclosures can be made direct to a journalist or parliamentarian. Corporations are required to ensure the identity of the whistleblower is not revealed. Certain corporate entities are required to develop a whistleblowing policy and make it available to officers and employees.[113]

Thus, the *Corporations Act* now gives ample room to corporate lawyers to fulfil their ethical duties. In-house corporate lawyers also have responsibility to *facilitate* legitimate whistleblowing. The Australian Association of Corporate Counsel ('ACC Australia') gives the following advice:

> In-house counsel are the legal gatekeepers for an organisation. They are often viewed as being the moral compass for their organisation. In-house counsel should actively encourage their organisations to put in place robust whistleblowing policies that provide a supportive environment for employees to express their good-faith and legitimate concerns regarding any unethical or illegal behaviour within the organisation.[114]

ACC Australia advises further that, while in-house counsel should not take on the role of the person nominated as a contact for whistleblowers, because this is likely to create a conflict of interests, they should educate the organisation about best-practice whistleblowing procedures. They should also raise any legal/ethical concerns they themselves have with senior decision makers, until they are satisfied that their concerns have been addressed. It is important that actual or perceived misconduct is address promptly and thoroughly, and to this end, in-house counsel should encourage periodic reviews of reporting procedures.[115]

Commonwealth public sector lawyers (and employees generally) have fewer whistleblower protections. The protections in the *Public Interest Disclosure Act 2013* (Cth) were reviewed in 2013 by Phillip Moss AM and found to be ineffectual. In 2016, Moss made 33 recommendations for reform, which were largely accepted by the Coalition Government in December 2020. At the time of writing the newly elected Labor Government had indicated it will introduce enacting legislation as a matter of priority, seeing it as 'is a significant matter because it is linked to the national anti-corruption commission', which is also a legislative priority.[116]

Outside of activities covered by the *Corporations Act* and the *Public Interest Disclosure Act*, lawyers are not well covered by whistleblower protections. There is no provision for whistleblower protection in legal profession legislation or conduct rules. A lawyer who finds their conscience troubled by client behaviour still faces an uphill internal battle in deciding what to do. They will need to weigh up the strength of their ethical preferences – for example, for either *responsible lawyering* or *moral activism* – before determining whether

112 *Corporations Act 2001* (Cth) s 1317AA(4).

113 See Rebecca Ananian-Welsh, Rose Cronin and Peter Greste, 'In the Public Interest: Protections and Risks in Whistleblowing to the Media' (2021) 44(4) *University of New South Wales Law Journal* 1242. The authors note that the protections in the *Corporations Act* are 'significant … but do not attach to every disclosure of misconduct in the private sector': at 1254.

114 ACC Australia, *Ethics Handbook* (2018) 16.

115 Ibid.

116 See 'Attorney General Mark Dreyfus Speaks to the Law Report', *Law Report* (ABC Radio National, 28 June 2022) <https://www.abc.net.au/radionational/programs/lawreport/attorney-general-mark-dreyfus/13949800>. See also Senate Environment and Communications References Committee, Parliament of Australia, *Inquiry into Freedom of the Press* (Report, May 2021), which recommended that 'the Australian Government expedite long-awaited reforms to the Public Interest Disclosure Act 2013' (recommendation 4.62). See, generally, Ananian-Welsh, Cronin and Greste (n 113).

the circumstances justify blowing the whistle. Knowing when to breach confidence requires ethical judgement, not just legal knowledge, because the circumstances in which the public interest or a client's 'fraud on justice' might justify or, indeed, demand whistleblowing can never be fully specified in the law. So it is appropriate to suggest that lawyers know something of the wider public debate about whistleblowing.

In the last few years, several 'public service' whistleblowers have been charged with criminal offences, even though the concerns about which they 'blew the whistle' have been shown to have substance. Richard Boyle, an employee of the Australian Taxation Office ('ATO'), initially raised concerns internally about the ATO's debt recovery practices that were aggressively targeting vulnerable small businesses. When his concerns were ignored, he contacted the media.[117] He was charged with 66 offences, 42 of which were dropped after a federal parliamentary report found the ATO's internal investigation into Boyle's complaint was 'superficial'. There have been calls for all charges to be dropped. Boyle has pleaded not guilty to the charges, on the basis that his disclosure to the media was in the public interest.[118]

David McBride is a former Australian Defence Force lawyer, who between 2014 and 2016 collated information (from classified documents) on war crimes committed by Australian soldiers in Afghanistan. McBride disclosed this information internally, and then to the Australian Federal Police, but no action was taken. He then made the information available to the Australian Broadcasting Corporation ('ABC'), which broadcast it in 2017. He was charged in 2018 with offences relating to disclosure of classified information. At the time, Major General Justice Paul Brereton was conducting a four-year inquiry into the allegations. His Honour's report, which was made public in November 2020, found 'credible information' that war crimes were committed by Australians.[119] McBride faces trial on theft of Commonwealth property, breaching the *Defence Act 1983* (Cth) and unauthorised disclosure of information.[120]

CASE STUDY 4.5 **WITNESS K AND HIS LAWYER**

In 2004, East Timor was newly independent from Indonesia after a brutal war; it was also one of the poorest countries in the world. At this time Witness K, a senior officer with the Australian Security and Intelligence Service ('ASIS'), was involved in bugging the meeting room of East Timor's Cabinet, to enable Australia to spy on East Timor ahead of negotiations

117 Christopher Knaus, 'Whistleblower Went Public After Tax Office's "Superficial" Inquiry into Concerns', *The Guardian* (online at 19 June 2020) <https://www.theguardian.com/australia-news/2020/jun/19/whistleblower-went-public-after-tax-offices-superficial-inquiry-into-concerns>.

118 Nassim Khadem, 'Prosecutors Proceed with Case Against ATO Whistleblower Richard Boyle', *ABC News* (online at 29 April 2021) <https://www.abc.net.au/news/2021-04-29/prosecutors-proceed-case-against-ato-whistleblower-richard-boyle/100105710>.

119 Inspector-General of the Australian Defence Force: Afghanistan Inquiry (Report, 2020).

120 Nick Xenophon, 'If Moral Courage Matters, This Whistleblower Needs Defending', *The Age* (online at 18 November 2020) <https://www.theage.com.au/national/if-moral-courage-matters-this-whistleblower-needs-defending-20201116-p56ey4.html>. (Nick Xenophon is a partner in the law firm Xenophon Davis, which is acting for David McBride. The above opinion piece was published as an open letter to the Chief of the Australian Defence Forces, General Angus Campbell.) The Senate Inquiry into Freedom of the Press recommended that the Commonwealth DPP 'urgently reconsider, on strong public interest grounds, whether the prosecution of Mr David McBride should be continued': Senate Environment and Communications References Committee, Parliament of Australia (n 116) recommendation 7.78.

over rights to oil and gas fields in the Timor Sea. The negotiations between Australia and East Timor resulted in 2006 in a treaty fairly heavily weighted in Australia's favour. Witness K was concerned that the bugging was an inappropriate activity for ASIS, particularly because it diverted funds from other important intelligence work and seemed to be advancing commercial, rather than national security, interests. In 2008 he raised his concerns internally; ASIS terminated his employment.[121] He lodged a complaint with the Inspector-General for Intelligence and Security, who authorised him to retain Bernard Collaery as his lawyer. Collaery, a former Attorney-General of the Australian Capital Territory, had a security clearance and had also been a legal adviser to the East Timorese for many years.

In 2008, East Timor's Prime Minister, Xanana Gusmao, was notified of the bugging[122] (presumably by Collaery on instructions from Witness K). In 2013, Gusmao confidentially raised the spying allegation with the Australian Government and proposed renegotiation of the treaty.[123] The Australian Government denied the allegations, so East Timor, assisted by Collaery and Witness K,[124] initiated proceedings in the Permanent Court of Arbitration in The Hague, alleging that the treaty was void because Australia had acted in bad faith. Witness K was scheduled to give crucial evidence in the proceedings, but in December 2013, ASIO searched his home and confiscated his passport. Collaery's home and chambers were also searched. When Collaery (who was already in Europe) heard about these searches, he contacted various ABC journalists and disclosed the substance of the spying allegations. These allegations were broadcast publicly via several ABC programs.[125] Collaery has adamantly denied that any of the information about the bugging disclosed by Witness K to East Timor names, or puts at risk, any ASIS officers or national security matters.[126]

The proceedings in The Hague stalled and in March 2018 a new treaty, more advantageous to East Timor, was eventually signed.[127] In May 2018 the then Commonwealth Attorney-General, Christian Porter, authorised the laying of charges against Witness K and Collaery. (The previous Attorney-General, George Brandis, had not given his approval to charges, even though he had first been briefed about the matter in 2015. It appears that the various national security agencies disagreed about the wisdom of proceeding with charges and that Brandis had had misgivings about a prosecution.)[128]

Witness K entered a plea of guilty to charges in 2019, having, according to Collaery, 'reached a conclusion he needs to exit the process' after 'six years of seclusion, harassment

121 Clinton Fernandes, 'Asia-Pacific: Espionage Against East Timor and the Need for Parliamentary Oversight' (2017) 42(1) *Alternative Law Journal* 71, 72.

122 Kim McGrath, *Drawing the Line: Witness K and the Ethics of Spying* (Schwartz Publishing, 2020) 69.

123 Ibid 70.

124 The first charge against Collaery is that in 2012–2013 he 'conspired with' Witness K to communicate information to East Timor about the ASIS operation: *R v Collaery (No 7)* [2020] ACTSC 165, [4].

125 'Drawing the Line', *ABC Four Corners* (Australian Broadcasting Corporation, 17 March 2014) <https://www.abc.net.au/4corners/drawing-the-line/5328634>; McGrath (n 122) 73.

126 'Drawing the Line' (n 125).

127 McGrath (n 122) 73. East Timor discontinued The Hague proceedings.

128 Steve Cannane and Peter Cronau, 'Former Attorney-General George Brandis Had "Misgivings" about Prosecuting Witness K and Collaery', *ABC News* (online at 26 August 2019) <https://www.abc.net.au/news/2019-08-26/brandis-had-misgivings-about-prosecuting-witness-k-and-collaery/11449758>. See also 'Secrets, Spies and Trials', *ABC Four Corners* (Australian Broadcasting Corporation, 30 August 2019) <https://www.abc.net.au/4corners/secrets,-spies-and-trials/11462842>.

and questioning'.[129] Collaery contested the charges against him. The Commonwealth argued that Collaery's trial should proceed largely in secret, given that it raised 'issues of national security'. This argument was largely accepted by the Supreme Court of the Australian Capital Territory[130] but was overturned on appeal in October 2021, the Court of Appeal noting the dangers of secrecy and the importance of open justice. The Commonwealth appealed (to the High Court) the decision to not suppress part of the reasons for judgment (not yet published).[131] In July 2022 the newly elected Labor Attorney-General directed the Commonwealth Director of Public Prosecutions to drop the charges against Collaery.[132]

The criminal proceedings against Richard Boyle, David McBride, Witness K and Collaery have been condemned by many, including the former New South Wales Department of Public Prosecutions, the former President of the Law Council of Australia, academics and civil society groups.[133] Apart from other issues, the charges against these whistleblowers raise questions about the exercise of discretion by the Commonwealth Director of Public Prosecutions in pursuing the charges.[134] While the charges against Collaery have been dropped, at the time of writing, the charges against Boyle and McBride remain. We deal with prosecutorial ethics in more detail in Chapter 5.

DISCUSSION QUESTIONS

1. What do you think empowered Richard Boyle, David McBride, Witness K and Bernard Collaery to blow the whistle, despite the ramifications for their careers and personal freedom (they face(d) gaol if found guilty)?

129 Paul Karp, 'Witness K to Plead Guilty in Timore-Leste Spying Case but Lawyer to Fight Charges', *The Guardian* (online at 6 August 2019) <https://www.theguardian.com/australia-news/2019/aug/06/witness-k-to-plead-guilty-in-timor-leste-spying-case-but-lawyer-to-fight-charges>.

130 *R v Collaery (No 7)* [2020] ACTSC 165; *R v Collaery (No 8)* [2020] ACTSC 200.

131 In an interlocutory decision – *Collaery v The Queen* [2021] ACTCA 1 – the Court noted at [17] that the Commonwealth Attorney-General's power under the *National Security Information (Criminal and Civil Proceedings) Act 2004* (Cth) to veto an accused person's choice of counsel (by denying that counsel access to sensitive information) is of an 'extraordinary nature' and must be exercised 'strictly for the purposes for which the power was given' and not 'exercised in order to gain a forensic advantage … Nor is it any part of the role of the Attorney-General to base his or her decision on whether he or she thinks that it is necessary for the accused to instruct that particular lawyer'. See Christopher Knaus, 'Open Justice v Secrecy: What is the Case Against Witness K Lawyer Bernard Collaery All About?', *The Guardian* (online at 31 January 2022) <https://www.theguardian.com/australia-news/2022/jan/31/open-justice-v-secrecy-what-is-the-case-against-witness-k-lawyer-bernard-collaery-all-about>.

132 'Attorney-General Mark Dreyfus Orders Commonwealth to Drop Charges Against Lawyer Bernard Collaery', *ABC News* (online at 7 July 2022) <https://www.abc.net.au/news/2022-07-07/attorney-general-orders-charges-dropped-against-bernard-collaery/101217272>.

133 Law Council of Australia, 'Law Council President, Pauline Wright, Support to Bernard Collaery' (Media Statement, 16 October 2020) <https://www.lawcouncil.asn.au/media/media-statements/law-council-president-pauline-wright-support-to-bernard-collaery>; 'Bernard Collaery 2020 Blueprint International Whistleblowing Prize', *Blueprint for Free Speech* (Web Page) <https://www.blueprintforfreespeech.net/en/prize/recipients/2020/bernard-collaery>.

134 Kieran Pender, 'The Cost of Courage: Australia Must Do More to Protect Whistleblowers', *Sydney Morning Herald* (Sydney, 17 December 2020) <https://www.smh.com.au/national/the-cost-of-courage-australia-must-do-more-to-protect-whistleblowers-20201217-p56odp.html>; Clinton Fernandes, 'Lawyer and Witness Face Charges Under Spy Laws, Raising Questions of Openness and Accountability', *The Conversation* (online at 29 June 2018) <https://theconversation.com/lawyer-and-witness-face-charges-under-spy-laws-raising-questions-of-openness-and-accountability-99143>.

2. Bernard Collaery and Witness K were charged with disclosing national security information to East Timor. Collaery was charged with disclosing national security information to journalists. Were Collaery's disclosures to the media justified, under the 'principle' of whistleblowing discussed above?
3. It is not clear whether Witness K instructed Collaery to disclose information to journalists. From a legal ethics perspective, is this relevant or important?

Conclusion

Although true privacy is increasingly unlikely for many people, it is critical for lawyers to recognise that impoverished clients are entitled to no less and no more privacy than those whose relative wealth, position or power allows them to contest intrusion into their private lives. Appropriate privacy, and the confidentiality that supports it, is essential to individuals' wellbeing, yet not at the cost of secrets that pervert the course of justice. The task of judging which secrets should remain secret falls to lawyers on an everyday basis, and *who* each lawyer is, at an ethical level, is central to that task. As law students and lawyers we must contemplate who we are (or would be) in these crises. Will we be unthinking zealous advocates for corporations and governments seeking to evade disclosure through excessive claims to CLP, or by denying freedom of information requests on the spurious basis of 'cabinet papers' or claims of 'commercial-in-confidence'? We need to apply our conscience to the integrity of our instructions. If zealous advocacy is our strongest instinct, we will have to decide on the limits to our zealotry and ask who benefits and who suffers if the client's instructions are pursued, and how the counter-balancing call of *responsible lawyering* might assist us. The lawyers acting for the clients discussed in the case studies above had such an obligation. Consider how they discharged it and how you would wish to behave in a similar situation, should it arise.

RECOMMENDED FURTHER READING

AJ Brown et al, *Clean as a Whistle: a Five Step Guide to Better Whistleblowing Policy and Practice in Business and Government* (ANU Research Publications, 2019) <https://openresearch-repository.anu.edu.au/handle/1885/204871>

Adrian Evans, *The Good Lawyer* (Cambridge University Press, 2014) ch 6

Selene E Mize, 'Should the Lawyer's Duty to Keep Confidences Override the Duty to Disclose Material Information to a Client?' (2009) 12(2) *Legal Ethics* 171

Christine Parker, Suzanne Le Mire and Anita Mackay, 'Lawyers, Confidentiality and Whistleblowing: Lessons from the *McCabe* Tobacco Litigation' (2017) 40(3) *Melbourne University Law Review* 999

William H Simon, 'Attorney-Client Confidentiality: A Critical Analysis' (2017) 30(3) *Georgetown Journal of Legal Ethics* 447

5

ETHICS IN CRIMINAL JUSTICE

Introduction

Television and movies often portray criminal practice as the most glamorous speciality within the legal profession. In fact, for many lawyers it is not an attractive option, probably because defending accused criminals can be seen as confronting and mostly low paying. Yet it is for these very reasons that the criminal defence advocate is usually taken as the paradigmatic example of why *adversarial advocacy* is necessary, is ethically justified and is fully deserving of our admiration. As one senior barrister put it:

> The quality of the system is tested by how it treats the worst … The worst, most revolting criminal or terrorist or whoever it happens to be, if you can get a fair trial for them then everyone else is guaranteed a good run. But if the system starts taking short cuts because somebody is so bad, then it's the system that's coming apart.[1]

Because the potential sanctions for criminal offences, such as deprivation of liberty, are so serious and the resources and capacity of the state to investigate and prosecute crimes so vast, our system insists that an accused should always have the opportunity to 'put the Crown to proof' of any charges brought against the accused. This effectively holds the state (including the police) accountable by making sure that the prosecution has strong enough evidence to justify a court/jury deciding to convict. It also maintains the integrity of the criminal justice system by making sure that the accused is treated fairly.

While there are unfortunately a few examples of dodgy lawyers in this area of the law, and this chapter includes reference to the cases that highlight these issues, we are completely convinced by examples set by the notable advocates who represent 'undesirable' or high-profile defendants in the interests of public confidence in the justice of the overall system. The lawyers who represent, for example, alleged terrorists, or alleged paedophiles, or those whom the media consider have protected these defendants, receive only limited support from the general public.[2] It is for this reason that they deserve the complete support of the wider legal profession. They are at the apex of a system that must insist on fairness to 'the worst' as much as to anyone, because who is sufficiently good or sufficiently bad can never be definitively known in advance.

The defence lawyer's task is to represent the interests of their client. If a client pleads not guilty, defence counsel's role is to ensure that their client is not convicted 'except by a competent tribunal and upon admissible evidence sufficient to support the offence charged'.[3] To advocate effectively, it is often argued that the defence lawyer must argue passionately, as if they really believe in their client's case.[4] On the other hand, the prosecutor

1 Lex Lasry QC quoted in Abbe Smith, 'Defending the Unpopular Down-Under' (2006) 30(2) *Melbourne University Law Review* 495, 508. Lasry was later appointed to the Supreme Court of Victoria and is now a reserve judge of that court.

2 For example, in 2021 New South Wales police officers targeted a small-town solicitor who was acting for a bikie gang member: Naomi Neilson, 'Defence Lawyers Call on A-G to Protect Lawyers from Further Police Harassment', *Lawyers Weekly* (13 April 2021) <https://www.lawyersweekly.com.au/biglaw/31122-defence-lawyers-call-on-a-g-to-protect-lawyers-from-further-police-harassment>.

3 Róisín Annesley and Victorian Bar Council, *Good Conduct Guide: Professional Standards for Australian Barristers* (2019) 136 [9.41].

4 Ibid.

in the criminal trial is probably the clearest example of lawyers being required to act as *responsible lawyers* – as 'ministers of justice' – rather than *adversarial advocates*:

> [T]he role of the prosecution is by evidence to prove all relevant facts to the court and (if appropriate) by moderately presented and reasoned steps to argue that by application of the law to those facts, the rational conclusion beyond reasonable doubt must be that the accused is guilty ... The prosecution must assist the court to arrive at the truth. It is probably the *only* role that an advocate can perform that is dedicated to the ascertainment of the truth.[5]

Prosecutors have special duties of fairness because the prosecutor is an agent of the state, and it is not appropriate for a prosecutor to be adversarial in pressing for conviction. We discuss prosecutors' ethical position in greater detail later in this chapter, but for now it is enough to recognise that as a state agent, the prosecutor generally has greater capacity and resources for investigating and prosecuting their case than has the defence.

The prosecution often has greater credibility with the jury. As representative of the state, it is the prosecutor's job to present a fair case for conviction based on good evidence, not to argue for conviction (and a high sentence) with adversarial zeal.[6] Indeed the prosecutor could be expected to have a role in checking the misconduct of the police or other state agents, by making sure that their own assertions are reasonably capable of supporting a finding of guilt and carry weight (*ASCR* r 29.4; *Barristers' Conduct Rules* r 86). Prosecutors also have various duties to share the evidence collected by the state with the accused in order to assist the accused and their lawyer to prepare a defence to the charges (*ASCR* rr 29.5–29.6, 29.8; *Barristers' Conduct Rules* rr 87–89).

Thus the prosecution and the defence have essentially complementary roles as 'officers of the court' in criminal trials – the prosecution's role is to present a fair case while the defence's role is to test and probe it adversarially. The prosecution must demonstrate judgement and the defence must have courage. It is the combination of these virtues that make for a fair trial and a fair justice system more generally.

It is important to remember, however, that both prosecutors and defence lawyers work within a very imperfect system that is still addressing historical racism and sexism, is subject to political pressures and is constrained by limited resources.[7] Further, a large number of criminal accused are afflicted by mental health and drug and alcohol problems; their actions reflect wider social problems as well as any criminal responsibility.[8] Some consider that criminal prosecution and defence are often better conceived as a matter of care as much as a matter of justice, and that our courts should, in many cases, adopt a more

5 Nicholas Cowdery, *Ethics and the Role of a Prosecutor* (1997) 32.

6 *ASCR* rr 29.1–29.3; *Barristers' Conduct Rules* rr 83–95.

7 See, eg, Simon Bronitt and Bernadette McSherry, *Principles of Criminal Law* (Thomson Reuters, 4th ed, 2017) 120, 121–5, 167–170, 700–2, 720, 767, 957, 1034–7; Andrew Boe, *The Truth Hurts* (Hachette Australia, 2021). See also 'The Long-Term Costs of Underfunding Legal Aid', *Law Council of Australia* (Web Page, 3 December 2021) <https://www.lawcouncil.asn.au/media/media-releases/the-long-term-costs-of-underfunding-legal-aid>.

8 Luke McNamara et al, 'Homelessness and Contact with the Criminal Justice System: Insights from Specialist Lawyers and Allied Professionals in Australia' (2020) 9(3) *International Journal for Crime, Justice and Social Democracy* 120–1.

'therapeutic jurisprudence'.[9] In addition, the victims of crime have only relatively recently been recognised as having a particular and legitimate interest in ensuring the system works fairly and treats all participants with dignity; more reform is necessary.

These challenges arguably make the ethics of the individual lawyer more important: the under-resourced criminal justice system and the high stakes of criminal trials will sometimes encourage the cutting of ethical corners. At other times the system will clearly work an injustice, and criminal lawyers will need to be involved in advocating for reform.[10] Even when the system works as it should, criminal law work sometimes involves dealing with extremely disturbing material, and/or traumatised clients/victims, and this can lead to the lawyers involved experiencing 'vicarious trauma'.[11] To remain competent and alert to ethical challenges, it is imperative that criminal lawyers (defence, prosecution and the judiciary) look after their mental health. Defence lawyers will also need to practise good client care, learning the skills of 'trauma-informed practice'.[12]

The criminal trial defence

Managing pleas of 'guilty' and 'not guilty'

A key task of defence counsel is to advise a client on the strength of the prosecution case against them. If counsel considers that case to be strong, they will advise their client accordingly, including advising on the sentencing discount available if the client pleads guilty early in the process.[13] If a client is minded to plead guilty, prosecution and defence will often engage in a process of 'plea bargaining', more aptly described as 'charge bargaining' or 'charge resolution', in which they negotiate the charges to which a defendant will agree to plead. Often, the prosecution will agree to less serious and/or fewer charges in return for a guilty plea. A guilty plea leads to a sentencing hearing before a court.

9 Liz Richardson, Pauline Spencer and David Wexler, 'The International Framework for Court Excellence and Therapeutic Jurisprudence: Creating Excellent Courts and Enhancing Wellbeing' (2016) 25(3) *Journal of Judicial Administration* 148; Wayne Martin, *Reflecting on the Practice of Non-Adversarial Justice* (Judicial Commission of New South Wales, 2018).

10 An example is Australia's shocking record of First Nations deaths in custody: see, eg, 'Joint Council Agrees to Accelerate Collective Efforts to Reduce Over-incarceration of Indigenous peoples … ', *Coalition of Peaks* (Web Page, 16 April 2021) <https://coalitionofpeaks.org.au/joint-council-agrees-to-accelerate-collective-efforts-to-reduce-over-incarceration-of-indigenous-peoples-as-first-annual-partnership-health-check-acknowledges-successes-and-challenges-of-historic-part/>; Law Council of Australia, 'Indigenous Justice Announcements Welcome, but Funding for Multi-faceted Response Needed' (Media Release, 15 April 2021) <https://lawcouncil.asn.au/media/media-releases/indigenous-justice-announcements-welcome-but-funding-for-multi-faceted-response-needed>.

11 Also known as 'secondary trauma'.

12 Colin James, 'Towards Trauma-Informed Legal Practice: A Review' (2020) 27(2) *Psychiatry, Psychology and Law* 275. See also 'Is Practising Criminal Law Bad for Your Mental Health?', *Law Report* (ABC Radio National, 11 July 2017) <https://www.abc.net.au/radionational/programs/lawreport/is-practicing-criminal-law-bad-for-your-mental-health/8697446>. There is an obligation on the organisations for which lawyers work to provide appropriate systems of work and support for employees exposed to traumatic material in their work: Anna Verney, *In Focus: Lessons on Vicarious Trauma and Wellbeing from a Royal Commission* (Law Society of New South Wales, 2018).

13 This is required under r 40 of the *Barristers' Conduct Rules*.

Unlike in the United States, where prosecution, defence and the court 'negotiate' a sentence on plea, in Australia the sentence remains solely a matter for the court.[14] It is now a requirement in most jurisdictions that courts give some sort of sentencing discounts for early guilty pleas.[15] In fact, the criminal justice system would likely collapse if all cases went to trial, or if defendants intending to plead guilty did so only at the door of the court after significant prosecution and defence/Legal Aid resources have been expended in preparation for trial.

Some have questioned the increasing move to 'managing justice' in this way. There are legitimate ethical concerns that sentencing discounts pressure a defendant into pleading guilty.[16] Further, why should a sentence be reduced *merely* because the defendant pleads guilty early? Why should the defendant be able to plead to a lesser charge (and so receive a lighter sentence) when the crime was horrendous? Over the past few decades in Australia these concerns have given way to (or, depending on your point of view, been balanced by) other competing concerns, explained by the guidelines for prosecutors in the NSW Office of the Director of Public Prosecutions ('ODPP NSW')[17] in this way:

> **4.2. Why charge resolution is important**
> The option of charge resolution in appropriate cases is necessary for the effective and efficient conduct of prosecutions. It relieves victims and other witnesses of the burden of having to give evidence, provides certainty of outcome and saves the community the cost of running trials. However, charge resolution must be based on principle and reason, not on expedience alone.
>
> … The law recognises the benefits to the criminal justice system of appropriate early guilty pleas, and sentencing discounts are available in most cases to reflect their utilitarian value. The earlier an appropriate plea is offered, the greater the benefits to the offender and the community in general.
>
> **4.3. When is it appropriate that charge resolution occur**
> A matter may only be dealt with by way of charge resolution if it is in the public interest to do so. In determining whether a charge resolution is in the public interest, the following factors are to be considered, in addition to the public interest factors outlined in Chapter 1[18] [of the *Prosecution Guidelines*]:

14 *Barbaro v The Queen* (2014) 253 CLR 58.

15 See, eg, *Penalties and Sentencing Act 1992* (Qld) s 13(2).

16 See Editorial, 'Sentence Discounts for Pleas of Guilty' (2005) 29 *Criminal Law Journal* 69; Kathy Mack and Sharyn Roach Anleu, 'Guilty Pleas: Discussions and Agreements' (1996) 6 *Journal of Judicial Administration* 8. Some legal ethicists in the United Kingdom have characterised the criminal justice system reforms in that jurisdiction as undermining the adversarial process by unduly pressuring the accused to plead guilty and co-opting defence lawyers as partners in the quest for efficiency at the expense of zealous advocacy on behalf of accused: Mike McConville and Luke Marsh, 'Adversarialism Goes West: Case Management in Criminal Courts' (2015) 19(3) *The International Journal of Evidence and Proof* 172; Ed Johnston, 'The Adversarial Defence Lawyer: Myths, Disclosure and Efficiency – A Contemporary Analysis of the Role in the Era of the Criminal Procedure Rules' (2020) 24(1) *The International Journal of Evidence and Proof* 35.

17 'Prosecution Guidelines', *ODPP NSW* (Web Page, 2021) <https://www.odpp.nsw.gov.au/prosecution-guidelines>.

18 Chapter 1.4 includes a non-exhaustive list of factors to be considered including 'Offence-related factors', 'Accused-related factors', 'Victim-related factors', 'Sentencing factors' and 'Other factors'.

> 1. the charge or charges to proceed appropriately reflect the essential criminality of the criminal conduct capable of being proven beyond a reasonable doubt and provide an adequate basis for sentencing
> 2. the evidence available to support the prosecution case is weak in a material way, even though it cannot be said that there is no reasonable prospect of conviction, and the public interest will be satisfied with an acknowledgment of guilt to certain lesser criminal conduct
> 3. the cost saving to the community is significant when weighed against the likely outcome of the matter if it went to trial
> 4. charge resolution will save a witness from having to give evidence in court proceedings, where the desirability of this is a particularly compelling factor in the case
>
> ...
>
> ..., the victim and the officer-in-charge must be consulted and their views properly considered, although the public interest is the overriding consideration.

Rule 40 of the *Barristers' Conduct Rules* endorses barristers advising a client 'in strong terms that the client is unlikely to escape conviction and that a plea of guilty is generally regarded by the court as a mitigating factor to the extent that the client is viewed by the court as co-operating in the criminal justice process'.

DISCUSSION QUESTIONS

1. Can you envisage a situation where an overworked defence lawyer puts the case for pleading guilty too strongly, so as to avoid having to prepare for a contested trial?
2. What ethical approach do you think is most likely to avoid this situation?
3. In most jurisdictions a sentencing discount is available on the grounds of administrative convenience (although courts retain a discretion as to whether to apply the discount).[19] Is pressure to plead guilty applied for utilitarian concerns about public resources acceptable?
4. Are you convinced that the system (as reflected in the NSW ODPP *Prosecution Guidelines*) has struck the right balance between the competing interests of a defendant, the community and the victim in relation to its practice of charge resolution?
5. What might undermine this balance in practice? Consider, for example, the view expressed when, in 2005, New South Wales moved to further encourage sentencing discounts for early guilty pleas: 'It is understandable that the NSW Government is keen to reduce the [high] number of pleas of guilty entered on the eve of trial ... However, great care should be taken in introducing a system which may put unconscionable pressure on accused persons to plead guilty before they receive proper legal assistance and fully appreciate the nature of the case against them.'[20]

19 LexisAdvance, *Halsbury's Laws of Australia* (online at 6 July 2022) 130 Criminal Law, 'Remorse and Plea of Guilty ' [130-17130].

20 Editorial, 'Sentence Discounts for Pleas of Guilty' (2005) 29 *Criminal Law Journal* 69.

Sometimes a client will maintain their innocence but insist on pleading guilty, to 'get the matter over with' or for some other reason important to them. Reflecting on his work as a barrister instructed by the Aboriginal Legal Service ('ALS'), Peter Hidden wrote in 1991:

> Many older Aborigines [sic], especially from rural areas, have a long history of appearing without representation in magistrates' courts, and their experience of the criminal justice system taught them that conviction follows arrest as the night follows the day. Even with legal representation, they cannot break the pattern of pleading guilty 'and getting it over with', regardless of the merits of their case; and it [is] understandable that they have no stomach for a fight which they are convinced they cannot win.[21]

'Convenience pleas' as they are known are not an uncommon occurrence in some areas of practice.[22] In 1995 the High Court held:

> A person charged with an offence is at liberty to plead guilty or not guilty to the charge, whether or not that person is in truth guilty or not guilty. … A Court will act on a plea of guilty when it is entered in open Court by a person who is of full age and apparently of sound mind and understanding, provided the plea is entered in exercise of free choice in the interests of the person entering the plea. There is no miscarriage of justice if a Court does act on such a plea, even if the person entering it is not in truth guilty of the offence.[23]

The NSW Court of Criminal Appeal explains that

> the accused person's exercise of free choice may 'extend beyond that person's belief in his guilt' and includes situations such as the avoidance of worry or inconvenience, the protection of one's family and even 'the hope of obtaining a more lenient sentence than [the accused] would if convicted after a plea of not guilty …[24]

The responsibilities of the defence barristers in this situation are now clearly set out in *Barristers' Conduct Rules* r 41:

> **41** Where a barrister is informed that the client denies committing the offence charged but insists on pleading guilty to the charge, the barrister:
> **(a)** must advise the client to the effect that by pleading guilty, the client will be admitting guilt to all the world in respect of all the elements of the charge,
> **(b)** must advise the client that matters submitted in mitigation after a plea of guilty must be consistent with admitting guilt in respect of all of the elements of the offence,

21 Peter Hidden, 'Plead Guilty and Get It Over With?' (1991) *Bar News* reproduced in Appendix 1 to Peter Hidden, 'Some Ethical Problems for the Criminal Advocate' (2003) 27(4) *Criminal Law Journal* 191.

22 Benjamin Bickford confirmed in 2011 that the circumstances described by Hidden were often faced by ALS lawyers in regional practice: 'Convenience Pleas', *Hunter Street Chambers* (Web Page, 18 February 2016) <https://www.hunterstreetchambers.com.au/convenience-pleas/>.

23 *Meissner v The Queen* (1995) 184 CLR 132 [141].

24 *Loury v The Queen* [2010] NSWCCA 158.

(c) must be satisfied that after receiving proper advice the client is making a free and informed choice to plead guilty, and
(d) may otherwise continue to represent the client.

CASE STUDY 5.1 GUILTY PLEAS

Some ethicists argue that it is sometimes naïve to characterise a defendant's choice as 'free and informed' in light of the institutional pressure (for example, in the form of sentencing discounts) to plead guilty.[25] Lee Bridges suggests that a defence lawyer should in some cases consider whether withdrawal of representation is necessary 'to avoid implication in a perversion of the course of justice or substantial risk of a miscarriage of justice'.[26] Bridges recognises that withdrawal may negate the principle of client autonomy, deny the client legal representation and also place the client at risk of a harsher sentence if the matter goes to trial. He thus emphasises the need for the lawyer to 'carefully … exercise professional judgement depending on the circumstances of each case'.[27]

Discussion question

Do you agree with Bridges's concern about guilty pleas? How workable is Bridges's suggested solution?

Defending the 'guilty' client

How does a lawyer defend the guilty client? Public incredulity over this issue usually points to a narrower question: can a lawyer ethically argue a 'not guilty' plea for a 'guilty' client? The profession says 'yes' on the basis that (1) in very few circumstances will a defence lawyer, faced with their client's denial, be able to be absolutely certain of the client's guilt and (2) guilt or otherwise is for the court to determine; it is the defence lawyer's task to challenge aspects of the prosecution's case with a view to uncovering any gaps in the evidence presented. One criminal defence lawyer described it this way:

> [T]he role is to go into bat for your clients. You're acting for them, you're acting in their best interest, and you leave it to other people to make decisions as to guilt or innocence … We're there for the accused people and to put their best case forward as best we can.[28]

25 In relation to guilty pleas by innocent people in the United States, the United Kingdom and Wales, see Rebecca Helm, 'False Guilty Pleas and the Post Office Scandal', *Evidence-Based Justice Lab*, University of Exeter Law School (Blog Post, 28 April 2021) <https://evidencebasedjustice.exeter.ac.uk/false-guilty-pleas-and-the-post-office-scandal>.

26 Lee Bridges, 'The Ethics of Representation on Guilty Pleas' (2006) 9(1) *Legal Ethics* 80, 100.

27 Ibid 99–100.

28 'The Ethics of Criminal Lawyers', *Law Report* (ABC Radio National, 12 November 2002) <http://www.abc.net.au/radionational/programs/lawreport/the-ethics-of-criminal-lawyers/3527274>. See also the discussion in Chapter 2 on the philosophical/ethical approaches to this issue.

In our system, a lawyer's view of their client's guilt or otherwise is not relevant to their role as defence advocate, *unless* the client admits guilt but still elects to plead *not guilty* – and in such a case, it is still possible to play a limited, legitimate role (discussed in more detail below) designed to put the prosecution to its proof beyond reasonable doubt. Where a client does not admit guilt and pleads not guilty, the lawyer is under a duty to defend the client *irrespective* of their opinion about the client's guilt or otherwise.[29] So, what is it like to represent a client who is pleading not guilty when you believe them to be guilty? Peter McGrath SC, who has worked as both defence and prosecution lawyer, answered this question as follows in a discussion on criminal practice and mental health on ABC Radio National's *Law Report*:

> You take the case that you're given and you do your professional, ethical best in that particular case … You do have your own belief about whether you think someone did it or not, it's impossible not to.
>
> Often it's easier in a way to represent someone who you think may be guilty, even if you are representing them and they are denying guilt. It is easier in that circumstance than to have the dreadful worry that, gosh … I really think this person didn't do it, and the consequences … for the conviction of a person that you think may be innocent are of course truly horrible. … Everyone has strategies [to help them cope], you think, okay, at the end of the day these are my instructions, this is the evidence, I'll do the best I can with it, and you take that professional step back and present things that way. But that too takes [its mental toll].[30]

There will be cases in which the role a defence lawyer plays sits very heavily with them. As we noted in Chapter 1, adversarial advocacy sees the suppression of one's own individual moral opinions and consideration of general ethical concerns as a moral act in itself. The lawyer must sometimes turn off these other ethical considerations in order to fulfill their proper moral role as advocate for their client. But continued suppression of one's own individual moral opinion comes at a personal cost. In the same *Law Report* discussion, psychiatrist Greg de Moore counselled lawyers to keep a broad perspective on the importance of the work they do when individual cases are particularly challenging.[31]

DISCUSSION QUESTIONS

1. How might a criminal lawyer/prosecutor keep in mind the larger ethical or social justifications for their work when working on challenging cases?
2. How else might the lawyer look after their mental health?

Overriding the defence lawyer's duty to their client is their primary duty to the court. A lawyer must not mislead the court, make up facts to assist a client's case or allow their client to deceive the court. The following rules make this clear.

---

29 Annesley and Victorian Bar Council (n 3) 136 [9.41].

30 'Is Practising Criminal Law Bad for Your Mental Health?' (n 12). McGrath was New South Wales Deputy Senior Public Defender at the time of the interview. He was appointed New South Wales Deputy DPP in 2018.

31 'Is Practising Criminal Law Bad for Your Mental Health?' (n 12).

ASCR rr 19, 20 and *Barristers' Conduct Rules* rr 24, 25, 79, 80

ASCR r 19. Duty to the court

19.1 A solicitor must not deceive or knowingly or recklessly mislead the court.

19.2 A solicitor must take all necessary steps to correct any misleading statement made by the solicitor to a court as soon as possible after the solicitor becomes aware that the statement was misleading.

ASCR r 20. Delinquent or guilty clients

20.1 A solicitor who, as a result of information provided by the client or a witness called on behalf of the client, learns during a hearing or after judgment or the decision is reserved and while it remains pending, that the client or a witness called on behalf of the client:

20.1.1 has lied in a material particular to the court or has procured another person to lie to the court;

20.1.2 has falsified or procured another person to falsify in any way a document which has been tendered; or

20.1.3 has suppressed or procured another person to suppress material evidence upon a topic where there was a positive duty to make disclosure to the court;

must –

20.1.4 (repealed)

20.1.5 refuse to take any further part in the case unless the client authorises the solicitor to inform the court of the lie, falsification or suppression and must promptly inform the court of the lie, falsification or suppression upon the client authorising the solicitor to do so but otherwise may not inform the court of the lie, falsification or suppression.

If a client refuses to authorise their lawyer to inform the court of a deceit in the circumstances envisaged by these rules, do all advocates simply depart from the case and keep silent? The answer is unknown, but, should an advocate pretend they know nothing after learning from their client of falsified evidence, they would leave themselves vulnerable to future blackmail by that client. The reputation of a criminal advocate within criminal circles is too important to leave to chance. The concern not addressed by this rule is that, by refusing to continue to act in the absence of instructions to inform the court of a deceit, the lawyer effectively schools a deceitful client about what not to reveal to their next lawyer.

There are precise restrictions in *ASCR* r 20.2 on what an advocate can and cannot do if their client actually confesses guilt to them before or during a trial.

ASCR r 20.2

20.2 A solicitor whose client in criminal proceedings confesses guilt to the solicitor but maintains a plea of not guilty:

20.2.1	may, subject to the client accepting the constraints set out in Rules 20.2.2–20.2.8, but not otherwise, continue to act in the client's defence,
20.2.2	must not falsely suggest that some other person committed the offence charged,
20.2.3	must not set up an affirmative case inconsistent with the confession,
20.2.4	must ensure that the prosecution is put to proof on its case,
20.2.5	may argue that the evidence as a whole does not prove that the client is guilty of the offence charged,
20.2.6	may argue that for some reason of law the client is not guilty of the offence charged,
20.2.7	may argue that for another reason not prohibited by Rule 20.2.2 or 20.2.3 the client should not be convicted of the offence charged, and
20.2.8	must not continue to act if the client insists on giving evidence denying guilt or requires the making of a statement asserting the client's innocence.

There are cogent *responsible lawyering* and fairness justifications for the restrictions set out in *ASCR* rr 20.1 and 20.2 (and *Barristers' Conduct Rules* r 79), as illustrated by the 1934 Northern Territory case of *Tuckiar v The King*.[32] In that case an Aboriginal elder was charged with the murder of a policeman in Arnhem Land. Tuckiar, or Dhakiyarr as he was and is now known in his community, had come upon the policeman as he (the policeman) was taking Dhakiyarr's wife away in chains, during a search for other Indigenous people who were suspected of killing some Japanese fishermen. The action of the policeman in forcibly taking the woman (very likely with the intention of committing sexual assault) was against tribal law. Dhakiyarr speared him.[33]

Dharkiyarr was captured and tried in Darwin. However, it was only during his trial that Dhakiyarr communicated to his counsel, through an interpreter, the circumstances of the spearing. Counsel reacted hastily and unwisely – the now infamous advocate got to his feet in front of the jury and stated that he was in 'the worst predicament he had encountered in all his legal career' (code for 'my client did it') and needed to speak to the judge.[34] Counsel did not argue any defence on Dhakiyarr's behalf throughout the case, and Dhakiyarr was subsequently convicted.

On appeal, the High Court unanimously held that advocates are bound to keep silent in such circumstances and continue with fully testing the prosecution case, although they must avoid putting their clients in the witness box to give affirmative evidence of innocence. Dhakiyarr won his appeal on the basis that his advocate's statement to the Court had produced

32 (1934) 52 CLR 335.

33 As explored in the documentary *Dhakiyarr vs The King* (Film Australia, 2004). See also Tom Murray, 'Dhakiyarr vs The King' (Study Guide, National Film and Sound Archive of Australia, 2004). The documentary makes the point that two systems of law operated in Arnhem Land at the time and that Dhakiyarr did not realise that his law was no longer dominant. See also Nicole Watson, 'In the Matter of Djappari (Re Tuckiar): Judgement' in Heather Douglas et al (eds), *Australian Feminist Judgments: Righting and Rewriting Law* (Hart Publishing, 2014) 442.

34 *Tuckiar v The King* (1934) 52 CLR 335, 341.

a substantial miscarriage of justice. He was released, never to be seen again.[35] As a result of the appeal, however, it is clear that the duty of confidentiality binds advocates' actions, provided the advocate does not actively mislead the court. The irony of Dhakiyarr's case is that his own evidence, had he been allowed to give it, might have caused a modern jury to consider him not guilty, though this result was probably most unlikely before a jury in 1930s Darwin.

As the High Court explained in the *Tuckiar* case, the principles set out in *ASCR* r 20 are designed to retain, for even the 'guilty' client, some representation before the court, in the interests of ensuring that the continuing prosecution is as fair as possible. *ASCR* r 20.2 and *Barristers' Conduct Rules* r 80 (in similar terms) properly allow the lawyer to continue to act providing they confine themselves to testing the prosecution's evidence (*ASCR* rr 20.2.4, 20.2.5) and avoid leading affirmative evidence of innocence (*ASCR* rr 20.2.2, 20.2.3, 20.2.8). Evidence (for example, DNA evidence of identity) must still be tested because it might be flawed. If such evidence is flawed, perhaps the alleged 'confession' was also contrived or misunderstood.[36] Advocates must not put such clients in the witness box and ask them whether they are innocent or not, knowing their assertion of innocence will be false, because that is equivalent to actively misleading the court.

While advocates must not knowingly mislead a court (*ASCR* r 19.1, *Barristers' Conduct Rules* r 24) they may be excused from doing so 'unknowingly', if correction is made 'as soon as possible' (*ASCR* r 19.2, *Barristers' Conduct Rules* r 25). But an advocate 'will not have made a misleading statement to a court simply by failing to correct an error in a statement made to the court by the opponent or any other person' (*ASCR* r 19.3). If a prosecutor fails, usually because their information is incomplete, to mention relevant prior convictions to a judge, the judge may give a lighter sentence to a defendant as a result. In fact, in *ASCR* r 19.10 and *Barristers' Conduct Rules* r 33 there is a specific reference to the prior conviction circumstance, which permits silence by defence counsel, providing they truly remain passive and do not specifically ask a prosecution witness whether there are relevant 'priors', in the expectation of receiving a negative answer. The defence lawyer must not give any indication that their client has a cleaner record than is the case.

DISCUSSION QUESTIONS

1. If a lawyer learns, *after* an acquittal of murder, of the guilt of a client, what should they do?

   Most (15 out of 20) lawyers in a 2003 study by Ben Clarke[37] considered they are bound to keep the confidence. Some lawyers would wisely decide not to act for the

35 Dhakiyarr's descendants have since claimed, though been unable to prove, that he was killed shortly after his release by those unhappy with the decision of the High Court: *Dhakiyarr v The King* (n 33). In 2003 there was a reconciliation ceremony between the descendants of Dhakiyarr and those of policeman McColl that culminated in the installation of nine *larrakitj*, or ceremonial log coffins, in the Supreme Court of the Northern Territory in Darwin.

36 It is important to note the possibilities of misunderstanding by advocates as to what is said to them, different cultural and religious understandings of guilt that allow a defendant to say one thing while meaning another, and the fact that what a client thinks of as guilt will occasionally be otherwise, as in the case of someone who commits a criminal act (actus reus) but has insufficient mens rea (generally because of some form of diminished mental responsibility).

37 Ben Clarke, 'An Ethics Survey of Australian Criminal Law Practitioners' (2003) 27(3) *Criminal Law Journal* 142.

person again, so as to ensure the client could not blackmail them on the basis of this confidence.[38] Chapter 4 mentioned the case of Alton Logan in the United States, where a considered concern for the confidences of a confessed murderer led to the imprisonment of an innocent person for 26 years.

2. What would you do if a client confessed to a heinous crime after acquittal? What might sway your decision one way or another?

Tactics in running a defence

While we accept that adversarial advocacy is generally the appropriate ethical perspective for defence work, some of the tactics supposedly 'justified' by reference to it are highly questionable.

Over-zealous conduct

While counsel are 'entitled and obliged to deploy such skill and discretion as the proper preparation of their client's interests demands',[39] they have a duty to the court to conduct proceedings expeditiously. In *R v Wilson*[40]– the trial and retrial of two businessmen charged with corporate fraud – the delaying actions of counsel for the defendant Wilson were considered by the Court to be responsible for the bulk of 22 months' court time, while the prosecution was 'deplored' in the retrial for *reading* to the jury, 'over some 10 calendar weeks,' the evidence of the defendants at their first trial.[41] This is surely one of the worst cases of *adversarial advocacy* dominating *responsible lawyering* in the hope of wearing down a jury. The appeal court in this case reminded counsel that 'whether the cost of legal representation be privately or publicly borne, counsel are to understand that they are exercising a privilege as well as fulfilling a duty in appearing in a court of law'.[42]

Under-zealous conduct

A variation on this problem (possibly pervasive in an under-resourced system where high caseloads are the norm) is that of the incompetent or inadequate defence, where advocates, for their own reasons, and despite *ASCR* r 4.1.1 ('must … act in the best interests of a client'), do not attend properly to their client's defence. For example, in *R v Kina*[43] there was a complete failure of defence counsel to aggressively or competently represent an Aboriginal woman who had killed her de facto husband after shocking and sustained provocation. Barrister Andrew Boe recounts another example: in one of the first criminal cases he worked on, neither he (then solicitor) nor the barrister were properly prepared, and the client was

38 'The Ethics of Criminal Lawyers', *Law Report* (ABC Radio National, 12 November 2002) <http://www.abc.net.au/radionational/programs/lawreport/the-ethics-of-criminal-lawyers/3527274#transcript>.

39 *R v Wilson* [1995] 1 VR 163, 180.

40 [1995] 1 VR 163.

41 David Parsons and Mark Taft, 'Review of Judgments' (1994) 68(9) *Law Institute Journal* 863.

42 *R v Wilson* [1995] 1 VR 163, 180.

43 *R v Kina* [1993] QCA 480.

convicted of a serious offence – unjustly it appears. He learnt that 'there are no shortcuts in criminal practice. Every case has to be attacked cover to cover.'[44]

Aggressive, 'win at all costs' tactics

Critics ask why defence advocates are allowed to attack, confuse and humiliate witnesses during cross-examination in order to defend someone. This question is particularly salient in relation to sexual assault trials, where guilt or otherwise will often be determined solely on the basis of whether the jury believes the complainant's word. Louise Milligan's book *Witness*[45] paints a disturbing picture of the cost of this practice on complainants in such trials: many are retraumatised by their experience, surely not an acceptable outcome for a 'justice' system and one that discourages many victims from pursuing complaints.

There *are* rules of conduct, common law principles and specific provisions of uniform Evidence Acts[46] addressing this issue, including the following.

ASCR rr 21.2, 21.8, 21.9 and *Barristers' Conduct Rules* rr 61, 62, 63

21.2 A solicitor must take care to ensure that decisions by the solicitor to make allegations or suggestions under privilege against any person:

- **21.2.1** are reasonably justified by the material then available to the solicitor;
- **21.2.2** are appropriate for the robust advancement of the client's case on its merits; and
- **21.2.3** are not made principally in order to harass or embarrass a person.

21.8 Without limiting the generality of Rule 21.2, in proceedings in which an allegation of domestic or family violence, sexual assault, indecent assault or the commission of an act of indecency is made and in which the alleged victim gives evidence:

- **21.8.1** a solicitor must not ask that witness a question or pursue a line of questioning of that witness which is intended:
  - **(i)** to mislead or confuse the witness; or
  - **(ii)** to be unduly annoying, harassing, intimidating, offensive, oppressive, humiliating or repetitive; and
- **21.8.2** a solicitor must take into account any particular vulnerability of the witness in the manner and tone of the questions that the solicitor asks.

21.9 A solicitor does not infringe Rule 21.8 merely because –

- **21.9.1** the question or questioning challenges the truthfulness of the witness or the consistency or accuracy of a statement made by the witness, or
- **21.9.2** the question or questioning requires the witness to give evidence that the witness could consider to be offensive, distasteful or private.

---

44 Boe (n 7) 80.

45 Louise Milligan, *Witness: An Investigation into the Brutal Cost of Seeking Justice* (Hachette Australia, 2020).

46 *Evidence Act 1995* (Cth) s 41.

However, it appears that prosecutors and judges are reluctant to intervene to insist on compliance with the rules, in the case of judges out of fear their intervention may give rise to an appeal.[47] Milligan has proposed that sexual assault complainants be represented by their own lawyer to help them navigate the system and to object on their behalf against overly intimidatory tactics. This proposal was supported by some of Milligan's lawyer interviewees, but others consider it would skew the trial process.[48] While the solutions may not be readily apparent, it is clear that the current system is working an injustice and needs reform.[49]

Some reform has occurred in trials involving child or 'vulnerable' adult witnesses. It is now *witness intermediaries* – independent and impartial participants who are speech specialists – who are drawing the line between acceptable and unacceptable cross-examination tactics in many Australian jurisdictions. Their task is to assess the witness and inform the prosecution, defence and the court about how to communicate with the witness in a way that is developmentally appropriate and most likely to elicit reliable evidence. Evaluation of the UK witness intermediary scheme shows that it has instigated a 'positive cultural shift' in the legal profession and has improved access to justice for vulnerable victims.[50] Experience in Australia of witness intermediary schemes has been positive.[51]

Jury nullification

Jury nullification is used as a defence tactic – that is, juries are distracted from considering cogent prosecution evidence by focusing them on emotive issues such as personal or racial intolerance of a prosecution witness or remote possibilities of crime-scene contaminants. Case study 5.2 illustrates how this problem can occur in practice.

Stereotypes

Abbe Smith quotes the following defence lawyers discussing some of the tactics they use to try to 'get their clients off':

> One lawyer was sceptical about her fellow lawyers' regard for the truth when it comes to advocacy:
>
> > I think lawyers are kidding themselves when they say they care about truth. If someone has a drop of Aboriginal blood, I'll milk it in court for all it's worth. I will play on female stuff. I will use stereotypes as part of advocacy. ... I know I'm not alone in this. ...

47 Russell Boyd and Anthony Hopkins, 'Cross-Examination of Child Sexual Assault Complainants: Concerns about the Application of s 41 of the Evidence Act' (2010) 34(3) *Criminal Law Journal* 149, 158–62; Milligan (n 45) 347, 354. We note that judges *are* in position to stop inappropriate cross-examination and should be supported by appellate courts in doing so.

48 Milligan (n 45) 362.

49 Ben Matthews, 'Review: Louise Milligan's *Witness* Is a Devastating Critique of the Criminal Trial Process', *The Conversation* (online at 27 October 2020) <https://theconversation.com/review-louise-milligans-witness-is-a-devastating-critique-of-the-criminal-trial-process-148334>; Adam V Chernov, 'Witness', *Law Institute Journal* (April 2021); Roy Williams, 'Louise Milligan's *Witness* and the High Price of Seeking Justice', *The Australian* (Sydney, 11 February 2021).

50 Natalia Anatolak-Saper and Hannah MacPherson, 'Vulnerable *Witnesses* and Victoria's Intermediary Pilot Program' (2019) 43(5) *Criminal Law Journal* 325, 335.

51 Ibid.

> [Another lawyer], and quite a few others, indicated that, as an advocate, he 'would do everything allowed by law', including 'exploit[ing] prejudice on behalf of a client'. He saw this as a 'tactical decision', not an ethical one:
>
> > If it was a weak, piddling point, I wouldn't make it. But if it was a decent point I would. ... If there were blacks or Asians on the jury I would exploit a point to get to them – if the facts were there. I wouldn't make it up. It's not my concern whether I am perpetuating prejudice or misogyny or whatever. Political correctness is not an issue for the Bar. ...[52]

DISCUSSION QUESTIONS

1. Is there a difference between a 'tactical' decision and an 'ethical' one?
2. Do jury nullification tactics break any rules? Does resort to stereotypes? What principles might apply to these situations?

   Note: In Chapter 1 we suggested a three-step approach to ethical decision-making: first, be aware of the ethical issues that arise in practice, and of your own values and predispositions; second, make a choice between the range of standards and values that are available to help resolve those ethical issues; and third, implement that choice in practice. In considering the above tactics, begin by considering which of your values are relevant here, and then consider whether the above tactics of advocates are fair and proper enough in the adversarial advocate's context, or whether they exceed this measure.
3. Is there a possibility such tactics might put the jury offside?
4. How do these practices fit with the idea of being an officer of the court and *responsible lawyering*?

Independence and integrity of advocates

Although many of the *ASCR* rules (rr 17–29) and the *Barristers' Conduct Rules* (rr 42–48) do not expressly refer to the prosecution or defence of criminal cases, their context and application make it clear that the obligations of defence counsel in criminal trials are a primary concern.

ASCR r 17.1 (and in virtually identical language, *Barristers' Conduct Rules* r 42) refers to the need for candour in its requirement for 'independence': 'A practitioner must not act as the mere mouthpiece of the client or of the instructing practitioner and must exercise the forensic judgments called for during the case independently.'

This means that it is not permissible to simply do as the client wants – for example, lead evidence of an alibi that counsel thinks is very likely to be false – if the effect of that action would be to ignore the requirement for candour with the court. This rule makes the need for integrity crystal clear and reflects the proper priority of *responsible lawyering* over *adversarial advocacy*.

52 Smith (n 1) 539, 545, 545 n 338 (citations omitted).

ASCR r 17 Independence – avoidance of personal bias

17.1 A solicitor representing a client in a matter that is before the court must not act as the mere mouthpiece of the client or of the instructing solicitor (if any) and must exercise the forensic judgments called for during the case independently, after the appropriate consideration of the client's and the instructing solicitor's instructions where applicable.

Another way that integrity and independence may be compromised is when a lawyer is in a position of conflict. We discuss conflicts of interest generally in Chapter 7, but it is important here to note that conflicts between the interests of two or more defendants in the same or related criminal matters are a real possibility. There may be no apparent conflict at the outset of a matter, but conflicts can easily arise during trials, which are 'notoriously unpredictable',[53] and also in sentence proceedings.

Nicola Gobbo is an infamous example of a barrister in a different type of conflict of interest – acting for clients while at the same time providing police with information disclosed to her during 'confidential' conversations with those clients. As discussed in Chapter 4, in acting in this way, Ms Gobbo engaged in what the High Court described as 'fundamental and appalling breaches' of her duties to her clients and to the court. The Victorian Director of Public Prosecution's ('DPP') submission to the Royal Commission investigating the conduct of Victorian Police and Ms Gobbo noted the need to address another conflict of interest concern – 'key criminal figures can control those around them by providing funds for, or briefing the same, legal counsel'.[54] The Victorian DPP recommended several changes to the ethical conduct rules, including:

- clarify that regardless of who pays the fees, instructions should only be obtained from the client (or the client's litigation guardian);
- provide that where there is a conflict between the interests of the client and the interests of those paying the fees, the practitioner should only act in the best interests of the client, and should inform both the client and the person paying the fees of this; and
- require that the practitioner return the matter or cease acting where there is a real possibility of conflict between the interests of the client and the interests of the person paying the fees.[55]

The Royal Commission has recommended 'that the Victorian Bar ... develops ethics guidance on specific conflict of interest issues and scenarios that can arise for criminal defence barristers'[56] and that the Law Council of Australia and Australian Bar Council develop specific guidance for solicitors and barristers on maintaining appropriate professional boundaries.[57]

53 *R v Pham* [2017] QCA 43, [59].

54 Director of Public Prosecutions (Victoria), *Submission to the Royal Commission into the Management of Police Informants: Disclosure Issues* (19 December 2019) [342].

55 Ibid [345].

56 *Royal Commission into the Management of Police Informants* (Final Report, 2020) recommendation 81.

57 Ibid recommendations 82, 83. There are unfortunately cases where lawyers abandon their professional ethics and boundaries completely and become complicit in the criminal behaviour of their clients. Money laundering is one example of this. For example, New Zealand lawyer Andrew Simpson set up a scheme for laundering money for the Comanchero motorcycle gang. He was convicted and subsequently struck off the roll: *National Standards Committee 1 v Simpson* [2020] NZLCDT 36.

DISCUSSION QUESTIONS

1. Would it concern you if your client (charged with serious offences) wants to pay your legal fees in cash (that is, dollar notes)?
2. Would it ever be okay to socialise with criminal law clients? Does the answer to this depend on your perspective as an adversarial advocate/officer of the court/moral activist/proponent of the ethics of care?

ASCR r 17.3 and *Barristers' Conduct Rules* r 44 require a practitioner to avoid making any submissions or expressing any views to a court 'on any material evidence or material issue ... which convey ... the practitioner's personal opinion on the merits of that evidence or issue'. This rule also supports lawyer independence by prohibiting lawyers from giving personal opinions about cases. It is no surprise that such a rule is needed, since we are all familiar with the stereotypical attorney who comments 'zealously' on witnesses and their evidence in closing addresses to a jury. But there is a fine line between negative comment on witnesses or evidence, having regard to objective criticisms that can be made of their credibility or recollections, and reflections on witnesses or their evidence that appear to target irrelevant matters or come from the private views of the advocate. The problem arises here not from the rule itself, but from its implementation.

ASCR r 17 Independence (cont'd) – avoidance of personal bias

17.3 A solicitor must not make submissions or express views to a court on any material evidence or issue in the case in terms which convey or appear to convey the solicitor's personal opinion on the merits of that evidence or issue.

It seems there is a tendency among some advocates not only to cross the line by implying a negative personal opinion of a witness but also to undermine an opposing police witness in front of a jury – 'to play the man, not the ball', as the (sexist) phrase goes – by repeatedly asking them to give opinions on matters of fact and then self-righteously correcting the process by insisting that they did not intend to put any opinion in front of the jury. On occasion an appeal court will comment negatively on this tendency but by then the consequences for the advocate concerned are minimal and only those with an intimate knowledge of the case are aware of the possible transgression. *ASCR* r 17.3 and *Barristers' Conduct Rules* r 44 suffer from a lack of comprehensive enforcement. We wonder whether the Council of Chief Justices ought to consider this point, recognising that the best witness to this sort of problem, and indeed all in-court conduct, is the trial judge.

The defence counsel's conduct in *R v Neilan* (Case study 5.2) is an example of giving an opinion on matters of fact.

CASE STUDY 5.2 *R v NEILAN*[58]

In the late 1980s, Mark Neilan was a successful veterinary surgeon in the Victorian town of Drouin, where he lived with his wife, Kathryn, and a young daughter, Sheridan. One night, according to Neilan, intruders broke in, took him outside and, while bundling him into the boot of his car, went to the main bedroom and apparently shot Kathryn, then four months pregnant, in the head. Sheridan was left undisturbed in bed. A neighbour found Neilan locked in the boot of his car the following afternoon. As soon as he was released from the boot, he entered the house and exclaimed, 'Oh Kathy, oh no', when he saw her body. A search for the intruders or any physical evidence of their presence in the house revealed nothing, though a break-in at Neilan's nearby veterinary practice in the town, which apparently occurred on the same night, resulted in some money and a small quantity of Valium disappearing.

Neilan later made various inconsistent statements about when he had first seen the intruders on the night of the murder. The police came to disbelieve his version of events, and charged him with his wife's murder. He was bailed, and then two strange things happened. First, some weeks after his release on bail, Neilan claimed to have positively identified one of the intruders at Chadstone shopping centre, prepared a sketch of the sighting at his own expense and advertised for anyone who might know the face. Second, about nine days after the advertisement appeared, one of Neilan's dogs, a Border Collie, was shot and killed while Neilan was apparently away from home. The bullets came from a semi-automatic .22 rifle, the same type of gun that had been used to kill Kathryn – a gun that had not then and has never since been found. Neilan asserted that his advertisement had provoked the murderers into killing his dog as a warning to him to leave the murder alone, but the police believed that the incidents were manufactured by Neilan to support his story that the intruders, looking for drugs and money in the area on the night of the offence, were responsible for the killing. The major difficulty for the police, however, was that they could not suggest, let alone prove, any motive at all for Neilan to murder his wife.

When Neilan was eventually brought to trial, he asserted through his counsel that he knew nothing more about the death of his wife than he had already indicated. He declined to give personal evidence in his own defence but did call other evidence. His counsel relied on the lack of motive, witnesses or confession, and concentrated on characterising the prosecution case as entirely circumstantial, even prejudicial and vindictive on the part of the police. Nevertheless, Neilan was convicted.

Of ethical significance in this case is the effort to which defence counsel went to criticise the police witnesses. Neilan was facing the real hurdle of persuading the jury that he was innocent, while at the same time declining to give evidence about a matter that only he could clarify: what happened on the night. A formidable task therefore lay ahead of defence counsel and a device of some sort was needed to capture, or rather divert, the jury's attention. Counsel attempted to persuade the jury that the police, lacking a motive, had been engaged in nothing more than a series of speculations about what really happened, leaving them with the impression that no one could be certain of events on the night of the murder. In the event, however, this strategy failed – possibly because the silence of the defendant was just too much for the jury to swallow.

58 [1992] 1 VR 57.

Neilan unsuccessfully appealed his conviction on a number of grounds and in the course of the Court of Criminal Appeal's judgment, their Honours referred to the defence strategy of distraction or nullification:

> A very strong attack was made by the defence on Noonan [a police witness]. It was suggested to him that he had shut his eyes to everything that was in favour of the applicant and assumed his guilt ... that he had put forward and acted upon theories with regard to the crime which were far-fetched ... It was not that Noonan sought argumentatively to support the Crown case or attempted to introduce tendentious matter: senior counsel for the applicant forced him to express opinions and in effect to debate with him a number of questions ... The cross-examination was highly unusual, amounting as it did on occasions to a debate between the police officer and counsel, and moreover a debate which was of counsel's making.[59]

There is a rule of evidence that witnesses, other than experts (and the police witness Noonan did not qualify as an expert in this case), must confine their evidence to factual observations of which they have personal knowledge. Knowing this rule only too well, counsel for Neilan invited the police witness to express an opinion on an issue of fact and, when the witness, after having been exposed to earlier questions of this type, duly provided that opinion, counsel immediately applied for discharge of the jury.[60] Although the request was refused by the trial judge, the seed could have been sown with the jury that, on the basis that opinion evidence had been given, there were other police theories about the crime and any of these theories, in the 'real' minds of the police, were all contenders. In other words, the jury was invited to reflect on the possibility that the police were not certain whether the defendant was the murderer.

The Court of Criminal Appeal considered whether the trial judge ought to have reined in defence counsel or done more to counter the effects of the cross-examination, before deciding on balance that the jury had other bases on which to determine that the defendant was guilty. However, the Court was most critical of the strategy of the defence and said so at length, because this strategy of persistent invitation to the police to give opinion evidence, knowing such evidence was arguably inadmissible, was designed only to poison the jury's mind as to the motives of the prosecution.

As with so many other cases where counsel take an ethically suspect stance, however, appeal courts tend to confine themselves to criticism within the case context and rarely refer matters to the legal profession regulators for investigation as to whether any misconduct that may warrant disciplinary action has occurred.[61]

59 In the reported version of *R v Neilan*, ibid, the comments of the Court of Criminal Appeal as to the conduct of defence counsel were edited out. However, the unreported version explains the matter fully: see *R v Neilan* (Victorian Court of Criminal Appeal, Young CJ, Brooking and Marks JJ, 5 April 1991) 67–8.

60 See *R v Neilan* (Victorian Court of Criminal Appeal, Young CJ, Brooking and Marks JJ, 5 April 1991) 68.

61 Advocates are not liable for any negligence in respect of their behaviour in court – see discussion of advocates' immunity from suit in Chapter 6.

DISCUSSION QUESTIONS

Imagine you were defence counsel for Neilan.

1. Given the facts set out above, what instructions do you think it is likely you would have received from your client?
2. What would have been your advice to the defendant as to the best approach to take to the defence of his case?

Assuming your client was insistent on pleading 'not guilty':

3. Would you think it appropriate to criticise the police for their lack of a motive for the killing?
4. Would you try to persuade the jury that the police were targeting your client unfairly or casting around for a defendant – any defendant – without any real idea as to who was responsible?

If you thought it appropriate to point out to the jury that the police had nothing absolutely 'concrete' on your client:

5. Would you think it acceptable to point to an ulterior motive by the police and to do so by highlighting their opinions, rather than the facts, about the evidence?
6. In representing Neilan, would you see yourself as an *adversarial advocate* (and obliged to make serious distracting allegations about the police in order to create doubt in the mind of the jury) or someone concerned to ensure that the jury deals only with admissible evidence in making their decision?
7. Is the second option consistent only with a *responsible lawyer*, or could an *adversarial advocate*, concerned not to overdo it with a jury, be content just to point firmly to the lack of both a motive and conclusive evidence of guilt?
8. Is it simply necessary for defence counsel (in both a consequentialist sense and in the interests of fairness when an individual is faced by state prosecution) to point to everything that might derail that prosecution?

Recognition of the social evil that would arise from undefended[62] criminal trials lies in large part behind the strength of *adversarial advocacy*. The paradoxical cultural reverence for the unflinching and fearless defence counsel who takes on the very unattractive or vulnerable client is cited again and again.[63] It is no surprise therefore that lawyers tend to think that *adversarial advocacy* is the preferred ethical type.[64] At its core, *adversarial advocacy* embodies a deep professionalism and a fervent passion for fairness for which lawyers are often justly praised, as we highlighted in the introduction to this chapter. The

62 It is not uncommon for a person charged with a minor offence to not have legal representation during a hearing before a magistrate.

63 See Smith (n 1).

64 In trials of the ethics self-assessment tool set out in the Appendix: Part 1, a small majority of respondents indicated a preference for *adversarial advocacy* over other types. See Adrian Evans and Helen Forgasz, 'Framing Lawyers' Choices: Factor Analysis of a Psychological Scale to Self-Assess Lawyers' Ethical Preferences' (2013) 16(1) *Legal Ethics* 134.

'cab rank' rule in the *Barristers' Conduct Rules* that obliges barristers to defend anyone charged with a criminal offence if they are competent in the area and available, and their fee can be met,[65] is regarded as a norm of practice: full-time advocates shall accept all comers as clients in all matters (civil as well as criminal).

Significantly, there is no equivalent 'cab rank' rule for solicitors set out in the *ASCR*, and the validity of this ethical norm is perhaps not as easily justified as it used to be, even when defending alleged criminals. In practice, a barrister who finds a defendant unattractive will be tempted to pretend that they are unavailable in order to avoid the 'cab rank' rule. A few barristers will openly say that they find the case repulsive and simply defy the rule, risking a disciplinary prosecution, although there are few, if any, disciplinary cases alleging breach of the rule. Without consistent enforcement, the 'cab rank' rule is really a guideline, even if its fundamental importance remains.[66]

Barristers who are compelled by their character to say that their values, ethical preferences or their mental health would not allow them to represent a particular client to the best of their ability are put in an unenviable position by the 'cab rank' principle. It would be psychologically and ethically healthier for the Bar and barristers to formally allow exceptions to the 'cab rank' rule where a barrister has a conscientious objection to representation of a particular defendant.

The prosecution

Prosecutors represent the Crown in criminal cases – that is, they present the case in court against an accused person.[67]

It is also the prosecutor's duty to hold the police accountable for the way they use their powers,[68] all the more so now that police and other agents of the state operate with ever-widening coercive powers of investigation.[69]

Prosecutors face choices in the exercise of the prosecutorial function and, as always, those choices are value-driven and ought to reflect the rule of law. For example, in deciding whether to prosecute, prosecutors exercise a discretion. In each case, they must be satisfied that:

1. there is *sufficient evidence* to prosecute the case; and

65 See *Barristers' Conduct Rules* rr 17–18.

66 See Janie Plant, 'The Cab Rank Rule' (2017) 44(1) *Brief* 20 for differing views on whether the 'rule' should remain a rule.

67 In Australia, cases involving minor criminal offences are prosecuted by police prosecutors (except in the Australian Capital Territory). More serious criminal offences are prosecuted by the various Commonwealth, State and Territory Directors of Public Prosecutions ('DPP').

68 Once he learnt of it, the Victorian DPP considered it his duty to disclose to several convicted persons the fact that Nicola Gobbo (their lawyer) had also been a police informant. This was opposed by the police, which led to court proceedings ruling in favour of disclosure: *Royal Commission into the Management of Police Informants* (n 56) 12–13.

69 Rebecca Ananian-Welsh and George Williams, 'The New Terrorists: The Normalisation and Spread of Anti-Terror Laws in Australia' (2014) 38(2) *Melbourne University Law Review* 362. See also David Brown, 'Breaking the Code of Silence' (1997) 22(5) *Alternative Law Journal* 220, 222 (asking why prosecutors and lawyers did not speak up about massive police corruption in New South Wales during the 1980s and 1990s).

2. it is evident from the facts of the case, and all the surrounding circumstances, that the prosecution would be in the *public interest*.[70]

CASE STUDY 5.3 PROSECUTING WHISTLEBLOWERS

The prosecutions of whistleblowers Richard Boyle, David McBride, Witness K and Bernard Collaery (see Chapter 4) have been critiqued for several reasons, including that they are not in the public interest. In relation to Witness K and Collaery, former NSW DPP Nicholas Cowdery publicly expressed his opinion that the prosecutors were wrong to deem prosecution to be in the public interest, and that the prosecutions harmed the public interest by undermining public trust in the justice system and encouraging people to turn a blind eye in the face of official misconduct.[71] Prominent human rights barrister Geoffrey Robertson has described the prosecutions as 'disgraceful'.[72] Likewise, prosecutors' decision not to drop charges against ATO whistleblower Richard Boyle has been described as 'profoundly wrong and unjust' and against the public interest.[73] As noted in Chapter 4, in July 2022 the newly elected Labor Commonwealth Attorney-General directed the Commonwealth Director of Public Prosecutions to drop the charges against Collaery, but as at the time of writing, the charges against Boyle and McBride remain.

DISCUSSION QUESTIONS

1. What do you think may have influenced the Commonwealth DPP ('Cth DPP') to proceed with charges against Witness K and Bernard Collaery? What may have convinced the Cth DPP that the prosecution was in the public interest? What about Commonwealth prosecutors in the case of Richard Boyle?

---

70 'Prosecution Policy', *CDPP* (Web Page) <https://www.cdpp.gov.au/prosecution-process/prosecution-policy>. 'Although both these elements exist in each [Australian] jurisdiction's guidelines, there are differences in how they are structured and whether they are framed positively or negatively. Additionally, some jurisdictions provide further guidelines relating to the decision to prosecute particular offences or offenders, and all the guidelines contain a list of factors that should not influence the decision to prosecute': Natalie Hodgson et al, 'The Decision to Prosecute: A Comparative Analysis of Australian Prosecutorial Guidelines' (2020) 44(3) *Criminal Law Journal* 155, 159.

71 Christopher Klaus, 'Commonwealth Prosecutors Wrong on Witness K Case, Former NSW DPP Says', *The Guardian* (online at 1 April 2021) <https://www.theguardian.com/australia-news/2021/apr/01/commonwealth-prosecutors-wrong-on-witness-k-case-former-nsw-dpp-says>.

72 Naomi Neilson, '"It Is a Disgraceful Prosecution": Geoffrey Robertson Condemns Australian Government for Secret Trials of Bernard Collaery and Witness K', *Lawyers Weekly* (online at 5 May 2021) <https://www.lawyersweekly.com.au/biglaw/31299-it-is-a-disgraceful-prosecution-geoffrey-robertson-condemns-australian-government-for-secret-trials-of-bernard-collaery-and-witness-k>.

73 Kieran Pender, Human Rights Centre quoted in Christopher Knaus, 'Prosecutors Refuse to Drop Case Against Tax Office Whistleblower Richard Boyle', *The Guardian* (online at 29 April 2021) <https://www.theguardian.com/australia-news/2021/apr/29/prosecutors-refuse-to-drop-case-against-tax-office-whistleblower-richard-boyle>.

2. The ATO must consent to a prosecution under the *Intelligence Services Act 2001* (Cth).[74] Would an indication of consent by the Attorney-General be relevant to the Cth DPP's decision to prosecute in the public interest? If so, in what way? Is the Attorney-General a more accurate arbiter of public interest than the Cth DPP?
3. Given that the prosecutions of Witness K and Collaery concerned alleged behaviour by a previous Coalition government, was the then Attorney-General, as a member of the successor Coalition Government, in a position of conflict of interest in relation to the decision to prosecute?
4. 'Witness J' is a former military intelligence officer who was charged with, and pleaded guilty to, the disclosure of confidential information. He was sentenced and served out a sentence in the ACT gaol 'without any public knowledge, due to secrecy imposed by the National Security Information Act (NSI Act) and orders agreed to by commonwealth [sic] prosecutors, the [Commonwealth] attorney general and Witness J's lawyers'.[75] The total secrecy surrounding this case, reminiscent as it is of totalitarian regimes, has shocked many observers. What ethical deliberations do you think might have persuaded the prosecutors, defence lawyers and judges involved that they should take part in this secret procedure?
5. In the United States the chief prosecutor in most states is elected in a public election. In what ways might this influence the exercise of the prosecutor's discretion? Is this a good thing?[76]

ASCR r 29 (and *Barristers' Conduct Rules* rr 83–86) deal specifically with prosecutors' duties during a trial or sentencing hearing. *ASCR* rr 29.1–29.3 set out the approach that a prosecutor should take in arguing their case.

ASCR r 29 Prosecutor's duties

29.1 A prosecutor must fairly assist the court to arrive at the truth, must seek impartially to have the whole of the relevant evidence placed intelligibly before the court, and must seek to assist the court with adequate submissions of law to enable the law properly to be applied to the facts.

29.2 A prosecutor must not press the prosecution's case for a conviction beyond a full and firm presentation of that case.

29.3 A prosecutor must not, by language or other conduct, seek to inflame or bias the court against the accused.

---

74 Section 41.

75 Christopher Knaus, 'Secret Australian Prosecution "Unprecedented" and Must Never Happen Again, Watchdog Told', *The Guardian* (online at 4 May 2021) <https://www.theguardian.com/australia-news/2021/may/04/secret-australian-trial-unprecedented-and-must-never-happen-again-watchdog-told>.

76 Siddhartha Bandyopadhyay and Bryan C McCannon, 'The Effect of the Election of Prosecutors on Criminal Trials' (2014) 161(1–2) *Public Choice* 141.

Some argue that the interests of the state and the safety of its citizens have never been so threatened (by organised crime, terrorism etc) and that a successful defence of almost any defendant is part of a social disease rather than a check on over-zealous state power. But we suggest there is a longer term and more significant threat to public security if the proper ethical balance between prosecution and defence is not maintained.

Whatever the current cultural push to achieve convictions at all costs, whatever the personal attraction of a successful prosecution, and regardless of popular pressure to 'safeguard' person and property, there is no alternative in a democratic society to a balanced prosecution process. If the prosecution function is allowed to become partisan, the burden of proof will subtly shift to the defence, and the power of the state will prove inexorably more difficult to check. Prosecutors are supposed to stop at a 'full and firm' presentation of the case; they must not 'inflame or bias the court' (including the jury) against a defendant; and they must 'believe on reasonable grounds' in the propriety of their arguments. All of these safeguards have been put in place because earlier generations have seen what can happen to individual autonomy and freedoms once the court system becomes just the instrument of the government of the day. Relatively successful democracies, embodying the principles of fairness, can become fragile quite quickly if these primary constraints on prosecutions are allowed to degrade.

The stereotypical pressure to get a conviction at all costs is not endorsed by the *ASCR* or the *Barristers' Conduct Rules* and is completely unacceptable in the Australian legal system. Just how careful a prosecutor must be to remain a prosecutor and – as cultural pressure can increasingly dictate – avoid becoming a *persecutor* is made clear by *ASCR* r 29 in the context of sentencing.

ASCR r 29.12

29.12 A prosecutor:

- **29.12.1** must correct any error made by the opponent in address on sentence;
- **29.12.2** must inform the court of any relevant authority or legislation bearing on the appropriate sentence;
- **29.12.3** must assist the court to avoid appealable error on the issue of sentence; and
- **29.12.4** may submit that a custodial or non-custodial sentence is appropriate.

Barristers' Conduct Rules r 95 has similar terms. All of these 'informing the court' functions are to be performed by prosecutors without inflaming the situation – that is, without becoming vindictive. Courts are not empowered by the rule of law to seek revenge but to impose proportionate punishment in a dispassionate atmosphere. Balance, judgement and proportion are required, not partisanship and retribution. Prosecutors with a clear sense of their role need to be wary of *adversarial advocacy* and pay consistent attention to nurturing these alternative ethical values in their advocacy. This is all the more important given that prosecutors are rarely disciplined for breaking the rules.

Courts will, however, censure prosecutors where appropriate. A case in point is *Hughes v The Queen*,[77] an appeal against conviction on sexual assault charges. The NSW Court of Criminal Appeal dismissed the appeal but criticised the prosecutor for some comments in her closing address.[78] The Court was particularly critical of the prosecutor's invitation to the jury to 'tell that man what he did to those girls was wrong and it was criminal':

> [I]t is quite inappropriate for a Crown prosecutor to invite a jury to 'tell that man' that what he has done is criminal. Indeed, the delivery of verdicts in criminal trials in Australia is not a matter of juries 'telling' any accused – or indeed anyone else – anything; rather, it is a matter of juries, acting as unemotional and unprejudiced judges of the facts, determining whether or not the Crown has proven its case beyond reasonable doubt on the evidence placed before them, and returning verdicts accordingly.
>
> Whilst one may accept that a Crown prosecutor, like any advocate, seeks to end his or her final address with a persuasive flourish, we consider that it was very wrong for the Crown prosecutor to conclude her address in that way. And if it happens to be the case that there is something of a practice of the final addresses of Crown prosecutors in New South Wales ending in that way, or in some similar way, it should cease immediately.[79]

Criminal advocacy generally

The values of criminal advocates are probably as diverse as those of the rest of the community. There is no empirical evidence to suggest that criminal advocates are all *adversarial* all the time or, on the other hand, all *responsible* all the time, let alone inclined to take a universal *morally activist* approach and decline to act for any clients who refuse to 'do the moral thing'.[80] It is more likely that experienced advocates will tend to take one ethical approach most of the time, varying their behaviour on occasion, when the complexity of the situation demands.

It is important to be aware of alternative ethical approaches to criminal trial work. Since the enforcement of rules of advocacy in Australia is more or less left by the courts to the legal professional associations, and advocates tend not to report one another, it is not unusual for their unethical behaviour to go unnoticed by the wider community – advocates are not very accountable for their ethical decisions.[81] Further, since the dominant ethic in criminal practice is adversarial, in the interests of a necessary fairness between a

77 *Hughes v The Queen* (2015) 93 NSWLR 474. See also *MG v The Queen* (2007) 69 NSWLR 20 where the prosecutor was enjoined by the Court of Appeal against conducting the retrial because of remarks made publicly about the former trial.

78 The Court of Criminal Appeal set out 10 basic principles governing prosecutors' conduct: (2015) 93 NSWLR 474, [265]–[275]. See also Kieran Fitzgerald, 'Case and Comment: Appellate Authority on the Role of the Prosecutor' (2018) 42(3) *Criminal Law Journal* 186.

79 *Hughes v The Queen* (2015) 93 NSWLR 474, [309]–[310].

80 See Smith (n 1).

81 As discussed in Chapter 7, advocates are immune from civil suit (ie negligence) under the doctrine of advocates' immunity and enjoy court privilege (ie they cannot be sued for defamation). They are still liable to professional discipline for breaches of conduct rules but this is rarely prosecuted.

powerful state and a single individual, it will often be the case that the alternatives – such as *responsible lawyering* and *moral activism* – will be invisible, unless lawyers explicitly bring ethical reflection to the foreground of their minds.

Discussion Questions

1. If you had the choice, would you prefer to be a prosecutor or a defence advocate? If the former, would you see yourself as entitled to prosecute with as much vigour and energy as an advocate for the defence?
2. Are you by nature more or less inclined to see the outcome of any contest as more important than the means used to get to that outcome? What implications does your answer have for the way in which you will tend to practise law?
3. Are you likely to have one set of values 'at home' and another set for 'the office'? Could you, for example, be keen to be fair at home but go along with necessity at work? If so, will the differences make it hard to lead an emotionally integrated life?

Ethics in criminal justice: from the local criminal trial to global justice

Global ethics and criminal justice

Both defence and prosecution lawyers and those involved in drafting criminal laws and procedures play an important part in global, as well as national and local, security and justice. Their role is to make sure the law works fairly, legitimately and effectively according to the rule of law, without ignoring fundamental human rights. There are dangers when lawyers face pressures from morally corrupt regimes to be involved in legal systems that take away those rights. Lawyers have been in the past and will again be required to draft unjust laws and, as prosecutors, judges and even defence counsel, to implement those laws. This occurred in apartheid South Africa, Stalinist Eastern Europe and Nazi Germany.[82] Even acting as defence lawyers in such a system might be seen as 'legitimating' a system that should only be resisted.

In liberal democracies the criminal justice system is under pressure as governments try to grapple with the threats of transnational crime, be it terrorism, drug or people trafficking, cybercrime or money laundering. Ethical challenges for lawyers in these situations are numerous.

One example is the 'torture memos' in the United States. In the aftermath of the 9/11 attack on the Twin Towers in Manhattan in 2001, government lawyers were instructed to provide written advice that it was legal under US law to conduct 'interrogations' of suspected terrorists in order to prevent further attacks. This advice was eventually disclosed[83] and discredited when it became clear that the interrogators had used it to justify torture, but this

82 See David Dyzenhaus, *Judging the Judges, Judging Ourselves: Truth, Reconciliation and the Apartheid Legal Order* (Hart Publishing, 1998); David Luban, 'Complicity and Lesser Evils: A Tale of Two Lawyers' (2021) 34(3) *Georgetown Journal of Legal Ethics* 613.

83 See, eg, Clare Keefe Coleman, 'Teaching the Torture Memos: "Making Decisions Under Conditions of Uncertainty"' (2012) 62(1) *Journal of Legal Education* 81.

episode exemplifies the pressure that government and military lawyers were under to come up with ways to justify practices that would otherwise be seen as human rights abuses.[84] Many essential elements of fairness in the US criminal process were deliberately set aside, and this occurred in Australia as well.[85] The Law Council of Australia was, to its credit, particularly critical of the Australian government's acquiescence in arrangements by the United States to establish 'military commissions'[86] in order to deal with non-citizens detained at Guantanamo Bay as suspected terrorists. The legislation establishing the commissions classified detainees as 'unlawful enemy combatants' so as to deny them the rights afforded to citizens in the US legal system (such as the right to silence, the prohibition of hearsay evidence) or the rights of 'prisoners of war' in the international legal system.[87] In 2006, despite both the Australian and US governments' insistence that these commissions were legitimate, the US Supreme Court finally ruled them illegal.[88] However, the US Government legislated shortly afterwards to establish commissions very similar to those deemed unconstitutional by the Court[89] and the detention of 'unlawful enemy combatants' at Guantanamo Bay has continued into 2022.[90] What ethical approach guided the lawyers who helped to establish the Guantanamo incarceration and who drafted the *Military Commissions Act of 2006*?[91]

With sporadic instances of violent extremism continuing across the globe,[92] the issue of whether public security is enhanced or undermined by treating alleged terrorists differently to 'normal' criminal defendants seems likely to remain contentious in the wider community. But in ethical terms it is and will remain a dangerous path to say that one class of defendant is entitled to more rights than another, or that some individuals, though not charged with anything, are nevertheless by mere implication 'guilty' of something 'bad'.[93]

84 For a brief summary see W Bradley Wendel, 'The Torture Memos and the Demands of Legality' (2009) 12(1) *Legal Ethics* 107. See also Jane Mayer, 'Annals of the Pentagon – The Memo: How an Internal Effort to Ban the Abuse and Torture of Detainees Was Thwarted', *The New Yorker* (New York, 27 February 2006) 32; W Bradley Wendel, 'Legal Ethics and the Separation of Law and Morals' (2005) 91(1) *Cornell Law Review* 67.

85 Ananian-Welsh and Williams (n 69).

86 See Law Council of Australia, 'Government Must Do More Over Mounting Criticism of Military Commissions' (Press Release, 3 August 2005).

87 See the discussion at the online Berkley Forum: see, eg, Carly Gordenstein, 'The Efficacy of the Guantánamo Military Commissions', *Berkley Center for Religion, Peace and World Affairs* (Web Page, 15 September 2020) <https://berkleycenter.georgetown.edu/responses/the-efficacy-of-the-guantanamo-military-commissions>.

88 *Hamdan v Rumsfeld*, 548 US 557 (2006).

89 Alissa J Kness, 'The Military Commissions Act of 2006: An Unconstitutional Response to Hamdan v Rumsfeld' (2007) 52(2) *South Dakota Law Review* 382.

90 President Biden has indicated that he plans to close the facility, but progress is slow: Associated Press, 'Why Half of Guantanamo Bay's Prisoners Could Be Set Free', *9 News* (online at 20 February 2022) <https://www.9news.com.au/world/guantanamo-bay-half-prisoners-could-be-released-usa/1b1ab0a5-d438-4154-b156-86b0e9143314>.

91 Consider also the issues raised in Dana Carver Boehm, 'Guantanamo Bay and the Conflict of Ethical Lawyering' (2012) 117 *Pennsylvania State Law Review* 283.

92 In Australia 'nationalist, racist and misogynous violence is the fastest growing threat, according to the head of the Australian Security Intelligence Organisation: '"A Salad Bar of Hate": Terrorist Attack Anticipated in the Next Year', *The Canberra Times* (Canberra, 30 April 2021) 11.

93 One of the Australian detainees at Guantanamo Bay, Mamdouh Habib, was returned to Australia after being released from three years' detention without charge. The Australian government tried to discourage, under a hastily enacted law, receipt by Habib of any payment for telling his story of incarceration and alleged torture: Michelle Grattan, 'Canberra Shackled and Shamed by Habib', *The Sunday Age* (Melbourne, 30 January 2005) 17.

The rule of law, under which *everyone* is supposed to be equally protected and accountable, and that underlies every piece of substantive law taught in law school, is only as good as is the will of each government and each lawyer to insist on continuing fairness in all trial processes. Without fairness the rule of law becomes a hollow edifice. Thus there may be an ethical duty upon the prosecution and the defence to protest and withdraw (as *responsible lawyers* and perhaps *moral activists*) when systemic political decisions have been taken to eliminate or limit overall fairness in the drafting of legislation or the management of a trial. Suspect processes emerge by inducing participation from the legal profession.

Consider the issue of genocide. Lawyers' ethics may be implicated in mass killings when lawyers (often employed by government) remain silent about or condone genocides and then participate in compromised prosecutions of the alleged perpetrators. The German state in the 1930s was perhaps the first to systematically involve elements of the legal profession in what we now know as 'ethnic cleansing'. Starting with the drafting of national legislation to progressively de-legalise 'non-Aryans' in the 1930s (as a precursor to the Holocaust), Germans were progressively acclimatised to categorising Polish, Jewish, Roma, homosexuals and others as less than human – that is, by degree, as 'cockroaches', 'insects' and finally, 'nothing'.[94] The apparatus of the German criminal law was completely subverted by a relentless legislative (and cultural) program so that, eventually, the Nazi transportation and extermination program became domestic, hygienic and even banal to the populace at large.[95] Lacking any institutional or global ethics of *moral activism*, and overwhelmed by the culture of obedience to National Socialist edicts, there were then many lawyers who were simply ethically overwhelmed.[96]

Hans Guggenheim, the Holocaust anthropologist, has written:

> We have no right to forgive the suffering inflicted on others, but we can show compassion for the suffering experienced by our enemies and thus lay the foundation for a better future … The lesson of Auschwitz is that without compassion our world is doomed … that it is the only way we can control our technologies of war, our greed for gold, our lust for power and domination and above all, the only way we can administer our Laws with justice for all.[97]

Guggenheim considers that for justice to be possible it must be based on the virtue of compassion.[98] This is why it is important to ask today's lawyers what values they hold and whether those values are evident in their behaviour. Furthermore, lawyers should never forget that accused persons have a right to be treated humanely. The key is for law students and lawyers to see that anyone may become a defendant and experience the potential

94 See Thérèse O'Donnell, '*Law After Auschwitz: Towards a Jurisprudence of the Holocaust*, by David Fraser' (2005) 15 *Law and Politics Book Review* 581.

95 See Hans Guggenheim, 'Lecture to GAJE at Auschwitz' (Conference Paper, Worldwide Conference of the Global Alliance for Justice Education, Krakow, 22 July 2004); Hannah Arendt, *Eichmann in Jerusalem: A Report on the Banality of Evil* (Viking Press, 1964).

96 See David Luban, 'Complicity and Lesser Evils: A Tale of Two Lawyers' (2021) 34(3) *Georgetown Journal of Legal Ethics* 613 for a moral biography of two lawyers in Nazi Germany.

97 Guggenheim (n 95).

98 Ibid. See also Lorana Bartels and Anthony Hopkins, 'Engaging Head and Heart: An Australian Story on the Role of Compassion in Criminal Justice Reform' in *Research Handbook on Law and Emotion* (Edward Elgar Publishing, 2021) 268.

degradation of that position. Lawyers must be conscious not to regard themselves as 'good' and defendants as 'bad'.

The lawyers (Indonesian and Australian) who represented Andrew Chan and Myuran Sukumaran, drug traffickers on death row in Indonesia, are an inspiring example of compassionate defence lawyers. Chan and Sukumaran were arrested in 2005 in Bali along with seven other Australians. Judged to be the ring leaders, they were sentenced in 2006 to death by firing squad, a sentence eventually carried out in 2015, despite many legal appeals and requests for clemency. Alongside the 'magnificent'[99] Indonesian criminal/human rights lawyer Todung Mulya Lubis, the Australian barrister Julian McMahon took up the case. Lex Lasry (who worked on the case before his appointment to the Victorian Supreme Court bench) describes the work McMahon and others did:

> Julian McMahon assembled a team of thoroughly committed Victorian lawyers to become involved in every aspect of the case. Each of these lawyers gave everything they had to the case. They displayed a commitment to saving Andrew and Myuran's lives that was extraordinary. In the finest traditions of the Victorian Criminal Bar, they demonstrated the force in the thesis that criminal lawyers defending clients are in every sense human rights lawyers. With Julian as the spiritual leader and inspiration of this group, they excelled in their devotion to their pro bono task.[100]

McMahon received the Victorian Australian of the Year Award in 2016 for his committed advocacy in this and other capital punishment cases and in opposing the death penalty. His work is a shining example of adversarial advocacy, responsible lawyering, moral activism and ethics of care.

Conclusion

Criminal justice in Australia is likely to retain its adversarial character, even if governments generally want to shift the goal posts in favour of greater prosecutorial power, heavier penalties and the criminalisation of more and more behaviour. The stakes for all lawyers involved in criminal justice are increasingly global and ethical: do they help draft repressive and dehumanising legislation? Do they succumb to the pressure to discard fair processes because of fear about terrorism? Do they exploit 'confessions' made by tired and fearful individuals after many hours of interrogation? Do they pressure defendants to simply plead 'guilty' and eliminate the stress of a trial on them and their families?

In fact, an ethical approach to criminal justice has never been so important for social confidence in our courts and the comprehensive security only the courts provide to society. After reviewing gross breaches of ethics in the Victorian criminal justice system, Commissioner McMurdo reminds us:

> Fairness underpins and fosters public trust and confidence in, and therefore the legitimacy of, the criminal justice system. The system cannot operate effectively if it does not command the public's trust and confidence.[101]

99 Lex Lasry, 'Vale Andrew Chan and Myuran Sukumaran' (2017) 152 *Victorian Bar News* 61.
100 Ibid.
101 In *Royal Commission into the Management of Police Informants* (n 56) 63.

Fairness will only be achieved if all lawyers (and other players) in the system act ethically. This requires criminal lawyers to regularly reflect on their own motives – that is, to look at *who* they are and *what* they value – as they engage in this important work.

RECOMMENDED FURTHER READING

Benjamin Bickford, 'Convenience Pleas', *Hunter Street Chambers* (Web Page, 18 February 2016) <https://www.hunterstreetchambers.com.au/convenience-pleas/>

Andrew Boe, *The Truth Hurts* (Hachett Australia, 2021)

Ben Clarke, 'An Ethics Survey of Australian Criminal Law Practitioners' (2003) 27(3) *Criminal Law Journal* 142

'Is Practising Criminal Law Bad for Your Mental Health?', *Law Report* (ABC Radio National, 11 July 2017) <https://www.abc.net.au/radionational/programs/lawreport/is-practicing-criminal-law-bad-for-your-mental-health/8697446>

Louise Milligan, *Witness: An Investigation into the Brutal Cost of Seeking Justice* (Hachette Australia, 2020)

Abbe Smith, 'Defending the Unpopular Down-Under' (2006) 30(2) *Melbourne University Law Review* 495

David B Wexler (ed), *Rehabilitating Lawyers: Principles of Therapeutic Jurisprudence for Criminal Law Practice* (Carolina Academic Press, 2008)

Richard Young and Andrew Sanders, 'The Ethics of Prosecution Lawyers' (2004) 7(2) *Legal Ethics* 190

6

ETHICAL CHALLENGES IN CIVIL DISPUTE RESOLUTION

Introduction

The previous chapter discussed how the different roles of criminal defence and prosecution are defined by the context of a criminal proceeding. As we describe, while criminal process has changed due to evolving notions of justice, lawyers are typically primarily engaged in representation around a court trial. In civil dispute resolution, there is a greater diversity of roles performed by lawyers. For instance, a lawyer may be on record in a civil trial with clear rules of evidence and procedure or they may be an advocate in a less regulated tribunal or a court-ordered mediation or adopt other alternative dispute resolution strategies for the client. They may be the deal-maker and representative in negotiating the legal structure of their client's business or commercial venture. These differing roles require a range of technical skills as well as ethical judgement to determine how best to act according to the context in which the lawyer is working.

There is a public interest in maintaining the fairness and justice of the court system and the legal decisions emanating from that system. Consequently, as key actors in this system, lawyers have a paramount duty to the administration of justice. This is a wider notion than simply observing duties to a court. It is increasingly recognised that there is a public interest in the encouragement of efficient and efficacious dispute resolution.[1] This is achieved by better observation of duties to assist efficient, as well as fair, processes in formal courts and tribunals as discussed in detail in the next part of this chapter. It is also achieved by recognising that many disputes can be effectively and justly resolved without recourse to the courts or tribunals. Indeed, the ethical rules applying to both barristers and solicitors expressly impose a duty to advise their clients about alternatives to litigation in court where appropriate.[2] And when acting in private negotiations and alternative dispute resolution, lawyers have comparable duties to those when acting in court, as discussed later in this chapter.

Lawyers are also representatives of their clients. There is a public interest in lawyers serving the legal interests of their clients so as to vindicate their clients' legal rights and to ensure clients are accorded procedural fairness. For the lawyer this involves, as examined in Chapter 4, fostering a relationship of trust and loyalty and observing duties of confidentiality. It also requires lawyers to be competent in their advocacy for a client. The same is required of the lawyer on the other side of the dispute. There is an assumption of equality of arms in the adversary system. In this sense, the system assumes an alignment of the duties of the lawyer to the client and to the administration of justice.

However, in practice, there are tensions that the lawyer must navigate in the civil dispute resolution context. Lawyers must balance the interests of the client with what might be competing duties that the lawyer owes to the administration of justice. Tensions can arise in a range of ways depending on the client, the case and the nature of representation.

At its most extreme this tension may manifest as a clash of interests – clients have a private interest in having disputes concluded in a certain way that might conflict with the proper process of a court or the public interest. When a person needs to use a lawyer, they

1 See Michael King et al, *Non-Adversarial Justice* (Federation Press, 2nd ed, 2014); *Aon Risk Services Australia Ltd v Australian National University* (2009) 239 CLR 175.

2 *ASCR* r 7.2.1. At the federal level, the *Civil Dispute Resolution Act 2011* (Cth) s 9 places an onus on lawyers to inform and assist their clients to take non-adversarial measures to resolve disputes *before* accessing some federal courts.

are often in the midst of conflict and not always at their most altruistic or rational. The work that clients ask their lawyers to do may be aimed at cutting across the interests and positions of other people. We need lawyers precisely because of the conflicts we face as we live together in society.[3] Surveys show that people tend to be critical of lawyers in general but very favourable towards their own lawyer: they condemn lawyers for doing for others what they praise them for doing for themselves – being adversarial advocates.[4] We do not like the idea of lawyers as hired guns until we feel that we ourselves need a hired gun! While this might be an understandable human reaction, this chapter begins by considering the many harms of 'excessive adversarialism' by lawyers in civil litigation.

Conversely, a lawyer can cause harm to a client and the administration of justice in *failing* to act zealously or competently in advocating for them in a civil dispute. Clients are justifiably upset when their lawyers delay work on their matter. Delay might result in a loss of legal rights, or a perception that lawyers lack an appreciation of their clients' needs and interests. There are a wide range of clients – from an individual seeing a lawyer for the first time in a proceeding in which they are deeply emotionally or financially invested, to an in-house counsel asking for assistance from an external lawyer in the arbitration of a corporate dispute. Understanding what is needed to act appropriately in the client's best interest will vary depending on the nature of the client and their case. Clients may lack capacity to provide good instructions or a lawyer might be concerned that client instructions are harmful to the client. In these cases what is in the 'best interests' of the client might be difficult to discern and a lawyer might have to make tough decisions about what is needed to safeguard the client's best interests or, in some cases, whether to continue to act. This chapter considers some of the impacts of a lack of care by the lawyer and the need for a fulsome notion of competence in providing legal services in dispute resolution.

The chapter then turns to how the law of lawyering attempts to balance or observe lawyers' obligations to the client and the administration of justice in each case. It is likely that the law of lawyering does not (and does not seek to) provide enough guidance as to how to act appropriately in all cases. We suggest that a *responsible lawyering* approach might temper the excessive adversarialism and/or a lack of care for the client often observed in civil litigation. Such an approach requires a lawyer to interpret the law and the rules of professional responsibility in accordance with the purpose of the substantive law. The responsible lawyer will not unhesitatingly use loopholes, procedural rules or barely arguable points to frustrate the substance and spirit of the law. Equally, the responsible lawyer will act diligently in the interests of the client, not in self-interest, and try to understand how the client's reasonable legal rights can be best served.

We go on to consider the possibility for lawyers to go beyond the legal minimum, to take responsibility for a more *moral activist* approach by engaging in a moral conversation with clients. We contend that in many cases this conversation with the client can be conceived of as squarely within the lawyer's role of carefully considering the context and impact of the law on the client in a holistic way. For an organisation this could mean discussing how a legal course of action might be inconsistent with its stated organisational goals or values and

3 Robert Post, 'On the Popular Image of the Lawyer: Reflections in a Dark Glass' (1987) 75(1) *California Law Review* 379.

4 Christine Parker, *Just Lawyers: Regulation and Access to Justice* (Oxford University Press, 1999) 11.

how acting against these might result in further legal risks. For an individual client it might be taking time to help them better understand the law and their rights.

In the final part of this chapter we turn to lawyers' roles in the administration of justice outside the courts, where they represent clients in alternative and more collaborative or non-adversarial forms of dispute resolution. We point to some of the dangers of approaching these roles as ethics-free zones. We suggest that an *ethics of care* approach might emphasise a holistic conception of client interest including dialogue with clients, as well as encouraging the participation of the client in deciding how their case will proceed and thinking realistically and appropriately about the outcomes they want to achieve.

The harms of excessive adversarialism

According to the *adversarial advocacy* approach, a lawyer's role is to advance clients' interests subject only to the lawyer's duty to obey the law, including professional conduct and procedural rules. In Australia, case law and conduct rules prioritise duties of truth and fairness owed to the court over the duty to the client where these duties are in conflict (discussed below). However, in practice, some lawyers may feel that an 'adversarial imperative' requires them to exploit any advantages the legal system allows for their clients:

> The adversarial imperative is the compulsion which litigants and especially their lawyers have to see the other side as the enemy who must be defeated; the 'no stone unturned mentality' is a compulsion to take every step which could conceivably advance the prospects of victory or reduce the risk of defeat. Both, in turn, increase the labour intensiveness and consequently the cost and delay of dispute resolution and, especially as between parties of unequal means, render it unfair.[5]

An adversarial mindset can extend to all aspects of a lawyer's practice even where this may be unnecessary or inappropriate in acting in the best interests of the client. The ethical justification for this adversarial attitude relies on the spectre of the courtroom. The standard conception of the lawyers' role, and the conduct rules, focus on advocacy on behalf of clients and responsibilities to the court. However, only a small proportion of lawyers devote a substantial amount of their practice time to litigation and most disputes do not go all or even part of the way to trial.[6] Nevertheless, lawyers have a 'pervading consciousness' that litigation is the potential conclusion and even *likely* outcome of any contract, trust or deed of conveyance, or any legal advice tendered. This leads to an attitude of precaution directed at covering every circumstance and eventuality, which might make legal advice (even outside of litigation) time-consuming, complex and costly.[7] While there have been reforms to the

5 GL Davies, 'Fairness in a Predominantly Adversarial System' in Helen Stacey and Michael Lavarch (eds), *Beyond the Adversarial System* (Federation Press, 1999) 102, 111.

6 For two classic socio-legal studies on this point, see William Felstiner, Richard Abel and Austin Sarat, 'The Emergence and Transformation of Disputes: Naming, Blaming, Claiming … ' (1981) 15 *Law and Society Review* 631 and Hazel Genn, *Paths to Justice: What People Do and Think About Going to Law* (Hart Publishing, 1999) 252.

7 Australian Law Reform Commission, *Review of the Adversarial System of Civil Litigation – Rethinking the Federal Civil Litigation System* (Issues Paper, 1997) [11.10]–[11.11]; Productivity Commission, *Access to Justice Arrangements* (Inquiry Report, 2014).

conduct rules that have attempted to address this issue by requiring lawyers to advise their clients about other options and exercise forensic judgement, as described below, concerns persist about lawyers' part in making the system ever more expensive.

Even when lawyers use negotiation, mediation or other alternative forms of resolution to settle disputes, this is often not a separate process to litigation. Rather, both can be seen as part of 'a single process of disputing in the vicinity of official tribunals that we might call *litigotiation*, that is, the strategic pursuit of a settlement through mobilizing the court process'.[8] Lawyers are likely to use legal rules and norms to shape the substance of the outcomes they seek to negotiate on behalf of their clients. And they can bring excessive adversarialism even into 'non-adversarial justice' forums.[9] Conventional but increasingly outmoded advice on negotiation tactics for lawyers (and often for business people) suggests that they should see their role as being to represent their client's position as aggressively as possible, using posturing (emotional displays and manipulation) and other misleading or bullying tactics, and making concessions only to the extent necessary to get greater concessions from the other side.[10]

Where such attitudes pervade within the civil dispute resolution system, we can observe individual 'wins' but arguably many more losses. The Chief Justice of Western Australia's Supreme Court, Peter Quinlan, recently observed:

> I have had, over the past couple of years, the nagging sense that, however much we might be aware of it, we, as a profession, don't acknowledge and are certainly not attentive to, the reality that our legal system, as a system, ***hurts*** people; really harms them in a variety of concrete lasting ways.[11]

We agree. We argue that, when lawyers within this system exhibit excessive adversarialism, we can observe a range of resulting harms. *Adversarial advocacy* is not necessarily always in the interests of clients. The adversarial advocate may feel that they must do whatever they can to protect, advance and expand a client's legal rights in the short term. Yet the adversarial advocate might not adequately take into account the costs of these actions to the client, particularly as litigation advances. As well as financial, there will be relational, emotional and reputational – even physical[12] – losses for the client in aggravating or pursuing a dispute, and these too will be greater the longer the dispute continues. Clients often feel cheated by their lawyer when costs are high as a result of a long trial (see discussion of fees and costs in Chapter 8). The client may also simply want someone to pay their bills now and give them some monetary recognition of their pain rather than waiting four to five years

8 Marc Galanter, 'Worlds of Deals: Using Negotiation to Teach About Legal Process' (1984) 34(2) *Journal of Legal Education* 268, 268.

9 The Productivity Commission's *Access to Justice Arrangements* report noted a 'creeping legalism', with the Victorian and Civil Administrative Tribunal's process 'often not much differently run from jurisdictions such as the Federal Court': Productivity Commission (n 7) 364, 367.

10 See Albert Z Carr, 'Is Business Bluffing Ethical?' in Carrie Menkel-Meadow and Michael Wheeler (eds), *What's Fair? Ethics for Negotiators* (Jossey Bass, 2004) 246.

11 Peter Quinlan CJ, '*Primum Non Nocere*: What Might the Justice System Learn from Hippocrates?' (Speech, Piddington Society, 4 June 2021) 6 <https://www.supremecourt.wa.gov.au/S/speeches_2018_2022.aspx> (emphasis in original).

12 Some studies have found that there might be correlations between poor health outcomes and participating in civil litigation in person injury cases: Clare E Scollay et al, 'Claimant Lawyer Use in Road Traffic Injury Compensation Claims' (2020) 43(1) *UNSW Law Journal* 82.

for courthouse justice. Some studies have shown that receiving an apology might be more valuable for a client than money, certainly compared to enduring a long, drawn-out trial.[13]

Moreover, adversarial behaviour by a lawyer on behalf of a client also affects the other side, and other parties. Adversarialism can lead to various misleading and deceptive tactics, as described in the next section of the chapter. It can also lead to highly technical and manipulative arguments about the facts or the law that evade the substance of, while paying lip service to the letter of, the law. This can increase the cost of cases for parties and delays in the system. There is also plain aggressive and bullying behaviour that is not only unpleasant but might prejudice just claims.

Some lawyers argue that each of these tactics is appropriate because each party is represented and can look after themselves. But frequently, one side cannot afford as much, or as skilful, legal representation as the other side. Since large business enterprises dominate many economic and social relationships, the fact that companies' legal expenses are tax deductible, while individuals' legal expenses generally are not, heightens this type of inequality.[14] For example, in the case of most personal injury litigation, the plaintiff is an individual who has been harmed and the defendant, more often than not, has the backing of an insurance company. In another context, recent studies have highlighted the prevalence of litigation being used to continue family violence. Applications for protection orders or family law disputes may be drawn out by a party refusing to comply with reasonable demands, thereby increasing costs and delays. There may be bullying or intimidation by one party or their lawyers.[15] This behaviour creates inequity between the parties where one party becomes unable to continue to afford representation or is simply frightened away from a case.

This leads to a further concern – that overly zealous advocacy can damage the fabric of the legal system itself. Excessive adversarialism makes the whole system more expensive and unfair for everyone, since it constantly increases expectations about the minimal level of representation. Adversarial advocates may create a system where each side believes they must do more to protect their own client, because of what they believe the other side is going to do, until ultimately the issues seem to revolve around procedure rather than substance, and the form of words rather than their purpose.[16] In *Expense Reduction Analysts Group Pty Ltd v Armstrong Strategic Management and Marketing Pty Ltd*,[17] the High Court considered an argument on waiver of client legal privilege claimed over 13 out of over 60,000 documents in the discovery process of a civil trial. The Court saw this as an unnecessary legalistic argument not going to the dispute between the parties – and named it a costly 'satellite interlocutory proceeding'. In other civil dispute contexts, there are reports

13 Jennifer Rubbenolt, 'Attorneys, Apologies, and Settlement Negotiation' (2008) 13(2) *Harvard Negotiation Law Review* 349.

14 Australian Law Reform Commission, *Managing Justice: A Review of the Federal Civil Justice System* (Report, 2000) [5.34]–[5.50]; Cameron Murphy, 'Tax Deductability [sic] and Litigation: Reducing the Impact of Legal Fees and Improving Access to the System' (2004) 27(1) *University of New South Wales Law Journal* 240.

15 Heather Douglas, 'Family Violence, Lawyers and Debt' (2020) 33(3) *Australian Journal of Family Law* 264.

16 William Simon, *The Practice of Justice: A Theory of Lawyers' Ethics* (Harvard University Press, 1998) 138–69; Geoffrey Davies, 'Fairness in a Predominantly Adversarial System' in H Stacey and M Lavarch (eds), *Beyond the Adversarial System* (Federation Press, 1999) 111.

17 (2013) 250 CLR 303.

that lawyers have put on a show of aggression in the courtroom to attract future clients who may be impressed by the destructive force of the hired gun.[18] Thus, in many ways, excessive adversarialism can make the civil legal system more complex and expensive, more daunting or unpleasant, yet more removed from the substantive justice concerns of ordinary people.[19]

The harms associated with lack of care and competence

We may also hold concerns about a lawyer's representation in civil dispute resolution that are quite different to the harms caused by excessive adversarialism. At the other end of the spectrum, disciplinary cases abound with examples of a lack of care and competence shown by lawyers in civil dispute resolution. For instance, in *Legal Services Commissioner v McHenry*[20] there were 30 separate disciplinary charges against the practitioner, many of which related to significant delays in advancing cases in which clients lost legal rights due to time limitations on bringing actions. In one case, this lawyer failed to take steps in progressing a matter for over eight years and made false representations to the client about its progress. Not only might a client suffer financial loss, but this type of behaviour is likely to significantly damage an individual's trust in lawyers. Equally, we know from cases where lawyers are in court as parties, rather than as advocates – where they are being sued for negligence or breach of contract[21] – that there are losses to the client and old stereotypes about self-interested and untrustworthy lawyers are reinforced.

There are many reasons why a lawyer might fail to act competently and diligently for a client. Often disciplinary cases document significant personal illness, addiction and financial distress.[22] Lawyers working in small and solo practices and in remote locations may struggle with isolation and poor access to resources.[23] A lack of (what the lawyer sees as) adequate remuneration might mean a lawyer doesn't devote enough time to a proceeding. Fryberg's comments in *Re N (A Solicitor)* illustrate this concern where a grant of legal aid is insufficient to cover all steps of a proceeding:

> I am left with the uncomfortable feeling that the errors on the part of both N and counsel for T would not have occurred had the matter not been funded by legal aid … It is a natural enough human reaction in such circumstances to seek to defer

18 Jerome Doraisamy, 'Overcoming Aggression (from Opposing Counsel and Their Clients)', *Lawyers Weekly* (online at 20 May 2021) <https://www.lawyersweekly.com.au/sme-law/31416-overcoming-aggression-from-opposing-counsel-and-their-clients>.

19 See Parker (n 4).

20 [2018] QCAT 417. The application for discipline, specifically to have the practitioner struck from the roll of lawyers, was brought by the Commissioner as a result of investigations from a referral from the Federal Circuit Court around forgery charges.

21 Failures in representation in settlement of disputes are a common example. For instance, in a long and bitterly fought family law dispute the lawyers failed to properly advise a client with failing mental health about the final settlement that resulted in a poor outcome for the client: *Goddard Elliott v Fritsch* [2012] VSC 87, [132].

22 See Stephen Tang, Tony Foley and Vivien Holmes, 'Ethical Misconduct by New Australian Lawyers: Prevalence and Prevention' (2020) 27(3) *International Journal of the Legal Profession* 245.

23 Leslie C Levin, 'The Ethical World of Solo and Small Law Firm Practitioners' (2004) 41(2) *Houston Law Review* 309.

> incurring cost; but that is a reaction that is apt to blur the sound exercise of professional judgment. Having accepted a retainer, a true professional does not let the quality of the work undertaken suffer because the available remuneration is inadequate. If lawyers are not prepared to bear the cost of all necessary steps in a legal aid matter, regardless of funding, they should not take on the work.[24]

While personal issues faced by the lawyer might be pressing and unavoidable, they must be recognised and addressed. If they go unmanaged, lawyers with the best intentions can cause significant harms to the client and the proper administration of justice.

Some lawyers might struggle rather with external factors such as the rapid advancement of technology in legal practice. In Australia the effects of the global pandemic have forced rapid changes in lawyers' practices in and around courts and tribunals.[25] As of writing, most decision makers have returned to largely in-person processes, which allow for open justice and traditional advocacy practices. However, some practices will have changed forever. Even before the pandemic forced us to work from home,[26] lawyers were increasingly using technology in courts. Australian courts had been relatively early adopters of technological approaches to civil processes as well as intensive judicial case management in many areas.[27] Lawyers have been required to respond to these reforms by developing relevant technological capabilities such as electronic filing and appearing by telephone or video-link in remote hearings. Where a lawyer is unable to adapt, they are likely to cause harm to their client and to the efficacy of the civil system.

Whether a lawyer displays excessive adversarialism or lack of competence, their approach to civil dispute resolution affects their clients, other parties and the legal system. We turn now to consider how the law of lawyering addresses these issues.

The law of lawyering for fair civil processes

The law of lawyering is clear that lawyers in litigation, and civil dispute resolution roles generally, have duties to the client and to the administration of justice. It accords with *adversarial advocacy* in assuming that the lawyer will seek to act as best as possible within the law for the client, including seeking and understanding their instructions. However, the conduct rules are also clear that when there is a conflict, the duty of the lawyer to the administration of justice *overrides* their duty to their clients – a *responsible lawyer* approach. Civil procedural law and disciplinary case law also suggests that caring for the client requires more than simply seeking a win at all costs for them.

24 [2010] QSC 267, [35]. While there are increasingly fewer aspects of civil law proceedings that are funded by legal aid across the country, eligible people may access this government-funded scheme for areas such as family law, migration, disability and mental health advocacy and employment disputes.

25 Anne Wallace and Kathy Laster, 'Courts in Victoria, Australia, During COVID: Will Digital Innovation Stick?' (2021) 12(2) *International Journal for Court Administration* 9.

26 The Australian Bureau of Statistics reported in 2021 that 41% of the Australian workforce regularly worked from home (up from 32% in August 2019): *Working Arrangements* (Catalogue No 6336.0, 14 December 2021).

27 Tom Bathurst, 'Three Contemporary Issues in Civil Litigation: Expert Evidence, Discovery and Alternative Dispute Resolution' (Speech, Annual Civil Litigation Seminar, 5 March 2016).

ASCR rr 3, 4 Overriding duty and other fundamental ethical duties

ASCR r 3. Paramount duty to the court and the administration of justice

3.1 A solicitor's duty to the court and the administration of justice is paramount and prevails to the extent of inconsistency with any other duty.

ASCR r 4. Other fundamental ethical duties

4.1 A solicitor must also:

- **4.1.1** act in the best interests of a client in any matter in which the solicitor represents the client;
- **4.1.2** be honest and courteous in all dealings in the course of legal practice;
- **4.1.3** deliver legal services competently, diligently and as promptly as reasonably possible;
- **4.1.4** avoid any compromise to their integrity and professional independence; and
- **4.1.5** comply with these Rules and the law.

The *ASCR* state as a matter of general principle that lawyers must act with independence exercising their own 'forensic judgment' when acting in advocacy contexts.

ASCR r 17 Independence – avoidance of personal bias

17.1 A solicitor representing a client in a matter that is before the court must not act as the mere mouthpiece of the client or of the instructing solicitor (if any) and must exercise the forensic judgments called for during the case independently, after the appropriate consideration of the client's and the instructing solicitor's instructions where applicable.

17.2 A solicitor does not breach the solicitor's duty to the client, and will not have failed to give appropriate consideration to the client's or the instructing solicitor's instructions, simply by choosing, contrary to those instructions, to exercise the forensic judgments called for during the case so as to:

- **17.2.1** confine any hearing to those issues which the solicitor believes to be the real issues;
- **17.2.2** present the client's case as quickly and simply as may be consistent with its robust advancement; or
- **17.2.3** inform the court of any persuasive authority against the client's case.

The conduct rules seek to provide some protection for clients and due administration of justice at the outset by prohibiting ambulance-chasing behaviours.[28] A court can use its own 'inherent' jurisdiction to control its 'officers' (that is, lawyers admitted to

28 *ASCR* r 36 prohibits false and misleading advertising and *ASCR* r 34.2 prohibits a lawyer seeking to enter into a lawyer–client relationship with a client in a position of disadvantage due to 'recent trauma or injury'.

practise in that court) and its own procedure.[29] Courts also have powers to address excessively adversarial conduct by parties and their lawyers by ordering them to take certain steps in litigation, to personally pay costs associated with the litigation to the other side if they have behaved inappropriately, or to find them guilty of contempt of court where they have breached their duties to the court. In a decision a judge can also comment on the behaviour of the lawyers appearing before them and recommend to a regulator that disciplinary action be taken against a lawyer for breach of the duty to the court on the basis of general principles or specific rules in the *ASCR* or *Barristers' Conduct Rules*.

Yet the law of lawyering does not frame the lawyer's duty to the court and the administration of justice as a clearly defined code. It is, rather, a set of broad principles that prescribe a *responsible lawyering* type role as officer of the court, independent from the client. This can make it difficult for lawyers to be sure about how to act in specific instances. The *adversarial advocacy* approach tends to suggest that the lawyer should closely follow the client's instructions and objectives, and it is up to the other side to complain about problematic tactics and behaviour to the court or to disciplinary authorities. We concede that this is no longer a tenable view given the principles now laid out in civil procedure rules and in conduct rules and statements of the courts.

We now look at key examples of how the law and conduct rules direct lawyers in their civil advocacy. First, we discuss lawyers' (and parties') 'overarching obligations' to ensure a just and efficient process in civil litigation, which is particularly strongly emphasised in Victorian and, to a somewhat lesser extent, NSW and federal, legislation. We also examine the common law approach that provides courts with powers to require a poorly behaving lawyer to pay costs. We then look at lawyers' obligations of honesty, fairness and competence, as reflected in general principles developed via the court's inherent jurisdiction to discipline lawyers and in the *ASCR*.[30]

Overarching obligations in civil litigation

Justice Ipp has argued that a lawyer is only required to do for a client what the client might 'fairly' do for him or herself, not to take every point and make every argument or allegation.[31] This is in tune with the Australian Law Reform Commission's recommendation some years ago that we should move 'away from the idea that litigation is only self-seeking activity in a private sphere with lawyers there merely to oil the wheels … [Rather,] the central role of the court as 'battleground' [should] be downplayed in favour of a notion of the court as a public forum in which, with the assistance of lawyers, rights and obligations of parties to litigation [are] determined according to law'.[32] As Chief Justice Quinlan recently commented,

29 See the discussion of admission and discipline in Chapter 3.

30 We also refer to the conduct rules governing barristers – the *Uniform Conduct (Barristers) Rules 2015* – where it is relevant to do so or there is a distinction.

31 DA Ipp, 'Lawyers' Duties to the Court' (1998) 114 *Law Quarterly Review* 63, 100.

32 Australian Law Reform Commission (n 1) [11.17], partially quoting Stephen Parker, 'Islands of Civic Virtue? Lawyers and Civil Justice Reform' (Speech delivered at the Inaugural Professorial Lecture, Griffith University, 1996) 38.

a failure to observe this approach might damage everyone: 'How often are even those people who have, on any objective analysis, "won" left worse off because of the cost, delay and disruption of the system?'[33]

To address these concerns, civil procedure legislation across Australia imposes obligations on parties, their lawyers and courts to observe 'just', expeditious or 'quick and cheap' litigation processes. It provides powers to courts to impose costs liability on parties and their lawyers for failure to observe these 'overriding' or 'overarching' purposes or obligations.[34] The NSW *Civil Procedure Act 2005* provides that parties to civil proceedings are 'under a duty to assist the court to further the overriding purpose' to 'facilitate the just, quick and cheap resolution of the real issues in the proceedings' and that solicitors and barristers must not by their conduct cause them to breach this duty (ss 56(3), (4)). The Victorian *Civil Procedure Act 2010* ('*CP Act*') goes further by setting out a number of 'overarching obligations' that go beyond meeting minimum advocacy expectations of honesty and diligence and to proceeding only on a proper basis (that is, in a manner not frivolous, vexatious or constituting an abuse of process). In Victorian courts, parties must take steps only to resolve or determine the dispute; to cooperate in the conduct of the civil proceeding; to use reasonable endeavours to resolve the dispute; to narrow the issues in dispute; to ensure costs are reasonable and proportionate; and to disclose the existence of documents.[35] These obligations must be complied with regardless of any conflicting duties owed to their clients[36] or any 'orders' given by those clients.

The *CP Act* recognises that some corporate clients are in an economically powerful position and can exert inappropriate pressure on their lawyers. Accordingly, clients (whether human or corporate), litigation funders, insurers and even expert witnesses are also bound by these provisions;[37] the parties must personally certify that they have read and understand the overarching obligations;[38] and lawyers must themselves personally certify in writing before cases commence that they and their clients assert that the litigation has a proper basis to proceed.[39] The Victorian provisions also provide the courts with powers to *sanction* a lawyer or firm (rather than compensate the other side) for a breach – from a costs award to apportioning fees and ordering the firm to show a damning judgment to the client. This sanction was imposed by the Victorian Court of Appeal in the case described in Case study 6.1.

33 Quinlan (n 11) 6.

34 There are different terminologies used in the various State and Territory schemes. For example, *Uniform Civil Procedure Rules 1999* (Qld) r 5 refers to 'overriding purpose'; *Civil Procedure Act 2005* (NSW) s 56 refers to an 'overriding purpose' of civil proceedings; *Civil Procedure Act 2010* (Vic) s 7(1) prescribes an 'overarching purpose' for civil litigation.

35 *Civil Procedure Act 2010* (Vic) ss 19–26.

36 Ibid ss 12–13.

37 Ibid ss 10, 14.

38 Ibid s 41(1).

39 Ibid ss 41, 42. The notion that the lawyer must certify that a case has merit – or 'reasonable prospects of success' – has long been part of the requirement for civil litigation in the Australian Capital Territory and New South Wales: see *Civil Law (Wrongs) Act 2002* (ACT) s 188(3); *Legal Profession Uniform Law Application Act 2014* (NSW) sch 2 cl 4(1).

CASE STUDY 6.1 THE CONSEQUENCES OF OVER-LAWYERING IN A VICTORIAN COURT

This case involved an application for leave to appeal a decision by a judge to set aside an order for security for costs in a case.[40] The main proceeding concerned a complex commercial dispute between the ANZ bank, insurance companies and a company selling fertilising products, with damages claimed of hundreds of millions of dollars. Multiple defendants each sought a security for costs order that was initially granted for between approximately $22,000 and $86,000. In the leave application on this minor part of the main case, there were five senior counsel, six junior counsel and five firms representing the parties. Submissions ran to over 2,700 pages. The Court, in refusing the appeal, observed that much of the material was unnecessary and not referred to in argument. It therefore asked the parties, including their lawyers, whether they had acted properly in bringing the leave application.

Under the Victorian *CP Act,* submissions and representation must be 'reasonable and proportionate to the complexity and importance of the issues and sums in dispute' (s 24(a)). In this case, overarching obligations of the appellants' lawyers were found not to have been observed. The appellants' lawyers were ordered to indemnify the other party for 50% of their costs, and to recover no more than 50% of their fees from their clients, and to show the judgment to their clients. The Court described this procedure as 'disciplinary' rather than the usual objective of compensating the client or other party for unnecessary losses though a wasted costs order.

DISCUSSION QUESTIONS

1. What aspect of the representation in this case do you think was most concerning for the court? Shouldn't each party be permitted to have as many lawyers and make all the submissions relevant to their case that they wish?
2. The Court stated:

> The [*CP Act*] is clearly designed to influence the culture of litigation through the imposition of sanctions on those who do not observe their obligations. Moreover, the power to sanction is not confined to cases of incompetence or improper conduct by a legal practitioner. Where there is a failure by the practitioner, whether solicitor or counsel, to use reasonable endeavours to comply with the overarching obligations, it will be no answer that the practitioner acted upon the explicit and

40 *Oswal v Australia and New Zealand Banking Group Ltd* [2012] VSC 356; *Yara Australia Pty Ltd v Oswal* (2013) 41 VR 302.

> informed instructions of the client. A sanction may be imposed where, ... the legal practitioner acts on the instruction of his or her client in breach of the overarching obligations.[41]

These comments indicate an intention to change litigation culture. Do you think such statements will have an impact on how lawyers behave in court for their clients?

3. How might you go about talking to a client about these overriding obligations when they provide instructions to do 'whatever it takes' to win?

For government lawyers there are other legal goalposts that similarly require fairness in litigation. *Model litigant* obligations require government to act fairly and honestly by dealing with claims promptly and not causing delay, paying legitimate claims without delay, using alternative dispute resolution where appropriate, keeping the costs of litigation to a minimum, not relying on technical defences, contesting liability if the dispute is really about a claim amount, not taking advantage of a claimant without resources and apologising where one of its officers has acted wrongfully or improperly.[42] It has also been suggested that large business corporations should act as model litigants due to their superior resources and power in relation to individual litigants.[43]

Legislation such as the Victorian *CP Act* or model litigant policies for government lawyers may change behaviours where these lawyers are repeat players in the system and heed the warnings of judges (as in the case above) about the need to confine their advocacy to efficient and proportionate approaches.[44] However, clients – even government ministers – might still wish to pursue marginal cases and push for the use of any tactical advantage. Lawyers must not become the instrument of the client's improper purpose – as their 'mere mouthpiece' (as in *ASCR* r 17.1) – in running the case. But how to run a case efficiently and fairly is often a matter of judgement. The vagueness of the Victorian legislation about minimising delay, 'steps' to resolve, cooperation, reasonable endeavours, narrowing the issues, and reasonable cost[45] still requires lawyers themselves to take responsibility for balancing the overriding duty to court against the duty to client in the context of the specific facts of each case. And in other jurisdictions, the legislative requirements around efficient litigation are even less precise, allowing for more variation in lawyer approach.[46] The following subsections explore further guidance provided by the conduct rules as to key ethical duties in conducting litigation.

---

41 *Yara Australia Pty Ltd v Oswal* (2013) 41 VR 302, [20].

42 The Commonwealth's obligation to act as a model litigant is imposed by the *Legal Services Directions 2017* (Appendix B) issued by the Attorney-General pursuant to the *Judiciary Act 1903* (Cth) s 55ZF. In States and Territories there are similar obligations imposed on government lawyers: see, eg, Victorian Department of Justice and Community Safety, *Victorian Model Litigant Guidelines* (2021); Gabrielle Appleby, 'The Government as Litigant' (2014) 37(1) *University of New South Wales Law Journal* 94. See further the discussion in Chapter 9.

43 Camille Cameron and Michelle Taylor-Sands, '"Corporate Governments" as Model Litigants' (2007) 10(2) *Legal Ethics* 154.

44 Francesca Bartlett, 'Educational Impacts of Civil Procedural Laws and Judicial Activism' in K Barker, K Fairweather and Ross Grantham (eds), *Private Law in the 21st Century* (Bloomsbury, 2017) 531.

45 These terms are all used in the *Civil Procedure Act 2010* (Vic) ss 17–26.

46 For instance, the Queensland *Uniform Civil Procedure Rules 1999* r 5(3) simply imposes the obligation on parties, including lawyers, 'to proceed in an expeditious way'.

Honesty – not misleading the court

The clearest curb on lawyers' adversarial behaviour on behalf of their clients is the principle that practitioners must not mislead the court.[47] *ASCR* r 4.2 states that solicitors must 'be honest and courteous in all dealings in the course of legal practice'. *ASCR* r 19 (which was discussed at length in Chapter 5 on ethics in criminal trials) states:

> A solicitor must not deceive or knowingly or recklessly mislead the court. A solicitor must take all necessary steps to correct any misleading statement made by the solicitor to a court as soon as possible after the solicitor becomes aware that the statement was misleading.[48]

In the aftermath of the United States' general federal election and shocking raid on the US Capitol building in Washington DC in January 2021, the former president launched a series of legal challenges to the election results. His lawyer, Rudy Giuliani, made public statements and court submissions alleging voter fraud without evidence to support these claims. The New York Supreme Court Appeals Court suspended Giuliani's licence to practise law in New York, on the basis that he breached rules comparable to those cited above by knowingly making false statements. This case illustrates the importance of lawyer honesty where the stakes are high. The Court was concerned not just with the damage done to the administration of justice but also that a lawyer had used his position to undermine governance of the country and rule of law: 'False statements intended to foment a loss of confidence in our elections and resulting loss of confidence in government generally damage the proper functioning of a free society.'[49]

In Australia the law of lawyering also makes it clear that where a lawyer knows that their client has been dishonest or misled the court, they must act.[50] For instance, where the lawyer knows that their client, or one of their witnesses, has perjured themselves, or has tendered evidence that is false, the lawyer must refuse to take any further part in the case unless the client allows the lawyer to correct the record (see *ASCR* rr 20.1–20.2 and Chapter 5). Similarly, it is clear that lawyers should 'not advise or suggest to a witness that false or misleading evidence should be given', or 'coach a witness by advising what answers the witness should give to questions which might be asked' (*ASCR* rr 24.1.1–24.1.2). As well as being clearly prohibited in the *ASCR*, such conduct could amount to a criminal offence and contempt of court.

However, the balance struck by the rules in laying down a process for withdrawal when the client lies might also be seen as morally questionable. Where the lawyer knows of their client's perjury and their client will not allow them to correct a misleading statement, *ASCR* r 20.1.5 preserves client confidentiality above the duty of truthfulness to the court

47 In this section we refer to 'court' for simplicity. However, the *ASCR* glossary of terms defined this very broadly to include tribunals, investigations or inquiries established or conducted under statute or by a parliament, royal commissions and arbitrations or mediations or any other form of dispute resolution. We will specifically turn to guidance for lawyers outside the courts in the final section.

48 *ASCR* rr 19.1–19.2.

49 *Matter of Giuliani*, 146 NYS 3d 266, 283 (2021).

50 Substantially similar conduct rules apply to barristers concerning duties of honesty to the court: *Legal Profession Uniform Conduct (Barristers) Rules 2015*.

by providing that the lawyer must withdraw 'but otherwise may not inform the court of the lie, falsification or suppression'. Because the lawyer withdraws without being able to alert the court to the deception, the best that can be said is that the lawyer is no longer directly a part of any deception of the court. Yet the lawyer has still allowed the court to be misled[51] (although it is quite possible the court will recognise that something untoward has occurred). Many laypeople would view this sort of 'silent withdrawal' as damning for the client and morally weak on the part of the lawyer. This issue is discussed in Chapter 5 in the context of criminal representation where the client is facing a criminal sanction and possibly loss of their liberty. Does it make a difference that the client has lied to the court in a civil claim? It might be thought to be less morally justified to allow the court to be misled in a context that involves a civil dispute between individuals. However, the impacts of civil litigation can still be very significant for parties.

Lawyers are under more onerous obligations to proactively inform the court of the law, even when it goes against the client's case. This includes informing the court of any binding legal authority, any authority decided by relevant superior and appellate courts (even if it is not binding on the court in question) and any decision (including first-instance decisions) on legislation similar to that at issue in a case, as well as any applicable legislation 'which the practitioner has reasonable grounds to believe to be directly on point' (*ASCR* r 19.6). This obligation extends to authority that comes to the lawyers' knowledge after argument in a case has concluded and while judgment is pending (*ASCR* r 19.8). There is no obligation to even consult the client about this. In these ways the lawyer is under a proactive duty to inform the court of the correct law – they cannot wash their hands of the problem by withdrawal or by saying nothing. The principle does not, of course, prevent lawyers from arguing that a contrary authority should not be applied for some reason.

According to the conduct rules, there is another area where the rules of conduct provide that lawyers are under a similarly proactive obligation to disclose *factual* information to the court even though it goes against their client's case. That is where they are making an ex parte application for interlocutory relief – where the other side is not present to argue their side of the case in relation to an injunction or other order that might make a big difference to the way their case progresses (*ASCR* r 19.4).[52]

However, for all other matters, for a lawyer to be professionally responsible for misleading the court on *factual* matters they must have been actively and knowingly, or at least recklessly, involved in misleading the court. *ASCR* r 19.3 provides:

> A solicitor will not have made a misleading statement to a court simply by failing to correct an error in a statement made to the court by the opponent or any other person.

Case study 6.2 sets out two examples that test the boundaries of lawyers' duties of honesty on the facts.

51 See the discussion of the 'perjury trilemma' (it is impossible for a lawyer to fulfil all three of their duties to know everything, keep it in confidence and reveal it to the court) in Monroe H Freedman and Abbe Smith, *Understanding Lawyers' Ethics* (LexisNexis, 3rd ed, 2004) 161.

52 A similar principle might apply where the lawyer is acting against a litigant who is not represented by a lawyer.

CASE STUDY 6.2 DISHONESTY IN LEGAL PRACTICE?

Example 1

A legal practitioner acting for a woman to settle the estate of her deceased husband decided that, even though the husband's will was not properly executed, it would probably be accepted by a court as valid. The husband had only signed a facsimile of the will and it had not been witnessed. The legal practitioner knew, however, that if the will was not accepted as valid, the siblings of the client's deceased husband would have a legal claim on the estate. The client was concerned that in negotiating the wrapping up of the estate between herself and her husband's siblings, the siblings might challenge the will if they knew it had not been properly executed. She therefore instructed the practitioner not to provide a copy of the will to her husband's siblings. The practitioner obeyed this instruction and the practitioner referred to the document as the husband's 'will' throughout the negotiations. The siblings later found out that no formal will had been executed.[53]

Example 2

The lawyer for the plaintiff mistakenly stated on a writ commencing an action that the amount owing was $25,000. The amount owing should have been stated as $250,000. The lawyer for the defendant (himself in this case) did not inform the plaintiff's lawyer of the mistake. Instead, the lawyer immediately filed terms of settlement and a consent judgment in the lesser amount to make it legally binding, while knowing about the mistake.[54]

DISCUSSION QUESTIONS

1. In both cases the lawyers were found to have stepped over the line and professional disciplinary findings were made. In both cases the lawyers purposely misled or created a misleading state of affairs by their own statements and actions. In the first case, would it have made a difference if the lawyer hadn't referred to 'the will' but used another way to describe it?
2. *ASCR* r 30.1 now provides that 'A solicitor must not take unfair advantage of the obvious error of another solicitor or other person, if to do so would obtain for a client a benefit which has no supportable foundation in law or fact'. The lawyer in the second case was dishonest in his behaviour and also exploited a tactical advantage, which, if

53 *Legal Practitioners Complaints Committee and Fleming* [2006] WASAT 352.

54 Adapted from the facts of *Chamberlain v Law Society of the Australian Capital Territory* (1993) 43 FCR 148. This case was decided prior to the introduction of *ASCR* rr 19.3 and 30.1, but the Federal Court found that the lawyer's behaviour constituted professional misconduct because he deliberately took unfair advantage of a mistake for his own advantage.

it happened today, would be a breach of this rule. Would it be a breach to simply allow the lower debt to be pursued rather than taking the initiative to bind the other side to receiving a lower amount?

3. Does this standard of honesty permitted by the law accord with your understanding of socially acceptable behaviour? Can you be dishonest by omission?

In general we can describe the balance to be observed by the lawyers as being wholly responsible for the *legal* argument in a case while clients, not lawyers, are largely responsible for the *facts* advanced in a case. Why should the lawyer not be obliged to argue the client's case on the basis of the full *facts* in the same way that they must argue the case on a full view of the relevant *legal authority*? This minimal requirement of honesty might contribute to a continued public belief in the lack of honesty of the profession.[55]

Fairness – abuse of process, unsupported or irrelevant allegations, hopeless cases, and unreasonable delay and expense

The principles relating to lawyers' obligations of fair use of court processes are more broadly defined than those relating to honesty to the court. There are four broad categories of conduct that are considered unfair uses of litigation processes for which a lawyer might be held responsible: (1) using legal processes for improper or ulterior purposes, (2) entering into proceedings without proper consideration for the prospects of success, (3) making unsupported or irrelevant allegations against a person or unnecessarily objectionable statements and (4) running a case in a way that gives rise to unreasonable delay or expense. These concerns apply to the *parties* to litigation, not just their lawyers. But the focus here is on the extent to which *lawyers* can be held personally responsible for these types of conduct.

Case study 6.3, *White Industries v Flower & Hart*, illustrates lawyers involved in conduct that falls into a number of these categories.

CASE STUDY 6.3 WHITE INDUSTRIES *v* FLOWER & HART[56]

In 1986, Queensland property developer George Herscu (through his company Caboolture Park) was building a new shopping centre and had hired White Industries to build it. After several months Mr Herscu was running out of money and felt that the cost of the project was blowing out. His solicitors, Flower & Hart, advised him that there were no grounds for refusing to pay the builder under the terms of the contract. But they suggested a legal strategy for buying time: an action for misleading or deceptive conduct in relation to the builder's quote.

55 Roy Morgan, *Image of Professions Survey 2021*, reported by Jerome Doraisamy, 'Lawyers' Perceived Honesty at Lowest Level in Over 20 Years', *Lawyers Weekly* (online at 4 May 2021) <https://www.lawyersweekly.com.au/biglaw/31293-lawyers-perceived-honesty-at-lowest-level-in-over-20-years>.

They also briefed Ian Callinan QC (who was later appointed to the High Court of Australia) and junior barristers for the case. Flower & Hart wrote a letter advising as follows:

> The strict legalities are against you and your contractual position is weak ... Is there anything that can be done to try to give you, at the very least, *a temporary bargaining stance?* ... Ian Callinan and I think that you should immediately start Section 52 proceedings (under the *Trade Practices Act*) in the Federal Court alleging deceptive conduct ... Fraud on the ground of recklessness may also be available to be pleaded against the builder ... I do have to make it clear to you however that you could not win any litigation if put to the test ...[57] [emphasis in original letter]

The fraud case went ahead, with White Industries cross-claiming for the money due under the contract.

After 150 hearing days (more than a year of trial, and almost three years from when the action was commenced), Caboolture Park had gone into liquidation and Flower & Hart and Mr Callinan had withdrawn from the case. Judgment was entered in favour of White Industries for more than $5 million including costs that were awarded to White. But with Caboolture Park in liquidation, White Industries had no prospect of recovering the amount from them, and still had their own very large legal bill to pay.

White Industries obtained the written advice and communications of Flower & Hart and Mr Callinan to their client as a result of the liquidator selling company assets. On the basis of this advice, White Industries sued Flower & Hart (not Mr Callinan[58]) for wasted costs. In 1998, Goldberg J held that Flower & Hart had alleged fraud without evidence to support it, that their purpose was to delay and frustrate the claims of their client's creditor for payment, and that 'abuse of process was exacerbated by the manner in which Flower & Hart conducted the proceeding and the obstructionist and delaying tactics in which it indulged'.[59] The obstructionist and delaying tactics had included making sure senior counsel was not present when White Industries tried to get a trial date set, so that 'awkward questions' could not be asked, and sending 700 pages of interrogatories to make matters more difficult for the other side.

Goldberg J observed:

> The fact that [Mr Herscu] had a robust approach to litigation, did not believe anything was impossible and was unconcerned about entering into litigation with limited prospects made it all the more important for Flower & Hart to have regard to the manner in which it instituted and conducted proceedings on his behalf and on behalf of his companies and to be conscious of its duty to the Court.[60]

56 *White Industries (Qld) Pty Ltd v Flower & Hart* (1998) 156 ALR 169 (Goldberg J), affd *Flower & Hart v White Industries (Qld) Pty Ltd* (1999) 87 FCR 134.

57 *White Industries (Qld) Pty Ltd v Flower & Hart* (1998) 156 ALR 169, 180–1.

58 This means Mr Callinan was not a party and it was not necessary to make any determination about whether he shared Flower & Hart's improper purpose in commencing the litigation: *Flower & Hart v White Industries (Qld) Pty Ltd* (1999) 87 FCR 134, 148, 149.

59 *White Industries (Qld) Pty Ltd v Flower & Hart* (1998) 156 ALR 169, 251.

60 Ibid 249–50.

Flower & Hart was ordered to pay White Industries $1.65 million in court costs.[61] The president of the Law Council of Australia asked the Attorney-General for an investigation into Mr Callinan's fitness to remain on the High Court.[62] The Attorney-General, Daryl Williams, refused, saying: 'I have decided that on the information available, no inquiry into the conduct of the judge is warranted. Any inquiry held inappropriately can endanger the independence of the judiciary, damage the standing of the courts and do harm to an individual judge.'[63] It was reported that Professor Greg Craven said 'lawyers did that sort of thing all the time'[64] and that if 'this is proved misbehaviour then we've just disqualified 95% of the commercial Bar from High Court appointment'.[65] Ian Barker QC (then president of the NSW Bar Association) replied: 'I have perhaps led a sheltered, forensic existence, but everybody does not do it.'[66]

DISCUSSION QUESTIONS

1. Why do you think the lawyers acted as they did in this case? How would you talk to such a client to explain your legal and ethical duties?
2. Do you think this sort of behaviour should be liable for professional discipline, in addition to, or instead of, wasted costs orders? Does it make any difference if it was a common practice as asserted above?
3. Unlike *White Industries*, most investigations of lawyers' conduct arise from complaints by clients, in which case the client has impliedly waived privilege. What problems does privilege create in hiding lawyer–client collusion in abuses of court process? How could courts and disciplinary authorities overcome this problem?

It is an abuse of process for a party to make allegations, bring proceedings, or argue a particular defence for an *ulterior purpose* – that is, for purposes for which they are not intended – or dishonestly. This is absolutely prohibited.[67] There does not have to be evidence of a malicious intent, as long as the party's purpose for using court proceedings and court processes is unrelated to the objectives the court process is designed to achieve. It is likely to be easier to prove an ulterior purpose where a case is 'arguable although weak',[68] but

61 On the basis of the actions of the lawyers, the Court ordered that they pay the costs of the other side: *White Industries (Qld) Pty Ltd v Flower & Hart (No 2)* (2000) 103 FCR 559; upheld on appeal: *Flower & Hart v White Industries (Qld) Pty Ltd* (1999) 87 FCR 134. The quantum of the costs order was decided in *White Industries (Qld) Pty Ltd v Flower & Hart (No 2)* (2000) 103 FCR 559, 561.

62 As reported by HP Lee and Enid Campbell, *The Australia Judiciary* (Cambridge University Press, 2nd ed, 2013) 123; Margo Kingston, 'Callinan Casts a Long Shadow', *The Sydney Morning Herald* (Sydney, 14 August 1998) 19.

63 Lee and Campbell (n 62) 124.

64 Margo Kingston, 'Behind the Myth of Lawyers' Ethical Duty; Analysis', *The Sydney Morning Herald* (12 June 1999) 11.

65 Kingston, 'Callinan Casts a Long Shadow' (n 62) 19.

66 Ibid.

67 *Williams v Spautz* (1992) 174 CLR 509.

68 *White Industries (Qld) Pty Ltd v Flower & Hart* (1998) 156 ALR 169, 251.

the prohibition applies also to stronger cases if the only purpose in bringing the case is an ulterior one, whether or not the client also knew of and approved the ulterior purpose. However, proving an ulterior purpose is often difficult. *White Industries* (Case study 6.3) is an unusual case, because the lawyers' communications with their client and the reason for the action became available to the other side (because of the liquidation of the client's company). Usually, such communications are protected by legal privilege and so are only available to the lawyer and their client. Even if the other side suspects a breach of the duty to the court, they are unable to access communications between lawyer and client on the other side to prove their case. Thus, decisions tend to occur only in cases where the action plainly has no merit.[69]

The abuse of process rules sanction lawyers for assisting in a misuse of the legal system. But from both an *adversarial advocacy* and *moral activist* perspective, and in pursuit of courageous lawyering, it is quite proper for lawyers to use the legal system to help clients challenge perceived injustices, existing precedent or common conceptions of how the law should be interpreted or to test government decision-making, even if there is little chance of success. In Australia today, test cases run as class actions are important methods to facilitate access to justice through cheaper access to lawyers and are seen as a relatively efficient way to litigate many difficult claims simultaneously, and often to address mass public wrongs.[70]

So where do we draw the line as to when a case is too weak to be brought or is pursued for an ulterior purpose? The *White Industries* case is an example of litigation commenced for an ulterior purpose that should be regarded as unethical for all lawyers. However, where the case is very weak but pursuing a genuine legal interest, this will need to be judged on a case-by-case basis with proper client consultation. In our view, *proper* but weak cases, and ones that might seek a change to law or its current interpretation, cannot be said to 'waste' the court's and other parties' time and money, as the legal system is available precisely for that purpose.[71] The law should not be expanded to prohibit lawyers taking on cases with apparently little or no prospects of success (as the law stands now) where there is a genuine issue of justice or rights to be resolved. For example, lawyers bringing novel cases under new human rights instruments[72] are likely to be unsure of the courts' interpretations and thereby the likely result for their client. Yet these might be important cases to protect the fundamental rights of vulnerable citizens. Climate change litigation is another example of this, as discussed in Chapter 10. What if personal costs orders or misconduct charges were pursued against those who sought to argue that the longstanding doctrine of terra nullius should be overturned in the *Mabo* case so that First Nations Peoples' native title claims could be recognised in Australian law?[73] This may have deterred good lawyers from taking on the case.

69 See the discussion below concerning competency in litigation.

70 Australian Law Reform Commission, *Integrity, Fairness and Efficiency: An Inquiry into Class Action Proceedings and Third-Party Litigation Funders* (Report 134, 2018) 22.

71 This has been strongly argued by many commentators in relation to the NSW *Uniform Law* sch 2 cl 5(1), which requires lawyers to assess 'reasonable prospects of success': Pam Stewart and Maxine Evers, 'The Requirement that Lawyers Certify Reasonable Prospects of Success: Must 21st Century Lawyers Boldly Go Where No Lawyer Has Gone Before?' (2010) 13(1) *Legal Ethics* 1.

72 *Charter of Human Rights and Responsibilities Act 2006* (Vic); *Human Rights Act 2004* (ACT); *Human Rights Act 2019* (Qld).

73 *Mabo v Queensland (No 2)* (1992) 175 CLR 1. See also Peter H Russell, *Recognising Aboriginal Title: The Mabo Case and Indigenous Resistance to English-Settler Colonialism* (University of New South Wales Press, 2006).

In the contentious case of asylum seekers stranded on a boat called MV *Tampa* off the Australian coast in 2001, government lawyers sought wasted costs orders against lawyers working pro bono, including the Victorian Council for Civil Liberties, upon winning an appeal.[74] Indeed, here we can see a perverse application of adversarialism where an argument about efficiency of court process might be used as a tactic to chill litigation in the public interest.[75] Such arguments can become further time and money wasters for the court.

The conduct rules warn against trying to effectively remove an opponent by making tactical threats against another lawyer to put them off litigating.[76] The most well-known Australian example of a failure to observe these standards is *Clyne v New South Wales Bar Association,*[77] where the barrister 'in this opening address ... launched ... an unrestrained and vicious public attack on [the solicitor on the other side], making allegations of the most serious and damaging nature, which, so far as any evidence which he had went, could not possibly be substantiated, and inviting inferences which could not possibly be drawn from any material which he had'.[78] The objective was to intimidate the other solicitor into dropping the case and in the hope that the opposing client would then settle on favourable terms. Clyne, the barrister, was struck off for professional misconduct because of this behaviour in court. As in this case, the case law and conduct rules are concerned that lawyers not be involved in using court proceedings to harass or embarrass people either intentionally, recklessly (also grounds for a wasted costs order), negligently (by making serious allegations against other people without an evidential basis for those allegations) or where the allegations are not necessary to the advancement of the case (*ASCR* r 21.1).[79]

These rules are considered especially important given that advocates are privileged from liability for defamation for what they say in court. So the courts consider that lawyers need to take responsibility for the 'common decency and common fairness' of what is said.[80] In 2012, in the highly politicised case of *Ashby v Commonwealth*,[81] the plaintiff claimed he had been sexually harassed by the second defendant, who at that time was the Speaker of the Australian House of Representatives. Substantially irrelevant allegations were made in the pleadings that were later dropped, the apparent intention being to injure the reputation of the second defendant. Rares J found that the lawyer representing the plaintiff was aware 'how damaging the making of the ... allegations as a whole would be' and found that the

74 *Ruddock v Vardarlis (No 2)* (2001) 115 FCR 229.

75 These might also arguably constitute a breach of the model litigant policies imposed on government lawyers.

76 *ASCR* r 32 provides that a lawyer must not make 'unfounded allegations against another Australian legal practitioner of unsatisfactory professional conduct or professional misconduct unless the allegation is made bona fide and the solicitor believes on reasonable grounds that available material by which the allegation could be supported provides a proper basis for it'. Similarly, *ASCR* r 34, among other things, prohibits lawyers from the use of 'tactics that go beyond legitimate advocacy and which are primarily designed to embarrass or frustrate another person'.

77 (1960) 104 CLR 186.

78 Ibid 9.

79 See also *Medcalf v Mardell* [2003] 1 AC 120; *Guo v Minister for Immigration and Multicultural Affairs* [2000] FCA 146.

80 *Clyne v New South Wales Bar Association* (1960) 104 CLR 186, 200.

81 *Ashby v Commonwealth* [2012] FCA 640.

'attack, in the form it was made, was a misuse of [the lawyer's] privilege as a lawyer', citing the authority of the *Clyne* case (described above).[82]

Ulterior purposes and baseless allegations are two areas where lawyers do have a clear *responsible lawyering*, 'gate-keeping' type of obligation to ensure they check the truthfulness and purpose of the case, as provided in *ASCR* r 21. This rule is complex and lengthy.

ASCR r 21 Responsible use of court process and privilege[83]

21.1 A solicitor must take care to ensure that the solicitor's advice to invoke the coercive powers of a court:

- **21.1.1** is reasonably justified by the material then available to the solicitor;
- **21.1.2** is appropriate for the robust advancement of the client's case on its merits;
- **21.1.3** is not given principally in order to harass or embarrass a person; and
- **21.1.4** is not given principally in order to gain some collateral advantage for the client or the solicitor or a third party out of court.

21.2 A solicitor must take care to ensure that decisions by the solicitor to make allegations or suggestions under privilege against any person:

- **21.2.1** are reasonably justified by the material then available to the solicitor;
- **21.2.2** are appropriate for the robust advancement of the client's case on its merits; and
- **21.2.3** are not made principally in order to harass or embarrass a person.

21.3 A solicitor must not allege any matter of fact in:

- **21.3.1** any court document settled by the solicitor;
- **21.3.2** any submission during any hearing;
- **21.3.3** the course of an opening address; or
- **21.3.4** the course of a closing address or submission on the evidence, unless the solicitor believes on reasonable grounds that the factual material already available provides a proper basis to do so.

21.4 A solicitor must not allege any matter of fact amounting to criminality, fraud or other serious misconduct against any person unless the solicitor believes on reasonable grounds that:

- **21.4.1** available material by which the allegation could be supported provides a proper basis for it; and
- **21.4.2** the client wishes the allegation to be made, after having been advised of the seriousness of the allegation and of the possible consequences for the client and the case if it is not made out.

---

82 *Ashby v Commonwealth of Australia (No 4)* (2012) FCA 1411, [185], [191]. After a number of appeals, costs orders in this case were vacated.

83 A substantially similar provision is contained in the *Legal Profession Uniform Conduct (Barristers) Rules 2015*. The *ASCR* rule cited is the amended rule in force in New South Wales and Victoria. This amendment only makes minor rather than substantive changes to the *ASCR* applying around the country except for the changes to r 21.8 and new r 21.9.

21.5 A solicitor must not make a suggestion in cross-examination on credit unless the solicitor believes on reasonable grounds that acceptance of the suggestion would diminish the credibility of the evidence of the witness.

21.6 A solicitor may regard the opinion of an instructing solicitor that material which is available to the instructing solicitor is credible, being material which appears to the solicitor from its nature to support an allegation to which Rules 21.1, 21.2, 21.3 and 21.4 apply as a reasonable ground for holding the belief required by those Rules (except in the case of a closing address or submission on the evidence).

21.7 A solicitor who has instructions which justify submissions for the client in mitigation of the client's criminality which involve allegations of serious misconduct against any other person not able to answer the allegations in the case must seek to avoid disclosing the other person's identity directly or indirectly unless the solicitor believes on reasonable grounds that such disclosure is necessary for the proper conduct of the client's case.

21.8 Without limiting the generality of Rule 21.2, in proceedings in which an allegation of domestic or family violence, sexual assault, indecent assault or the commission of an act of indecency is made and in which the alleged victim gives evidence:

21.8.1 a solicitor must not ask that witness a question or pursue a line of questioning of that witness which is intended:

(i) to mislead or confuse the witness; or

(ii) to be unduly annoying, harassing, intimidating, offensive, oppressive, humiliating or repetitive; and

21.8.2 a solicitor must take into account any particular vulnerability of the witness in the manner and tone of the questions that the solicitor asks.

21.9 A solicitor does not infringe rule 21.8 merely because:

21.9.1 the question or questioning challenges the truthfulness of the witness or the consistency or accuracy of a statement made by the witness, or

21.9.2 the question or questioning requires the witness to give evidence that the witness could consider to be offensive, distasteful or private.

While the intention of the rule is for constraint in advocacy, an adversarial advocate could take a minimal approach to compliance with the rules that might avoid professional sanction. For instance, the rules do not give much express guidance as to what level of active inquiry lawyers should make about the truthfulness of what their client tells them, or what is required for a 'reasonable belief' as to the existence of the evidential basis for the allegations to be made. What if the lawyer purposely turns away from finding out? At what point should a lawyer be put on inquiry as to whether what the client is telling them is true?

The common law approach to 'recklessness' requires a subjective inquiry – whether the lawyer was indifferent to the truth of the statement.[84] Thus it depends on the level of knowledge of the lawyer when they 'turn away' from finding out the truth. In one case in

84 *Giudice v Legal Practitioners Complaints Committee* [2014] WACA 115.

the Supreme Court of Queensland, the defendant client had falsified documents and her solicitor had unknowingly presented these to the Court as true in a personal affidavit.[85] However, the solicitor was found to be reckless in failing to recognise the obvious falseness of the client's documents over some time and had wasted the Court's time. The Court found that the solicitor was under an obligation to the Court to take all necessary steps to correct the record as soon as possible, which may have included withdrawing the personal affidavit. He was under an obligation to seek permission from his client to correct the misleading statement and to cease acting, if he was not given this permission (as described above: *ASCR* r 20.1). The case was referred to the Legal Services Commissioner but was not prosecuted.

ASCR r 17.2.1 supports the independence of *responsible lawyering* by releasing solicitors from an obligation to obey their client when they decide to emphasise the 'real issues' only, or present a case in a concise manner, or actually inform the court of an authority that might persuade the court against their client. These freedoms are important since each of them helps a court to get to a prompt and arguably correct result. But, with the exception of alerting a court to contrary authority or decision, which must be disclosed (see *ASCR* r 19.6.1), there is no positive injunction to conduct the case having regard to these factors. The rule simply *permits* a solicitor advocate to take this approach in the face of client demands to do the opposite. Accordingly, the rule operates in a passive, defensive role (primarily for the benefit of the advocate). Compare this with a rule in the conduct rules for barristers that provides a positive duty to ensure they exercise proper forensic judgement.[86]

The *ASCR* include guidance on dealing with other lawyers that may be relevant to civil disputes. In the case of *Expense Reduction Analysts Group Pty Ltd v Armstrong Strategic Management and Marketing Pty Ltd*,[87] described earlier, the High Court referred to *ASCR* r 31, which prohibits the disclosure or use by a lawyer of confidential material inadvertently disclosed by the other side.[88] While acknowledging the rule's relevance to the facts before it, the Court was clearly of the opinion that such a rule should not be necessary – it codifies what should be standard professional behaviour. The *ASCR* contains other rules prohibiting specific behaviours that can be characterised as opportunistic trickery. Perhaps none of these rules would be required if a *responsible lawyering* approach was adopted. Consider Case study 6.4.

---

85 *Perpetual Trustee Co Ltd v Cowley* [2010] QSC 65.

86 *Legal Profession Uniform Conduct (Barristers) Rules 2015* r 58:

> A barrister must seek to ensure that work which the barrister is briefed to do in relation to a case is done so as to:
> (a) confine the case to identified issues which are genuinely in dispute,
> (b) have the case ready to be heard as soon as practicable,
> (c) present the identified issues in dispute clearly and succinctly,
> (d) limit evidence, including cross-examination, to that which is reasonably necessary to advance and protect the client's interests which are at stake in the case, and
> (e) occupy as short a time in court as is reasonably necessary to advance and protect the client's interests which are at stake in the case.

87 (2013) 250 CLR 303.

CASE STUDY 6.4 PURSUING CLAIMS THAT EXCEED LEGITIMATE RIGHTS

A solicitor acting for a video rental company (which allowed customers to borrow videos or DVDs from a store and then return them in a few days) is responsible for ensuring debts are recovered from customers who have not returned their videos on time. Each customer owes only a small amount (in the hundreds of dollars or less), but across the whole chain of stores many thousands of dollars are owing. Over a number of years, the solicitor develops a strategy of writing letters of demand to these customers, pointing out that not only is a certain sum of money owing, but that if the video store took action in court the customer would have to pay additional legal costs. The letter includes a notice similar in format to a court order. In reality, in small claims courts legal costs are generally only awarded in rare circumstances, the letters are merely letters of demand and no legal action has been commenced or decided.[89]

DISCUSSION QUESTIONS

1. What is wrong with the actions of the lawyer in this case?
2. *ASCR* r 34 prohibits a lawyer from communicating with another person in a way that 'grossly exceeds the legitimate assertion of the rights and entitlements' of their client. What do you think the threshold is for deciding whether such a communication is 'grossly' beyond the client's entitlements?

Although it is arguable that (solicitors') conduct rules and disciplinary decisions do not require active *responsible lawyering* obligations, the previous discussion of civil procedure legislation shows that courts are now using their own powers through practice directions, rules of court and interlocutory decisions on procedural matters to require that cases are brought with a proper purpose. Other regulators such as the Australian Competition and Consumer Commission might use powers to police lawyer behaviour where it breaches consumer protection provisions, as in Case study 6.5.[90] Yet, the adversarial imperative might produce strained interpretations of the law of lawyering, or a simple lack of interest in compliance. Thus, we emphasise the importance of lawyers' general willingness to reflect on who they are as moral agents, and what type of practitioner they ought to be, before they make tactical decisions in litigation. Strained interpretations of the conduct rules risk possible disciplinary action and/or sanction by the court, and can cause the harms described in the first section of the chapter.

88 This rule is described further in Chapter 4.
89 Based on *Legal Services Commissioner v Sampson* [2013] VCAT 1439.
90 *Australian Competition and Consumer Commission v Sampson* [2011] FCA 1165.

The need for a lawyer to be competent in civil dispute resolution

ASCR r 4 expects solicitors to act in the best interests of a client and deliver legal services competently, diligently and promptly. There is an implied expectation of competency in any retainer or costs agreement with a client.[91] However, for their work in court, or where that work has an 'intimate' or 'functional' connection to the judge's decision, lawyers are immune from civil suit because of the doctrine of advocates' immunity.[92] We believe this is another reason why it is important for lawyers to observe their commitment to *responsible lawyering* where the lawyer is the agent of promoting justice even where they might not have legal liability. As described above, failure to observe the conduct rules, or perhaps taking a narrow construction of them, can obstruct the proper administration of justice. Equally, a failure to care for the client, through inactivity, technical incompetence or lack of appreciation of their proper interests can endanger the client's legal entitlements as well as perpetrate other harms to the client and the system. However, there is not much guidance in the conduct rules about what is expected of lawyers as a matter of general competency, and the advocacy rules are focused on an appropriate balance between client interests and duties to the administration of justice.

Nevertheless, there might be an overlap of concerns where, for instance, a lack of competency causes a lawyer to assist a client to commence an action doomed to fail. In a recent disciplinary decision against a Western Australian lawyer, the State Administrative Tribunal was concerned about a lawyer commencing an unmeritorious action and seeking costs because 'to do so squanders valuable court time and resources and results in the practitioners' own client incurring unnecessary costs'.[93] The Tribunal specifically noted that legislation in the Australian Capital Territory and New South Wales 'provides that the provision of legal services without a reasonable prospect of success is capable of being unsatisfactory professional conduct or professional misconduct'.[94] While not the relevant standard in Western Australia, the Tribunal found that the lawyer's conduct fell short of a standard of competence and diligence that a member of the public is entitled to expect. Where a client wishes to pursue an action without merit, the lawyer can and should decline to do so.

The common law standard of competence expected of lawyers in delivering legal services generally is described briefly in Chapter 3 and in terms of duties of confidence in Chapter 4. Importantly, that standard is now guided by the conduct rules requiring that lawyers exercise independent judgement (*ASCR* r 17), with lawyers needing to 'avoid a compromise to their professional integrity and independence' (*ASCR* r 4.1.5). There are minimum expectations

91 *Groom v Crocker* [1939] 1 KB 194.

92 *Attwells v Jackson Lalic Lawyers Pty Ltd* (2016) 259 CLR 1. This doctrine, which is unique to Australia (and Scotland), provides that a lawyer cannot be sued for anything they do in this forensic context in order to stop collateral attacks on decided cases: *D'Orta-Ekenaike v Victoria Legal Aid* (2005) 223 CLR 1. Nevertheless, settlement advice that does not lead to a judgment will not be covered by the immunity.

93 *Legal Profession Complaints Committee and Metaxas* [2021] WASAT 82, [45].

94 Ibid. The provisions are *Civil Law (Wrongs) Act 2002* (ACT) s 188(3); *Legal Profession Uniform Law Application Act 2014* (NSW) sch 2 cl 4(1).

of technical competence and an attitude of care and attention to the client[95] that must be balanced against protection of the administration of justice (*ASCR* r 3). We also note that, as a matter of professional ethics and common law, a lawyer can make a mistake without attracting liability.

Consider the case presented in Case study 6.5 where arguably a mixture of lack of competence and inappropriate adversarialism was displayed.

CASE STUDY 6.5 A LAWYER OUT OF HIS DEPTH

A lawyer and his junior colleague and a barrister met with their client at the lawyer's firm. The client had a personal injury claim for psychological injury against Comcare that was due to be heard in the Administrative Appeals Tribunal ('AAT') the following day. The barrister advised that it was not a strong claim and that it would be best to try to settle the matter. The client did not like this advice and fired the barrister. Unable to hire new counsel, the lawyer wrote to the AAT for an urgent hearing to request an adjournment and informed a doctor due to give evidence that they were no longer needed. At the hearing that afternoon, the lawyer appeared by telephone and asked for an adjournment because they no longer had a barrister to appear in the case the following day. When asked by the AAT Member why the lawyer (a solicitor) could not represent the client, he said: 'My family and I need to take my daughter to a medical appointment and that's been scheduled. So I'm personally not available.' The AAT Member suggested that the matter could be heard at another time in the day to allow for this medical appointment, but the lawyer said he wasn't available all day. None of this was true. No adjournment was granted on the basis that another solicitor from the law firm could appear.

The lawyer then told the client that he wasn't available to appear at the hearing because of his daughter's (fictitious) medical appointment. He told the client that the junior solicitor was too inexperienced to appear. He said that if the client terminated the lawyer–client relationship and appeared as a self-represented litigant at the hearing, there would be more likelihood of getting an adjournment. He later described this as a 'strategic' approach. The adjournment was granted when the client appeared alone. The client faced the cost of hiring another lawyer and had to foot the bill for the doctor who was supposed to, but didn't, give evidence in the client's case the next day.

The client complained about the lawyer. When the lawyer's behaviour was prosecuted by the Law Society of the Australian Capital Territory, the lawyer initially lied about what he had said to the AAT. The ACT Civil and Administrative Tribunal (as a disciplinary tribunal) observed:

95 *Heydon v NRMA Ltd* (2000) 51 NSWLR 1; *Civil Liability Acts* around the country. The standard is judged by the peer professional opinion. As described in Chapter 3, legislative regulation of lawyers has also set expected minimum standards of competence by way of the disciplinary charges of professional misconduct and unsatisfactory professional conduct. These require a reasonable standard of competence and diligence, and the standard of competence and diligence is that which a member of the public, rather than a lawyer, is entitled to expect.

> The first lie was unplanned and only occurred when the practitioner was suddenly faced with the prospect of running a case himself that he was unprepared for and that he thought he was not up to. That was situational stress. The matters that occurred on that day and the next were a product of this first response. They are indicative of not dealing with the matter in a structured way.[96]

The disciplinary tribunal went on to say that subsequent dishonest behaviour displayed when a complaint was made by the client related to the lawyer's poor mental health and financial stress.[97]

DISCUSSION QUESTIONS

1. If you were the lawyer in the above case, what would you have done when the client dismissed the barrister the day before the first hearing?
2. Misleading a court or another dispute resolution body is considered to be a serious breach of professional ethics (see, for example, *ASCR* r 19). If we assume that the lawyer was well aware of this professional expectation (as well as a moral one not to lie), what do you think motivated him to act in the way he did?
3. In Chapter 9 we discuss, in the context of corporate legal work, how influential the culture of an organisation can be in shaping how you perform your work as a lawyer and how you relate to your clients, other practitioners and courts and tribunals. What message would this incident have sent to the junior lawyer in this case?

The intersecting responsibilities of appropriate care for the client and their case and assisting the due administration of justice can be observed in how lawyers are expected to adapt to new practices and challenges within their professional lives. For instance, the 'I'm not a cat' video that has circulated widely on the internet shows a lawyer accidentally appearing in a virtual proceeding in the 394th Judicial District Court (in Texas, United States) with a filter of a kitten and unable to remove it.[98] This video was posted by the presiding judge as an educational 'reminder' for lawyers working, since the COVID-19 pandemic, in the rapidly evolving environment of online court proceedings. An inability to navigate a virtual hearing can result in costs orders and delays in settling a client's matter. The principle-based duties in *ASCR* r 4, and general law described above, arguably require that lawyers have a minimum understanding of common technological developments in the legal community in order to be competent in their work.[99] However, others argue that there should be more prescriptive guidance

96 *Council of the Law Society of the Australian Capital Territory v Legal Practitioner 201920 (Occupational Discipline)* [2020] ACAT 31, 180.

97 As cited in the appeal in *Council of the Law Society of the Australian Capital Territory v LP 201920 (Appeal)* [2021] ACAT 16.

98 394th District Court of Texas, 'Kitten Zoom Filter Mishap' (YouTube, 10 February 2021) <https://www.youtube.com/watch?v=KxlPGPupdd8>.

99 Amy Salyzyn, 'Courtroom Technology Competence as a Lawyer's Ethical Duty: What Should Regulators Do About It?' in Karim Benyehklef et al (eds), *eAccess to Justice* (uOttawa Press, 2016) <https://ssrn.com/abstract=2697796>.

about the level of technological competence required, as in the commentary to the US *Model Rules of Professional Conduct*.[100]

When lawyers are required to appear for their clients virtually, there are a range of ways in which a lawyer might make a mistake about how to appropriately conduct themselves. For instance, courts and tribunals have recently begun to warn against lawyers appearing with a level of informality not observed in in-person appearances.[101] It might seem harmless to appear in a shirt and suit jacket, or a robe for a barrister, together with pyjama pants on when 'appearing' remotely. Yet this might signal a lack of care for the seriousness of the client's case or respect for the process. More concerning is where a lawyer conducts themselves in a way that might invite a perception of, or might contribute to, a lack of procedural fairness. *ASCR* r 18 prohibits a lawyer from dealing with a 'court on terms of informal personal familiarity which may reasonably give the appearance that the solicitor has special favour with the court'. The professional actors (judges and lawyers) in our civil system should be aware of how they are perceived by the parties and the public when they do their daily work. Not only might there be a risk of a legal argument of apprehended bias[102] but perceived bias can diminish trust in the system.

Similarly, the conduct rules reflect a concern about the proper administration of justice in requiring honesty and courteousness of a lawyer (*ASCR* r 4.1.2). This refers not only to expectations of formality but also avoidance of rude or bullying behaviours. Numerous reports have shown that junior and female lawyers experience such behaviour, or sexual harassment, in civil courts and tribunals at the hands of other lawyers and judicial officers.[103] Such behaviour is clearly a breach of anti-discrimination laws, the conduct rules,[104] and judicial ethics; it also creates an unacceptable workplace environment and endangers the proper administration of justice.

Competence also entails care for a client. Clients may find that the civil justice system is a scary and overwhelming environment. Clients might have no idea what a civil proceeding entails. Care for a client will require providing them with information so that they can make informed choices for themselves.

100 *Model Rules of Professional Conduct* (2004) r 1.1 (Competence), Comment 8 provides that lawyers are expected to keep up with 'the benefits and risks associated with relevant technology'.

101 See, eg, the detailed guide to online appearances provided by Federal Court of Australia, *National Practitioners/Litigants Guide to Online Hearings and Microsoft Teams* <https://www.fedcourt.gov.au/online-services/online-hearings/National-Practitioners-and-Litigants-Guide-V5.pdf>.

102 A majority of the Full Court of the Family Court held that regular contact between a barrister acting for a party in an ongoing case and the presiding judge, including exchange of text messages and coffee meetings, was not enough to justify a conclusion of apprehended bias: *Charisteas v Charisteas* [2020] FamCAFC 162. This was emphatically rejected by the High Court in *Charisteas v Charisteas* (2021) 393 ALR 389.

103 Kieran Pender, *Us Too? Bullying and Sexual Harassment in the Legal Profession* (IBA Legal Policy and Research Unit, Report, 2019) 87; Law Council of Australia, *Addressing Sexual Harassment in the Profession* (Discussion Paper, 2019).

104 *ASCR* r 42 (as amended in 2022). See Suzanne Le Mire and Rosemary Owens, 'A Propitious Moment? Workplace Bullying and Regulation of the Legal Profession' (2014) 37(3) *University of New South Wales Law Journal* 1030.

ASCR rr 7, 8 Communication of advice and client instructions

7.1 A solicitor must provide clear and timely advice to assist a client to understand relevant legal issues and to make informed choices about action to be taken during the course of a matter, consistent with the terms of the engagement.

8.1 A solicitor must follow a client's lawful, proper and competent instructions.

The conduct rules expect that lawyers will converse regularly with their client about a matter. Good lawyers help clients understand everything they can about the costs, benefits and risks of each legal course of action they might take.[105] Lawyers generally have a greater experience and knowledge of the wide-ranging costs and consequences of different legal strategies than their clients do. Nevertheless, there are no specific client-care rules that set out exactly what a lawyer needs to tell a client or what inquiries a lawyer should make about what a client knows. Lawyers may face clients who cannot provide good instructions.[106] Acting for aging clients – for example, drafting their will or a power of attorney – can be difficult if the lawyer must also assess the client's capacity for legal decision-making.[107] A lawyer might act as an advocate in hearings that assess whether compulsory treatment orders for mental illness should be made where their client is known to be lacking in capacity. In some situations a lawyer will need to be alert not only to the abilities of their client to express their legal wishes but also to any forms of abuse that may be occurring, such as where family members might be exerting unacceptable emotional or financial pressure on an older relative. There is an increasing array of guidance about how to assess a client's capacity (from asking basic general knowledge questions to seeking medical assessment)[108] and how to screen for other legal issues that may impact them. A minimum level of cultural competency when working with certain communities might be required. However, the law of lawyering does not provide any concrete requirements relating to assessment of client capacity to provide proper and lawful instructions. While the lawyer should not assume a client does not have capacity, and must seek to understand their instructions, there will be times when a lawyer must not act if the client cannot provide instructions. To do so would be to go beyond the lawyer's role as agent of the client and could be imposing the will of the lawyer on their client. However, to leave a vulnerable client in the middle of a case is a difficult decision.

Conversely, can a lawyer refuse to follow client instructions (that are lawful) when to do so might result in a bad outcome for the client – for example, discontinuing an action

105 See David A Binder, Paul Bergman and Susan Price, *Lawyers as Counselors: A Client-Centered Approach* (West Publishing Co, 2nd ed, 2004); Avrom Sherr, *Client Care for Lawyers: An Analysis and Guide* (Sweet & Maxwell, 2nd ed, 1999).

106 Lawyers are likely to be expected to assess capacity to the common law standard for other professionals as capacity to understand the nature of the transaction when it is explained: *Gibbons v Wright* (1954) 91 CLR 423.

107 Lisa Barry, '"He Was Wearing Street Clothes, Not Pyjamas": Common Mistakes in Lawyers' Assessment of Legal Capacity for Vulnerable Older Clients' (2018) 21(1) *Legal Ethics* 3.

108 For instance, the NSW Government provides a 'Capacity Toolkit' for assessing client capacity for a range of professionals: 'Capacity Toolkit', *NSW Government, Communities & Justice* (Web Page, 2022) <https://www.justice.nsw.gov.au/diversityservices/Pages/divserv/ds_capacity_tool/ds_capacity_tool.aspx>.

designed to provide safety for the client or to protect their legal entitlement to their family home?[109] On the basis of the conduct rules, the lawyer may have no choice but to follow these instructions if they are provided by a client who is competent (*ASCR* r 8). Where the client requests that the lawyer lie to the court, there is clear legal and moral guidance about how to respond (as set out above the lawyer must not mislead a court: *ASCR* r 19.1). However, in other cases a lawyer might be troubled by being professionally expected to simply follow instructions, thereby likely causing financial, physical or emotional harms to their client. A *responsible lawyering* approach might take a wide interpretation of the conduct rules so as to enable the lawyer to continue to help the client as long as they can. An *ethics of care* approach might involve a lawyer being more creative, such as by looking for extra-legal assistance, or by perhaps setting aside more time or deciding to continue to act without instructions.[110] But caution is needed because acting without instructions might work against the administration of justice or simply be treating the client paternalistically.

The preceding subsections examining the law of lawyering provide some guidance to lawyers in acting well for clients and the justice system, but the current regime leaves much to the judgement of the lawyer. Different ethical approaches can produce quite different answers in many of the cases described above. Lawyers need to understand their own values and character, as well as the rules, before they make ethical decisions in the contexts of specific cases. We believe that lawyers need to take ethical responsibility for *their own conduct on behalf of clients* in litigation and dispute resolution. We argue that as a matter of ethics and good practice, lawyers may also need to take a *moral activist* or *ethics of care* approach, to which we now turn.

Moral activism: what sort of conversations do lawyers need to have with their clients?

The previous paragraphs discussed the legal and moral importance of lawyers engaging in meaningful conversations with their clients so as to give them enough knowledge to decide how their case will proceed and whether litigation or alternative dispute resolution will be needed. This approach may also provide a client with a sense of agency or vindication as well as establishing lines of communication so there are no misunderstandings. The conversation might also take the form of *counselling* where the lawyer discusses the outcomes of the case with the client and possibly tries to persuade the client to take a different course.

A purely *adversarial advocacy* approach to the lawyer's role in litigation suggests that lawyers need not encourage clients to consider any ethical issues. It would be even worse, according to adversarial advocacy, for a lawyer to unilaterally decide to limit what they are willing to do for a client by reference to ethical considerations where the course of action is

109 Paul Tremblay provides an example of a client with declining mental fitness who provides instructions that the lawyer believes will diminish his legal rights: Paul Tremblay, 'On Persuasion and Paternalism: Lawyer Decision Making and the Questionably Competent Client' (1987) (3) *Utah Law Review* 515.

110 Margaret Castles, 'Mind the Gaps: Ethical Representation of Client with Questionable Mental Capacity' (2015) 18(1) *Legal Ethics* 24.

not clearly prohibited by law.[111] In grey areas, the adversarial advocacy approach sees it as up to the other side to complain, and for the courts to order the conduct to stop, if a lawyer is doing something wrong.

Adversarial advocacy can undermine the capacity of both the client and the lawyer to take moral responsibility for the way legal representation is carried out:

> Lawyers often justify their misdeeds as necessary to protect the interests of their client. Whether and when the adversary system or the protection of client rights can justify lawyers in committing lawful acts that would otherwise be unethical is a familiar subject of debate. If the justification holds, it transfers blame from the lawyer to the client. This presupposes the lawyer has actually placed the choice before the client. Too often, lawyers assume that clients would do anything lawful to prevail, while clients rely on their lawyers' judgment on the propriety of their tactics. The attorney-client relationship thus fosters mutual avoidance of responsibility, making it easier for lawyers to use professional rules unethically with a clear conscience.[112]

Neither lawyer nor client has inherent authority within *adversarial advocacy,* because the lawyer is only an agent of the client, and the client is permitted by the adversarial approach to hide behind the lawyer when necessary. Clients can easily allow their case to be handed to their lawyer while the lawyer can be equally comfortable with leaving moral choices about strategy to their clients. This can lead to a situation where choices are made that neither lawyer nor client would have chosen by themselves on their own account, or that are in no one's longer term interests.

Consider the example of how legal advice shaped the response of Catholic Church leaders to child sexual abuse, in Case study 6.6.

CASE STUDY 6.6 **PRIESTS AND LAWYERS**[113]

All over the world, inquiries have been undertaken into institutional child sexual abuse in churches, schools, residential homes and so on. A common theme has been concern that even when victims of abuse later complained about the abuse, their complaints were not adequately handled or were covered up and the abuse continued. Often it seems that the institution was protected at the expense of children. For example, priests the subject of complaint were moved from parish to parish and not reported to the police, while complainants were offered counselling and cash settlements in return for silence, making it more difficult for other victims to pursue justice.

In March 2014 the Australian Royal Commission into Institutional Responses to Child Sexual Abuse heard evidence about how lawyers for the Catholic Church may have assisted

111 We discuss this further in Chapter 2. Tim Dare has argued strongly against the lawyer imposing their own moral sensibilities on their clients: Tim Dare, 'Mere-Zeal, Hyper-Zeal and the Ethical Obligations of Lawyers' (2004) 7 *Legal Ethics* 24.

112 John Leubsdorf, 'Using Legal Ethics to Screw Your Enemies and Clients' (1998) 11 *Georgetown Journal of Legal Ethics* 831, 836–7.

and even encouraged the Church to take an unduly narrow and legalistic approach to child sexual abuse claimants.[114] The Royal Commission questioned both Cardinal Pell and two lawyers from the Church's law firm (Corrs) as to how the decision had been made to deny that abuse of John Ellis had occurred, even though the abuse had been confirmed by the Church's own internal report (the Eccleston Report). Rather than admit the abuse, the decision was made instead to cross-examine Ellis at some length about his claim of abuse. Commission Chair Justice McClellan put to both Cardinal Pell and the Corrs partner who managed the case that the decision was made to dispute the abuse for tactical reasons, despite the Church's earlier acceptance of the Eccleston Report's finding that the abuse had in fact occurred. Putting the abuse in issue meant that the Church could argue that the limitation period for Ellis' action should not be extended, because witnesses would have to be called to establish the facts. If the Church accepted the abuse, then there would be little reason not to extend the limitation period. Putting the abuse in issue also opened up the possibility for the Church to cross-examine Ellis (at great length) about the facts during the proceedings concerning the extension of the limitation period. After a finding in its favour in the substantive case, the Archdiocese pursued Ellis for payment of its costs (exceeding $500,000), causing him great emotional distress.

Vivien Holmes describes the litigious path taken by the Church and its lawyers as

> a merry-go-round of rationalisations. Pell was 'acting on legal advice' and protecting the church's assets. The lawyers were 'acting on client's instructions' and holding senior counsel responsible for how the case was prosecuted in court.[115]

Yet, as Holmes and Tony Foley point out, the decision to advise the Church that mediation was no longer a viable option and to vigorously litigate was not the only, or indeed the best, legal advice possible. Cardinal Pell's former lawyers, Monahan & Rowell, would have 'unhesitatingly and strongly recommended' that the Archdiocese engage in mediation. In the end there was recognition that significant negative publicity would result if Ellis went bankrupt or his psychiatric condition worsened. Indeed, in the end the Archdiocese dropped its claim for costs and made some ex gratia payments to Ellis, including for counselling.

Foley notes that the adversarial approach fitted with the interest in protecting the Church from liability, but it cut completely and totally against a pastoral morality that would have placed a higher value on victim wellbeing.[116] When asked if he believed that the Church had acted honestly and fairly in relation to the Ellis litigation, Cardinal Pell said that

113 This case study is based on the account given by Tony Foley, 'Institutional Responses to Child Sexual Abuse: How a Moral Conversation with Its Lawyers Might Contribute to Cultural Change in a Faith-Based Institution' (2015) 18(2) *Legal Ethics* 164.

114 For a more detailed summary, see Vivien Holmes, 'Compounding the Abuse: Lawyers for the Catholic Church in the Ellis Case' (2014) 17(3) *Legal Ethics* 433, 433–5 (references omitted).

115 Vivien Holmes, 'Pell Was Wrong to Blame the Lawyers, but They Aren't Blameless', *The Conversation* (online at 3 April 2014) <https://theconversation.com/pell-was-wrong-to-blame-the-lawyers-but-they-arent-blameless-25016>.

116 Foley (n 113) 176.

he now understood this distinction between legal ethics and 'Christian' or pastoral ethics: 'In a legal sense, we always acted honestly, and I believe in a legal sense there was nothing done that was improper, and that any reservations I might have about particular stands of our lawyers, I would not want to suggest that they did anything improper. But from my point of view, from a Christian point of view, leaving aside the legal dimension, I don't think we deal [sic] fairly [with Mr Ellis].'[117]

DISCUSSION QUESTIONS

1. In response to this case, Foley suggests that lawyers should 'explicitly open to scrutiny moral dimensions of the legal approaches they are proposing their clients pursue' and that they should 'advise clients that they may need to explore the morality of these approaches and take their counsel about how the approaches align with their avowed personal or institutional values'.[118] This approach assumes a broadly *moral activist* or *ethics of care* approach to lawyering.

   In what circumstances, if any, do you think lawyers should help clients consider the moral, ethical and relational dimensions of how to respond to legal problems? Does it make a difference what ethical stance the client has? Should lawyers take some ethical responsibility for the advice they give regardless of the values and ethical positions of their clients?
2. To what extent do you think organisational clients intentionally choose between different ethical stances by choosing their law firm?[119] What difference might this make to how you choose which law firm to work for?
3. The Royal Commission into Institutional Responses to Child Sexual Abuse recommended that both government and non-government institutions that receive or expect to receive civil claims for child sexual abuse, including the Catholic Church, should adopt responsibilities similar to those that the Commonwealth government has to act as a 'model litigant' in litigation.[120] What do you think about this recommendation and would it be enough in this situation? Model litigant approaches reflect a *responsible lawyering* type approach, but should a church be engaging in litigation against their members at all? Should they take an *ethics of care* approach? What would this require?

117 Cardinal George Pell, response to question at Royal Commission into Institutional Responses to Child Sexual Abuse, Public Hearing – Case Study 8 (Day 62), Sydney, 26 March 2014 (at 6494). Before the Chair: Justice Peter McClellan AM and Commissioner Prof Helen Milroy and Mr Andrew Murray <http://www.childabuseroyalcommission.gov.au/case-study/6c8c5e48-5c11-4902-a5e3-7f5988493fcf/case-study-8,-march-2014,-sydney>. See also Foley (n 113) 180.

118 Foley (n 113) 180.

119 See Christine E Parker, Robert Eli Rosen and Vibeke Lehmann Nielsen, 'The Two Faces of Lawyers: Professional Ethics and Business Compliance with Regulation' (2009) 22(1) *Georgetown Journal of Legal Ethics* 201.

120 Foley (n 113) 179–80. See the explanation of what a 'model litigant' is under 'Overarching obligations in civil litigation' above.

Lawyers should, by any account of lawyering, talk to their clients about their case, what the clients want from it and any associated risks and harms. Lawyers might also encourage some clients to seek other professional advice from counsellors, financiers and accountants, public relations consultants, family and friends on the likely impact and the wisdom of different courses of action. A good oncologist will advise a patient to think about and discuss with family and counsellor the consequences of chemotherapy or radical surgery, in responding to a cancer, in relation to their total wellbeing. They do not expect patients to treat this type of decision as a purely medical matter. Good lawyers should be no less holistic in the way they advise their clients. Since legal options are generally about how to resolve disputes with other people, there is likely to be an ethical dimension to a holistic consideration of different options for litigating or resolving a dispute.

It should always be part of the lawyer's role, as an officer of the court, to at a minimum inform the client of the minimum standard of appropriate adversarial behaviour – in terms of both honesty to the court and fair use of process – and to advise them of possible consequences of courses of action. A lawyer should also seek to establish with clients the ethical considerations that the clients themselves would see as important in resolving a dispute and engage in dialogue with the clients about the lawyer's view of the situation including ethical, legal and practical dimensions.[121]

An ethics of care for lawyers in negotiation and mediation?

Many lawyers have become disillusioned with traditional legal practice based on *adversarial advocacy* and the way it requires them to behave as aggressive warriors rather than problem-solvers for their clients. Many lawyers see the possibility of being involved in collaborative negotiation and alternative dispute resolution ('ADR') as a welcome opportunity to bring an *ethic of care* into their representation of clients.[122] They may be able to act in collaborative, problem-solving mode to help their clients prevent or resolve disputes. It may equally be that lawyers inevitably find themselves involved in ADR through the flourishing of mediation as mainstream dispute resolution adopted by Australian courts and tribunals. Many civil courts refer parties to mediation – prior to commencement of litigation as in most family law cases, or at some stage in the litigation. In many cases this might not be a choice or tactic of the parties or their lawyers.

On the other hand, it is sometimes suggested that tactics such as posturing, strategic misrepresentation, taking advantage of the other side's mistakes or ignorance, and even bullying and threats are just part of the 'rules of the game' for *negotiation*, as if negotiation

121 For a good case study and ethical analysis of this dynamic, see William H Simon, 'Lawyer Advice and Autonomy: Mrs Jones's Case' in Deborah L Rhode (ed), *Ethics in Practice: Lawyers' Roles, Responsibilities, and Regulation* (Oxford University Press, 2000) 165.

122 Note that in this chapter we only consider the role of lawyers as representatives in the ADR process, not as facilitators of ADR (for instance, as mediators). When lawyers become mediators then they take on a different role, and different standards will be applicable to that role.

has a different set of ethics to everyday life, or even to court. Some lawyers (and clients) use ADR processes, such as court-ordered mediation, as 'just another stop in the "litigotiation" game', another 'opportunity for the manipulation of rules, time, information and ultimately, money'.[123] ADR may be used as a delaying tactic[124] or to 'mask' and contain wider social and political conflicts.[125]

The law of lawyering as it currently stands assumes that lawyers owe exactly the same obligations of truthfulness and fairness in negotiations with other parties and in ADR processes as they owe in litigation. All the rules discussed in this chapter previously concerning misleading statements to 'the court', client perjury, the need for serious allegations to be based on evidence, and the need for competence apply equally to lawyer behaviour on behalf of clients in all ADR processes and negotiations. However, acting for a client in a civil dispute outside the formal confines of a court might obscure these duties in the lawyer's mind. Consider Case study 6.7 where the lawyer did not reveal a factual truth in a mediation.

CASE STUDY 6.7 **ETHICS IN MEDIATION**

A few days before the mandatory mediation in a motor vehicle accident case was due to occur, the plaintiff informed his barrister that he had been diagnosed with a serious cancer that was unrelated to the accident and likely to reduce his life expectancy. The plaintiff was claiming damages for serious personal injuries (quadriplegia) based in part on estimated life expectancy. An agreed report detailing assumptions about life expectancy, lost income and future care needs had already been prepared and was relied upon as correct by both parties. The cancer diagnosis would change the basis of these estimates and significantly reduce the amount the plaintiff would receive. At first, the barrister advised that in his preliminary view the cancer should be disclosed to the insurer on the other side. The client plaintiff instructed that he did not want to reveal his cancer unless legally obligated to do so, and that he wanted the mediation to proceed as scheduled.

The barrister went away, did some research and consulted a senior practitioner, and decided that the cancer did not have to be proactively revealed to the other side as long as the plaintiff and his lawyer made no inconsistent positive assertions during the mediation. The relevant insurance legislation provided that such matter would have to be disclosed to the insurer within a couple of weeks – but not at the time of the mediation. The lawyer and this client hoped that the mediation could simply proceed on the basis of the agreed report. They knew that the insurer was relying on its truthfulness.[126]

123 Carrie Menkel-Meadow quoted in Tania Sourdin, *Alternative Dispute Resolution* (Lawbook Co, 2nd ed, 2005) 235.

124 Grant Dearlove, 'Court-Ordered ADR: Sanctions for the Recalcitrant Lawyer and Party' (2000) 11(1) *Australian Dispute Resolution Journal* 12, 16.

125 Tania Sourdin, *Alternative Dispute Resolution* (Thomson Reuters, 6th ed, 2020).

126 Based on *Legal Services Commissioner v Mullins* [2006] LPT 012.

DISCUSSION QUESTIONS

1. Is this a case where proactive honesty was required of the lawyer and his client?
2. During the disciplinary hearing, the lawyer argued that he considered such a dispute resolution context as an 'honesty free zone'. The disciplinary tribunal disagreed (see below). Why do you think his assertion is incorrect as a matter of professional ethics?
3. In this case the client and his lawyer had been involved in long-term discussions with the insurer to secure a payout to provide needed funds for medical care and loss of wages for an emphatic injury (quadriplegia). The diagnosis of an existing cancer shortly before the mediation was a stroke of terrible fate. Given this context, including how much this payout meant to the welfare of the client, would you, as the lawyer, consider simply staying quiet?
4. Do you think that proceedings occurring privately (not in open court or presided over by a judge) raise different responsibilities for the lawyers? Do lawyers need to be fairer in their approach?

In the above case the disciplinary tribunal found that the lawyer knowingly misled the other side. The *ASCR* include a rule specifically prohibiting solicitors from 'knowingly' making 'a false or misleading statement to the opponent in relation to the case (including its compromise)' and requiring solicitors to correct any false or misleading statements made as soon as possible (*ASCR* rr 22.1 and 22.2). As with the rules relating to misleading statements in court, however, *ASCR* r 22 (making a false or misleading statement to the opponent) explicitly provides that it is not making a false or misleading statement 'simply by failing to correct an error on any matter stated to the solicitor by the opponent' (*ASCR* r 22.3). Yet if the solicitor and their client rely on, or in any way put forward as the truth, any false or misleading statement (including a statement that has become untrue) then they have breached *ASCR* r 22.

Furthermore, misleading and deceptive conduct and bullying behaviour in negotiating contracts will generally be contrary to federal and State legislation as well as general principles of contract and tort law. If lawyers knowingly participate in such misbehaviour on the part of their clients, they (as well as their clients) may be liable under general principles of law.[127] However, as already described, current conduct rules only minimally limit untruthfulness and unfairness, and lawyers are free to act as adversary advocates even in ADR. Yet, where ongoing relationships between the parties are at stake, it is likely that zealous approaches based only on rights will miss the mark completely. As Tania Sourdin comments, 'a rights-based [approach] is increasingly clumsy in managing conflict that involves continuing relationships or interests that lie outside a clearly articulated rights-based framework'.[128] Should lawyers steeped in traditional adversarial ways of practice be involved with ADR at all?

Many practitioners and theorists argue (and we agree) that the purpose of negotiating a settlement to a dispute is to avoid the adversarialism of a trial in which each side defends

127 Warren Pengilley, '"But You Can't Do That Anymore!" – The Effect of Section 52 on Common Negotiating Techniques' (1993) 1(1) *Trade Practices Law Journal* 113, 118–19.

128 Tania Sourdin, *Alternative Dispute Resolution* (Thomson Reuters, 4th ed, 2012) ix.

a position, and one side's position must win. The advantage of negotiating or mediating is that parties can come to a voluntary, mutually agreed resolution rather than handing their dispute over to a court that will generally make one party the winner in terms of a financial award; both parties might be losers when it comes to time, cost and stress.[129]

Many ADR processes, including mediation, are aimed at facilitating this vision of principled, collaborative or problem-solving negotiation. The mediator, negotiator or collaborative lawyer is supposed to help the parties identify their interests, see the problem from the other side's point of view and work together to identify options and creative solutions. The policy statements and contracts governing many ADR processes usually explicitly state that it is expected that the parties and their lawyers will enter into the process in a 'good faith' effort to work together to identify interests and options and resolve their dispute.[130] Even court rules and court decisions requiring court mediation as part of the pre-litigation process recognise that the object of mediation is that the parties should 'communicate effectively with each other about the dispute' in an 'endeavour to resolve their differences'.[131] Or in the memorable words of Gray J to the litigants in one case, 'you can go and make love before you make war'.[132]

We might therefore expect that where parties and their lawyers are utilising negotiation, collaboration or ADR to resolve their dispute, relationships will be more open and collaborative than in litigation. The lawyer ought to consult with the client about their interests and capabilities. Collaborative lawyering or practice – a 'process involving confidential and transparent negotiations that take an interest-based, team approach, as opposed to one that is rights-based or adversarial'[133] – is an increasingly prevalent approach in family law and other areas of civil dispute resolution. This is arguably the furthest from an adversarial approach and poses difficulties in complying with conduct rules that assume strict client confidentiality and (at least some) partisanship. Nevertheless, there is evidence that this approach, particularly where it has evolved to be 'interdisciplinary collaborative practice' that involves working with a team of experts, is highly effective to preserve relationships and achieve satisfactory outcomes.[134]

The ethical standards that apply to lawyer conduct in this context ought to reflect these approaches. *Ethics of care* type values, such as interests-based approaches, fair dealing and open disclosure, are likely to be more appropriate than the conventional combination of *adversarial advocacy* and *responsible lawyering* reflected in the professional conduct standards.[135] Carrie Menkel-Meadow suggests that any ethical rules applying to lawyers'

129 See, eg, Roger Fisher, William Ury and Bruce Patton, *Getting to Yes: Negotiating Agreement Without Giving In* (Penguin Books, 2nd ed, 1991); Carrie Menkel-Meadow, 'Whose Dispute Is It Anyway? A Philosophical and Democratic Defense of Settlement (in Some Cases)' (1995) 83(7) *Georgetown Law Journal* 2663.

130 Bobette Wolski, 'The Truth About Honesty and Candour in Mediation: What the Tribunal Left Unsaid in Mullins' Case' (2012) 36(2) *Melbourne University Law Review* 706, 724–7.

131 *Australian Competition and Consumer Commission v Lux Pty Ltd* [2001] FCA 600, [26], [28].

132 Ibid [28].

133 Caroline Counsel, 'What Is This Thing Called Collaborative Law?' (2010) (85) *Family Matters* 77.

134 Rosemary Hunter, Anne Barlow, Janet Smithson and Jan Ewing, 'Law, Discretion, Gender and Justice in Out-of-Court Financial Settlements' (2018) 32(1–2) *Australian Journal of Family Law* 189.

135 Carrie Menkel-Meadow, 'The Limits of Adversarial Ethics' in Deborah L Rhode (ed), *Ethics in Practice: Lawyers' Roles, Responsibilities, and Regulation* (Oxford University Press, 2002) 123; Michelle Wills, 'The Use of Deception in Negotiations: Is It "Strategic Misrepresentation" or Is It a Lie?' (2000) 11(4) *Australian Dispute Resolution Journal* 220.

conduct in ADR (as representatives or facilitators) should reflect five generally accepted underlying goals or principles of ADR, as presented below. These are different to and complementary to adversarial litigation.

1. 'Party consent' – 'outcomes should not be coerced' and 'parties should be given a fair chance to make their own choices';
2. 'Democratic participation (of clients vis-à-vis lawyers and multiple parties when disputes involve more than two dyadic players)' – parties should be given a fair opportunity to participate in their own dispute resolution, and third parties should be neutral and show no partisanship;
3. 'Responsive and particularized solutions to legal disputes and transactions, which do no worse harm to the parties (or other parties) than non-resolution of the dispute';
4. 'An orientation to joint, not individualized, problem-solving'; and
5. '"Problem-solving," rather than "adversarial" orientation to legal disputes and transactions'.[136]

These principles reflect the ideal of ADR as an equitable process where people communicate freely, understand each other, settle differences and perhaps even change their behaviour rather than have a judgment (usually financial damages) imposed on them in the alien, adversarial setting of the court.[137]

But ADR has some limits. In collaborative practice, lawyers must be careful not to impose pressure on their clients to settle. This is particularly a concern because parties will normally agree that, where a settlement is not reached, their lawyers are precluded from representing them in subsequent litigation.[138] Lawyers need to trust each other in the 'collaborative' process, but, as we have described throughout the chapter, a culture of adversarialism might be hard to shake, making such trust available only where both have lawyers truly committed to the practice. Critics also argue that ADR approaches are prone to perpetuation of the domination and oppression of everyday life, as they are designed to empower disputants to participate in resolving their own problems. Inappropriate mediation in family law, particularly where there is domestic violence, can return disputes to families already imbued with imbalances of power, give unaccountable power to mediation professionals, and detour victims (usually women and children) away from enforceable decisions of courts.[139] Consumer complaint schemes in a bank or phone company can send pacified customers away unaware that their problem confronts thousands of others who may or may not complain, and leave exploitative company policies untouched. Internal dispute resolution in a workplace can change issues of institutional bias and discrimination into individual management problems for particular work areas to deal with.[140]

136 Carrie Menkel-Meadow, 'Ethics in Alternative Dispute Resolution: New Issues, No Answers from the Adversary Conception of Lawyers' Responsibilities' (1997) 38(2) *South Texas Law Review* 407, 453.

137 Parker (n 4), 36–8, 60–1; Genn (n 6) 225 (on the anxiety and stress people feel on 'entering the alien world of the court').

138 Ralph Peeples and John Sarratt, 'Sinn Fein Amhain: Taking Collaborative Law Beyond Divorce' (2017) 52(2) *Wake Forest Law Review* 139.

139 Rachael Field, 'Using the Feminist Critique of Mediation to Explore "The Good, The Bad and The Ugly" Implications for Women of the Introduction of Mandatory Family Dispute Resolution in Australia' (2006) 20(1) *Australian Journal of Family Law* 45.

140 Parker (n 4) 61–3.

We have seen from the above discussion that collaborative practice and mediation require lawyers representing parties to be centrally concerned with doing what they can to ensure that *processes* of negotiation are open, honest, fair and cooperative. Should lawyers and ADR facilitators also be concerned about whether the *outcomes* decided in ADR processes are fair as between the parties, and whether the interests of third parties and the public interest are appropriately protected? Where settlements are negotiated between the parties and their lawyers without third-party assistance, the lawyers will often be 'god' in deciding what an appropriate settlement is. As one of the specialist plaintiff's solicitors in Hazel Genn's research said:

> The fact is, when you settle a case, who can argue? The client's happy. I mean, most clients will settle for tuppence. You know, you tell them that that's all they're going to get – they'll settle ... So all you've got is you and your conscience to actually play with and it depends where your conscience leads you.[141]

The standard *adversarial advocacy* conception of lawyers' ethics and professional conduct obligations says that lawyers have a responsibility to make sure their own clients get the best deal they can in negotiations. But how do they balance the desire to get justice for their client against the need to compromise in order to get anything at all? The client will generally rely on the lawyer to advise them as to whether to accept a deal that gives them less money than they think they deserve (that is, less than their idea of justice) or whether to risk getting nothing at all, except a huge bill for legal costs, if they go to court. A lawyer might also have considerable discretion as to how hard to press the other side in negotiations for a public apology or admission of liability, as opposed to a confidential settlement. A good lawyer should not simply advise their client to agree to anything that gets the matter resolved cooperatively; but nor should they refuse any deal that does not conform exactly with what they believe the courts would, or should, give their client. Lawyers will often need to take responsibility for developing their own ethical opinion about what is a 'good' deal for their clients – taking into account their duty to represent their client's needs and desires, the other side's interests, and legal principle.

Legal professional practice inspired by an *ethics of care* can be criticised because it is not primarily aimed at protecting people's rights (unlike *adversarial advocacy*) or advancing legal or social justice (unlike *responsible lawyering* and *moral activism*, respectively). Even the strongest advocates of the use of *ethics of care* values and ADR by legal practitioners emphasise that ADR and cooperative negotiation can only work fairly where people still have realistic access to courts and lawyers to vindicate their rights if necessary, and law and lawyers are vigilant in promoting justice more broadly.[142] In the end, in our view it is likely that those lawyers who seek to develop a close understanding of *who* they are and what they want to achieve in their practice will be best placed to balance these complementary ethical values.

141 Hazel Genn, *Hard Bargaining: Out of Court Settlement in Personal Injury Actions* (Clarendon Press, 1987) 129.

142 Menkel-Meadow, 'Whose Dispute Is It Anyway?' (n 129); Parker (n 4).

Conclusion

Lawyers should thoroughly assess with their clients what dispute resolution option is likely to best suit their needs and circumstances. An astute lawyer knows that a focus on cost-effective outcomes is the only way to keep clients over the long term. Equally, a lawyer who is failing to meet basic standards of competence is unlikely to retain clients.

Lawyers should also help clients to prevent disputes arising in the first place. ADR processes could be established at the beginning of major projects even before any disputes have arisen, including mediation or arbitration clauses in contracts. For organisational clients, this could involve setting up internal dispute-resolution schemes and joining external complaints resolution and ombudsman schemes. The lawyer might equally assist individuals to make appropriate decisions for themselves that might predict and plan to avoid future interactions with the law. This might involve assisting the client to access services beyond what the lawyer can provide.

Once a client's matter does proceed to litigation, negotiation or ADR, the appropriate ethics for the process should relate to the purpose of the process. Litigation in court must be conducted honestly and fairly, as well as competently, in line with *responsible lawyering* obligations. The law of lawyering reflects this, but lawyers also need to work out for themselves the parameters of their obligations to the court and administration of justice on the one hand and their client on the other. Even in litigation, lawyers should engage their clients in conversation about what they want from the case, their underlying ethics and the consequences of taking action.

Where lawyers are involved in ADR and collaborative deal-making or problem-solving, the lawyer's role is rarely to aggressively represent the client's position. It is to assist the client in working with the other side to attempt to solve their problem through open interest-based negotiation. Where parties are represented, it is a very important part of a lawyer's role to explain to their clients how the ADR process will work and what their obligations are in that process, and to prime them to participate effectively. Again, ethical and practical conversation will be necessary here.

Lawyers need to remember that they are repeat players in the system. Their efficacy for their clients rests to a large extent on their reputation within the profession with which they must deal (see also *ASCR* r 5), either in appearing in court before a judge or negotiating with another practitioner. Acting in a way that exploits every advantage, or fails to provide competent representation for a client will impede their ability to act effectively for their clients and do justice in the future.

RECOMMENDED FURTHER READING

Camille Cameron, 'Hired Guns and Smoking Guns: McCabe v British American Tobacco Australia Ltd' (2002) 25(3) *University of New South Wales Law Journal* 768

Margaret Castles, 'Mind the Gaps: Ethical Representation of Clients with Questionable Mental Capacity' (2015) 18(1) *Legal Ethics* 24

Tony Foley, 'Institutional Responses to Child Sexual Abuse: How a Moral Conversation with Its Lawyers Might Contribute to Cultural Change in a Faith-Based Institution' (2015) 18(2) *Legal Ethics* 164

Michael King, Arie Freiberg, Becky Batagol and Ross Hyams, *Non-Adversarial Justice* (Federation Press, 2nd ed, 2014)

Carrie Menkel-Meadow, 'The Limits of Adversarial Ethics' in Deborah L Rhode (ed), *Ethics in Practice: Lawyers' Roles, Responsibilities, and Regulation* (Oxford University Press, 2000) 123

Lola Akin Ojelabi and Mary Anne Noone (eds), *Ethics in Alternative Dispute Resolution* (Federation Press, 2017); also published as *Law in Context Special Issue* 35(1)

Bobette Wolski, 'The Truth About Honesty and Candour in Mediation: What the Tribunal Left Unsaid in Mullins' Case' (2012) 36(2) *Melbourne University Law Review* 706

7

CONFLICTING LOYALTIES

Introduction

As discussed in previous chapters, the touchstones of lawyers' professional obligations to their clients are confidentiality and care. These duties can be understood as key elements in a relationship of trust and loyalty between client and lawyer. This chapter is chiefly concerned with this relationship of loyalty, and how it can be strained by, or overlooked because of, conflicting or competing interests and duties.

The relationship of loyalty requires lawyers to avoid situations involving a *conflict of interest* between a lawyer's personal interest and their duty to a client.[1] This means that, in addition to avoiding a situation where the lawyer's interest may compete with or harm a client interest, a lawyer must refrain from using their relationship as a means of making any personal gain except the receipt of reasonable fees.[2] This strict conception of lawyer loyalty is reflected in the common law concept of a fiduciary and, to a certain extent, in the ethical rules described in this chapter.

A relationship of loyalty exists for each client. Lawyers and law firms rarely just have one client and so there can be competing client duties that give rise to conflicts of interest. The law and ethical rules require that lawyers observe their duties to every client equally and do not prefer one over the other. This relationship of loyalty to a current client may also be tested where it conflicts or competes with a lawyer's duties of confidentiality to a former client. There will be a conflict of interest if confidential information is known or held for the former client, and it is relevant or material to a current client's legal matter. Loyalty to the current client[3] usually obliges the lawyer to reveal information relevant to the client's case, but where this information is confidential to a former client, it may be impermissible to tell the current client. This gives rise to an inherent conflict for the lawyer.

These situations apply not just to the individual lawyer but to the whole firm. For instance, if a lawyer cannot act for a potential client because of a conflict of interest, then usually the whole firm cannot act. The onus is on the lawyer or the firm to proactively avoid conflicts of interest as opposed to waiting until they arise and then acting. Equally, lawyers must fully disclose to their clients any potential conflicts of interest. As we discuss below, while the common law and ethical conduct rules contemplate that client knowledge and consent might negate any harm arising from competing interests and duties in some situations, some conflicts go to the heart of the relationship of loyalty and must simply be avoided.

A lawyer's obligation of loyalty is a 'fiduciary' obligation, which is enforceable in the law of equity. The notions of loyalty and care are also implied in a lawyer–client contract and are imposed as professional ethical standards in ethical conduct rules. The duty of

1 While courts have spoken about a duty of loyalty, generally the fiduciary is conceived of as a relationship of trust and care. It has been described as proscriptive in nature. In *Breen v Williams* (1996) 186 CLR 71 Gaudron and McHugh JJ stated: 'the law of this country does not … impose positive legal duties on the fiduciary to act in the interests of the person to whom the duty is owed' (at 113). The fiduciary is therefore prohibited from being disloyal.

2 The conduct codes also contemplate that solicitors may ethically earn other financial gains that are not payment for professional services, such as commission fees: *ASCR* r 12. This is discussed further in the text below.

3 As described below, Victorian courts have also held that there is an enduring duty of loyalty to former clients in certain contexts.

confidentiality and the evidential rule of client legal privilege have a related justification of protecting the relationship of trust and confidence between lawyer and client.[4] Thus, a breach of loyalty could result in a lawyer being sued by a client for breach of equitable or common law obligations, being enjoined from acting for a client and being disciplined for misconduct.

Observing a relationship of loyalty is consonant with both *adversarial advocacy* and *responsible lawyering*. *Adversarial advocacy* assumes that clients need to be able to trust their lawyers to provide advice and represent them in the legal system completely uninfluenced by any concern other than the client's interests. A narrow adversarial advocacy conception of loyalty would see the client's interest as the touchstone of the duty. As long as the client's interests are not actually harmed, then it might be possible to 'cure' a potential conflict through measures such as client consent or information barriers (discussed further below). On an adversarial advocacy approach, the relationship of loyalty would not survive the ending of the lawyer–client relationship as the lawyer is no longer obligated to further the client's interests. As we describe in the first part of this chapter, the *Australian Solicitors' Conduct Rules* ('*ASCR*') and *Barristers' Conduct Rules* arguably align with an adversarial advocacy approach as they contemplate that any sort of conflict of interest can be cured by client consent or other administrative means that seek to prevent actual client harm.

A *responsible lawyering* approach might conceive of the lawyer's loyalty differently. While still interested in advancing the client's interest, the relationship is understood as shaped by the lawyer's role as officer of the court. In this conception, any appearance of bias or disloyalty is considered important as a matter of procedural fairness – for determining whether justice is done and seen to be done. On this account, acting against the client might be concerning, even if the client consents to the conflict and there is no evidence that their interest has in fact been harmed. Here, the lawyer's role as officer of the court requires a broader obligation to justice than merely serving this client in this case according to what this client will consent to. The equitable remedy of an injunction can be understood to embody this idea: a court may prevent a lawyer from acting in a matter in order to protect, or prevent negative perceptions of, the administration of justice.

The final section of this chapter traces how the different conceptions of the lawyer's role might produce diverse legal principles, such as whether loyalty is or is not imposed beyond the end of the legal relationship. As a matter of professional ethics, there are differing views about whether to allow certain conflicts to arise and be managed by the lawyer or law firm, and whether such management of conflicts should be done with or without client consent. We argue that the *ASCR* and *Barristers' Conduct Rules* do not necessarily reflect an adequate and clear approach to assessing and dealing with conflicting interests and loyalties.

While client loyalty is essential, lawyers also need to be sensitive to the fact that zeal on behalf of clients cannot be the only ethical goal. It must be tempered by considerations of the proper administration of justice, and even other personal and moral considerations. However, lawyers must balance their personal interests carefully so as not to prefer,

4 There are strong policy arguments for confidentiality as engendering a relationship of trust and confidence between lawyer and client in order that the client 'make full and frank disclosure of the relevant circumstances' to their lawyer: *Grant v Downs* (1976) 135 CLR 674; *Glencore International AG v Commissioner of Taxation (Cth)* (2019) 265 CLR 646, [27].

consciously or unconsciously, their own interests above either the client's interests or their duties to the proper administration of justice. This chapter traces many of the frequent variations of these conflicting interests and duties. Given the balancing of duties required in legal practice, lawyers will inevitably face conflicts between legitimate loyalties. The ethically significant thing is how each lawyer responds to these conflicts when they occur, or whether they even notice them. As Davies AJA observed in *Alexander v Perpetual Trustees WA Ltd*, a conflict of interest is an 'insidious thing' that can cast well-known duties in a 'hazy light'.[5] Being clear about how they arise and the dangers they pose is essential.

What do we mean by a relationship of loyalty?

In this principal section of the chapter we critically analyse the principles of professional conduct set out in the *ASCR* that relate to conflicts between solicitors' own interests and their duty to their clients, conflicts between the duties owed to two or more current clients, and the situation where a solicitor proposes to act against a former client for a new client or where a former client's confidential information might be material to a current client. The *Barristers' Conduct Rules* largely mirror the *ASCR* except where barristers' limited practice does not require a rule[6] or there is another difference indicated later in the text. As we shall see, for both branches of the profession, some of the obligations are not set out as clearly as we might expect. There are grounds to criticise the ethical rules for a tendency to strengthen lawyers' capacity to generate additional fees, or prefer self-interest, by defining unacceptable conflicts in the narrowest possible terms.[7]

However, there are significant dangers for a lawyer or law firm applying a narrow or technical construction. In injunction proceedings to restrain lawyers or firms from acting, the courts arguably apply a test more rigorous than the *ASCR* concerning competing client duties and firms might find themselves without a client.[8] We also consider the scope of a court's power to restrain lawyers from acting when there are clashes of personal or client interests that might cast doubt on the proper administration of justice. Here, lawyers' higher loyalty to the functioning of the justice system is enforced.

5 [2001] NSWCA 240, [125] (Stein JA, Davies and Ipp AJJA).

6 As described in Chapter 3, barristers fulfil a more limited role, being mostly confined to advocacy and advice work. Therefore, certain conflicts that might arise for solicitors in their wider field of work simply do not arise for barristers.

7 There is less scope for barristers as solo practitioners to manage a conflict through the implementation of information barriers. However, as described in Case study 7.4, a barrister might still define what constitutes a conflict very narrowly with the apparent aim of taking on a related client.

8 See, eg, the decision of the Federal Court in *Dyer v Chrysanthou (No 2) (Injunction)* [2021] FCA 641 (affirmed on appeal). A court may grant an injunction for misuse of a client's confidential information, breach of a lawyer's fiduciary duty of loyalty and the inherent jurisdiction of the court over its officers: *Kallinicos v Hunt* (2005) 64 NSWLR 561. See Sandro Goubran, 'Conflicts of Duty: The Perennial Lawyers' Tale – A Comparative Study of the Law in England and Australia' (2006) 30(1) *Melbourne University Law Review* 88.

Lawyer–client conflict

ASCR r 12 concerns situations where the lawyer's interest might clash with their client's interest or with the lawyer's obligation of loyalty to the client.[9] At the outset the rule insists that where this occurs solicitors 'must not act'. The *ASCR* go on to provide specific examples of types of interest–duty conflicts that must be avoided or properly managed. The first concerns exerting pressure on a client to agree to pay unreasonable fees or provide other benefits to the solicitor.

ASCR r 12 Conflict concerning a solicitor's own interests

12.2 A solicitor must not do anything –

(i) calculated to dispose a client or a third party to confer on the solicitor, either directly or indirectly, any benefit in excess of the solicitor's fair and reasonable remuneration for legal services provided to the client, or

(ii) that the solicitor knows, or ought to reasonably anticipate, is likely to induce a client or third party to confer such a benefit and is not reasonably incidental to the performance of the retainer.

ASCR r 12.2 implicitly recognises that a lawyer's interests are in conflict with their client's interests 'the minute they begin work for a client, since their interest in making a larger income conflicts with the client's interest in paying as little as possible for solving his or her legal [problems]'.[10] As discussed in Chapter 8, lawyers have a duty to only charge 'fair and reasonably' for their professional services. *ASCR* r 12.2 (as amended in 2022) provides more detailed guidance about behaviour that must be avoided because it might induce or dispose a client into paying more. However, there may be a range of reasons why a lawyer may fail to appreciate this obligation where their self-interest seems more pressing. For instance, lawyers employed by law firms may intentionally or unintentionally elevate the interests of their employer in making profits above their ethical and fiduciary duties to their client.

The courts have sanctioned lawyers where they seek to receive a higher fee from the client than is 'fair and reasonable' or exert undue pressure to increase their remuneration. In *Council of the Queensland Law Society Inc v Roche*,[11] for example, a practitioner negotiated a substantial increase in fees with an existing 'no-win, no-fee' client in a personal injuries matter. The client was in financial difficulties, did not fully understand how charges were being incurred under the original fee agreement and was anxious for the legal practitioner to take on a second case on his behalf. The Court found the practitioner guilty of professional

9 For barristers, see, eg, *Legal Profession Conduct (Barristers) Rules 2015* r 101(b): 'A barrister must refuse to accept or retain a brief or instructions to appear before a court if the client's interest in the matter or otherwise is or would be in conflict with the barrister's own interest or the interest of an associate'.

10 Larry May, *The Socially Responsive Self: Social Theory and Professional Ethics* (University of Chicago Press, 1996) 126.

11 [2004] 2 Qd R 574.

misconduct for 'preferring his own interest to that of his client'.[12] He had breached his fiduciary obligations to the client by failing to fully inform the client of the way the client's rights under the fee agreement and the fees payable would change. He should also have advised the client to obtain independent legal advice before signing the new agreement, even though the client gave evidence that he would not have sought out that independent advice.[13] (See Chapter 8 for further discussion of the case and lawyers' fees and billing arrangements.)

The common law assumes that the lawyer is in a position of power and influence over the client.[14] Thus, there are many lawyer–client conflicts where an uncompromising stand is resolutely (and properly) applied as a matter of law and the ethical rules follow this approach. The courts and legal profession regulators consistently denounce and sanction obvious, direct conflicts of interest such as financial or property dealings between lawyers and clients,[15] including borrowing[16] or lending money to one another, as well as situations where the client invests in a scheme or business run by the lawyer.[17] *ASCR* rr 12.1 and 12.2 support these prohibitions in general terms. *ASCR* r 12.3 specifically prohibits borrowing from a client or former client, even if the client has consented.[18] This sets the ethical standards higher than fiduciary law, where borrowing from a client may be permissible if informed consent is given and the lawyer has advised the client to obtain independent legal advice.[19]

ASCR r 12.4, however, provides for several exceptions that appear designed to permit, tolerate and regulate certain lawyer–client conflicts rather than to prohibit and prevent them.

ASCR r 12 (cont'd) Conflict concerning a solicitor's own interests

12.4 A solicitor will not have breached this Rule merely by –

12.4.1 drawing a Will appointing the solicitor or an associate of the solicitor as executor, provided the solicitor informs the client in writing before the Will is signed:

(i) of any entitlement of the solicitor, or the solicitor's law practice or associate, to claim executor's commission,

---

12 Ibid 576 (de Jersey CJ). This case was decided before *ASCR* r 12.2 applied, but the Court was nevertheless clear that this behaviour was unethical.

13 Ibid.

14 The lawyer–client relationship is a fiduciary one and a presumed category of undue influence that must be rebutted by evidence of client consent and advice to receive independent legal advice: *Powell v Powell* [1900] 1 Ch 243; *Johnson v Buttress* (1936) 56 CLR 113.

15 *Legal Services Commissioner v McQuaid* [2018] QCAT 342 found a breach of *ASCR* r 12 where the lawyer and a client had pursued a business venture within the lawyer–client relationship.

16 *Legal Services Commissioner v Janes* [2015] QCAT 84, concerning borrowing money held in trust for a client to use to cover the costs of running another client's case.

17 See, eg, *Law Society of New South Wales v Harvey* [1976] 2 NSWLR 154; *Reilly v Law Society of New South Wales* (1988) 24 NSWLR 204.

18 Except for when the lender is a bank, trustee company, managed investment scheme, an associate of the lawyer providing fully informed consent, or their employer. It is arguable that this relationship of lender and borrower is also concerning because the lawyer may feel that their ability to provide independent advice is compromised.

19 *Maguire v Makaronis* (1997) 188 CLR 449.

(ii) of the inclusion in the Will of any provision entitling the solicitor, or the solicitor's law practice or associate, to charge legal costs in relation to the administration of the estate, and

(iii) if the solicitor or the solicitor's law practice or associate has an entitlement to claim commission, that the client could appoint as executor a person who might make no claim for executor's commission,

12.4.2 drawing a Will or other instrument under which the solicitor (or the solicitor's law practice or associate) will or may receive a substantial benefit other than any proper entitlement to executor's commission and proper fees, provided the person instructing the solicitor is either:

(i) a member of the solicitor's immediate family,

(ia) a member of the immediate family of the solicitor's spouse, or

(ii) a solicitor, or a member of the immediate family of a solicitor, who is a partner, employer, or employee, of the solicitor,

12.4.3 receiving a financial benefit from a third party in relation to any dealing where the solicitor represents a client, or from another service provider to whom a client has been referred by the solicitor, provided the solicitor advises the client:

(i) that a commission or benefit is or may be payable to the solicitor in respect of the dealing or referral and the nature of that commission or benefit,

(ii) that the client may refuse any referral, and

the client has given informed consent to the commission or benefit received or which may be received,

12.4.4 acting for a client in any dealing in which a financial benefit may be payable to a third party for referring the client, provided the solicitor has first disclosed the payment or financial benefit to the client.

ASCR r 12.4 provides for exceptions to the overarching ethical standard imposed by *ASCR* r 12.1 that a solicitor must not act where there is a lawyer–client conflict. *ASCR* rr 12.4.1 and 12.4.2 address conflicts of interest inherent in lawyers earning fees from their clients in the specific environment of will-making. As discussed in Chapter 6, acting for a client where there might be concerns about their capacity to provide proper and lawful instructions (which will also go to testamentary intent) is a complex undertaking. Lawyers must be careful to assess the specific situation and client capacity in order to act with competence and in the client's best interests.[20] As in the case of lawyers' trust

20 Solicitors have a duty to ensure a testator's capacity when there is a doubt: *Makripoulias v Arhontovasilis* [2022] VSC 53. This case concerned a conflict arising for the lawyer acting for a party seeking probate – the lawyer had drafted the will and was the executor of the deceased estate. The Court enjoined the lawyer from acting in the case because there was a possibility of the lawyer being called as a witness (to attest to the validity of the will) in the case.

accounts,[21] wills and estates is an area of practice where the accessibility of considerable funds provides a significant opportunity and temptation to prefer the lawyer's interest. For instance, in one disciplinary case a lawyer deliberately and repeatedly misled beneficiaries of the estate about the amount of money that had been withdrawn by the lawyer, purportedly for legal costs and his executor's commission.[22] In this case the solicitor had a personal connection to the client and was therefore particularly trusted and relied upon by the client's children (beneficiaries of her will) who had no knowledge of the provision in the will for the lawyer to draw a fee as executor.

ASCR r 12.4.2 prevents a lawyer from drafting a will 'under which the solicitor (or the solicitor's law practice or associate) will or may receive a substantial benefit' (in addition to normal fees and any executor's commission), unless the client is a family member or a close associate. This rule contemplates that a lawyer may be acting for a family member or close colleague in drawing their will and could be a beneficiary under this instrument. As discussed below, while the rules anticipate that solicitors may act for someone close to them, and simply provide limits on doing so in certain circumstances, we caution against it in most cases. There are many reasons why this is ethically dangerous.

ASCR r 12.4.1 requires lawyers to disclose in writing to the client any right to a commission and/or legal fee that they will be entitled to claim under the will. For example, a solicitor drawing a will for a client might also be appointed in that will as the executor of the estate and have a right to claim a commission and legal fees for administering the estate upon the death of the client. Following the common law expectation, the ethical rules require informed consent of the client to these payments (in addition to the client attesting to the will) as this is an extra benefit flowing to the lawyer than just the legal fees for drawing the will. *ASCR* r 12.4.1 also requires the lawyer to inform the client that they could appoint another executor who might not charge a fee to administer the estate. This rule recognises and accepts a long tradition of lawyers acting both as executors and solicitors for deceased estates. However, it is debatable whether we should even permit a lawyer to claim a sizeable executor's commission from the estate when also acting as the lawyer for the estate. As in the above example, the client and future beneficiaries may be easily misled about the distinction of each of these roles occupied by the lawyer and what would be reasonable to pay for them. Good practice would require that a lawyer advise the beneficiaries of the provision in the will appointing the lawyer as executor, the fees to be charged and the beneficiaries' right to have a court assessment of the executor's commission.[23] We note that courts have frequently expressed concern about the potential for conflict where a solicitor

21 Solicitors frequently maintain a firm trust account to hold money received during a lawyer–client relationship. Law firm trust accounts around the country hold many millions of dollars to which others are beneficially entitled. However, this money is relatively easily accessible to solicitors. While there is detailed and strictly enforced regulation around how solicitors take and deal with trust money in this context, there are a multitude of disciplinary cases documenting how solicitors routinely succumb to temptation to steal or borrow client money.

22 *Victorian Legal Services Commissioner v McBain (Legal Practice)* [2015] VCAT 1545; *Legal Services Commissioner v Rhoden* [2016] VSC 67.

23 In *Victorian Legal Services Commissioner v McBain (Legal Practice)* [2015] VCAT 1545 this was part of the concern of the Tribunal that there was limited disclosure of the charges as executor.

acts as both lawyer to the estate and executor and have advised: 'It is not a position the solicitor should seek.'[24]

Lawyers have been disciplined for receiving a profit or commission for referring clients to other service providers (for example, to a financial adviser or real estate agent) where the referral has not been fully disclosed to the client and the client's fully informed consent has not been provided.[25] Indeed, receiving a secret profit in this way can even amount to the commission of a crime by the lawyer[26] (and is clearly unethical under *ASCR* rr 12.4.3 and 12.4.4). Nevertheless, the ethical rules are not explicit as to whether the lawyer must disclose the amount of payment. Should the ethical rules prohibit receiving referral fees with or without client consent?[27] The practice seems contrary to the fiduciary responsibility not to receive an extra profit from the relationship. Indeed, some jurisdictions have identified referral fees as a particular temptation for the lawyer to prefer their own interests at the expense of vulnerable clients. Thus, referral fees and receipt of benefits by lawyers in personal injury matters are prohibited in several jurisdictions.[28] Should the *ASCR* at least be clear that the lawyer may only make or receive a referral where it is in the best interests of the client? This might be an important reminder to lawyers that their judgment could be impaired by personal interest or third-party influence.[29]

Under the ethical rules most lawyers would readily identify that they face a conflict of interest if they or any associate are holding shares in a company that is in dispute with, or possibly even on the other side of a proposed transaction with, the lawyer's client. Most lawyers would probably consider it standard ethical practice to disclose to a client any interests of their own of this nature, and perhaps any immediate family member's interests that they are aware of, and allow the client to decide whether the lawyer can continue to act.[30] *Financial* conflicts of interest between a lawyer and their 'associates' and client are, however, only the most obvious of the many ways in which a lawyer's personal interests may conflict with acting in the best interest of the client or client loyalty. Lawyers might have personal, social or political interests that need to be considered in the context of any

24 See, eg, *Re Will and Estate of Mary Irene McClung* [2006] VSC 209, [34].

25 See, eg, *Law Society of the Australian Capital Territory v Lardner* [1998] ACTSC 187.

26 *Criminal Code 2002* (ACT) s 353(1); *Crimes Act 1900* (NSW) s 249B(1); *Criminal Code Act 1983* (NT) s 236; *Criminal Code Act 1899* (Qld) ss 442A–442M; *Criminal Law Consolidation Act 1935* (SA) s 150; *Criminal Code* (Tas) s 442B; *Crimes Act 1958* (Vic) s 266(1); *Criminal Code* (WA) s 529.

27 Barristers are prohibited from receiving or giving referral fees. For an interesting reminder to Victorian barristers of the *Legal Profession Uniform Conduct (Barristers) Rules 2015* r 46: 'A barrister may not make a payment or gift to any person by reason of or in connection with the introduction of professional work by that person to the barrister', see 'Ethics Committee Bulletin No 3 of 2018 – Operation of Rule 26', *Victorian Bar* (Web Page, 14 December 2018) <https://www.vicbar.com.au/news-events/ethics-committee-bulletin-no-3-2018-operation-rule-46>.

28 See, eg, *Motor Accidents Compensation Regulation 2015* (NSW) reg 24; *Legal Profession Act 2006* (NT) s 293(1); *Personal Injuries Proceedings Act 2002* (Qld) s 68(1); *Liability Act 2002* (WA) s 20(1).

29 This specific requirement for the lawyer to ensure independence from third-party influence was explicit in a previous version of the *Model Rules of Professional Conduct and Practice* (r 33.2) by the Law Council of Australia.

30 *ASCR* r 12 defines a conflict of interest broadly as where the lawyer or an 'associate' of the lawyer has a conflicting interest to the duty to the client. An associate is defined in the Glossary to the *ASCR* (r 44) as including any immediate family member of the lawyer, or a partner or employee in the lawyer's law firm, or any immediate family of the lawyer's partner.

lawyer–client relationship. For example, there may be a concern raised where the lawyers on opposing sides of a case are close friends or family members.

CASE STUDY 7.1 LAWYERS WITH RELATIONSHIPS TO OTHER LAWYERS AND JUDGES

In a criminal trial it became known that the prosecutor and the defence barrister had resumed their sexual relationship (they had lived together as a de facto couple over the course of nearly a year, an arrangement that had ended only two or three months before the trial). The lawyers did not inform their clients or the court of their relationship.[31] The Queensland Court of Appeal found that despite there being no evidence of any actual detriment to the client in the proceedings, 'a fair minded, reasonable observer' would 'entertain a reasonable suspicion that justice had miscarried'.[32] Thomas J explained that the perception might be that 'defence counsel had "run dead" or colluded with the Crown prosecutor contrary to the interests of the accused' to make it a miscarriage of justice.[33] The client deposed that, had he known of his lawyer's recent past sexual relationship with the prosecutor, he would have changed barrister. The Court set aside the convictions and ordered a retrial.

The Court was clear that the concern did not derive from the mere fact that the lawyers on opposing sides were in an intimate relationship but that they had not disclosed this. Nevertheless, Thomas J went on to consider a range of circumstances where the public might be concerned about the personal interests of the lawyers conflicting with their loyalty to clients or the due administration of justice:

> Applying these principles to the present circumstances, one immediately has to consider whether it is proper for persons in particular relationships to act for contrary interests. Would it be improper for a husband and wife to oppose each other as counsel for different parties in the same case? I am not aware of any general reason of public policy why this should be prohibited, although individual factors may arise in particular instances which make it undesirable. There is no current rule of conduct approved by the Bar Association of Queensland that addresses such a problem. Speaking generally there does not appear to be any sufficient reason to think that by reason of their relationship such persons would not each do their best on behalf of their respective clients. There is of course a risk that counsel living in the same house or with access to each other's property could improperly read the other's brief, although the risk hardly seems any greater than in the case of counsel in the same group of chambers. A client with particularly valuable information might

31 *R v Szabo* [2001] 2 Qd R 214.

32 Ibid [59]. This finding was said to be aligned with, but not based upon, the doctrine of apprehended bias applied to judicial officers.

33 Ibid.

however choose not to take such a risk if notified of the relationship. That is one of the reasons that lead me to consider that in such a situation there is at the very least an ethical duty upon counsel to disclose to the client that such a relationship with opposing counsel exists. I do not think that a similar duty necessarily arises in relation to a case involving counsel in the same group of chambers. While this distinction may not seem entirely logical, its justification is the greater suspicion arising from sexual intimacy and an assumption that persons in a sexual relationship are more likely to be prepared to do a favour for the other than persons not in such a relationship.[34]

DISCUSSION QUESTIONS

1. Do you agree that opposing lawyers in an intimate relationship should disclose their relationship to their respective clients when they act against each other in a case?
2. What difference does it make to tell the client about this relationship? Might there be other competing interests and duties for the lawyer to consider?
3. Can you think of other personal relationships that might raise concerns about actual or perceived conflicts between the personal interest of a lawyer and loyalty to the client? What about where the lawyer is in an intimate or sexual relationship with the client? What about where the lawyer's partner has a financial interest in the client's business?
4. The High Court has found apprehended bias in a case[35] where the presiding judge and a lawyer for one of the parties exchanged text messages and phone calls and met for coffee or a drink on a number of occasions during the trial or when judgment was reserved. This was not disclosed to the other party and their lawyers until a later time. While this judgment related to the judge in that case, is there an ethical concern arising for the lawyer? If so, could this be avoided? Should a lawyer ever be friends with a judge?

Another category of personal relationship that may raise a concern about conflicts of interests is a sexual relationship between a lawyer and client. There is no rule in the *ASCR* or *Barristers' Conduct Rules* explicitly prohibiting such a relationship. However, in these situations the lawyer might find it difficult to act with the professional independence expected under the rules (*ASCR* r 4.1.4). Similarly, there are no rules addressing situations where the lawyer's client is a relative, friend or social associate of some kind (whether spouse or indeed enemy). However, law societies generally advise their members to avoid these situations, so as to prevent current or future conflicts arising. It may be that a lawyer's insurance policy may not cover work for a family member or at least require that the insurer be notified of the representation. In a recent Guidance Statement, the Queensland

34 Ibid [61].
35 *Charisteas v Charisteas* (2021) 393 ALR 389.

Law Society identifies a range of dangers in practice when working for friends and family including personal loyalties and undue influence leading to a poor perception of issues and even a temptation to act outside of expertise.[36]

The lawyer's personal interest in receiving a higher fee, pursuing satisfying and career-enhancing cases, or advocating certain political, ethical or ideological interests might also have a tendency to influence the way the lawyer performs their duty to the client. Yet the potential for these conflicts is unavoidable. Lawyers naturally have their own concerns and interests that they bring to the lawyer–client relationship. It would be naive to assume that complete client loyalty in all one's thinking and acting as a lawyer can be guaranteed, and that all conflicts can be completely avoided. Indeed, the more broadly we define the lawyer's 'interests', beyond the direct financial interests of the lawyer personally, the more likely we are to discover other conflicts between the lawyer's interests (and their associates' interests) and their duty to the client. Lawyers cannot be expected to be completely immune to these other interests or pressures. A reasonable self-interest in work-life balance and an enjoyable career is also to be encouraged.

Lawyers need to reflect on their own motives and interests and how these could improperly impact on how they act for the client, and if they do, avoid this or simply end the relationship. As the ethical conduct rules and common law expect, lawyers should clearly explain any conflicts and what this might mean for the client, so that the client can make up their mind about whether or how they want the lawyer to act for them. The existing conduct rules give lawyers little indication of the degree of openness and honesty about their own interests that might be required to fully apprise the client of the extent of lawyer–client conflicts of interest.[37] Where the lawyer is in doubt, recourse to the relationship of loyalty may assist to recognise that there is a conflict and to decline to act, or to seek informed consent. As Megarry J stated in the well-known case of *Spector v Ageda*:

> The solicitor must be remarkable indeed if he can feel assured of holding the scales evenly between himself and his client. Even if in fact he can and does, to demonstrate to conviction that he has done so will usually be beyond possibility in a case where anything to the client's detriment has occurred. Not only must his duty be discharged, but it must manifestly and undoubtedly be seen to have been discharged.[38]

In the following two subsections we consider conflicts between the duties owed to two or more clients – in other words, in client–client conflicts. As we shall see, lawyer–client conflicts can magnify client–client conflicts. It will often be in the interests of a lawyer or law firm to keep acting for two or more clients with conflicting interests to earn more fees

36 'No 23 Acting for Family and Friends', *Queensland Law Society* (Web Page) <https://www.qls.com.au/Guidance-Statements/No-23-Acting-for-Family-and-Friends>. See also 'Lawyers Who Sleep with Their Clients', *Law Report* (ABC Radio National, 23 August 2005) <https://www.abc.net.au/radionational/programs/lawreport/lawyers-who-sleep-with-their-clients/3367908>.

37 Eli Wald argues that there should be an ethical duty to engage in in-depth conversations with clients – what he calls 'a materiality-based communication' requirement where the client receives all information the client would consider relevant to make a decision in their case. See Eli Wald, 'Taking Attorney-Client Communications (and Therefore Clients) Seriously' (2008) 42(3) *University of San Francisco Law Review* 747.

38 [1973] Ch 30 [47].

or maintain a relationship with a client who provides steady and interesting work. Such concerns may influence lawyers' ethical judgement about how to handle the equally difficult client–client conflicts.

Balancing competing relationships of loyalty, ongoing duties of confidentiality and the duty to the administration of justice

There are two main situations where *client–client conflicts* can arise.

- *Current client conflicts:* The lawyer or law firm has two current clients with conflicting interests. The extreme version of this would be where a lawyer acts on either side of a dispute. This situation might arise less obviously for a large law firm where someone in the banking section acts for a bank suing a building firm in liquidation, and someone in the insolvency section acts on behalf of that building firm. If the firm acted on both sides of a dispute, this would be a concurrent client conflict of the most concerning type. However, conflicts can also arise where the law firm acts for two clients in unrelated matters but holds confidential information about one client that is material to the case of another client.
- *Former client conflicts:* The lawyer faces a conflict between the interests of a current client and a former client. There are a range of situations that might give rise to this type of conflict for a lawyer or law firm. Lawyers frequently move between firms, which might mean that the lawyer is asked to act against a client still represented by their former firm, or they may know confidential information of their former client that is relevant to the new firm's client (see Case study 7.3). Another example might be where a lawyer acts for a client and provides some advice and then seeks to act for a new client and the former client's confidential information is relevant to the prospective client (see Case study 7.4).

For former client conflicts, the ethical concern generally relates to a continuing duty of confidentiality. However, we also consider whether some continued duty of loyalty to, or obligation not to harm, a former client persists that might give rise to a conflict for the lawyer.

The *ASCR* (rr 10 and 11) prohibit both concurrent client conflicts and conflicts of interests relating to former clients, as discussed below. This will generally mean that it would be unethical for a lawyer to act in these situations. A client might also seek an injunction to prevent the lawyer or law firm from acting for another client.

However, under the *ASCR* and common law approaches to injunctions, client consent and use of information barriers may permit a lawyer or law firm to ethically continue to act despite a client–client conflict. Information barriers (once commonly called 'Chinese Walls') are arrangements within a firm designed to manage or minimise conflicts, so that a law firm can continue to act for both clients (described further below). Many firms use information barriers, but it is questionable whether they are effective, or indeed appropriate, in many of the situations in which they are currently employed.

This subsection considers the differing types of conflicting duties to clients that arise and whether a firm should continue to act for one or either of its clients, including in a context where the ethical rules indicate that this is permissible. We examine the ethical conduct rules and common law cases that are concerned with preventing a breach of loyalty or duty of confidentiality to a client. A court may also decide that there is a conflict of interest that prevents a lawyer from acting, on the basis that it gives rise to a perception of an injustice. As discussed in Case studies 7.1 and 7.3, courts will intervene where it is necessary to ensure that justice is done and is seen to be done. Such intervention is based on the court's inherent jurisdiction to control its own officers. This 'administration of justice' ground for preventing a lawyer from acting in breach of a conflict is very broad, and the court will make a contextual judgement. This ground for intervention can apply to current client conflict scenarios, former client conflict scenarios and in situations such as where a lawyer has acted repeatedly against one party.[39]

Current clients

ASCR r 11.1 requires a practitioner to '*avoid* conflicts between the duties owed to two or more current clients' (our emphasis). However, this clear standard is immediately followed by several other rules which allow legal practitioners to act for more than one party in a matter, even though this might give rise to conflicts of interest.

ASCR r 11 Conflicts of duties concerning current clients

11.1 A solicitor and a law practice must avoid conflicts between the duties owed to two or more current clients.

Duty of loyalty

11.2 If a solicitor or a law practice seeks to act for two or more clients in the same or related matters where the clients' interests are adverse and there is a conflict or potential conflict of the duties to act in the best interests of each client, the solicitor or law practice must not act, except where permitted by Rule 11.3 and 11.4.

11.3 Where a solicitor or law practice seeks to act in the circumstances specified in Rule 11.2, the solicitor or law practice may, subject always to each solicitor discharging their duty to act in the best interests of their client, only act if each client:

11.3.1 is aware that the solicitor or law practice is also acting for another client; and

11.3.2 has given informed consent to the solicitor or law practice so acting.

The values expressed in *ASCR* rr 11.1 and 11.2–11.3 are contradictory. *ASCR* r 11.1 requires lawyers to *avoid* any conflict of interest. The common law also expects that a fiduciary be proactive in avoiding conflicts before they arise. Acting for different clients with opposing interests in the same matter has been described as 'the very heartland of fiduciary law'[40] and should not be cured by client consent, because there will be 'some circumstances in which it is impossible, notwithstanding … disclosure for any solicitor to act fairly and adequately for both'.[41] Indeed, even obtaining informed consent appears to be difficult in

39 *Asia Pacific Telecommunications Ltd v Optus Networks Pty Ltd* [2007] NSWSC 350.
40 *Beach Petroleum NL v Kennedy* (1999) 48 NSWLR 1, 47–8.
41 *Farrington v Rowe McBride & Partners* [1985] 1 NZLR 83, 90.

this circumstance, because duties of confidentiality to each would restrict what the lawyer can tell the other client.

One might expect that, if it is the lawyer's purpose to *avoid* conflicts of interest between clients, they should also avoid situations, such as joint representation, that are likely to give rise to a conflict of interest. The joint representation of criminal accused is a case in point. It may be convenient for the one lawyer to represent both accused, but the danger is that facts and arguments that emerge during preparation and trial mean that the two clients may benefit from having inconsistent defences argued on their behalf, or even blaming each other for the crime, as described in Case study 7.2. Yet *ASCR* rr 11.2–11.3 implicitly allow a firm to act for two or more clients to a matter, even though this joint representation could involve a conflict of interest. Indeed, *ASCR* r 11.3.1 contemplates that the lawyer, or law firm, may well already be in possession of information that will benefit one client and hurt the other, but they are still allowed to represent both. *ASCR* r 11.3 attempts to reconcile the inconsistency by allowing joint representation only where the lawyer has disclosed the conflict to both clients, and both clients consent. The rule does also provide that this is 'subject always to each solicitor discharging their duty to act in the best interests of their client'. This seems to contemplate that even where a client consents to the lawyer acting, if the lawyer cannot act for one or both of the clients competently, then it would be unethical to do so.

CASE STUDY 7.2 ACTING FOR CO-ACCUSED – A FORESEEABLE CONFLICT?

Two men were convicted of attempted possession of a commercial quantity of unlawfully imported border-controlled drugs. Another co-offender had pleaded guilty.[42] One of the men convicted appealed his conviction on a number of grounds, including that his solicitors had an actual or apparent conflict of duties caused by them also acting for his co-defendants and that this had deprived him of a fair trial. The convicted man and his two co-defendants were all represented by Bosscher Lawyers, and two solicitors from the same firm acted for the three co-defendants.

The co-accused knew that the same firm represented them all. There had been little discussion of evidence with the solicitors or the barrister. The solicitors asked the client to sign a standard typed form confirming that he wanted the lawyers to represent him at trial. However, he wasn't told that the evidence of his co-accused might implicate him or not support his story. Nevertheless, the Court found that there was no evidence that the appellant would have acted differently, if he had known about the evidence to be given by his co-accused. The appeal failed and there was no finding that justice had miscarried. However, President McMurdo raised a general concern about the representation of co-accused:

> As the appellant submits and the ASCR recognise, [co-representation] is a practice fraught with danger.

42 *R v Pham* [2017] QCA 43.

Even if there is no immediately apparent conflict of duties concerning the co-defendants, conflicts can easily arise during trials, which are notoriously unpredictable. They can also arise in sentence proceedings. Unanticipated evidence or submissions can result in a conflict of the duties owed to co-defendants, with a risk of real prejudice to one or all co-defendants. Substantial costs to parties and the community result where lawyers withdraw because of an arising conflict, causing adjournments or even mis-trials. One or a number of defendants may be more culpable than others. By having the same legal practitioner acting for all, more dominant co-defendants may manipulate those less dominant to give instructions to their detriment and to the advantage of the dominant co-defendants. Where co-defendants are faced with a strong prosecution case, their lawyers should advise them of the value of a guilty plea and co-operation with the authorities in mitigation of penalty. That course may be against the interests of other co-defendants. This list of potential conflicts of duties when acting for co-defendants is far from exhaustive.[43]

DISCUSSION QUESTIONS

1. Do you agree with McMurdo P that the *ASCR* recognise that this is a 'practice fraught with danger'? Should we consider changing the *ASCR* to provide better guidance or prohibit lawyers acting in this situation?
2. *ASCR* r 11.3 seems to allow for representation of co-accused with their informed consent. However, are there any concerns about being able to obtain informed consent of a client when they are in this situation (facing a serious criminal charge)?

There are a range of other contexts that are well known to involve foreseeable competing interests of concurrent clients such as acting for a borrower and lender, a vendor and purchaser, and an insurer and insured.[44] In some of these cases, the lawyer or law firm will be acting on both sides of a contentious matter and should not act even where it is possible to obtain informed consent.

Some clients may want the same lawyer to represent them in relatively simple transactions, because they see it as more convenient and less expensive.[45] Even in more complicated, commercial transactions where there is greater chance of competing interests arising over time, two clients may be happy for different partners (in different offices) of the same large law firm to represent them both – perhaps a lawyer who is familiar with their business, or a

43 Ibid [58]–[59].

44 While there are no current ethical rules regulating acting in these specific cases, previous conduct rules in various jurisdictions indicated caution or prohibited acting on both sides of land dealings: *Legal Profession (Solicitors) Rules 2007* (ACT) r 7; *Legal Profession (Solicitors) Rules 2007* (Qld) r 8.6; *Professional Conduct and Practice Rules 2005* (Vic) r 8.6. All are no longer in force.

45 See commentary to *ASCR* r 11: Law Council of Australia, *Australian Solicitors' Conduct Rules 2011 and Commentary* (2013) 15 <https://www.lawcouncil.asn.au/files/web-pdf/SolicitorsConductRulesHandbook_Ver3.pdf>.

lawyer who specialises in a particular area. It is also common practice for law firms to seek client consent to continue to act in the event of certain foreseeable conflicts arising.[46]

ASCR rr 11.2 and 11.3 see client consent as the 'cure-all' for a potential conflict in joint representation. The consent process appears to be tight and protective: it insists on a high level of disclosure of the (potential) conflict, and its likely impact, to both clients, followed by their informed consent. However, a client's understanding of the potential conflict, its likely impact on them and whether they should consent to it will depend very much on what their lawyer tells them. Even so-called 'sophisticated' clients are prepared to rely on advice that they are paying for. The whole point of prohibiting conflicts of interest is that the lawyer's own judgement, and ability to fully inform and advise the client about the conflict, might be clouded by the conflict. The case law on breach of fiduciary obligations generally requires that independent advice be obtained before someone can consent to a conflict of interest. For lawyers and clients, this means that the client should be advised to go to a second, independent lawyer to receive reliable advice as to whether to consent to the first lawyer acting in a potential conflict situation.[47] Yet the professional obligations of the *ASCR* do not appear to reflect this requirement of the general law.

ASCR r 11 (cont'd) Conflicts of duties concerning current clients

Duty of confidentiality

11.4 In addition to Rule 11.3, where a solicitor or law practice acts for two or more clients in the same or related matters and the solicitor or law practice is in, or comes into, possession of information which is confidential to one client (the first client) which might reasonably be concluded to be material to the other client's or clients' matter and detrimental to the interests of the first client if disclosed, the solicitor and the solicitor's law practice may not act or continue to act for the other client or clients unless each client's informed consent:

- **11.4.1** permits the disclosure and use of that information for the benefit of the other client or clients; or
- **11.4.2** requires the establishment and maintenance at all times of an effective information barrier to protect the confidential information of each client.

ASCR r 11.4 seeks to go further than the general law and challenges it by permitting a firm to act for two or more clients where they hold confidential information for one or more that is material and adverse to the interests of another client, providing there is informed consent from all parties. Rule 11 (as amended in 2022) provides for two sorts of informed consent. First, a client can provide consent to the disclosure and use of their confidential information for the other client's benefit. Second, both clients can agree to the erection of an

46 Michael DiLernia, 'Advance Waivers of Conflicts of Interest in Large Law Firm Practice' (2009) 22(1) *Georgetown Journal of Legal Ethics* 97.

47 See *Clark Boyce v Mouat* [1993] 3 NZLR 641.

information barrier so that neither client may learn of the other's confidential information, nor may that information be used for the other's case.

The previous version of this rule (still in force at the time of writing in jurisdictions apart from New South Wales, Victoria and Western Australia) did not provide any conjunction between r 11.4.1 (informed consent) and 11.4.2 (information barriers), allowing a possible reading that it is ethically permissible to act where there is an information barrier erected, but no client has been informed or given consent. We note, though, that the Law Council's Commentary to the previous version of the *ASCR* suggests that the lack of conjunction was a drafting omission; the expectation is that informed consent is always obtained.[48] We believe that informed client consent is a minimum requirement for any lawyer continuing to act in this conflict situation.

The last part of *ASCR* r 11, sub-r 11.5, refers to an 'actual' conflict arising while acting for two or more clients.

ASCR r 11 (cont'd) Conflicts of duties concerning current clients

Actual conflict arising between current clients in the course of the matter

11.5 If a solicitor or a law practice acts for more than one client in a matter and, during the course of the conduct of that matter, an actual conflict arises between the duties owed to two or more of those clients, the solicitor or law practice may only continue to act for one of those clients (or for two or more of those clients between whom there is no conflict) in the following exceptional circumstances:

- **11.5.1** any client for whom the solicitor or law practice ceases to act has given informed consent to the solicitor or law practice continuing to act for the remaining clients; and
- **11.5.2** the duty of confidentiality owed to all of the clients, both those for whom the solicitor or law practice ceases to act and those for whom the solicitor or law practice continues to act, is not put at risk.

In this subrule, a distinction is drawn between an 'actual' conflict, which must be avoided, and a 'potential' conflict (referred to in *ASCR* r 11.2) that may be managed so long as it does not crystallise into an actual conflict. But the purpose of rules requiring lawyers to avoid conflicts of interest should be to proactively prevent conflicts arising, as has long been the common law requirement. As Justice Cummins of the Supreme Court of Victoria commented at an ethics seminar:

> What bedevils the prohibition of a conflict of interest is a confusion of purposes. The purpose of prohibition of conflict of interest is not to remedy an offence or a failure. The purpose of prohibition of conflict of interest is to prevent an offence or a failure. Prohibition of conflict operates upstream of offence or failure. It is preventative. It is prophylactic. Thus it is no answer to breach of conflict to say that in fact no harm occurred,

48 Law Council of Australia, *Australian Solicitors' Conduct Rules 2011 and Commentary* (n 45) 14.

> that the client was not harmed. If harm, a loss, a failure, an offence occurred, you would be dealt with for a consequential matter. Prohibition of conflict is an antecedent matter. That also is why the phrase 'potential conflict of interest' is tautologous.[49]

Similarly, courts in injunction cases have described the responsibility of the lawyer as a prophylactic one to avoid the conflict in the first place. Where a foreseeable conflict does in fact arise, 'it is [the lawyer's] own fault, and [the lawyer] cannot use his own discomfiture as a reason why his duty to either client should be taken to have been modified'.[50]

Even if we accept that a lawyer or law firm may act for two clients in the same matter with client consent, and something unforeseeable arises, *ASCR* r 11.5 remains questionable. The rule provides that the lawyer may then choose which client to retain as long as duties of confidentiality to both are not endangered and the client for whom the firm ceases to act consents. As the commentary to the previous version of the *ASCR* contemplates,[51] it seems unlikely that any client would agree to the firm ceasing to act for them but continuing to act for the other, if their confidential information is likely to be very material to the other client. Still, the rule may be taken as a concerning indication that lawyers may choose which client they would prefer to work for should a conflict arise.

On the other hand, the common law allows consideration of what is described as a public interest in clients being able to have their 'lawyer of choice'.[52] This might be seen as consistent with the emphasis on personal liberty underpinning an adversarial advocate approach. Alternatively, a moral activist or ethics of care approach may suggest that we should be cautious in removing lawyers from representing certain clients where access to adequate representation might be constrained, especially where there might be a shortage of lawyers with relevant specialist expertise. The strong supply of lawyers in the Australian market in urban areas makes this a thin suggestion. It is arguable that the rules have been crafted to enable lawyers and law firms to preserve their ability to earn fees from multiple clients rather than to facilitate access to rare expertise. However, there are access to justice concerns relating to lawyer conflicts in regional and remote area contexts,[53] and to situations where clients' only options for representation are free legal services from community law firms or Legal Aid.[54] Small firms must observe the standards set in the *ASCR* but might be far less able to manage conflicts through implementing information barriers.[55] As discussed in the final section of chapter where we consider the moral activist approach, these important concerns are a basis for exceptions to the application of conflict rules. An amendment in

49 Justice PD Cummins, 'An Ethical Profession: Dealing with Ethical Dilemmas' (Speech, Law Institute of Victoria Continuing Legal Education seminar, 28 February 2002).

50 *Hilton v Barker Booth and Eastwood (A Firm)* [2005] 1 WLR 567.

51 Law Council of Australia, *Australian Solicitors' Conduct Rules 2011 and Commentary* (n 45) r 11.5.

52 In some cases, this is a consideration made by the court as to whether to grant the equitable remedy of an injunction. This situation arose in Case study 7.4.

53 See, eg, reports from the Law Council of Australia's Justice Project: 'The Justice Project', *Law Council of Australia* (Web Page) <https://www.lawcouncil.asn.au/justice-project>.

54 See Helen McGowan, 'Transpiration', Public Submission on Appearance, Productivity Commission Public Inquiry Melbourne Hearing, Access to Justice Arrangements <https://www.pc.gov.au/inquiries/completed/access-justice/submissions/submissions-test2/submission-counter/subdr284-access-justice.pdf>.

55 Louise Kyle, Richard Coverdale and Tim Powers, *Conflicts of Interest in Victorian Rural and Regional Legal Practice* (Deakin University, 2014).

2022 to the *ASCR* (r 11A) allows for lawyers or law firms (which now specifically include community legal services – *ASCR* Glossary) not to screen for conflicts of interest when providing short-term assistance to ensure access to justice, and time constraints prohibit screening. This amendment might facilitate access to services such as representation by court duty lawyers. However, the new rule is not a licence to just ignore a known conflict, and clients must give informed consent to the provision of services. Even for short-term, possibly pro bono, legal assistance services, the rules will not simply allow a lawyer to act in a conflict situation. But the new rule does allow lawyers or law firms to act for multiple clients without an 'effective information barrier', recognising a different context of practice. It allows for representation by different solicitors in a law practice of two clients with adverse interests, provided there is client consent and an effort to preserve client confidentiality.

ASCR r 11 (cont'd) Conflicts of interest between current clients

11A.1 If a solicitor providing short-term legal assistance services forms a reasonable belief that the solicitor cannot screen for conflicts of interest due to circumstances where it is not reasonably practicable as the time required to do so may result in a real risk of the client being denied access to legal assistance, the solicitor must ensure, to the extent reasonably practicable, that –

11A.1.1 the solicitor has disclosed the nature of the services to the client, and

11A.1.2 there is no actual or potential conflict between the duties owed to the client and one or more other clients, and

11A.1.3 the client has given informed consent to the provision of the services.

11A.2 A solicitor must not provide, or continue to provide, short-term legal assistance services to a client if the solicitor:

11A2.1 is or becomes aware that the interests of the client are adverse to the interests of a current client of the solicitor or the solicitor's law practice, or

11A2.2 is aware that the solicitor has, or while providing the short-term legal assistance services obtains, confidential information of a current or former client that might reasonably be concluded to be:

11A2.2.1 material to the client's matter, and

11A2.2.2 detrimental to the current or former client, if disclosed.

11A.3 A solicitor who is a partner, associate, employee, officer or employer in a law practice through which another solicitor is providing short-term legal assistance services, may act for another client of the law practice whose interests are adverse to the interests of the client receiving the services if:

11A.3.1 each client has given informed consent, and

11A.3.2 measures are in place to ensure confidential information will not be disclosed.

11A.4 In this Rule:

short-term legal assistance services means services offered by a solicitor to a client, whether through a legal assistance service provider or on a pro bono basis, with the expectation by the solicitor and the client that the solicitor will not provide continuing legal advice or representation in the matter.

In another area of practice, conflicts arise in a quite different context. The very *size* of large law firms – each with hundreds of partners and employee practitioners – requires that they be constantly on guard in case one of those partners takes on a client who is involved in a dispute or transaction with a client already represented by another partner. The relationship of loyalty to the client is owed by the firm in most cases. Therefore, it is essential to maintain and comply with protocols for conflict checks (which is a process of checking potential new clients against a list of all current clients and, especially, their opposing parties). In Case study 7.3 in the next subsection, we see how easily conflicts of interest can arise in the large law firm context, particularly concerning former clients.

We now consider how the *ASCR* and *Barristers' Conduct Rules* apply to situations where the conflict is between a former client and a current client. This is the most frequently encountered, and troubling, conflict for all lawyers (law firms and barristers).

Former clients and information barriers

ASCR r 10 provides for the situation where a lawyer or law firm is considering representing one client in a matter where they would be acting against a former client.[56]

ASCR r 10 Conflicts concerning former clients

10.1 A solicitor and law practice must avoid conflicts between the duties owed to current and former clients.

10.2 A solicitor or law practice who or which is in possession of confidential information of a former client where that information might reasonably be concluded to be material to the matter of another client and detrimental to the interests of the former client if disclosed, must not act for the current client in that matter UNLESS –

10.2.1 the former client has given informed consent to the disclosure and use of that information, or

10.2.2 an effective information barrier has been established.

In this rule, which closely reflects the position at common law, the conflict only arises where a former client's confidential information is both 'material' to the current client matter and could be used to the detriment of the former client. Applying the leading House of Lords decision in *Bolkiah's* case,[57] a series of Australian cases have held that the former client may be granted an injunction to prevent their former lawyer, or their former lawyer's law firm, acting if there is a 'real, not fanciful' risk or a 'real possibility' of disclosure of their confidential information.[58] Recent Australia cases have considered whether this test is satisfied by considering the following questions:

56 There are provisions for barristers which are substantially identical to *ASCR* r 10.2: *Legal Profession Uniform Conduct (Barristers) Rules 2015* r 101(a).

57 *Prince Jefri Bolkiah v KPMG (A Firm)* [1999] 2 AC 222.

58 Ibid. This has also often been expressed as where there is 'a real and sensible possibility of the misuse of confidential information': *Dealer Support Services Pty Ltd v Motor Trades Association of Australia Ltd* (2014) 228 FCR 252, 3 [4]; *Sent v John Fairfax Publication Pty Ltd* [2002] VSC 429, [33]; *Nash v Timbercorp Finance Pty Ltd* (2019) 137 ASCR 189, [62].

- What is the relevant information?
- Is that information confidential?
- Does the legal practitioner have possession of that information?
- Is the legal practitioner proposing to act 'against' the former client in the requisite sense?
- Is there a real risk that the confidential information will be relevant?
- Is there no real risk of misuse of the confidential information?[59]

The party seeking the injunction must prove at least the first five points, and there must be some precision about the confidential information that is said to be held by the lawyer to be enjoined and why it is material to another client. However, as is illustrated in Case study 7.4, injunctions will be granted to avoid inadvertent or subconscious use of confidential information, even if the lawyer claims that they have no documents and do not recall a former client's matter.

ASCR r 10.2 reflects this case law by suggesting that there is an ethically unacceptable conflict, and the lawyer cannot act, if confidences 'might reasonably be concluded to be material to the matter of another client and detrimental to the interests of the former client'. It seems appropriate that a breach of confidentiality alone would be seen as being to the client's detriment.[60] However, there are exceptions or management strategies available for this conflict under the rules. For example the firm may act when a former client gives informed consent to the practitioner or firm acting. The *ASCR* do not explicitly require that the *current* client be informed and consent to the firm continuing to act.

ASCR r 10.2 *alternatively* provides that the lawyer or law firm may act in a situation where a former client's confidential information is material to a new client even without the consent of either *or* both former or current client, if the firm establishes an 'effective information barrier'. Information barriers are not legal instruments but administrative systems that law firms have used to separate individual or teams of lawyers to 'ensure' (prove) that there is no real risk of slippage of confidential information. There are a range of practical concerns about this approach that are discussed further below.

The value expressed by these *ASCR* exceptions is less than strict adherence to client confidentiality. Many former clients might feel that *any* confidential information their lawyers acquired from them could be material. They might expect that if a lawyer or law firm holds their confidential information, the lawyer or firm should not act against them. Even the remote possibility that their former lawyer might not need to ask their permission before acting against their interests would give most former clients pause to reflect on the values of their former lawyer and the profession in general. This reality would seem to be inconsistent with the very strict, almost sacrosanct, protections for lawyer–client confidentiality based on lawyer–client trust and care.[61]

59 *Dyer v Chrysanthou (No 2) (Injunction)* [2021] FCA 641, [76]; *Mumbin v Northern Territory (No 1)* [2020] FCA 475, [38].

60 As discussed in Case study 7.4, the courts appear to also take the view that the likelihood of the lawyer using confidential information of a former client to assist a new client is enough 'detriment' without the need to show some other harm to the former client.

61 See generally Chapter 5.

INFORMATION BARRIERS – IMPENETRABLE WALLS OR POTENTIALLY POROUS INVENTIONS?

Law firms have sought to prevent a range of conflicts of interest from arising or to manage what would otherwise be an impermissible concurrent or former client conflict, through the use of information barriers. As discussed above, the *ASCR* contemplate that most conflicts faced by lawyers or firms can be managed with an effective information barrier.

An effective information barrier would include established, documented protocols for setting up and maintaining barriers or screens between those with relevant confidential information from current or former clients and those working on matters for other clients. These would include:

- undertakings by lawyers not to talk to each other, and procedures to ensure that people on either side of the information barrier have no, or limited, contact with one another;
- physical separation of people and files on each side of the information barrier from one another;
- restricted access to electronic files;
- programs to educate all staff on their responsibility in relation to confidentiality and the firm's protocols for information barriers;
- monitoring of effectiveness of the protocols by a compliance officer; and
- disciplinary sanctions imposed on any staff who breach the protocols.[62]

Information barriers are used to separate sections of a firm that might work on the same or related matters. Alternatively, they might be implemented where a lawyer within the law firm had nothing to do with the representation of the earlier client but wants to act for the new client. This may be permissible as long as adequate ('effective') safeguards are in place to make sure the lawyer cannot access any confidential information from those who did act for the former client. Finally, an information barrier might be used where a lawyer new to the firm has confidential information about a former client – the barrier would separate the lawyer from others in the firm who wish to work against that former client, as in Case study 7.3. As in that case, courts have found that information barriers can be effective in preventing or managing conflicts. They are particularly commonplace in large law firm practice to address a variety of conflicts.

Why are such measures needed if only certain individual lawyers have confidential information within an organisation? The law provides that generally if one lawyer is disqualified from acting because they have confidential information of one client that is material to another client, the whole firm is disqualified. The reason is that there is a rebuttable presumption, or imputation, of knowledge shared within a firm.[63] An information barrier is evidence that this sharing has not actually occurred in this firm in this case. In the same way, the knowledge of a lawyer new to a firm is not automatically assumed to be known by other lawyers in that firm. An information barrier might then quite effectively provide a shield for confidential information of former clients known to the new lawyer,

62 GE Dal Pont, *Lawyers' Professional Responsibility* (Thomson Reuters, 7th ed, 2021) 322–3. See also Law Society of New South Wales, *Information Barrier Guidelines* (2015) <https://www.lawsociety.com.au/sites/default/files/2018-03/Info%20barriers.pdf>.

63 *Mallesons Stephens Jaques v KPMG Peat Marwick* (1990) 4 WAR 357, 374.

so that it cannot be passed on to the new firm or its clients (again, this arose in Case study 7.3).[64] The *ASCR* imply that the rebuttable presumption of shared knowledge holds for ethical duties as well, as r 10 applies not just to the lawyer but to the law practice.

Courts have traditionally been sceptical about information barriers because of a concern about the casual and inevitable sharing of information within a firm. In *Mallesons Stephen Jaques v KPMG Peat Marwick*, Ipp J observed of the term 'information barrier': 'The derivation of the nomenclature is obscure. It appears to be an attempt to clad with respectable antiquity and impenetrability something that is relatively novel and potentially porous.'[65] Thus courts have been clear that the requirement is not just that the firm *tries* to protect information but that it is actually successful in doing so. One difficulty with this is that an information barrier might be impossible in anything but a large, well-resourced law firm. It might not be feasible to provide for physical separation of lawyers in a small office or have permanent procedures in place. The discussion in Case study 7.3 illustrates the specific requirements that might be expected for this procedure to be effective. In light of these, the *ASCR* seem tailored for the large law firm sector while making such 'management' of conflicts impossible for smaller firms (except when acting in short-term legal assistance contexts, as per *ASCR* r 11A). This might not only be perceived as inequitable across the sector but might pose access to justice concerns.

CASE STUDY 7.3 THE MOBILITY OF MODERN LAWYERS AND CONFIDENTIAL INFORMATION[66]

A relatively junior solicitor was employed by a large law firm for two years. During that time she worked on a range of insurance law matters for a client. She spent approximately 260 hours on insurance and employee indemnity related issues relevant to a commercial dispute the client was involved in. She then moved firms.

The following year another large civil claim was commenced against her former client (the 'Coinmach case'). Her new employer firm was acting for the plaintiff in the Coinmach case. It was another year later before her former law firm realised that there might be a conflict of interest in her working at her new employer firm. They wrote to the new employer firm setting out the concerns about the solicitor acting in this matter; her new employer firm advised that it saw no conflict of interest for either the solicitor or the firm. An application was made to the court to restrain the firm and the solicitor from acting in the Coinmach case.

After the first hearing the Court ordered the solicitor to provide an undertaking that she would not disclose any confidential information acquired during her employment at her

64 *Bureau Interprofessionel des Vins de Bourgogne v Red Earth Nominees Pty Ltd* [2002] FCA 588, [34]. It is unclear how far the rebuttable presumption might apply – for example, whether it captures non-legal staff who move between firms.

65 (1990) 4 WAR 357, 371.

66 The case is *Babcock & Brown DIF III Global v Babcock & Brown International Pty Ltd* [2015] VSC 612.

former firm, and that she was not to be involved in the conduct of the Coinmach matter. She had already been taken off the file by this time and the new employer firm proposed to establish an information barrier to prevent any future breach of confidentiality in her speaking to other lawyers in the firm. However, the parties could not agree to consent orders as to a sufficient information barrier and her former firm went back to the Court asking it to restrain both the solicitor and her current firm from acting in the Coinmach matter.

One of the arguments of the former employer was that under the information barrier protocols proposed to be implemented, the solicitor was to remain working in close physical proximity to lawyers working on the case. However, the solicitor had been physically moved and files were kept away from her and she had no access to electronic versions of the files. The current employer also argued that there was no problem because the Court had already ruled that there was only a 'theoretical risk' of breach of confidential information in this case given the solicitor had 'scant recollection of details of alleged confidential information'.

The Court found that the solicitor had received confidential information of her former client but that it was of a limited nature. It also noted that when she was employed at the former employer, she was a very junior solicitor with limited exposure to, or understanding of, the matter and was working on only very discrete issues. The Court accepted that confidential information of the former client had not been disclosed to the new employer. While the Court found that she didn't recall information, it noted that this may not be sufficient to remove the prospect of a future conflict because she could later recall information. However, she had been removed from the case and so was not in a position to recall facts and then use them against the former client. In any event, even if she did recall information the Court found that it would be unlikely to be of a nature that was useful in the current case:

> [T]he fragmented nature of the manner in which she was exposed to the confidential information renders the possibility of the recollection amounting to any more than fragments, which would cause no detriment to the [former client], is negligible.[67]

On this basis the Court refused to grant an injunction for a potential breach of duties of confidence or for the protection of the administration of justice. The Court expressly weighed the following consideration:

> In modern times, the flow of lawyers between large firms, as has occurred in this case, is extremely common. Lawyers taking up positions with new firms will invariably possess information, acquired from their previous position, which they are required to keep confidential. It is not in the public interest for the courts to disqualify the new firm from acting in a matter unless there is a real risk of disclosure of the confidential information that will be relevant to the action.[68]

67 Ibid [82].
68 Ibid [83].

Discussion questions

1. Do you agree with the Court's decision that the lawyer here was unlikely to have passed on information or used it against her former client already? Who should have to establish that there is no information sharing among lawyers in a firm (former client or the law firm)?
2. Most law firms have systems for checking for conflicts of interest before taking on a new matter, such as database searches for names related to the new matter to see if the same names are on any files relating to existing matters. What do you think went wrong here, given that the possible conflict was not discovered for some time?
3. In deciding whether to grant the injunction, the Court quoted an article that stated:

   > Lawyers transferring between firms have become a significant feature of modern legal practice. Many courts have shown awareness of this change in the legal profession by considering the impact that vicarious disqualification has on the mobility of lawyers. Adopting a disqualification rule that is too strict has the potential to seriously curtail the careers of lawyers simply because of a temporary association with a large firm.[69]

   Do you agree that this is an important consideration for the court? Is there a counterargument?

A potential problem with the widespread use of information barriers in parts of the legal industry is that lawyers and law firms are likely to have an interest in believing that there will be an effective way of 'managing' potential conflicts in a much wider range of circumstances than is appropriate. For example, courts have generally said that information barriers are only relevant for protecting the confidential information of *former* clients who are no longer clients of the firm.[70] They are not appropriate where there is an active duty to promote the interests of two current clients in contentious cases, though, as we have seen, *ASCR* r 11.4.2 provides that their use is ethical in these situations. The Law Council has indicated that client assent is also necessary,[71] but the poor drafting of the *ASCR* r 11.4 might indicate to law firms that these arrangements will be acceptable without even consulting affected clients or former clients.

Continued loyalty to a client and interest conflicting with the administration of justice

While Case study 7.3 shows that courts are becoming more tolerant of law firms 'managing' conflicts in large commercial law contexts, we need to consider does this risk losing sight of the relationship of loyalty to clients and continued duties of confidentiality to past and present clients? Should lawyers have more wide-ranging duties to remain loyal to their former clients? In the Full Court of the Supreme Court of Victoria's decision in *Spincode*

69 David Coull, 'Typhoid Marys: The Ethical Dilemma of Lawyers Who Switch Firms' (1998) 28(1) *Victoria University of Wellington Law Review* 41, 55.

70 But see *Australian Liquor Marketers Pty Ltd v Tasman Liquor Traders Pty Ltd* [2002] VSC 324.

71 Law Council of Australia, *Australian Solicitors' Conduct Rules 2011 and Commentary* (n 45) r 11.

Pty Ltd v Look Software Pty Ltd[72] Brooking JA somewhat controversially stated that case law and legal principle indicate that lawyers do have a wider duty. Brooking JA suggested that lawyers have an ongoing obligation of loyalty not to act against a former client and in the interests of a preferred client in relation to the same matter, regardless of whether there is any issue about disclosure of confidential information. Brooking JA argued that a solicitor's obligation of loyalty cannot be 'extinguished by the mere termination of the period of [the lawyer's] retainer' and that public policy 'gives a special relationship to the relationship of solicitor and client that the law will not generally permit to be stained by the appearance of disloyalty'.[73] He went on to say there was a 'public interest in reassuring the community … that even the appearance of improper behaviour will not be tolerated', and that the lawyer's conduct in this case was 'offensive to common notions of fairness and justice'.[74] The case concerned the not uncommon problem of a lawyer who was supposed to be acting for a company but in fact preferred the interests of one individual officer of the company. In short, the lawyer provided covert advice to two shareholders while still acting for the company and while there were disputes between the company's shareholders. The lawyer then acted for one of the shareholders in proceedings to wind up the company. The Court restrained the lawyer from continuing to act for the shareholders on the basis that the lawyer possessed confidential information from the client company that was at risk of being disclosed to the detriment of the company in the winding-up proceedings. The comments of Brooking JA were obiter, as it was clear that there was relevant company information held by the law firm. Indeed, the facts of the case were such that the Court was unsurprisingly concerned about the ethicality of the conduct of a lawyer in changing sides in a dispute.

While Brooking JA's decision might suggest that a lawyer cannot ever act against a former client, the principle is likely to be more confined. For instance, in Case study 7.3 the lawyer moving between firms was found to owe an ongoing duty of loyalty to the former client (the Court followed the Victorian approach), but as the lawyer was no longer working on the Coinmach case (the case concerning her former client) there were no breach of loyalty concerns. Thus, loyalty to a client owed by her former firm was not imputed to her new firm. However, if the lawyer had remained in her former firm and had been simply removed from the case, the ongoing assumption of loyalty may have applied in the Victorian context.

Courts in most jurisdictions outside of Victoria have not accepted Brooking JA's suggestion that a lawyer or law firm can be restrained from acting against a former client on the basis of the obligation of ongoing loyalty alone. Courts outside Victoria do, however, accept the *responsible lawyering* perspective of the court's inherent jurisdiction over solicitors as officers of the court to prevent the appearance of impropriety.[75] Disciplinary decisions such as in *Fordham v Legal Practitioners Complaints Committee*[76] have also found that causing harm to a former client can be unethical conduct.

72 (2001) 4 VR 501.

73 Ibid 517.

74 Ibid. Note that Brooking JA's approach has been followed in numerous cases in Victoria: see, eg, *Sent v John Fairfax Publication Pty Ltd* [2002] VSC 429, [98]–[104]; *Santin v Sfameni* [2020] VSC 26, [37] (Moore J).

75 *Dealer Support Services Pty Ltd v Motor Trades Association of Australia Ltd* (2014) 228 FCR 252; *Re IPM Group Pty Ltd* [2015] NSWSC 240; *Berengo v Berengo* [2014] VSC 667.

76 (1997) 18 WAR 467.

In many cases across Australia courts have exercised their inherent jurisdiction to disqualify a lawyer or firm from acting for a client to preserve the appearance of justice. This is most often applied in the context of concurrent representation as arose in Case study 7.1. In Case study 7.4 a court enjoined a lawyer from acting on the basis of a real possibility of misuse of confidential information *and* to protect the integrity of the judicial process. The test is whether a 'fair-minded reasonably informed member of the public would conclude that the proper administration of justice requires' that the lawyer should be prevented from acting.[77] An injunction is said to be applied exceptionally and with regard to 'the public interest that litigants should not be deprived of their choice of counsel without good cause'.[78] Here, the issue is not client loyalty but rather the role of the lawyer in the proper conduct of a case. As Beach J explains, the court is concerned

> not just with private fiduciary relationships and *inter-partes* fiduciary obligations, but rather the administration of justice, the public and the appearance of propriety of officers of the court.[79]

CASE STUDY 7.4 A BARRISTER WITH KNOWLEDGE AND A HIGH-PROFILE CASE

On 9 November 2020 the Australian Broadcasting Corporation ('ABC') broadcast the investigative television news program *Four Corners* with an episode called 'Inside the Canberra Bubble'. The episode addressed the conduct of some federal politicians, including the then Attorney-General, Christian Porter. Joanne Dyer had been interviewed for the episode on 8 July 2020. Only part of the interview with Ms Dyer was broadcast. What was not aired included her knowledge of an allegation made by Ms Dyer's friend, AB, that Mr Porter had raped AB in January 1988 when they both attended a debating tournament held at the University of Sydney. On 14 November 2020, *The Australian* newspaper published an article written by Janet Albrechtsen entitled 'Vested interests cornered by shoddy ABC hatchet job' that commented on the *Four Corners* episode.

Shortly afterwards, a friend of Ms Dyer's, James Hooke, approached her to suggest that she seek advice about whether the article was defamatory of her. In November 2020, Ms Dyer (assisted by Mr Hooke) instructed Marque Lawyers to act for her. Her solicitor, Mr Bradley, suggested briefing a senior barrister who specialises in defamation law, Sue Chrysanthou. Mr Hooke also suggested talking to Matthew Richardson, a longstanding friend of Mr Hooke and a barrister with expertise in defamation law. On 20 November 2020, Ms Dyer, Mr Hooke and Mr Bradley attended a conference with Mr Richardson and Ms Chrysanthou. Before the conference, Mr Richardson provided Ms Chrysanthou with a copy

77 This test is applied across the country: *Kallinicos v Hunt* (2005) 64 NSWLR 561, 582 [76].

78 *Fruehauf Finance Corporation Pty Ltd v Fez Ruthning (A Firm)* [1991] 1 Qd R 558, 566.

79 *Dealer Support Services Pty Ltd v Motor Trades Association of Australia Ltd* (2014) 228 FCR 252, [96].

of the article from *The Australian.* He also provided a copy of the police statement that had been prepared by AB when she went with her friend to the police station to make a report in June 2020 concerning Mr Porter.[80] The conference was found by a court to be a wide-ranging discussion about what Ms Dyer knew about the allegations against Mr Porter and the context of the ABC investigations.[81]

AB committed suicide in September 2020. The South Australian Coroner is investigating her death.

In late November 2020 a 'concerns notice' was drafted by the legal team for Ms Dyer to issue to *The Australian* about the article it had published. Ms Chysanthou provided feedback on this concerns notice and also acted for Ms Dyer in responding to the lawyers for the newspaper in late January to February 2021.

On 26 February 2021 the ABC published an article by Louise Milligan about a letter to the Prime Minister containing allegations against a senior cabinet minister having committed a rape in 1988. Although he was not named, the article was about Mr Porter, as he later himself revealed in a press conference on 3 March 2021.[82]

On 10 March 2021, Mr Porter briefed Ms Chrysanthou to act for him in defamation proceedings he wished to commence against the ABC in response to the Mulligan article. On 15 March, Mr Porter commenced the proceedings in the midst of intense media attention.

Ms Dyer's lawyers spoke to Ms Chrysanthou and told her it was a 'bad idea' for her to represent Mr Porter given her previous work for Ms Dyer. Ms Chrysanthou said 'she searched her emails and also spoke to Mr Richardson. She was unable to find any documents or emails in relation to Ms Dyer's matter, except for the concerns notice. Ms Chrysanthou stated in cross-examination that she deletes emails every few days.[83] It was on this basis that she felt she did not have a conflict in taking on Mr Porter's case. She claimed that she was obliged to take on the case as she was 'bound by the cab rank rule'.[84] She did not at any time ask for permission from Ms Dyer to act for Mr Porter.

After some discussions with Ms Chrysanthou about whether she faced a conflict, Ms Dyer initiated an application to restrain Ms Chrysanthou from continuing to act in the Porter defamation proceedings. The two grounds were that there was a danger that Ms

80 The police opened a file but did not investigate the matter at that time, citing insufficient evidence.

81 *Dyer v Chrysanthou (No 2) (Injunction)* [2021] FCA 641. Much of the judgment's coverage of the conversation and other documents relating to the allegations against Mr Porter has been redacted. The account of the case in this case study is principally taken from the judgment. An appeal by the barrister was dismissed by the Federal Court: *Porter v Dyer* [2022] FCAFC 116.

82 Elizabeth Byrne, 'Federal Court of Australia to Decide Whether ABC's Defence in Christian Porter Case Should Be Made Public', *ABC News* (online, 9 July 2021) <https://www.abc.net.au/news/2021-07-09/decision-to-be-made-on-abc-defence-in-christian-porter-case/100279250>.

83 *Dyer v Chrysanthou (No 2) (Injunction)* [2021] FCA 641, [42].

84 Ibid [46].

Chysanthou would use confidential information received from Ms Dyer in the course of acting in the defamation proceedings, and that she ought to be restrained from acting to protect the integrity of the judicial process and the proper administration of justice. The Court found that Ms Chrysanthou should be enjoined from acting for Mr Porter on both grounds.

The Court considered the relevant authorities in some detail and applied the five-stage set of questions provided earlier in this chapter. Despite the submissions made by Mr Porter, it found that a lawyer–client relationship had existed between the barrister and client that was also fiduciary. It appears to be assumed that this relationship had come to an end sometime prior to Ms Chrysanthou acting for Mr Porter. Nevertheless, a duty of confidence persisted.

Ms Chrysanthou argued that she did not recall any conversations with or information passed to her by Ms Dyer and had no documentary evidence except the concerns notice originally sent to *The Australian* newspaper. She said anything she knew was now in the public realm and so there was no relevant duty of confidence. The Court disagreed. It stated that 'the question whether confidential information has entered the public domain to such an extent that it loses its character as such is a question of fact and degree'.[85] It also found that a lawyer may face a conflict regarding confidential information even when the information exchange is impressionistic and may have been forgotten:

> Ms Chrysanthou is relevantly in possession of confidential information irrespective of whether or not she presently recalls the content of it. Further, Ms Chrysanthou's assessment of Ms Dyer as a witness, and of the credibility of Ms Dyer's account of the facts, is confidential information. Ms Chrysanthou denies she made such an assessment. Accepting that Ms Chrysanthou did not make any formal assessment of such matters, that does not gainsay that impressions were inevitably formed by her and formed in connection with particular facts, some of which were confidential. It is a part of human nature to assess what one is told by reference to the way in which it is said and the impression one forms, often if not generally subconsciously, of the person making the statement. Barristers are no exception; indeed they readily engage in such assessments out of professional necessity. This kind of confidential information has been rightly described as 'highly confidential'. Amongst other reasons, this is because the course of litigation, including whether it should be settled, and the result of litigation, can turn on whether or not a particular witness should be called and the credibility or reliability of witnesses.[86]

This information could be used even inadvertently for Mr Porter in drafting pleadings and in argument, because the matters were so closely related.

85 Ibid [95]–[96].
86 Ibid [100]–[101] (references omitted).

While this was not a case of acting on the other side of a contentious matter, the Court still found a conflict where the danger was a real risk of confidential information being used for Mr Porter without the consent of Ms Dyer:

> [T]he defamation proceedings ought not be conducted by a barrister who has already obtained information on a confidential basis about those matters. A part of the reason for this is that knowledge of the confidential information might affect, even subconsciously, the manner in which those proceedings are conducted, including with respect to interrogatories and discovery.[87]

The Court also considered the question of the maladministration of justice and found:

> Ms Chrysanthou acted for Ms Dyer in circumstances in which fair minded members of the public would think that it was likely that material was disclosed to Ms Chrysanthou which would be relevant to the proceedings instituted by Mr Porter against the ABC and Ms Milligan, and that Mr Porter might gain an advantage from his barrister possessing such information. It would not matter whether Ms Chrysanthou in fact had confidential information.[88]

Further the Court noted that the 'public might have less faith in the result of the defamation proceedings' if Ms Chrysanthou was allowed to act.

DISCUSSION QUESTIONS

1. In *Sent v John Fairfax Publication Pty Ltd*[89] a barrister was restrained from acting against a party with whom he had had a conference 14 years earlier. The Court considered that the barrister's recollection was liable to be revived when preparing for a new case with like facts. Do you agree that barristers should be restrained from acting where they have received information in same or related cases and yet do not recall anything?
2. The Court in the *Dyer* case found that a barrister's 'impressions' of a client are confidential information. Do you think we should be concerned about a lawyer acting for another party on the basis of the lawyer's own thoughts about the former client?
3. Would it have made a difference if Ms Chrysanthou had sought the consent of Ms Dyer to act for Mr Porter?
4. Do you think the public would be concerned about Ms Chrysanthou acting for Mr Porter in terms of the proper administration of justice even if all the information was in the public domain? Was she effectively changing sides in a dispute? Do you think the very public nature of the case, and that one of the parties was the first law officer of Australia, is relevant to this assessment?

87 Ibid [125].
88 Ibid [140].
89 [2002] VSC 429.

Client loyalty and the ideal of adversarial advocacy

The *ASCR*'s approach to client loyalty is largely based on the ideal of *adversarial advocacy*. Adversarial zeal for single clients is, however, undermined by efforts to generate fees from multiple clients. In relation to *lawyer–client conflicts*, adversarial advocacy assumes that in their role as professional advocates, lawyers can and should divest themselves of human temptations and all other concerns apart from their obligation to further their client's interests. But this is more difficult than the *ASCR* assume. Some conflicts – such as receiving commissions without providing clear written advice to the client about the exact nature of the lawyer interest – can be evaded under the rules. Some conflicts are not addressed in the *ASCR* at all – these include avoiding sexual relationships with clients or where lawyers have personal relationships with other lawyers or judicial officers in a case. Other conflicts cannot be so easily prohibited and avoided – for example, the inevitable conflict of interest between lawyer and client in negotiating the lawyer's fee, and the time and priority devoted by the lawyer to clients' work as against personal and family commitments. Handling these sorts of conflicts well is likely to be more a matter of lawyers being ethically reflective and aware of the influences on their own thinking and action, rather than merely following rules.

In relation to *client–client conflicts*, the *ASCR* themselves undermine their own apparently absolute commitment to client loyalty and confidentiality. The duty to avoid conflicts between current clients or former and current clients is expressed subject to conditions and qualifications that appear to be based on commercial expediency rather than on principle. As discussed in Chapter 2, the ideal of adversarial advocacy developed particularly as a rationale for the role of lawyers representing individual (not corporate) clients in criminal proceedings. The *ASCR* appear to represent a particular version of this orientation that relates not to criminal practitioners but to large law firms. In both contexts the rules equally rely on clients understanding and consenting to law firms acting in conflict situations. In some cases, such as where there is a criminal co-accused, informed consent might be questionable. Where the rules allow the firm to unilaterally decide to manage a conflict without disclosing it to the client (under r 10), the principle of acting only in the client's best interest seems to have been lost sight of entirely.

Alternative ethical approaches to client loyalty

In this section we consider how the *adversarial advocacy* picture of unadulterated loyalty to the client is made richer, and more complex, by considering the insights of the other three ethical approaches introduced in Chapter 2: *responsible lawyering*, *moral activism* and *ethics of care*. We have argued above that the *ASCR* seem to allow exceptions to the adversarial advocacy duty of pure loyalty and strict duties of client confidentiality to clients for commercial rather than ethical reasons. As discussed in Case study 7.3, the courts have also given significant weight to commercial and practical concerns about the movement of lawyers around the legal industry. The three alternative approaches give principled and ethical justifications for the extent and limits of the relationship of trust and loyalty between lawyers and their current and former clients. Alternative ethical approaches challenge the current rules and the way they are applied to legal practice.

The responsible lawyer

The *responsible lawyering* approach takes the lawyer's obligation of loyalty to the client very seriously because it is derived from the lawyer's role as an officer of the court who must be available to represent and advocate for clients. Client representation and advocacy is seen as a public obligation, not just a private matter between lawyer and client. A responsible lawyering approach to conflicts between clients would therefore likely be consistent with Brooking JA's view in *Spincode* that a lawyer should not act in a situation where there would be an appearance of disloyalty and impropriety in the administration of justice, regardless of a risk of disclosure of confidential information.[90] Similarly, responsible lawyering would see the lawyer's obligation to avoid personal conflicts as absolute and going well beyond avoiding direct, financial conflicts. While in cases where the courts have raised concerns about personal relationships clouding the judgment of a lawyer, such as Case study 7.1, client knowledge and consent are seen as the antidote. A responsible lawyering approach might question whether the client's interest should be the chief concern.

For concurrent client representation in all contexts, the *ASCR* imply that there is little distinction to be made between contentious and non-contentious matters, as both can be managed by client consent. However, the law has long been concerned about a lawyer acting on both sides of a dispute, because this may be more likely to harm the client *and* to impede the appropriate administration of justice. Responsible lawyering might be concerned that lawyers and clients make private arrangements in which clients consent to waive their rights to full loyalty. Arguably, it is not up to clients to decide how much loyalty they are willing to accept from their lawyer. There is also a public interest in requiring lawyers to show full loyalty to the client every time, so as not to damage the appearance of justice being done by lawyers performing their role properly in the legal system.[91] Responsible lawyering is therefore highly suspicious of information barriers and other arrangements by which law firms try to garner client consent for continuing to act in conflict situations.

Alongside the duty of loyalty to the client there will also be an equal ethical concern that lawyers do not show 'too much' loyalty to clients. According to the responsible lawyer, because the duty of loyalty to clients is derived from the lawyer's role as officer of the court, the lawyer's loyalty to the client must be confined and constrained by the lawyer's loyalty to the court and the legal system. We have already considered what this might mean in the criminal and civil litigation context (in Chapters 5 and 6) in terms of the lawyer seeking to dissuade a client from any action that goes against the lawyer's duty to the administration of justice. In Chapter 9 we will also consider lawyers' responsibilities in relation to legal or ethical misconduct by corporate and government clients, including lawyers' whistleblowing capacities and obligations.

Thus, discernment of a conflict can be difficult where lawyers have become used to seeing things from their client's point of view. Even more difficult issues are raised if we consider that lawyers, in at least some circumstances, might also owe an obligation of loyalty to the public interest that overrides their duty to their client, and perhaps even to the administration of justice. This is the concern of the *moral activist*.

90 *Spincode Pty Ltd v Look Software Pty Ltd* (2001) 4 VR 501. See also *A-G (NT) v Maurice* (1986) 161 CLR 475, 490 (Deane J); *Baker v Campbell* (1983) 153 CLR 52, 120 (Deane J).

91 See Duncan Webb, 'Autonomy, Paternalism, and Institutional Interest: Why Some Conflicts Can't Be Waived' (2005) 12(2) *International Journal of the Legal Profession* 261.

Moral activism

Moral activism encourages lawyers to have other ethical priorities beyond their loyalty to the client, which may impinge on what those lawyers will and will not do for their clients. This does not mean that moral activism gives lawyers an excuse for allowing self-interest or personal taste to limit their loyalty to client interests. Rather, moral activism says that lawyers must critically examine their own inclinations and commitments in each situation in terms of what justice requires.

The moral activist might say that lawyers should be encouraged to actively seek out and choose clients and causes to whom they can ethically devote their services so that loyalty is assured. A moral activist approach would also urge lawyers to explicitly discuss their own values and ethical commitments with their clients, to inform the client as to the likely limits of their loyalty, and also more importantly to try to persuade the client to share their ethical commitment.

Consider, for example, the situation where a lawyer has a personal or political commitment that goes against a position they are asked to argue: perhaps a committed animal lover and vegetarian is asked to defend a fast food company that claims it has been defamed by suggestions that the chickens it cooks have been treated inhumanely.[92] The law of lawyering generally seems to assume the adversarial advocacy view that a lawyer will automatically be able to do their best for the client regardless of their personal opinion of them and their case. But a broader, more holistic view of the principle of avoiding lawyer–client conflict suggests that the lawyer ought to disclose to their client their personal position and opinion and the way these might affect the lawyer's representation of the client's case.

In serious circumstances, where a client cannot be persuaded to do what the lawyer believes (on principled grounds) to be the right thing, the moral activist would consider ending the relationship or even breaching client loyalty and confidentiality to prevent harm (as discussed in Chapter 2).[93] Thus, the commitment to loyalty is tempered by a broader conception of personal morality and impact on society and the justice system. This does not mean that the moral activist rejects loyalty and confidentiality to clients, as there is general agreement that these are usually necessary for the justice system to operate fairly. As discussed in Chapter 4, the *ASCR* and the law itself recognise that there are limited exceptions to lawyers' obligations of confidentiality when clients are acting illegally or dangerously. These exceptions give lawyers some legal discretion and even permission to behave in a moral activist way to blow the whistle and breach confidentiality and loyalty where a greater public interest demands it.[94]

A moral activist stance might also take a view that seems somewhat contrary to client loyalty, where the object is to enhance access to justice. The Productivity Commission has noted the great value to access to justice of lawyers providing discrete services, such as

92 See *McDonald's Corporation v Steel* [1997] EWHC QB 366; *Steel v McDonald's Corporation* [1999] EWCA Civ 1144.

93 Sissela Bok, *Secrets: The Ethics of Concealment and Revelation* (Pantheon Books, 1983) 129–30; David Luban, *Lawyers and Justice: An Ethical Study* (Princeton University Press, 1988) 177–205.

94 See Paul Finn, 'Professionals and Confidentiality' (1992) 14 *Sydney Law Review* 317, 323; Karen Koomen, 'Breach of Confidence and the Public Interest Defence: Is It in the Public Interest?' (1994) 10 *Queensland University of Technology Law Journal* 56, 86–8; Christine Parker, Suzanne LeMire and Anita Mackay, 'Lawyers, Confidentiality and Whistleblowing: Lessons from the McCabe Tobacco Litigation' (2017) 40(3) *Melbourne University Law Review* 999.

advice and duty lawyer services.[95] Community organisations and Legal Aid bodies that provide many of these services have made submissions to reviews of the *ASCR* arguing for a less rigorous approach to some conflicts, so as to foster access to justice.[96] These organisations often argue that the one-size-fits-all approach to ethical governance should be rejected. For instance, community law firms mostly provide discrete services that might not require the rigour of a full conflict screening, or information barriers (which might be impossible in small organisations). They contend that 'it is not practical or even reasonably necessary to obtain consent in the case of one or more current clients where only discrete service provision is contemplated'.[97] The National Association of Community Law Centres recommended that the *ASCR* be amended to 'provide a limited exception to rules 10 and 11 for unbundled, discrete legal assistance services provided to individual clients' by community sector law services.[98] While these requests have been partially implemented in *ASCR* r 11A, as described above, there is still a requirement that lawyers obtain client consent.

Regional legal practitioner Helen McGowan has argued for a diverse approach to conflicts that places ethical discretion with the lawyer in the context of their practice. She argues:

> [J]ustice delivery requires lawyers to develop an adaptive ethical stance to respond effectively to the context of their law practice, and this adaptive practice should be moderated by professional peers through participation within professional communities of practice.[99]

The 'ethical acuity' (her words) that McGowan demands may mean that certain lawyers act for clients as best they can, notwithstanding a conflict of duties applying.[100] McGowan notes that such an approach requires a process of reflection on the public interest inherent in access to lawyers. It also requires consultation within the local profession. This relational perspective of personal reflection within a community of lawyers might also be seen as an *ethics of care* approach.

Ethics of care approach

Adopting an *ethic of care*, like *moral activism*, means a lawyer is aware of and acts on their own ethical commitments in practising law. But an ethics of care approach values personal and relational commitments. This might include care for oneself. For example, rather than viewing work-life balance as an impediment to acting in the best interests of a client who

95 Productivity Commission, *Access to Justice Arrangements* (Report No 72, September 2014) vol 2 ch 19.

96 See, eg, Law Council of Australia, *Review of the Australian Solicitors' Conduct Rules* (February 2018) 57.

97 Ibid.

98 Ibid 3. The Law Council of Australia published a Consultation Paper in 2020 seeking responses to this proposal: Law Council of Australia, *Australian Solicitors' Conduct Rules – Short-Term Legal Assistance Services* (Public Consultation Paper, November 2020).

99 Helen McGowan, 'Adapt, Improvise and Overcome: Engaging with Conflict of Interest in the Bush' (PhD Thesis, The Australian National University, 2018) 5.

100 Compare this to the opinion of the Court in *Seidler v Seidler* [2010] FMCAfam 1394, [59]: in considering an argument about a lack of supply of lawyers in regional towns, it stated that legal principles should not be overlooked.

expects 24-hour attention, an ethic of care values the needs of the client *and* the lawyer. There is no conflict between these two interests/needs – they are seen as aligned, because care for oneself will provide better care for the client. While other ethical approaches may agree that overwork to meet the demands of a client (or employer) is not necessary to act competently and loyally for the client, an ethic of care might more readily identify this issue.

Equally, an ethic of care recognises lawyers' humanity, fallibility, and susceptibility to pressure and temptation, even when trying to act ethically. Conflicting interests and obligations will inevitably be a part of the lawyer–client relationship, for good and for ill. According to an ethic of care, lawyers need to be open and honest with their clients about the factors that might influence their judgement, so that clients can judge their lawyer's advice for themselves, and even persuade their own lawyer to a different point of view on ethical issues.[101] Thus they might take a much more consultative approach to considering conflicts than is contemplated in the *ASCR*.

An ethic of care holds a strong commitment to resolving disputes amicably rather than adversarially, ensuring all parties' interests are valued and openly discussed. This approach could equally be understood as a conflict of interest in itself. Where the lawyer values, or even considers, the interests of parties other than the client in a dispute, this could be characterised as a lack of client loyalty. Indeed, the adversarial ethic underlying the *ASCR* (as discussed in Chapters 5 and 6) might suggest that this is an unacceptable professional approach.

However, like adversarial ethics, an ethics of care approach would value the client's views and may therefore consider a client as able to consent to their lawyer continuing to act in a situation of conflict of interests, or potential conflict, as long as the lawyer has put the client in a position to fully understand the conflict and its possible implications for them.

An ethic of care might take a different approach to lawyering for two or more clients where there is a positive relationship between them, by emphasising achievement of a 'common goal' – for example, in putting together a deal, arranging matters amicably after a separation or divorce, or mediating a dispute between business partners.[102] Of course, joint representation can only be justified where the clients genuinely want to work together, can be equal partners without power imbalances and are in a position to understand what joint representation involves.

Conclusion

Understanding and anticipating the ethical challenges raised by conflicting duties is arguably one of the most difficult processes for lawyers, because conflicts can be obscured by a range of contextual and personal factors, as we have seen above.

Lawyers can easily become occupationally desensitised to the implications of conflict. They can come to see the process of living with different competing interests – that is, owing different loyalties to different people and different institutions – as merely one of

101 See, eg, Donald Nicolson and Julian Webb, *Professional Legal Ethics: Critical Interrogations* (Oxford University Press, 1999) 146–56 on the concept of 'autonomy-in-relation'.

102 Janine Griffiths-Baker, *Serving Two Masters* (Hart Publishing, 2002) 115 refers to solicitors' firms as differentiating 'common goal' conflicts as one type of conflict.

'operational management' associated with maximising the number of lucrative and desirable clients. Equally, human factors applying to us all can obscure good ethical decision-making. It is essential that an ethical lawyer be vigilant in their practices to screen for, and anticipate, conflicts. The earlier it is understood that loyalty or other legal and ethical duties are being compromised, the more capacity lawyers have to do something about it. Where there is a possibility of a compromise of loyalty to the client or the administration of justice, the best ethical decision may be to simply refuse to act. On the other hand, exercising ethical reflection in each case might produce differing responses depending on the context – it might be in the interests of justice to work for a client where a conflict persists, if the lawyer can still act with competency and care, and the fully informed client agrees.

RECOMMENDED FURTHER READING

Sandro Goubran, 'Conflicts of Duty: The Perennial Lawyers' Tale – A Comparative Study of the Law in England and Australia' (2006) 30(1) *Melbourne University Law Review* 88

Janine Griffiths-Baker, *Serving Two Masters: Conflicts of Interest in the Modern Law Firm* (Hart Publishing, 2002)

Law Society of New South Wales, *Information Barrier Guidelines* (2015) <https://www.lawsociety.com.au/sites/default/files/2018-03/Info%20barriers.pdf>.

Eli Wald, 'Taking Attorney-Client Communications (and Therefore Clients) Seriously' (2008) 42(3) *University of San Francisco Law Review* 747

Duncan Webb, 'Autonomy, Paternalism, and Institutional Interest: Why Some Conflicts Can't Be Waived' (2005) 12(2) *International Journal of the Legal Profession* 261

8

LAWYERS' FEES AND COSTS: COMMUNICATING WELL WITH CLIENTS AND AVOIDING OVERCHARGING

Introduction

Lawyers' fees are one of the main causes of complaint by clients[1] and of continued public concern about the ethicality of the profession.[2] Charging 'fairly and reasonably' and in compliance with the detailed legislative requirements imposed on a practitioner can be tricky. Even the most honest and conscientious lawyers may have trouble explaining fees to clients and controlling their increase. Organisational pressures and adversarial approaches can lead to questionable billing practices and place pressure on individual lawyers to behave unethically.

Deliberate 'gross' or excessive overcharging, withdrawal of costs from a client's trust account without their permission or other legal entitlement, or the deduction of fees in the absence of a proper bill or costs agreement are the most easily recognisable types of unethical practice. These often result in a client complaint to a regulatory authority, may result in professional discipline and draw considerable negative comment from the public. For instance, in a well-publicised case in New South Wales the principal solicitor of a firm was struck off for charging a client with a personal injuries claim a quarter of her $3.5 million settlement in fees and charges, where the bill contained errors and duplications and charged for work that was not done.[3] Such conduct can also be subject to civil claims against law firms for negligence, breach of fiduciary duty and breach of contract, as well as constitute breaches of the *Australian Consumer Law*.[4]

Individual clients are especially vulnerable to costs abuses. People may have to use a lawyer for the first time when they are in a vulnerable social, emotional and financial situation and need legal help quickly because of a disputatious relationship breakdown or criminal charges against them. Many clients who have not previously engaged a lawyer will be at a disadvantage in negotiating the services to be provided and costs to be paid. The

1 In one study considering complaints over 10 years until 2015, around 40% of complaints related to overcharging: Stephen Tang, Tony Foley and Vivien Holmes, 'Ethical Misconduct by New Australian Lawyers: Prevalence and Prevention' (2020) 20(1) *International Journal of the Legal Profession* 1, 8. This remains the case in that jurisdiction in 2021, with 41% of complaints relating to costs and overbilling and 7% of complaints relating to defective costs disclosure: Victorian Legal Services Board and Commissioner, *2021 Annual Report* (2021) 31. This is replicated in reports of regulators around the country as described later in the chapter.

2 See, eg, the discussion in Chapter 3 of public scandals that led to legislative reform regulating the legal profession.

3 *Legal Services Commissioner v Keddie* [2012] NSWADT 106. The disciplinary case associated with this firm's billing practices is discussed further in Case study 8.1. This case was widely reported in the Australian media: see, eg, 'The Law Firm, Their Clients and the Legal Fees', *Background Briefing* (ABC Radio National, 22 July 2012) <https://www.abc.net.au/radionational/programs/backgroundbriefing/4139052>.

4 In *Liu v Barakat* (District Court of New South Wales, Curtis J, 8 November 2011) there was a finding against Keddies of a breach of s 18 of the *Australian Consumer Law* (*Competition and Consumer Act 2010* (Cth) sch 2), being misleading or deceptive conduct by the firm. Items charged included three-line letters that would take a few seconds to read but were billed for 12 minutes of time at a senior litigation lawyer's rate of $435 an hour. Secretaries in the firm were being billed out at partners' rates of $460 an hour and there was charging for 'perusing and considering' two-line letters: cited in Richard Ackland, 'Small Cases, Big Bills: Keddies Working Overtime to Kill Complaints', *The Sydney Morning Herald* (Sydney, 18 November 2011).

frequent imbalance of power between lawyer and client[5] (in the lawyer's favour) can mean that the lawyer influences the client about the nature of the retainer and the costs involved. Indeed, the law treats this imbalance as a category of assumed undue influence, and the *ASCR* prohibit activities that the common law has found to be a breach of fiduciary duty.[6] For instance, a lawyer was suspended for 12 months for gross overcharging of a 'no-win, no-fee' client who was suing in relation to a birth injury of his child.[7] The charges were billed under a second costs agreement, more favourable to the lawyer, that had been agreed to by the client under pressure from the lawyer. Such conduct is a breach of the fiduciary relationship between lawyer and client, and it was found to be unethical.

Many of the disciplinary and civil cases against lawyers in relation to their costs occur where the lawyer or firm is charging on the basis of the time spent working on a client's matter. Time billing is the predominant method of billing in Australian legal practices. The ethical challenges posed for lawyers by time billing are discussed in detail in this chapter. Indeed, it is not just because of unethical practices by *individual* lawyers that cost abuses might occur. Cultural and structural factors in the legal *organisation* often lead to excessive costs. In the next section of the chapter we describe how time-based billing as a way of charging clients and managing lawyers' performance within firms can magnify incentives for poor billing practices (and produce unhealthy workplaces).

There are a range of other ways lawyers and law firms can charge for their services. This chapter begins by explaining the most common approaches and their ethical pitfalls. There is no one way of billing that is universally agreed to be free from risk of abuse. Individual factors (such as personal pressures[8]) and organisational demands might lead to overcharging or other abuses relating to billing. The predominance of an ethical approach of *adversarial advocacy* can also exacerbate costs to clients and diminish access to justice.

While some charges are obviously excessive, illegitimate or even fraudulent, others might be more debatable due to differing understandings between a lawyer and client. Working out when lawyers' fees are legally and ethically acceptable can be a tricky exercise, and lawyers and clients are bound to disagree. This chapter considers the legal requirements and ethical guidance for lawyers about billing appropriately. Ethical lawyers need to be aware of the career, financial and personal pressures to increase a bill but nonetheless act according to the legal requirements to charge only for what is 'fair and reasonable'. This will mean managing from the outset *how and what* work is performed.

The legal and ethical requirements around billing emphasise informed consent by the client, gained through disclosure about costs. The legislative requirements of costs disclosure are considered later in this chapter. We argue that ethical billing practice requires much more than the specific disclosures legally required. Lawyers and law firms must communicate with

5 There are a range of studies that have attempted to assess whether such an imbalance of power or asymmetry of information exists, and if so in what contests. This will vary depending on the nature of the client, but in most cases the law firm has more power and information: Alice Woolley, 'Time for Change: Unethical Hourly Billing in the Canadian Profession and What Should Be Done About It' (2004) 83 *La Revue Du Barreau Canadien* 859.

6 *Re Morris Fletcher & Cross' Bill of Costs* [1997] 2 Qd R 228. *ASCR* r 12.2, set out in full later in the chapter, proscribes acting in a way to influence a client to pay more than is fair and reasonable.

7 *Council of the Queensland Law Society Inc v Roche* [2004] 2 Qd R 574.

8 Described in more depth as applying to all aspects of practice in Chapter 3.

the client effectively and honestly about how the legal services will be delivered and the implications of this for the quantum of their bill (and perhaps all parties' costs).

Nevertheless, disputes between lawyers and clients will invariably arise. The regulatory regime covering costs sets out specific ways these disputes are dealt with, including resolution of disputes about the quantum of a bill, and the situations in which the lawyer's costs are suspect enough to be seen as unethical practice and subject to professional discipline.

Methods of charging for legal services

One reason that clients complain so often about their legal bills is that legal costs are often unpredictable and difficult to understand. There are many approaches to charging for legal services and, we argue, no one method of calculating legal fees seems to be perfect. We begin by introducing the main ways in which lawyers calculate their fees – item remuneration, time-based billing, contingent fees, and lump sum and value billing – and the different ethical issues that these methods of billing raise.

All methods of billing have their advantages and detriments, but time billing has the most potential for client disillusionment, confusion *and* lawyer wrongdoing. Time billing is therefore the most contested approach; most of the disciplinary cases relating to ethical behaviours around costs relate to charging on the basis of time, and consequently there are periodically calls for this charging method to be prohibited. Despite this, time billing remains the predominant method of charging in the legal industry. A common version of billing by time in certain areas of legal practice is on a contingent basis – what is often called 'no-win, no-fee'. Under this arrangement the client does not have to pay for legal services unless and until they are successful in their case. While this might contribute to access to justice by allowing a poor person to hire a lawyer, there are a range of ethical concerns about this approach that have led regulators to prohibit no-win, no-fee arrangements in certain areas.[9]

Otherwise, how a lawyer charges for legal services, including what tasks are undertaken and how they are undertaken, is largely at the hands of the lawyers.[10] Some clients, such as large organisations or wealthy individuals, have enough purchasing power and experience dealing with lawyers to dictate terms. They will often require law firms to tender for a package of services where the successful tenderer agrees to a lump sum for all work done, regardless of the problems that might later occur in providing the contracted services. This passes to the law firm the risk of accurately assessing the cost to the firm (in time, resources and wages) of delivering competent services in the matter. However, most clients have no alternative but to accept the billing method proposed by their lawyer (although there are legislative protections explained later in this chapter). Nevertheless, there are other approaches to charging for legal services becoming more available, such as 'value billing', that appear to allow more client participation and align more with client interest rather than lawyer profit.

9 No-win, no-fee arrangements are not permitted for criminal or family law matters.

10 As described later in the chapter, the legislative regimes applying to lawyers do not prescribe a particular method of charging for legal services but do provide constraints on certain practices.

Item remuneration billing

Lawyers can charge on an *item remuneration* or *task-completed* basis, which means they apply a predetermined 'scale' or schedule that specifies the amount of money that may be claimed for each subcategory of legal work, or task, in a larger case or transaction. Item remuneration allows lawyers to be specific about what they have done for their client and to produce a bill itemising the amount charged for each task in the case. Thus, drafting a letter may be charged to the client – say $30 per 'folio' (a folio = 100 words). It makes no difference *how long* the lawyer takes to draft the letter of 100 words, the lawyer will still be paid the same amount for the *task*. The actual amount charged per item usually varies upwards according to how much money is being claimed (or defended), to recognise the extra 'skill, care and responsibility' associated with a larger claim.[11]

Historically, legislation governing the legal profession and legal work allowed the legal profession and the courts to set minimum fee scales for all legal work.[12] These scales were considered justified because they were thought to protect unsophisticated clients from being exploited by lawyers in situations where clients could not judge the quality and appropriate price for legal services. Nor would clients necessarily be able to negotiate and bargain effectively with their prospective lawyer to get the best deal. It was considered better to highly regulate lawyers' fees by scales set for the whole profession on the assumption that the profession would act in the public interest and ensure that all lawyers conformed to the same high quality and charged fair fees. These 'scale fees' set by the profession were abolished in the 1990s because they were considered anticompetitive.[13] They effectively allowed the profession to set a minimum floor for their own prices and prevented clients from 'shopping around' for a better price. As one lawyer commented about the impact of abolition of scales:

> [Before] the mid-80s pretty much everything was done on scale, so you got paid per item, and nobody particularly cared how long it took you as long as you billed enough items. And the conveyancing scales, for example, were so generous that, if you had the clients, you could work maybe 15 hours a week … But all that's changed … Things are getting measured more precisely; the overseers have become crueller.[14]

Despite the abolition of scales as a required method of charging, the courts have continued to publish fee scales for the purposes of assessing disputes about costs in litigation. And since individual lawyers and law firms are free to set their own fees on an item remuneration

11 There are different scales for different levels of courts and tribunals.

12 Michael Legg and Justine Rogers, 'Lawyers' Fee Arrangements and Their Wellbeing' in M Legg, P Vines and J Chin (eds), *The Impact of Technology and Innovation on the Wellbeing of the Legal Profession* (Intersentia, 2020) 267; Gino Dal Pont, 'Contextualising Lawyer Overcharging' (2016) 42(2) *Monash University Law Review* 283.

13 Trade Practices Commission, *Study of the Professions: Legal* (Final Report, 1994) ch 8; Christine Parker, *Just Lawyers: Regulation and Access to Justice* (Oxford University Press, 1999) ch 3, 38–41. A change of regulatory approach to apply competition policy to lawyer regulation is described in detail in Chapter 3.

14 Lawyer interviewed and quoted by Iain Campbell and Sara Charlesworth, 'Salaried Lawyers and Billable Hours: A New Perspective from the Sociology of Work' (2012) 19 *International Journal of the Legal Profession* 89, 98–9.

basis, many lawyers use these 'court scales' as a basis for their own charging. Clients have the comfort of knowing that, even if the lawyer is a bit slow in completing the task, it is the lawyer not the client who carries the cost of the extra time spent. There are, however, a number of potential ethical disadvantages in item remuneration billing for clients.

This approach diminishes competition and therefore pressure for reduction of price. Lawyers set the cost of specific tasks or items performed. This cost might be set by the firm in the costs agreement with the individual client or according to the court scale. But the scale amounts are set by committees and, although those committees may be diligent and conscious of their wider responsibilities, they are dominated by lawyers rather than being comprised of a mix of lawyers and consumers. Court scales of costs generally only specify a *minimum* fee because the cost committees that set the scales have always leaned towards lawyers' arguments that fees for individual items under the scales may be increased if the circumstances justify this.

Despite these concerns, the method of charging is relatively transparent and often allows a straightforward comparison with the fees charged by other lawyers providing like services. Indeed, courts determining whether a costs agreement is fair and reasonable in a dispute have pointed to these scales as a transparent benchmark of fairness.[15] This is to be contrasted with the predominant method of charging for legal services, which is billing for the time spent by lawyers working on the case.

Time-based billing

Time-based billing is generally thought to have been first used by law firms in the 1950s as a management tool.[16] After that time it was eagerly adopted by the profession and remains the main method of charging legal fees despite some disruptions (described below).[17] The approach – often called the 'billable hour' – is based on charging according to the time spent by the lawyer on the legal task. The lawyer specifies an hourly rate – say $350[18] – and the client agrees to pay that rate multiplied by however many hours the task takes.

There are variations to this approach, such as billing according to time but postponing payment until the client secures a 'win' (being a legal settlement or judgment) – this is called a 'conditional costs agreement' and described further below. The time-based method is also often accompanied by a percentage charge on top of the calculated fee according to hours spent on the matter.[19] At the outset we warn that charging an additional percentage on top of agreed fees for time spent working on a client's matter, even where there is complexity or significant skill, is ethically questionable. The base rate of legal fees usually already takes

15 See GE Dal Pont, *Law of Costs* (LexisNexis, 5th ed, 2021).

16 Herbert Kritzer, 'Lawyers' Fees and the Holy Grail: Where Should Clients Search for Value?' (1994) 77 *Judicature* 186.

17 Legg and Rogers (n 12) 271; Stuart Pardau, 'Bill, Baby, Bill: How the Billable Hour Emerged as the Primary Method of Attorney Fee Generation and Why Early Reports of Its Demise Might Be Greatly Exaggerated' (2013) 50(1) *Idaho Law Review* 1.

18 Choice reported median rates are between $350 and $650: Rebecca Douglas, 'Legal Fees: How Much Should They Cost?' *CHOICE* (Web Page, 1 August 2018) <https://www.choice.com.au/shopping/shopping-for-services/services/articles/legal-fees>.

19 There are two common approaches to this: care and consideration and an 'uplift fee' that can apply to conditional arrangements. These are discussed in the next subsection.

into account the seniority of the lawyer doing the work and the costs of them doing business (such as having an office). The minimum ethical expectation is that lawyers are competent in their area of work (*ASCR* r 4.1) and so charging more for doing a good job is questionable.

Time-based billing is attractive to the profession because it normally results in a higher level of fees than item remuneration. It might also reflect lawyers' sense that they are being paid for their professional advice rather than for a product. Time-based billing is also a useful way for law firms to keep track of what individual lawyers are doing and how much they are earning for the firm. As Iain Campbell and Sara Charlesworth argue: 'The billable hours system came to prominence as a billing method but its primary function is no longer billing; instead its primary function is as a mechanism of management control, which acts to transmit pressure on salaried solicitors.'[20] This aspect of lawyers' costs as a consequence or symptom of poor organisational cultures is considered later in the chapter (and in Case study 8.3).

Time billing is not as transparent to the client as other ways of charging because it is difficult for clients to imagine the full cost of obtaining legal services at the outset and it can be hard to compare a firm's pricing when there is considerable discretion as to how time is spent working on the matter. Time billing is also far less certain because legal work need not be as precisely itemised in the bill,[21] there is discretion about who performs the task at what rate, and further charges can be added to the bill on top of charging for time spent on legal work. In many cases the notion that the client is billed according to time might be somewhat arguable where the agreement specifies that a lawyer charges a minimum unit of time – typically six minutes. This means that where a task performed for a client takes less than six minutes, the client will be billed for the full cost of six minutes.

Thus, critics increasingly regard the opacity and unpredictability of time billing as both inefficient and unfair, since there is not necessarily any upper limit on the total hours appearing on the time sheet.[22] Some critics also note that the drive to generate more billable hours reduces the time spent on developing professional skills.[23] Former Chief Justice Spigelman went so far as to say that much of the problem with lawyers' fees centres on time-based billing:

> [I]t is difficult to justify a system in which inefficiency is rewarded with higher remuneration ... [because] the legal practitioner does not have a financial incentive to do the service as quickly as possible. The control is of course, the practitioner's sense of professional responsibility.[24]

20 Campbell and Charlesworth (n 14) 112.

21 Legislators around the country have addressed this by requiring that an itemised bill be provided to the client on request (and a lawyer cannot charge for this task): *Uniform Law* s 187; *Legal Profession Act 2006* (ACT) s 292; *Legal Profession Act 2006* (NT) s 327; *Legal Profession Act 2007* (Qld) s 332; *Legal Practitioners Act 1981* (SA) sch 3, cl 34; *Legal Profession Act 2007* (Tas) s 316.

22 Woolley (n 5). Further discussion of the basis on which overcharging can occur is provided below. See also Colin James, 'Legal Practice on Time: The Ethical Risk and Inefficiency of the Six Minute Unit' (2017) 42(1) *Alternative Law Journal* 61.

23 Legg and Rogers (n 12) 290.

24 Chief Justice Jim Spigelman, 'Opening of Law Term Dinner, 2004' (Speech, Opening of Law Term Dinner, Sydney, 2 February 2004).

Time-based billing will be in a client's interest if the lawyer completes the task quickly and so charges less than if fees were calculated on an item remuneration basis. Yet, as described in the next section, personal financial and organisational management structures might present much greater pressures to overcharge the client than to be efficient.

There are a range of ways in which time billing might lend itself to overcharging a client. Lawyers may spend more time on tasks than required, perform unnecessary tasks or even add time to their timesheet that was not spent on the client matter (often called 'padding').[25] Some accounts have cited the exploitation of minimum time provisions. For instance, a lawyer might wait until a time when people are unlikely to be in their office (such as lunchtime) and then make 30 (unanswered) phone calls, recording each one as a separate six-minute task, or by doing tiny tasks on a number of files in one six-minute timeslot so that work done on each file can be recorded as a separate time unit.[26]

Absent unethical intention, time billing is often accused of inaccuracy. Humans being fallible, all time might not be accurately recorded to the correct client's file. As one lawyer commented:

> I'd never understood it until I did it, until I had to. I used to think: 'oh what's the big deal about a timesheet'. But until you go, oh you know: 'Remember to start the clock, turn off the clock, start it at this point, turn it off at that point' ... Or [you] come to the end of the day and think: 'God, what did I do today and how long did it take me?' I used to try and write things down but it didn't always work – nightmare.[27]

There are increasingly better tools to improve accuracy in recording time – for example, using time-recording software rather than writing things down on a file note. But technology does not necessarily remove overcharging. Automated billing is the norm. These systems better capture the length and purpose of phone calls, allow lawyers to swap between matters quickly and record their time spent, permit easily generated interim bills, and allow for remote recording in the cloud while lawyers are on the move. Yet, human error or poor firm practices, and outright fraud, will always be a risk. Consider Case study 8.1 (mentioned earlier), where inaccuracy in creating a bill for a client resulted in excessive charges.

CASE STUDY 8.1 **THE MANY WAYS TO OVERCHARGE A CLIENT**

In a disciplinary case against the principal of a firm, the then NSW Legal Services Commissioner argued that an excessive amount was charged through a variety of inaccuracies and errors: 'charges were made representing work in excess of the work performed; there were charges for work which was not performed; and, there were charges

25 See, eg, Case study 8.2.

26 See Lisa G Lerman, 'Gross Profits? Questions About Lawyer Billing Practices' (1994) 22(3) *Hofstra Law Review* 645 for reports of similar practices in the United States.

27 Lawyer interviewed and quoted by Campbell and Charlesworth (n 14) 104.

for work undertaken and time spent on the file that included steps that were excessive and unnecessary'.[28] It was also alleged that 'work was undertaken and charged for by persons of inappropriate seniority or qualification; and, unnecessary work was undertaken in relation to the file'. An itemised bill provided to the client also revealed that 'the narrative bill duplicated charges for work performed'.[29]

The bill sent to the client was 132 pages in length and contained approximately 1,766 items. In addition to the time spent on the matter, a further 25% uplift was added. The disciplinary tribunal found that the firm had overcharged the client by $215,074.65.[30]

The firm used a time-recording system called 'Locus System' that could be and was accessed by all employees and was set to the minimum unit of a six-minute activity. Employees of the firm would record work done on the matters by themselves or others in the system by providing a brief description of that work and the time taken to do it. An employed lawyer gave evidence that he received only a 'fairly elementary' description of how to use the computerised time-recording system but there was 'considerable pressure on employed solicitors and other fee earners to ensure, so far as possible, that all work that was properly chargeable was correctly captured and entered on the computer system so that it could be fully charged'.[31]

Discussion questions

1. Can you list the ways in which the lawyers unacceptably added to the cost of legal services in this case?
2. The principal, Mr Keddie, was reported to have told lawyers working on the matter to look for any 'leakage' – that is, work performed but not entered into the firm-billing software that could relate to the matter and be included in the bill.[32] Do you think this is a questionable direction? Why or why not?
3. The Tribunal found that the Locus System was a seriously flawed way to account for legal work performed because, for instance, it produced multiple entries for the same work. What should be the process for the law firm prior to sending out a bill to a client? Do individual lawyers have responsibility to ensure their time entries are accurate?
4. The Tribunal did not find that the billing was deliberately fraudulent but rather that the culture around billing and the billing system was seriously flawed. It found that there was a failure by the principal of the firm to properly or adequately supervise the work done and charged for.[33] What would have been adequate supervision in this context?

28 *Legal Services Commissioner v Keddie* [2012] NSWADT 106, [34].
29 Ibid.
30 Ibid [80].
31 Ibid [20].
32 From the accompanying disciplinary proceeding against the employee lawyer: *Scroope v Legal Services Commissioner* [2013] NSWCA 178.
33 *ASCR* r 37 requires principals to provide 'reasonable supervision' to employees of the firm in providing legal services.

Case study 8.1 concerns a case where there was an 'uplift fee' of 25% charged on a conditional arrangement, described next. This was accepted as lawful but it certainly added to the cost of an already inflated bill.

Conditional and contingent agreements, and uplift fees

One way in which some lawyers attempt to make justice more affordable and accessible for clients who cannot afford litigation is by charging on a *conditional* basis. This means the client pays only if they are successful in a case. As discussed above, this is often known as a 'no-win, no-fee' arrangement. It is a way of assisting litigants who cannot afford to pay lawyers' fees in advance, and is easily understood. Conditional fees are, however, ethically ambiguous. On the one hand, these types of fees may help clients access legal and substantive justice in line with all four ethical perspectives discussed in Chapter 2. On the other hand, conditional arrangements are ethically questionable if they damage the probity and integrity of, as well as the care for, the lawyer–client relationship. They have the potential to distort the litigation or dispute resolution process by giving lawyers a personal stake or interest in the litigation, which may conflict with their ability to advise as to the clients' best interests or even to obey their duty to the court.[34]

Conditional costs agreements are those in which the lawyer and client agree that the lawyer will only be paid if the client is 'successful' (being a damages award, settlement or some other agreed outcome for the client). Conditional agreements include those that merely provide that the lawyer will charge their ordinary base fee (usually calculated on a time basis) if the client succeeds. Most conditional costs agreements, however, allow the lawyer to charge an 'uplift' of their fee (see below) if their case succeeds. These arrangements can promote access to justice but might also result in a temptation to charge higher fees where there is limited risk (the case is sure to succeed).

Conditional costs agreements have been accepted by the Australian courts[35] and are explicitly allowed under legislation around the country, with certain safeguards around express client consent and a cooling-off period.[36] This regulation seeks to ensure that clients understand the nature of the agreement, including that they may be liable to pay certain costs – such as barristers' fees and court costs – even if they do not win their case.[37]

---

34 *Re Robb* (1996) 134 FLR 294, 300. Concerns about this billing practice leading to an increase in litigation in areas of personal injury resulted in further regulation of advertising banning promoting services as 'no-win, no-fee'. This regulation has been largely repealed around the country (except Queensland).

35 *Clyne v New South Wales Bar Association* (1960) 104 CLR 186, 203.

36 The *Uniform Law* is provided here as an example. Conditional costs are permitted in other jurisdictions: *Legal Profession Act 2006* (ACT) s 283; *Legal Profession Act 2006* (NT) s 318; *Legal Profession Act 2007* (Qld) s 323; *Legal Practitioners Act 1981* (SA) sch 3, cl 25; *Legal Profession Act 2007* (Tas) s 307.

37 Regulators have warned lawyers not to be misleading in their advertising concerning no-win, no-fee arrangements, and there have been disciplinary prosecutions such as *Legal Practitioners Complaints Committee and Browne* [2006] WASAT 201 where the words 'no compensation = no legal fees' were found to be misleading and amounted to unprofessional conduct.

Legal Profession Uniform Law

181 Conditional costs agreements

(1) A costs agreement (a ***conditional costs agreement***) may provide that the payment of some or all of the legal costs is conditional on the successful outcome of the matter to which those costs relate.

(2) A conditional costs agreement must –
  (a) be in writing and in plain language; and
  (b) set out the circumstances that constitute the successful outcome of the matter to which it relates.

(3) A conditional costs agreement must –
  (a) be signed by the client; and
  (b) include a statement that the client has been informed of the client's rights to seek independent legal advice before entering into the agreement.

(4) A conditional costs agreement must contain a cooling-off period of not less than 5 clear business days during which the client, by written notice, may terminate the agreement, but this requirement does not apply where the agreement is made between law practices only.

(5) If a client terminates a conditional costs agreement within the cooling-off period, the law practice –
  (a) may recover only those legal costs in respect of legal services performed for the client before that termination that were performed on the instructions of the client and with the client's knowledge that the legal services would be performed during that period; and
  (b) in particular, may not recover any uplift fee.

(6) A conditional costs agreement may provide for disbursements to be paid irrespective of the outcome of the matter.

(7) A conditional costs agreement may relate to any matter, except a matter that involves –
  (a) criminal proceedings; or
  (b) proceedings under the *Family Law Act 1975* of the Commonwealth; or
  (c) proceedings under legislation specified in the *Uniform Rules* for the purposes of this section.

Contingent fee arrangements, in contrast, allow a lawyer to take a *percentage* of the actual judgment or settlement sum, if the client is successful. The more a client recovers in a judgment, the more their lawyer is paid. The terminology is confusing, as 'conditional' and 'contingent' are synonyms outside this legal context. The term 'proportional' fee agreements better describes contingent arrangements. Contingent or proportional fees have the advantage of certainty, as the client knows that their lawyer will never take more than a certain percentage of their 'winnings'. However, contingent fees are *prohibited* in Australia and charging them will lead to professional disciplinary consequences.[38] The rationale for banning contingent fees is that they create an incentive for the lawyer to seek to maximise the settlement sum while minimising the amount of work they do. Accordingly, the lawyer might not advise settlement early on, even though this might be better for the client, in the

38 *Uniform Law* s 183; *Legal Profession Act 2006* (ACT) s 285; *Legal Profession Act 2006* (NT) s 320; *Legal Profession Act 2007* (Qld) s 325; *Legal Practitioners Act 1981* (SA) sch 3, cl 25; *Legal Profession Act 2007* (Tas) s 309. If the agreement attempts to recover a contingency (proportional) fee, the practitioner can face criminal and disciplinary proceedings: *Legal Services Commissioner v Barrett* [2012] VCAT 1800. No costs can be recovered under the agreement (see later in the chapter about getting paid).

hope of holding out for a higher fee. Equally the lawyer will not want to go ahead with the actual trial, even though this might give the client a better chance at a higher amount, if there is a settlement offer and there might be diminishing returns for the lawyer for the work required in going to trial. However, proportional fees are permitted in most other common law jurisdictions[39] and justifications for the blanket ban have been seriously questioned in a range of Australian reviews,[40] including the recent recommendation by the Australian Law Reform Commission that a limited contingency billing arrangement be allowed in the interests of supporting access to justice in class actions.[41]

Further, there is a lawful way of charging a percentage – a modified contingency fee – in the form of an *uplift fee*. An uplift fee means that the practitioner charges up to 25% of their normal fee as an addition, or uplift, to their normal fee, if they are successful. An uplift fee is not based on the settlement sum, as with the contingency fee, but on the lawyer's ordinary fee for the same work. The argument is that the lawyer should be compensated for the risk of financing a speculative 'no-win, no-fee' case and a bonus if they win. This creates an incentive to take on the matter in the first place.

Legal Profession Uniform Law[42]

182 Conditional costs agreements involving uplift fees

(1) A conditional costs agreement may provide for the payment of an uplift fee.

(2) If a conditional costs agreement relates to a litigious matter –

- **(a)** the agreement must not provide for the payment of an uplift fee unless the law practice has a reasonable belief that a successful outcome of the matter is reasonably likely; and
- **(b)** the uplift fee must not exceed 25% of the legal costs (excluding disbursements) otherwise payable.

(3) A conditional costs agreement that includes an uplift fee –

- **(a)** must identify the basis on which the uplift fee is to be calculated; and
- **(b)** must include an estimate of the uplift fee or, if that is not reasonably practical –
- **(i)** a range of estimates for the uplift fee; and
- **(ii)** an explanation of the major variables that may affect the calculation of the uplift fee.

(4) A law practice must not enter into a costs agreement in contravention of this section or of the Uniform Rules relating to uplift fees.

Civil penalty: 100 penalty units.

39 See, eg, the American Bar Association's *Model Rules of Professional Conduct* r 1.5(c). More recently, contingent or 'damages-based agreements' have been permitted in England and Wales for litigation: *Courts and Legal Services Act 1990* (UK) s 58AA (amended in 2012).

40 Productivity Commission, *Access to Justice Arrangements* (Report No 72, 2014) recommendation 18.1; Victorian Law Reform Commission, *Access to Justice: Litigation Funding and Group Proceedings* (Report, March 2018) recommendation 7.

41 Australian Law Reform Commission, *Integrity, Fairness and Efficient: An Inquiry into Class Action Proceedings and Third Party Litigation Funders: Final Report*, (Report 134, 2018). This report also considered third parties that fund the litigation who *can* charge the client as a percentage of their winnings, and recommended that these activities be further regulated. Lawyers cannot be funders for cases they act in as this would be a conflict of interest.

42 *Legal Profession Act 2006* (ACT) s 284; *Legal Profession Act 2006* (NT) s 319; *Legal Profession Act 2007* (Qld) s 324; *Legal Practitioners Act 1981* (SA) s 26; *Legal Profession Act 2007* (Tas) s 308.

Although no litigation is risk free, the uplift fee may often be used simply as a means of charging higher fees where there is no great risk of an action failing.[43] Case study 8.1 appears to be an example of this. Legislation around the country requires that conditional costs agreements be signed by the client and must define the circumstances that constitute a 'success', but these provisions only moderate the conflict of interest between lawyer and client; they do not remove it.

Alternative fee arrangements – 'value' billing, lump sum or fixed fees

There are a range of what are often called 'alternative fee arrangements' that have been employed to address concerns about conflicts of interest or lawyer-centred time-billing approaches. Over 15 years ago, the then NSW Legal Services Commissioner suggested 'flexible, fixed-fee or value billing' as a better approach that attracts few complaints about costs in both court and transaction work.[44]

Most simply, fixed fee or lump sum arrangements provide that the lawyer will work for the client for a specified fee irrespective of the time it takes. This approach is common in some areas such as in conveyancing and in wills and estates matters, as well as employment contracts and corporate compliance tasks. Lump sum or fixed fees have the advantage of being transparent and comparable to the fees of other legal service providers in the market. Thus, a client can shop around for the best price and this might bring the general cost of legal services down.[45] However, it is still relatively difficult to compare most legal services, even with the rise of online marketplace websites, due to the complexity of much legal work – this might mean different components of services in any specific matter are charged for on a task or lump sum basis.

There are also potential downsides with these arrangements. These methods of charging are less desirable for law firms in complex matters because of the unpredictability of the legal work needed. For clients, there is a potential of being charged more than would be chargeable on a normal time-cost basis. For instance, given the rapid uptake of technology in the Australian legal profession, what were once time-consuming tasks for lawyers can now be done quickly by a computer.[46] Competency may suffer where there is a temptation to reduce the time spent or quality of work – for example, by assigning a junior lawyer to the task. Of course, it needs to be remembered that there are common law and ethical requirements of competency to be observed by law firms and individual lawyers (see the

43 Indeed, under the *Uniform Law* (s 182) and, in the Australian Capital Territory, *Legal Practitioners Act 2006* (ACT) s 284, an uplift fee is only acceptable where the firm has a reasonable belief that success is reasonably likely. In some States, it is also lawful to charge for 'care and consideration' – another percentage top-up without a legislative cap – that might not relate to a costs agreement on a contingency basis. While legislation is silent, it would seem excessive and thereby unethical to charge a client for work performed with both a percentage charge for care and consideration *and* an uplift fee.

44 Steve Mark, 'The Cost of Justice or Justice in Costs: The Experience of the OLSC in Handling Costs Complaints' (2004) 27(1) *University of New South Wales Law Journal* 225.

45 Vicky Waye, ML Verreynne and J Knowler, 'Innovation in the Australian Legal Profession' (2018) 25(2) *International Journal of the Legal Profession* 213, 203.

46 Legg and Rogers (n 12) 267, 301. Of course, the amount of technology used, particularly use of machine learning for tasks such as disclosure or due diligence, will depend on the size and approach of the firm.

discussion in Chapter 6). On the other hand, this method of charging can provide cost savings, and it allows for lawyers to work together on a matter without worrying about billing the client excessively for their time.[47]

Value billing as an alternative approach relies on discussion between lawyer and client to set the fees chargeable in reference to what the value of the service is to the client. This approach aims to develop a trust relationship between practitioner and client where they meet early and negotiate as to the value of the project or case to the client. This might be expressed in the lawyer's initial question: 'What do you hope to achieve by this process/transaction?' Value billing focuses on defining a measurable stage in a case and assigning a particular fee amount to the achievement of that stage. Value billing is not a distinct method of charging – as it can be a fixed fee, a contingency fee or by the hour. Rather, it focuses on what is best value for the client.

Lump sum and value-based billing have gained adherents in recent years, particularly among corporate clients who have the market power to require large and medium-sized law firms to, in effect, quote competitively for the provision of specialised legal services.[48] 'NewLaw' firms – which are organisations set up in contrast to the traditional 'bricks and mortar' firms, such as 'legal process outsourcing firms, lawyer secondment firms and fixed fees service firms that leverage on demand lawyers'[49] – favour alternative billing to help create a new market that doesn't rely on large profits to cover expensive overheads (such as corporate offices).[50] These law firms point to the considerable benefits of lump sum and value billing, which foreground client interest and participation. That is not to say that these methods cannot be abused. Value billing has been critiqued as opaque and ill-defined.[51] If the lawyer–client relationship is unequal, lump sum arrangements can allow the lawyer to simply quote a higher price than is reasonable.

There are of course diverse areas of legal practice and lawyers charge differently according to what types of service they provide. A firm providing conveyancing services is likely to charge on a task or lump sum basis due to the competitiveness of that area of practice, whereas litigation is usually costed on a time-billing basis. There is particular pressure to provide affordable services in areas such as family law.[52] Debate continues about the merits of 'unbundling' legal services, which involves lawyers being engaged to undertake specific tasks only within a matter. This might provide a way to keep costs down for impecunious clients, but may present significant ethical dangers for lawyers (such as providing sub-standard services and being sued in negligence[53]) and may not result in good outcomes for clients.

47 Craig Hollett, 'Taking the Step, Banning Six-Minute Units and Embracing Fixed-Price Billing' (2013) 40 (December) *Brief* 11, 26–8.

48 Sean Corrigan, 'Alternative Fee Arrangements' (2021) 44(2) *Manitoba Law Journal* 134.

49 Margaret Thornton, 'Towards the Uberisation of Legal Practice' (2019) 1(1) *Law, Technology and Humans* 46.

50 Benjamin Barton, 'A Glass Half Full Look at the Changes in the American Market' (2014) 38 *International Review of Law and Economics* 29.

51 Woolley (n 5).

52 Australian Law Reform Commission, *Family Law for the Future – An Inquiry into the Family Law System* (Final Report No 135, 2019).

53 *Sharon Minkin v Lesley Landsberg (Practising as Barnet Family Law)* [2015] EWCA Civ 1152 is an English case where the Court of Appeal considered the importance of the availability of lawyers in family law matters but also the difficulties associated with providing fulsome legal advice or drafting in a small part of a dispute.

Having considered the range of approaches to charging for legal services, this section concludes with Case study 8.2, which invites reflection on the relative merits of each in different contexts.

CASE STUDY 8.2 WORKING OUT HOW TO ETHICALLY BILL: THREE SCENARIOS[54]

Example 1

A first client, Arturo, asks you to prepare a contract. The fee, calculated on a time basis, is $15,000. Later, a second client, Brahma, wants a contract for a similar transaction. As a result of your work for Arturo, you now have a precedent that covers most of Brahma's requirements. Only a small percentage of the document needs to be altered.

DISCUSSION QUESTIONS

1. If you were in legal practice, would you charge Brahma less than Arturo or the same $15,000? Would it be acceptable to do so on a time-cost basis?
2. How would you explain your fee structure to your two clients? For example, if you decided to charge $15,000 for the second contract, would you attempt to discuss the value of your work to the client's project as a basis for justification of the higher fee? Or would you simply say that $15,000 is the fixed fee?

Example 2

Now imagine that Arturo retains your firm to draft another contract on the basis that he will be charged an hourly rate. Your partner provides an estimate of work for $10,000. At the conclusion of the matter, the account comes to $5,000 on a time costing basis. Your partner charges the client $9,000, as the work performed by the firm was, in his view, of a high quality and the outcome exceptional.

54 The first scenario is from Legal Fees Review Panel (NSW), *Lawyer's Costs and the [sic] Time Billing* (Discussion Paper, November 2004), 20–21 [2.59], which in turn drew on Stuart Kay, 'Cost, Value and ROI for Knowledge Management in Law Firms', *LLRX.com* (online at 31 August 2003). The second two scenarios are from the Queensland Legal Services Commission billing practices survey described in Christine Parker and David Ruschena, 'The Pressures of Billable Hours: Lessons from a Survey of Billing Practices Inside Law Firms' (2011) 9(2) *University of St Thomas Law Journal* 619, 647–9.

DISCUSSION QUESTIONS

1. Do you think this is ethically acceptable?[55]
2. Would Arturo feel deceived if he found out what had happened?

Example 3

Now imagine a third scenario: You are taking a two-hour flight from Brisbane to Melbourne to conduct an interview in a matter involving client Arturo. While on the plane, you review materials for another file you are working on for client Brahma for the following week. Your firm has a billing procedure whereby you normally bill clients for your time spent travelling or waiting on their behalf.

DISCUSSION QUESTIONS

1. Would you bill Arturo and Brahma each for two hours? What are the arguments for and against?[56]
2. What would represent true value for each client?

   For all of the case studies above:
3. To what extent do different billing methods suit different contexts: for example, different practice contexts (solo practitioner, large firm) or different types of cases (litigation, preparing and advising on a contract, writing a will)?

Since the economic downturn late in the first decade of the 2000s (the Global Financial Crisis), law firms have experienced pressure from corporate clients to cut costs and be more transparent in their charging. Nevertheless, in Australia and across the common law world, time billing is the predominant billing method.[57] And, while there are a range of disruptors to modern practice such as technological innovation and the COVID-19 pandemic, the Australian legal industry is reported to have increased its profitability.[58] Thus there might be little pressure to further innovate around fees.

In the next section of the chapter, we examine other reasons why we might want to keep pressure on the legal industry to carefully consider its billing practices – not only might this give clients more participation in negotiating their fees and receiving fairer bills, but the

55 The regulatory regimes are explained later in this chapter. You might refer back to your initial response to this question after you have considered what the law provides.

56 See further the discussion of this issue later in this chapter. *Bechara v Legal Services Commissioner* (2010) 79 NSWLR 763 suggests this might be a questionable approach.

57 For instance, the Macquarie Bank 2017 'Legal Benchmarking' report found that time billing is dominant in every area except conveyancing and wills and estates: Macquarie Bank, *An Industry in Transition: 2017 Legal Benchmarking Results* (2017) 16–17.

58 '2021 Australia: State of the Legal Market Report', *Thomson Reuters* (Web Page) <https://insight.thomsonreuters.com.au/legal/resources/resource/2021-australia-state-of-the-legal-market-report>.

lawyers themselves might need a break from the pressures of time billing. Indeed, the cost of the justice system is also at stake when lawyers' bills are too high.

Wider ethical problems with lawyers' fees and billing practices

The many costs of time billing within firms

Case study 8.1 illustrates how a law firm with a poor billing practice, and lack of both training for junior staff and supervision by partners, can have terrible outcomes. Many studies in Australia and other common law countries where lawyers employ similar billing practices suggest that abuses are as much related to the organisational culture as to individual ethical failings.[59] Poor firm cultures can lead to overcharging clients, no matter the billing method.

However, time billing is most implicated in overcharging for the reasons discussed earlier, such as the ease with which bills can be increased. Time-based billing also encourages its own destructive psychology inside certain firms. Most law firms set targets of numbers of hours to be billed by each lawyer each year. About six and a half hours per day is standard practice in Australia; however, eight to eight and a half hours is sometimes required. Billable hours are those that clients can be billed for. Non-billable hours include coffee and meal breaks, toilet breaks, general training sessions, administration meetings and associated paperwork. Lawyers generally need to work about 10 hours per day to generate six to eight billable hours.

Some US estimates of associates' (the most junior employee lawyers in a firm) time-billing expectations put the number of expected annual billable hours at 2,500. This expects nine billable hours every working day of the year, which would take about 3,300 hours in the office to achieve.[60] No surprise then, that larger law firms with high-end billing expectations can tend to employ more new graduates than they really need, because they know that up to 30% of them will leave within five years.[61] Recent inquiries by SafeWork NSW have classified law as a high-risk profession due to the prevalence of long hours and 'unrealistic demands'.[62] These inquiries were sparked by claims that staff were sleeping in

59 Adrian Evans and Josephine Palermo, 'Australian Law Students' Perceptions of Their Values: Interim Results in the First Year – 2001 – of a Three-Year Empirical Assessment' (2002) 5 *Legal Ethics* 103; Adrian Evans and Josephine Palermo, 'Zero Impact: Are Lawyers' Values Affected by Law School?' (2005) 8 *Legal Ethics* 240.

60 Legal Fees Review Panel (NSW) (n 54) 24–5 [3.7]. Another recent report indicates there might be more pressure to work long hours due to the pandemic, with one report of United States associates working 2,400 hours per year: Sindhu Sundar, 'Junior Lawyers Share What It's Really Like to Bill 2,400 Hours Per Year, with Normal Days from 6.30am Until Midnight', *Insider* (online at 17 December 2021) <https://www.businessinsider.com/big-law-associates-what-its-like-to-bill-2400-hours-2021-12>.

61 Sara Charlesworth and Iain Campbell, *Scoping Study for an Attrition Study of Victorian Lawyers: Report to Victoria Law Foundation* (Report, Centre for Applied Social Research, RMIT University, July 2010) 2, 9. More recent reports have confirmed this attrition trend: Law Council of Australia, *National Attrition and Re-engagement Study* (2014).

62 Hannah Wooton, 'Law Deemed "High-Risk" Job' *The Australian Financial Review* (online at 10 June 2021) <https://www.afr.com/companies/professional-services/long-hours-high-demands-makes-law-a-high-risk-job-safework-20210607-p57yrz > (paywall).

their offices and took supplements to stay awake and keep working. It is reported that SafeWork NSW's Director of Health and Safe Design noted particularly that 'the requirement workers are hyper-vigilant on accounting [for] their time attached to fees for service' added to the other demands.[63]

As discussed elsewhere, the impact of excessive hours can have a range of negative impacts on practitioners, from disproportionately disadvantaging those with caring responsibilities[64] to mental and physical ill-health.[65] It might also exacerbate the current trend of lawyers leaving the profession – what has been called the 'great resignation'.[66] While billing is not the only cause of excessive expectations on lawyers to work long hours, a high billable target can require a lawyer to work for as long as it takes to meet the target, however unrealistic.

In this environment, billing can seem all-important, particularly in the many firms where a legal practitioner's budget – that is, the number of chargeable (billable) hours per month that they must achieve if they are to retain their job (let alone be promoted) – is the ever-present personal watchdog. It can also make it extremely difficult for lawyers to spend time away from the office fostering their own relationships, interests and community involvements. One lawyer commented in a billing practices survey of large and medium firms in Queensland undertaken in 2011:

> Here's the thing … you can do all of the surveys of this nature that you want to. The firms can produce pretty policies which say all of the right things. However, while the driving force behind a lawyer's advancement is time recording, you will always have an issue with time sheet padding and 'time theft'. Younger lawyers in a firm, despite all their high ideals, will always fall into line with what the firm wants, and will not be empowered to do anything differently.[67]

Such pressures can eat away at possibilities for trust and collegiality between lawyers. This can create a sense of being surveilled by clients and other lawyers, increasing anxiety and diminishing the quality of relationships.[68] Some consider such organisational approaches to be unethical because of the unrealistic demands on employee lawyers – which could be perceived as a form of bullying.[69]

Organisational pressures can lead to unethical practices such as intentional over-billing. The pressure to simply cheat on a bill can be enormous; as one United States associate

63 Ibid.

64 Margaret Thornton and Joanne Bagust, 'The Gender Trap: Flexible Work in Corporate Legal Practice' (2007) 45 *Osgoode Hall Law Journal* 773; Law Council of Australia, *National Attrition and Re-Engagement Study* (2014).

65 See generally Chapter 3.

66 Thomson Reuters Institute and Georgetown Law, *2022 A Report on the State of the Legal Market: A Challenging Road to Recovery* <https://www.thomsonreuters.com/en-us/posts/wp-content/uploads/sites/20/2022/01/State-of-Legal-Market-Report_Final.pdf>.

67 Parker and Ruschena (n 54) 658.

68 L Krieger and K Sheldon, 'What Makes Lawyers Happy? A Data-Driven Prescription to Redefine Professional Success' (2015) 83(2) *George Washington Law Review* 554.

69 Joanne Bagust, 'The Culture of Bullying in Australian Corporate Law Firms' (2014) 17(2) *Legal Ethics* 177; Susan Le Mire and Rosemary Owens, 'A Propitious Moment? Workplace Bullying and Regulation of the Legal Profession' (2014) 37(3) *University of New South Wales Law Journal* 1030.

stated: 'the 2000 billable hour requirement is an impossible task for an HONEST and hardworking attorney'.[70] In an extreme case in Australia, a lawyer who had added 914 false hours in electronic timesheet entries described himself as becoming 'obsessed' with overcharging to increase his profit margins.[71]

Even those lawyers who are not padding their bills to make billable hour targets may believe that others must be, leading to a situation where everyone thinks everyone else is probably cheating, and wondering whether they may as well cheat themselves – an 'everyone does it' mentality. Parker and Ruschena's analysis of lawyers' experiences of ethics and billing practices in their firms found that lawyers in the firms that did not have clear, explicit and enforced ethical billing policies were more likely to believe that their colleagues were engaging in unethical practices such as padding bills.[72]

In other words, the imposition of targets for number of hours billed on individual lawyers and overly profit-oriented work groups can provide incentives for lawyers to artificially increase bills. While the well-known Australian case covered in Case study 8.3 is around 30 years old, we believe it remains relevant while the conditions of practice leading to pressure to excessively bill clients continue.

CASE STUDY 8.3 THE *FOREMAN* CASE: OVERCHARGING AND FALSIFYING EVIDENCE UNDER PRESSURE OF LAW FIRM BILLING PRACTICES[73]

In 1994, Carol Foreman, former family law partner at a large law firm, was struck off the roll of solicitors for deception of other practitioners and the court. Her deception occurred in the course of a dispute with a former client, Mrs Avidan, about the firm's bill (based on time billing) of more than $500,000 for Mrs Avidan's divorce arrangements. Ms Foreman swore that she had given Mrs Avidan a standard costs agreement at their first interview and then again a few months later. However, the costs agreement could not be found and nor was there any record in Ms Foreman's file relating to the case that the costs agreement had ever been given to the client. The costs dispute was going to a hearing in the Family Court, and without evidence that it had entered into a costs agreement with the client, the firm would not be able to prove any basis for demanding such high fees from the client.

Ms Foreman rewrote her timesheet in her own client file to make it appear that she had recorded giving the costs agreement to the client at the beginning of the relationship with

70 Susan Fortney, 'The Billable Hours Derby: Empirical Data on the Problems and Pressure Point (2005) 33(1) *Fordham Urban Law Journal* 3, 108.

71 *Legal Services Commissioner v McDonald* [2018] QCAT 82, [13].

72 Parker and Ruschena (n 54).

73 Based on *Law Society of New South Wales v Foreman* (1994) 34 NSWLR 408. Other material for this case study is from Ann Daniel, *Scapegoats for a Profession: Uncovering Procedural Injustice* (Harwood Academic Publishers, 1998) 71 and Christine Parker, 'Law Firms Incorporated: How Incorporation Could and Should Make Firms More Ethically Responsible' (2004) 23(2) *The University of Queensland Law Journal* 347.

the client. Later, when the matter was about to go to the Family Court, she discovered that another copy of the original (unaltered) time sheet was about to be submitted to the Court by her firm. Ms Foreman destroyed this copy of the original timesheet and forged a new version to be submitted to the Court.

When this was revealed, Ms Foreman faced disciplinary action because she had knowingly misled the Court and her colleagues, as well as the lawyers and client on the other side.

In her disciplinary hearing Ms Foreman accepted that she had acted inappropriately but argued that she had done so because she was working under great pressure to meet the billing targets for her section of the firm. Ms Foreman was a very successful family lawyer who had been a partner at another law firm before being headhunted. However, by the time of the Avidan dispute, she had been told that her firm was going to close its family law practice because it was not making enough money, and that she and another specialist family law partner would have to work for a more junior partner. She was allowed to run the family law division on a trial basis for six months, at which point its financial performance would be assessed. Her evidence to the Court indicated that during that time she was totally cost-driven, working 12.5 hour days in the office close to breakdown.[74] One of the judges, Kirby P, commented:

> Astonishingly, the evidence revealed that she and some staff members even slept at the office on occasion after working very late. Many, like [Ms Foreman], were highly stressed by the pressure under which they worked. Part of the stress would appear to have arisen from the obligation to meet budgeted requirements of fee production established by the firm. This was allegedly done by reference to the standards set by the Tobacco Institute, an amply funded client well able to pay its monthly accounts upon presentation.[75]

Originally Ms Foreman had been charged with 'gross overcharging'. However, this aspect of the case was dropped because the Family Court found that there was a costs agreement to which the changes related. The Tribunal accepted that this meant there could be no basis for a finding of overcharging, and this issue was not reopened in the Court of Appeal.

DISCUSSION QUESTIONS

1. Kirby P pointed out that 'those charges were rendered not by Ms Foreman alone but by her firm'; that Ms Foreman's own 'charging strategy was, to say the least, influenced by a system of time charging and by budget requirements within the firm which were not of her individual making'; and that he was 'not satisfied that this matter has been as

74 Parker (n 73) 347–80.

75 *Law Society of New South Wales v Foreman* (1994) 34 NSWLR 408, 414. See the judgments of Mahoney JA at 433–8 and Giles AJA at 462–3 for descriptions of the firm (the threat to close down the family law section because of its lack of profitability) and budget pressures that Foreman was under.

fully and properly investigated as it should have been'. He suggested that perhaps the law firm itself should have been held responsible for overcharging.[76] To what extent was the firm responsible for the fees charged in this case? Do you think that the firm should have been disciplined for overcharging?

2. Kirby P also commented, 'it seems virtually impossible to credit that legal costs in a dispute between a married couple for the most part over their matrimonial property could properly run up legal costs in the figures that are mentioned here [that is, half a million dollars]'.[77] Do you agree that the quantum of the bill compared to the value to the client is enough to say that it was unfair or excessive?
3. Do you think the context in which Foreman found herself is any justification for how she acted? What should Foreman have done to manage the situation?

Legal fees diminishing access to justice in court

While time billing has been implicated in a range of abuses, many commentators have also argued that costs abuse (on a time-based system) is a symptom rather than a cause – that it is not the billing method but an unethical culture of the firm that is the problem.[78] In any case, the client receives a higher bill than should be the case.

One might argue that doing all you can as a lawyer to advance the client's interests within the law 'requires lawyers to charge their client as little as possible', but zealous advocacy 'also requires a lawyer to leave no stone unturned in the advancing of their client's case', which might increase their costs.[79] This tension is usually resolved in favour of 'no stone unturned'. While corporate clients are in a good position to control their costs, because of their greater capacity to deny ongoing work to a lawyer who is seen to be price gouging, excessive adversarial advocacy might result in excessive costs even for these clients. As described in Chapter 6, an appeal court was scathing of three major law firms' willingness to prepare unnecessary and voluminous documents in an interlocutory matter, and substantial costs orders were made against the three firms.[80]

Costs can be inflated not only for the wealthy client. *Adversarial advocacy* may require a lawyer to proceed on the basis of acting in pursuit of the client's aims, which can increase the cost for both the client and the other side, particularly in disputes. As we have seen in Chapter 6, the adversarial litigation system creates high, and unpredictable, costs, putting at risk the fundamental values of fair and equal access to justice for all.[81] Firms working for defendants in litigation can delay or even completely frustrate a case by devices such as overburdening plaintiffs with documents in discovery, contesting every step of the pretrial

76 *Law Society of New South Wales v Foreman* (1994) 34 NSWLR 408, 422–3.
77 Ibid 422.
78 Indeed, there are still advocates for time billing as an ethical approach as it allows for efficiencies: Brian Bartley, 'Fair Trade? Why We Need to Rethink Time Billing' (2010) 30(8) *Proctor* 12.
79 Richard Moorhead, 'Filthy Lucre: Lawyers' Fees and Lawyers' Ethics – What Is Wrong with Informed Consent?' (2011) 31(3) *Legal Studies* 345, 352.
80 See *Yara Australia Pty Ltd v Oswal* (2013) 41 VR 302.
81 See, eg, Australian Law Reform Commission, *Managing Justice: A Review of the Federal Civil Justice System* (Report No 89, 2000) ch 4.

process and then arguing every point during trial.[82] A litigant with 'deep pockets' thereby has the capacity 'to increase the threat of litigation costs being paid by the other party as a result of complications and elaborations of the dispute and the procedure for deciding it'.[83] Where lawyers act on such instructions, or advise these forensic tactics, they assist to cripple possibilities for access to justice precisely *because* such tactics increase costs in unpredictable ways.

As part of the final court orders in litigation, the court will usually decide who should pay what legal costs, on the basis of what is fair and equitable between the parties.[84] A client who wins a legal action is normally entitled to have costs that are reasonably incurred and are reasonable in amount[85] paid by the losing party. These costs are generally known as *standard* or *ordinary costs*. *Reasonable* costs are all those costs that the lawyer was justified in incurring in running the case and attending to their client's needs for information. A successful party can also recover from the losing party all their reasonable expenses ('disbursements'), such as court filing fees, medical report fees and barristers' fees, provided they are reasonable in amount.

However, standard costs generally cover only 60–80% of the total costs that the winning party actually owes their lawyer, whether the total costs are calculated on an item- or time-based process.[86] The extra 20–40% of costs *cannot* be recovered from the losing party, unless the court makes an 'indemnity costs' order. Such an order is only available in a limited range of circumstances, such as where the other party has pursued a hopeless case. In order to understand what legal fees and costs they might have to pay in relation to litigation, a client therefore needs to understand that, even if they win the case, they will also need to personally pay, say, 30% of the costs charged by their lawyer. In order to go ahead with litigation, they would need to be confident that they will win and that paying that 30% of their own costs will not unacceptably reduce their net receipts from the case.

If this is confusing for law students and lawyers, consider how clients feel when they first hear about the effect of the system of costs on what they think is their just entitlement? Figure 8.1 describes the relationship between these concepts.

It is not surprising that clients complain that the case they thought was worth $10,000 produces a meagre result. Unless the amount in dispute is substantial, having the court determine the dispute will often be uneconomic for the client and benefit only the lawyers. In many cases, even clients who are very likely to succeed in court may feel forced to agree to negotiation or mediation to resolve their disputes, regardless of how suitable their case is for mediation (see Chapter 6).[87] This makes the prospect of equal access to justice in the

82 This approach can be seen in cases discussed in Chapter 6.

83 Bret Walker, 'Proportionality and Cost-Shifting' (2004) 27(1) *University of New South Wales Law Journal* 214, 216–17.

84 In civil tribunals, the Federal Circuit and Family Court of Australia and various Land and Environment Courts each party ordinarily pays their own costs.

85 See, eg, *Civil Procedure Act 2005* (NSW) s 98(1); *Supreme Court (General Civil Procedure) Rules 2005* (Vic) s 63.30.

86 Victorian Law Reform Commission, *Civil Justice Review* (Report No 14, 2008) ch 11, 648 [3.2.1].

87 An alternative would be for the trial judge to control the costs process. This happens in New Zealand where the successful party must make an application to the trial judge for a fixed, lump sum costs order as a part of the substantive judgment, and the judge makes that decision after

Figure 8.1 Relationship between standard costs and total legal costs

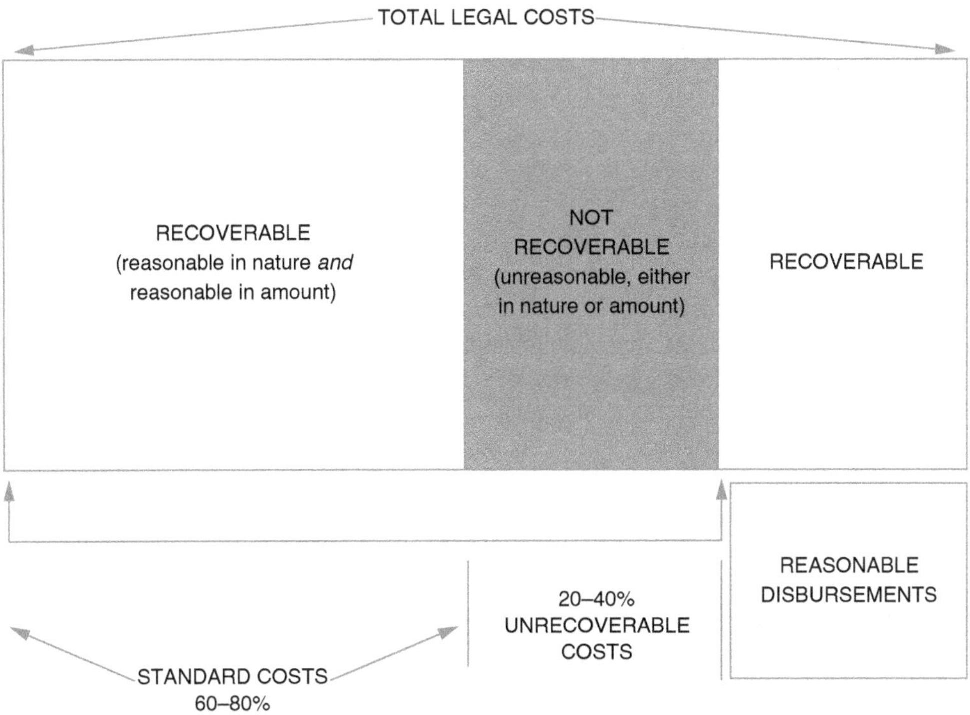

Note: *Standard costs* are costs that are reasonably incurred and are reasonable in amount. *Unrecoverable costs* are costs that are not reasonably incurred or are higher than reasonable in the circumstances.

court system recede further and further and makes it more likely that matters will be settled unjustly. Access to justice, on which lawyers depend for much of their social legitimacy, is at risk even when lawyers are candid in fully apprising potential clients of the financial risks of their proposed court action, and discussing the alternatives, such as mediation.

Curbing billing excesses and providing guidance to the profession

Rapacity in the legal profession is an old adage, and more recently the many critiques of corporate legal culture add to the assumption that the profession is increasingly 'corporatised' rather than professional (see discussion of the approach to law as a business in regulating the profession in Chapter 3). Legislatures have responded to the deregulation of costs with consumer protective legislation that requires greater disclosure of costs and 'fair and

receiving evidence from the parties as to their costs. See Deborah Vine Hall, 'Present Difficulties with the Assessment System' (2004) 27(1) *University of New South Wales Law Journal* 206.

reasonable' billing. Despite continued calls, regulatory intervention has not gone so far as to prohibit time-based billing.

Costs disclosure and consumer protection

In the usual time-based billing relationship, clients might have little power to negotiate the lawyers' fees, no understanding that such negotiation is possible, or may agree to an excessively high hourly rate. Many potential plaintiffs, perhaps one-off litigants anxious to prove a point or recover what they think will be many thousands of dollars in a judgment, may be unwilling to think about the legal costs of their claim. This is not to say that the price of legal services is unimportant to consumers. Across the country, legislation assumes price competition is to be encouraged through giving consumers information to shop around. Thus, regulation seeks to address a potential lack of information about lawyers' costs by requiring lawyers to provide an estimate of total legal costs and other information about client rights to negotiate both methods of billing and the quantum of the final bill, including disbursements, and disputing costs.[88] This information must be in writing and in 'plain language', and there is an obligation to update costs disclosure as a matter progresses.[89]

Costs disclosure obligations around the country vary somewhat. For instance, the *Uniform Law* applying to New South Wales, Victoria and Western Australia contains a stricter requirement for the lawyer to provide a client with an accurate understanding of total costs rather than merely an estimated costs range as in other jurisdictions.[90] However, the *Uniform Law* (as below) has fewer express requirements of disclosure about a range of aspects of billing, such as rates of interest on overdue bills, intervals of bills, right to progress reports or an estimate of a range of costs at the end of a litigation, whether successful or unsuccessful.

Legal Profession Uniform Law

Part 4.3 div 3 – Costs disclosure

174 Disclosure obligations of law practice regarding clients

(1) Main disclosure requirement

A law practice –

(a) must, when or as soon as practicable after instructions are initially given in a matter, provide the client with information disclosing the basis on which legal costs will be calculated in the matter and an estimate of the total legal costs; …

88 It is commonly misunderstood that the costs of a legal action are only the solicitor's fees. However, fees for a solicitor engaging a barrister on behalf of the client, paying for evidence such as medical reports or other court costs such as filing fees are payable by the client. These must be disclosed to the client at the outset. In the case of barristers engaged during the matter, the solicitor will need to negotiate an appropriate fee on behalf of the client and provide disclosure: *Farrah v Julian-Armitage* [2015] QCA 289. There are exceptions to disclosure obligations where the costs of the legal service are likely to be less than a prescribed amount. This varies from $750 under the *Uniform Law* s 174 to $1,500 in some jurisdictions such as Queensland: *Legal Profession Act 2007* (Qld) s 311. Under the *Uniform Law*, s 170 excludes 'commercial and government clients' and third-party payers from the compulsory disclosure obligations.

89 *Uniform Law* s 290.

90 *Uniform Law* s 174; *Legal Profession Act 2006* (ACT) s 269; *Legal Profession Act 2006* (NT) s 303; *Legal Profession Act 2007* (Qld) s 308; *Legal Profession Act 2007* (Tas) s 291.

(2) Additional information to be provided
Information provided under –
(a) subsection (1)(a) must include information about the client's rights –
(i) to negotiate a costs agreement with the law practice; and
(ii) to negotiate the billing method (for example, by reference to timing or task); and
(iii) to receive a bill from the law practice and to request an itemised bill after receiving a bill that is not itemised or is only partially itemised; and
(iv) to seek the assistance of the designated local regulatory authority in the event of a dispute about legal costs; …

(3) Client's consent and understanding
If a disclosure is made under subsection (1), the law practice must take all reasonable steps to satisfy itself that the client has understood and given consent to the proposed course of action for the conduct of the matter and the proposed costs.

Disclosure obligations apply to all lawyer–client relationships whether involving a barrister or a solicitor, solo practitioner or large law firm. They also provide for a diverse range of clients and demand that the lawyer ensure that each client (whatever their level of education or English proficiency) understands the agreement.[91] The aim is to provide clients with enough information to make good choices, as Bell J explained:

> The protective policy of requiring disclosure by lawyers and enhancing freedom of informed choice by clients underpins this legislation, reflecting the modern conception that clients are not just clients but also consumers who are typically in a position of negotiating disadvantage, that lawyers are not just professionals but also suppliers of legal service and that the provision of legal services is not just an indispensable ingredient of the system of justice but also a (national) market in which information and bargaining power are imperfectly distributed.[92]

This view of legal services within a market might not match notions of law as a profession or an aspect of the justice system. However, regulators and consumers increasingly believe external restraints and accountability are necessary. As described above, the lack of information about the full cost of hiring a lawyer, particularly where it might require an understanding of the workings of the court system in awarding costs, means that some clients simply do not know what they are signing up for. The requirement to provide an estimate of total costs (even if this is not binding or must be later revised should the case become more complicated) is an effective way of addressing this.

Unfortunately, law firms can take a technical approach to these requirements, negating their protective purpose. For instance, in one case a law firm provided legal services to a client over several years. It claimed that there was an outstanding debt due to the firm of

91 *Uniform Law* s 174 imposes an obligation on the lawyer to satisfy themselves that the client understands and consents; *Legal Profession Act 2006* (ACT) s 275; *Legal Profession Act 2006* (NT) s 309; *Legal Profession Act 2007* (Qld) s 314(2); *Legal Practitioners Act 1981* (SA) sch 3 cl 16 and *Legal Profession Act 2007* (Tas) s 298(2) require translation in some instances or to read the agreement to the client.

92 *Russells v McCardel* [2014] VSC 287, [10].

$14,823.60 in unpaid legal fees and had lodged a caveat on the property of the client for the debt.[93] The caveat was said to be enforceable on the basis of an equitable lien (lawyer's lien) for the outstanding fees.[94] However, when the Court considered the law firm's claim, it was not satisfied there was evidence of a valid costs agreement (described further below) or the necessary disclosure about costs to the client. The Court described the costs disclosure as 'incomprehensible' because it stated that the 'total estimate of costs and disbursements' would be 'between $2,200 – $55,000'. The Court concluded that 'on its face, [the disclosure is] so wide a range as to provide no guidance to any client and is not, on any rational basis to be described as an "estimate of the total legal costs" that complies with the legislation'.[95]

While this case provides some assurance that a court is looking for costs disclosure that is meaningful for clients, it also indicates that some firms might not observe the intention of the legislation, treating it as a box-ticking exercise. The onus will be on the client to take care in negotiating a costs agreement or disputing a bill when it arrives. Unfortunately, recent reports of disciplinary authorities confirm that a failure to adequately disclose costs is a common consumer complaint.[96]

Costs agreements and getting paid – legislative and common law principles

Where, as is usually the case, lawyers wish to make specific arrangements with a client for the amount and method of payment, a written costs agreement must be created and delivered to the client (as regulated by the relevant jurisdiction's legislation). The example above of a law firm that failed to ensure that a costs agreement was in place that corresponded to the legal services provided and billed for[97] is no longer a satisfactory way to act for and charge a client. Lawyers across the country must have a written document explaining to clients how the lawyers will charge (other than billing on the default basis of scales of costs for litigation) for their services.[98] For example, the *Uniform Law* requires:

93 *Frontier Law Group Pty Ltd v Robert Glenn Barkman* [2016] NSWSC 1542.

94 Lawyers have historically had a right to secure payment of a legitimate outstanding fee by asserting a lawyer's lien. This legal right allows a lawyer to hold property, often the client's file, until their costs are paid. This prevents the client from 'in effect getting solicitors' work done for nothing by the simply expedient of changing his solicitor as often as he choose [sic], leaving a trail of unpaid costs in his wake and demanding papers without payment when he had no just cause to complain of the conduct of the solicitors instructed and discarded': *Hughes v Hughes* [1958] 3 All ER 179, 180–1. This practice is also ethical, but the *ASCR* provide some practical requirements around holding client documents hostage to unpaid bills: *ASCR* r 15.

95 *Frontier Law Group Pty Ltd v Robert Glenn Barkman* [2016] NSWSC 1542, [38].

96 See, eg, Office of the Legal Services Commissioner (NSW), *Annual Report 2020–21* (Report, 2021) 12.

97 In this case there were 'multiple retainers and costs agreements [between the law firm and the client] ... as he was a regular client of the solicitor over several years': *Frontier Law Group Pty Ltd v Robert Glenn Barkman* [2016] NSWSC 1542, [26]. It was asserted that there were oral and written contracts that formed the relationship.

98 *Uniform Law* s 179; *Legal Profession Act 2006* (ACT) s 282(2); *Legal Profession Act 2006* (NT) s 317; *Legal Profession Act 2007* (Qld) s 322; *Legal Practitioners Act 1981* (SA) sch 3 cl 24(1); *Legal Profession Act 2007* (Tas) s 306(1).

Legal Profession Uniform Law

Part 4.3 div 4 – Costs agreements

179 Client's right to costs agreement

A client of a law practice has the right to require and to have a negotiated costs agreement with the law practice.

180 Making costs agreements

(1) A costs agreement may be made –

- **(a)** between a client and a law practice retained by the client; or
- **(b)** between a client and a law practice retained on behalf of the client by another law practice; or
- **(c)** between a law practice and another law practice that retained that law practice on behalf of a client; or
- **(d)** between a law practice and an associated third party payer.

(2) A costs agreement must be written or evidenced in writing.

(3) A costs agreement may consist of a written offer that is accepted in writing or (except in the case of a conditional costs agreement) by other conduct.

(4) A costs agreement cannot provide that the legal costs to which it relates are not subject to a costs assessment.

Legislation in each jurisdiction renders a costs agreement void if it contravenes these legislative requirements. Where contravention occurs, the lawyer cannot bill under the costs agreement and may be subject to professional discipline for doing so. However, it may still be possible for the lawyer or law firm to charge for work done, even where the costs agreement is rendered void, or there is no costs agreement at all. Legislative regimes provide that the lawyer can charge on an applicable scale (as described above) or for work performed *after* a costs assessment is made (described later in the chapter).[99] At common law and under legislation in some States, it is possible to claim *quantum meruit* for work performed under an oral contract, but common law has assumed a lawyer–client agreement is a complete contract and requires completion of work before an entitlement to be paid.[100]

Barristers have traditionally had no common law right to charge for fees as they did not have a legal relationship with the client or solicitor.[101] Model laws introduced around the country, and the *Uniform Law* in New South Wales, Victoria and Western Australia now regulate their professional relationships as discussed further in Chapter 3. Barristers typically enter into a costs agreement with a solicitor and have a right to sue a solicitor for

99 *Uniform Law* ss 178, 194; *Legal Profession Act 2006* (ACT) s 279; *Legal Profession Act 2007* (Qld) s 319; *Legal Practitioners Act 1981* (SA) s 41; *Legal Profession Act 2007* (Tas) s 303.

100 *Olympic Holdings Pty Ltd v Lochel* [2004] WASC 61. As discussed later in the chapter, there are disciplinary implications associated with charging for fees when there is no entitlement to them. This might occur in a range of circumstances but is often the case where there is no costs agreement.

101 *Moor v Row* (1629) 1 Ch Rep 38; 21 ER 501; *Thornhill v Evans* (1742) 2 Atk 330; 26 ER 501.

fees, while the client is usually ultimately responsible for paying these costs (described as 'disbursements' and the solicitor must disclose the arrangement to the client).[102]

In most parts of Australia, legislative regimes set out a process for challenging a costs agreement, whereby a court or tribunal decide if the agreement is 'unfair and unreasonable'.[103] The decision maker looks to the circumstances in which a costs agreement was made – such as whether it was made by fraud or misrepresentation. If the decision maker sets aside a costs agreement, it must then decide what would be a reasonable way to charge, any reasonable fees payable and what was reasonable work to perform. The legislation prescribes certain practical considerations such as the following:[104]

- how the law firm advertised its costs;
- the skill, labour and responsibility displayed by the lawyer responsible for the matter;
- the retainer and whether the work done was within the scope of the retainer;
- the complexity, novelty or difficulty of the matter;
- the quality of the work done; and
- the time and the place where, and circumstances in which, the work was done.

Under the *Uniform Law* s 172 there is a proactive obligation imposed on lawyers to charge only what is fair and reasonable. A practitioner fulfils this obligation by considering matters similar to those listed above. But there is an additional aspect in the *Uniform Law* which requires practitioners to consider what tasks need to be performed, and to what degree, with reference to the specifics of the client matter. There is a related obligation expressed negatively – to *not to act in a way that increases costs*.[105] Put another way, only the *Uniform Law* jurisdictions expressly require that lawyers proactively consider whether the work performed and their bill reflects the value of the matter to the client. Any costs agreement is presumed to reflect this.

While the regulatory schema across the country differs, it is unclear how much substantive difference this makes to clients: aggrieved clients must generally contest a bill or complain about their agreement, or the size of their bill. It is reasonable to say that, under all regimes, lawyers and law firms may only charge what is fair and reasonable in each matter and lawyers should comply with the spirit of being a fiduciary (including when entering into

102 Although High Court authority indicates that this does not impute legal liability to the client should the solicitor fail to pay the fees: *Legal Services Board v Gillespie-Jones* (2013) 249 CLR 493. Barristers' fees should also be 'fair and reasonable' by implication of the *Legal Profession Uniform Conduct (Barristers) Rules 2015* r 47: 'A barrister must not in any dealings with a client exercise any undue influence intended to dispose the client to benefit the barrister in excess of the barrister's fair remuneration for the legal services provided to the client.'

103 *Legal Profession Act 2006* (ACT) s 288(3); *Legal Profession Act 2006* (NT) s 323; *Legal Profession Act 2007* (Qld) s 328; *Legal Practitioners Act 1981* (SA) sch 3 cl 30; *Legal Profession Act 2007* (Tas) s 312. In the Northern Territory and Tasmania a costs assessor has power to set aside a costs agreement applying similar considerations to a court or tribunal in other states. Under the *Uniform Law* s 199 this assessment is also made by a costs assessor (described in the last section of the chapter) as a first step in deciding the disputed bill between lawyer and client.

104 *Uniform Law* s 172(2). Similar considerations are prescribed in legislation in other jurisdictions in provisions cited in the above note. For a more in-depth discussion see Dal Pont, *Law of Costs* (n 15) 50–61.

105 *Uniform Law* s 173 ('Avoidance of increased costs').

a relationship with a client). The ethical rules for solicitors reinforce this legislative and common law expectation[106] and place the temptation to overcharge a client within the context of a lawyer–client conflict.

ASCR r 12.2 Charging excessive fees a conflict of lawyer and client interest

12.2 A solicitor must not do anything:

(a) calculated to dispose a client or a third party to confer on the solicitor, either directly or indirectly, any benefit in excess of the solicitor's fair and reasonable remuneration for legal services provided to the client, or

(b) that the solicitor knows, or ought reasonably to anticipate, is likely to induce the client or third party to confer such a benefit and is not reasonably incidental to the performance of the retainer.

Despite this, in many Australian jurisdictions, the question in professional discipline cases is not only whether there has been adequate costs disclosure or an unfair contract, but also whether the lawyer has deliberately charged 'grossly excessive' legal costs.[107] In contrast, the *Uniform Law* expressly provides that a 'contravention of a requirement … that a law practice must not charge more than fair and reasonable legal costs is capable of constituting unsatisfactory professional conduct or professional misconduct'.[108] While this seems to represent a different ethical standard, we contend that in any jurisdiction it would be dangerous and unethical to take a narrow reading of the law and to bill above what is genuinely believed to be fair and reasonable.

The question then is what is fair and reasonable in any particular case. Assessment of what is fair and reasonable will be dependent on the context in which the legal services were provided, as set out in the considerations listed above.[109] However, there are some principles that can guide us. Deceptive conduct (such as adding time not spent on the matter) or undertaking tasks that are obviously unnecessary or excessive are clearly wrongful practice. In a recent Victorian case, five lawyers were found to have engaged in a fraudulent scheme to illegitimately claim more that $19 million in legal costs associated with representation in a class action. Unsurprisingly, Dixon J found that these actions were breaches of the lawyers'

106 There is a presumption of undue influence in favour of the lawyer that will be found in any excessive gain. This legal presumption can be rebutted by full disclosure to the client.

107 *Legal Profession Act 2006* (ACT) s 389(b); *Legal Profession Act 2006* (NT) s 466(1)(b); *Legal Profession Act 2007* (Qld) s 420(b); *Legal Practitioners Act 1981* (SA) sch 3, cl 50(1); *Legal Profession Act 2007* (Tas) s 422(1)(b). This replicates the common law test of 'charging fees that grossly exceeds that which would be charged by a practitioner of good repute and competency': *D'Alessandro v Legal Practitioners Complaints Committee* (1995) 15 WAR 198, 214.

108 *Uniform Law* s 207.

109 This is reinforced in many disciplinary cases: see, eg, *De Pardo v Legal Practitioners Complaints Committee* (2000) 97 FCR 575, [45].

ethical duties and duties to the court, and ordered them to pay costs personally.[110] In another case, a solicitor acted for three clients in separate personal injury claims against the same defendant. It was agreed that the three matters would be heard together in the New South Wales District Court and each was successful. When the solicitor prepared bills, she charged each client for her own and a junior solicitor's time in the court, thereby tripling the amount received for their time. This practice was found to be professional misconduct because she failed to apportion the time between each client. The NSW Court of Appeal set down the clear principle that 'one unit of time cannot be charged more than once'.[111]

Other aspects of time billing might be more ethically arguable. Charging for things that are not legal costs, such as photocopying, might be acceptable if contemplated in the agreement but should be pointed out to the client and not done excessively. It seems unreasonable to charge for undertaking 'self-education' not required in the case,[112] and tasks not requiring legal skill undertaken by a lawyer might need to be billed at a lower rate.[113] Time-based charging where the lowest unit of time charged is six minutes is also contentious. Where the client has agreed to this it may be legally enforceable.[114] However, many argue that this amounts to billing fraud where a law firm charges one six-minute unit for work that took less than six minutes.[115] Costs agreements are enforced as ordinary contracts under legislation and therefore bind the parties to their terms. This means that when clients agree to pay at a particular rate or a fixed sum, or with a minimum unit of charging, they are stuck with this, unless there is a common law principle that applies to indicate a lack of consent,[116] or duress, or a legislative protection applies.

Where a firm charges for work that is not legal in nature or unlikely to have been contemplated by the client, this can be unethical. In *Council of the Queensland Law Society Inc v Roche*[117] a law firm argued that its costs agreement allowed for certain charges that were being contested by the client. The Court considered the work performed and the bill in detail and found some charges to be obviously unfair, such as charging 12 minutes (at $300 an hour) for a secretary wrapping a box of chocolates to be given to a reporting doctor's secretary as thanks for correcting a report, and another 12 minutes discussing the purchase of the chocolates. The original disciplinary tribunal concluded of the entire file: 'No fairminded practitioner would be justified in charging his or her client at what the Tribunal regards as an unusually high rate across the large number of hours involved, including the significant time on the mundane matters of the kind described.'[118]

110 *Bolitho v Banksia Securities Ltd (No 18) (Remitter)* [2021] VSC 666.

111 *Bechara v Legal Services Commissioner* (2010) 79 NSWLR 763, [138].

112 *Legal Services Commissioner v Challen* [2009] QCAT 273.

113 This was a finding by the Victorian Legal Services Commissioner in a binding determination: *Commissioner Determination (Overcharging)* [2018] VLSC 20.

114 Indeed, in *Steicke v Pederick* [2017] 5 SASC 98 the Court found that not only was this lawful if provided for in a costs agreement but could be regarded as 'fair and reasonable' because it was a 'common method of charging' that had been used 'since the last century': at [15].

115 Stephen Warne, 'On Rapacity' (2012) 110 (May/June) *Precedent* 14. See also *Legal Profession Complaints Committee and O'Halloran* [2013] WASAT 105 where a solicitor was suspended for only ever rounding up.

116 Undue influence as in *Council of the Queensland Law Society Inc v Roche* [2004] 2 Qd R 574.

117 *Council of the Queensland Law Society Inc v Roche* [2004] 2 Qd R 574.

118 Ibid [16]. The practitioner was struck off.

As Katzmann J has observed, the key to charging ethically is to honestly reflect on the bill sent in each case:

> Determining the amount to be charged is not a mere arithmetical calculation. Nor is it sufficient for the lawyer to check that the charges accord with the terms of the costs agreement. It is invariably necessary to consider whether the amounts charged may be excessive. The ultimate question should always be whether the charges are fair and reasonable.[119]

Negotiating fair and reasonable costs agreements and disputes about costs

Given the complexity of charging for legal services, it is imperative that lawyers understand their legal and ethical responsibilities and clearly communicate to clients what is involved in undertaking legal work and the costs of it. This final section of the chapter considers the practicality of communicating effectively with clients about costs, in the context of the legislative requirements and case law so far. However, despite the best communication, disputes will invariably arise in relation to the nature and quantum of lawyers' bills. The final section considers how costs disputes are regulated in Australia.

Communicating with the client to avoid misunderstandings and disputes

Clients' perceptions of the worth of their lawyers' work often depend a lot on the quality of information and communication they receive from their lawyer. This means that good lawyering requires excellent communication between lawyer and client about the work to be done, the anticipated time for the work and likely fees. The written costs disclosures – often running to tens of pages – required by legislation are not clear enough for many clients to properly understand. Lawyers should sit down with their prospective clients and walk them through the way they will be charged, making sure the client understands. This is also a way of building trust between client and lawyer. An important aspect of client trust in their lawyer is confidence: 'Can I trust my lawyer to tell me the truth in their assessment of the merits of my case and how much it will cost me?' This trust then lends itself to important communication throughout the representation including telling the lawyer all relevant information to allow the lawyer to act competently.[120]

Communicating well about costs might require a careful consideration of the nature of the client and whether further explanation is needed for them to fully comprehend the agreement. The NSW Office of the Legal Services Commissioner reported in 2021 that costs disputes and complaints in family matters were the most prevalent (around 30%), indicating

119 *Hudson v Sigalla (No 2)* [2017] FCA 339, [54].

120 See Chapter 4 on confidentiality and the assumption of a relationship of trust between lawyer and client.

that there are certain areas of practice and clients that might require specific strategies of communication.[121] Lawyers could suggest that another family member or friend be present to help clarify things when a costs agreement is discussed, if they have any doubts about a client's cognition.[122] Lawyers who want to communicate well with clients and make a fair agreement will go to much greater lengths than those required by legislation to explain as much as possible to each and every client about what must be done, the risks and associated costs.

In sum, fair costs agreements – and how they are negotiated with clients – are the linchpin of many successful legal practices and can be a powerful expression of both an *ethic of care* and respect for client autonomy because they depend on lawyers giving clients information and receiving informed instructions. Few problems will surface at the end of a case if the lawyer engages in the complaint prevention practices outlined in Figure 8.2.[123]

Disputing lawyers' costs

Despite good communication, lawyers and clients might disagree about the quantum of the bill and even whether certain work should have been performed and at what cost. Clients can dispute the substance of a bill, or request an itemised bill, within 30 days of receiving a bill.[125] The client can ask for someone to assess the fairness of the bill through a process of costs assessment (described below). In New South Wales, Victoria and Western Australia, under the *Uniform Law*, complaints about 'costs disputes' for less than $100,000 can be made to the Legal Services Commissioner in the respective jurisdictions for informal resolution.[126] Finally, clients across the country can complain about overcharging to their local regulator. The latter may result in a disciplinary prosecution on the basis of overcharging.

There is some variation between *Uniform Law* States and other jurisdictions around how costs disputes are handled. For instance, in New South Wales the Office of the Legal Services Commissioner will assist to resolve disputes informally. If this is not possible, the Commissioner has power to make binding determinations on costs (up to $12,880). In Victoria the regulator has similar powers; however, no matter what the quantum of the bill, the dispute can also be heard by the Costs Court for 'taxation' of the bill. In other jurisdictions such as South Australia, a court can decide disputes, but the regulator will also assist in mediation of costs disputes as a voluntary process.[127] These processes of assisting informal resolution of disputes are increasingly favoured across the country to reduce the

121 Office of Legal Services Commissioner (NSW) (n 96) 11.

122 As discussed in Chapter 6, this might be an expectation for a minimal level of competency.

123 Law societies also provide assistance for lawyers on compliance with disclosure requirements and developing good communication approaches.

124 The *Uniform Law* provisions cited in Figure 8.2 are replicated in other legislation around the country.

125 *Uniform Law* ss 194, 272(3); *Legal Profession Act 2006* (ACT) s 292 (30 days for an itemised bill); *Legal Profession Act 2006* (NT) s 324(1); *Legal Profession Act 2007* (Qld) ss 329, 332; *Legal Practitioners Act 1981* (SA) sch 3 cl 31; *Legal Profession Act 2007* (Tas) s 313.

126 *Uniform Law* ss 287–291. In New South Wales the cap for the regulator handling disputes is $128,760.

127 However, in this jurisdiction the Commissioner has power to make binding determinations of overcharging where the complaint is no more than $50,000: *Legal Practitioners Act 1981* (SA) s 77N(7)(a).

Figure 8.2 Complaint prevention practices[124]

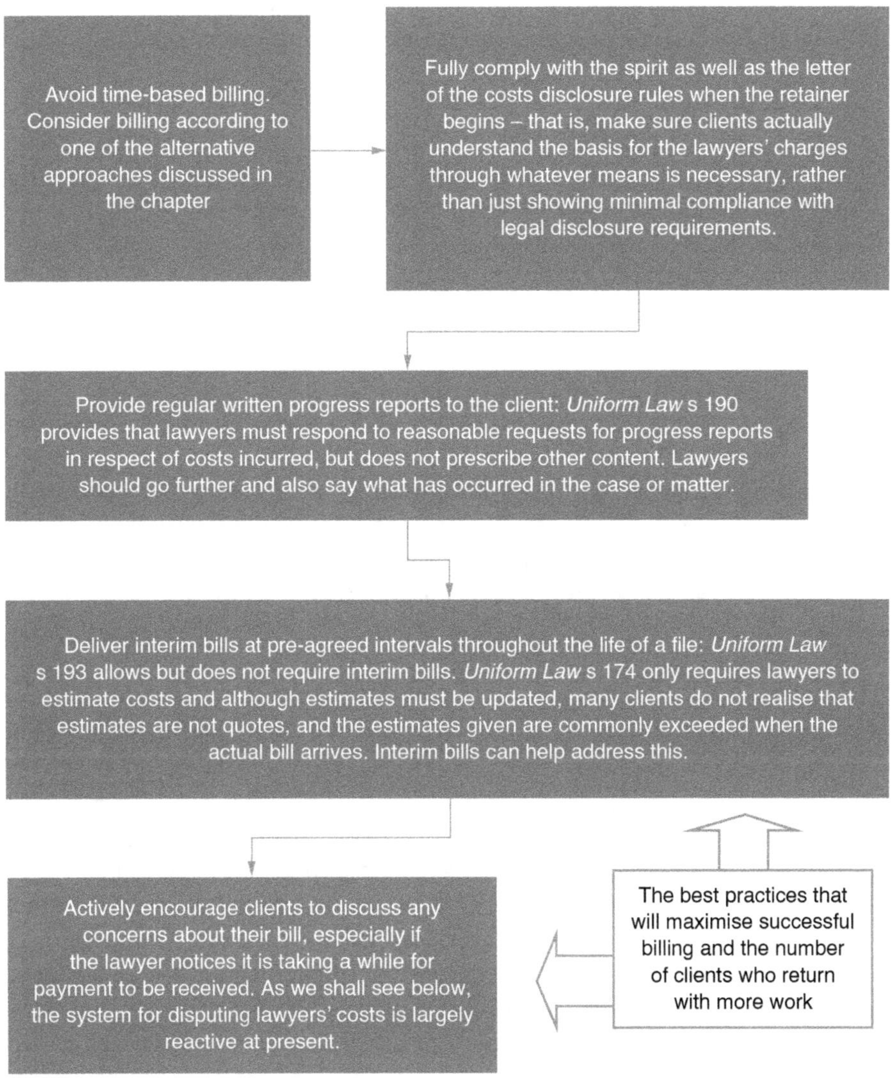

stress and cost for the client, and burden on the civil justice system. Regulators also publish case examples of costs disputes, lack of costs disclosure or overcharging to educate the profession and public, and to demonstrate how many are effectively resolved through mediation (usually by the lawyer reducing the bill).[128]

In most jurisdictions another regime applies to resolve costs disputes whereby an independent costs assessor (a court official or appointed lawyer) assesses the bill for its fairness

128 See, eg, Office of Legal Services Commissioner (NSW) (n 96) 36–40.

and reasonableness when a client or losing party to litigation (who must pay the winner's costs) complains. For simplicity we describe the most common form of costs assessment. The criteria for assessment of the lawyer's bill in this scheme is the same as described above in relation to setting aside a costs agreement under s 172 of the *Uniform Law*.

Legal Profession Uniform Law

199 Costs assessment

(1) Assessments of legal costs are to be conducted by costs assessors ...

(2) On a costs assessment, the costs assessor must –

- **(a)** determine whether or not a valid costs agreement exists; and
- **(b)** determine whether legal costs are fair and reasonable and, to the extent they are not fair and reasonable, determine the amount of legal costs (if any) that are to be payable.

200 Factors in a costs assessment

(1) In considering whether legal costs for legal work are fair and reasonable, the costs assessor must apply the principles in section 172 so far as they are applicable.

(2) In considering whether legal costs for legal work are fair and reasonable, the costs assessor may have regard to the following matters –

- **(a)** whether the law practice and any legal practitioner associate or foreign lawyer associate involved in the work complied with this Law and the Uniform Rules;
- **(b)** any disclosures made, including whether it would have been reasonably practicable for the law practice to disclose the total costs of the work at the outset (rather than simply disclosing charging rates);
- **(c)** any relevant advertisement as to the law practice's costs or the skills of the law practice or any legal practitioner associate or foreign lawyer associate involved in the work;
- **(d)** any other relevant matter.

The timing of applying for resolution of a costs dispute is set by legislation, and is generally within 12 months of the delivery of the bill *or* payment of any costs.[129] In some cases where the client is unhappy with the bill, the law firm may have already issued proceedings to recover its costs.[130] However, once an application for a costs assessment is made, the law firm must not commence any court proceedings to recover the legal costs. Equally, law firms might be tempted to draw on money held in trust for a client on account of legal costs. Trust money is not the lawyer's or law firm's money and can only be claimed when they are entitled to be paid.[131]

---

129 *Uniform Law* s 198; *Legal Profession Act 2006* (ACT) s 302(2); *Legal Profession Act 2006* (NT) s 350(3)(b); *Legal Profession Act 2007* (Qld) s 342(2); *Legal Practitioners Act 1981* (SA) sch 3 cl 49; *Legal Profession Act 2007* (Tas) s 331(2).

130 This process might be through a civil debt claim but there are statutory limitations on when this can be commenced (generally not until 30 days after the client has received the bill).

131 Trust accounting duties are briefly described in Chapter 3. Money that is intended to eventually pay the lawyer is often held by the law firm in trust for the client while the legal services are being performed. There are specific and detailed provisions in the *Uniform Law* and other legislation around the country about dealing with trust money and the way in which a lawyer can pay themselves from trust. For the moment, the relevant point is that it is unethical for a lawyer to draw on trust money before being entitled to it; such a breach often leads to a serious disciplinary finding.

The costs assessment process, like the regulator mediation approach, is aimed at swift and cheap resolution of disputes without the need to go through formal civil court proceedings. However, complaints usually come only after the client relationship has already been badly damaged. If a client seems ready to complain, then the smart firm will have clear processes in place to discuss the bill with their client and to mediate the final figure as soon as possible, so that they get paid promptly and avoid the delays and risk to reputation that can come with a formal costs assessment. Moreover, the assessment process is itself expensive.[132] It might lead to a disciplinary result, if the lawyer is found to have significantly overcharged or failed to follow their statutory obligations in costs disclosure.

On the other side of the coin, some complaints about costs are generated by clients who seize upon a minor issue because they do not wish to pay for legal services fairly provided, or simply misunderstand the cost of legal services. It is very hard to predict which clients will fall into this category, so the best protection for both clients and lawyers is to strike a fair costs agreement and to communicate openly, including providing updates about any changes in the case that have cost consequences.

Conclusion

A key ingredient of successful legal practice is lawyers' understanding of the genuine worth of the work performed and their capacity to communicate that worth and recover its value both ethically and in a timely manner. Lawyers will be most effective in the billing process when their clients are fully aware of likely costs well in advance and are never surprised. Clear, timely and accurate information about what the client will have to pay at the end of the day, and prompt attention to any sign that a client does not understand, are key. A few clients will exploit lawyers' failures around fees and costs, but the huge majority only want to be treated with respect and diligence.

Nevertheless, if the bill is not fair and reasonable, or there has been no costs disclosure, the client has every right to complain. For a range of reasons canvassed in this chapter, lawyers and their firms might lose sight of the need to be fair in charging for work reasonably performed. Legislation reminds lawyers of the need to speak to clients about the real cost of legal services and how to properly bill for services. It permits a range of methods of charging for time that can be crafted to best suit the nature of the work and the client and their interests.

Time billing persists as the predominant method of charging for services. It provides the most scope for lawyers to overcharge and has been implicated in the most wrongdoing associated with billing a client. In many cases these ethical failings are an aspect of poor law firm culture. In some cases, engaging in unethical approaches to billing might be difficult to avoid when working in a firm context that encourages this. Early awareness of these possibilities and the effect that the climate of legal practice can have on lawyers personally

132 If the bill complained of is reduced by at least 15% in a costs assessment or taxation, the law practice, not the client, will ordinarily have to pay the costs of the assessment process: *Uniform Law* s 204; *Legal Profession Act 2006* (ACT) s 294A(2); *Legal Profession Act 2006* (NT) s 322(5); *Legal Profession Act 2007* (Qld) s 335(5). In South Australia it must be made within six months: *Legal Practitioners Act 1981* (SA) sch 3 cl 37(4).

may be important for new lawyers' decisions about the type and structure of legal practice they intend to pursue. Such awareness should also lead law students and young lawyers to ask questions (of the firm, and also of colleagues and contacts in the profession more widely) about the values and ethical climate of practice in any law firm they are thinking of joining.

We suggest also that law students and lawyers should continue to pressure regulators and their professional leaders to make changes so that no billing system is contributing to poor mental health in legal workplaces.[133]

RECOMMENDED FURTHER READING

Iain Campbell and Sara Charlesworth, 'Salaried Lawyers and Billable Hours: A New Perspective from the Sociology of Work' (2012) 19(1) *International Journal of the Legal Profession* 89

GE Dal Pont, 'Contextualising Lawyer Overcharging' (2016) 42(2) *Monash University Law Review* 283

GE Dal Pont, *Law of Costs* (Lawbook, 5th ed, 2021)

Richard Moorhead, 'Filthy Lucre: Lawyers' Fees and Lawyers' Ethics – What is Wrong with Informed Consent?' (2011) 31(3) *Legal Studies* 345

Christine Parker and David Ruschena, 'The Pressures of Billable Hours: Lessons from a Survey of Billing Practices Inside Law Firms' (2011) 9(2) *University of St Thomas Law Journal* 619

133 As recognised in Hannah Wootton, 'Tough Demands, Long Hours Make Sector "High-Risk"', *The Australian Financial Review* (Sydney, 11 June 2021): 'Lawyers on billable hour arrangements were particularly vulnerable to fatigue, as "the requirement [that] workers are hyper-vigilant on accounting their time attached to fees for service" added to the other demands.'

9

CORPORATE AND GOVERNMENT LAWYERS

Introduction

The ethics of both corporate and government lawyers are critically important to the proper functioning of democratic societies. Both groups advise and act for powerful clients: corporations are among the most powerful actors in our society because of the potentially far-reaching impact of their activities; governments have 'powers and obligations which far exceed those of the normal citizen'.[1] In this chapter we discuss the ethical responsibilities and challenges facing lawyers who act for these clients. We focus predominantly on corporate lawyers but then turn our attention to lawyers working in government. While government legal work may seem a far cry from the work of corporate lawyers, in fact in-house corporate and in-house government lawyers face some similar challenges and opportunities.

'Corporate lawyers'

We use the term 'corporate lawyer' throughout this chapter to refer both to lawyers employed in-house in business corporations and those in law firm practice who are retained as external lawyers to advise or represent corporate clients, noting differences where appropriate. Traditionally it was thought that the *external* lawyers for a company were automatically more independent and more capable of giving fearless, ethical advice to corporate clients than were *internal or in-house* lawyers employed inside the company and whose whole job depended on the company. But today external law firm lawyers can be almost as financially dependent on, and closely involved in, their corporate clients' businesses as in-house lawyers. And, like in-house legal staff, most external corporate lawyers are themselves also employed in large, profit-oriented organisations, whether it is a law firm or a consultancy or accounting firm. Further, the status and power of in-house counsel has increased dramatically over recent decades, and their place in the corporate structure gives them an overview and potential influence greater than that accorded outside counsel.[2] Many general counsel (the most senior in-house legal role) also hold the role of company secretary, making them one of the core company decision-makers.

Corporate lawyers play an important part in facilitating almost every economic activity in our society. They negotiate and draft business deals. They often advise what representations can or should be made in advertising campaigns, financial statements and disclosure documents for investors. They advise as to how to comply with the host of laws that apply to business, including environmental, health and safety, employment, intellectual property, competition and fair-trading regulation. They are also a source of information for their clients about whether and how other businesses are complying with the law, and thus about social norms of legal compliance. Tanina Rostain and Mitt Regan's study of elite US lawyers' involvement in creating and marketing tax shelters that pushed or overrode the limits of the law showed that clients are more likely to comply with tax obligations when they believe

1 Bradley Selway, 'The Duties of Lawyers Acting for Government' (1999) 10(2) *Public Law Review* 114.

2 The number of lawyers working in-house in the Australian corporate sector has also increased dramatically. There was an 82% increase from 2011 to 2020: Urbis, *2020 National Profile of Solicitors* (Final Report, July 2021).

others are doing so and are less likely to comply if they believe others are not cooperating. Their study illustrates that lawyers' advice on norms can be crucial to how well the law works in society.[3] And, of course, corporate lawyers also advise businesses on a day-to-day basis as to when to litigate, when to settle disputes and when to advise that a corporation might need to change the way it designs its products or governs itself in response to plaintiff suits.[4]

Corporate lawyers, whether in-house or external, are subject to professional regulation and have the same ethical responsibilities as other lawyers. This means that, in theory, their duty to the court and the administration of justice is paramount and their duty to the client secondary. The importance of ethical conduct by corporate lawyers is recognised by the international Association of Corporate Counsel ('ACC'). The ACC has endorsed the General Counsel Oath,[5] which urges general counsel to 'go beyond stated rules, codes and guidance to act with integrity, honesty, and … the highest ethical and professional values'.[6] The Oath, developed by Simon Zinger,[7] has been described by the ACC as 'a timely, critical reminder of [the] responsibilities [of] corporate counsel to [their] clients, … colleagues, and … communities'.[8] It reflects a belief that the work of corporate lawyers should be 'underpinned by ideals of fairness, justice and professional responsibility'.[9] As we discuss below, this ideal can be challenged by the reality of corporate practice, but this makes promotion of the Oath all the more important.

Corporate lawyers have been criticised for using their legal skills uncritically to enable misleading, illegal or unethical corporate conduct. We identify here three main ways in which this may play out and then turn to alternative, more ethical approaches to corporate lawyering.

(a) Reactive corporate lawyering: narrow legalism that ignores ethical issues

Lawyers can adopt a narrow legalistic approach to their work and the advice they give. After interviewing 57 corporate finance lawyers in global law firms based in London, Stephen Vaughan and Emma Oakley concluded that 'there is an apathy – a lack of concern or interest – about ethics'[10] on the part of the lawyers interviewed. Common themes from the interviews include lawyers 'taking the deal at "face value" [not probing about ethical

3 Tanina Rostain and Milton C Regan, *Confidence Games: Lawyers, Accountants and the Tax Shelter Industry* (MIT Press, 2014) 339–43.
4 Robert Eli Rosen, 'The Sociological Imagination and Legal Ethics' (2016) 19 *Legal Ethics* 97.
5 Simon Zinger, 'The General Counsel Oath,' *The General Counsel Oath* (Web Page, 2022) <https://generalcounseloath.com/>.
6 'ACC Endorsed General Counsel Oath', *ACC – Association of Corporate Counsel* (Blog Post, 29 September 2020) <https://www.acc.com/about/newsroom/news/acc-endorses-general-counsel-oath>.
7 Simon Zinger, 'About', *The General Counsel Oath* (Web Page, August 2020) <https://generalcounseloath.com/about/>.
8 'ACC Endorsed General Counsel Oath' (n 6).
9 Ibid.
10 Steven Vaughan and Emma Oakley, '"Gorilla Exceptions" and the Ethically Apathetic Corporate Lawyer' (2016) 19 *Legal Ethics* 50, 73.

implications], being the lawyer-technician who uses the law to effect the client's wishes, and not "pushing" ethics'.[11] Vaughan and Oakley suggest that this apathy about ethical considerations stems from several sources, including adherence to *adversarial advocacy*, with its insistence that it is not the lawyer's role to enquire into the morality (as opposed to the legality) of the client's instructions, even in transactional (not litigious) work.[12] Lawyer interviewees justified this approach with beliefs that the corporate client itself will have made an ethical assessment before asking the lawyer to act, and that their own law firm will not take on completely unethical clients.[13]

It can be in the interests of both external lawyers and their corporate clients to keep the scope of the work given to the lawyer very narrow so as to exclude the possibility that the lawyer might find out about, or need to turn their mind to, any unethical or illegal aspects of corporate plans. In Case study 9.2 the lawyers for James Hardie Industries Ltd ('JH') gave detailed technical legal advice (over a number of years) about how JH could separate itself from its liabilities to compensate those who had suffered disease or died as a result of exposure to the asbestos that the company had included in the manufacture of various products. At one point during the government-commissioned inquiry into JH's actions, Commissioner David Jackson QC commented in relation to the lawyers' advice, 'Why didn't someone stand back and say: "This is just too hot"?'[14] Journalist and observer of the Australian legal profession Richard Ackland analysed the JH situation in terms of 'plausible deniability' for both the lawyers and the corporate client:

> Boards of directors and senior directors have schemes that need implementation. Lawyers are hired to get the client over the line. When things go wrong, as they often do, the directors and executives invariably say, 'We acted on advice'. The standard retort of the [legal] advisers is[:] 'We were not given all the information, so the advice was necessarily limited'. This reliable formulation usually saves a lot of bacon.[15]

This type of plausible deniability can be seen as an example of a narrow, reactive approach in which the corporate lawyer avoids consideration of issues that might give rise to ethical obligations:

11 Ibid.

12 Ibid.

13 Ibid. See also Richard Moorhead and Victoria Hinchly, 'Professional Minimalism? The Ethical Consciousness of Commercial Lawyers' (2015) 42(3) *Journal of Law and Society* 387.

14 David F Jackson (Commissioner), 'Statement in the Hearing Before the Special Commission of Inquiry into the Medical Research and Compensation Fund' (7 July 2004) 2. (In his report Jackson concluded that he found it 'disturbing' that none of JH's professional advisers and officers, especially its solicitors, 'expressed any view of the merits [or rightness] of the underlying transaction'. But he did not find that JH's law firm breached any legal or professional conduct obligation on this issue: New South Wales, Special Commission of Inquiry into the Medical Research and Compensation Foundation, *Report of the Special Commission of Inquiry into the Medical Research and Compensation Foundation* (Report, 2004) vol 1, 548 [29.16]. (The inquiry report is hereinafter referred to as '*Report of the Special Commission of Inquiry into the MRCF*'.) Eventually the in-house counsel for JH was found to have breached the *Corporations Act 2001* (Cth) by failing to advise the Board of certain matters: *Shafron v Australian Securities and Investments Commission* (2012) 247 CLR 465.

15 Richard Ackland, 'Irresistible Charms', *Business Review Weekly* (Melbourne, 29 September 2004) 50.

> Legal departments adopting the narrow view sharply distinguish legal from business advice and confine the lawyer's role to the strictly legal; their advice is reactive, neutral risk analysis, given only when sought, accepting as the 'client' whatever manager at whatever level consults it, and accepting the 'problem' and the corporation's 'interest' as defined by the manager. They don't ask what happens when the 'client' leaves their office – unless required to perform monitoring or auditing functions, in which case they will confine themselves to formal questions and formal responses. Under attack by regulators or civil adversaries, they will see their function as simply minimizing liability in every case ...[16]

(b) Proactive corporate lawyering: commercial savvy that consciously uses law to achieve unethical goals

Most business clients want their lawyers to take a proactive, 'commercial' approach. This entails lawyers taking into account the social and political contexts of their work. Lawyers are expected to understand their clients' business goals and advise on how to use law to achieve them. Indeed, in some businesses it is now anticipated that, rather than being a mere 'cost centre', an in-house legal department should generate profits or 'value-add' through strategies such as aggressive tax planning, intellectual property protections and takeover litigation.[17] More constructively, lawyers might be expected to implement corporate governance systems that improve corporate decision-making processes and corporate social responsibility systems and, in turn, the businesses' credibility with the public and therefore their brand value.

Corporate lawyers have been criticised for legal manipulation and innovation that produce legal devices and techniques to achieve client goals but without regard to the spirit and ethical substance of the law or the community's ethical expectations. Clients may expect lawyers to understand and address the company's broader commercial, political and ethical context, and not just its technical legal needs, but also expect them to come up with strategies to achieve the client's goals by 'managing' this context. Corporate lawyers may help companies engage in 'creative compliance'[18] by avoiding and evading the imposition of law before it becomes a problem. Or these lawyers may create legal techniques that make it look like companies are complying with the law and addressing social and governmental expectations of ethical behaviour when in actual fact they are making as little real change as possible. They may also devise legal techniques that abuse the law by achieving corporate goals regardless of the real purpose of the law involved.[19] The following are examples of the latter.

---

16 Robert Gordon and William Simon, 'The Redemption of Professionalism' in Robert Nelson, David Trubek and Robert Solomon (eds), *Lawyers' Ideals / Lawyers' Practices: Transformations in the American Legal Profession* (Cornell University Press, 1992) 230, 252, summarising Robert Eli Rosen, 'The Inside Counsel Movement, Professional Judgment and Organizational Representation' (1989) 64(3) *Indiana Law Journal* 479.

17 Robert Eli Rosen, '"We're All Consultants Now": How Change in Client Organizational Strategies Influences Change in the Organization of Corporate Legal Services' (2002) 44 *Arizona Law Review* 637, 650–60, 675–9; G Richard Shell, *Make the Rules or Your Rivals Will* (Crown Business, 2004).

18 Christopher J Whelan, 'Some Realism about Professionalism: Core Values, Legality, and Corporate Law Practice' (2006) 54(4) *Buffalo Law Review* 1067, 1113.

19 Whelan (n 18).

The 'litigation option'

Corporate lawyers sometimes advise their clients to use the 'litigation option' as a tactic to put commercial pressure on their opponents in takeover battles and other corporate disputes.[20] One of Australia's 1980s 'corporate cowboys' used litigation in this way in the *White Industries* case (see Case study 6.3). Of course, such action is an abuse of process. As we discuss in Chapter 6, legislation that now requires clients to certify that they are aware of their overarching obligations[21] (including not to issue proceedings that are an abuse of process), and strong judicial condemnation of breaches of the Act, may go some way to deterring lawyers from using this tactic.

'Regulatory entrepreneurship'

'Regulatory entrepreneurship' refers to the use of the law to further corporate interests. Some companies adopt a goal of changing the law as part of their business plan. Lawyers are key to the success of such behaviour – they advise and facilitate it. Regulatory entrepreneurship is not always a negative for society – sometimes it results in changes to 'inefficient or otherwise flawed laws'.[22] However, as Elizabeth Pollman and Jordan Barry point out, regulatory entrepreneurs are profit-seeking entities that will use their political power to pursue their own interests, with little regard to other stakeholders or society.[23] Philip Morris Australia's legal challenge to Australia's plain packaging legislation under an Australia–Hong Kong investment treaty is an example of this.[24] Philip Morris International had changed its corporate structure in an attempt to gain protection under the treaty. The Tribunal hearing the challenge agreed with Australia's argument that this restructure amounted to an abuse of rights because it took place at a time when a dispute was foreseeable. The Tribunal found in favour of Australia. But, as Janani Shanthosh and colleagues explain, in other instances corporations have successfully used regulatory entrepreneurship to weaken the impact of laws that could protect health, even where health is not the focus of these laws. Such laws include 'trade agreements, planning legislation, and environmental or industrial relations legislation'.

> For example, large liquor outlets in Australia regularly use the courts to dispute failed development applications for bottle shops, hotels, pubs and clubs. Even in locations where the police, social services and the community have argued strongly against new alcohol outlets, a review of Australian case law found the rulings were overwhelmingly in favour of industry interests.
>
> Under our existing planning legislation, public health evidence regarding potential harm to health has had little or no influence in local courts, which are bound by laws that preference other considerations including market freedoms, amenity and existing planning controls. The result is high densities of fast food, alcohol outlets, tobacco retailers, and poor health outcomes in some areas – especially low-income areas.

20 Roman Tomasic and Stephen Bottomley, *Directing the Top 500* (Allen & Unwin, 1993) 3.
21 See, eg, *Civil Procedure Act 2010* (Vic) s 41.
22 Elizabeth Pollman and Jordan M Barry, 'Regulatory Entrepreneurship' (2016) 90(3) *Southern California Law Review* 383, 445.
23 Ibid 443.
24 Sera Mirzabegian, 'Big Tobacco v Australia: Challenges to Plain Packaging' (2019) 4(1) *Business and Human Rights Journal* 177.

> Even when industry does not mount legal action, the threat of doing so has been used successfully to delay legislation. Scare tactics and the fear of having to defend expensive legal action can be enough to derail the best intentions of our legislators and deter the introduction of innovative new policy that could create healthier communities.[25]

(c) Abusing lawyer–client confidentiality protections to cover up misconduct and obstruct justice

The final and most serious criticism of the ethics of corporate lawyers is that they sometimes aid their clients by helping them obstruct justice where civil litigation or regulatory investigation and prosecution is occurring or likely.

In the case of *McCabe v British American Tobacco Australia Services Ltd*[26] the Supreme Court of Victoria at first instance found that Clayton Utz, the solicitors for the defendant, British American Tobacco Australia Services Ltd ('BATAS'), had advised the company on a 'document retention policy' that intentionally resulted in the destruction of thousands of documents as part of the preparation for an anticipated wave of litigation against the tobacco industry.[27] These documents would have been relevant and favourable to Rolah McCabe's negligence case against the company for her terminal cancer. Documentary evidence was clearly critical to support or undermine the claim that the company had access to scientific evidence, held knowledge of the health effects of tobacco products, and crafted marketing strategies to enlist child smokers and conceal the health consequences of smoking. Eames J struck out BATAS's defence on the basis that the destruction of documentary evidence relevant to the claim had made a fair trial impossible. The Victorian Court of Appeal reversed this decision and remitted the case for trial: it accepted the defence's contentions that the handling of the documentary evidence was within the bounds of appropriate document management despite the likelihood the documents would be relevant to inevitable future litigation.[28] Rolah McCabe died after the appeal was heard.

Le Mire has argued:

> As a result of the *McCabe* case it appeared that, while lawyers could not advise the destruction of documents without risking sanction for the breach of their professional duties [due to professional conduct obligations], corporations could destroy documents almost at will up until the time litigation commenced [as long as they could show some document management purpose in doing so].[29]

---

25 'How Multinationals Are Using the Law to Damage Our Health', *Lawyers Weekly* (online at 20 June 2021) <https://www.lawyersweekly.com.au/politics/31662-how-multinationals-are-using-the-law-to-damage-our-health>. See also Belinda Townsend et al, 'How Does Policy Framing Enable or Constrain Inclusion of Social Determinants of Health and Health Equity on Trade Policy Agendas?' (2020) 30(1) *Critical Public Health* 115.

26 [2002] VSC 73 (Eames J).

27 This material on the *McCabe* case is taken from Christine Parker, 'A Critical Morality for Australian Lawyers and Law Students' (2004) 30 *Monash University Law Review* 49–74; Christine Parker, Suzanne Le Mire and Anita Mackay, 'Lawyers, Confidentiality and Whistleblowing: Lessons from the *McCabe* Tobacco Litigation' (2017) 40 *Melbourne University Law Review* 999.

28 *British American Tobacco Australia Services Ltd v Cowell* (2002) 7 VR 524, 592–3 [191].

29 Suzanne Le Mire, 'Document Destruction and Corporate Culture: A Victorian Initiative' (2006) 19(3) *Australian Journal of Corporate Law* 304, 308 (citations omitted).

This loophole led the Victorian government to pass legislation in 2006 making it an indictable offence to intentionally destroy or conceal a 'document or other thing of any kind [that] is, or is reasonably likely to be, required in evidence in a legal proceeding'.[30] Some of the activities attributed to BATAS and its lawyers may have been criminal had the legislation been in place at the time.

One very important way in which business corporations can use lawyers to obstruct justice is where corporate lawyers are able to use their professional responsibilities in relation to confidentiality and client legal privilege to protect corporate activities from scrutiny, and cover up evidence of any wrongdoing.[31] Case study 4.3 discusses the way in which tobacco industry lawyers in the United States devised schemes to claim client legal privilege over reports that showed smoking was dangerous. Another example of client legal privilege being invoked to prevent public scrutiny of alleged organisational wrongdoing is the response by the Australian Wheat Board ('AWB') to the Commission of Inquiry into the payment of 'kickbacks' (a form of bribe) to former Iraqi dictator Saddam Hussein (see Case studies 4.4 and 9.1). Rather than cooperate with the Inquiry, AWB chose to claim privilege over a large number of documents, a claim that was referred to the Federal Court, resulting in significant delays to the Inquiry. The Federal Court found that privilege did not attach to a substantial number of the documents, including those 'brought into existence in furtherance of a fraud or other impropriety'.[32]

What is so disturbing about the conduct of the lawyers in these case studies is not merely that they committed technical infractions by using confidentiality and privilege inappropriately – it is that the lawyers were used by their client companies to shut down the proper operation of the adversary system and therefore legal scrutiny of their conduct. While one can make a very good case that tobacco companies are systematically immoral, because they market and sell a product that they know is addictive and lethal to a large proportion of their customers,[33] the ethical problem in the *McCabe* case, and other tobacco cases, was that the company and its lawyers made sure that the legal system could not clearly see and determine this substantive moral and legal issue. The lawyers allowed large, powerful organisations to manipulate the law to avoid scrutiny of their conduct. This is not a problem of lack of professional conduct/civil procedure rules, or even of non-compliance with those rules.

Ethically unreflective corporate lawyering can sometimes occur not so much due to failures of personal ideals but due to narrow legalistic training and workplace cultures that do not equip corporate lawyers to know how to put ethics into action, or even to recognise ethical issues when they arise. The loss of ethical discernment is often a subtle and gradual progression, especially in the context of complex corporate decision-making.[34] It is easy to ignore the interests of investors, the public, the courts and the law, without even noticing

30 *Crimes Act 1958* (Vic) s 254, as inserted by *Crimes (Document Destruction) Act 2006* (Vic) s 3.

31 William H Simon, 'The Confidentiality Fetish: The Problem with Attorney-Client Privilege' (2004) 294(5) *Atlantic Monthly* 113.

32 *AWB Ltd v Cole (No 5)* (2006) 155 FCR 30, [236].

33 See Jonathan Liberman and Jonathan Clough, 'Corporations That Kill: The Criminal Liability of Tobacco Manufacturers' (2002) 26 *Criminal Law Journal* 223.

34 See Robert Eli Rosen, 'Problem-Setting and Serving the Organizational Client: Legal Diagnosis and Professional Independence' (2001) 56(1) *University of Miami Law Review* 179, 182.

that is what we are doing, where it is psychologically more comfortable to do so, or the issues have become so complex that we subconsciously screen out uncomfortable facts. In particular, when lawyers become financially dependent on their clients, spend a lot of their time with clients and try to see things from their clients' point of view in order to provide a good service, they will naturally, and often subconsciously, tend to identify with those clients and their purposes.

In Chapter 1 we briefly discuss the effect of organisational culture on lawyers on lawyers wellbeing and ethics. Here we consider the effects of the cultures in which corporate lawyers work, and also the human tendency to rationalise unethical behaviour.

Commercial immersion of corporate lawyering

It has been suggested that uncritical corporate lawyering has become more ethically problematic, more widespread and more deeply entrenched as the market for legal services has become increasingly competitive and fragmented. Big companies (and also government departments) shop around for the 'right legal advice at the right price'. They have unbundled their legal services so that no one firm, not even their own in-house legal department, is necessarily guaranteed a steady flow of legal work or is aware of all legal matters in which the company is involved. Yet, at the same time there is also more demand for corporate lawyers to be embedded in (employed by, or seconded to) business sub-units within corporate clients so that they can provide commercially realistic advice and anticipate, avoid or resolve legal problems for that unit. While there is demand for a closer relationship between lawyers and business, that relationship is also less secure for the lawyer as lawyers can easily be sacked if their advice does not suit. This is one reason that lawyers will come under pressure to please individual managers, executives or work teams (who control the purse strings) rather than consider their obligation to the corporation as a whole, let alone any duty to the law or the public interest.[35]

The ethical dangers posed by businesses' increasingly commercial approach to legal advice are compounded by the fact that law firms themselves are being managed more and more like large business corporations. Corporate lawyers rarely operate as independent solo practitioners or work together in equal partnerships. Rather, a large number of lawyers today work as employees subject to detailed direction and supervision, especially in large national and global law firms. These firms are vastly more profitable, and more profits-driven, than smaller firms.

The *McCabe* case provides a good example of the extent of this commercial immersion of corporate lawyers. As the judge described the facts:

> The relationship between the defendant [BAT] and its retained solicitors was so close that solicitors employed by private [law] firms sometimes became employees of Wills [a company in the BAT corporate group] and then continued to work alongside members of their former firm, and employees of one of the legal firms sometimes spent months working on the premises of Wills. Private practitioners and in-house lawyers travelled together to conferences of litigation lawyers, organised by companies in the BAT Group,

35 Rosen, '"We're All Consultants Now"' (n 17) 672–3.

> to discuss litigation tactics … The longstanding and very close association between in-house lawyers and private practitioners had the potential for blurring the roles and responsibilities of the lawyers.[36]

The danger of too close a relationship between in-house and external counsel was more recently illustrated during the Royal Commission into Misconduct in the Banking, Superannuation and Financial Services Industry. The financial services company AMP Ltd instructed the law firm Clayton Utz to prepare an 'independent' report for the corporate regulator (the Australian Securities and Investment Commission, or 'ASIC') about a 'fees for no service' scandal that the Commission was investigating. AMP's executive team, including its general counsel (who was a former Clayton Utz solicitor), requested Clayton Utz to make changes to the 'independent' report, the initial draft of which was changed 22 times before being delivered to the Australian Securities and Investments Commission ('ASIC'). The Royal Commissioner considered that AMP may have misled ASIC about the independent nature of the report. He made no findings in relation to Clayton Utz;[37] however, it is worth noting the following commentary in relation to the external lawyers:

> [A] corporate governance expert at UTS Business School [noted that] Clayton Utz … helped AMP mislead the corporate regulator.
>
> 'Unless at some stage they have withdrawn their claim to ASIC [that] it was an independent report, they were complicit,' he said.
>
> He said while historically, consultants, audit firms and law firms had always been criticised for being too influenced by very generous consulting fees on offer, this instance stood out because the report was destined for a regulator.
>
> 'It doesn't get more serious in terms of questioning the professional integrity of both the law firm itself and AMP,' he said.
>
> …
>
> Sydney Law School professor David Kinley said it was 'rich' for AMP to call the report independent and AMP sought to mislead ASIC by presenting it as an independent report.
>
> 'If this was to be presented by AMP to ASIC as an independent report then both AMP and Clayton Utz have an obligation to ensure that it is worthy of that name,' he said.
>
> A managing partner at a commercial law firm, who declined to be named, said the Clayton Utz report was not a normal practice for a law firm.
>
> 'There is no way whatsoever that the report should have been labelled "independent", because it clearly wasn't,' he said.
>
> He said while it was not uncommon for external lawyers to amend a report at the client's instructions, they should not have agreed to be identified as operating independently.[38]

36 *McCabe v British American Tobacco Australia Services Ltd* [2002] VSC 73, [284]–[286] (Eames J).

37 *Royal Commission into Misconduct in the Banking, Superannuation and Financial Services Industry* (Interim Report, 2018) vol 2, 144–51.

38 Misa Han, 'Clayton Utz Complicit in AMP Misleading ASIC', *The Australian Financial Review* (Sydney, 19 April 2018).

Competitive, high-stress environments

Another cultural factor to consider in some large/global law firms is the competitive, high-stress environment in which lip service is paid to work-life balance. A 2021 global survey of almost 2,500 private practice partners reported that 'Forty-nine percent of senior lawyers do not think they should set any boundaries when it comes to being available for contact … A quarter of partners feel unable to discuss boundaries with any of their clients.'[39] In Australia, junior lawyers have queried the culture of overwork at large firms, some of which have been found to be significantly underpaying their junior legal staff: the expectation of working very long hours means the staff end up being paid below the minimum wage.[40] Donald Langevoort describes the ethical danger of this type of work environment:

> Research shows that being ethical is harder cognitive work than giving in to temptation. Resisting temptation depletes energy over time; tiredness and stress, in turn, increase the likelihood of further cheating. And corporate lawyers, by all accounts, inhabit workplaces filled with stamina-challenging workloads, along with many other competitive stressors tied to promotion, status, and compensation.[41]

Lack of work-life balance has negative impacts on lawyers' own wellbeing, including their ability to engage in caring relationships with their friends and families and to spend time cultivating their own personal ethical and political beliefs. It also means they have little free time and thought to devote to learning about and coming to an opinion on important social, environmental and justice issues and getting involved in pro bono action on those causes.

Rationalisation in a general and moral sense

We all want to believe the best of those we identify with, including the clients we serve. If we notice any sign of dishonesty or other conduct that goes against our own personal ethical standards and social values among our friends or colleagues, this causes what psychologists call 'cognitive dissonance' – the uncomfortable feeling of lack of fit between our belief in ourselves as an ethical person on the one hand, and our involvement or

39 Thomson Reuters Institute, *Stella Performance: A Survey of Stand Out Talent* (Report, June 2021) Executive Summary, 3. See also, in relation to hyper-competitive environments, Margaret Thornton, 'Hypercompetitiveness or a Balanced Life? Gendered Discourses in the Globalisation of Australian Law Firms' (2014) 17(2) *Legal Ethics* 153; Richard Collier, 'Wellbeing in the Legal Profession: Reflections on Recent Developments (or, What Do We Talk About, When We Talk About Wellbeing?)' (2016) 23(1) *International Journal of the Legal Profession* 41.

40 Naaman Zhou, 'Young Lawyers Push Back Against Culture of Overwork in Top Law Firms', *The Guardian* (online at 3 December 2018) <https://www.theguardian.com/law/2018/dec/03/young-lawyers-push-back-against-culture-of-overwork-in-top-law-firms>; Hannah Wootton and David Marin-Guzman, 'Freehills Under Paid Juniors $20,000', *The Australian Financial Review* (Sydney, 25 September 2020).

41 Donald C Langevoort, 'Gatekeepers, Cultural Captives, or Knaves? Corporate Lawyers through Different Lenses Colloquium: Corporate Lawyers' (2020) 88(5) *Fordham Law Review* 1683, 1693 (citations excluded). See also Milton C Regan and Lisa H Rohrer, *BigLaw: Money and Meaning in the Modern Law Firm* (University of Chicago Press, 2020).

identification with unethical activity on the other. Psychologists have shown that people often use subconscious strategies to avoid this sort of cognitive dissonance: they either subconsciously strive to 'not notice' unethical activity or rationalise it as soon as they do notice it. Thus corporate lawyers

> will often unconsciously dismiss or discount evidence of misconduct and its impact on third parties. The risks of such dissonance are exacerbated when lawyers bond socially and professionally with the client's management team. The more that [the lawyer] blends with the culture of corporate insiders, the greater the pressures of cohesiveness. That, in turn, encourages lawyers to underestimate risk and to suppress compromising information in order to preserve internal solidarity.[42]

Where it is in the client's interest to keep information about unethical conduct from the lawyer, it is even easier for lawyers to choose to remain ignorant of their client's misconduct.

Rationalisation in a general sense is something we all do – for both good and bad. As Kath Hall and Vivien Holmes explain:

> In the Oxford Dictionary, the general definition of rationalising is: *the act of rendering something comfortable to reason, to explain it on a rational basis*. This definition reflects the common idea that rationalisation is an acceptable process of bringing forth the most logical and compelling reason in support of our actions and beliefs.[43]

We all need to rationalise our life experiences and plans in order to preserve a coherent sense of personal identity and meaning for ourselves. However, as Hall and Holmes go on to explain, there is a second form of rationalisation that we might describe as 'moral rationalisation', because it creates excuses and denies responsibility for behaviour. Hall and Holmes summarise rationalisation in this second negative sense which:

- involves self-serving explanations, and these assist in making behaviour appear more acceptable to both self and others;
- entails a degree of self-deception;
- often occurs outside the realm of the conscious mind;
- can reduce feelings of responsibility and/or anxiety for the negative aspects of behaviour; and
- can neutralise the impact of legal or ethical issues involved in a decision.[44]

'Moral rationalisation' is described in the psychological literature negatively, as

> a self-serving process designed to preserve self-image, legitimate behaviour and facilitate decision making. In this context, the Oxford Dictionary defines rationalisation

42 Deborah Rhode and Paul Paton, 'Lawyers, Ethics, and Enron' (2002) 8(1) *Stanford Journal of Law, Business & Finance* 9, 32. See also Kenneth Mann, *Defending White-Collar Crime: A Portrait of Attorneys at Work* (Yale University Press, 1985) for evidence of lawyers purposely remaining ignorant of their clients' guilt so that they can zealously defend them.

43 Kath Hall and Vivien Holmes, 'The Power of Rationalisation to Influence Lawyers' Decisions to Act Unethically' (2008) 11 *Legal Ethics* 137, 138 (emphasis in original).

44 Ibid 140.

> as: *(psychol) a justification of behaviour to make it appear rational or socially acceptable by (subconsciously) ignoring, concealing or glossing over its real motive.*[45]

Common rationalisations for illegal and unethical conduct include:[46]

- *Denial of responsibility – 'It wasn't my fault … I didn't mean it':* My behaviour was caused by forces outside of me and beyond my control such as a poor upbringing and education, bad companions or a bad situation that I was helpless to change.
- *Denial of injury – 'I didn't hurt anyone':* My behaviour may have been wrong but it did not cause any great harm to anyone. If the victim is physically absent, unknown or a vague abstraction then it is easier to deny the injury, because there is only a weak awareness of any human victim.
- *Denial of the victim – 'They had it coming to them':* My behaviour may have caused injury but the injury is justified as a form of rightful retaliation, punishment or recompense against some individual or group who has done me or society wrong.
- *Condemnation of the condemners – 'Everybody's picking on me':* My behaviour may be wrong but the motives and behaviours of those who condemn me are no better or are even worse than mine. My condemners are hypocrites, deviants in disguise, or impelled by personal spite.
- *Appeal to higher loyalties – 'I didn't do it for myself':* I know I did what was wrong according to society, but I had to do it for the sake of an individual or group to whom I owe a particular obligation of loyalty such as my family, friendship clique, business partner or client. I found myself in an ethical dilemma and I had to break the law in order to resolve it.

It is possible that the adversarial lawyer mindset is particularly attuned to rationalisation. One account of the adversarial advocate's role is to rationalise client conduct through 'creative interpretation of rules and fashioning plausible arguments in support of their interpretations'.[47] Therefore, lawyers may be both particularly comfortable and skilled at using their role in the adversary system to rationalise away any need to be aware of, consider, and come to a judgement on the broader ethical and social implications of their work – that is, how ordinary people would morally evaluate their work.[48] In Case study 9.1 you are asked to consider how these rationalisations might be used by lawyers in a situation of commercial misconduct.

45 Ibid 138 (emphasis in original) (citations omitted).

46 This list is based on the authors' reworking of Gresham M Sykes and David Matza, 'Techniques of Neutralisation: A Theory of Delinquency' (1957) 22 *American Sociological Review* 664, 667–9.

47 Kath Hall, 'Mind the Gap: Psychological Jurisprudence and the Professional Regulation of Lawyer Dishonesty' (PhD Thesis, Australian National University, 2011) 63, referring to Milton C Regan, 'Risky Business' (2006) 94(6) *Georgetown Law Journal* 1957, 1972. See also Doreen McBarnet, 'Legal Creativity: Law, Capital and Legal Avoidance' in Maureen Cain and Christine Harrington (eds), *Lawyers in a Postmodern World: Translation and Transgression* (New York University Press, 1994) 73; Maureen Cain, 'The Symbol Traders' in Maureen Cain and Christine Harrington (eds), *Lawyers in a Postmodern World: Translation and Transgression* (New York University Press, 1994) 15.

48 See Hall (n 47) 73. Hall identifies three rationalisations that are part of this account for lawyers: 'This is just the way things are done'; 'If I had not done it, someone else would have'; 'I didn't know what was really going on': at 101. See also Terri L Orbuch, 'People's Accounts Count: The Sociology of Accounts' (1997) 23 *Annual Review of Sociology* 455.

Moral rationalisation is an inherently unstable and unsustainable way of dealing with the world. Nevertheless, it is a common approach to dealing with stressful and uncertain situations and the cognitive dissonance of being in a situation where a person wants to believe they are an ethical person but it would be easier to engage in unethical behaviour. People rationalise their own behaviour to make it easier to live with themselves rather than dealing with the problem of the dissonance between ethical principles and behaviour. This can be particularly dangerous in groups and organisations, where mutual reinforcement between individual and group behaviour can transform self-serving rationalisations into organisational facts.[49] Since moral rationalisation involves lying to oneself and others, it is psychologically stressful and ultimately can lead to depression.

Psychological experiments suggest that quite often we do not even notice that we are rationalising. This might be because, at the individual level, our unconscious might cut in and 'save' our conscious mind from troubling thoughts through self-deception. However, people can come to recognise when they are rationalising and reduce its impact and potential to produce apathy and immoral decisions. Developing sensitivity to one's own thought processes is a first step and is also an important aspect of developing the type of reflection on action and moral judgement that is part of professional competency. Becoming aware of the different types of rationalisation and the cognitive, perceptual and self-deceptive tricks our minds play on us (in our own self-interest) can also be helpful.[50] Such awareness is the purpose of this discussion. Indeed, it has been suggested that ethics training about the rules is no use if people are not also trained to recognise the mechanisms by which they are likely to rationalise away the rules.

Another reason that we might not notice that we are engaging in rationalisation is because situational factors 'frame' the way we think about our decision-making and behaviours in different contexts. In some contexts we might be primed to see the situation as involving ethical dimensions – for example, when conducting the conflicts of interest check in relation to a new client, or while sitting a legal ethics exam! But there are other situations in which ethical issues have been framed out of the picture. The way our workplaces are set up and even the whole profession – their habits and cultures – can either help us see or blind us to the ethical dimensions of particular situations.

Thus, in Case study 9.1 we are clearly told that the situation in which AWB found itself involved 'bribing' Saddam Hussein. We are told various factors that might be used to rationalise that bribery, but we are alerted by the mention of bribery (and the fact that the story is told in a legal ethics book) that there is an issue of ethics and quite possibly illegality involved. Of course, ethical decisions do not often announce themselves in this way in real life. Compare the first and second version of the story of AWB in Case study 9.1. In the second version, more of the story is told about the way the ethical issues became more difficult for the lawyers, because the executives in AWB attempted to frame the judgement about what to do as a business decision that had already been made.

49 Hall and Holmes (n 43) 138.

50 Jennifer K Robbennolt and Jean R Sternlight, 'Behavioural Legal Ethics' (2013) 45(3) *Arizona State Law Journal* 1107; Robert A Prentice, 'Behavioral Ethics: Can It Help Lawyers (and Others) Be Their Best Selves?' (2015) 29 *Notre Dame Journal of Law, Ethics & Public Policy* 35.

CASE STUDY 9.1 RATIONALISATION AND THE LAWYERS FOR AWB

It is 2002. You are an in-house lawyer with the Australian company AWB, which sells Australian wheat overseas – it is one of the largest wheat exporters in the world. You are asked to help draft a contract for selling wheat to Iraq under the United Nations' Oil-for-Food Programme (international sanctions are in place against direct trade with Iraq). Selling wheat to Iraq would involve paying a bribe to Saddam Hussein to make sure Australian wheat was chosen. There is a way to do this that will likely keep it secret. If AWB does not clinch this 'deal' via this contract, the Australian wheat price will take a dive and Australian wheat growers will suffer – some may be forced off their land – and your own future might also be uncertain. The AWB executive responsible for sales to Iraq has not asked you for your opinion on whether to enter into the contract or not. He has just asked you to draft the contract and inflate the price to be paid for the wheat by the amount of the 'trucking fees' and 'port charges' that will be paid to offload and transport the wheat once it gets to Iraq. He has made it clear implicitly that these amounts will in fact be paid to Saddam Hussein's government.

DISCUSSION QUESTIONS

1. Is the decision to enter into the contract an ethical decision, a legal decision or a commercial decision? Who should make the call on this decision? (The executive? The lawyer?)
2. If the lawyer was inclined to help draft the contract, how might they rationalise their decision?

Now consider the following more detailed version of the AWB scenario.

The majority of Australian wheat is exported and these exports count for a significant amount of the world's wheat trade and of Australian exports. Among the 50 or so countries to which Australian wheat has historically been exported was Iraq. But trading to Iraq was suspended in 1990 when the UN Security Council imposed trade sanctions on Iraq in response to its invasion of Kuwait. Food trade was allowed in 'humanitarian' circumstances, but Iraq had no hard currency to buy wheat even for humanitarian purposes. In 1995 the United Nations set up the Oil-for-Food Programme to soften the impact of the sanctions. It allowed Iraq to sell its oil, keep the income in a UN escrow account and use that income to buy humanitarian goods, including wheat, to alleviate famine and hunger caused by the trading sanctions. Only contracts favourably reviewed by the United Nations could be paid from the escrow account. By 1999 about 10% of Australia's annual wheat export was going to Iraq, and this represented about 90% of all wheat sales to Iraq. AWB was the largest single exporter of any humanitarian item to Iraq.[51]

In 1999, Iraq introduced a requirement that AWB pay a fee for the transportation of the wheat from the Iraqi port to the inland silos. These fees were factored into the wheat price in the official contract documentation that was given to the United Nations for approval of payments from the escrow accounts. The price to be paid for the wheat coming out of the account was inflated by the amount of the transportation fees. The Cole Royal Commission later found that these amounts were paid back to the Iraqi government in hard currency through 'trucking fees' and 'port charges', and that AWB executives knew this.

Between November 1999 and March 2003 the Iraqi government, headed by Saddam Hussein, obtained US$224 million in 'fees' by this means. Although these payments breached UN resolutions and the provisions of the Oil-for-Food Programme, they did not directly amount to a breach of Australian law. The UN resolutions applied to the Australian state, not to private companies, and the Australian government had not legislated to make it an offence for private companies and individuals to act in breach of the UN trading sanctions on Iraq.

Nevertheless, as the Cole Royal Commission later found, these payments were essentially corrupt payment (or 'kickbacks') to ensure Iraq maintained its contract with AWB for Australian wheat. They were also akin to money laundering, because they allowed the Iraqi regime to access some of the income it had obtained from selling oil under the Oil-for-Food Programme to use for its own purposes, rather than only for humanitarian purposes approved by the United Nations.

Around the same time that Australia was paying 'transportation fees' to Iraq, Australia, together with the United States and United Kingdom, was accusing Iraq of possessing weapons of mass destruction and preparing to invade it.[52]

After an inquiry by the United Nations into AWB's payment of trucking fees, AWB commissioned accounting and auditing firm Arthur Andersen to investigate the existence of any unethical or illegal conduct in AWB. The United Nations did not follow up on its inquiry about the trucking fees until 2005, but Arthur Andersen's 2001 report pointed out that the culture of AWB required review as far as ethical dealing was concerned, and that the payment of trucking fees in Iraq was of concern.

AWB employed several in-house lawyers. These lawyers did not settle the contracts that included the surcharges and so it is unclear when they found out about the surcharges. But one of the lawyers did meet regularly with the executives responsible for the contracts to sort out any legal issues that arose, and one was present at the meeting that discussed the Arthur Andersen report.

51 This paragraph and the following paragraphs are based on Hall and Holmes (n 43) and Linda Courtenay Botterill and Anne McNaughton, 'Laying the Foundations for the Wheat Scandal: UN Sanctions, Private Actors and the Cole Inquiry' (2008) 43(4) *Australian Journal of Political Science* 583.

52 Weapons of mass destruction were never found and the US, UK and Australian governments were heavily criticised for their stance on Iraq, and even for breaching international law conventions and UN Security Council resolutions by invading Iraq.

Imagine that you are that lawyer. In mid-2002, AWB executives approach you with an urgent problem. A few weeks ago, the Iraqi Minister for Trade halved the amount of wheat Iraq planned to buy from Australia because of concern that Australia was supporting the United States' pro-invasion stance on Iraq. Now Iraq has alleged that a shipment of wheat from AWB is contaminated with iron filings and is seeking US$2 million in compensation. An AWB delegation in Iraq has already agreed to pay the compensation rather than lose the remaining contracts, and Iraq has now responded to this agreement by reinstating its original order.

The problem, however, is how to structure the reinstated contract so as to conceal from the UN Oil-for-Food Programme the payment of the compensation, since this payment would breach the rules of the Oil-for-Food scheme. You are well aware that AWB, your client, is under tremendous pressure to maintain its sales of wheat to Iraq, as the sale of wheat to Iraq has been portrayed in the media by the government as a huge success story for Australian wheat growers and the Australian economy. Indeed, the Prime Minister, John Howard MP, himself congratulated the AWB on its success in exporting wheat to Iraq. You are also aware of the trucking fees and the fact that they are essential to maintaining AWB's exports to Iraq. The executives of AWB tell you that it is your job to write a contract for them that enables the contracts they have already entered into to go ahead.

Discussion questions

3. Can you identify the different rationalisation strategies mentioned above that the AWB in-house counsel might have used when they went ahead and drafted the contracts without protest?
4. Were there any other options available to the in-house counsel other than simply obeying the instructions of their client to draft the contract or refusing to do so?
5. How do you think the lawyers' role as in-house counsel (as opposed to external legal adviser) might have contributed to what happened in the AWB scenario?

Corporate lawyers as corporate citizens

Adversarial advocacy and responsible lawyering: hired gun or independent counsellor?

In our view, *adversarial advocacy* is rarely suited to the corporate counselling context. Most of the matters on which a corporate lawyer advises will never be aired in a court or any other public forum. Moreover, while the power imbalance between the individual criminal defendant and the state means that criminal defence lawyers might be justified in zealous advocacy that protects their clients' autonomy to the limits of the law, large corporate clients are not generally the victims of any power imbalance. Indeed, many corporate clients can afford hordes of lawyers to work out ways to interpret the law and to present the company to others (regulators, investors, customers) as legally compliant. Therefore, the justification for legal advocacy that goes to the limits of the law and ethics on behalf of corporate clients is correspondingly reduced. Further, as noted in Chapter 2, the *adversarial advocate* approach assumes that lawyers practise within the rule of law, where the 'limits of the law' are a reasonable guide to accepted societal norms. This assumption does not hold when corporations operate across the globe, including in countries where the rule of law is fragile or almost nonexistent.

In most situations, then, we do not consider the *adversarial advocacy* approach to be justified for corporate lawyers.[53] When lawyers advise business, they are most often not just advocating 'after the fact' as to how something the client has done should be interpreted. They are actually helping the client decide whether to comply with the law and if so how. The ideal of *responsible lawyer* as trusted, independent counsellor expresses this role better than *adversarial advocacy*:

> In giving advice, [the *responsible lawyer*] refers not only to specific rules of black-letter law, but also to general principles of equity, fair dealing, and public policy in dealing with inchoate or potential legal problems. By advising businesses about the legal risks, constraints and requirements associated with proposed actions, the corporate lawyer plays a crucial role in pushing business toward socially responsible behavior ... By telling business executives how to avoid antitrust suits, civil rights suits, and regulatory prosecutions, and by insisting on knowing the truth about financial weaknesses that might affect the accuracy of representations in disclosure statements, license applications, or opinion letters signed by the law firm, the lawyer necessarily forces corporations to be more honest and to establish internal systems for ensuring compliance with the law. The corporate lawyer, from this perspective, is an autonomous agent of social control and enforcement.[54]

In the following subsection we explore this alternative ethical approach for corporate lawyering in more detail and also suggest ways in which corporate lawyers may need to go beyond *responsible lawyering* to embracing elements of *moral activism* in order to avoid unethical conduct.

The corporate lawyer as responsible lawyer

Much discussion of corporate lawyers' ethics emphasises the need to strengthen their gatekeeping responsibilities by expecting lawyers to act in the interests of the corporation as a whole, including its investors and other stakeholders, to clearly counsel clients against illegal behaviour and behaviour at the margins of legality, and to report corporate misconduct

53 Robert Gordon, 'A New Role for Lawyers? The Corporate Counselor After Enron' (2003) 35 *Connecticut Law Review* 1185, 1204–7.

54 Robert A Kagan and Robert Eli Rosen, 'On the Social Significance of Large Law Firm Practice' (1985) 37 *Stanford Law Review* 399, 409–10. See also Robert Gordon, 'Corporate Law Practice as a Public Calling' (1990) 49 *Maryland Law Review* 255; David Luban, *Lawyers and Justice: An Ethical Study* (Princeton University Press, 1988) 206–34; Brian Preston, 'Climate Conscious Lawyering' (2021) 95 *Australian Law Journal* 51.

to appropriate authorities within the organisation or outside it, if they cannot otherwise prevent it occurring.[55] This reflects a *responsible lawyering* approach.

In fact, in Australia at least, the general principles set out in current professional conduct rules, the law of lawyering, and criminal and regulatory law *already* give corporate lawyers many obligations to act as 'independent counsellors' (*responsible lawyers*). Legal profession regulators in Australia have so far not done much to enforce these obligations in the corporate lawyering context. These obligations are not set out very specifically or clearly in the *Australian Solicitors' Conduct Rules* ('*ASCR*') but they are covered in the Australian Association of Corporate Counsel's ('ACC') *Ethics Handbook*.[56]

Corporate lawyers have legal and professional conduct obligations (a) to the law, and (b) to the corporate entity as a whole, as well as (c) capacities and obligations in relation to whistleblowing (as shown below).

(a) Duty to the law

We have seen in Chapter 6 that lawyers owe general obligations to the law and justice, including obligations not to assist in any abuse of process or misleading of the court (see *ASCR* rr 3, 4 and 5, set out below). Disciplinary action and other sanctions are available if these obligations are breached. These obligations apply equally to lawyers' work for corporate clients as to other clients, and to non-litigious work as to litigious work. In fact, it is all the more important for lawyers engaged in, for example, transactional or advisory work outside the purview of the court, to remember that they are no less bound by ethical rules than are their litigator colleagues. And, just like those colleagues, they should try to dissuade their clients from illegal or improper courses of action and withdraw from representing them, if the client insists on that course of action.[57] For an in-house lawyer, withdrawal from representation may, however, mean resigning from their job – a very serious decision.

ASCR rr 3–5 Fundamental duties of solicitors

ASCR r 3 Paramount duty to the court and the administration of justice

3.1 A solicitor's duty to the court and the administration of justice is paramount and prevails to the extent of inconsistency with any other duty.

ASCR r 4 Other fundamental ethical duties

4.1 A solicitor must also:

4.1.1 act in the best interests of a client in any matter in which the solicitor represents the client;

55 See, eg, John C Coffee, *Professional Gatekeepers: The Professions and Corporate Governance* (Oxford University Press, 2006); Gordon, 'A New Role for Lawyers?' (n 53). For a more nuanced discussion of independence and the gatekeeper role for in-house counsel, see Richard Moorhead, Steven Vaughan and Cristina Godinho, *In-House Lawyers' Ethics: Institutional Logics, Legal Risk and the Tournament of Influence* (Bloomsbury, 2019) and, in relation to external lawyers, see Regan and Rohrer (n 41) 200–31.

56 ACC Australia, *Ethics Handbook* (2018).

57 See Gino Dal Pont, *Lawyers' Professional Responsibility* (Thomson Reuters, 7th ed, 2021) 654 [19.10].

4.1.2 be honest and courteous in all dealings in the course of legal practice;

4.1.3 deliver legal services competently, diligently and as promptly as reasonably possible;

4.1.4 avoid any compromise to their integrity and professional independence; and

4.1.5 comply with these Rules and the law.

ASCR **r 5 Standard of conduct – dishonest or disreputable conduct**

5.1 A solicitor must not engage in conduct, in the course of legal practice or otherwise, which –

5.1.1 demonstrates that the solicitor is not a fit and proper person to practise law, or

5.1.2 is likely to a material degree to –

(i) be prejudicial to, or diminish the public confidence in, the administration of justice, or

(ii) bring the profession into disrepute.

Similarly, general principles of liability in criminal law and most areas of business regulation prohibit lawyers from helping their clients, if this would amount to aiding and abetting illegality, or conspiring to break the law.[58] The Australian Competition and Consumer Commission, Australian Securities and Investments Commission and Australian Taxation Office have all taken action against lawyers on these grounds.[59]

As previously discussed, lawyers (both corporate lawyers and those who act for individual clients) who adopt an *adversarial advocate* approach have argued that they are not morally responsible or legally accountable for their clients' misconduct unless they are knowingly and intentionally involved in initiating or assisting the misconduct.[60] But it is often hard to prove that the lawyer had the requisite knowledge and intention to establish this type of liability.[61] As we have seen, lawyers and executives are expert at plausible deniability in many corporate ethical scandals, and the language of the relevant rules themselves often gives them numerous excuses to avoid liability.[62]

Moreover, this type of liability will of course only apply to client conduct that is itself illegal. Much of the 'genius' of corporate lawyering is to contrive ways in which unethical conduct can be performed 'legally'. Emphasising corporate lawyers' duty to the law is not

58 Russell Lyons and David Handelsmann, 'Corporate Misconduct and Legal Professional Responsibility' (2003) 41(4) *Law Society Journal* 60; Dal Pont (n 57) 425–6.

59 See, eg, *Australian Competition and Consumer Commission v Real Estate Institute of Western Australia Inc* (1999) 161 ALR 79 (solicitor assisted in drafting agreement that amounted to price-fixing); *Australian Securities and Investments Commission v Somerville* (2009) 77 NSWLR 110 (solicitor assisted in 'phoenixing' a company so that directors could avoid debts). See also Dal Pont (n 57) ch 19.

60 Lyons and Handelsmann (n 58).

61 William H Simon, 'Wrongs of Ignorance and Ambiguity: Lawyer Responsibility for Collective Misconduct' (2005) 22 *Yale Journal on Regulation* 1.

62 Ibid. Simon analyses this in terms of lawyers (wrongfully) being able to avoid liability for corporate misconduct on the grounds of 'ignorance' and 'ambiguity'.

enough where the law itself has proven to be easily manipulated, unless the duty to the law encompasses an obligation to consider what ethical concerns the law applying to corporations *should* embrace, and to act accordingly – a more *moral activist* conception of lawyers' ethics.

(b) Duty to the corporation as a whole

It is quite clear that lawyers acting for a corporation owe their obligations of care and loyalty to the corporation as a whole, not to individual managers, executives or work teams, since it is the corporation that is the client, not individual officers (see Chapter 7).[63] Much of lawyers' complicity in corporate wrongdoing amounts to conflicts of interest, where lawyers defy their duty to the corporation as a whole to follow the instructions and wishes of individual managers, executives or work teams, at the expense of shareholders and other stakeholders. It will usually be in the interests of the corporation as a whole to comply with the law and therefore avoid the legal sanctions and reputational losses that come with breach of the law. Breaches of the obligation to the corporation as a whole could amount to a basis for disciplinary action or actions for breach of duty by the corporation in negligence or contract. Often where management or the Board has breached its duties and a company has collapsed or suffered severe losses as a result, the new management, the shareholders or the liquidator will sue the previous management and/or Board to recover the losses. Lawyers who have contributed to the previous management's wrongful conduct can be sued.[64]

Corporate lawyers, of course, deal with individual corporate officers who define the scope of their work, and whose concerns and goals can influence corporate lawyers' consciences. Comprehending and acting on the duty to the corporation as a whole requires lawyers to actively look beyond the instructions they receive from the individuals they are dealing with, in order to consider whether the interests of the corporation as a whole are being followed properly. This requires a degree of ethical discernment.

(c) Taking active responsibility

The duty to the corporation as a whole does not mean that corporate lawyers need to substitute their own moral judgement for that of the corporation. What it does mean is that they need to take their share of responsibility for making sure that the broad interests of the company as a whole are pursued, including the corporation's interest in behaving legally and ethically. A persuasive literature in business ethics suggests that corporate decisions can become immoral, illegal or just bad because, although many individuals are involved in making them, none feels personal responsibility for the ultimate outcome – it's a 'corporate' decision, not a personal one.[65] Everybody has their own role within the corporation – whether it is as lawyer, marketer, sales agent or financial controller – but

63 William H Simon, 'Whom (or What) Does the Organization's Lawyer Represent? An Anatomy of Intraclient Conflict' (2003) 91(1) *California Law Review* 57.

64 See Milton C Regan, 'Teaching Enron' (2005) 74(3) *Fordham Law Review* 1139. This is an article based on the Enron liquidator's assessment of what causes of action might be available against Enron's various lawyers.

65 Christine Parker, *The Open Corporation: Effective Self-Regulation and Democracy* (Cambridge University Press, 2002) 31–7.

often no one feels that it is their job to understand the whole context, including the ethical context, of decision-making, or to access all the relevant information for understanding that context. Lawyers, and other corporate advisers and employees, can allow their sense of personal responsibility to be subsumed by their role in an organisational system, so that they see themselves as disposable actors hired to play bit parts. This analysis holds good even though in-house lawyers very often have the breadth of information and forensic skill needed to be the ethical watchdogs of the corporation. So they take their instructions as they find them rather than actively taking responsibility for working out whether they have been given all the relevant information to understand a problem or decision in its full context.[66] This is compounded if legal services are 'unbundled' and given to a number of lawyers.

Rob Rosen has shown how this unbundling or 'siloing' influenced the General Motors ('GM') ignition switch scandal in which GM delayed recalling cars that had a fatal ignition switch fault. The fault could cause the car to turn off while driving, leaving drivers with little control over steering and braking and no air bags. Even though some engineers in GM were aware of the issues, they saw it as a matter of driver awareness and education, not a fault that had to be remedied via a recall. As a result of the delayed recall, many people were killed or injured in accidents. However, the lawyers who handled the product liability actions brought by victims of the faulty ignition switches did not raise the alarm or act to help GM prevent more accidents. Rather, as Rosen suggests, they

> saw themselves as defence lawyers. Their responses to the claimed accidents was not to see them as problems requiring perhaps creative solutions, but as cases to be defended, whether because they blamed the drivers [as Rosen argues, engineers did], or because they thought plaintiff lawyers were making up claims hoping for fat settlements. Between 2006 and 2014, GM lawyers raised every possible defence against liability.[67]

Rosen comments that the way the legal department and its settlement process was organised implicitly made it clear that the objective for the lawyers was to 'settle as cheaply as possible' with suits 'to be treated as cases, and not as revealing problems in particular products'.[68]

By contrast, a more *responsible lawyer/moral activist approach* would require lawyers to clearly flag potential ethical and legal problems that might otherwise be ignored or overridden, even if they are not directly within the scope of the particular jobs they have been assigned by individual officers. Having flagged these legal and ethical issues, corporate lawyers should then go on to make sure that the corporation as a whole uses proper decision-making processes, and proper substantive principles, to decide what to do about them. This may entail the lawyer disclosing potential misconduct up the corporate hierarchy or even outside the company, as we set out in Chapter 4 in relation to whistleblowing. More constructively, corporate lawyers could take active responsibility to help organisational clients notice and come up with creative solutions to potential problems.

66 Rosen, 'Problem-Setting and Serving the Organizational Client' (n 34).
67 Rosen, 'The Sociological Imagination and Legal Ethics' (n 4) 110.
68 Ibid.

It is easy to understand why lawyers might often prefer not to notice, or to rationalise, unethical corporate conduct instead of reporting misconduct up the hierarchy and whistleblowing outside the organisation. As we saw in Chapter 4, the content of the current law on confidentiality gives ample room to corporate lawyers to fulfil their ethical duties. But knowing when to breach confidence requires ethical judgement, not just legal knowledge, because the circumstances in which the public interest or a client's 'fraud on justice' might justify and, indeed, demand whistleblowing can never be fully specified in the law. The way the legal profession tends to treat confidentiality as an absolute value (see Chapter 4) may discourage lawyers from this type of ethical judgement, but it need not do so.

Legal ethics and business ethics

It would certainly be helpful if the *ASCR* and professional regulators spelled out more clearly the ethical obligations of corporate lawyers, and actually enforced them. But, as we have seen, when ethical failures in corporate lawyering occur, the problem might be more in the attitude and style of corporate lawyering than in the content of the current rules. Lawyers advising business today need to demonstrate proactive responsibility for appreciating and advising on the broader ethical and legal consequences of their advice. While corporate lawyers' particular ethical responsibility will relate mainly to their legal expertise and role, they cannot avoid responsibility for having a substantive ethical view about the situations they are called to advise on and participate in merely because they are lawyers and supposedly independent of the corporate client. This means that corporate lawyers should be business ethicists, and this is likely to require them to use the following three strategies.

Strategy 1: Identifying the client correctly

Corporate lawyers regularly participate in, or at least help facilitate, business decisions that affect the wealth and wellbeing of hundreds and thousands of business stakeholders. Most of the key ethical issues for businesses concern potential conflict between their different stakeholders. Indeed, corporations are basically entities made up of, and exercising power over, different stakeholders.[69] These stakeholders include people who have invested their wealth in the organisation – shareholders, banks, superannuation funds, etc – and those who have invested their time, skill and labour in it – employees and managers.

When a lawyer acts for a corporation, they are supposed to act for the entity as a whole, not for individual managers or work teams. This means that ethical issues are likely to be unavoidable for corporate lawyers. They must constantly keep one eye on whether the managers from whom they take instructions are adequately taking into account the interests of all the corporation's stakeholders, or whether they are asking their lawyers to help them prefer their own interests over those of, say, the shareholders, or even employees.

Where the lawyer thinks management may not be appropriately pursuing the interests of the entity as a whole, the lawyer, as a participant in corporate decision-making, should

69 Parker, *The Open Corporation* (n 65) 3–7; James E Post, Lee E Preston and Sybille Sachs, *Redefining the Corporation: Stakeholder Management and Organizational Wealth* (Stanford University Press, 2002).

be able to initiate discussion and resolution of the issue within the company.[70] This is not the lawyer deciding *for* the corporate client what is the appropriate thing to do; but the lawyer should be in a position to activate an appropriate decision-making process within the corporation. As we have seen, debate and controversy over the role of lawyers in corporate misconduct has focused on whether corporate lawyers should (or already do) have a 'whistleblowing' obligation to raise such matters within the organisation and outside it. However, ideally, this role of raising ethical issues should not be seen as extraordinary whistleblowing but rather as a natural part of the legal role. This means that in-house lawyers, particularly the chief in-house lawyer in each organisation, need to have a certain degree of power and respect so that, if necessary, they can question corporate activities, goals and commitments, and can ensure that ethical issues are resolved properly at an appropriate place in the corporate decision-making process.

Most commentators on ethics for in-house lawyers acknowledge the fact that in-house lawyers should have a degree of influence and power within the organisation by having the possibility of dotted-line reporting[71] direct to the chief executive officer ('CEO') and to the board of directors itself, and by having the authority to investigate and intervene at any level of a company.[72] The ACC Australia *Ethics Handbook* recommends that in-house lawyers report to a member of the senior management team, such as general counsel, the CEO or the chair of the board.[73] It further notes:

> The ultimate duty owed by in-house counsel to the organisation is to the board of directors. Of course, from a day-to-day management perspective, in-house counsel may be advising the chief executive officer or other members of the senior executive team. However, in-house counsel must always keep in mind where their ultimate client duty lies.
>
> ...
>
> Acting in the best interests of the client may not always be aligned with the best interests of the CEO, the chairperson, an individual board member or different entities within an organisational group. In these situations, there should be documented arrangements between all the parties setting out who is being advised; on what basis the advice is being given; how differences in the interests or duties between entities will be handled; and what the in-house counsel's obligations are to each entity should a conflict arise.[74]

Strategy 2: Framing the problem to include ethical issues

Lawyers advising business need to be aware of the ways in which the business context is likely to shape their own view of the ethics of each situation on which they are asked to advise. Their own judgement is likely to be affected by their relationship to the organisation – what

70 See Simon (n 61).

71 'Dotted-line' reporting means that in addition to your everyday obligation to report up the line to your direct superior, you also have the capacity to bypass that superior to a higher level. It is a safeguard for where your direct superior may be acting unethically, obstructively or incompetently.

72 Gordon and Simon (n 16) 253.

73 ACC Australia (n 56) 7.

74 Ibid.

information comes to them, how it comes to them, how the politics of the organisation work, and what influence they themselves have within that organisation. Lawyers ought to take special care and responsibility to make sure that they see the questions and problems brought to them in a holistic context – this will enable them to take ethical and legal responsibility for those problems rather than simply allowing the organisation (with its politics and bureaucratic pathologies) to present problems to them as isolated events or concepts.[75] Taking on responsibility in this manner requires substantive ethical analysis.

One way of trying to make sure that corporate decisions are always made in an ethical way is for the company (client) to put in place internal controls or management programs that seek to make sure that the whole organisation meets its legal and ethical responsibilities, and guard against those responsibilities being forgotten or trampled on. These internal controls and management programs are a way of trying to create a conscience within business organisations.[76] Lawyers might be particularly suited to helping businesses with this.

Many legal ethicists have suggested that corporate lawyers should take a more proactive or positive role in making sure adequate internal controls and whistleblowing protections are in place so that companies can police themselves to make sure they comply with the law and with ethical obligations. Thus ACC Australia's *Ethics Handbook* suggests that in-house counsel promote ethical corporate behaviour, including the adoption of an attitude of compliance and other procedures and policies that consider the legitimate interests of all of the organisation's stakeholders and the community.[77] As discussed in Chapter 4, in-house counsel should educate the organisation about best practice whistleblowing procedures. They should also raise any legal/ethical concerns they have themselves with senior decision makers until they are satisfied that their concerns have been addressed.[78]

The *Sarbanes-Oxley Act*[79] requirements in the United States and the Australian Securities Exchange's ('ASX') *Corporate Governance Principles and Recommendations*[80] (also introduced in response to corporate collapses and scandals) both seek to encourage companies to make sure they have adequate internal controls, codes of conduct and whistleblowing protections in place to ensure that obligations to the corporation as a whole, including its shareholders and stakeholders, are protected. These institutional safeguards complement rather than replace 'bottom-up' cultural change that originates when employees lower down the corporate ladder push for ethical development.

It is to be hoped that taking a broad view of corporate ethics will become a core element of corporate lawyers' work. There is increasing pressure from the public for the corporate sector to take account of environmental, social and governance ('ESG')[81] concerns in business operations. As Gerry Bean, a partner in the global firm DLA Piper, explains:

75 Rosen, 'Problem-Setting and Serving the Organizational Client' (n 34).

76 See Parker, *The Open Corporation* (n 65).

77 ACC Australia (n 56) 6.

78 Ibid 10.

79 *Sarbanes-Oxley Act of 2002*, Pub L No 107–204, 116 Stat 745.

80 ASX Corporate Governance Council, *Corporate Governance Principles and Recommendations* (4th ed, 2019).

81 For an explanation of what ESG covers (a broad canvas of concerns) see International Finance Corporation, *Who Cares Wins: Connecting Financial Markets to a Changing World* (2004) <https://www.ifc.org/wps/wcm/connect/topics_ext_content/ifc_external_corporate_site/sustainability-at-ifc/publications/publications_report_whocareswins__wci__1319579355342>.

> There is a shift from analysing directors' duties through a legalistic prism to considering whether their actions promote positive ESG outcomes. It is a move from 'Can we legally do this?' to 'Should we be doing this?'
>
> Consumers, investors, providers of debt, and activist shareholders are forcing directors to embrace ESG. Directors now understand that consumers won't buy their products if they come from a company with a bad ESG record; investors won't invest in or provide finance to a company with a bad ESG record – they will 'vote with their money'; and companies that have a bad ESG record won't attract the best employees.[82]

If directors are increasingly required to adopt a broader focus that includes ESG concerns, their legal advisers also need to be cognisant of those concerns and advise their clients accordingly. This means taking a broader view of ethics and of what the client's 'best interests' entail. It will often mean renouncing an adversarial advocate/technical legal expert mindset in favour of a much more constructive approach to corporate lawyering. There are some positive signs that this is happening. In 2021 the global firm Herbert Smith Freehills interviewed 20 general counsel at large organisations (most of which were listed companies) to gauge their approach in relation to ESG factors: 'we sought to explore the specific role and contribution of GCs and in-house legal teams in grasping what promises to be the defining business transformation challenge of the next 20 years.'[83] All those interviewed placed ESG at the top of the corporate agenda and expected increasing pressure to prioritise ESG factors over the next decade.[84] As Langevoort comments, 'the corporate social licence is increasingly difficult to earn and easily put at risk'.[85] He notes further that '[a] good general counsel is a prized commodity in managing that risk'.[86] Langevoort suggests that 'the norms of corporate governance [may] shift to favor firms with genuinely influential general counsel who speak both law and ethics'.[87]

Some recent corporate scandals exemplify the dangers of overlooking ESG factors – two are outlined below. While we are, of course, not privy to the legal advice received by the companies involved, it is clear that those making decisions took a narrow, legalistic view of the corporation's best interests, which in each case had serious repercussions for the company.

AMP: sexual harassment incidents

AMP is a global financial services company. In 2017 an AMP senior executive, Mr Pahari, harassed his much younger and junior colleague, Ms Szlakowski. After a complaint by Ms Szlakowski, an investigation by a London QC found that Pahari's actions 'added up to a relatively modest breach of the AMP Workplace Behaviour and Equal Opportunity Policy'.[88] (In parenthesis, we doubt many women would agree with this characterisation.) The QC's

82 Gerry Bean, 'Directors' Duties: At Your Peril' (2021) 95(7) *Law Institute Journal* 24.

83 Herbert Smith Freehills, *Responsibility Incorporated: General Counsel and the Dawning ESG Revolution* (2021) <https://insights.hsf.com/esg-report-2021/p/1>.

84 Ibid.

85 Langevoort (n 41) 1698.

86 Ibid.

87 Ibid.

88 Richard Baker, 'AMP Harassment Victim's Allegations Credible, Investigation Finds', *The Sydney Morning Herald* (online at 31 August 2020) <https://www.smh.com.au/business/companies/amp-harassment-victim-told-the-truth-but-harassment-minor-review-20200826-p55piv.html>.

advice further noted that the behaviour 'involved a senior manager who ought to have been observing a high standard of equality and diversity practice'.[89] As 'punishment', Pahari's annual bonus was reduced by 25%, while Szlakowski left the company. When Pahari was later promoted to CEO of AMP Capital,[90] it appeared to many that Pahari's 'punishment' was nominal. The matter made news when Szlakowski alleged that AMP had downplayed the severity of the harassment against her. It seems that AMP's shareholders agreed with these allegations: 'The board's decision [to promote Pahari] not only caused the company reputational damage, but investor outcry so strong that … AMP chairman David Murray and fellow board member John Fraser resigned.'[91]

Rio Tinto's destruction of the Juukan Gorge rock shelters

In 2020, Australian mining company Rio Tinto destroyed two Aboriginal rock shelters estimated to be 46,000 years old, as part of a mine expansion. Prior to the destruction the company's in-house counsel confirmed that Rio had the legal right to do this under (outdated) heritage laws. Senior managers were aware of opposition to this plan by local Aboriginal elders, and external lawyers had been instructed to defend any injunction proceedings brought by the Traditional Owners.[92] The interim report of the Commonwealth Parliamentary Inquiry into the destruction of the Gorge, *Never Again*, noted that Rio Tinto's conduct reflected a corporate culture 'which prioritised commercial gain over the kind of meaningful engagement with Traditional Owners that should form a critical part of their social licence to operate'.[93] After a public and shareholder outcry over the incident, the CEO and two other executives resigned. At the first shareholder meeting after the incident, proposed bonus payments to the executive team, including a very large payout to the former CEO, were voted down by 60% of shareholders.[94]

Strategy 3: Building ethics into law firms

It is also very important that business lawyers engage substantively with business ethics in relation to their own practice structures. The disciplinary provisions and ethical conduct rules in most jurisdictions have generally been directed only at individual practitioners, not at law

89 Ibid.

90 Ibid.

91 Nassim Khadem, 'AMP's "MeToo" Moment Raises Bigger Questions for Corporate Australia About Sexual Harassment', *ABC News* (online at 25 August 2020) <https://www.abc.net.au/news/2020-08-25/amp-sexual-harassment-metoo-corporate-culture/12589602>.

92 Calla Wahlquist, 'Juukan Gorge: Rio Tinto Hired Lawyers for Potential Injunction Against Blasting of Aboriginal Site', *The Guardian* (online at 5 September 2020) <https://www.theguardian.com/business/2020/sep/05/juukan-gorge-rio-tinto-hired-lawyers-for-potential-injunction-against-blasting-of-aboriginal-site>; Lorena Allam, 'Rio Tinto Condemned by Shareholders for Seeking Legal Advice Before Blowing Up Juukan Gorge', *The Guardian* (online at 8 September 2020) <https://www.theguardian.com/business/2020/sep/07/rio-tinto-condemned-by-shareholders-for-seeking-legal-advice-before-blowing-up-juukan-gorge>.

93 Commonwealth of Australia, Joint Standing Committee on Northern Australia, *Never Again: Inquiry into the Destruction of 46,000 Year Old Caves at the Juukan Gorge in the Pilbara Region of Western Australia* (Interim Report, 2020) 7.

94 Sue Lannin and Rachel Pupazzoni, 'Rio Tinto Hit by Huge Protest Vote on Executive Pay over Juukan Destruction', *ABC News* (online at 7 May 2020) <https://www.abc.net.au/news/2021-05-07/rio-tinto-investor-revolt-over-juukan-caves-destruction/100122824>.

firms.[95] This reflects the traditional assumption that once a person qualifies as a lawyer they will become an independent practitioner who is able and competent to take responsibility for the quality and ethics of their own work. But the majority of lawyers no longer operate as independent professionals. They are employed by law firms, as well as accounting firms and in-house corporate legal departments. One of the biggest challenges for the ethical regulation of lawyering is to understand that law firms (and other organisational practice contexts) have their own ethical character and culture, for good or for ill.[96] In some law firm divisions the climate can be almost family-like, with supportive partners, an atmosphere of collegiality, and a shared excitement in pursuing intellectually challenging cases and transactions. But there is also evidence that inside some law practices new lawyers are likely to be under pressure to prioritise business values and to discount – or ignore entirely – traditional professional values.[97]

Since the organisational (law firm) context of legal practice has such an important influence on unethical behaviour, some commentators have suggested that law firms should consciously implement 'ethical infrastructures'.[98] A law firm ethical infrastructure means formal and informal management policies, procedures and controls, work team cultures, and habits of interaction and practice that support and encourage ethical behaviour.[99] It means having a managing partner who lives out the values of integrity and fidelity and provides ethical leadership. It might include the appointment of an ethics partner and/or ethics committee; written policies on ethical conduct in general, and in specific areas such as conflicts of interest, billing, trust accounting, opinion letters, litigation tactics; specified procedures for ensuring ethical policies are not breached and to encourage the raising of ethical problems with colleagues and management; the monitoring of lawyer compliance with policies and procedures; and ethics education, training and discussion within the firm. We have already seen the importance of internal responsibility and management/ethics systems within law firms for explaining fees and communicating about problems with bills and costs (Chapter 8) and avoiding and managing conflicts of interest (Chapter 7).

95 See Ted Schneyer, 'Professional Discipline for Law Firms?' (1991) 77(1) *Cornell Law Review* 1; Elizabeth Chambliss and David B Wilkins, 'Promoting Effective Ethical Infrastructure in Large Law Firms: A Call for Research and Reporting' (2002) 30(3) *Hofstra Law Review* 691. In England and Wales there is a requirement that all law firms have a Compliance Officer for Legal Practice and a Compliance Officer for Finance and Administration who are responsible for ensuring their firms have systems and controls in place to ensure ethical compliance: see Joan Loughrey, 'Accountability and the Regulation of the Large Law Firm Lawyer' (2014) 77(5) *Modern Law Review* 732; Sundeep Aulakh and Joan Loughrey, 'Regulating Law Firms from the Inside: The Role of Compliance Officers for Legal Practice in England and Wales' (2017) 45(2) *Journal of Law and Society* 254.

96 See Lillian Corbin, 'How "Firm" Are Lawyers' Perceptions of Professionalism?' (2005) 8(2) *Legal Ethics* 265. See also Regan and Rohrer (n 41).

97 See Corbin (n 96); Regan and Rohrer (n 41); Bruce A Green, 'Professional Challenges in Large Firm Practices' (2005) 33(1) *Fordham Urban Law Journal* 7; Stephen Tang, Vivien Holmes and Tony Foley, 'Ethical Climate, Job Satisfaction and Wellbeing: Observations from an Empirical Study of New Australian Lawyers Symposium: Attorney Regulation: Ethical Implications of a Changing Profession' (2020) 33(4) *Georgetown Journal of Legal Ethics* 1035.

98 This paragraph and the following paragraphs are partly based on Christine Parker et al, 'The Ethical Infrastructure of Legal Practice in Larger Law Firms: Values, Policy and Behaviour' (2008) 31(1) *University of New South Wales Law Journal* 158, 172, 174–5.

99 Schneyer (n 95); Chambliss and Wilkins (n 95).

Large law firms are increasingly using bureaucratic management practices that incorporate commercial pressure into legal practice by, for example, requiring lawyers to meet certain billable hour targets, having client relations partners with the explicit job of ensuring that other lawyers (including other partners) are making clients happy, and implementing performance criteria and in-firm professional development all aimed at making sure lawyers meet client needs. If these new bureaucracies are not led by CEOs or managing partners who prioritise ethics, and do not incorporate controls explicitly aimed at promoting ethical behaviour, they may in fact undermine ethical behaviour by putting pressure on lawyers to cut corners or do 'too much' for clients, and thereby undermine the value of the firm's 'organisational capital'.

Now that legal practices are allowed to incorporate, and some law firms have even listed on the stock exchange (see Chapter 3), there is even greater pressure on professional ethical responsibilities as incorporated legal practices adopt increasingly commercial business structures, and encourage outside investors and non-lawyer staff to become shareholders in the law practice.[100] For this reason the legislative provisions that first allowed law firms to incorporate also required incorporated legal practices to have 'appropriate management systems' in place to deal with ethical issues – in effect, a requirement that incorporated legal practices consciously implement an ethical infrastructure as part of their new business structure. The NSW Legal Services Commissioner developed '10 commandments' that incorporated legal practices' management systems must follow, and a system for self-assessment and external audit to measure how effectively incorporated legal practices are implementing them.[101]

Unfortunately, with the move to the *Uniform Law* in New South Wales and Victoria in 2015, the statutory provisions and rules underpinning this regulatory regime in New South Wales and the equivalent version in Victoria were not carried over into the new national regulatory regime.[102] However, the legal profession regulators in New South Wales and Victoria continue to encourage and educate all legal practices to have appropriate management systems in place and to self-audit in accordance with the 10 objectives for strong law firm governance, based on the '10 commandments' first developed in New South Wales (see the 10 objectives set out below).[103]

100 See Christine Parker, Tahlia Gordon and Steve Mark, 'Regulating Law Firm Ethics Management: An Empirical Assessment of an Innovation in Regulation of the Legal Profession in New South Wales' (2010) 37(3) *Journal of Law and Society* 466; Susan Fortney and Tahlia Gordon, 'Adopting Law Firm Management Systems to Survive and Thrive: A Study of the Australian Approach to Management-Based Regulation' (2012) 10(1) *University of St Thomas Law Journal* 152.

101 Parker, Gordon and Mark (n 100); Fortney and Gordon (n 100). Other jurisdictions have also introduced this such as Queensland.

102 See Justine Rogers, Dimity Kingsford Smith and John Chellew, 'The Large Professional Service Firm: A New Force in the Regulative Bargain' (2017) 40(1) *University of New South Wales Law Journal* 218, 245–6.

103 See 'Legal Practice Self-Assessment Audit', *Victorian Legal Services Board* (Web Page, 2020) <https://lsbc.vic.gov.au/resources/legal-practice-self-assessment-audit>; 'Practice Management', *Office of the Legal Services Commissioner* (NSW) (Web Page, 18 September 2015) <https://www.olsc.nsw.gov.au/Pages/lsc_practice_management/lsc_practice_management.aspx>; *Guide to Appropriate Management Systems* (Queensland Law Society, 2017) <https://www.qls.com.au/Content-Collections/Guides/Guide-to-appropriate-management-systems>.

TEN OBJECTIVES FOR SELF-ASSESSMENT OF LAW PRACTICE GOVERNANCE AND ETHICAL MANAGEMENT

1. Competent work practices to avoid negligence
2. Effective, timely and courteous communication
3. The timely delivery, review and follow-up of legal services to avoid delay
4. Acceptable processes for liens and file transfers
5. Providing for a shared understanding and appropriate documentation from commencement through to termination of engagement covering costs disclosure, billing practices and termination of engagement
6. Timely identification and resolution of conflicts of interest
7. Safe and secure records management
8. Timely compliance with undertakings, orders and rulings
9. The effective supervision of the practice and its staff
10. Avoidance of any failure to account for trust monies.

As law firm management and business structures evolve, 'a crucial question is whether law firms will be able to sustain a distinctive culture' that balances duty to client and duty to court 'rather than becoming purely market-driven organizations'.[104] This concern with the internal management structures within law firms is consistent with an increasing focus on similar structures within *business* firms to improve corporate ethics, social responsibility and regulatory compliance.[105] The crucial combination required is ethical business structures led by morally responsible CEOs. Those leaders may be lawyers, but more often they will be advised by company secretaries who are lawyers. Indeed many large commercial law firms in Australia have lawyers who specialise in advising their business clients on how to implement regulatory and ethical compliance systems, and who sell educational and management tools to clients for this purpose.[106] It is logical that large law firms might apply the same principles to themselves, and that regulators, insurers,[107] clients[108] and lawyers should all be interested in understanding and improving the ethical climate of law firms.

104 Milton C Regan, 'Taking Law Firms Seriously' (2002) 16(1) *Georgetown Journal of Legal Ethics* 155, 172. See also Regan and Rohrer (n 41).

105 See, eg, Parker, *The Open Corporation* (n 65).

106 See Tanina Rostain, 'The Emergence of Law Consultants' (2006) 75(3) *Fordham Law Review* 1397.

107 In the United States and United Kingdom some legal insurers, especially the US insurer Attorneys' Liability Assurance Society, have promoted in-house ethical compliance efforts within law firms by giving discounts for firms with ethics partners and similar roles: see Elizabeth Chambliss and David B Wilkins, 'The Emerging Role of Ethics Advisors, General Counsel, and Other Compliance Specialists in Large Law Firms' (2002) 44(3–4) *Arizona Law Review* 559, 590.

108 For example, the Victorian government has extensive ethical, pro bono and equal employment opportunity requirements that need to be met by law firms that do work for it: see 'Legal Services Panel Contract', *vic.gov.au* (Web Page) <https://www.vic.gov.au/legal-services-panel-contract#key-benefits>. See also Suzanne Le Mire and Christine Parker, 'Keeping It In-House: Ethics in the

In Australia, legal professional associations have been encouraging law firms to voluntarily institute ethics programs and other internal controls, such as ethics partners who can be 'the first contact when someone in the firm has an ethical question or problem'.[109] They might also review internal ethical decisions and rule on internal differences of opinion on ethical matters. Ethics programs in law firms and companies can be very helpful, if they evidence a real commitment to ethical responsibility; however, they can also be dangerously thin. Research has shown that senior lawyers and junior lawyers in larger law firms may have very different views of these ethics programs. Law firm partners often believe they have very good ethics programs and an open door for the discussion of ethical issues. Junior lawyers in the same firm might not necessarily even be aware of the existence of ethics partners and ethics policies within their firms or may not feel empowered to use them openly.[110] Lawyers in a firm may live in a culture of mutual suspicion where everyone believes that everybody *else* is padding their bills, cutting corners and generally gaming the system to meet billable hours requirements and please clients.[111] Moreover, even where law firms do implement in-house ethics programs, they are largely directed at ensuring ethical client service in relation to issues such as billing, communication and avoiding conflicts of interest rather than grappling with the broader social, economic and environmental implications of lawyers' work for corporate clients.

In Chapter 1 we note that the ethical climate in which lawyers work affects not just their ethics but also their mental health and job satisfaction. It seems that new lawyers have clear perceptions of their practice's (un)ethical norms.[112] New lawyers' sense of professional wellbeing is enhanced in ethical climates characterised by both integrity and an ethic of care. However, this suffers significantly when they are in workplaces where they perceive important decisions are determined by considerations of power and self-interest, or alternatively in workplaces with little ethical awareness or relational engagement. Ethics, wellbeing and job/career satisfaction appear to be inextricably linked.[113] These findings underline how important it is to build ethics into law firms and indeed all legal practices.[114]

Relationship Between Large Firm Lawyers and Their Corporate Clients Through the Eyes of In-House Counsel' (2008) 11(2) *Legal Ethics* 201.

109 See, eg, Kim Cull, 'Ethics and Law as an Influence on Business' (2002) 40(9) *Law Society Journal* 50, 50–1; John Cain, 'Good Ethics Requires Constant Vigilance' (2002) 76(8) *Law Institute Journal* 4, 4.

110 Christine Parker and Lyn Aitken, 'The Queensland "Workplace Culture Check": Learning from Reflection on Ethics Inside Law Firms' (2011) 24(2) *Georgetown Journal of Legal Ethics* 399. But for evidence of the positive impact of ethics audits and international ethics management systems in law firms, see Parker, Gordon and Mark (n 99); Fortney and Gordon (n 100).

111 Christine Parker and David Ruschena, 'The Pressures of Billable Hours: Lessons from a Survey of Billing Practices Inside Law Firms' (2012) 9(2) *University of St Thomas Law Journal* 619.

112 Tang, Holmes and Foley (n 97).

113 See also Vivien Holmes, 'Values. The Flip Side of the Well-Being Coin' in *Educating for Well-Being in Law. Positive Professional Identities and Practice* (Routledge, 2019) 27.

114 See also, eg, Collier (n 39); Law Council of Australia, *National Attrition and Re-engagement Study* (Report, 2014); Kieran Pender, *Us Too? Bullying And Sexual Harassment in the Legal Profession* (International Bar Association, 2019).

DISCUSSION QUESTIONS

1. Do you think an ethics partner would be an effective tool for improving ethics generally in law firm practice? Consider again the four ethical approaches introduced in Chapter 2: what would a whole law firm need to do in order to ensure that its legal practice meets the values of its chosen approach, or combination of approaches?
2. Critically assess the 10 objectives for self-assessment of law practice governance and ethical management set out in the list above. Which types of ethical issues are they likely to effectively address? Which types do they not address? Would they have been effective to prevent the various types of ethical misconduct and scandals discussed throughout this chapter? How do they fit with each of *adversarial advocacy*, *responsible lawyering*, *moral activist* and *ethics of care* conceptions of legal ethics? How would you change them to make sure they take into account general morality and cover a broader range of responsibilities to clients, the law and the public interest in relation to social and environmental responsibilities?

We conclude our discussion of corporate lawyers with a case study. Case study 9.2 is an extended case study examining in detail James Hardie's attempts to separate itself from its asbestos liabilities, and the role its lawyers played in that series of events mentioned above. This case study provides a vivid example of the ways in which lawyers can become an important part of corporate decision-making, and the way the law can be used to manage rather than resolve a company's ethical problems. It illustrates well the opportunities that corporate lawyers have to contribute, for good or for ill, to the ethical climate within corporate decision-making and ultimately to the impact of corporate activities on thousands of individuals.

CASE STUDY 9.2 JAMES HARDIE'S ATTEMPTS TO SEPARATE ITSELF FROM ITS ASBESTOS LIABILITIES[115]

James Hardie ('JH') opened its first Australian asbestos factory in 1916. The first known death of a JH employee due to asbestos occurred in about 1960, and the first asbestos compensation claims were filed against JH and other Australian companies in 1977. JH stopped manufacturing asbestos in 1987 and focused on other businesses, including expansion into the United States and Europe. However, JH management realised that it

115 The material for this case study is drawn from the following: *Report of the Special Commission of Inquiry into the MRCF* (n 14); Gideon Haigh, *Asbestos House: The Secret History of James Hardie Industries* (Scribe, 2006) 269–70; Elizabeth Sexton, 'Hardie Writhes in Self-Made Circles of Hell', *The Age* (Melbourne, 21 August 2004) 8; Ackland (n 15). See also Suzanne Le Mire, 'The James Hardie Case and Its Implications for the Teaching of Ethics' in Bronwyn Naylor and Ross Hyams (eds), *Innovation in Clinical Legal Education: Educating Lawyers for the Future* (Legal Services Bulletin Cooperative, 2007) 25.

would be facing significant asbestos liabilities for years to come – its asbestos manufacturing business had been enormously successful and Australians were the highest per capita users of asbestos in the world. By 2001 approximately 2,000 asbestos compensation claims had been made against JH, but asbestos diseases can have a latency period of up to 40 years. At the time of writing there are still new diagnoses of mesothelioma (a deadly cancer of the pleural lining of the lungs caused only by asbestos) and other asbestos-related lung cancer being diagnosed.[116]

By 2001, JH management was keen to 'resolve' the ongoing liability to compensate asbestos victims so that it could 'focus entirely on growing the company for the benefit of all shareholders'.[117] Over the period from February 2001 to March 2003, management restructured the JH group of companies with the ultimate result that all the group's asbestos liabilities were vested in the Medical Research and Compensation Foundation ('MRCF') together with a set amount of funding for compensation. However, it soon became evident that the money would run out after three years, with a shortfall of between $800 million and $1.5 billion for future liabilities after that time. The MRCF had no legal recourse against the rest of the group for further funds to pay compensation, the parent company moved from Australia to the Netherlands and there was a public outcry. The NSW government set up a Special Commission of Inquiry, under David Jackson QC, into these events.

The facts set out below explain, in summary, the legal manoeuvres through which the JH group tried to separate itself from its asbestos liabilities, and the role played in this process by JH's external law firm, Allens Arthur Robinson. JH and Allens had a relationship going back 100 years, and one of the principal Hardie executives who orchestrated the events (the chief in-house counsel and later company financial officer at JH) was a former Allens partner.[118]

February 2001

Before February 2001 the JH group's main legal responsibilities for asbestos compensation related to claims against two subsidiary companies owned by the parent company, James Hardie Industries Ltd ('JHIL'). These two companies, Amaba Pty Ltd and Amaca Pty Ltd, had made asbestos products from 1937 until 1987. In February 2001, JHIL transferred ownership of Amaba and Amaca to a new trust, the MRCF. They also gave the MRCF $293 million to meet future compensation claims. At the same time, Amaba and Amaca

116 'Mesothelioma in Australia Statistics', *Australian Government, Cancer Australia* (Web Page) <https://www.canceraustralia.gov.au/cancer-types/mesothelioma-cancer/statistics>.

117 Quoted words are from JH's 16 February 2001 media release upon the establishment of the Medical Research and Compensation Fund (see explanation below): James Hardie, 'James Hardie Resolves Its Asbestos Liability Favourably for Claimants and Shareholders' (Press Release, 16 February 2001), included as an annexure in *Report of the Special Commission of Inquiry into the MRCF* (n 14) vol 2, 333–4.

118 He later lost his job at JH, as did Chief Executive Officer Peter Macdonald: Ean Higgins, 'Hardie Dumps Asbestos Chiefs', *The Australian* (Sydney, 16 May 2006) 2.

indemnified JHIL for any further asbestos liabilities.[119] This meant that JHIL would not be liable in the future in relation to asbestos.[120]

The JHIL Board's decision in February 2001 to create the MCRF with $293 million was based on an actuarial report on the likely amount of claims that would need to be paid out in relation to asbestos liability (the Trowbridge Report). However, this report was based on out-of-date data and other inaccurate methodologies. In fact, $293 million would be nowhere near enough money to pay out all of Amaba's and Amaca's asbestos liabilities. JHIL's chief in-house counsel had a more up-to-date 'draft' report and was aware of other problems in the Trowbridge Report but chose not to make this information available to the Board of JHIL. Allens lawyers were involved in advising on the preparations for the creation of the MRCF, and the Allens lawyers raised concerns about the fact that the report to be given to the Board did not include more up-to-date data, but were assured by the chief in-house counsel and the CEO that the report was adequate and that the MRCF would be sufficiently funded.[121] The role of the Allens lawyers in relation to this Board meeting (at which it was decided to hive off JH's asbestos liabilities to MRCF) was described as follows by Gideon Haigh:[122]

> Through this, too, sat the advisers ... the lawyers staved off concern about the data whose absence had made them so anxious that morning. [One of the Allens solicitors present] contemplated raising the subject, but chose not to after asking his superior: 'We were available for questions to be asked of us. No questions were asked of us and so we did not say – we did not raise it.' ... Yet it may not only be in what they did or did not do that the advisers in this transaction were influential. The impression of having the best advice at one's beck is a reassuring one. The advisers here were by now familiar faces at Hardie, and this was a board culture that placed heavy reliance on them. Recall [the chief in-house counsel's] acid comment on directors in July 2000: 'I don't think we should underestimate the value the Board will place on *outside* third party advisers (as insulting as that is to the company's internal advisers – myself included)'. Yet these same advisers were by now so close to the company as to be almost indistinguishable from corporate officers.[123]

JH put out a media release and report to the Australian Stock Exchange on 16 February 2001 announcing the creation of the MRCF, and stating that '[t]he Foundation [MRCF] has sufficient funds to meet all legitimate compensation claims anticipated from people injured

119 The net assets of Amaca and Amaba were $214 million, with JHIL adding the rest: *Report of the Special Commission of Inquiry into the MRCF* (n 14) vol 1, 8 [1.7].

120 There is controversy about the exact extent to which JHIL, as the holding company (that is the company that owned Amaca and Amaba at the time asbestos liabilities arose, but was legally a separate entity to them) might be liable in relation to asbestos claims where the asbestos was produced and sold by its subsidiaries (Amaca and Amaba), but JHIL had accepted that it had some responsibility to provide for asbestos compensation claims at least as long as it still owned Amaba and Amaca.

121 Haigh (n 115) 262–3, 269–71, 281–2; *Report of the Special Commission of Inquiry into the MRCF* (n 14) vol 1, 547 [29.14], 399–400 [24.25]–[24.28].

122 See Haigh (n 115) and accompanying text.

123 Haigh (n 115).

by asbestos products that were manufactured in the past by two former subsidiaries of JHIL'. The announcement also stated that all asbestos-related costs would be removed from JHIL's future balance sheets and that '[n]o future provisions are expected to be required'.[124]

Commissioner Jackson later described this announcement as 'seriously misleading'[125] on the provision of funds for asbestos victims, and also stated that, in his view, the CEO and chief in-house counsel had breached their duties as JHIL officers 'by encouraging the Board to act on the Trowbridge Report in forming the view that the Foundation would be fully funded'.[126]

Between February and October 2001

The directors of the MRCF realised that they were facing a shortfall in funds to meet the asbestos liabilities of Amaba and Amaca, and began to insist that JHIL needed to do something about this. It was conceivable that the MRCF might sue JHIL. However, JHIL 'was adamant that no further substantial funds would be made available to the Foundation, and that it had taken all proper steps at the establishment of the Foundation'.[127]

Allens advised Hardie that the Foundation would have no compensable legal claim against Hardie. Commissioner Jackson later commented:

> There was no *legal* obligation for JHIL to provide greater funding to the Foundation, but it was aware – indeed, very aware because it had made extensive efforts to identify and target those who might be 'stakeholders', or were regarded as having influence with 'stakeholders' – that if it were perceived as not having made adequate provision for the future asbestos liabilities of its former subsidiaries there would be a wave of adverse public opinion which might well result in action being taken by the Commonwealth or State governments (on whom much of the cost of such asbestos victims would be thrown) to legislate to make other companies in the Group liable in addition to Amaca or Amaba.[128]

October 2001

The Hardie group restructured. The assets of the Australian parent, JHIL, were transferred to a new parent company based in Amsterdam, James Hardie Industries NV ('JHINV'). JHIL was left as a non-operating 'shell' company with net assets of $20 million. As part of the restructure, JHIL issued partly paid shares to JHINV. The partly paid shares gave JHIL the ability to call on funds up to the value of $1.85 billion from JHINV (the new Dutch parent). Allens continued to act for JHIL. In the lead-up to the restructure Allens and JHIL discussed the possibility that the partly paid shares would be cancelled at some time in the future.

124 James Hardie (n 117).

125 *Report of the Special Commission of Inquiry into the MRCF* (n 14) vol 1, 10 [1.15]. See also at vol 1, 13 [1.26].

126 Ibid vol 1, 420 [24.82].

127 Ibid vol 1, 12 [1.22].

128 Ibid vol 1, 8–9 [1.8] (emphasis in original).

Jackson found that while there was no 'fixed intention' to cancel the partly paid shares at this stage, 'it was, in effect, the "operating assumption" on which both management and the Board were proceeding' that it would occur within a year or so of the restructure.[129]

The 2001 restructure had to be approved by the NSW Supreme Court (Justice Kim Santow) in order to ensure that the interests of shareholders and creditors in the company were adequately looked after (as a 'scheme of arrangement'). As part of this process JHIL stated that the $20 million and the funds available from the partly paid shares would be available to the MRCF to meet the asbestos liabilities of JHIL's former subsidiaries, Amaba and Amaca, if necessary.[130] Allens and JHIL did not tell Justice Santow about the concerns relating to the MRCF's solvency, or the possibility that the partly paid shares would be cancelled. Permission for the restructure was granted.

Jackson later found Allens and JHIL were in breach of their duty of disclosure to the Court by not telling the Court that cancellation of the partly paid shares was 'almost inevitable', a view that should have been held by 'anyone familiar with JHIL's internal strategic planning' including the JHIL Board, senior management and Allens lawyers.[131] However, he found that this failure was not deliberate. He also thought Allens might have breached its duty of care to JHIL in failing to make sure disclosure occurred.[132]

March–July 2002

After October 2001 the MRCF directors became increasingly worried about their lack of funds. MRCF's relationship with JHINV (now standing in the place of JHIL) deteriorated further as MRCF asked for extra funding and JHINV refused. In March 2002 JHINV sought advice from Allens about the possibility of cancelling the partly paid shares. At the meeting where this was discussed, Allens lawyers discussed the possibility that it was 'too soon' to cancel the partly paid shares because it might look like the company had had the intention to cancel the partly paid shares at the time of having the restructure arrangement approved by the Court, and therefore misled the Court by not disclosing that intention in the scheme documents at the time.[133]

Records from the meetings also indicated that the lawyers considered that if this were true, there would be nothing that the court could do about it, as the failure to disclose had already occurred. However, the Australian Securities and Investment Commission might be

129 Ibid vol 1, 453 [25.80].

130 Haigh (n 115) 286; *Report of the Special Commission of Inquiry into the MRCF* (n 14) vol 1, 431 [25.21], 432–3 [25.22].

131 *Report of the Special Commission of Inquiry into the MRCF* (n 14) vol 1, 455–6 [25.87]. One of the options that JH had considered before entering into the October 2001 scheme of arrangement was an option in which no partly paid shares would be issued to link JHINV and JHIL. Rather, JHIL would be completely separated from the group, possibly even liquidated. That option was explicitly rejected by the JHIL Board in favour of the 'more flexible' option of issuing the partly paid shares that could later be cancelled or called in to bring further funds into JHIL.

132 Ibid vol 1, 456–7 [25.91]. They also unintentionally failed to disclose the existence of a put option that would in effect require MRCF to buy all the shares in JHIL, having the same effect as cancelling the partly paid shares.

133 Ibid vol 1, 479–82 [26.60]–[26.71], 485–8 [26.82]–[26.87]; Haigh (n 115) 303–6.

able to prosecute for failure to disclose, and there would also be a 'commercial and political risk' in JH being seen to have misled the Court.[134]

15 March 2003

JHIL (now known as ABN 60 and wholly owned and controlled by JHINV) cancelled the partly paid shares, which were all held by JHINV, for no consideration. The cancellation of these shares meant JHINV no longer had any legal liability to give any funds to JHIL (ABN 60), and therefore JHIL had no capacity to fund MRCF, beyond JHIL's own $20 million in assets. The JH group's asbestos liabilities were effectively 'owned' by MRCF, while the group's main assets were owned by JHINV, separate legal entities from one another with no clear legal responsibilities between them. The JHINV chief financial officer, who was also a director of JHIL, was responsible for executing this plan. At the Commission of Inquiry he claimed to rely on advice from Allens that JHIL was not liable to the MRCF for anything.[135]

Discussion questions

1. In his findings Commissioner Jackson commented that he was surprised that the lawyers from Allens did not raise the question of the adequacy of the funding for the MRCF earlier than just before the fateful Board meeting of February 2001. He also thought that it was 'disturbing' that JHIL's advisers had failed to say that 'separation was unlikely to be successful unless the Foundation *was* fully funded, and that this was required to be rigorously checked'.[136] Why do you think Hardie's lawyers did not provide this advice more forcefully and earlier? Why did they not speak up about this issue and the adequacy of the Trowbridge Report at the Board meeting? Do you think they participated in deception of the Board by saying nothing at the Board meeting about their concerns?[137]
2. Commissioner Jackson described JHIL's chief in-house lawyer as 'a man who seemed determined to control the course of events, and the activities of the participants'.[138] He also commented that '[i]t may well be, however, that this was a case where the JHIL management were determined, so far as possible, to deal with the matter in-house as far as possible [sic] and that outside advice touching the merits of the proposal was

134 One Allens lawyer did attempt to communicate these concerns to JHINV in a letter of advice, but the letter was substantially edited while he was on holidays, and there is no evidence that it received any attention at JHINV anyway: Haigh (n 115) 310–12.

135 *Report of the Special Commission of Inquiry into the MRCF* (n 14) vol 1, 511–12 [27.67].

136 Ibid vol 1, 547 [29.14], 547–8 [29.15] (emphasis in original).

137 Gideon Haigh's view is that, even in saying nothing at all, the external lawyers participated in the management's (the CEO and in-house lawyer's) plan to separate off the MRCF, and the Board's acquiescence in that plan. By saying nothing about the missing data, which they were aware of, the external lawyers also played their part in the deception of the Board: Haigh (n 115) 269–79.

138 *Report of the Special Commission of Inquiry into the MRCF* (n 14) vol 1, 546 [29.9].

unwelcome'.[139] Jackson seems to be suggesting that JHIL management (particularly the CEO and chief in-house lawyer) may have intentionally discouraged the Allens lawyers from looking more broadly at the arrangements for setting up the MRCF in their advice. If you were the external lawyer, how would you feel about this? Should you accept these types of limitations on the way your work is framed? What other options do you have? What would happen if you attempted to bypass the chief in-house lawyer and CEO and go straight to the Board with any concerns? (In answering these questions, think about what the four different ethical approaches would say about how you should respond to this sort of situation.)

3. Jackson found that JHIL and Allens misled the Court about JHIL's plans in relation to the cancellation of the partly paid shares (although not intentionally). At the Commission of Inquiry, Allens and JHIL attempted to make a distinction between what was the 'intention' of JHIL at the time and what was in 'contemplation'. (Cancellation was in contemplation but there was no fixed intention to cancel.)[140] Is this type of distinction justified? Could the lawyers have done anything differently to make sure that the court was fully informed of the likely cancellation in the future? (Again, think about how the four different ethical approaches would help you answer these questions.)
4. After the MRCF became aware of its lack of funds and began to demand that JHIL do something about it, Allens provided advice on several occasions that there was little likelihood of JHIL (the parent company) being held legally responsible for the asbestos liabilities of its former subsidiaries, Amaca and Amaba. Yet JHIL, as parent of the group, had previously acted as if it had moral responsibility at least to compensate asbestos sufferers on behalf of the whole group. Moreover, as Jackson commented, regardless of the precise legal situation in relation to JHIL's liability, there was a real possibility that if JHIL failed to adequately provide for the group's asbestos victims, the government would step in and legislate to make them responsible. This is in fact what happened. As a result of the Commission of Inquiry, the NSW government threatened to legislate to make the James Hardie group liable unless they were able to negotiate a satisfactory arrangement for compensation of everyone. They suffered much bad publicity before an arrangement was finally negotiated.[141] In hindsight, should the external lawyers have more strongly advised JHIL about ethical and political considerations? What do you think the duty to the corporation as a whole required? Would you have felt capable of giving this sort of 'hard' advice to JHIL in all the circumstances?
5. These events occurred two decades ago. Given the 'ESG Revolution' happening today, do you think a similar situation might play out differently?

139 Ibid vol 1, 547–8 [29.15]. Yet later the CEO used Allens' name when journalist Ben Hills raised concerns that the fund may not be adequate – the CEO pointed out that they had received 'in-depth advice from a large number of specialist firms with noted, long-standing experience in relevant areas': Haigh (n 115) 276–7. See also at 282–3 (Allens was concerned about its name being used in this way).

140 Haigh (n 115) 303.

141 On 1 December 2005 the company effectively agreed to undo its 2001–02 restructuring and re-establish its liability to compensate victims of asbestos: Marcus Priest, 'Buck Stops with New Local Unit', *The Australian Financial Review* (Sydney, 2 December 2005) 5.

Government lawyers

The term 'government lawyer' covers many different types of lawyers – from those working within specific government departments and executive agencies (including prosecution and legal aid work) to those within the Government Solicitor's practice. Our focus here is on lawyers giving legal advice to government and/or being involved in transactional or litigious work for government.[142] As noted in the introduction to this chapter, corporate practice and government practice can throw up similar ethical challenges, from losing sight of the real client to rationalising dubious behaviour.

In a speech to government lawyers in 2017, then Victorian Chief Justice Marilyn Warren, reminded her audience:

> Government lawyers are advisers to the government but not part of it. The role is fundamental to the rule of law. While closely associated with government, government lawyers remain fundamentally separate from it and provide the first check on any abuse of executive power …
>
> … The role of the government lawyer is important. It matters. Governments may make 'political' mistakes with legal consequences. The role of the government lawyer is to provide strong, sometimes courageous, accurate and independent legal advice.[143]

Like corporate lawyers, government lawyers need to keep in mind who their client is. In theory, the client for all government lawyers is the 'Crown' or 'the government', but in practice government lawyers act for the organisation that employs them (or in the case of Legal Aid or the Government Solicitor, for the clients of those organisations). While government lawyers take their instructions from employees or officers of the organisations for which they work, or from the relevant Minister, they do not act for those individuals. Similarly, as we have seen, in-house corporate lawyers may take instructions from officers of their employer corporation but do not act for those individuals. So it is critical to keep the actual client in mind.

Kathleen Clark[144] details how lawyers in the US Department of Justice ('DOJ') during the Trump presidency mistook the President for their client. The DOJ lawyers (both those who were political appointees and those who were career lawyers)[145] adopted an interpretation of the *United States Constitution*'s Foreign Emoluments Clause[146] that was at odds with the DOJ's own interpretations of that Clause over the preceding 150 years, in favour of an interpretation that served President's Trump's personal financial interests. The Clause had historically been interpreted broadly, to protect the United States against foreign government influence. After President Trump's inauguration, an anti-corruption group filed a lawsuit alleging that the

142 We discuss the role of prosecutors in Chapter 5.

143 Marilyn Warren CJ, 'Being a Government Lawyer' (Speech, Government Lawyers Conference, 23 June 2017) <https://www.supremecourt.vic.gov.au/about-the-court/speeches/being-a-government-lawyer>.

144 Kathleen Clark, 'The Lawyers Who Mistook a President for Their Client' (2019) 52(2) *Indiana Law Review* 271.

145 Ibid 290.

146 *United States Constitution* art I § 9 cl 8: 'No Person holding any Office of Profit or Trust under [the United States], shall, without the Consent of the Congress, accept of any present, Emolument, Office, or Title, of any kind whatever, from any King, Prince, or foreign State.'

acceptance by Trump's personal business enterprises of funds and other benefits from foreign governments was a violation of the Emoluments Clause. In response, President Trump's personal lawyers argued for a narrow, technical interpretation of the Clause that ignored its underlying purpose and would allow the President to continue to receive such money. The DOJ adopted this narrow interpretation. In doing so, DOJ chose 'to protect the personal financial interests of Donald Trump instead of the institutional interests of the United States', leading Clark to note that DOJ lawyers had 'mistaken this President for their actual client, the United States'.[147]

Government lawyers are gatekeepers of the rule of law. It is well accepted that government lawyers are required to take a *responsible lawyer* approach to their work: their conduct must 'both be, and be seen to be, above reproach. It is critical that the government should, in all its legal endeavours, be seen to uphold the law.'[148] They are 'custodians of the public trust not only in the legal profession and the administration of justice, but also in the administration of government.'[149] The model litigant rules operating in several jurisdictions make it very clear that government lawyers are required to adopt a responsible lawyer approach to litigation: for example, 'not taking advantage of a claimant who lacks the resources to litigate a legitimate claim'; 'not relying on technical defences unless the [Government's] interests would be prejudiced by the failure to comply with a particular requirement'.[150] In relation to advice work, Richard Painter, former chief ethics lawyer to US President George W Bush, underlines the need for a *responsible lawyering* approach:

> [Government lawyers] have an ethical obligation to go beyond advising compliance with a minimal interpretation of the letter of the law, but to consider both the law's letter and its spirit. Government lawyers should not go along with government actors when a course of action is one that technically is permissible under the law, but which undermines the actual purpose of the law. Instead, government lawyers have an obligation to encourage government officials to act with integrity in upholding laws, rather than trying to get away with technical compliance while eviscerating public interest purposes underlying those laws.[151]

Failure by government lawyers to act as gatekeepers leads to an erosion of government's integrity and legitimacy, and harm to its citizens. As Margaret Tarkington notes:

> Where government lawyers should be defenders of due process and the rule of law, they can instead become instruments of state oppression when they countenance, advise, or assist in unlawful and unethical actions of government officers or agencies.[152]

147 Clark (n 144) 272.

148 Dal Pont (n 58) 470 [13.80].

149 Ibid.

150 See, eg, 'Victorian Model Litigant Guidelines', *Victoria State Government* (Web Page, 22 July 2021), 2(j), (k) <https://www.justice.vic.gov.au/justice-system/laws-and-regulation/victorian-model-litigant-guidelines>.

151 Margaret Tarkington, 'Introduction: The Ethics of Lawyers in Government' (2019) 52(2) *Indiana Law Review* 265, 267.

152 Ibid 269. For a fascinating discussion of 'whether to stay on the job or quit' when the government is one a lawyer finds 'morally abhorrent', see David Luban, 'Complicity and Lesser Evils: A Tale of Two Lawyers' (2021) 34(3) *Georgetown Journal of Legal Ethics* 613; Leora Bilsky and Natalie R Davidson, 'Legal Ethics in Authoritarian Legality: Response' (2021) 34(3) *Georgetown Journal of Legal Ethics* 665.

Comprehensive research into the in-house legal role (both corporate and government), conducted by Richard Moorhead, Steven Vaughan and Cristina Godinho in the United Kingdom, found that both categories of lawyers are subjected to 'ethical pressure':

> [A]bout 10 per cent of our respondents were asked to advise on ethically or legally debatable actions frequently or very frequently; and about 40 per cent were asked to so advise at least sometimes. Interestingly … lawyers working in a public sector organisation showed significantly *higher* ratings of ethical pressure than those working in a business.[153]

It is possible that the higher ratings of ethical pressure reflects an increased sensitivity to ethical issues by lawyers who have chosen to work in the public sector. Certainly, pressure to tailor one's advice to a particular political agenda should be resisted. As the NSW Law Society's *Handy Hints for Government Legal Practitioners* explains:

> You must not compromise the provision or quality of your legal advice in any way, particularly if your superior requests, either expressly or impliedly, that your advice should be revised, rewritten or 'more delicately worded' to accommodate a stated position or policy. The reasons are twofold. First, your role as a government legal practitioner, whose paramount duty to the Court is to always uphold and respect the rule of law obliges you to provide full and frank advice on the 'best view of the law', not merely 'what is plausible or arguable'. The second, being that to do otherwise will seriously erode your standing and reputation as a source of authoritative, objective and credible legal analysis.[154]

Ethical pressure can be insidious. As we have seen in relation to corporate lawyers, close identification with employees or officers of the client can mean a lawyer loses sight of their real client, and may find themselves serving the interests other than those of their client. This is what happened to some Australian Defence Force lawyers working in Afghanistan with the Special Operations Task Force.

CASE STUDY 9.3 **SPECIAL FORCES LAWYERS IN AFGHANISTAN**

The Inquiry by Major General Paul Brereton into allegations of serious misconduct (including war crimes) by Australian Special Forces in Afghanistan (the 'Brereton Inquiry')[155] found that certain lawyers defended the interests of the Special Forces ('SF') rather than those of the Commonwealth. This led them, for example, to denigrate civilian complaints about SF's

153 Moorhead, Vaughan and Godinho (n 55) 67.

154 The Law Society of New South Wales, *Handy Hints for Government Legal Practitioners* (2019) 10 <https://www.lawsociety.com.au/sites/default/files/2019-09/LS3240_Policy_Handy-hints-gov-sol_v3.pdf>.

155 Commonwealth of Australia, *Inspector General of the Australian Defence Force Afghanistan Inquiry Report* (2020).

behaviour rather than deal with them impartially[156] and to 'polish' reports of events that were in fact unlawful killings by the SF:

> As the [more senior, Joint Operations Command] lawyers started to become more 'troublesome' [in questioning actions by the SF], the SF unit started to rely more on their own lawyers, 'with the promise of being inside their 'elite tent', doing cool stuff in return for legally polishing their version of events and the truth in a way that created enough doubt as to exonerate them ... Ultimately, the After Action Reports [reports on incidents], rather than being part of the oversight and institutional understanding process, in some cases became a way of removing scrutiny for wrongdoing. This would have added to the insidious corrosive effect of some people believing that they were untouchable thanks to the legal whitewashing of their activities.[157]

DISCUSSION QUESTIONS

1. How do you think the Special Forces lawyers might have rationalised their 'legal whitewashing' of the After Action Reports? How does this differ from the rationalisations likely to have been operating in the Department of Justice during the Trump presidency in relation to interpretation of the Emoluments Clause?
2. Why is an invitation to 'be inside the tent, doing cool stuff' so enticing? How might we counter an inclination to accept the invitation?

It may be tempting to categorise these actions by the SF lawyers as occurring in extreme circumstances (for example, 'the fog of war') and unlikely to happen elsewhere.[158] But an invitation to be 'inside the tent, doing [unethical] cool stuff' can occur in many environments. As discussed, it is likely that many of the ethical failures by James Hardie's external lawyers occurred because they were 'inside the tent' and did not step outside it to look more objectively at the whole situation. Lawyers need to be alert to organisational cultures (whether in government or private enterprise) that encourage and facilitate unethical behaviour, and to consider how they might take action to fulfil their duty to the law and their client(s) while maintaining their own integrity.

Conclusion

The work of corporate and government lawyers differs in many respects, but the ethical challenges each face can be surprisingly similar. The primary duty of both corporate and government lawyers is owed to the legal system and the administration of justice. Both types

156 Ibid 383–4.

157 Ibid 458–9.

158 Brereton makes it clear that a 'combination of factors led to a normalisation over time of behaviours that should never have been considered normal and ultimately, the effective covering up of, or wilful blindness to, the perpetration of war crimes': ibid 526.

of lawyer need to keep in mind who their client is – this focus can be a useful compass when there is pressure to act in the interests of officers or ministers instead. Leaders in both corporate and government legal practices assist their staff to act ethically and stay mentally well when they build ethical infrastructures within their organisations. And all lawyers would do well to remember humans' tendency to rationalise unethical requests. The challenge for lawyers in the face of ethical pressures is to sensitise themselves to the rationalising processes that they and others may use to dull their moral sense. Once exposed, rationalising is less powerful as a controlling tool and it becomes possible to assert alternative models for appropriate corporate and government lawyering.

RECOMMENDED FURTHER READING

Kath Hall and Vivien Holmes, 'The Power of Rationalisation to Influence Lawyers' Decisions to Act Unethically' (2008) 11(2) *Legal Ethics* 137

Donald C Langevoort, 'Gatekeepers, Cultural Captives, or Knaves? Corporate Lawyers through Different Lenses Colloquium: Corporate Lawyers' (2020) 88(5) *Fordham Law Review* 1683

Suzanne Le Mire and Christine Parker, 'Keeping It In-House: Ethics in the Relationship Between Large Firm Lawyers and Their Corporate Clients Through the Eyes of In-House Counsel' (2008) 11(2) *Legal Ethics* 201

David Luban, 'Complicity and Lesser Evils: A Tale of Two Lawyers' (2021) 34(3) *Georgetown Journal of Legal Ethics* 613

Richard Moorhead et al, *In-House Lawyers' Ethics: Institutional Logics, Legal Risk and the Tournament of Influence* (Bloomsbury, 2019)

Richard Moorhead and Victoria Hinchly, 'Professional Minimalism? The Ethical Consciousness of Commercial Lawyers' (2015) 42 (3) *Journal of Law and Society* 387

Christine Parker et al, 'The Ethical Infrastructure of Legal Practice in Larger Law Firms: Values, Policy and Behaviour' (2008) 31(1) *University of New South Wales Law Journal* 158

Milton C Regan and Lisa H Rohrer, *BigLaw: Money and Meaning in the Modern Law Firm* (University of Chicago Press, 2020)

Stephen Tang, Vivien Holmes and Tony Foley, 'Ethical Climate, Job Satisfaction and Wellbeing: Observations from an Empirical Study of New Australian Lawyers' (2020) 33(4) *Georgetown Journal of Legal Ethics* 1035

Steven Vaughan and Emma Oakley, '"Gorilla Exceptions" and the Ethically Apathetic Corporate Lawyer' (2016) 19(1) *Legal Ethics* 50

10

LAWYERS' ETHICS IN THE ANTHROPOCENE

Introduction

We are now in the Anthropocene, a time in the earth's four-billion-year history when human activities are affecting the planet to such an extent that humans have become a 'significant geological force'.[1] The burning of fossil fuels, deforestation and land use changes have combined to cause dangerous climate change. Alongside extreme climate change, humanity faces several other key threats, such as food insecurity and environmental degradation.[2]

These challenges intersect and compound. Climate change will lead to more frequent wildfires, longer droughts, and an increase in the number, duration and severity of tropical storms.[3] This in turn will worsen food insecurity and biodiversity loss/extinction. Biodiversity and ecosystem loss (which is caused by climate change, pollution, deforestation and overpopulation) can lead to economic downturn: according to analysis by the global insurance company Swiss Re, a fifth of countries worldwide are at risk from ecosystem collapse because at least 55% of global GDP depends on high-functioning biodiversity and ecosystems.[4] Economic downturn results in widespread poverty. The UN Special Rapporteur on Extreme Poverty and Human Rights warns:

> Climate change will have devastating consequences for people in poverty. Even under the best-case scenario, hundreds of millions will face food insecurity, forced migration, disease, and death. Climate change threatens the future of human rights and risks undoing the last fifty years of progress in development, global health, and poverty reduction.[5]

The risks facing humanity also challenge the rule of law. Ideally, law operates to help keep a society stable, peaceful and ordered. But its 'rule' is challenged by social breakdown. Justice Francois Kunc of the NSW Supreme Court writes:

> Inadequately mitigated climate change could undo our social order and the rule of law itself ... It is no longer either difficult or alarmist to imagine a day when, in extremis, the defence, external affairs and immigration powers of the Commonwealth are invoked to support measures not seen since World War II to deal with the social, political, economic and physical effects of climate change.[6]

---

1 Paul J Crutzen, 'The "Anthropocene"' in Eckart Ehlers and Thomas Krafft (eds), *Earth System Science in the Anthropocene* (Springer-Verlag, 2006) 13, 13.

2 Commission for the Human Future (Web Page) <https://www.humanfuture.net/>. See also Toby Ord, *The Precipice: Existential Risk and the Future of Humanity* (Bloomsbury Academic, 2020); Corey JA Bradshaw et al, 'Underestimating the Challenges of Avoiding a Ghastly Future' (2021) 1: *Frontiers in Conservation Science* 615419.

3 Intergovernmental Panel on Climate Change, *Climate Change 2021: The Physical Science Basis. Contribution of Working Group I to the Sixth Assessment Report of the Intergovernmental Panel on Climate Change*, eds V Masson-Delmotte et al (Cambridge University Press, forthcoming).

4 Anna Retsa et al, *Biodiversity and Ecosystem Services* (Swiss Re Management Ltd, 2020).

5 Human Rights Council, United Nations General Assembly, *Climate Change and Poverty* (Report of the United Nations Special Rapporteur on Extreme Poverty and Human Rights, 17 July 2019).

6 Francois Kunc, 'Current Issues. Climate Change and the Law' [2018] (92) *Australian Law Journal* 745, 745.

While the risks to humanity are interconnected, so are their solutions. Both the risks and their solutions pose huge public policy questions, and, since law is 'the principal means of implementing public policy',[7] law must evolve to play its part. Lawyers have a key role to play in assisting that evolution, and the ethics that govern lawyers' work will play a large part in determining its success.

This chapter focuses on the work of lawyers in addressing climate change and environmental damage. Such work raises important issues about lawyers' role generally and the values and ethics underpinning that role. As the International Bar Association says:

> A global response to the climate crisis will undoubtedly give rise to increased disputes, with lawyers representing the legal interests and rights of all sides. Parties to these disputes will include states, corporations, communities, civil society organisations and individuals who are the most vulnerable to the impacts of the climate crisis. The legal profession must be prepared to play a leading role in maintaining and strengthening the rule of law and supporting responsible, enlightened governance in an era marked by a climate crisis.[8]

The Australian Pro Bono Centre believes that

> [l]awyers have the skills, opportunities and resources to tackle [the climate change] challenge. While our individual actions may seem small, collectively the legal profession can show leadership – and have a substantial impact on the climate crisis.[9]

In this chapter we consider how the different ethical approaches (*adversarial advocacy*, *responsible lawyering*, *moral activism* and *ethics of care*) are informing lawyers' actions on behalf of the planet. Of course, many lawyers will draw from several ethical approaches in their work. Likewise, all four approaches can support efforts at law reform, which we discuss later in the chapter.

Moral activist

There are multiple aspects of justice involved in addressing climate change, such as intergenerational justice, racial justice, gender justice, human rights and other species' rights. We know that climate change and environmental degradation disproportionately affect developing nations and poor communities.[10] Add to this the 'business as usual' approach taken by many governments and corporations, it is no surprise that many lawyers adopt a *moral activist* approach to addressing climate change, applying legal pressure in an attempt to hasten the evolution of policy and law to fill the gap left by inaction. Examples of the moral activist approach include the World Lawyers Pledge on Climate Action, its signatories promising to 'initiate, foster, and sustain the change necessary to avert climate catastrophe,

7 Ibid.

8 International Bar Association, 'Climate Crisis Statement' (5 May 2020) <https://www.ibanet.org/LPRU/Climate-Crisis>.

9 Australian Pro Bono Centre, *Pro Bono Guide to the Climate Crisis* (2020) 4.

10 Sarah Krakoff, 'Parenting the Planet' in Denis G Arnold (ed), *The Ethics of Global Climate Change* (Cambridge University Press, 2011) 145, 152.

and transition our societies and laws towards a sustainable future'.[11] Lawyers are organising for climate action and climate justice.[12]

One of the most high-profile avenues for *moral activist* legal work is *strategic litigation,* which employs existing law in an attempt to raise public consciousness of climate change and force governments to take stronger action. The Sabin Centre for Climate Change Law at Columbia Law School maintains a database of climate change litigation.[13] The Centre tracks cases against governments and corporations around the world – both decided cases and cases on foot. Its database contains details on over 2,000 climate change lawsuits, including from Australia.

Justice Rachel Pepper describes three 'waves' of climate litigation: the first wave comprising cases seeking compliance with existing environmental and planning legislation; the second based on arguments about constitutional or human rights; and the third using corporate law to hold corporate players to account for failure to avoid or mitigate 'transactional' risks of climate change.[14] Initially, this litigation has been undertaken by the classic *moral activist* lawyer/legal practices, such as the Australian non-government organisation ('NGO') Environmental Defenders Office ('EDO') and the international NGO Client Earth. The EDO describes itself as 'the largest environmental legal centre in the Australia-Pacific region, dedicated to protecting our climate, communities and shared environment by providing access to justice, running groundbreaking litigation and leading law reform advocacy'.[15] Client Earth is 'dedicated to protecting life on Earth. [It] work[s] in over 50 countries, ingeniously using the law to create systemic change'.[16] But private lawyers also take on such cases. We look at the example of one firm in Case study 10.1.

CASE STUDY 10.1 A CLIMATE ACTIVIST LAWYER

According to its website, Equity Generation Lawyers combine 'expertise in climate change risk and a flair for innovative legal action that has international reach'.[17] This firm has run several groundbreaking cases, including these two:

- Mark McVeigh sued his superannuation fund, REST, over its failure to disclose how it was managing climate risk in its investment portfolio. The case settled in 2020,

11 'World Lawyers' Pledge on Climate Action', *World Lawyers' Pledge on Climate Action* (Web Page) <https://lawyersclimatepledge.org/>.

12 See, eg, 'Using the Law to Ensure a Better Future', *Lawyers for Climate Action, NZ, Inc* (Web Page) <https://www.lawyersforclimateaction.nz/>.

13 Sabine Centre for Climate Change Law, *Climate Change Litigation Databases* (Web Page) <http://climatecasechart.com/>.

14 Rachel J Pepper, 'Turning a Ripple into a Torrent: Riding the Waves of Climate Change Litigation' (Presentation, Clayton Utz seminar, Climate Change Litigation, Sydney, 16 March 2021) 2 <https://www.lec.nsw.gov.au/lec/publications-and-resources/judicial-speeches-and-papers.html#Current1>. See also Corey Byrne, 'Environmental Class Actions in Australia: A Coming Storm?' (2020) 37(2) *Environmental and Planning Law Journal* 186.

15 'About', Environmental Defenders Office (Web Page) <https://www.edo.org.au/about/>.

16 'About', *Client Earth* (Web Page) <https://www.clientearth.org/about/>.

17 'About Us', *Equity Generation Lawyers* (Web Page) <https://equitygenerationlawyers.com/about/>.

with REST accepting that climate change poses a direct financial risk to the fund and that REST has a responsibility to manage that risk.[18]

- In the 2021 case of *Sharma v Minister for the Environment*[19] eight teenagers and a nun (as litigation guardian) sued the Minister for the Environment, arguing that she would be in breach of a duty of care to protect future generations from harm if she agreed to expansion of the Whitehaven Coal mine in the Hunter Valley. At first instance Bromberg J found that the Minister does owe such a duty. This decision was overturned on appeal, the three members of the Court of Appeal giving different reasons why a duty of care should not be imposed.[20] The Court, however, accepted Bromberg J's extensive findings about climate change and the dangers it poses to the world and humanity.

Lawyer David Barnden established Equity Generation Lawyers in 2019. '"It was risky", he admits. "I had many sleepless nights, wondering if it was the right thing to do."'[21] Public interest litigation is costly for clients. Even if lawyers work pro bono, clients need to pay court fees, travel costs etc and be prepared to pay the defendants (substantial) costs if they lose. Barnden is inspired by his clients, most of whom are young:

> They inspire me … They are incredibly aware, intelligent, articulate and passionate. If these young people are tomorrow's leaders, I have a lot of hope for the future … It is easy to be despondent about climate change, to feel helpless … But we pride ourselves on offering our clients the chance to make a difference. It is a privilege be able to do this work.[22]

DISCUSSION QUESTIONS

1. Do you think that it is the role of lawyers to run cases about climate change? Or should climate change policy be a matter for government?
2. As discussed in Chapter 2, *moral activist* lawyers can be tempted to subordinate client interests to 'the cause'. Do you think this is a concern in environmental litigation and, if so, how might a lawyer such as David Barnden guard against it?

18 'Mark McVeigh v Retail Employees Superannuation Pty Ltd', *Equity Generation Lawyers* (Web Page) <https://equitygenerationlawyers.com/cases/mcveigh-v-rest/>.

19 *Sharma by her Litigation Representative Sister Marie Brigid Arthur v Minister for the Environment* (2021) 391 ALR 1.

20 *Minister for the Environment v Sharma* (2022) 400 ALR 203. See also 'Sharma v Minister for Environment', *Equity Generation Lawyers* (Web Page) <https://equitygenerationlawyers.com/cases/sharma-v-minister-for-environment/>.

21 Quoted in Kieran Pender, 'Suing for Climate Action: Can the Courts Save Us from the Black Hole of Political Inaction?', *The Guardian* (online at 15 November 2020) <https://www.theguardian.com/australia-news/2020/nov/15/suing-for-climate-action-can-the-courts-save-us-from-the-black-hole-of-political-inaction>.

22 Ibid.

Lawyers in the 'Global South' have also been active in climate litigation.[23] Jolene Lin and Jacqueline Peel describe the legal actors in this litigation as the 'hero litigator' – that is, moral activists. The legal actor may be a local or foreign lawyer –

> a lawyer-activist who is passionate about the use of litigation and other legal tools to champion for climate justice. She is a dominant figure who has a high-profile role in relation to the litigation, often raising publicity for the case (and climate litigation more broadly), through press conferences and media appearances. The hero litigator drives the litigation strategy and process.[24]

The authors note:

> As climate litigation develops in the global South, some cases following the Hero Litigator model are likely to emerge. In India, for example, … [i]t would not be surprising to witness the emergence of a number of hero litigators who seek climate justice, particularly for the most vulnerable and marginalized sectors of Indian society. It is also noteworthy that some international organizations working in the global South seek to cultivate 'environmental law champions'.[25]

It is important to remember, however, that litigation involves cost and risk. As Peel notes, courts 'are not a panacea … for the ills of climate change inaction'.[26] Courts rule on the particular case before them rather than making broad policy decisions. They are 'followers, not leaders, of broader social movements'.[27] The Law Council of Australia's ('LCA') Climate Change Policy Statement likewise notes: 'Litigation should not be relied on as the primary tool for resolving emerging gaps, uncertainties and inconsistencies in the law as litigation is an imperfect, costly and time-consuming method of driving a response to climate change.'[28]

Other lawyers are using alternative legal means to promote sustainability, with many adopting a *responsible lawyering* approach.

---

23 Jacqueline Peel and Jolene Lin, 'Transnational Climate Litigation: The Contribution of the Global South' (2019) 113(4) *American Journal of International Law* 679. The authors note that the term 'Global South' is contested. They use the term to denote the 'developed/developing country divide that is widely applied in international environmental and climate law scholarship, and which underpins the UNFCCC's differentiation between Annex I (developed countries and former Soviet Union states) and non-Annex I (developing country) parties': at 682.

24 Joelene Lin and Jacqueline Peel, 'The Farmer or the Hero Litigator? Modes of Climate Litigation in the Global South', *OpenGlobalRights* (28 June 2020) <https://www.openglobalrights.org/farmer-or-hero-litigator-modes-of-climate-litigation-in-global-south/>.

25 Ibid.

26 Jacqueline Peel, 'Can Legal Action Force Governments and Businesses to Respond to Climate Change? *ABC News* (online at 13 February 2020) <https://www.abc.net.au/news/2020-02-13/climate-change-legal-action-solve-global-warming/11943146>.

27 Ibid.

28 Law Council of Australia, *Climate Change Policy Statement* (27 November 2021) [48].

Responsible lawyering

Sustainable development and law

The concept of sustainable development became widely known after its use in the 1987 UN report *Our Common Future*,[29] which placed environmental concerns squarely on the global political agenda. The interconnected nature of global crises was evident; the report argued that economic and social development must be 'sustainable development' – that is, it must meet 'the needs of the present without compromising the ability of future generations to meet their own needs'.[30]

Sustainable development principles are increasingly important in, and relevant to, numerous areas of law and legal practice. In 2015 the American Bar Association's Task Force on Sustainable Development recognised that '[t]he transition to sustainability in both governmental and private sector decision making is inevitable, and will profoundly affect the legal profession'.[31] In 2019 the LCA adopted a Policy on Sustainable Development and made several commitments, including to 'support the scrutiny of new legislation for consistency with the key principles' of Sustainable Development and 'to promote respect for and implementation of [the UN's] Sustainable Development Goals by government, corporations and other entities'.[32]

US lawyer and scholar John Dernbach has reflected extensively on a 'sustainable development' approach to legal practice. Dernbach understands 'sustainable development' as a decision-making framework for the promotion of environmental protection, social justice and economic/financial responsibility, with the ultimate goal of promoting human wellbeing in both the present and future.[33] The framework can be applied to a wide variety of legal matters, as is borne out by his interviews with 26 US lawyers who bring a sustainable development perspective to their work. The interviewees worked in a variety of legal fields, ranging from land law, corporate law and finance through to corporate social responsibility and human rights. Their clients ranged from global corporations, banks and developers through to government and NGOs,[34] and their work involved counselling, litigating, transactions and drafting. The lawyers understood sustainability 'as a lens for productively addressing all legal problems and for helping clients make better decisions'.[35] Dernbach notes that the results of the lawyers' work are sometimes modest, sometimes far-reaching: 'helping

29 Gro Harlem Brundtland, *Report of the World Commission on Environment and Development: Our Common Future* (United Nations, 1987).

30 Ibid [27].

31 American Bar Association, *Final Report of the ABA Task Force on Sustainable Development* (2015) 4 <https://climate.law.columbia.edu/sites/default/files/content/docs/others/final_sdtf_aba_annual_08-2015.authcheckdam.pdf>.

32 Law Council of Australia, *Policy on Sustainable Development* (14 September 2019) 6 <https://www.lawcouncil.asn.au/media/news/sustainable-development-policy>. See also 'Do You Know All 17 SDGs?', *United Nations Department of Economic and Social Affairs* (Web Page) <https://sdgs.un.org/goals>; Margaret A Young, 'Climate Change and Law: A Global Challenge for Legal Education' (2021) 40(3) *University of Queensland Law Journal* 351, 356–62. The latter provides an excellent overview of how climate change is now a critical issue in many areas of legal practice.

33 John C Dernbach, 'Sustainable Development in Law Practice: A Lens for Addressing All Legal Problems' (2017) 95(1) *Denver Law Review* 123, 125.

34 Ibid 132.

35 Ibid 123.

companies, businesses, and governments to achieve their ambitious sustainability goals, or nudging them to understand how a sustainability perspective can reduce the environmental and social harms they would otherwise create and even create economic, environmental, and social benefits.'[36]

The lawyers interviewed by Dernbach are engaged in what Chief Judge Brian Preston might call 'climate conscious lawyering' (noting, though, that the sustainable development framework is not limited to matters involving climate change). Preston calls for a 'climate conscious' rather than 'climate blind' approach to daily legal practice. He encourages lawyers to provide 'holistic legal advice' that addresses not just legal issues but also many non-legal consequences of different courses of action.[37] He also suggests they have the opportunity to interpret laws and legal rules in a way that 'promotes or better implements climate change goals' where such an interpretation is consistent with established principles of interpretation.[38] Preston argues that these practices are consistent with 'responsible lawyering' because they 'uphold and advance the fundamental values and integrity of the legal system, including climate justice'.[39] He believes that responsible lawyering requires a lawyer's advice and actions to be consistent with the goals of UN Sustainable Development Goal 16 in promoting 'peaceful and inclusive societies, ... including a just transition to carbon neutrality, and promoting access to justice for all, including people who have suffered or will suffer harm due to climate change'.[40] Preston also calls on lawyers to adopt the following 'personal ethical approaches':

1. moral counselling with clients, including addressing the climate change consequences of the client's proposed activity;
2. promoting human rights in business;
3. encouraging clients to adopt sustainable business models;
4. encouraging action by government and the judiciary to address the climate crisis;
5. engaging in intellectual activism, including law reform; and
6. working pro bono or at a reduced fee in climate change matters.[41]

This list is perhaps more reminiscent of *moral activist* lawyering than *responsible lawyering*, as we use the terms in this book. But we note that behaviour that was once considered *moral activist* may in time be accepted as mainstream *responsible lawyering*. David Morris, the CEO of the EDO, has compared the increase in climate litigation with litigation against tobacco companies as the health effects of smoking became more widely known:

> Ten years ago, these sorts of [climate] cases seemed wild. People would have thought 'how can you possibly have a case like that' ... Now, I think it's going to become increasingly normal.[42]

36 Ibid 189.
37 Brian Preston, 'Climate Conscious Lawyering' (2021) 95 *Australian Law Journal* 51, 52.
38 Ibid 56.
39 Ibid 62.
40 Ibid 29.
41 Ibid 63–4.
42 Adam Morton, '"A Duty of Care": Australian Teenagers Take Their Climate Crisis Plea to Court', *The Guardian* (online at 2 March 2021) <https://www.theguardian.com/environment/2021/mar/02/a-duty-of-care-australian-teenagers-take-their-climate-crisis-plea-to-court>.

We discuss Preston's call for lawyers to engage in law reform below, but next we consider his call for lawyers to offer 'moral counselling' and to encourage the adoption of sustainable business models.

Moral counselling and sustainable business models

Unlike the Australian ethical conduct rules (the *ASCR* and *Barristers' Conduct Rules*), the American Bar Association's ('ABA') *Model Rules of Professional Conduct* ('*Model Rules*') explicitly permit lawyers to 'counsel' clients on the 'moral, economic, social and political factors'[43] that the lawyer believes are relevant to the client's situation. We believe that this type of counselling in the context of business exposure to climate and biodiversity risk is today simply an aspect of competent lawyering. As we explore in Chapter 9, consideration of environmental, social and governance ('ESG') factors is increasing important in commercial law work. Further, it is clear that, while climate change and environmental concerns were once considered a niche area of practice, today lawyers in very many areas of practice need to be across developments in climate-related law (and, we would argue, the social and political context of those developments) in order to give competent advice. The LCA's Climate Change Policy Statement underlines the need for lawyers to be aware of the many impacts climate change is having across multiple practice areas and to understand the context in which their advice will be applied. The Statement stops short of endorsing 'moral counselling', but we note that moral issues relevant to 'reputation' can have significant implications for legal advice:

> 53. Lawyers should be alive to the unfolding legal implications of climate change and its consequences, and they should be informed, skilled and ready to assist clients on climate change-related legal matters, within their areas of skill and competence.
> 54. Lawyers should be responsive to the broad spectrum of clients across the Australian community facing new legal risks, liabilities and challenges in light of the physical and transition risks of climate change.
>
> ...
>
> 56. Lawyers should also be aware that advice regarding a legal problem should be provided in a manner which meaningfully addresses any identified climate change issues and related consequences, including the possible risks, liabilities and reputational damage which may flow from activity that has a negative impact on climate change. It is not suggested that lawyers should offer advice on matters unconnected to legal issues or outside the scope of their retainer, but rather, that legal advice should take into account the full range of contextual circumstances in which it is given, consistently with professional obligations.[44]

The Statement makes it clear that all lawyers (including those taking an adversarial advocate approach to their work) must now keep climate change and its consequences front of mind, in order to give competent legal advice. We look in more detail at the *adversarial advocate* approach next.

43 ABA Model Rule 2.1 'Advisor'.
44 Law Council of Australia, *Climate Change Policy Statement* (n 28).

Adversarial advocate

In Chapter 5 we suggest that the most justifiable context for an adversarial advocate approach to legal ethics is criminal defence work: we note the importance of defence lawyers acting zealously (that is, not half-heartedly) for a client charged with serious offences (all within ethical boundaries). We believe that some lawyers will find *adversarial advocacy* an empowering approach when defending clients charged with offences designed to stifle environmental protests. The State governments of New South Wales and Tasmania have legislated anti-protest laws with 'broad police powers, vague offences and severe penalties' that, according to Benjamin Richardson, 'signal the prioritization of business operations over the rights of individuals to peacefully protest'.[45] In 2019 the Queensland Government legislated to ban lock-on devices that are used by protestors to attach themselves to machinery or structures.[46] This legislation has been critiqued as breaching Australia's obligations under the *International Covenant on Civil and Political Rights*.[47]

Some environmental activists in Australia and overseas argue that non-violent civil disobedience is a necessity in the face of the climate emergency. This defence has been accepted in England and Wales by a jury but rejected in Queensland[48] (although on appeal, the Queensland District Court significantly reduced the sentence, noting 'the sincerity of the appellants' beliefs, grounded in conscience and seeking to communicate disapproval of government policy').[49] We suspect that civil disobedience in relation to environmental concerns will increase in the future, and that defendants charged with 'public order' offences will require lawyers willing to zealously advocate on their behalf, including raising human rights concerns where appropriate.[50]

As we discuss in Chapter 2, some lawyers who adopt an *adversarial approach* to their work consider it acceptable to use loopholes, procedural points or spurious arguments to frustrate the spirit of the law. In his call for lawyers to be 'climate conscious' Chief Justice Preston counsels against such an approach[51] and, as in Chapters 2 and 6, we argue that

45 Benjamin J Richardson, 'Editorial: Climate Strikes to Extinction Rebellion: Environmental Activism Shaping Our Future' (2020) 11(3) *Journal of Human Rights and the Environment* 1, 2. The NSW Government in 2022 passed the Roads and Crimes Legislation Amendment Bill against fierce opposition from a coalition of civil society organisations. The legislation undermines freedom of protest: Kieran Pender, 'Curbing Our Freedom: The NSW Bill that Should Never Have Become Law', *The Sydney Morning Herald* (online at 4 April 2022) <https://www.smh.com.au/national/nsw/curbing-our-freedom-the-nsw-bill-that-should-never-have-become-law-20220402-p5aaat.html>.

46 *Summary Offences Act 2005* (Qld), inserting a new s 14C(1).

47 Toby Hemmings and Azadeh Dastyari, 'A Danger to Protest: The Freedom of Peaceful Assembly and Disruptive Protest under the *Summary Offences and Other Legislation Amendment Act 2019* (Qld)' (2021) 27(2) *Australian Journal of Human Rights* 330.

48 Richardson (n 45) 2.

49 *EH v Queensland Police Service; GS v Queensland Police Service* [2020] QDC 205, [77].

50 See also Royce Kurmelovs, 'Extinction Rebellion Activist Has Chalk Message Case Thrown Out by Perth Magistrate', *The Guardian* (online at 12 January 2022) <https://www.theguardian.com/environment/2022/jan/12/extinction-rebellion-activist-has-chalk-message-case-thrown-out-by-perth-magistrate>. The defendant's barrister, Anthony Eyers, stated: 'any prosecution would have set a bad precedent by criminalising the act of being near protest actions … If these prosecutions are allowed to stand, they will invariably generate precedents affecting fundamental freedom of expression and freedom of movement, and association.'

51 Preston (n 37) 62.

often such an approach is not legal under either the ethics rules or legislation such as the *Civil Procedure Acts*. Case study 10.2 considers the historical actions of lawyers advising fossil fuel companies on public relations ('PR') campaigns and asks whether these lawyers overstepped the ethical line in their adversarial advocacy.

CASE STUDY 10.2 CORPORATE LAWYERS' ETHICAL RESPONSIBILITIES IN THE FACE OF THE CLIMATE DISINFORMATION CAMPAIGN[52]

In the 1980s, when the science on human-induced climate change became increasingly clear, several global corporations began a major corporate disinformation campaign to discredit that science.[53] The campaign was designed to mislead the public about the climate science, so as to influence public policy to the benefit of fossil fuel interests. Exxon Mobil Corporation ('Exxon') was a lead player in the campaign.[54] According to Lissa Griffin and Katrina F Kuh:

> Any argument that Exxon did not understand the link between its actions and climate change is not plausible. Numerous analyses have traced how Exxon exploited the scientific concept of uncertainty in a misleading fashion; sought out, funded, greatly magnified the attention afforded to, and overlooked serious criticisms of the work of contrarian scientists and studies; and, most tellingly, promoted a public message about the state of climate science inconsistent with what it understood to be accurate.[55]

The disinformation campaign in the United States involved several techniques including advertorials in *The New York Times* and other publications (designed to look very much like a newspaper editorial but written by Exxon). The campaign funded multiple groups whose mission was to raise doubt in the public's mind about the existence, causes and severity of climate change: '[t]he Union of Concerned Scientists estimates that between 1998 and 2005, Exxon gave over $15 million to 43 groups involved in spreading disinformation on climate science'.[56]

Although the results of this campaign are difficult to quantify, it clearly had an impact. Public concern about climate change lessened: '[T]he correlation of the timing of the

52 This case study is based on Lissa Griffin and Katrina F Kuh, 'Professional Responsibility and the Corporate Hoodwink: Using the Climate Disinformation Campaign to Examine the Ethical Responsibilities of Attorneys When Corporate Clients Mislead the Public to Avoid Government Regulation' in Keith Hirokawa and Jessica Owley (eds), *Environmental Law, Disrupted* (Environmental Law Institute, 2021) 101.

53 Marian Wilkinson, *The Carbon Club: How a Network of Influential Climate Sceptics, Politicians and Business Leaders Fought to Control Australia's Climate Policy* (Allen & Unwin, 2020) 7.

54 Ibid 19–20.

55 Griffin and Kuh (n 52) 107.

56 Ibid 110.

climate disinformation campaign with shifts in public belief and inertia or agnosticism in [government] policy suggest that the … campaign … affected public beliefs, mitigation policy and adaption policy'.[57] The Australian campaign, involving Australian fossil fuel interests, politicians and climate-science sceptics, had clear links to the US campaign and had similar effects. Marion Wilkinson's *The Carbon Club* chronicles its impact: 'The more the climate science was questioned, the more politicians lost the imperative to act.'[58]

Griffin and Kuh explore the likely role of Exxon's lawyers in the disinformation campaign. While there is no direct evidence that the lawyers were involved in the campaign, they argue that it is common for corporate lawyers to be involved in clients' PR activities. They posit that, given the extent, the cost and the importance of Exxon's campaign, it is very likely that lawyers were involved and that those lawyers knew the campaign was designed to mislead the public.[59]

In support of this conclusion, Griffin and Kuh cite the work of Michele DeStefano Beardslee whose empirical study found that corporate counsel are deeply involved in PR. DeStefano suggests that it is in the public interest to have lawyers involved in PR related to legal controversies because they 'can help ensure messages to the public are accurate, understandable and informative',[60] but she also notes that 'lawyers are under great pressure to manipulate information about legal controversies in a way that misleads' which 'is unethical whether done as the spokesperson or behind the scenes'.[61]

Griffin and Kuh analyse the likely role of Exxon lawyers in the climate disinformation campaign though the lens of lawyers' ethical responsibilities, as set out below. (While they note relevant rules in the ABA *Model Rules*, we note relevant *ASCR* rules and Australian legal principles.)

1. Lawyers may not make false statements in public

It is clear that lawyers must not make false statements in the service of a client or otherwise.

ASCR r 4.1 provides that a solicitor must 'be honest … in all dealings in the course of legal practice' and 'avoid any compromise to their integrity and professional independence'. Rule 5 forbids 'dishonest and disreputable conduct', which, according to the LCA commentary,[62] would include 'lack of integrity' and 'dishonest, deceitful or fraudulent conduct'.

57 Ibid 104.

58 Wilkinson (n 53) blurb.

59 Griffin and Kuh (n 52) 113.

60 Michele DeStefano Beardslee, 'Advocacy in the Court of Public Opinion, Installment One: Broadening the Role of Corporate Attorneys' (2009) 22(4) *Georgetown Journal of Legal Ethics* 1259, 1258–9.

61 Ibid 1303.

62 Law Council of Australia, *Australian Solicitors' Conduct Rules 2011 and Commentary* (2013) 15 <https://www.lawcouncil.asn.au/files/web-pdf/SolicitorsConductRulesHandbook_Ver3.pdf>.

2. A lawyer may not assist a client in fraudulent or criminal conduct

It is clear that a lawyer must not knowingly assist a client to engage in conduct that is criminal or fraudulent. Fraud comprises a knowing 'material misrepresentation of fact, opinion, intention or law for the purpose of inducing another to act or refrain from acting'.[63] A lawyer must counsel a client against such conduct. A lawyer is also prohibited from assisting client conduct that would 'violate criminal and civil securities, mail or wire fraud, truth in advertising, or consumer protection requirements'.[64]

Further, a lawyer for a corporation must act in the best interests of the corporation. If the lawyer becomes aware that a corporate employee intends to act against the best interests of the corporation, then the whistleblowing requirements discussed in Chapter 9 come in to play.

Applying these principles to the (assumed) actions of Exxon lawyers, Griffin and Kuh argue that legal advice condoning the misinformation campaign would have been in breach of ethics rules if the lawyers knew that the campaign statements were fraudulent. Fraud is hard to prove, but

> [w]hile misleading the public to forestall regulation may not itself meet the traditional definition of fraud, Exxon's public statements may have violated state and federal laws governing deceptive representations to shareholders and consumers ... A verdict against a client would go far to establishing fraudulent conduct, that, if assisted by counsel, would establish an ethical violation. In addition, counsel may well have an obligation to report internally and possibly externally upon learning of the client's intentions. Given this ethical minefield, corporate counsel advising a client in a public relations campaign should be extremely cautious to avoid being subject to discipline or accusations of malpractice.[65]

3. Norms of professionalism may limit a lawyer's role in public disinformation

The norms of professionalism require a lawyer to act in a way that does not mislead the public. Those norms would include integrity and honesty, as discussed above, as well as compliance with relevant corporate disclosure obligations and, more generally, the duty to the administration of justice. As discussed in Chapter 3, the key professional value identified within admission and discipline is lawyer honesty. Griffin and Kuh conclude that ethics rules are one tool for preventing lawyers from being complicit in corporate disinformation campaigns. Heeding the rules and their broader professional obligations, lawyers need to

63 Griffin and Kuh (n 52) 119.

64 Ibid. These principles also apply in Australia.

65 Ibid 119. In relation to current claims against Exxon for misleading practices, Massachusetts State Attorney General Maura Healey filed a lawsuit in 2021 accusing Exxon of misleading consumers and investors about its role in climate change: Jonathan Stemple, 'Exxon Must Face Massachusetts Lawsuit Alleging Climate Change Deceit', *Reuters* (online at 24 June 2021) <https://www.reuters.com/business/exxon-must-face-massachusetts-lawsuit-alleging-climate-change-deceit-2021-06-23/>.

be very careful when advising on such campaigns. However, Griffin and Kuh also argue that the ABA *Model Rules* are not clear enough about the ethical obligations of lawyers in this area and suggest that the rules should very clearly prohibit lawyer participation in misleading the public in this way.[66]

DISCUSSION QUESTIONS

1. Assume the Exxon lawyers were aware that the climate disinformation campaign was misleading and were involved in advising on the campaign.
   a. Do you agree that they breached ethical duties? Which duties?
   b. How might the lawyers have rationalised their involvement in such a campaign?
   c. How might you counter such rationalisations?
2. Do you think the *ASCR* are currently clear enough to prohibit lawyers' involvement in corporate disinformation campaigns? If not, what addition to the rules would you suggest?
3. Although fossil fuel companies now 'accept the science' on climate, some are promulgating more subtle messages to delay action on climate change or shift responsibility for it away from fossil fuel companies onto individuals,[67] including by claiming that their products are more environmentally friendly than they actually are ('greenwashing').[68] What do you see as corporate counsel's ethical responsibilities in light of these developments?

Ethics of care

Brian Preston writes that 'climate conscious lawyers have compassion for people and planet wounded by climate change and are, in their daily legal practice providing advice and taking action to heal these wounds'.[69] Such compassion is based on an *ethic of care* that puts relationships between people, and between people and planet, at the centre of legal practice. We suspect that many 'sustainable development' lawyers are motivated by these values, as are other lawyers looking to preserve relationships via non-adversarial methods of dispute resolution.

66 Ibid 120–1.

67 William F Lamb et al, 'Discourses of Climate Delay' (2020) 3 *Global Sustainability* e35 1–2; Trevor Culhane, Galen Hall and J Timmons Roberts, 'Who Delays Climate Action? Interest Groups and Coalitions in State Legislative Struggles in the United States' (2021) 79 *Energy Research and Social Science* 102114.

68 Kim Sheehan, 'This Ain't Your Daddy's Greenwashing: An Assessment of the American Petroleum Institute's Power Past Impossible Campaign' in Matthew Rimmer (ed), *Intellectual Property and Clean Energy* (Springer Singapore, 2018) 301. See also 'The Greenwashing Files', *Client Earth* (Web Page) <https://www.clientearth.org/projects/the-greenwashing-files/>.

69 Preston (n 37) 66.

As noted, litigation is often not the best way to address environmental concerns. Rather, extensive and careful consultation with a community, and negotiation with government and other land/resources users may be the most productive approach. For example, given the importance of relationship to First Nations communities (both relationships with people and with Country), lawyers working with these communities to assist them to care for Country would be wise to adopt an *ethics of care* and *empowerment* approach to their work. We note the EDO's commitment to its Aboriginal clients: 'We will use our expertise, professionalism and deep commitment to assist and stand with our Aboriginal clients as they protect and promote their Country, culture and heritage through law.'[70] The verbs 'assist' and 'stand with' are important. Marianne Endgleman Lado and Kenneth Rumelt's analysis of the work of lawyers involved in campaigns against fossil fuel pipelines in the United States emphasises the importance of lawyers supporting, rather than supplanting, community-led action on environmental issues.[71]

Ethics of care lawyering also supports a restorative justice approach to environmental offending on a local scale. Restorative justice involves a conferencing process between the offender, the victim(s) and any other relevant stakeholders (supported by a trained facilitator) with the aim of reaching a mutually acceptable resolution. Haneed Al-Alosi and Mark Hamilton describe its many benefits: it 'provides a forum for the participants to discuss the offence, its impact, and allow the parties to provide input into formulating ways to remedy the harm caused to the environment. Conferencing can also empower victims and repair ruptured relationships.'[72]

An *ethic of care* is also central to some law reform efforts. We consider law reform below.

Law reform

Reform of legal ethics rules

Some lawyers argue that the ethical conduct rules should more clearly support lawyers advising against environmental harm and in favour of a healthy environment. US lawyer Tom Lininger makes the case that the ABA *Model Rules* should be amended to explicitly require lawyers to promote environmental health. He notes that the ethical codes of other professionals, such as doctors and engineers, address the importance of 'environmental stewardship' and that lawyers' professional code should do likewise. Lininger lists the inroads made over recent years into the partisan (adversarial advocate) model behind the *Model Rules*, citing recent rules authorising lawyers to 'blow the whistle' if they discover their

70 'Aboriginal Engagement and Cultural Heritage', *Environmental Defenders Office* (Web Page) <https://www.edo.org.au/aboriginal-engagement-cultural-heritage/>.

71 Marianne Engelman Lado and Kenneth Rumelt, 'Pipeline Struggles: Case Studies in Ground up Lawyering Symposium' (2021) 45(2) *Harvard Environmental Law Review* 377.

72 Hadeel Al-Alosi and Mark Hamilton, 'The Ingredients of Success for Effective Restorative Justice Conferencing in an Environmental Offending Context' (2019) 42(4) *University of New South Wales Law Journal* 1460, 1488. The authors cite Australian and New Zealand cases where this approach has been successfully used, and suggest that the process could be more widely adopted in cases involving environmental crimes: Hadeel Al-Alosi and Mark Hamilton, 'The Potential of Restorative Justice in Promoting Environmental Offenders' Acceptance of Responsibility' (2021) 44(2) *University of New South Wales Law Journal* 487.

client is engaged in financial crime or fraud. (The Australian rules have been reformed in a similar way: see Chapter 4.) Lininger believes it is time for ethics rules to take into account non-human interests and to include the environment as a third party whose interests must be protected. He advances several modest and more radical proposals for changes to the ABA *Model Rules*. His modest proposals include permitting disclosure of confidential client information 'to prevent imminent, substantial and irremediable environmental damage' and adding 'environmental' to the list of factors that a lawyer may counsel a client about under Model Rule 2.1, while his more radical proposals include an environmental scorecard for law firms that holds firms accountable 'on certain criteria measuring their efforts to protect the environment'.[73]

Lininger emphasises the purpose of an ethical code, which

> is to ensure that practitioners attend to issues of transcendent importance – issues that practitioners might neglect if they focused narrowly on their day-to-day tasks. Scientists have informed us that environmental protection is one of the most urgent challenges facing humanity today. It should not be a distraction from lawyers' ordinary ethical duties: it should be a central part of those duties.[74]

We agree, as does Joshua Gostel. Like Lininger, Gostel notes the ethical requirements imposed on other professions to protect the environment and believes that lawyers should be subject to similar requirements. Gostel argues that the most effective way of implementing such an obligation would be through legislation to *require* a lawyer to disclose environmental harm caused by a client's actions, where 'environmental harm' is defined as 'detrimental harm to the environment caused by pollution or other methods that increase the impact of climate change'.[75] The US *Sarbanes-Oxley Act*, which requires lawyers to report violations of securities law, is precedent for this type of legislation. This proposal – to impose a *duty to report* – is significantly stronger than an extension of the exceptions to confidentiality under ethics rules.

As we discuss in Chapter 4, there is no positive legislative obligation on lawyers in Australia to 'blow the whistle' on corporate (or government) wrongdoing; however, there is now some legislative protection for lawyer corporate employees who choose to do so. While we would support legislation such as that proposed by Gostel, we doubt that it will be forthcoming in Australia in the near future. We agree with Lininger that the exceptions to confidentiality (in *ASCR* r 9) warrant expansion to cover disclosure 'to prevent imminent,

---

73 Tom Lininger, 'Green Ethics for Lawyers' (2016) 57(1) *Boston College Law Review* 61, 77–82, 106. A group of US law students has developed such a scorecard: Law Students for Climate Accountability, *The 2021 Law Firm Climate Change Scorecard* <https://static1.squarespace.com/static/5f53fa556b708446acb4dcb5/t/611dba29c5ad3077663d4947/1629338162366/2021+Law+Firm+Climate+Change+Scorecard.pdf>.

74 Lininger (n 73) 115. Lininger also argues forcefully for extension of the US crime-fraud exception to attorney–client privilege to include civil violations of environmental law, particularly the knowing emission of listed pollutants: Tom Lininger, 'No Privilege to Pollute: Expanding the Crime-Fraud Exception to the Attorney-Client Privilege' (2020) 105(1) *Minnesota Law Review* 113. We consider Australian common law and statute on this exception is already broad enough to cover violations of environmental law facilitated by lawyer–client communications (see Chapter 4).

75 Joshua Gostel, 'Ethics, Energy and the Environment: A Proposal to Hold Attorneys to Certain Standards in Protecting Our Planet' (2017) 30(4) *Georgetown Journal of Legal Ethics* 819, 835.

substantial and irremediable environmental damage'. The current exemptions (*ASCR* rr 9.2.4 and 9.2.5) are not wide enough to cover environmental harm that is not a serious crime (even if it should be!) or likely to result in imminent serious harm to a person. We strongly support the call by both Lininger and Gostel for ethical rules to specifically address lawyers' duties in relation to environmental protection.

Law reform generally

Law reform is a critical area of activity for 'climate conscious lawyers', whatever their usual ethical approach to practice. As the LCA observes in its Climate Change Policy Statement, 'law reforms will increasingly be required to respond to climate-related gaps, uncertainties and unfolding novel situations'. In his address to the ABA in 2021, the US Climate Envoy, John Kerry, emphasised the crucial role lawyers need to play in expediting the transition to clean energy and in finding innovative solutions for decarbonisation.[76] Many lawyers are stepping up to this task. The following initiatives are good examples:

- In the United States, law firms, law school clinics and individual lawyers are working pro bono to draft model laws to facilitate decarbonisation of the US economy. These laws and other resources are available on the website Model Laws for Deep Decarbonization,[77] a collaboration of Columbia Law School's Sabin Center and Widener University Commonwealth Law School's Environmental Law and Sustainability Center.
- The Chancelry Lane Project has brought together legal professionals from many countries (including Australia) to draft contractual clauses designed to 'deliver climate solutions' that can be incorporated into law firm precedents and commercial agreements. The Project has developed a 'Net Zero Toolkit' with clauses and tools to enable lawyers to 'align their work with a decarbonised economy, and a safe and habitable planet for us all'.[78]
- A campaign for the reform of international law seeks to have ecocide (destruction of large areas of the natural environment as a consequence of human activity)[79] recognised as a crime at international law. This campaign builds on the work of UK barrister Polly Higgins, who was the archetypal *moral activist* – she gave up her high-flying job and sold her house to finance her life's work on ecocide.[80] In her book *Eradicating Ecocide: Law and Governance to Prevent the Destruction of Our Planet*,[81] Higgins outlined the legal mechanisms for holding to account perpetrators of widespread environmental

76 Karen Sloan, 'You're All Climate Lawyers Now, John Kerry Tells ABA', *Reuters* (online at 6 August 2021) <https://www.reuters.com/legal/litigation/you-are-all-climate-lawyers-now-john-kerry-tells-aba-2021-08-05/>.

77 'Model Laws for Deep Carbonization in the United States', *LPDD* (Web Page) <https://lpdd.org/>.

78 'Net Zero Toolkit', *Chancelry Lane Project* (Web Page) <https://chancerylaneproject.org/net-zero-toolkit/>.

79 Merriam-Webster (online at 12 April 2019) <https://www.merriam-webster.com/dictionary/ecocide> 'ecocide'.

80 Gloria Dickie, 'Sustainability: Politicians and CEOs Could Face Criminal Charges for Environmental Destruction', *Huffpost* (online at 12 April 2019) <https://www.huffpost.com/archive/au/entry/politicians-ceos-could-face-criminal-charges-environmental-destruction_au_5de860f8e4b0d50f32ae20dd>.

81 Polly Higgins, *Eradicating Ecocide: Laws and Governance to Prevent the Destruction of Our Planet* (Shepheard-Walwyn, 2010).

damage. Tragically, she died of cancer at the age of 50, but many other lawyers and activists continue her work: Stop Ecocide International is now an international NGO, working to establish ecocide as an international crime.[82] The campaign has gained support from a number of states and the European Union,[83] thereby becoming a more mainstream *responsible lawyering* campaign. An expert panel of international lawyers convened by the NGO has drafted a definition of ecocide for incorporation in the Statute of Rome.[84] If incorporated, the provision allows for the prosecution of individuals (corporate executives and government ministers) before the International Criminal Court for widespread damage to ecosystems.

Lawyers rethinking 'Law'

An *ethic of care* is at the heart of more radical approaches to the law reform deemed by some to be necessary to address the predicaments facing humanity. With his 2002 book *Wild Law: Governing People for Earth*,[85] the South African lawyer Cormac Cullinan draws attention to the anthropocentricism of the Western common law system, which treats the non-human world as a resource to be exploited and fails to see humans as part of the whole web of life. Cullinan calls for a new vision of 'Law' – 'Wild Law' or 'Earth Jurisprudence' – that understands the purpose of law and legal systems as supporting mutually beneficial relationships between humans and 'other members of the Earth Community'.[86] Of course, in many ways this is an old vision of law, reflecting the legal systems of many First Nations Peoples, which have underpinned the sustainable custodianship of land and seas for thousands of years.[87]

Along with Cullinan, many lawyers now believe that tinkering with current environmental laws is not enough – we need more radical change to our legal orientation.[88] The Australian Wild Law Judgements Project exemplifies such a change in outlook: for this project legal scholars wrote/rewrote legal judgments, placing 'Earth and the greater community of life at the centre' of those judgments, and in the process interrogating 'the anthropocentric and property rights assumptions embedded in existing common law'.[89]

82 'Who We Are', *Stop Ecocide International* (Web Page) <https://www.stopecocide.earth/who-we-are->.

83 'Leading States – Key Dates', *Stop Ecocide International* (Web Page) <https://www.stopecocide.earth/leading-states>.

84 'Legal Definition of Ecocide Completed', *Stop Ecocide International* (Web Page) <https://www.stopecocide.earth/expert-drafting-panel>.

85 Cormac Cullinan, *Wild Law: Governing People for Earth* (Siber Ink in association with the Gaia Foundation & EnACT Intl, 2002).

86 'Cormac Cullinan', *Wild Law Institute* (Web Page) <https://www.wildlaw.net/board-of-directors-and-team/cormac-cullinan>.

87 See also Jacqueline McGlade, 'A Just and Rights-Based Framework for Nature' (Gresham College lecture, 27 April 2021) <https://www.gresham.ac.uk/lectures-and-events/nature-rights>. McGlade draws attention to the chthonic legal tradition, one of the oldest legal traditions, which situates people in nature.

88 See, eg, Keith Hirokawa and Jessica Owley, *Environmental Law, Disrupted* (Environmental Law Institute, 2021); Leonie Kelleher, 'The Future of Environmental Law' (2019) 93(3) *Law Institute Journal* 30; Leonie Kelleher, 'Environmental Law: No Longer Unprecedented' (2020) 94(12) *Law Institute Journal* 78.

89 Nicole Rogers and Michelle Maloney (eds), *Law As If Earth Really Mattered: The Wild Law Judgment Project* (Routledge, 2017) Abstract <https://www.taylorfrancis.com/books/9781317210580>.

The theory of earth jurisprudence has become all the more compelling as scientific research continues to emphasise the fact that human thriving depends on a healthy biosphere. Earth jurisprudence proposes that we rethink our legal, political, economic and governance systems[90] so that they support, rather than undermine, the integrity and health of all living beings. In light of the environmental calamity we are facing, the concept of earth jurisprudence may quickly move from (what some see as) naivety or idealism to necessity. An indication of changing norms is that several governments around the world have legislated to accord legal rights to Nature.[91] In Australia the Blue Mountains City Council has adopted this approach.[92] The work of lawyers, in negotiating, drafting, enforcing and improving these laws, is key to their success.

Conclusion

As the law evolves to better address the dangers of climate change and environmental degradation, the advice lawyers give clients will change. Eventually, we surmise (and hope), lawyers will be advising even recalcitrant clients that to act legally they must act in ways that do not harm the environment. Until such time, a lawyer's ethical approach will influence their advice and their daily legal practice. Lawyers can draw on the strengths of several or all of the ethical approaches discussed to empower them to step up to the task ahead. We cannot avoid this task. As the US Special Presidential Envoy for Climate, John Kerry, told the General Assembly of the ABA in 2021: 'You are all climate lawyers now'.[93] Esteemed Australian environmental lawyer Leonie Kelleher reminds us:

> There is no magic wand. It is the sustained efforts lawyers take now that will create the … future of our planet. This challenge demands forward thinking, creativity and invention. It requires personal responsibility and self-discipline. It will likely transform the world, and the law itself.[94]

RECOMMENDED FURTHER READING

Law Institute Journal, Jan/Feb 2022 Environmental Law Special Edition:

Hubert Algie, 'Climate Lawyers of the Future' (2022) 96(1–2) *Law Institute Journal* 48

Gerry Bean, 'Litigating for Change' (2022) 96(1–2) *Law Institute Journal* 35

Leonie Kelleher, 'A Climate Conscious Approach' (2022) 96(1–2) *Law Institute Journal* 44

90 See also the work of Australian Earth Laws Alliance: <https://www.earthlaws.org.au/>.

91 Craig M Kauffman and Pamela L Martin, 'Constructing Rights of Nature Norms in the US, Ecuador, and New Zealand' (2018) 18(4) *Global Environmental Politics* 43.

92 'Blue Mountains City Council First in Australia to Adopt "Rights of Nature"' (Media Release, Blue Mountains City Council, 29 April 2021) <https://www.bmcc.nsw.gov.au/media-centre/blue-mountains-city-council-first-australia-to-adopt-%E2%80%98rights-of-nature%E2%80%99>.

93 ABA News, 'John Kerry to ABA: "You Are All Climate Lawyers Now"' (11 June 2021) <https://www.americanbar.org/news/abanews/aba-news-archives/2021/08/john-kerry-to-aba–you-are-all-climate-lawyers-now-/>.

94 Kelleher (n 88) 33.

Brian Preston, 'Call for New Ways to Understand Changing World' (2022) 96(1–2) *Law Institute Journal* 23

Chris Primmer, 'The Race to Net Zero: A Junior Lawyer's Perspective' (2022) 96(1–2) *Law Institute Journal* 52

Jody Williams, 'Nature Positive Outcomes' (2022) 96(1–2) *Law Institute Journal* 40

Margaret Young, 'Climate Change and Law: A Global Challenge for Legal Education (2021) 40(3) *University of Queensland Law Journal* 351

11

CONCLUSION: VALUES AND LEGAL PROFESSIONALISM

Introduction

At the start of this book we introduced four ways of thinking about ethical behaviour for lawyers. Zealous, client-focused lawyering – *adversarial advocacy* – was contrasted with *responsible lawyering* – lawyering that counterbalances client advocacy with upholding the responsibilities and duties of lawyers to society. A third approach, *moral activism*, sees the ethical duties of lawyering as being not so much in vigorously asserting clients' rights, or the rule of law, as in actively doing one's best in the interests of justice. Finally, an *ethics of care* approach sees the ethical virtues of all three of the preceding approaches as overrated and emphasises instead the importance of the lawyer caring for and respecting the needs and moral aspirations of each client, each witness and even each opponent with whom they come in contact, as well as attending to their own needs and aspirations.

Underpinning each of these approaches are the general moral categories of consequentialism, Kantian ethics and classical virtue ethics. An understanding of general morality enriches our grasp of the strengths and limitations of our four lawyer-specific approaches to ethical decision-making, such that carefully considered decisions are likely to involve both general morality and one or more of the four approaches.

In practice, of course, lawyers can and do move around among these ideal types and their general moral sensitivity. The *adversarial advocate* might still be dominant, but even the determined and courageous criminal barrister can also be the quiet and despairing *carer*, standing, if they are so permitted, near their condemned client when the trapdoor drops. Consider the case of Nguyen Tuong Van, aged 25, of Melbourne. He was hanged in Singapore on 2 December 2005 for smuggling 496 grams of heroin through Changi Airport in 2002. His Australian lawyers, Justice Lex Lasry (then a QC) and Julian McMahon AC,[1] represented him fearlessly and expertly throughout his trial and helped foster international pleas for mercy. When those pleas were rejected by Singapore, the two lawyers, who had always acted pro bono out of compassion, applied without success simply to be present at the hanging, for no other purpose but to stand alongside their client.

There is no advantage in any lawyer rigidly following just one of these four ideals of ethical lawyering all the time. But it seems likely that, just as individuals have preferred comfortable psychological types,[2] so also ethically aware lawyers will tend to identify more often than not with one ethical type that expresses their values for lawyering and shapes their practice. All lawyers and law students are likely to benefit from identifying their own values and reflecting on the ethical behaviour that they might derive from those values. In each of the previous chapters we have examined how the values represented by the different approaches would apply to certain specific situations and contexts that commonly arise in legal practice. In this chapter we examine more closely the significance of personal values-awareness for lawyers' ethics. The book concludes with a suggested method for self-assessing one's ethical type/preference.

1 As discussed in Chapter 5, McMahon subsequently represented Andrew Chan and Myuran Sukumaran, drug traffickers on death row in Indonesia.

2 See, eg, the Myers-Briggs Type Indicator ('MBTI'), a psychological categorisation instrument developed from the work of the Swiss psychologist and psychiatrist Carl Jung (1875–1961): see Isabel Briggs Myers and Peter B Myers, *Gifts Differing: Understanding Personality Type* (Davies-Black, first published 1980, 1995 edn).

The significance of personal values in legal professionalism

Underlying our analysis of the four ethical approaches to lawyering and ethics in legal practice are personal value commitments by scholars and practising lawyers. Consider, for example, the continuing debate among lawyers and ethicists about lawyers' proper role, if any, in securing justice where law does not do so. The issues of contention between the *responsible lawyer* and the *moral activist* are not merely academic. Rather, each participant in this scholarly and practical debate conscientiously asserts the moral superiority of their own viewpoint because of the values reflected in that viewpoint – for example, loyalty in the adversarial advocate, resilience in the responsible lawyer, determination in the moral activist or compassion in the carer.

For example, ethicists like Stephen Pepper, Alice Woolley and Bradley Wendel argue that the 'liberal', or neutral, model of legal partisanship, which favours the primacy of legal rules as the major reference point in resolving ethical quandaries, is the proper framework for determining lawyers' ethics.[3] Broadly speaking, they ground their powerful advocacy of their positions on the personal conviction that there is no greater guarantee of individual fairness or justice than that provided by the rules – in effect, by the rule of law.[4] Their argument is not new, although it is developed by each writer with great care, sophistication and an integrity that demands respect, even if we disagree with it. The essence of the argument is that true security comes from definable rules or, at least, from rules that are capable of flexible interpretation, as circumstances and developing moral dialogues require.[5]

In contrast, the equally impassioned injunction of ethicists like Donald Nicolson, Julian Webb and David Luban is first to look at the justice and fairness of the context of the lawyer's choice about how to act, regardless of any apparently applicable rules.[6] They suggest that deep-seated social inequality governs the major Western economies and that to rely on the rule of law (that is, to have blind confidence that the rules are fair and are administered fairly) as an ethical guideline is naive, or worse, complicit in the perpetuation of that inequality. With profound and rapidly growing gaps in wealth and access to justice the world over, Nicolson, Webb and Luban have never been more entitled to ask about the

3 See, eg, Stephen L Pepper, 'Lawyers' Ethics in the Gap Between Law and Justice' (1999) 40 *South Texas Law Review* 181; Stephen L Pepper, 'Counseling at the Limits of the Law: An Exercise in the Jurisprudence and Ethics of Lawyering' (1995) 104 *Yale Law Journal* 1545; Stephen L Pepper, 'The Lawyer's Amoral Ethical Role: A Defense, a Problem, and Some Possibilities' (1986) 11 *American Bar Foundation Research Journal* 613; W Bradley Wendel, 'Civil Obedience' (2004) 104 *Columbia Law Review* 363. Alice Woollley, 'Is Positivist Legal Ethics an Oxymoron?' (2019) 32(1) *Georgetown Journal of Legal Ethics* 77. See also Daniel Markovits, 'Legal Ethics from the Lawyer's Point of View' (2003) 15 *Yale Journal of Law and the Humanities* 209.

4 See W Bradley Wendel, 'Pluralism, Polarization, and the Common Good: The Possibility of *Modus Vivendi* Legal Ethics' (2021) 131 *Yale Law Journal Forum* 89.

5 Pepper, 'Lawyers' Ethics in the Gap Between Law and Justice' (n 3).

6 Donald Nicolson and Julian Webb, *Professional Legal Ethics: Critical Interrogations* (Oxford University Press, 1999); David Luban, *Lawyers and Justice: An Ethical Study* (Princeton University Press, 1988)

moral context: whether the client is, directly or indirectly, behaving oppressively to those more vulnerable than themselves, or being unfairly oppressed.

The important point is not that Pepper, Woolley and Wendel (who might be said to defend *adversarial advocacy* and *responsible lawyering*) and Nicolson, Webb and Luban (*moral activists*) disagree but that they disagree respectfully, and with an open-mindedness and willingness to be scrutinised. These ethicists write with energy and conviction because they believe lawyers' ethics matters, and think that others need to believe and act as if it matters too. Their actual ethical judgements are almost secondary. Their commitment to the integrity of open discussion of passionate positions is the essential quality that all lawyers, indeed all law students, can seek to identify with as one way to assist in strengthening their own virtues and working out their own ethical choices.

Inside lawyers' ethics in practice there are many very personal dilemmas. Feelings about what is right and wrong can lurk beneath the surface without being expressed. Law students are still too often told to 'think like a lawyer' and discouraged from linking their values and their feelings to what they are learning.[7] Many go into practice finding it difficult to recognise the importance of their often-confused feelings for ethical decision-making, and lawyers can be particularly poor at this skill. We often gloss over the personal dimensions of ethical conflicts by using rules as our only guide, ignoring the fact that rules are often full of overriding principles, qualifications and provisos, and discounting our 'gut feelings' about what is right.

As we have seen in the previous chapters of this book, all sorts of arguably unethical things are possible if bare rules are the start and finish of decision-making about ethical conduct: whether acting for the tobacco company that is intent on selling its product according to law but manoeuvring to avoid liability for its past deceit about the fatal effects of tobacco smoke; overcharging a client because time-billing remains a prevalent practice and allows for ambiguity as to what is a 'fair and reasonable' bill; structuring a global corporation's tax affairs so as to conceal indefinitely the income earned in one country or declare it in another with ultra-low taxes;[8] keeping client secrets, the disclosure of which might assist in avoiding an injustice or a public wrong; or even acting for two clients who have competing interests.

Rules should be only one part of the complex jigsaw of factors that lawyers consider in taking any ethical decision. The other jigsaw pieces are far more numerous than just the practice rules and even the common law rules and legislation.

More than anything, the jigsaw piece that must be explicitly identified and taken into account in each of these dilemmas is the individual lawyer's values – the personal, and

7 Molly Townes O'Brien, Stephen Tang and Kath Hall, 'Changing Our Thinking: Empirical Research on Law Student Wellbeing, Thinking Styles and the Law Curriculum' (2011) 21(2) *Legal Education Review* 149; Melanie Poole, *The Making of Professional Vandals: How Law Schools Degrade the Self* (Research Paper No 12–13, College of Law, Australian National University, 6 June 2011).

8 Luke Harding, 'Panama Papers Source Breaks Silence Over "Scale of Injustices"', *The Guardian* (online at 6 May 2016) <https://www.theguardian.com/news/2016/may/06/panama-papers-source-breaks-silence-over-scale-of-injustices>. See also International Consortium of Investigative Journalists and Elise Worthington, 'Panama Papers: Why "John Doe" Risked Their Life for the Mossack Fonseca Leak', *ABC News* (online at 5 April 2016) <http://www.abc.net.au/news/2016-04-05/why-the-panama-papers-mossack-fonseca-leaks-really-matters/7300262>.

often quite private, set of characteristics and priorities that are the bedrock for each person's beliefs, attitudes and behaviours. These qualities do not necessarily determine our behaviour, but they are the starting point in understanding that lawyers are as human as the rest of the species, and can and should make choices about what they actually do.[9]

As mentioned in Chapter 1, it is also important to be aware of our emotions: Hugh Brayne emphasises the importance of feelings in understanding values for everyone, including law students, quoting Daniel Goleman in *Emotional Intelligence*:

> While strong feelings can create havoc in reasoning, the *lack* of awareness of feeling can also be ruinous, especially in weighing the decisions on which our destiny largely depends: what career to pursue, whether to stay in a secure job or switch to one that is riskier but more interesting, whom to date or marry, where to live, which apartment to rent or house to buy – and on and on through life. Such decisions cannot be made through sheer rationality; they require gut feeling ...[10]

An individual lawyer may or may not be fully aware of their values or, more precisely, of the interplay between their ethical reasoning, emotional (feeling) processes and professional practice, but awareness of personal values is an important aid to ethical practice.[11] It is easier for a lawyer who knows what they truly value to decide, whether, for example, to

- assist a company to restructure to avoid significant liabilities to individuals who have been wronged by the company;
- refuse to change legal advice to make it more politically salient;
- use an 'attack dog' approach in cross-examining a fragile witness; or
- find legal loopholes to justify/rationalise a client's greenwashing PR campaign.

Lawyers may have some inkling of the right thing to do, but if they have not delved into their values very much and all this ethics and 'psychology' seems a bit too hazy or suspect, and they can find a rule – whether of substantive law or procedure – that just might allow them not to think about it too much, that rule will, all too often, be located and relied upon. For this reason the emphasis of this book is on exploring the values that underlie the traditional approach to many ethical dilemmas, and then suggesting possible alternatives, as well as setting out key formal rules of conduct as one point of reference in decision-making.

For many lawyers, knowing what they truly *value* will be the starting point not just for workplace survival but for longer term satisfaction in the legal world. Below we consider how our personal values might express themselves in preference for one ethical approach over another. But first we discuss another important reason to clarify our values.

9 Hugh Brayne, 'Learning to Think Like a Lawyer: One Law Teacher's Exploration of the Relevance of Evolutionary Psychology' (2002) 9(3) *International Journal of the Legal Profession* 283, 301. In contrast to our hopeful view of lawyers' autonomy, consider Markovits's argument that there is a sense in which lawyers can't make those choices – they are forced by their role in helping apply the law to be 'unethical ... due to historical forces beyond their control': see Markovits (n 3) 293.

10 Brayne (n 9) 298, quoting Daniel Goleman, *Emotional Intelligence: Why It Can Matter More Than IQ* (Bloomsbury, 1996) 53.

11 Brayne (n 9) 298. See also Donald A Schön, *The Reflective Practitioner: How Professionals Think in Action* (Basic Books, 1983).

Wellbeing, values and professionalism[12]

Our values, our wellbeing and our happiness are inextricably linked. Research tells us that wellbeing/true happiness does not come from the 'mere pursuit of pleasure, but from living in accordance with [values] that create a sense of meaning, connection and self'.[13] Psychology's self-determination theory ('SDT') helps explain this relationship. SDT holds that to live a satisfying life, we require certain basic psychological needs to be met: our needs for autonomy, competence and relatedness.[14] If our need for autonomy is met, we feel that we are able to live in a way that reflects our true self. Our competence need is met if we feel capable and competent in our endeavours. And if we are experiencing 'relatedness', we feel a meaningful connection to the important people in our lives.[15] These three needs are more likely to be met if we live by certain 'pro-social' values: self-understanding, good relationships with others, helping others and building community.[16] (These values are 'pro-social' because they support actions that benefit other individuals, our community or society as a whole.)

Our motivations, which are underpinned by our values, also influence our wellbeing.[17] If our motivations reflect a focus on 'extrinsic' values such as wealth, status or the desire to impress others, we can undermine our wellbeing because we are not prioritising activities that meet our psychological needs.[18] But if, for example, we are intrinsically motivated to work as a lawyer because we genuinely enjoy our work and find it fulfilling, our psychological needs are likely being met by our work, and we are thus more likely to experience satisfaction and wellbeing.

Research by Lawrence Krieger and Kennon Sheldon emphasises the importance for lawyers of these connections between values, motivation, psychological needs and happiness. The authors surveyed lawyers practising in four US states and found that lawyer happiness (which they defined as subjective wellbeing and life satisfaction) was very strongly predicted by whether a lawyer's basic psychological needs were met and whether the lawyer was intrinsically motivated in their work.[19] Lawyers in public service jobs reported better

12 This section draws on Vivien Holmes, 'Values: The Flip Side of the Well-Being Coin' in Caroline Strevens and Rachael Field (eds), *Educating for Well-Being in Law: Positive Professional Identities and Practice* (Routledge, 2019) 27.

13 Kathryn E Williams, Joseph Ciarrochi and Patrick CL Heaven, 'Relationships Between Valued Action and Wellbeing across the Transition from High School to Early Adulthood' (2015) 10(2) *The Journal of Positive Psychology* 127, 127. The authors explain that subjective wellbeing (wellbeing) has an affective component (the net balance between someone's positive and negative affect) and a cognitive component: at 132.

14 Lawrence S Krieger, 'The Most Ethical of People, the Least Ethical of People: Proposing Self-Determination Theory to Measure Professional Character Formation' (2011) 8(2) *University of St Thomas Law Journal* 168, 170.

15 Ibid 171.

16 Ibid 172–3.

17 Tim Kasser and Richard M Ryan, 'Further Examining the American Dream: Differential Correlates of Intrinsic and Extrinsic Goals' (1996) 3(22) *Personality and Social Psychology Bulletin* 280; Tim Kasser, 'Materialistic Values and Goals' (2016) 67(1) *Annual Review of Psychology* 489.

18 Yuval Feldman, 'The Complexity of Disentangling Intrinsic and Extrinsic Compliance Motivations: Theoretical and Empirical Insights from the Behavioural Analysis of Law' (2011) 35 *Washington University Journal of Law and Policy* 11, 12. As Feldman writes: 'Extrinsic motivation is linked to actions that are driven by external commands or incentives. Conversely, intrinsic motivation is found when the behaviour is chosen from within the individual, usually out of a sense of moral or civic duty' (at 12).

wellbeing and life satisfaction than did lawyers in prestigious, well-paid jobs. This research establishes that prestige, high incomes and other external benefits do not 'compensate a lawyer who does not experience autonomy, integrity, close relationships, and interest and meaning in her work'.[20]

Krieger and Sheldon also observed that, while their survey did not measure professionalism or ethics,

> it did measure psychological factors that are virtually certain to be important sources of ethical and professional behaviour for lawyers – authenticity (which is essentially identical to integrity), competence, relating well to others, helping and community values, and valuing self-understanding and growth. These factors also include the strongest predictors of well-being in our subjects.[21]

Other work by Krieger explains further these links between professionalism, ethics/values and psychological needs: a professional exhibits integrity (which is connected to autonomy), competence and service, and displays interpersonal skills when relating to colleagues and clients (relatedness to others).[22]

Attention to values is thus critically important: pro-social values underpin both our wellbeing/happiness and our professionalism. But attention to values is important not only for individuals. As discussed in Chapter 1, we (as legal practitioners and as a profession) also need to pay attention to *workplace* values, which influence lawyers' ethicality and wellbeing.

The next section includes an exercise designed to help clarify one's professional values and ethical preferences.

Measuring awareness of ethical preference[23]

The values that can be said to underlie ethical decision-making may appear well developed by the time a student is in law school, but the assumption of this book is that an individual law student's ethical preferences in relation to legal professionalism are still in formation and may undergo some change when the student is presented with possible alternatives.[24] If this is correct, then law students' early knowledge of their basic legal ethics preferences, and

19 Lawrence S Krieger and Kennon M Sheldon, 'What Makes Lawyers Happy? A Data Driven Prescription to Redefine Professional Success' (2014) 83(2) *George Washington Law Review* 554.

20 Ibid 623.

21 Ibid.

22 Krieger (n 14) 170.

23 This section draws on and modifies material originally published in Adrian Evans and Josephine Palermo, 'Preparing Australia's Future Lawyers: An Exposition of Changing Values Over Time in the Context of Teaching About Ethical Dilemmas' (2006) 11(1) *Deakin Law Review* 103; Adrian Evans and Helen Forgasz, 'Framing Lawyers' Choices: Factor Analysis of a Psychological Scale to Self-Assess Lawyers' Ethical Preferences' (2013) 16 *Legal Ethics* 134. See also Richard Moorhead et al, 'The Ethical Identity of Law Students' (2016) 23 *International Journal of the Legal Profession* 235.

24 See generally Adrian Evans and Josephine Palermo, 'Zero Impact: Are Lawyers' Values Affected by Law School?' (2005) 8 *Legal Ethics* 240; JD Droddy and C Scott Peters, 'The Effect of Law School on Political Attitudes: Some Evidence from the Class of 2000' (2003) 53 *Journal of Legal Education* 33.

of the possibilities and challenges of change, may promote earlier ethical development and more satisfactory working lives. Some might realise sooner that they would be better off following a different career path. Some will understand that they have a legal vocation and not just an occupation. Ethics awareness earlier on might also help law students and lawyers make better choices at the beginning of their careers about what area of practice to pursue.[25] Further, greater clarity about ethical choice could lead to a clearer sense of professionalism and contribute to better public regard for those professionals.

Complete transformation is most unlikely, but an ethics awareness process can assist in strengthening students' (and lawyers') resolve to behave ethically. We suggest the following process:

1. Complete (individually) the Appendix: Part 1 – 'Self-Assessment of Legal Ethical Preferences', following the instructions in the appendix, and then Appendix: Part 2 – 'Scale to Self-Assess Legal Ethical Preferences', strictly in that order. This instrument – technically described as a 'scale' – has been developed in an Australian legal profession setting[26] but can be used elsewhere with appropriate cautions. We emphasise that the instrument will only be useful if approached honestly and in good faith.
2. Discuss whether, on reflection, the number you obtained for each ethical preference appears realistic to you. Were you surprised by the result or are you confirmed in your earlier opinions or guesses?
3. Apply your recently discovered preference(s) to a hypothetical, but realistic, practice scenario to consider whether your preference or preferences ring true or not in the context of the scenario. The case studies in this chapter, in this book and elsewhere[27] are appropriate for this purpose. Remember that reflection on the scenarios is in itself both the process and the objective, and that there is rarely a 'correct' answer. The discussion itself tends to raise the various competing values at stake.
4. Consider any rules of conduct, legislation and case law that apply to the scenario, and revisit the choice of ethical approach with which you feel most comfortable. Note any differences between what the ethical rules and law say should be done in the scenario and what the different ethical approaches say should be done.
5. Consider how you might act consistently with your ethical preferences, when the issues in the scenarios come before you in real life.

---

25 Andrew M Perlman, 'A Career Choice Critique of Legal Ethics Theory' (2001) 31 *Seton Hall Law Review* 829.

26 Based on work by Evans and Forgasz (n 23).

27 Other resources include: the scenarios in the Australian Lawyers' Values Study in, eg, Evans and Palermo (n 24); Debra Lamb, 'Appendix: Case Studies' in Stephen Parker and Charles Sampford (eds), *Legal Ethics and Legal Practice: Contemporary Issues* (Clarendon Press, 1995) 237 (case studies collected from interviews with Australian lawyers about their real experiences); Philip B Heymann and Lance Liebman, *The Social Responsibilities of Lawyers: Case Studies* (Foundation Press, 1988). See also Robert Eli Rosen, 'Ethical Soap: *LA Law* and the Privileging of Character' (1989) 43(5) *University of Miami Law Review* 1229 (this is an excellent discussion of the use of TV shows and popular culture for ethics teaching and the limitations of using only short hypothetical scenarios to explore issues of ethical character). Finally, see the wide range of general moral scenarios provided by The Ethics Centre (Web Page) <https://ethics.org.au/consulting-and-leadership/ethi-call/>.

CASE STUDY 11.1 CONFIDENTIALITY IN THE FACE OF LIKELY CHILD ABUSE

The issue of child abuse has a very high profile in Australia. The media frequently covers incidents of the injury or death of young children at the hands of family members and institutions. In their work, lawyers may be privy to information that relates to the abuse of a child. This is likely to be information received from a client about a perpetrator or victim and therefore subject to the legal and ethical duty of confidentiality. Confidentiality could be described as one of the 'core' values of the Australian legal profession and, despite some policy concerns that question the utility and justice of strict confidentiality, it remains undeniably crucial as a linchpin of common law systems of legal representation. Consider again the scenario from Chapter 2, which raises many of the issues we have discussed concerning values and rules and professional conduct:

> You are acting for a mother of three small children in a divorce and intervention order matter. Your client has previously shown you some old photographs of bruises and marks on the children that she claims were inflicted not by their father but by her new boyfriend.
>
> One of the children now has blurred vision. Your client now instructs you to stop all legal proceedings as she intends to return to the children's father with her children. You believe the children will be at risk if this happens but your client tells you, as she leaves, to do nothing.[28]

DISCUSSION QUESTIONS

1. What are your reactions to the scenario? Have you seen anything or heard of anything similar in your work experience environments or those of your friends that you are willing to outline in general terms? What were your reactions to those events?
2. In reflecting on your decision about what to do here, which of the ethical approaches discussed in this book is most attractive to you? Does this choice 'fit' with the number you have identified for different ethical preferences? If not, why does there appear to be a difference? How would you answer the question posed in this scenario?
3. Would you break client confidentiality and inform the relevant welfare agency of your fears for the safety of the child?
4. If you thought that a report to the welfare authorities would result in an investigation (into the breach of confidence) by the legal professional regulator, would you still proceed and make the report?

28 Adrian Evans and Josephine Palermo, 'Australian Law Students' Perceptions of Their Values: Interim Results in the First Year – 2001 – of a Three-Year Empirical Assessment' (2002) 5(1–2) *Legal Ethics* 103, 115, 114.

5. Would your answers be different if, upon later, more thorough questioning of your client, you discovered that your client has an old history of drug abuse and was not, in the past, always reliable in what she said?
6. *ASCR* r 9.1 provides:

   > A solicitor must not disclose any information which is confidential to a client and acquired by the solicitor during the client's engagement to any person who is not … a solicitor who is a partner, principal, director, or employee of the solicitor's law practice …

   ASCR r 9.2 provides that lawyers do not have to maintain confidentiality where the practitioner discloses information in circumstances in which the law would probably compel its disclosure, or the disclosure is for the sole purpose of avoiding the probable commission of a serious criminal offence, or for the purpose of preventing *imminent* serious physical harm (our emphasis) (as discussed in Chapter 4).

   Does the *ASCR* exception affect your choice as to what to do in this scenario? Does it change your preferred ethical approach? Do you think the rule, together with its exception, reflects an appropriate ethical approach to this issue?

Case study 11.2 raises a different sort of values conflict.

CASE STUDY 11.2 THE LONG WEEKEND

You have been working long hours at a new law firm for over a year now, in an effort to establish yourself as a competent and willing employee. Your (life) partner was happy to support you in this at first but has started to express concerns that you are overworking and burning yourself out. They have also noted that you are often so tired when you actually go out together on the rare occasion during the week (to a play or concert), that it's hardly worth the effort. You sense that the relationship could be on rocky grounds because of these issues: you both want to have children, but your partner says they need to be sure that you will take on your fair share of child raising.

You agree with your partner that you are getting burnt out, and you notice that you're enjoying work less as a result. You're also a bit worried about missing important issues in a case because you're worn out. You have promised your partner that you'll turn over a new leaf, starting with a long weekend away and then a conversation with the firm's managing partner. You have booked lovely accommodation and promise your partner that you'll be home early so you can avoid some of the holiday traffic.

At 3 pm on Friday a firm partner (Bill Shelford) asks to see you. Shelford explains that a colleague with carriage of a large litigation matter has been pulled off the file at the client's request. Since you have proven your mettle, the file is being transferred to you. Shelford tells you that you'll need to spend the weekend getting up to speed on the file, ready for a meeting with the client on Tuesday. The client is very demanding, and the firm can't afford to lose it. The firm will provide any support you need.

DISCUSSION QUESTIONS

1. What values are in conflict here?
2. Are there any rules or principles of professional conduct relevant to the situation?
3. Assume that you decide that the most important thing to you is to keep your promise to your (life) partner and go away with them for the weekend. However, you do not want to lose your job or the firm's good opinion. You decide to have a conversation with Shelford, using a GVV approach (see Chapter 1). (You might have this conversation immediately, or ask him if you can come to see him in 15 minutes or so.) You consider:[29]
   - Whose interests are affected;
   - What is at stake for the key stakeholders;
   - Whether there is anything making you disinclined to have this conversation with Shelford, and, if so, how you might reframe the issue so that you feel more likely to speak up, keeping in mind your values;
   - What might happen if you do not speak up in this situation and how this might affect you, your partner, the firm, the client; and
   - Whether there are alternative ways of approaching this issue (that is, the work that needs to be done on the file) that might satisfy all the stakeholders.

   Practise the conversation with a colleague. Remember that having had a practice conversation makes it more likely we will speak up in a similar 'real-life' situation.

Conclusion

As will be clear throughout this book, we believe it is important that lawyers are aware of their values and of what really motivates them, and that they regularly reflect on these matters in their practice of law. This chapter explores the links between values and wellbeing, noting that lawyers who are intrinsically motivated by work that they value and enjoy are more likely to be happy (mentally well) and ethical. It also provides readers with a tool to help clarify their values.

As we have seen, legal practice serves up a proportion of clients whose objectives, strategies and tactics are morally questionable. Sometimes clients are just difficult to deal with or to understand. All clients are entitled to competence and care from their lawyers. Lawyers will be much better placed to represent their clients professionally, and to deal well with the ethical challenges arising from the pressures of practice, if they have a clear sense of their values and motivations and a sound understanding of the ethical underpinnings of legal practice. The question for the reader is, therefore: have you, in reading this book, developed a stronger sense of what might be important to you if you work as a lawyer, and of the ethical context of legal practice in Australia? If so, have you considered how you might act on these insights throughout your professional (and personal) life?

29 Vivien Holmes, '"Giving Voice to Values": Enhancing Students' Capacity to Cope with Ethical Challenges in Legal Practice' (2015) 18(2) *Legal Ethics* 115, 130.

APPENDIX: SELF-ASSESSMENT OF LEGAL ETHICAL PREFERENCES

Part 1: What do you think about these statements?[1]

Instructions

This exercise can be undertaken online using the online resources at www.cambridge.org/highereducation/isbn/9781009045636/resources or by completing a hard-copy version of the tables in this appendix. If this exercise is for a classroom setting, participants could be asked to complete Part 1 (the first table) prior to the class and to bring in their table and results to class to complete Part 2 and discuss the results.

1. There are 20 statements in the table below.[2] Consider each statement and whether or not you agree with it. The reliability of this instrument depends on your candour and willingness to honestly represent your level of agreement with each statement.
2. Please indicate your degree of support for each statement by giving it a score from 1 to 5, where 1 is strongly disagreeing and 5 is strongly agreeing.
3. Keep this table with your results. These results will be used in a second table to complete the exercise.

1 This scale is an amended version of the self-assessment tool included in previous editions of this textbook. A version of this tool was devised and tested by Adrian Evans and Helen Forgasz in 'Framing Lawyers' Choices: Factor Analysis of a Psychological Scale to Self-Assess Lawyers' Ethical Preferences' (2013) 16(1) *Legal Ethics* 134.

2 These statements are expressed in an abstract form to assist comparability. Please keep in mind that how we consider abstractions and how we actually act on them are two different things.

Statement	1	2	3	4	5
1. If I heard my client or my witness lie in court, I would correct the lie as soon as possible.					
2. Public interest lawyering is very attractive to me.					
3. I prefer dialogue, mediation and a focus on principled negotiation in resolving disputes for my clients.					
4. Achieving what my client wants is my main priority.					
5. I might do more than just refuse to act if my client insisted on an illegal course of action.					
6. The context and circumstances of an individual's suffering are more important than universal legal principles.					
7. Sometimes it's necessary to think less about your client's personal circumstances and more about what their case could do to improve justice.					
8. I put my client's interests first regardless of who the client is or the applicable law.					
9. I would much rather take a collaborative or restorative approach to problem-solving, than a combative stance.					
10. My aim is to do all for my client that my client would do for themselves, if they had my knowledge and experience.					
11. I find I can do a better job for my clients by helping them navigate beyond 'pure' legal considerations into the realm of policy and purpose behind legislation.					
12. My clients' enterprises ultimately depend upon their acceptance of the purpose and not just the letter of the law.					
13. I think of law reform and better access to justice as my chief interests.					

Statement	1	2	3	4	5
14. Saying 'no' to clients is sometimes necessary in order to preserve the system on which their own ultimate welfare depends.					
15. I find it hard to practise within 'the rules' when my clients demand something else.					
16. Clients need to know that I am not in their pocket.					
17. Social reform and the careful redistribution of wealth through the law are more important than my personal contentment.					
18. Apology, reconciliation and the acceptance of moral responsibility is more important than the 'just' and rigorous enforcement of legal rights.					
19. Concerns for justice and service are all very well, but if 'push comes to shove', what my client wants has to come first.					
20. I believe that it is important to ensure that participating in a legal process does not make my client unwell.					

Now turn to the next part of the self-assessment (Part 2) to learn your legal ethical preference(s) based on how you have responded to these statements.

Part 2: What is your ethical preference?

This exercise can be undertaken online using the online resources at <www.cambridge.org/highereducation/isbn/9781009045636/resources> or by completing a hardcopy version of the tables in this appendix. Please complete the following steps in the table below (Part 2) to reveal your overall legal ethical preference(s) based on your responses in the first table (Part 1).

1. Refer to the first table where you have given a score (1–5) next to each of the 20 statements. Now turn to the table below. Write the corresponding score next to the relevant statement.

   Note that in the table below the same 20 statements are set out but they are not listed in the same order; they have been grouped according to one of four legal ethical preferences.[1] To assist you to locate your previous rating, the statements in the second table have the same number as in the first table.

2. When you have entered a score of 1–5 next to each of the (5) statements in each category (moral activism, zealous advocacy, responsible lawyering and ethics of care), add them up to get a total score.
3. Compare the total scores you have given for each of the categories. If one or more have a higher score, this indicates your legal ethical preference(s).

Moral activism	Values
13. I think of law reform and better access to justice as my chief interests.	
7. Sometimes it's necessary to think less about your client's personal circumstances and more about what their case could do to improve justice.	
11. I find I can do a better job for my clients by helping them navigate beyond 'pure' legal considerations into the realm of policy and purpose behind legislation.	
2. Public interest lawyering is very attractive to me.	
17. Social reform and the careful redistribution of wealth through the law are more important than my personal contentment.	
Total – add up the numbers you have given to each of the five statements above for a total number for this category.	

Zealous advocacy	Values
19. Concerns for justice and service are all very well, but if 'push comes to shove', what my client wants has to come first.	
4. Achieving what my client wants is my main priority.	
15. I find it hard to practise within 'the rules' when my clients demand something else.	

1 In the first table, the statements are in random order to assist you to pay attention to the statements and not to prejudge your overall ethical preference.

8. I put my client's interests first regardless of who the client is or the applicable law.	
10. My aim is to do all for my client that my client would do for themselves, if they had my knowledge and experience.	
Total – add up the numbers you have given to each of the five statements above for a total number for this category.	

Responsible lawyering	Values
1. If I heard my client or my witness lie in court, I would correct the lie as soon as possible.	
12. My clients' enterprises ultimately depend upon their acceptance of the purpose and not just the letter of the law.	
5. I might do more than just refuse to act if my client insisted on an illegal course of action.	
16. Clients need to know that I am not in their pocket.	
14. Saying 'no' to clients is sometimes necessary in order to preserve the system on which their own ultimate welfare depends.	
Total – add up the numbers you have given to each of the five statements above for a total number for this category.	

Ethics of care	Values
3. I prefer dialogue, mediation and a focus on principled negotiation in resolving disputes for my clients.	
18. Apology, reconciliation and the acceptance of moral responsibility is more important than the 'just' and rigorous enforcement of legal rights.	
6. The context and circumstances of an individual's suffering are more important than universal legal principles.	
9. I would much rather take a collaborative or restorative approach to problem-solving, than a combative stance.	
20. I believe that it is important to ensure that participating in a legal process does not make my client unwell.	
Total – add up the numbers you have given to each of the five statements above for a total number for this category.	

The higher the score for a legal ethical preference, the more you identify with it. It is very possible that no single or overwhelming preference will emerge for you from the above table. Whether you have one preference or your preference is for more than one ethical perspective, your understanding of the relative strength of different preferences is useful for your future decision-making.

Discuss! To maximise the benefit of self-assessment, it is important that you debrief about your results. This conversation might involve discussing your reaction to your results and what you have learnt. This conversation does not require that you reveal to anyone your specific preferences according to the results of the scale. Rather, the conversation can be a starting point for you to become aware of your preferred ethical approach(es) and to develop a lifelong reflective practice.

Some questions you could discuss

- Are you surprised at your result?
- What do you think has influenced your ethical preference(s)?
- Do you think you would/will act on these preferences in legal practice? What might help or prevent you from doing so?

INDEX

For EU product safety concerns, contact us at Calle de José Abascal, 56–1°, 28003 Madrid, Spain or eugpsr@cambridge.org.

www.ingramcontent.com/pod-product-compliance
Lightning Source LLC
LaVergne TN
LVHW080013210926
848481LV00011B/3013

* 9 7 8 1 0 0 9 0 4 5 6 3 6 *